Instructor Wraparound Edition

GREGG

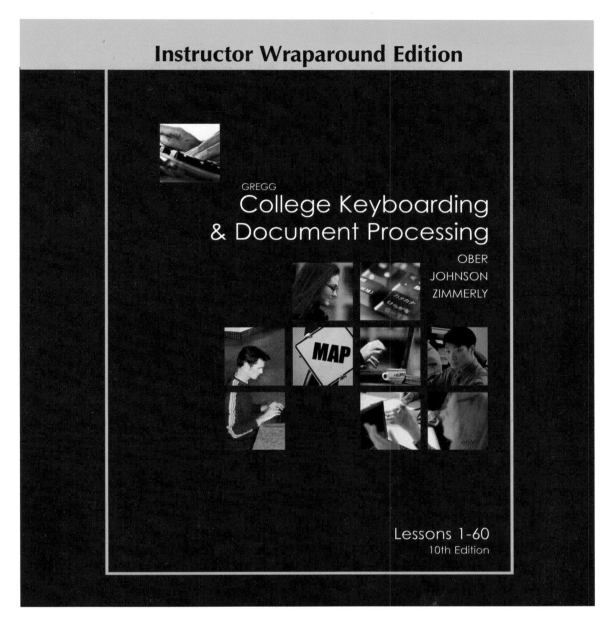

College Keyboarding & Document Processing

OBER
JOHNSON
ZIMMERLY

Lessons 1-60

10th Edition

Scot Ober
Ball State University

Jack E. Johnson
State University of West Georgia

Arlene Zimmerly
Los Angeles City College

Visit the *College Keyboarding* Web site at **www.mhhe.com/gdp**

Boston Burr Ridge, IL Dubuque, IA Madison, WI New York San Francisco St. Louis
Bangkok Bogotá Caracas Kuala Lumpur Lisbon London Madrid Mexico City
Milan Montreal New Delhi Santiago Seoul Singapore Sydney Taipei Toronto

Professional Handbook

GREGG
College Keyboarding

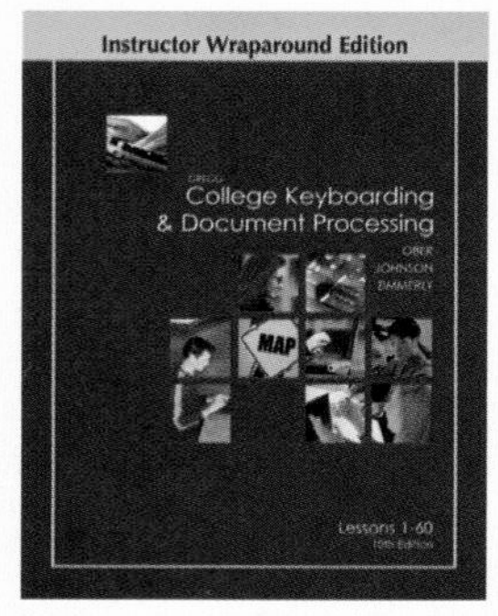

Methods of Teaching

& Document Processing

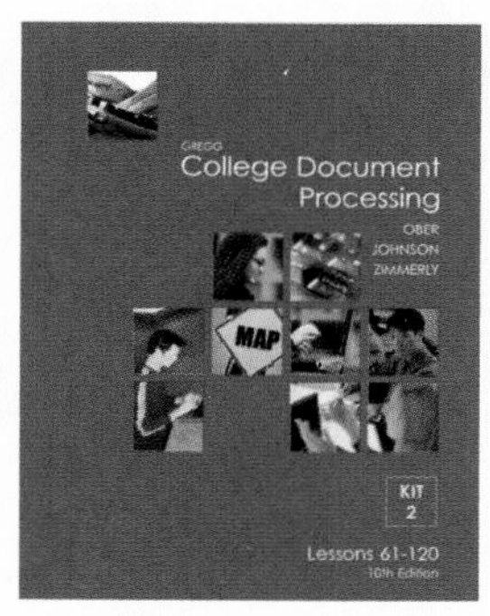

GREGG COLLEGE KEYBOARDING & DOCUMENT PROCESSING:
INSTRUCTOR WRAPAROUND EDITION, LESSONS 1–60
Published by McGraw-Hill/Irwin, a business unit of The McGraw-Hill Companies, Inc., 1221 Avenue of the Americas, New York, NY, 10020.

This book is printed on acid-free paper.

1 2 3 4 5 6 7 8 9 0 DOW/DOW 0 9 8 7 6 5

ISBN 0-07-296344-1

Editorial director: *John E. Biernat*
Publisher: *Linda Schreiber*
Sponsoring editor: *Doug Hughes*
Developmental editor: *Tammy Higham*
Developmental editor: *Megan Gates*
Marketing manager: *Keari Bedford*
Lead producer, Media technology: *Victoria Bryant*
Lead project manager: *Pat Frederickson*
Freelance project manager: *Rich Wright, Omega Publishing*
Senior production supervisor: *Michael R. McCormick*
Lead designer: *Matthew Baldwin*
Photo research coordinator: *Lori Kramer*
Senior supplement producer: *Susan Lombardi*
Senior digital content specialist: *Brian Nacik*
Cover design: *Subtle Intensity*
Interior design: *Matthew Baldwin*
Typeface: *11/12 Times Roman*
Compositor: *Seven Worldwide™ Publishing Solutions*
Printer: *R. R. Donnelley*

www.mhhe.com

Instructor Wraparound Edition

CONTENTS

The Gregg Philosophy

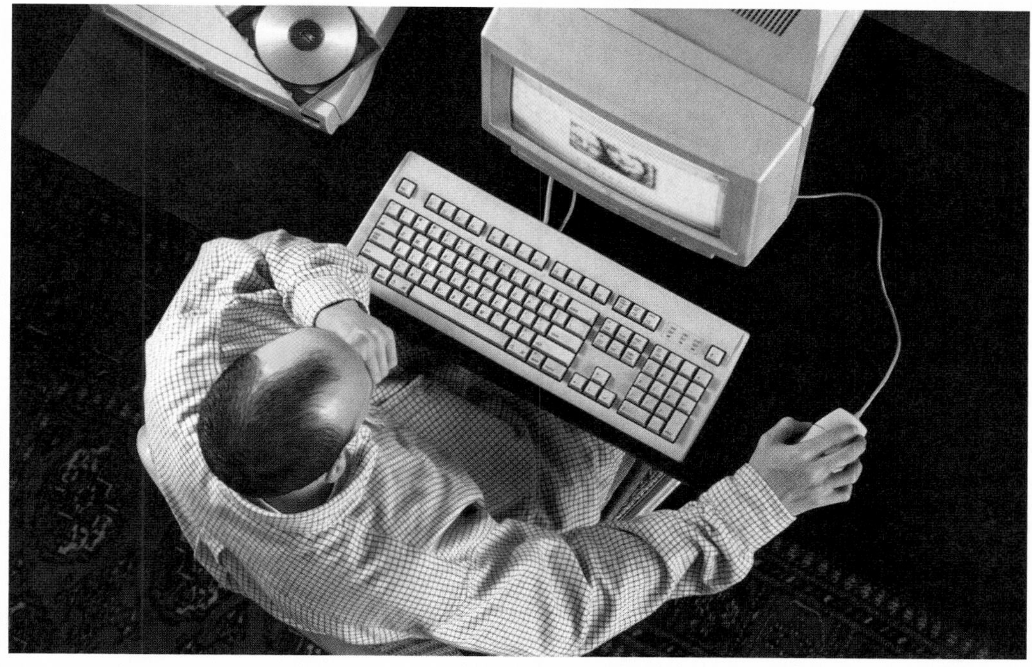

Despite technological advances being made in areas such as voice, optical-character, and handwriting recognition, it is likely that the fingertips will remain the primary means of data entry for the foreseeable future. And with keyboards on practically every desktop, keyboarding has become a primary means of basic communication—and keyboarding skills more important than ever.

Gregg College Keyboarding & Document Processing (GDP) reflects the latest research findings in a number of areas: the principles of learning, especially those relating to the acquisition of psychomotor skills; current business practices as they relate to the office environment; technological developments in providing instruction via software and the Internet; and the skills and knowledge needed for office employment. Thus, the current edition of this program is based on the following fundamental principles.

GENERAL

PRINCIPLE 1. The role of the instructor is paramount.

A few instructors teach keyboarding and document processing in a traditional classroom, with only textbook, computer, and a word processing program available but with no additional software or technology. Currently, however, most instructors add to this mix a correlated educational software program designed specifically to increase not only the efficiency with which students learn but also the level of skill they are able to attain. And an increasingly large number of instructors teach keyboarding and document processing in a distance-learning environment, using the Internet as the connection between student and instructor.

No matter. In every educational or training environment one can imagine, the *instructor* is the one critical element that determines the success or failure of the endeavor. In some situations, the instructor assumes a traditional role, introducing the new learning, guiding the students' practice, and assessing the results. In other situations, the instructor must become familiar with the features and operation of the correlated educational software being used, adapt his or her teaching methodology as needed, and use the software's scoring and recordkeeping features to increase the effectiveness and efficiency of skills assessment. In still other situations, the instructor must become an instructional designer and Webmaster, completely reconceptualizing the course so that instruction will be effective in an essentially noninstructor delivery system.

As has been true since the dawn of formal education, the effective instructor determines the goals of instruction, assesses the resources available, and analyzes the preparation, motivation, and maturity of his or her students to create an effective, efficient teaching and learning system.

The Professional Handbook section of the Instructor Wraparound Edition (IWE) contains, in effect, a mini-methods course in teaching keyboarding and document processing. Instructor notes on each student text page provide specific help on each lesson. The purpose of both unique features is to help instructors—especially part-time and adjunct faculty—perform their vital function more effectively.

PRINCIPLE 2. The use of appropriate computer technology for skill development should be an essential component of all keyboarding instruction.

Correlated software provides an additional avenue of learning, enhances student interest, provides flexibility, promotes individualized progress, and frees the instructor for other classroom management and instructional duties.

The GDP software offers one-click access to all aspects of the contemporary keyboarding classroom, including:

- Keyboard introduction
- Skillbuilding
- Language arts instruction
- Word processing
- Document checking
- Instructor management
- Distance learning

This sophisticated, pedagogically sound, and easy-to-use software component helps students gain keyboarding and document processing skills efficiently and effectively.

PRINCIPLE 3. The keyboard should be taught rapidly and logically.

The entire keyboard (including letters, numbers, and symbols) is taught within the first 20 lessons. All alphabetic keys are presented in eight lessons, the number keys are presented in three lessons, and the symbol keys are presented in three lessons.

Keys are introduced in a logical sequence. Keys using the stronger fingers are introduced before those using the weaker fingers; keys requiring shorter reaches are introduced before those requiring longer reaches; and keys are introduced in a sequence that makes it possible to type words and sentences early in the course.

In each lesson there is a balance between the new keys controlled by the left hand and those controlled by the right hand. Color is used throughout to help students identify correct finger reaches.

PRINCIPLE 4. Consistent, correct technique should be stressed at every level of instruction.

Good keyboarding technique is critical not only for high productivity but also for health reasons. Today, repetitive strain injuries such as carpal tunnel syndrome are the fastest-growing occupational injuries. Carpal tunnel syndrome comes about from hour after hour of straight keyboarding—making fast, repetitive motions that strain the tendons of the wrists and arms. The condition is exacerbated by the use of improper technique at the keyboard. Thus, at every stage of instruction, students must be taught to practice and maintain proper finger, hand, wrist, arm, and body position in order to remain healthy and productive.

SKILLBUILDING

PRINCIPLE 5. Straight-copy skillbuilding should be stressed at every level of instruction.

Most office employment tests require speed and accuracy at the keyboard. This means that students who cannot pass a straight-copy typing test will not even get the opportunity to demonstrate their well-developed word processing skills.

Straight-copy keyboarding skill is becoming increasingly important in today's automated office. One of the benefits of word processing is that document production becomes more like straight-copy typing because many decision-making and machine adjustments are automated.

Many typists and typing instructors, for example, remember the numerous *nontyping* steps involved in manually creating report footnotes or in creating tables. Contemporary word processors now handle these tasks with ease. This means that the typist can spend most of the time *keystroking;* and, as a result, straight-copy keystroking skill becomes even more important.

Thus, skillbuilding activities are included in every lesson in the text; moreover, a Skillbuilding section at the back of the text provides "anytime" individualized exercises. In addition, a balance between speed and accuracy development throughout the course is maintained. Students should acquire keyboarding skill that incorporates both speed and accuracy because both are essential for using the skill efficiently.

Finally, using the GDP software, students can access all of the skillbuilding routines at any time. Students are always "just a click away" from improving their straight-copy speed and accuracy.

PRINCIPLE 6. Students learn best by using a systems approach to skill development.

Keyboarding is a *psychomotor* skill; that is, it involves both mental and motor processes. Benefiting from the massive amount of evidence drawn from research in educational psychology, industrial psychology, and human anatomy, students learn to keyboard using a *systems* approach.

A *system* is a group of interacting elements forming a complex whole. Straight-copy speed and accuracy are developed systematically in GDP. Every skillbuilding routine has a specific objective (either speed or accuracy). These routines are cycled systematically throughout the program of study. There is scant time in the typical class for random, one-shot, cure-all approaches when the scientific approach to skillbuilding is used.

PRINCIPLE 7. The typist should always be working toward an attainable goal.

It makes no educational sense (or any other kind of sense) to assume that *all* students need to work on accuracy as opposed to speed at any given point, that *all* students need to work toward achieving a speed goal of 34 wpm, or that *all* students need remedial practice on accurately typing up reaches.

Students vary; their individual weaknesses vary. Even though end-of-term goals are established for straight-copy typing, students build toward these goals by pursuing short-term *individual goals*. They are always competing against their previous best effort—not some arbitrary "one-size-fits-all" goal.

PRINCIPLE 8. The analysis of keystroking errors must precede the correction of keystroking errors.

Just as physicians prescribe specific medicines for specific illnesses, the "typing doctor" should prescribe specific remedies for specific typing weaknesses. There is no "tonic" that cures all ills.

Only by analyzing a student's specific *pattern* of errors can effective remediation be achieved. Included in this edition is MAP (Misstroke Analysis and Prescription), a one-of-a-kind software program that analyzes the types of errors students make and then prescribes unique remediation drills to correct the most serious error patterns. Types of errors identified and remediated include concentration errors, errors on individual keys, errors on function keys, and reach errors—75 types of errors in all (see page PH-14 for a more detailed discussion of MAP).

PRINCIPLE 9. Timed writings used to assess skill should have a consistent format, length, and difficulty level.

Exercises designed to *build* straight-copy skill can have varying formats, lengths, and difficulty levels, depending upon the specific purpose of the drill. However, timed writings used to *measure* skill should be consistent.

This means that once students are able to complete 5-minute timed writings (Lesson 52), they should be graded only on 5-minute timed writings from then on, since most employment tests require a 5-minute timed writing.

All timed writings in GDP are in a consistent format as an aid to evaluation. Having a consistent format and difficulty level means that any change in a student's score can be attributed to a change in skill rather than merely to a change in the format of the timed writing; thus, more valid grading results.

All timed writings are shown double-spaced in monospaced font, all contain all letters of the alphabet (but no numbers or symbols other than common punctuation marks), and all have a similar syllabic intensity.

DOCUMENT PROCESSING

PRINCIPLE 10. The sequence of training activities should be based on a systematic spiral approach.

Most units in GDP (a unit consists of five lessons) are topical; that is, all the lessons in a unit stress a single topic, such as preparing correspondence. In this way, students cycle through the important document processing tasks (for example, correspondence, reports, and tables) and then repeat the cycle. The topical repetitions should spiral upward into levels of increasing difficulty and complexity. Such a plan is based upon the principle that learning proceeds most effectively when the learner participates in a continuously expanding pattern of behaviors.

The topical repetition of the units serves several functional purposes. First, whatever the length of a student's course, the student will achieve a balance of skillbuilding and document processing. Students whose schedule might limit them to a single semester of keyboarding will still achieve a functional level of skill and receive an introduction to basic office and personal-use documents.

In addition, because the spiral approach introduces a new topic to students every week, constant refreshment and renewal of interest take place. Thus, the spiral approach avoids boredom. Finally, students need "growing time" between the rungs of the ladder of document processing skill development.

PRINCIPLE 11. Competent language arts skills should be an essential component of competent document processing skills.

What good is it if a typist can type fast and has competence in word processing if the typist consistently makes errors in English or fails to proofread and correct his or her drafts? A document containing grammatical or typographical errors is unmailable—whether it is sent as an electronic file or as a paper document.

In GDP, students improve their language arts skills through a systematic series of exercises in proofreading, spelling, punctuation, capitalization, number expression, subject/verb agreement, abbreviations, and word choice. These skills are then reinforced in the document processing exercises in that lesson. Remedial instruction in the form of tutorials is also available in the GDP software.

PRINCIPLE 12. Word processing skills should not be taught in isolation.

Competence in one or more popular word processing software programs is an *enabling* skill—not a *terminal* skill. This means that typists learn word processing for one reason only—to produce typical office and personal documents as efficiently and correctly as possible.

Thus, formatting skills should be taught on the basis of *document requirements,* not on the basis of *word processing capabilities*. Formatting skills should be taught on a "need-to-know" basis, not on the basis of word processing features. It is not the word processing features themselves that are important; instead, it is the ability to produce a finished document efficiently and correctly that is important.

Word processing skills should not be taught as a course separate from keyboarding courses. Instead, they should be integrated into the keyboarding courses, with each word processing feature introduced as it is needed in order to format a particular job efficiently.

In GDP, students don't even start word processing instruction until after they have mastered the keyboard. Then, they have a four-lesson orientation unit on Microsoft Word, the most popular word processing software program. After this unit, word processing features are introduced systematically—never more than two or three in any one lesson—as they are needed to format the specific document introduced in the lesson.

PRINCIPLE 13. The formatting standards taught should achieve a delicate balance between reflecting industry practices and promoting office productivity.

As the long-time overwhelming leader in sales, *Gregg College Keyboarding & Document Processing* has had a tremendous impact on industry practice and office proficiency. The majority of students taking postsecondary keyboarding and document processing have learned their formatting standards from this text, and they carry these standards into the workplace. At the same time, the contemporary office is a dynamic environment—with new document types, new needs, and new pressures to increase productivity.

Gone, for example, are the days when clerical workers would estimate the number of words in the body of each letter they were about to type and then adjust the side margins and vertical spacing on the basis of letter length. Today's competitive environment requires high-efficiency formatting conventions. The simplified formats standardized in GDP promote office efficiency by requiring fewer hardware or software adjustments and less decision making.

Here's an example: Traditionally, the second page of a document contained a heading consisting of the name of the recipient, date, and page number. Typing the three-line page 2 heading was simple enough on the typewriter—because typists knew precisely when they removed the first page and inserted the second page into the machine. Not so with computers. Computer operators either had to learn to use the header/footer feature of their word processing program—or risk positioning the information in the wrong place on the page. Now, GDP recommends that a consistent format be used for the second page of *all* business documents—simply use the word processing feature to insert the page number at the top right on the second and subsequent pages. Nothing could be simpler—or more efficient.

Throughout the text, GDP maintains a careful balance between reflecting current formatting standards in industry and promoting more efficient standards.

CONCLUSION

When Alex Haley, the author of *Roots,* was asked what he would have done differently had he known that his book would be so successful, he replied, "I would have typed faster." By following the principles recommended in this program, business instructors will help their students also achieve success.

Teaching Strategies

Gregg College Keyboarding & Document Processing, 10th edition, is a multicomponent instructional system designed to prepare students for the business world, where keyboarding and word processing skills are essential for success. The components of this easy-to-use program, including software, textbooks, and manuals, are completely integrated and designed to work together as a complete system.

This section describes effective instructional methods for teaching from this program, including the following:

- Presenting the new keys
- Developing keyboarding technique
- Building straight-copy skill
- Building number-typing skill
- Building document processing skill
- Building language arts skills

PRESENTING THE NEW KEYS

Lessons 1–20 present all the new keys: the alphabetic keys in Lessons 1–10, the number keys in Lessons 11–15, and the symbol keys in Lessons 16–20. By the end of these 20 lessons, students should be able to touch-type at a rate of at least 28 wpm on a 2-minute timed writing, with no more than 5 errors.

THE FIRST DAY AT THE KEYBOARD

The first day students are sitting at the keyboard ready to begin learning is typically *not* the first day of class, but more often the second. The first day of class is generally spent on course management—finalizing class enrollment, introducing the course, and going over the course syllabus, needed supplies, and the like. Students will not typically come to the first class with textbooks, disks, and so on, in hand. On the first day of class you should, however, assign as homework for students the reading of the Introduction to the textbook.

As soon as students have their supplies (textbooks, blank disks, and the like) on hand, first familiarize them with their textbooks. Let students know that each text lesson is presented in the software, so that most students will use the software rather than their textbooks to navigate through each lesson. The software will *always* let students know when they need to refer to their texts.

Then, flip to a typical new-key lesson (for example, Lesson 2 on pages 5–6) and point out the usual elements of each new-key lesson.

- The lesson goals identify the new keys introduced in that lesson and the speed (number of words per minute) that the student should be typing by touch at the end of the lesson.
- The keyboard chart highlights the keys introduced in that lesson, identifies keys previously learned, and leaves yet-to-be-learned keys blank. The chart is color-coded to show which fingers control which keys.
- The warmup is 2 or 3 lines of text that review the new-key reaches introduced in the previous lessons. Students should type each line of the warmup 2 times by touch to be sure that they are ready for the new lesson.
- Each new key is introduced in 4 lines. The first line practices the reach from the home row. Students should look as their fingers make the reach to the new letter the first several times; thereafter, they should make the reach by touch. Lines 2–4 of the new-key drill move quickly to having students type words, phrases, and then sentences.
- Each of the first 20 lessons ends with a 1- or 2-minute timed writing. Each timed writing contains the same number of words as the speed goal, so if students finish the timed writing, they have met their speed goal for the lesson.

Next, walk students through the process of logging on to the GDP software, explain the main menu, and point out the major features of the software. Show students how they can always return to the main menu and how they exit the program. Encourage the students to access the audio tutorial within the program to become familiar with the main features of the GDP software.

CORRECT STROKING

Keys should be operated only by finger motion. The shoulders, arms, and wrists should be almost motionless. Poor technique when reaching for the keys pulls the hands from the proper position and causes errors.

Losing one's place when typing results in decreased speed and accuracy. Students must therefore pay close attention to the material being typed without glancing at their fingers or the screen. (*Exception:* Typists should look at their fingers when first learning each new key reach and at their screen when composing at the keyboard.)

LEVELS OF RESPONSE

There are three levels of response at which students are called upon to perform. The first, *letter response,* is developed in the very early stages of keyboarding. Each letter in a word is typed as a separate unit; that is, the student sees and thinks each letter of the word, as in *t–h–e*. This level of response is common during the learning of each new key.

In the second level, *word response,* students type short, familiar words as complete units without sounding out each letter. For example, the student sees the word *the* and types it without spelling out each letter.

The third level is a combination *word/letter response*. Everyone at one time or another types at this level. Whenever a new or difficult word is encountered, part of the word may be typed at the word level and the other part may be typed letter by letter; for example, *the–a–t–e–r*.

DEVELOPING KEYBOARDING TECHNIQUE

To build good keyboarding skills, students must develop, improve, and refine a number of basic techniques.

TECHNIQUE DEVELOPMENT

Students should learn and practice correct techniques for efficiency and physical well-being:

- Position the chair so that the upper and lower legs form a 90-degree angle and the lower back is supported.
- Position the keyboard even with the front of the desk.
- Position the text on either side of the monitor as close to the monitor vertically and horizontally as possible to minimize head and eye movement and to avoid neck strain.
- Position the mouse on a pad at the side of the monitor opposite the text.
- Center the body opposite the keyboard.
- Lean forward slightly from the hips, with the base of the spine touching the back of the chair and the feet flat on the floor.
- Keep the elbows alongside the body in a relaxed position.
- Curve the fingers naturally over the home position, with the back of the hand at the same angle as the keyboard.
- Keep the forearms horizontal and raise the hands slightly when typing so that the wrists do not touch the keyboard while typing. (Hands may rest at the bottom of the keyboard—away from the keys—during nontyping intervals.)
- Make quick, snappy strokes using the correct fingers.
- Return the finger immediately to the home position or move to the next position after each stroke.
- Operate all keys by touch, keeping the eyes on the copy most of the time while typing.

TECHNIQUE PRACTICE

Although most of the students' efforts are devoted to increasing skill on the printing keys, students must also develop facility on the nonprinting operational keys. Most typists quickly learn to strike the large ENTER key by touch, but the typist who has to interrupt his or her production to stop and manually locate the ENTER, LEFT or RIGHT SHIFT, BACKSPACE, or TAB keys cannot develop top-level proficiency.

These operational keys are systematically practiced in GDP, with every unit containing a special technique practice routine. In addition, the *10th* edition includes a Technique Practice on the BACKSPACE key that provides intensive practice on this frequently used nonprinting reach.

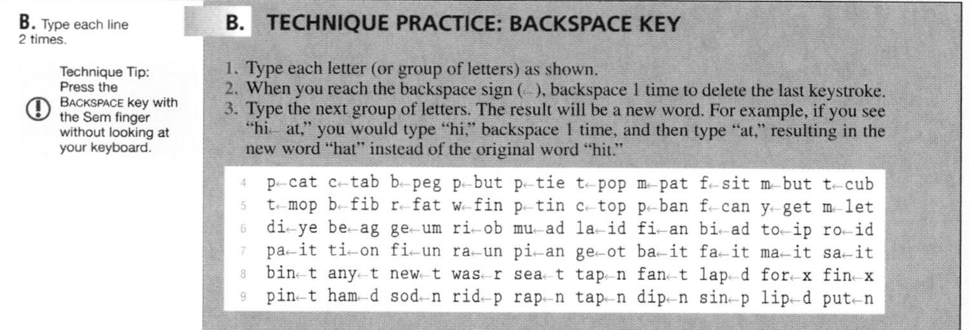

B. Type each line 2 times.

Technique Tip: Press the BACKSPACE key with the Sem finger without looking at your keyboard.

B. TECHNIQUE PRACTICE: BACKSPACE KEY

1. Type each letter (or group of letters) as shown.
2. When you reach the backspace sign (←), backspace 1 time to delete the last keystroke.
3. Type the next group of letters. The result will be a new word. For example, if you see "hi← at," you would type "hi," backspace 1 time, and then type "at," resulting in the new word "hat" instead of the original word "hit."

```
p←cat c←tab b←peg p←but p←tie t←pop m←pat f←sit m←but t←cub
t←mop b←fib r←fat w←fin p←tin c←top p←ban f←can y←get m←let
di←ye be←ag ge←um ri←ob mu←ad la←id fi←an bi←ad to←ip ro←id
pa←it ti←on fi←un ra←un pi←an ge←ot ba←it fa←it ma←it sa←it
bin←t any←t new←t was←r sea←t tap←n fan←t lap←d for←x fin←x
pin←t ham←d sod←n rid←p rap←n tap←n dip←n sin←p lip←d put←n
```

TECHNIQUE EVALUATION

Both the instructor and the student should use the Technique Evaluation Form for evaluating students' typing techniques. A sample form is provided on the College Keyboarding Web site at http://www.mhhe.com/gdp.

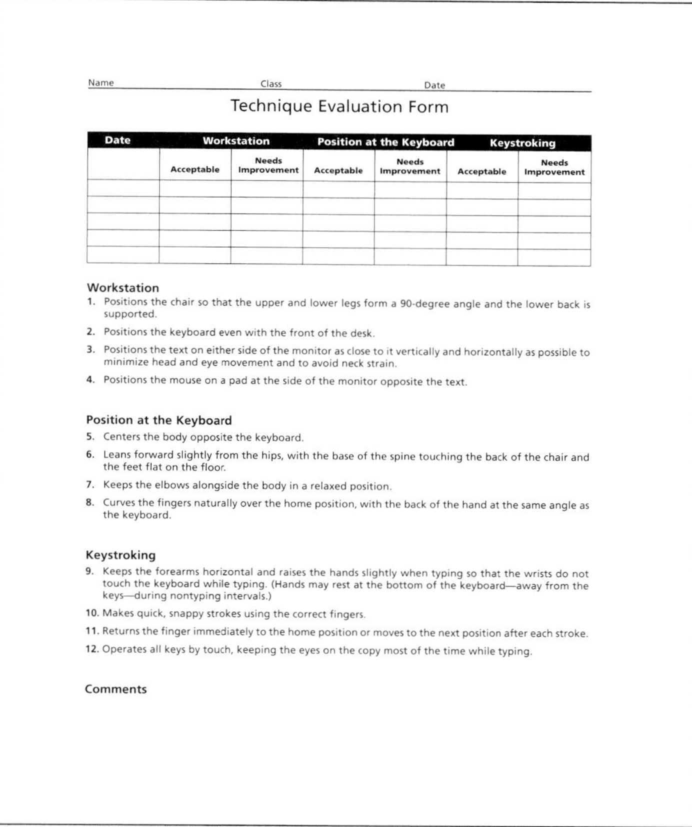

Name ______ Class ______ Date ______

Technique Evaluation Form

Date	Workstation		Position at the Keyboard		Keystroking	
	Acceptable	Needs Improvement	Acceptable	Needs Improvement	Acceptable	Needs Improvement

Workstation

1. Positions the chair so that the upper and lower legs form a 90-degree angle and the lower back is supported.
2. Positions the keyboard even with the front of the desk.
3. Positions the text on either side of the monitor as close to it vertically and horizontally as possible to minimize head and eye movement and to avoid neck strain.
4. Positions the mouse on a pad at the side of the monitor opposite the text.

Position at the Keyboard

5. Centers the body opposite the keyboard.
6. Leans forward slightly from the hips, with the base of the spine touching the back of the chair and the feet flat on the floor.
7. Keeps the elbows alongside the body in a relaxed position.
8. Curves the fingers naturally over the home position, with the back of the hand at the same angle as the keyboard.

Keystroking

9. Keeps the forearms horizontal and raises the hands slightly when typing so that the wrists do not touch the keyboard while typing. (Hands may rest at the bottom of the keyboard—away from the keys—during nontyping intervals.)
10. Makes quick, snappy strokes using the correct fingers.
11. Returns the finger immediately to the home position or moves to the next position after each stroke.
12. Operates all keys by touch, keeping the eyes on the copy most of the time while typing.

Comments

The form should be used frequently during the early stages of instruction and occasionally thereafter. At no point in the development of keyboarding and document processing skill should proper typing technique be ignored.

Students are rated as either acceptable or in need of improvement on three separate factors:

- Workstation
- Position at the keyboard
- Keystroking

One way to use the form is to have each student rate himself or herself; then the instructor rates each student. Periodically, have students simply read through the Technique Evaluation Form so that they are reminded of proper techniques. During these sessions, the instructor might want to demonstrate proper technique and discuss the role technique plays in terms of speed and accuracy as well as in avoiding fatigue and physical injury.

BUILDING STRAIGHT-COPY SKILL

As discussed earlier (see Principle 5 on page PH-8), straight-copy skillbuilding should be stressed at every level of instruction, primarily for two reasons: (1) most office workers must pass a straight-copy typing test for initial employment; and (2) word processing software makes document production much like straight-copy typing because it automates much of the decision making and machine adjustments.

CONCEPTS FOR BUILDING STRAIGHT-COPY SKILL

A number of factors serve as the basis for building, maintaining, and improving speed and accuracy. These factors should be stressed heavily during the initial stages of instruction and should be reinforced as needed thereafter.

Early Accuracy. At the very outset, a respectable level of accuracy (perhaps no more than 3 errors per minute) should be the goal. If that level can be attained within the first few weeks, refining it to an even higher level will not be difficult.

Learners developing any new skill will make inaccurate responses during their initial attempts, and you should focus on proper typing technique during the early lessons. However, the instructor who says that errors do not matter in the early lessons will surely regret those words later.

Systematic Push for Speed. Typing speed does not come naturally as a by-product of something else. It comes only by intention, conscious effort, thought, and practice.

The push for speed must be gradual; the speed goals themselves should increase gradually. For example, in most five-lesson units in GDP, the speed goal increases by only 1 word per minute.

Some aspect of typing should be timed (and recorded) every day—if only to keep students time-conscious and speed-conscious.

Also, it should be remembered that fatigue affects speed just as it affects accuracy. Speedbuilding routines are best administered during the first part of the class period to minimize the adverse effects of fatigue.

Intent. Speed and accuracy require conscious effort. No one ever typed quickly or accurately by accident; one must *intend* to type quickly or accurately. Thus you must constantly keep the goals of speed or accuracy before students.

However, you should realize that students cannot stress speed and accuracy simultaneously during their skill drives. Every skillbuilding routine should have as a goal speed *or* accuracy—not both.

Grading Emphasis. One of the easiest and most effective strategies that you can use to encourage speed or accuracy is to vary the weight of the speed or accuracy portion of the score on document processing jobs. If students are putting too much stress on speed to the detriment of accuracy, increasing the accuracy standards is the way to let your students know how important you consider accuracy to be. Similarly, if students are "obsessing" on accuracy to the detriment of speed, increase your speed standards.

Another way of letting your students know the importance you attach to accuracy or speed is the manner in which you ask for timed writing results. Instructors who want students to be more conscious of accuracy will ask for accuracy scores first; those who want students to be more conscious of speed will ask for speed scores first—always in the form of "Who increased his or her speed during that timed writing?" (but not "Who typed at least 40 words per minute?"—since speed goals should always be attainable and, therefore, individualized).

MAP (Misstroke Analysis and Prescription)

The MAP program is a highly sophisticated, individualized error analysis and remediation software program that is comprehensive and simple to use. MAP was introduced in the *9th* edition of GDP and has no counterpart anywhere else in keyboard publishing.

The following is a brief discussion of the format, procedure, and benefits of using MAP. A more detailed discussion of the manner in which MAP analyzes errors and the types of errors analyzed, as well as a sample error analysis and a review of related literature and research, is provided on the College Keyboarding Web site at www.mhhe.com/gdp.

Format. The heart of the program is the Error MAP (shown below), a one-shot identification of all the errors made on the pretest paragraph and the recommended prescriptive drills to correct these errors.

MAP identifies and remediates 75 different types of misstrokes that are included in Table 1 on page PH-15.

Procedure. The student begins by typing a random passage of 2 paragraphs (there are 16 passages in all). Each passage contains at least two occurrences of each letter and at least one occurrence of each punctuation mark and nonprinting character.

The program then analyzes the student's typing and displays the Error MAP. In the sample screen shown below, student Kate Gates made 44 errors on the pretest paragraph (0 misstrokes and 42 concentration and 2 nonprinting errors). Each error is identified either on the keyboard or in the boxes to the right of or below the keyboard.

The student can click any labeled key or box on the Error MAP to receive intensive practice on that reach. However, the software program recommends up to four remedial drills (in order of need). Students can click on any one of the recommended drills to immediately move to the selected

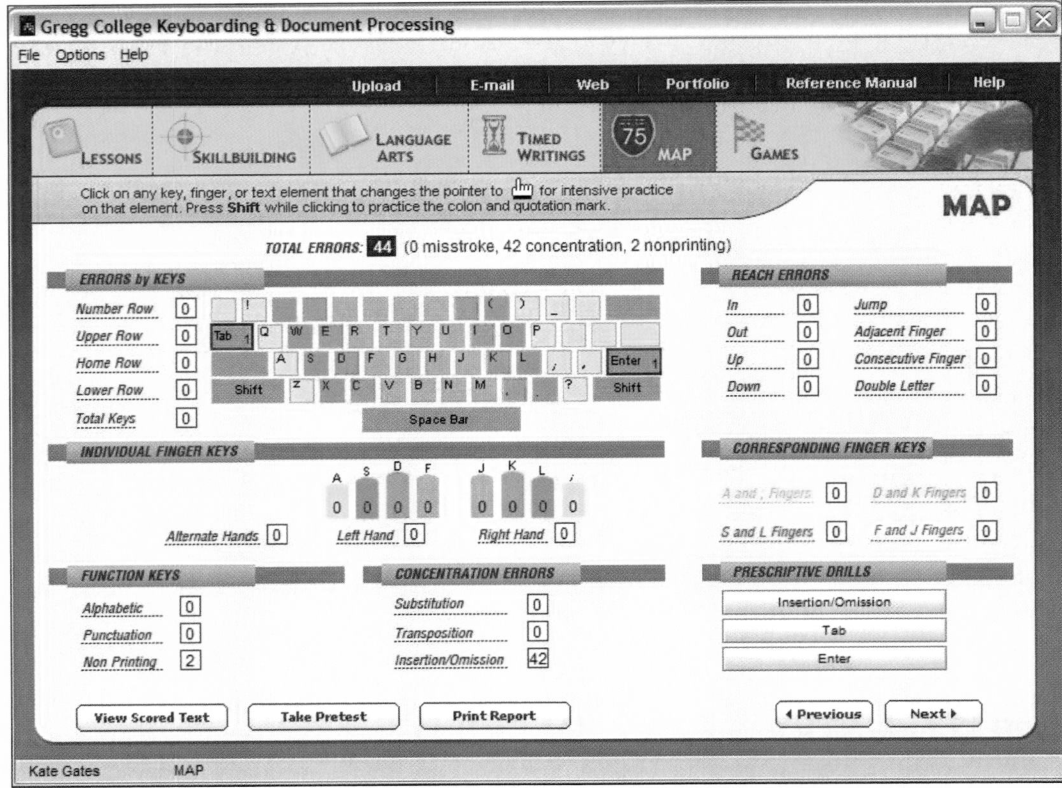

Table 1. TYPES OF MISSTROKING ERRORS IDENTIFIED IN MAP (N = 75)

Type	*Error*	*Explanation*		
Concentration (N = 3)	Insertion/Omission	Adding or leaving out a character or word.		
	Substitution	Making one of the following most common substitution errors: *R* for *T*, *M* for *N*, *I* for *O*, *A* for *S*, *D* for *S*, *E* for *R*, or *V* for *B* (or vice versa).		
	Transposition	Typing two consecutive characters correctly but in the wrong order.		
Keyboard (N = 1)		Mistyping any printed character.		
Individual Character (N = 37)	Alphabetic	Misstroking one of the 26 alphabetic characters: *A B C D E F G H I J K L M N O P Q R S T U V W X Y or Z.*		
	Punctuation	Misstroking one of the 11 punctuation marks: *! ( ) - ; : ' " , .* or *?.*		
Individual Finger (N = 8)	*Finger:*	*Misstroking:*	*Finger:*	*Misstroking:*
	A	*! Q A* or *Z*	J	*Y U H J N* or *M*
	S	*W S* or *X*	K	*I K* or *,*
	D	*E D* or *C*	L	*(O L* or *.*
	F	*R T F G V* or *B*	;	*) - P ; : ' "* or *?*
Corresponding Finger (N = 4)		*Making one of the following mirror-image errors:*		
	A and Sem	*A* for Sem or *Q* for *P* (or vice versa)		
	S and *L*	*S* for *L*, *W* for *O*, or *X* for period (or vice versa)		
	D and *K*	*D* for *K*, *E* for *I*, or *C* for comma (or vice versa)		
	F and *J*	*G* for *H*, *F* for *J*, *T* for *Y*, *R* for *U*, *B* for *N*, or *V* for *M* (or vice versa)		
Hand (N = 3)	Left	Misstroking *! Q W E R T A S D F G Z X C V* or *B*.		
	Right	Misstroking *( ) - Y U I O P H J K L ; : '* or *"*.		
	Alternate-hand	Misstroking the second of two consecutive keys controlled by fingers of opposite hands.		
Row (N = 4)	Number, upper home, and lower rows	Misstroking any key located on that particular row of the keyboard.		
Function (N = 7)	*Printing:*	Misstroking any of the printing keys.		
	Nonprinting:	Incorrectly pressing or failing to press the nonprinting keys.		
Reach (N = 8)	In	Misstroking the second of two consecutive same-hand alphabetic keys that move from the outside of the keyboard toward the inside.		
	Out	Misstroking the second of two consecutive same-hand alphabetic keys that move from the inside of the keyboard toward the outside.		
	Up	Misstroking the second of two consecutive same-hand alphabetic keys that move from one row to the next-higher row.		
	Down	Misstroking the second of two consecutive same-hand alphabetic keys that move from one row to the next-lower row.		
	Jump	Misstroking the second of two consecutive same-hand alphabetic keys that move from the lower alphabetic row to the upper alphabetic row (or vice versa).		
	Adjacent	Misstroking the second of two consecutive same-hand alphabetic keys that are immediately to the right or left of the previous key but typed with a different finger.		
	Consecutive finger	Misstroking the second of two consecutive same-hand alphabetic keys that are typed consecutively by the same finger (excluding double letters).		
	Double letter	Misstroking either double letter.		

exercise. For example, if the student clicked the ENTER key, an exercise similar to the one below would appear.

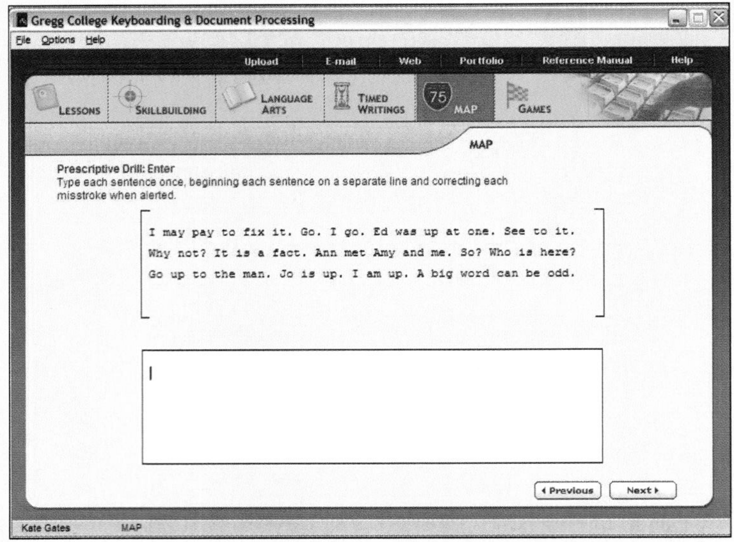

Because the drill lines are composed randomly by the software program, based upon specially developed dictionaries, every time the student accesses a prescriptive drill, new drill lines appear.

Student Benefits. MAP provides the following unique benefits:

- ***Simple.*** A single menu provides one-click access to all accuracy drills.
- ***Comprehensive.*** A total of 75 different accuracy problems are identified and practiced.
- ***Individualized.*** The prescriptive drills are based on the student's demonstrated accuracy deficiencies.
- ***Fast and Efficient.*** Each drill is made up of three lines of words—all crammed with examples of the problem reach.
- ***Motivational.*** The drills change with every access. No matter how many times students access the same prescriptive drill, *new* drill lines appear.
- ***Research-Based.*** Scientific error analysis has a long history in psychology and education. (Refer to the GDP Web site referenced earlier for a discussion of numerous research reports and journal articles that help provide a theoretical basis for the study of keyboarding accuracy and support for the use of MAP in developing keyboarding skill.)

Error analysis has many supporters. Here are some of their comments.

Most writers agree that diagnosis must precede cure. . . . The typing teacher must diagnose her students' difficulties and determine the nature and causes of errors before she can cure her students.

E. G. Blackstone and Sofrona L. Smith,
Improvement of Instruction in Typewriting

By recording the number and kinds of errors made by his students, a teacher may ascertain the exact kind of difficulties which cause them the most trouble and apply a remedy that will prevent or correct them at once.

William F. Book, *Learning to Typewrite*

There is but one intelligent approach to errors. It lies in your asking, "Why have I made this particular mistake?" . . . With the error as your cue, you will first look for your underlying difficulty. After finding the real trouble, you will plan to remove it.

August Dvorak et al., *Typewriting Behavior*

An analysis of errors must be made by and for each pupil. It is absolutely essential that the individual pupil's errors be studied in order that corrective drill work may be given for these particular difficulties.

D. D. Lessenberry,
Teacher's Manual, 20th Century Touch Typewriting

Practice in and of itself does not make perfect. It is correct *practice that makes perfect. One must practice the* correct *thing, the* correct *way, at the* correct *time in order to achieve the* correct *results.*

Cortez Peters, *Championship Keyboarding Drills*

Analysis of errors on timed writings will provide all the data necessary for a determination of needed remedial practice for a student.

Allien B. Russon and S. J. Wanous,
Philosophy and Psychology of Teaching Typewriting

PROGRESSIVE PRACTICE

The Progressive Practice program is designed to build straight-copy speed and accuracy in short, easy steps using individualized goals and immediate feedback. This program can be used at any point after Lesson 9, when all the alphabet keys have been introduced.

Format. Each passage contains the exact number of words needed to reach a particular 30-second speed goal *with no errors*. The passages range from 16 to 104 wpm.

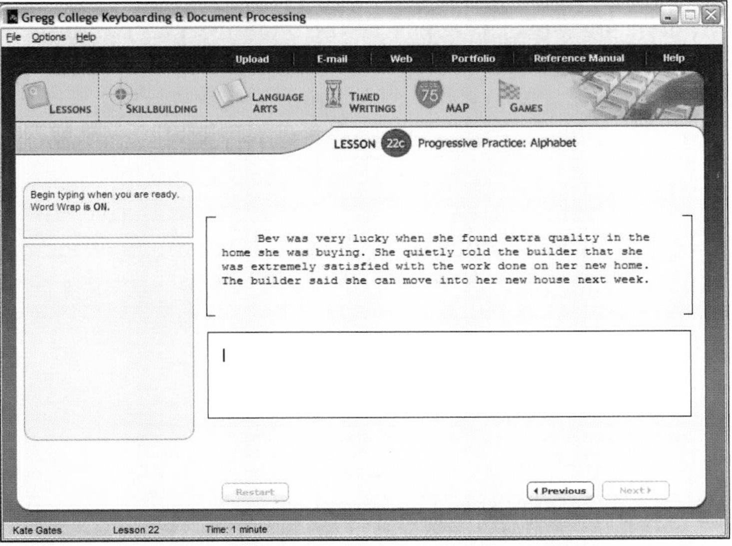

Procedure. The first time the Progressive Practice program is used, the student takes a 1-minute timed writing test to establish his or her base rate. The software then automatically displays a passage that is 2 or 3 wpm higher than the speed achieved on the test passage. Students then take a series of six 30-second timed writings. They repeat each passage until they can complete it within 30 seconds with no errors. Then they progress to the next, slightly longer passage.

The software automatically keeps track of progress and either redisplays the same passage (if the goal was not met) or displays the next passage. When students access the Progressive Practice program the next time, the appropriate passage is displayed, based on the student's last best performance.

Student Benefits. The Progressive Practice program enables each student to work at his or her own speed. The program also encourages self-competition. Students compete against themselves rather than against the class; thus the goals are motivational and realistic. Finally, this type of speed forcing is a proven way to break students of the habit of looking at the keys as they type.

PACED PRACTICE

The Paced Practice program is an individualized skill-development program designed to help students alternate between speed and accuracy improvement. The program can be used at any point after Lesson 9.

Format. Each passage contains the exact number of words needed to reach a particular 2-minute goal. The passages range from 16 to 96 wpm.

Procedure. The first time the Paced Practice program is used, the student takes a 1-minute timed writing test to establish his or her base rate. The software then automatically displays the appropriate passage with *either* a speed or an accuracy goal. Note in the illustration below, for example, that this particular student is working toward a *speed* goal of 50 wpm.

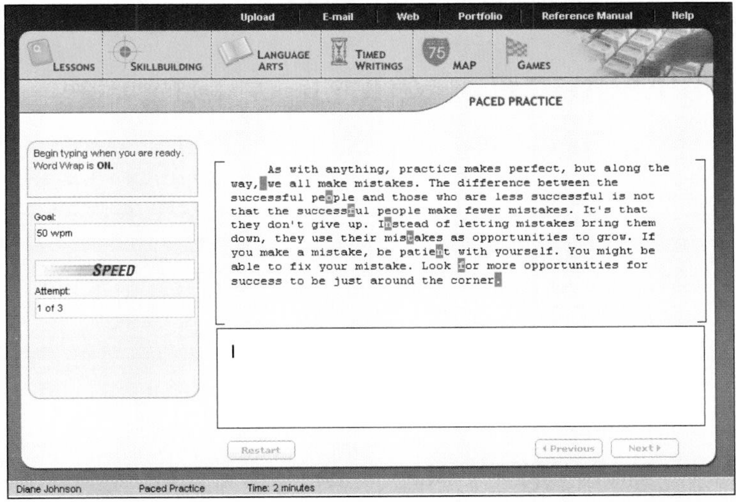

Speed Goal. When speed is the goal, students type the passage until they can complete it within 2 minutes without regard to the number of errors made. Then they switch and work on accuracy.

Accuracy Goal. To type accurately, students need to slow down—*just a bit*. Therefore, to reach their accuracy goal, the software drops back 2 wpm to the previous passage. Students type the passage until they can complete it within 2 minutes with no more than 2 errors. Then the software moves forward 4 wpm and works for speed again.

Note that, when completing a Paced Practice exercise using the GDP software, some of the characters in the passage are highlighted. These highlighted characters indicate how much text should be typed every 15 seconds to achieve the speed goal. Every 15 seconds the next highlighting disappears. Students should pace their typing to reach the highlighted character just before the highlighting disappears—typing neither too fast nor too slow. When a goal has been reached, the software automatically advances to the next timed writing.

Student Benefits. To increase speed, students should speed up—just a little. To increase accuracy, they should slow down—just a little. Any extreme variation in speed—either typing grossly faster or slower than a normal, comfortable speed—is detrimental to skill development.

The problem, of course, is knowing just how much "a little" change in speed is. Students should be instructed to pace their typing so that they are within a couple of characters before or after the highlighted character when the highlighting disappears. By the end of the 2-minute timed writing, students should be able to pace their speed accurately, thereby enhancing their chances of achieving their goal.

DIAGNOSTIC PRACTICE

The Diagnostic Practice program is designed to diagnose and then correct students' keystroking errors in two different environments: (1) symbols and punctuation copy and (2) number copy.

Format. The practice portion consists of 18 sets of drills (for symbol or punctuation copy) or 10 sets of drills (for number copy). Note in the illustration below that each drill line provides practice in typing a specific symbol, punctuation mark, or number key.

PRACTICE: **Symbols and Punctuation Reaches**

```
frf fr4 f4f f$f f$f f$f $40 $44 $44 f$f f4f $ff $45 $54 $$$
$40 and $82 and $90 and $13 and $33 and $56 and $86 and $25
$214 plus $882 plus $900 plus $718 plus $910 plus $112 plus
$1,937.53 plus $337.89 tax $3,985.43 minus $150.75 discount
```

PRACTICE: **Number Reaches**

```
2 sw sw2 sw2ws 222 sets 242 steps 226 salads 252 saddles s2
The 272 summer tourists saw the 22 soldiers and 32 sailors.
Your September 2 date was all right for 292 of 322 persons.
The 22 surgeons said 221 of those 225 operations went well.
```

Procedure. The student types a practice paragraph that contains at least one occurrence of each symbol or punctuation mark or each number reach. The software scores the typing and indicates how many errors were made on each character. For any key on which students made more than 1 error, they must type the appropriate drill twice. For any key on which they made 1 error, they must type the entire drill once. Finally, students retype the practice paragraph and note any progress made.

Student Benefits. The Diagnostic Practice program provides individualized practice by focusing students' efforts on their demonstrated weaknesses.

One benefit of using the program over a period of time is that students can easily see which reaches initially caused them problems but have now been mastered and which reaches continue to present problems. The record of their improvement builds confidence; the record of their continuing problems provides the motivation to try harder.

PRETEST/PRACTICE/POSTTEST

The Pretest/Practice/Posttest (PPP) program is designed to build straight-copy speed and accuracy through a three-step program that focuses on either speed or accuracy, depending on pretest performance.

Format. The program consists of three sections:

1. The Pretest is the preliminary effort to determine the learner's initial skill level.
2. The Practice section consists of intensive drills to improve the reaches focused on in the Pretest.
3. The Posttest measures the effect of the practice.

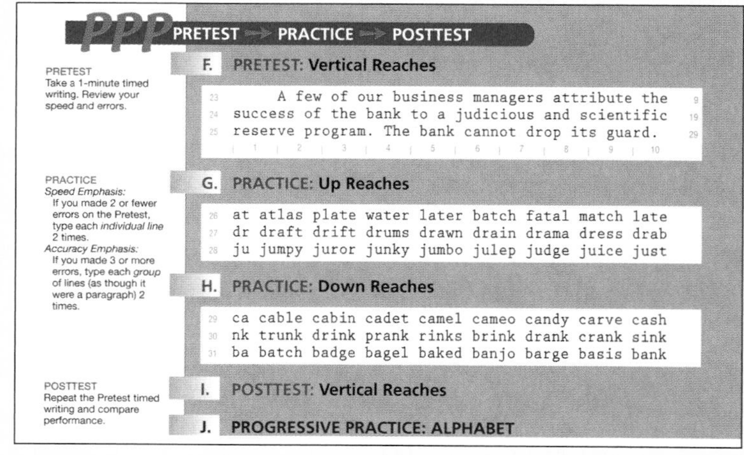

Procedure. The student takes a 1-minute timed writing on the Pretest, and the software determines the speed and errors. If the student made 2 or fewer errors on the Pretest (no more than

1 error in Lessons 61–120), he or she types each *individual* line 2 times. If 3 or more errors were made (2 or more in Lessons 61–120), the student types each *group* of lines (as though it were a paragraph) 2 times. Finally, students repeat the Pretest timed writing and compare performance.

Student Benefits. Each time, students work on either accuracy or speed, depending on their Pretest results. In addition, PPP provides intensive practice on six different types of reaches:

- Horizontal reaches
- Vertical reaches
- Close reaches
- Alternate- and one-hand words
- Common letter combinations
- Discrimination practice

12-SECOND SPEED SPRINTS

The 12-Second Speed Sprints foster speed improvement through the use of fast, repetitive typing on short, easy sentences without an error limit.

Format. Each drill consists of four 1-line sentences made up of easy words to type.

B. 12-SECOND SPEED SPRINTS

A good neighbor paid for these ancient ornaments.
Today I sit by the big lake and count huge rocks.
The four chapels sit by the end of the old field.
The signal means help is on its way to the child.
5 10 15 20 25 30 35 40 45 50

Procedure. Students take three 12-second timed writings on each line. Although the software automatically computes the typing speed, the scale below the last line shows the wpm speed for a 12-second timed writing. The goal is to increase one's speed on each successive typing of the line.

Student Benefits. Students enjoy these speed sprints because they can achieve much higher speeds by typing for just 12 seconds on easy copy. Thus, the practice is motivational. Because the software automatically times the student, instructors don't have to worry about students trying to squeeze in an extra letter or two (on a 12-second timed writing, each extra letter typed increases the wpm speed by 1 word).

SUSTAINED PRACTICE

The Sustained Practice program develops increased speed. Students are challenged to maintain or exceed their initial speed level on copy of increasing difficulty.

Format. The practice lines consist of four paragraphs of the same length. Each paragraph is more difficult than the preceding one, based on one of several difficulty factors:

- Syllabic intensity
- Numbers and symbols
- Punctuation
- Rough-draft symbols
- Alternate-hand words
- Capital letters

For example, in the illustration shown below, each paragraph is more difficult than the preceding one, based on syllabic intensity (average number of syllables per word):

Para. 1: SI = 1.35
Para. 2: SI = 1.47
Para. 3: SI = 1.62
Para. 4: SI = 1.88

C. SUSTAINED PRACTICE: SYLLABIC INTENSITY

Taking care of aging parents is not a new trend. This 11
issue has arisen more and more, since we are now living 22
longer. Companies are now trying to help out in many ways. 34
Help may come in many ways, ranging from financial aid 12
to sponsoring hospice or in-home respite care. Workers may 24
find it difficult to work and care for aging parents. 35
Why are employers so interested in elder care? Rising 11
interest is the result of a combination of several things. 23
The most notable is a marked increase in life expectancy. 34
Another trend is the increased participation of women, 11
the primary caregivers, in the workforce. Businesses are 22
recognizing that work and family life are intertwined. 33
1 2 3 4 5 6 7 8 9 10 11 12

Procedure. Students take a 1-minute timed writing on the first paragraph to establish their base speed. Then they take four 1-minute timed writings on the remaining paragraphs. As soon as they equal or exceed their base speed on one paragraph, they advance to the next, more difficult paragraph.

Student Benefits. This drill is different from others in that the goal is to *maintain* speed rather than to *increase* speed. The "catch," of course, is that the copy in each paragraph gets more difficult to type. As always, the drill is individualized, with students competing against their previous best efforts. Thus, the goal is always attainable.

A SKILLBUILDING *SYSTEM*

No matter how effective individual skillbuilding routines are, they lose much of their effectiveness if they are not used in a *systematic* and scientific manner to build skill. As illustrated in Table 2, GDP systematically cycles these skillbuilding routines throughout the 120 lessons (24 units) to provide maximum benefit, constant refreshment of skill, and motivation.

BUILDING NUMBER-TYPING SKILL

A competent typist should be able to use all the keys on the keyboard, including the number keys, with both speed and accuracy. Considering the importance of numerical data in the contemporary office, it is easy to understand why management expects typists to be proficient in number typing.

Whether a person is typing dates, telephone numbers, social security numbers, order numbers, inventory numbers, or

Table 2. A SKILLBUILDING *SYSTEM*

Routine Unit:	3	4	5	6	7	8	9	10	11	12	13	14	15	16	17	18	19	20	21	22	23	24
Warmups (5 per unit)	■	■	■	■	■	■	■	■	■	■	■	■	■	■	■	■	■	■	■	■	■	■
MAP (1 per unit)	■	■	■	■	■	■	■	■	■	■	■	■	■	■	■	■	■	■	■	■	■	■
Diagnostic Practice:																						
Symbols and Punctuation			■	■	■	■	■	■	■	■	■	■	■	■	■	■	■	■	■	■	■	■
Numbers		■		■		■		■		■		■		■		■		■		■		■
Progressive Practice:																						
Alphabet (1–2 per unit)	■	■	■	■	■	■	■	■	■	■	■	■	■	■	■	■	■	■	■	■	■	■
Numbers	■		■		■		■		■		■		■		■		■		■		■	
Pretest/Practice/Posttest:																						
Vertical Reaches	■						■						■						■			
Alternate/One-Hand Words		■						■						■						■		
Common Letter Combinations			■						■						■						■	
Close Reaches				■						■						■						■
Discrimination Practice					■						■						■					
Horizontal Reaches						■						■						■				
12" Sprints (1–2 per unit)	■	■	■	■	■	■	■	■	■	■	■	■	■	■	■	■	■	■	■	■	■	■
Sustained Practice:																						
Syllabic Intensity	■						■						■						■			
Numbers and Symbols		■						■						■						■		
Capitals			■						■						■						■	
Punctuation				■						■						■						■
Alternate-Hand Words					■						■						■					
Rough Draft						■						■						■				
Paced Practice (1–2 per unit)	■	■	■	■	■	■	■	■	■	■	■	■	■	■	■	■	■	■	■	■	■	■
Technique Practice:																						
Space Bar	■						■						■						■			
Enter Key		■						■						■						■		
Tab Key			■						■						■						■	
Concentration				■						■						■						■
Backspace Key					■						■						■					
Shift and Caps Lock						■						■						■				
Timed Writings (2–3 per unit)	■	■	■	■	■	■	■	■	■	■	■	■	■	■	■	■	■	■	■	■	■	■

amounts of money, accuracy is essential. An error that occurs in typing numbers could be much more serious than an error on alphabetic copy. For example, typing *$5,800* instead of *$8,500* can be a much more costly error than typing *teh* for *the*.

INTRODUCING THE NUMBER KEYS

The top-row number keys are taught in Unit 3 (Lessons 11–15), immediately after the alphabet keys are learned.

Your role in motivating students during this unit is critical. Impress upon them the importance of touch-typing numbers accurately. Your enthusiastic and positive introduction of the top-row keys will help students develop confidence that they can, indeed, master these keys.

The text and GDP software follow the same procedure in introducing the number keys as in introducing alphabet keys. Each new key is introduced in four lines. The first line provides practice in the reach from the home row. Students should look as their fingers make the reach to the new letter the first several times; thereafter, they should make the reach by touch. Lines 2–4 of the new-key drill move quickly to having students type words, phrases, and then sentences.

Throughout the unit, stress (and demonstrate, if possible) the importance of good technique to the students. Ensure that no parts of lessons are skipped. Indeed, some parts may be repeated if needed for number-typing mastery.

NUMBER-TYPING PRACTICE

GDP provides ample opportunity for students to maintain and increase their number-typing skill in every unit following the number-key introduction.

Warmups. Every warmup exercise contains numbers. In fact, every numeral occurs three to five times in the warmups for each unit.

Diagnostic Practice—Numbers. Every even-numbered unit contains a Diagnostic Practice emphasizing numbers. (See the discussion of Diagnostic Practice on page PH-18 for further information.)

Progressive Practice—Numbers. Every odd-numbered unit contains a Progressive Practice emphasizing numbers. (See the discussion of Progressive Practice on pages PH-16 and PH-17 for further information.)

Sustained Practice—Numbers and Symbols. Four units (4, 10, 16, and 22) contain a Sustained Practice emphasizing numbers and symbols. (See the discussion of Sustained Practice on page PH-19 for further information.)

Additional Practice. For instructors wishing even more number-practice exercises, three pages of number drills that can be duplicated for classroom use are provided at the GDP Web site (www.mhhe.com/gdp).

TEACHING THE NUMERIC KEYPAD

Most computer keyboards contain a separate numeric keypad located to the right of the alphanumeric keyboard. With a keypad students can learn to type numbers by placing the J, K, and L fingers on the 4, 5, and 6 keypad keys. This method can be very efficient if only numbers are being typed. If numbers are mixed with words, however, students should use the regular keyboard, with the numbers on the top row.

The GDP software program contains a separate module for teaching the ten-key numeric keypad by touch.

BUILDING DOCUMENT PROCESSING SKILL

The development of document processing skill is the *terminal* goal of keyboarding instruction (straight-copy skill is an *enabling* goal). Students must be able to apply their straight-copy skills to various real-life personal and office document processing tasks that they will encounter when their classroom days have ended.

Straight-copy skillbuilding, the study of technical information, and assessment strategies are the means by which the objective of possessing competent document processing skills is achieved. Both speed and accuracy are, of course, critical prerequisites (or corequisites) of competent document processing skill. Students should be able to type at least 25 wpm on a 2-minute timed writing before beginning their study of document processing.

The instructor is *absolutely critical* in the document processing stages of skill development. Use the instructional techniques discussed later in this section to assist students in applying creative judgments in a correct and efficient manner.

A DOCUMENT PROCESSING *SYSTEM*

As explained in Principle 10 on page PH-9, the sequence of document processing activities should be based on a systematic spiral approach. The major types of documents are cycled systematically throughout the GDP program. This unique organizational plan prevents boredom (lesson after lesson of the same type of document) and permits a smooth, easy-to-complex flow of learning. As illustrated in Table 3 on page PH-23, students first learn how to format simple reports in Unit 6. They then switch to learning how to format simple correspondence and tables and then return to more complex reports in Unit 9 and again in Units 14 and 17.

Similarly, word processing commands are introduced systematically. They begin with the most basic commands in the first document processing unit (Unit 5). More advanced commands are then introduced systematically, on a need-to-know basis, as they are needed to format documents. After the orientation lessons, no more than two word processing commands are introduced in any one lesson.

STAGES OF DOCUMENT PROCESSING INSTRUCTION

When introducing document processing, the competent instructor does more than simply make the assignments in the text and turn students loose on their own. Students will develop their document processing skills most efficiently if the instructor supplements the text and software instruction with effective classroom instruction and management procedures.

The three stages of document processing instruction discussed below assume an in-class environment. Instructors teaching in a distance-learning environment will need to make appropriate adjustments. (See pages PH-54 to PH-59 for instruction on teaching in a distance-learning environment.)

Directed Document Processing. When students are introduced to a particular formatting job (a business letter, for example), you should provide a good deal of control over the learning activities. Directed activities, therefore, are those in which you tightly control the learning experience. The goals and techniques are explained, and the pace, as well as the starting and stopping times, is established. You direct each step—to the point of dictating instructions, providing formatting commands, explaining the placement of the text on the page, and calling the beginning and ending times so as to force the pace while students type.

Students must be taught to form associations between one step and the next. For example, an association must be formed between typing the date for a letter and spacing down 6 times to type the salutation. These associations are most rapidly made when there is minimal time between the stimulus and the response.

Table 3. A DOCUMENT PROCESSING *SYSTEM*

Unit	*Content*	*Word Processing*
1	Keyboarding—The Alphabet	
2	Keyboarding—The Alphabet	
3	Keyboarding—The Numbers	
4	Keyboarding—The Symbols	
5	E-Mail and Orientation to Word Processing	Start Your Word Processor Choose a Command Open a File Quit Your Word Processor Navigate in a File Save a File Close a File New Select Text Bold Undo/Redo a Command Help Preview Pages Before Printing Check Spelling and Grammar Show Formatting Print
6	Reports	Alignment Font Size Page Numbering Page Break Bullets and Numbering Line Spacing Indent Cut, Copy, and Paste
7	Correspondence	Insert Date Envelopes Labels Italic Underline
8	Tables	Table—Create Table—AutoFit to Contents Table—Merge Cells Table—Borders Table—Center Horizontally Table—Center Page Table—Align Text in a Column
9	**Reports**	Footnotes Margins Headers and Footers Hanging Indent Tab Set—Dot Leaders
10	Correspondence	Ruler Tabs and Tab Set
11	Employment Documents	Fonts Table—Change Column Width Saving in Text-Only Format
12	Skillbuilding and In-Basket Review	
13	Skill Refinement	
14	Reports	Hyphenation Columns
15	Correspondence	Sort Shading Find and Replace
16	Tables	Table—Text Direction Table—Insert or Delete Rows or Columns Page Orientation Repeating Table Heading Rows Table—AutoFormat
17	Formal Report Project	Styles Insert Clip Art and Files
18	International Formatting	Paper Size Insert Symbol
19	Medical Office Documents	
20	Legal Office Documents	Line Numbering
21	Using and Designing Business Documents	Templates Small Caps Text Box Print Options
22	Designing Office Publications	Word Art Table—Move
23	Designing Web Pages	
24	Skillbuilding and In-Basket Review	

Directed production is recommended for a new experience in any document processing activity. Disregard tasks that students have already mastered. Concentrate instead on what is *new*—for example, the first subject line in a letter, the first open table, or the first endnote in a report.

The primary objective for directed formatting activities is to teach students the proper format for each type of document processing task—for example, the correct layout for a letter or a memo.

These directed formatting activities are designed to increase the rate of document processing.

Guided Document Processing. Guided document processing activities are a natural follow-up to the directed document processing activities described above. With guided activities, all the information the students need to complete the task is previewed. The objectives are explained, the work to be typed is previewed with the students, and the steps are discussed in detail. Then students are free to complete the formatting assignment.

It is vital that you observe the work process, reinforcing correct responses and offering suggestions as needed. One way that you can accomplish this is by walking up and down the aisles, making constructive comments while students work. (*Remember:* Competent keyboarding instructors teach from their *feet*—not from their seat.)

In addition, you may want to instruct students to place a printed copy of each completed job on their desks. You continue walking about, reviewing the format of the document at each student's desk and indicating approval by initialing. If the format is not correct, you may either offer comments directly to the students or write corrective comments in the margins of their documents. (For this activity, there is no need to be concerned with keystroking errors.)

Guided document processing is the pattern for much of the work in the introductory stages of formatting. For example, in the lesson in which business letters are introduced, students first receive directed practice in typing the various parts of a business letter; then they receive guided practice in typing the first letter; finally, they receive supervised practice in typing the second letter in the lesson.

Supervised Document Processing. Students must have an abundance of independent practice as they develop formatting skills. Therefore, you should move away from guided activities into supervised activities, where students work under your observation and supervision but without detailed assistance. While using this technique, you need to be aware of performance results so that you can provide remedial guidance if difficulties arise.

Decision-making skills essential for real-life activities can be acquired only through unguided practice, so quickly and constantly encourage students to "look it up." The *10th* edition of GDP contains a detailed Reference Manual at the beginning of the text—where sample documents of most kinds students will be formatting can be found. These same model documents can be found in the online Reference Manual—available from both the GDP software and within Microsoft Word when students are creating documents.

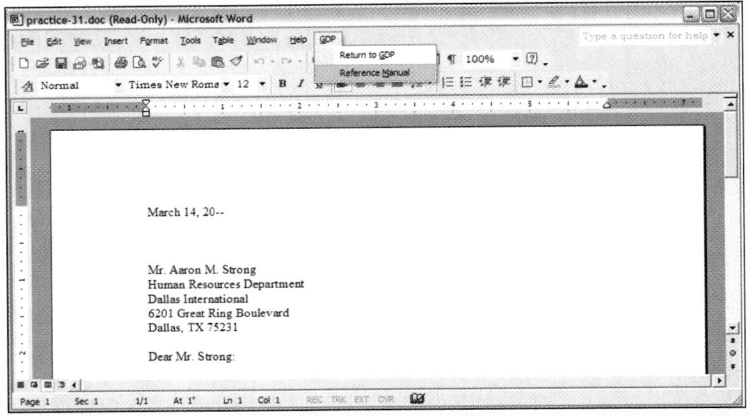

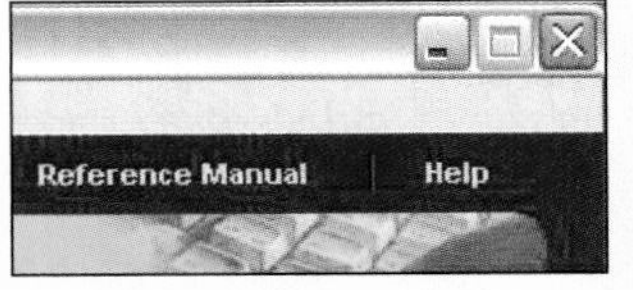

By requiring students who have questions to reread the lesson directions or refer to the text or online Reference Manual, you can help them quickly assume responsibility for their own correct document processing.

Later units in the second course of GDP (for example, Units 21–23) require *creative* document processing, with students being asked to design office forms, office publications, and Web pages.

COMPONENTS OF DOCUMENT PROCESSING

The real objective of your class is the development of formatting skills that enable the learner to quickly and accurately accomplish realistic document processing tasks, whether for personal use or for vocational purposes.

As the instructor, you are responsible for planning the classroom activities and conducting them in a manner that results in the accomplishment of this objective. Basic straight-copy skills are essential, of course, for efficient formatting. However, whereas straight-copy typing consists solely of keystroking, there are three basic components in performing a document processing task.

Planning. The first component is planning for the task. Because planning is a necessary part of the activity, instruction must be provided. Attention must be given to the need to quickly gather required materials. If a task deviates from the routine typing of copy, students must plan the formatting steps that will result in the correct layout of the finished job on the page.

Keystroking. The second component of document processing is the actual keystroking, or typing of copy. If proper attention has been given to planning, this step should proceed without undue delays and interruptions.

Proofreading. The third component is one that can be too easily overlooked. You should provide instruction and drill in proofreading. Microsoft Word has a spell-checker to aid in proofreading, and the GDP software will score the document for keystroking errors. On the job, however, students will not have their documents scored for them.

Right from the start of document processing, require students to assume final responsibility for proofreading all documents they submit. You can do this by limiting the number of attempts students have to complete a particular job. For example, the last document processing job in each unit is labeled a Progress Check/Proofreading Check. Here, students are allowed only one attempt to finish the job; that is, they cannot rely on the software to locate their errors for them to correct. They must correct all errors before exiting the word processor.

Mailable copy is a term that is often used to describe formatted copy that, in the opinion of the author of the job, is acceptable and can be sent to the intended recipient or distributed as desired. In building mailable-copy skills, GDP systematically leads students through the progressive steps of typing from properly formatted copy and then typing from copy that reflects the nature of realistic office tasks—unarranged, rough-draft, and handwritten copy.

BUILDING LANGUAGE ARTS SKILLS

As noted in Principle 11 on pages PH-9 to PH-10, competent language arts skills are an essential component of competent document processing skills.

Suppose, as happened to the senior author of this text, a student sent you an e-mail stating, in part, "im leaving for home early this weekend, so hear is all my homework jobs early." Instantly, the student has turned what should have been a good-news message into, at best, a *mixed*-news message. You are probably thinking, "If this student made four errors in a one-sentence e-mail, how many errors can I expect to find in the documents themselves?"

In short, if students can't *write* correctly, they can't *type* correctly. Thus, competent language arts skills are essential for success in the contemporary office. GDP provides systematic instruction in language arts rules, proofreading, spelling, and composing.

LANGUAGE ARTS RULES

GDP systematically teaches, practices, and reinforces 50 "must-know" language arts rules for business.

- 22 punctuation rules
- 14 grammar rules
- 14 mechanics rules

These rules are provided on pages R-15 to R-22 of the Reference Manual. They are also systematically introduced two or three at a time starting in Unit 5. First, the rules are presented in the text lesson. Then, students practice the rules by editing sentences in the software.

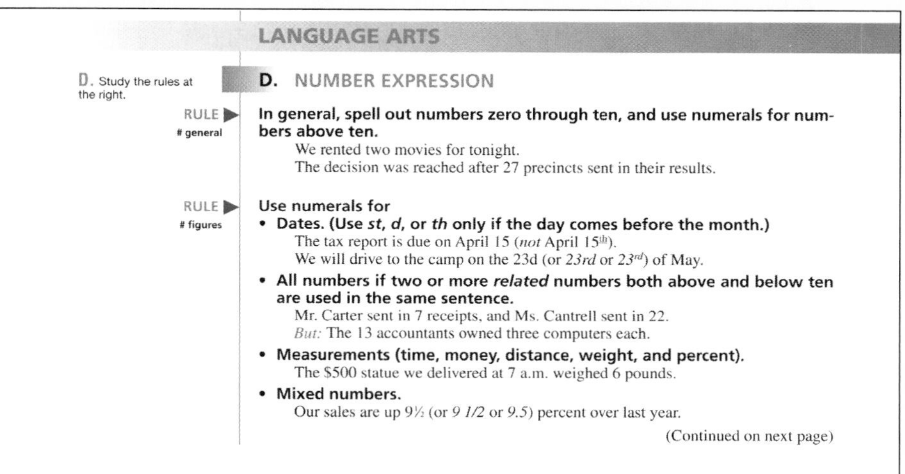
LANGUAGE ARTS

D. Study the rules at the right.

D. NUMBER EXPRESSION

RULE ▶ # general

In general, spell out numbers zero through ten, and use numerals for numbers above ten.

We rented two movies for tonight.
The decision was reached after 27 precincts sent in their results.

RULE ▶ # figures

Use numerals for

- **Dates. (Use *st*, *d*, or *th* only if the day comes before the month.)**
  The tax report is due on April 15 (*not* April 15th).
  We will drive to the camp on the 23d (or *23rd* or *23rd*) of May.
- **All numbers if two or more *related* numbers both above and below ten are used in the same sentence.**
  Mr. Carter sent in 7 receipts, and Ms. Cantrell sent in 22.
  But: The 13 accountants owned three computers each.
- **Measurements (time, money, distance, weight, and percent).**
  The $500 statue we delivered at 7 a.m. weighed 6 pounds.
- **Mixed numbers.**
  Our sales are up 9½ (or *9 1/2* or *9.5*) percent over last year.

(Continued on next page)

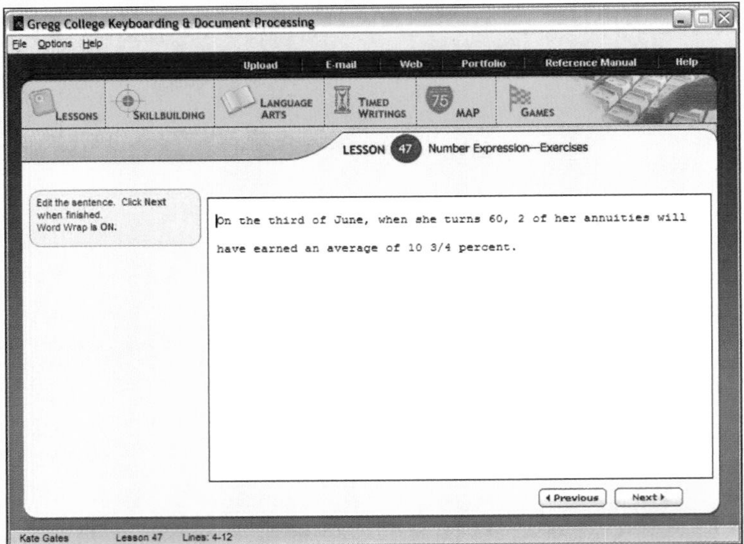

If a student makes one or more errors on the exercise, a tutorial appears that provides an in-depth, graphic discussion of the rules being presented:

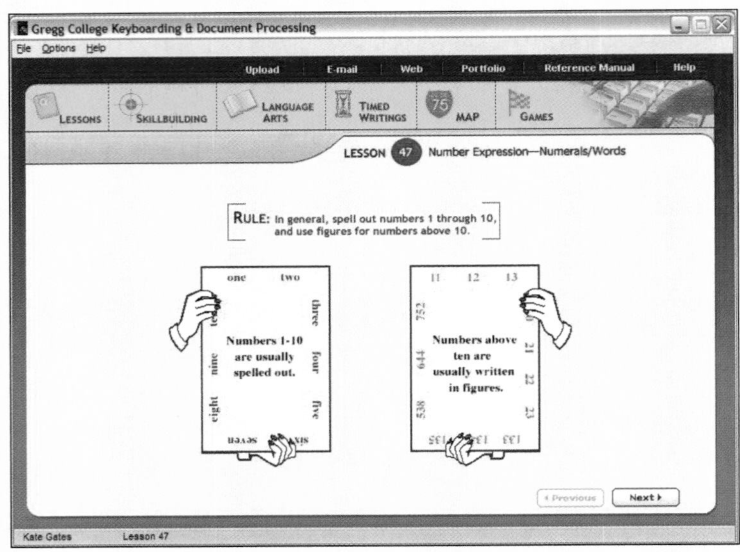

Finally, the rules presented in the lesson are reinforced in the document processing jobs in that lesson.

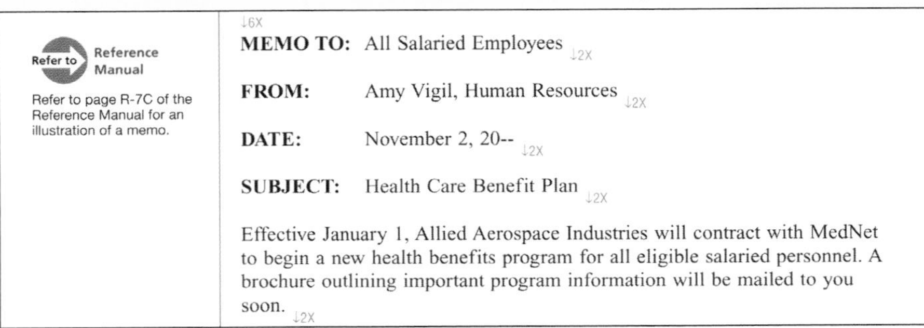

Refer to Reference Manual

Refer to page R-7C of the Reference Manual for an illustration of a memo.

↓6X

MEMO TO: All Salaried Employees ↓2X

FROM: Amy Vigil, Human Resources ↓2X

DATE: November 2, 20-- ↓2X

SUBJECT: Health Care Benefit Plan ↓2X

Effective January 1, Allied Aerospace Industries will contract with MedNet to begin a new health benefits program for all eligible salaried personnel. A brochure outlining important program information will be mailed to you soon. ↓2X

Ensure student competence on the language arts rules by requiring perfect completion of all exercises. When introducing the document processing jobs in lessons that present language arts rules, take the time to point out the application of each rule in the documents.

PROOFREADING

As stated earlier, competent proofreading skills are necessary for competent document processing skills.

In addition to proofreading every job they type, in every second unit in GDP students get an opportunity to practice their proofreading skills in special exercises in the skillbuilding section of the lesson. These exercises alternate between *comparing* (that is, comparing a typed version of a document with the original version and correcting all discrepancies) and *editing* (correcting all typing and formatting errors in a paragraph):

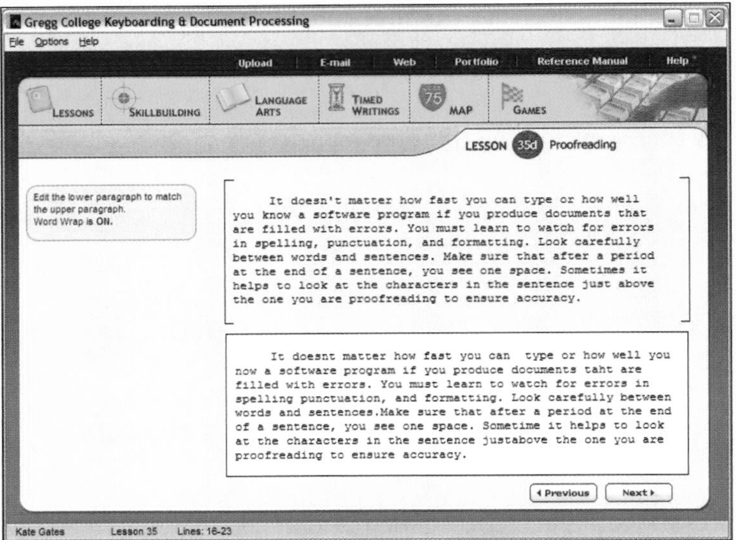

SPELLING

The English language is notorious for its spelling inconsistencies. For every spelling rule, it sometimes seems as if there are as many exceptions as there are examples of the rule.

In an effort to provide the most efficient practice of spelling skills, every second unit in GDP provides a list of 30–35 commonly misspelled business words for students to type. As with the language arts rules, students first study the words, then practice them, and later encounter them in the document processing jobs in that lesson.

The 328 words selected are taken directly from Ober's massive study of the most frequently occurring and the most frequently misspelled words in contemporary business writing (Scot Ober, "The Spelling Problems of First-Year Typewriting Students," *The NABTE Review,* Vol. 13, 1986, pages 43–47).

Considering the importance of competent spelling skills, some typing instructors elect to give a spelling test, based on the spelling words covered in that section, along with each Part Assessment Test.

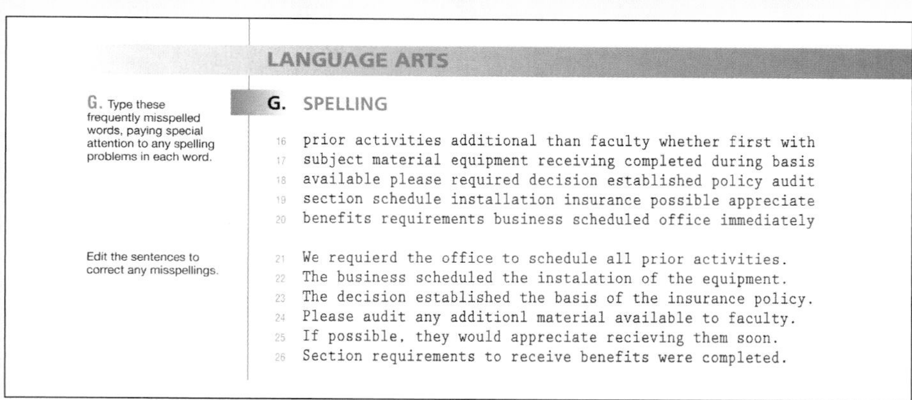

LANGUAGE ARTS

G. SPELLING

G. Type these frequently misspelled words, paying special attention to any spelling problems in each word.

prior activities additional than faculty whether first with
subject material equipment receiving completed during basis
available please required decision established policy audit
section schedule installation insurance possible appreciate
benefits requirements business scheduled office immediately

Edit the sentences to correct any misspellings.

We requierd the office to schedule all prior activities.
The business scheduled the instalation of the equipment.
The decision established the basis of the insurance policy.
Please audit any additionl material available to faculty.
If possible, they would appreciate recieving them soon.
Section requirements to receive benefits were completed.

A LANGUAGE ARTS *SYSTEM*

As shown in Table 4, the language arts rules, the proofreading and composing activities, and the business spelling words are presented systematically throughout the program. This cyclical approach prevents boredom by providing instruction in small segments.

Table 4. A LANGUAGE ARTS *SYSTEM*

Unit	Rules	Proofreading	Composing	Spelling
5. E-mail and Orientation to Word Processing	, dir ad frag run-on	Comparing	Sentences *(personal)*	
6. Reports	, ind , intro			Spelling
7. Correspondence	≡ sent ≡ prop ≡ time	Editing	Sentences *(personal)*	
8. Tables	' sing ' plur ' pro		Spelling	
9. Reports	" quote " title <u>*title*</u> , quote	Comparing	Sentences *(business)*	
10. Correspondence	# gen # fig			Spelling
11. Employment Documents	, date , place	Editing	Paragraphs *(personal)*	
12. Skillbuilding and In-Basket Review	# words - num			Spelling
13. Skill Refinement	, ser , tran	Comparing	Paragraphs *(personal)*	
14. Reports	- adj agr sing/plur abb no			Spelling
15. Correspondence	, non , adj	Editing	Paragraphs *(business)*	
16. Tables	≡ noun # ≡ region			Spelling
17. Formal Report Project	agr pro agr inter	Comparing	Documents *(personal)*	
18. International Formatting	abb meas abb lc abb ≡			Spelling
19. Medical Office Documents	: expl . req	Editing	Documents *(business—e-mail)*	
20. Legal Office Documents	; no conj ; ser			Spelling
21. Using and Designing Office Forms	adj/adv agr near	Comparing	Documents *(business—memo)*	
22. Designing Office Publications	nom pro obj pro			Spelling
23. Designing Web Pages	≡ org ≡ course	Editing	Documents *(business—letter)*	
24. Skillbuilding and In-Basket Review	Word Usage			Spelling

COURSE PLANNING GRID

PART 2, BASIC BUSINESS DOCUMENTS

Lesson	*Formatting*	*Word Processing*	*Documents*
Unit 5, E-MAIL AND WORD PROCESSING			
21. Orientation to Word Processing—A		Start Your Word Processor Choose a Command Open a File Quit Your Word Processor	
22. Orientation to Word Processing—B		Navigate in a File Save a File Close a File New	
23. Orientation to Word Processing—C		Select Text Bold Undo/Redo a Command Help	
24. Orientation to Word Processing—D		Preview Pages Before Printing Check Spelling and Grammar Show Formatting Print	
25. E-Mail Basics	Basic Parts of an E-Mail Message Formatting and Composing an E-Mail Message	E-Mail a Document	Correspondence 25-1, E-Mail Message Correspondence 25-2, E-Mail Message
Unit 6, REPORTS			
26. One-Page Business Reports	Basic Parts of a Report Business Reports Reports With Side Headings	Alignment Font Size	Report 26-1, Business Report Report 26-2, Business Report
27. Multipage Rough-Draft Business Reports	Basic Proofreaders' Marks Multipage Business Reports Business Reports With Paragraph Headings	Page Numbering Page Break	Report 27-3, Multipage Business Report Report 27-4, Multipage Business Report
28. Business Reports With Lists	Bulleted and Numbered Lists Business Reports With Lists	Bullets and Numbering Decrease Indent	Report 28-5, Business Report With Lists Report 28-6, Business Report With Lists
29. Academic Reports	More Proofreaders' Marks Academic Reports	Line Spacing	Report 29-7, Multipage Academic Report Report 29-8, Multipage Academic Report
30. Academic Reports With Displays	Academic Reports With Lists Academic Reports With Indented Displays	Increase Indent Double Indent Cut, Copy, and Paste	Report 30-9, Multipage Academic Report With List and Displayed Paragraph Report 30-10, Multipage Academic Report With List

Lesson	Formatting	Word Processing	Documents
Unit 7, Correspondence			
31. Business Letters	Basic Parts of a Business Letter Business Letters in Block Style	Insert Date	Correspondence 31-3, Business Letter in Block Style Correspondence 31-4, Business Letter in Block Style Correspondence 31-5, Business Letter in Block Style
32. Business Letters With Enclosure Notations	Enclosure Notation		Correspondence 32-6, Business Letter in Block Style Correspondence 32-7, Business Letter in Block Style Correspondence 32-8, Letter in Block Style
33. Envelopes and Labels	Envelopes Folding Letters Labels	Envelopes Labels	Correspondence 33-9, Envelope Correspondence 33-10, Envelope Correspondence 33-11, Mailing Labels Correspondence 33-12, Mailing Labels Correspondence 33-13, Envelope
34. Memos	Memos		Correspondence 34-14, Memo Correspondence 34-15, Memo Correspondence 34-16, Memo
35. Correspondence Review	Attachment Notation	Italic and Underline	Correspondence 35-17, Memo Correspondence 35-18, Memo Correspondence 35-19, Business Letter in Block Style
Unit 8, Tables			
36. Boxed Tables	Basic Parts of a Table	Table—Insert Table—AutoFit to Contents	Table 36-1, Three-Column Boxed Table Table 36-2, Two-Column Boxed Table Table 36-3, Three-Column Boxed Table Table 36-4, Three-Column Boxed Table
37. Open Tables With Titles	Table Heading Block	Table—Merge Cells Table—Borders	Table 37-5, Two-Column Open Table Table 37-6, Three-Column Open Table Table 37-7, Two-Column Open Table
38. Open Tables With Column Headings	Column Headings	Table—Center Horizontally Table—Center Page	Table 38-8, Two-Column Open Table Table 38-9, Two-Column Open Table Table 38-10, Two-Column Open Table Table 38-11, Two-Column Open Table
39. Ruled Tables With Number Columns	Ruled Tables With Number Columns	Table—Align Text in a Column	Table 39-12, Three-Column Ruled Table Table 39-13, Four-Column Ruled Table Table 39-14, Three-Column Ruled Table

COURSE PLANNING GRID

Lesson	Formatting	Word Processing	Documents
40. Formatting Review			Report 40-11, Academic Report With List Correspondence 40-20, Business Letter in Block Style With Envelope Table 40-15, Three-Column Boxed Table
TEST 2. Skills Assessment on Part 2			Correspondence Test 2-21, Business Letter in Block Style With Envelope (rough draft) Report Test 2-12, Multipage Academic Report With Side Headings and Paragraph Headings Table Test 2-16, Three-Column Boxed Table

PART 3, REPORTS, CORRESPONDENCE, AND EMPLOYMENT DOCUMENTS

Unit 9, REPORTS

Lesson	Formatting	Word Processing	Documents
41. Business Reports With Footnotes	Reports With Footnotes Long Quotations	Footnotes	Report 41-13, One-Page Business Report With Footnotes Report 41-14, Two-Page Business Report
42. Reports in APA Style	Reports Formatted in APA Style Author/Year Citations	Margins Headers and Footers	Report 42-15, Academic Report in APA Style With Author/Year Citations and Main Headings Report 42-16, Academic Report in APA Style With Author/Year Citations, Main Headings, and Subheadings
43. Reports in MLA Style	Reports Formatted in MLA Style		Report 43-17, Academic Report in MLA Style with Citations Report 43-18, Academic Report in MLA Style
44. Report Citations	Bibliographies Reference List Pages in APA Style Works-Cited Pages in MLA Style	Hanging Indent	Report 44-19, Bibliography Report 44-20, References in APA Style Report 44-21, Works Cited in MLA Style
45. Preliminary Report Pages	Title Page Table of Contents	Tab Set—Dot Leaders	Report 45-22, Title Page Report 45-23, Table of Contents Report 45-24, Title Page Report 45-25, Table of Contents Report 45-26, Business Report With Side Headings and Footnotes

Unit 10, CORRESPONDENCE

Lesson	Formatting	Word Processing	Documents
46. Personal Titles and Complimentary Closings in Letters	Personal Titles in Correspondence Complimentary Closings in Correspondence		Correspondence 46-22, Business Letter in Block Style With Enclosure Notation Correspondence 46-23, Business Letter in Block Style With Enclosure Notation

Lesson	Formatting	Word Processing	Documents
47. Personal-Business Letters	Personal-Business Letters		Correspondence 47-24, Personal-Business Letter in Block Style With Standard Punctuation Correspondence 47-25, Personal-Business Letter in Block Style With Standard Punctuation Correspondence 47-26, Personal-Business Letter in Block Style With Standard Punctuation
48. Memos With Lists	Lists in Correspondence		Correspondence 48-27, Memo With a Single-Line Bulleted List Correspondence 48-28, Memo With a Multiline Numbered List Correspondence 48-29, Memo With a Single-Line Bulleted List
49. Letters With Copy Notations	Copy Notations		Correspondence 49-30, Business Letter in Block Style With Copy Notation Correspondence 49-31, Business Letter in Block Style With Enclosure and Copy Notations
50. Letters in Modified-Block Style	Modified-Block Style Letters	Ruler Tabs Tab Set	Correspondence 50-32, Business Letter in Modified-Block Style With Enclosure and Copy Notation Correspondence 50-33, Business Letter in Modified-Block Style With Numbered List Correspondence 50-34, Business Letter in Modified-Block Style With Enclosure and Copy Notation Correspondence 50-35, Personal-Business Letter With Bulleted List, Enclosure, and Copy Notation
Unit 11, EMPLOYMENT DOCUMENTS			
51. Traditional Resumes	Traditional Resumes	Fonts Table—Changing Column Width	Report 51-27, One-Page Resume in Traditional Style Report 51-28, One-Page Resume in Traditional Style
52. Electronic Resumes	Electronic Resumes	Saving in Text-Only Format	Report 52-29, One-Page Resume in Electronic Style Report 52-30, One-Page Resume in Electronic Style
53. Letters of Application	Letters of Application		Correspondence 53-36, Application Letter in Modified-Block Style With Enclosure Notation Correspondence 53-37, Application Letter in Block Style With Enclosure Notation

Lesson	Formatting	Word Processing	Documents
54. Follow-Up Letters	Follow-Up Letters		Correspondence 54-38, Follow-Up Letter in Block Style Correspondence 54-39, Follow-Up Letter in Modified-Block Style Correspondence 54-40, Follow-Up Letter in Modified-Block Style
55. Integrated Employment Project			Report 55-31, Resume in Traditional Style Correspondence 55-41, Application Letter in Block Style Correspondence 55-42, Follow-Up Letter in Modified-Block Style Correspondence 55-43, Application Letter in Block Style With Enclosure Notation Correspondence 55-44, Follow-Up Letter in Modified-Block Style
Unit 12, SKILLBUILDING AND IN-BASKET REVIEW			
56. In-Basket Review (Insurance)			Correspondence 56-45, Business Letter With Bulleted List Correspondence 56-46, Memo With Bulleted List and Enclosure Notation Table 56-17, Two-Column Boxed Table
57. In-Basket Review (Hospitality)			Table 57-18, Four-Column Open Table Correspondence 57-47, Letter in Modified-Block Style With Enclosure and Copy Notations Report 57-32, Business Report With Bulleted List, Side Headings, and Paragraph Headings
58. In-Basket Review (Retail)			Correspondence 58-48, Business Letter in Block Style Correspondence 58-49, Memo With Numbered List Table 58-19, Three-Column Boxed Table
59. In-Basket Review (Nonprofit)			Report 59-33, Business Report With Bulleted List and Footnotes Table 59-20, Four-Column Boxed Table
60. In-Basket Review (Manufacturing)			Correspondence 60-50, Business Letter in Block Style With Bulleted List, Enclosure, and Copy Notations Table 60-21, Four-Column Boxed Table Correspondence 60-51, Memo With Numbered List Correspondence 60-52, Business Letter in Modified-Block Style With Numbered List and Enclosure Notation Table 60-22, Three-Column Boxed Table

Lesson	Formatting	Word Processing	Documents
TEST 3. Skills Assessment on Part 3			Correspondence Test 3-53, Business Letter in Block Style With Bulleted List and Copy Notations Correspondence Test 3-54, Memo With Bulleted List and Attachment Report Test 3-34, Business Report With Side Headings, Paragraph Headings, and Footnotes

PART 4, ADVANCED FORMATTING

Unit 13, SKILL REFINEMENT

Lesson	Formatting	Word Processing	Documents
61. Skillbuilding and Report Review			Report 61-35, Business Report With Side Headings and Paragraph Headings Report 61-36, Multipage Academic Report With Side Headings and Footnotes Report 61-37, Multipage Business Report
62. Skillbuilding and Letter Review			Correspondence 62-55, Personal-Business Letter in Modified-Block Style Correspondence 62-56, Business Letter in Modified-Block Style Correspondence 62-57, Business Letter in Block Style
63. Skillbuilding, Memo, and E-Mail Review			Correspondence 63-58, Memo With Attachment Correspondence 63-59, E-Mail Message Correspondence 63-60, Memo With Attachment and Copy Notation Correspondence 63-61, Memo
64. Skillbuilding and Table Review			Table 64-23, Three-Column Boxed Table Table 64-24, Three-Column Open Table Table 64-25, Three-Column Ruled Table
65. Skillbuilding and Employment Document Review			Report 65-38, Traditional Resume Correspondence 65-62, Application Letter in Block Style Correspondence 65-63, Follow-Up Letter in Block Style

Unit 14, REPORTS

Lesson	Formatting	Word Processing	Documents
66. Itineraries	Itineraries		Report 66-39, Itinerary Report 66-40, Itinerary Report 66-41, Itinerary
67. Agendas and Minutes of Meetings	Agendas Minutes of Meetings	Hyphenation	Report 67-42, Agenda Report 67-43, Agenda Report 67-44, Minutes of a Meeting Report 67-45, Minutes of a Meeting

COURSE PLANNING GRID

Lesson	Formatting	Word Processing	Documents
68. Procedures Manual	Procedures Manual		Report 68-46, Procedures Manual Report 68-47, Procedures Manual Report 68-48, Procedures Manual
69. Reports Formatted in Columns	Magazine Articles	Columns	Report 69-49, Magazine Article Report 69-50, Magazine Article Report 69-51, Magazine Article
70. Report Review			Report 70-52, Agenda Report 70-53, Minutes of a Meeting Report 70-54, Magazine Article
Unit 15, CORRESPONDENCE			
71. Multipage Letters	Multipage Letters		Correspondence 71-64, Multipage Business Letter in Modified-Block Style Correspondence 71-65, Multipage Business Letter in Block Style Correspondence 71-66, Multipage Business Letter in Modified-Block Style
72. Special Letter Features	Multiple Addresses On-Arrival Notations Subject Lines	Sort	Correspondence 72-67, Business Letter in Block Style Correspondence 72-68, Multipage Business Letter in Block Style With Multiple Addresses and Bulleted Lists Correspondence 72-69, Personal-Business Letter in Block Style
73. More Special Letter Features	Tables Within Documents Company Name in Closing Blind-Copy Notation Delivery Notation Postscript	Shading	Correspondence 73-70, Business Letter in Block Style With Open Table Correspondence 73-71, Business Letter in Block Style With Boxed Table Correspondence 73-72, Multipage Business Letter in Modified-Block Style
74. Multipage Memos With Tables		Find and Replace	Correspondence 74-73, Multipage Memo With Open Table and Postscript Correspondence 74-74, Multipage Memo With Open Table and Postscript Correspondence 74-75, Memo With Boxed Table
75. Memo Reports	Report Headings in Memos		Report 75-55, Memo Report Report 75-56, Memo Report Report 75-57, Memo Report
Unit 16, TABLES			
76. Tables With Footnotes or Source Notes	Tables With Footnotes or Source Notes	Table—Text Direction Table—Insert or Delete Rows or Columns	Table 76-26, Seven-Column Boxed Table Table 76-27, Seven-Column Boxed Table Table 76-28, Five-Column Boxed Table
77. Tables With Braced Column Headings	Braced Column Headings		Table 77-29, Six-Column Boxed Table Table 77-30, Four-Column Boxed Table Table 77-31, Four-Column Boxed Table

Lesson	Formatting	Word Processing	Documents
78. Tables Formatted	Page Orientation	Page Orientation	Table 78-32, Seven-Column Boxed Table Table 78-33, Seven-Column Boxed Table Table 78-34, Seven-Column Boxed Table
79. Multipage Tables	Multipage Tables	Repeating Table Heading Rows	Table 79-35, Multipage Boxed Table Table 79-36, Multipage Boxed Table Table 79-37, Five-Column Boxed Table
80. Using Predesigned Table Formats		Table—AutoFormat	Table 80-38, Three-Column Table Table 80-39, Three-Column Table Table 80-40, Four-Column Table
TEST 4. Skills Assessment on Part 4			Correspondence Test 4-76, Memo Report With Boxed Table Correspondence Test 4-77, Business Letter in Block Style Table Test 4-41, Four-Column Boxed Table

PART 5, SPECIALIZED APPLICATIONS

Unit 17, FORMAL REPORT PROJECT

Lesson	Formatting	Word Processing	Documents
81. Formal Report Project		Styles	Report 81-58, Multipage Business Report With Side Headings and a Bulleted List
82. Formal Report Project			Report 81-58, Continued
83. Formal Report Project		Insert Clip Art and Files	Report 81-58, Continued
84. Formal Report Project			Table 84-42, Three-Column Boxed Table Report 81-58, Continued
85. Formal Report Project			Report 85-59, Title Page Report 85-60, Table of Contents Report 85-61, Bibliography

Unit 18, International Formatting

Lesson	Formatting	Word Processing	Documents
86. International Formatting (Canada)	Metric Paper Size Metric Envelope Size International Addresses in Letters Day/Month/Year Format	Paper Size	Correspondence 86-78, Business Letter in Modified-Block Style With Copy Notations and Postscript Notation Table 86-43, Five-Column Boxed Table Table 86-44, Five-Column Boxed Table
87. International Formatting (Mexico)	International URLs	Insert Symbol	Correspondence 87-79, E-Mail Message Report 87-62, Business Report With Boxed Table
88. International Formatting (France)	Dot-Style Telephone Numbers International Telephone Access Codes		Correspondence 88-80, Business Letter in Block Style With Enclosure and Copy Notations Table 88-45, Three-Column Table With Cell Shading Correspondence 88-81, E-Mail Message

Lesson	*Formatting*	*Word Processing*	*Documents*
89. International Formatting (Germany)	Metric Units of Measurement		Correspondence 89-82, E-Mail Message Correspondence 89-83, Business Letter in Block Style Report 89-63, Multipage Business Report With Boxed Table and Bulleted List
90. International Formatting (Japan)			Correspondence 90-84, Business Letter in Block Style With Copy Notations Correspondence 90-85, E-Mail Message Correspondence 90-86, Business Letter in Block Style With Illustration Table 90-46, Two-Column Boxed Table Correspondence 90-87, Business Letter in Block Style With Enclosure
Unit 19, Medical Office Documents			
91. Medical Office Documents			Correspondence 91-88, Business Letter in Block Style With Enclosure Notation Table 91-47, Boxed Table With Shaded Cells Correspondence 91-89, Memo With Copy Notations
92. Medical Office Documents			Report 92-64, Multipage Business Report With Side Headings and Lists Table 92-48, Five-Column Boxed Table
93. Medical Office Documents			Correspondence 93-90, Business Letter in Modified-Block Style With Enclosure and Postscript Notation Report 93-65, Multipage Business Report With Side Headings and Paragraph Headings
94. Medical Office Documents			Table 94-49, Two-Column Boxed Table Correspondence 94-91, Business Letter in Block Style Table 94-50, Two-Column Boxed Table
95. Medical Office Documents			Table 95-51, Two-Column Boxed Table Report 95-66, Business Report With Numbered and Bulleted Lists Correspondence 95-92, E-Mail Message Correspondence 95-93, Memo With Copy Notations
Unit 20, Legal Office Documents			
96. Legal Office Documents	Legal Documents	Line Numbering	Report 96-67, Affidavit of Possession Correspondence 96-94, Business Letter in Block Style With Enclosure and Copy Notations

Lesson	Formatting	Word Processing	Documents
97. Legal Office Documents			Report 97-68, Warranty Deed Table 97-52, Two-Column Boxed Table Correspondence 97-95, E-Mail Message
98. Legal Office Documents			Report 98-69, Summons Correspondence 98-96, Memo With Enclosure Notation and Copy Notation Table 98-53, Four-Column Boxed Table
99. Legal Office Documents			Report 99-70, Last Will and Testament- Correspondence 99-97, Business Letter in Block Style With Subject Line, Bulleted List, Enclosure, and Copy Notations
100. Legal Office Documents			Report 100-71, Complaint Report 100-72, Judgment Report 100-73, Affidavit
TEST 5. Skills Assessment on Part 5			Correspondence Test 5-98, Letter in Block Style With Copy Notations Table Test 5-54, Boxed Table Report Test 5-74, Summons

PART 6, USING AND DESIGNING BUSINESS DOCUMENTS

Unit 21, Using and Designing Office Forms

Lesson	Formatting	Word Processing	Documents
101. Using Correspondence Templates	Filling in Forms	Correspondence Templates	Form 101-1, Memo Template Form 101-2, Letter Template Form 101-3, Memo Template
102. Using Report Templates		Report Templates	Form 102-4, Report Template Form 102-5, Report Template
103. Designing Letterheads	Designing a Form	Small Caps Text Boxes	Form 103-6, Letterhead Form Form 103-7, Letterhead Form Form 103-8, Letterhead Form
104. Designing Notepads		Print Options	Form 104-9, Notepad Form Form 104-10, Notepad Form Form 104-11, Notepad Form
105. Designing Miscellaneous Office Forms			Form 105-12, Directory Form Form 105-13, Sign-In Form Form 105-14, Memo Template

Unit 22, Designing Office Publications

Lesson	Formatting	Word Processing	Documents
106. Designing Cover Pages		Word Art	Report 106-75, Cover Page Report 106-76, Cover Page Report 106-77, Cover Page
107. Designing Announcements and Flyers		Table—Move	Report 107-78, Announcement Report 107-79, Flyer Report 107-80, Announcement or Flyer

COURSE PLANNING GRID

Lesson	Formatting	Word Processing	Documents
108. Designing Newsletters: A	Newsletter Design		Report 108-81, Newsletter Report 108-82, Newsletter
109. Designing Newsletters: B			Report 109-83, Newsletter (continued) Report 109-84, Newsletter
110. Designing Newsletters: C			Report 110-85, Newsletter (continued) Report 110-86, Flyer
Unit 23, Designing Web Pages			
111. Creating, Saving, and Viewing Web Pages	Basic Parts of a Web Page Web Site Design Guidelines	Web Page—Saving and Viewing	Report 111-87, Web Site Report 111-88, Your Web Site
112. Creating Frames			Report 112-89, Web Site (continued) Report 112-90, Your Web Site (continued)
113. Creating and Saving More Web Pages	Hyperlinks	Web Page—Hyperlinks	Report 113-91, Web Site (continued) Report 113-92, Web Site (continued) Report 113-93, Your Web Site (continued) Report 113-94, Your Web Site (continued)
114. Creating Web Pages With Hyperlinks			Report 114-95, Web Site (continued) Report 114-96, Web Site (continued) Report 114-97, Your Web Site (continued) Report 114-98, Your Web Site (continued)
115. Formatting Web Pages	More Web Site Design Guidelines	Web Page—Design Themes	Report 115-99, Web Site (continued) Report 115-100, Web Site
Unit 24, Skillbuilding and In-Basket Review			
116. In-Basket Review (Insurance)			Form 116-15, Letter Template Table 116-55, Three-Column Boxed Table Form 116-16, Letterhead Form
117. In-Basket Review (Hospitality)			Report 117-101, Web Site Report 117-102, Web Site
118. In-Basket Review (Retail)			Form 118-17, Memo Template Report 118-103, Agenda Report 118-104, Cover Page
119. In-Basket Review (Government)			Correspondence 119-99, Business Letter in Block Style With Postscript Notation Correspondence 119-100, Business Letter in Block Style With Postscript Notation Correspondence 119-101, E-Mail Message
120. In-Basket Review (Manufacturing)			Report 120-105, Multipage Business Report With Side Headings and Paragraph Headings Correspondence 120-102, Multipage Business Letter in Block Style With Table
TEST 6. Skills Assessment on Part 6			Form Test 6-18, Memo Template Report Test 6-106, Web Page Report Test 6-107, Flyer

Assessment Strategies

EVALUATION AND GRADING

Evaluation in the keyboarding course is an appraisal of progress or the lack of it and is a continuous process. Particularly during the first weeks of keyboarding, students should be made to feel confident that they can learn to type, and they should know exactly what is expected of them at the beginning of each class. Constant encouragement and correction will provide the feedback that students need to progress successfully.

Three factors should be considered in analyzing skill development: typing technique, performance on straight-copy timed writings, and document processing.

Practice is important for skill development, and students should be commended for doing extra work. However, it is not appropriate to grade in-class practice work or to give extra credit for doing additional practice work outside of class. Grades should reflect the skill level at which students are able to perform.

TYPING TECHNIQUE

As students begin to type, they will exhibit different typing behaviors that should be watched carefully so that skill can develop as easily and in as relaxed a fashion as possible. You should constantly observe students by moving about the classroom as they type.

Most experts agree that the development of proper typing technique should be a major priority during the first few weeks of instruction. The Technique Evaluation Form (download at www.mhhe.com/gdp) provides multiple opportunities for rating technique in three categories.

Students are rated on each of the three categories; they see whether their skills are acceptable or in need of improvement. Space is provided on the form for five rating periods.

One way to use the form is to have students rate themselves first; then you rate the students. Peer evaluation can also be used; that is, you can have students work in pairs. As one student types, the other observes and evaluates the performance; then they switch roles.

The Technique Evaluation Form should be used for each student at least once a week during the early stages of instruction. Less frequent evaluations may indicate to students that typing technique is not important; more frequent evaluations tend to build tension in students and place an additional burden on you. Following each written evaluation, you should discuss with students the areas that need improvement.

Although less time should be spent analyzing papers than observing students during the first few weeks of keyboarding, some weaknesses in technique can be detected by examining student papers.

Use the following list of different kinds of errors and their possible causes to help diagnose students' weaknesses.

1. Omitted spaces may indicate that students rested their hands on the keyboard.
2. Omitted letters may indicate that students are typing too rapidly or may not be watching the copy attentively enough.
3. Omitted words may indicate that students are not yet accustomed to reading stroke by stroke (their eyes get ahead of their fingers). Omitted words may also mean that students looked up and lost their place.
4. Extra spaces within and between words may indicate that students' thumbs or palms are putting slight pressure on the SPACE BAR.
5. Extra letters in words might mean that students were distracted or did not fully release a key after striking it.
6. Transposed letters could mean that students are confused about fingering or that they are not accustomed to reading letter by letter.

Periodically during document processing sessions, have your students simply read through the Technique Evaluation Form so that they are reminded of proper typing technique. During these sessions, you may wish to demonstrate proper technique and discuss the role technique plays in terms of speed and accuracy of typing as well as fatigue.

TIMED WRITINGS

Students want to know how well they can type, and frequent timed writings with continuous encouragement will fulfill that need and provide you with an additional variable for evaluation.

In Lessons 1–20, students are learning the touch system of typing and have the opportunity to type the first of many timed writings. Because of the learning load in these initial lessons, the authors do not recommend grading Part 1 (Lessons 1–20). If you believe that a grade is necessary, use the General Information Test (available in the Tests and Solution Keys Booklet) or any of the timed writings.

In all lessons, students are provided with both speed and accuracy goals for timed writings. These goals are recommended minimums for average students, and you may want to modify the goals to reflect the ability levels of your students.

Although all sections of the textbook may be used for practice to develop skill, only the timed writing passages should be used for grading. There are several reasons for this. All these passages are in the same format and at the same level of difficulty. In Lessons 21–60 the timed writings have a syllabic intensity (SI) of 1.30 to 1.40; in Lessons 61–120 they have an SI of 1.40 to 1.50; and in Lessons 121–180 they have an SI of 1.50 to 1.60. In addition, the timed writings contain all the letters of the alphabet but no numbers or symbols (other than hyphens and common punctuation marks). Thus, they provide a valid and consistent measure of progress in straight-copy typing.

No involved calculations are necessary to compute scores. If you are using the GDP software, it will compute speed and count errors automatically.

As discussed earlier, any timed writing may be used effectively for skillbuilding. However, in order to receive meaningful scores for evaluation, you should not test students on copy that they have been practicing. Students will naturally receive higher scores on practiced copy than on unpracticed copy. Students' timed writing grades at the end of the semester should be based on the average of the best three timed writings during the final week of the course, including the timed writing taken in the last part test, for this is the skill level that the student will have when he or she applies for a job.

DOCUMENT PROCESSING

The measurement of document processing skills is an ongoing process. Whether done formally—through graded classroom assignments, tests, and end-of-semester grades—or informally—through your daily constructive comments—it is an integral part of the learning process.

Students must be aware of their progress on a daily basis, for such awareness serves as motivation for the next lesson in both straight-copy skillbuilding and document processing development. But this type of evaluation can be done informally in the classroom without your having to grade stacks of papers every evening.

In addition, formal student evaluation is important to the instructor. Students must be assigned grades, and instructors need data with which to assess both their students' and their own classroom performance. A number of techniques for evaluating document processing performance have been advocated. No matter which technique you choose, you must be able to justify your choice on the basis of two criteria: validity of measurement and ease of administration. In order for a measurement of document processing performance to be valid, both the speed with which the typing is done and the accuracy of the document(s) must be assessed.

Mailability. In later stages of learning, an excellent measurement technique is the determination of whether a document is mailable. In other words, is the document of such quality that an executive would be willing to mail it to someone without further revisions? Students earn a rating of mailable, mailable after correction, or not mailable on their papers.

The meaning of *mailability* varies from instructor to instructor and from office to office; therefore, it is important that you establish categories of errors so that the ratings can be assigned uniformly, quickly, and accurately. For example, studies have shown that among the errors that would make a letter unmailable are misspelled words, word errors that change the meaning, poor horizontal or vertical placement, and dirty or crumpled stationery.

Using the mailability method, you determine grades either by the total number of mailable papers produced within the grading period or by the total number of points accumulated, with perhaps 3 points being awarded for mailable papers, 2 points for papers mailable after correction, and 1 point for unmailable papers. (The rationale for awarding 1 point for unmailable papers is that students who type a document should receive more credit than students who do not type a document.)

Line Measure. Some word processing centers have adopted the method of counting the number of lines correctly produced in a certain period of time as their primary tool for measuring operator productivity. Line-count measures may be used when evaluating document processing work.

In industry, the total number of lines typed is often multiplied by some factor to account for the varying levels of difficulty in typing different jobs (for example, it takes longer to format a report with rough-draft annotations than it does to format a report without handwritten corrections). However, because all students in the class will be typing the same jobs, using a straight line count is probably just as valid as using a weighted line count, and it is much easier to apply the straight line count method.

If you decide to use a line measure in grading, the easiest and most valid way to determine the number of correct lines typed is to subtract the number of lines that contain errors from the total number of lines in the job. This procedure relieves you of the necessity of counting the total number of correct lines in each student's job (the assumption being that the number of correct lines will far exceed the number of incorrect lines).

Although line measure may be used at any time during the three semesters of the *10th* edition, the method can more realistically be used in the simulated settings of the integrated office projects.

10TH EDITION TESTS

An integral part of measuring a student's progress is evaluating achievement throughout a course. This *10th* edition provides a series of tests for instructors to use.

OBJECTIVE TESTS

A General Information Test is provided for Parts 1–6. This test is in reproducible format in the Tests and Solution Keys Booklet.

PART TESTS

Beginning with Part 2, each of the part tests can be used to evaluate a student's success in meeting the goals of the part. Each test contains a timed writing and several document processing tasks based on skills taught in the part.

For each of the part tests provided in the textbook, there is an alternate test in the Tests and Solution Keys Booklet. Each of these alternate tests is parallel to its corresponding version in the textbook with regard to the types of jobs and their length, format, and difficulty. The alternate tests are available and scored within the software. The only difference between the two test versions is the content.

You may decide to use the textbook tests for practice and the alternate tests for actual grading, or you may choose to use the textbook tests for grading and the alternate tests for retests or makeup work. Finally, you can give the textbook tests at the end of each part and use the alternate tests for an intensive review at the end of the semester.

GRADING STANDARDS

The authors suggest the following grading standards. These standards are also the default standards in the Instructor Management program. However, you may want to use these standards only as guidelines to determine your own standards for your courses and students. (The default settings of the Instructor Management program can be easily changed. Follow the instructions in the Software User's Guide.)

Because of the heavy learning load in the early lessons, it is recommended that grades not be assigned to Part 1. However, if a grade is absolutely necessary, use the grade for the General Information Test or the grades for any timed writings. You may also choose to include technique grades during the first six weeks of instruction.

For grading Parts 2–6, there should be two letter grades for each part: one for the timed writings (the average of the three best timed writings in the part) and one for document processing (the average of all jobs completed in the part tests). If you desire, include technique grades with timed writings and document processing for Part 2.

The timed writing in a part test is not graded as a component of the part test. It becomes a part of the sequence of timed writings taken within the part. The timed writing grade for each part is determined by averaging the three best timed writings within the part. The following straight-copy standards are suggested; however, you may wish to alter the standards to meet your students' abilities and course requirements.

PART 2

Error tolerance: 4 or fewer

WPM		*Grade*
41+	=	A
37–40	=	B
32–36	=	C
28–31	=	D
0–27	=	F

PART 3

Error tolerance: 5 or fewer

WPM		*Grade*
45+	=	A
41–44	=	B
37–40	=	C
33–36	=	D
0–32	=	F

PART 4

Error tolerance: 5 or fewer

WPM		*Grade*
48+	=	A
44–47	=	B
40–43	=	C
36–39	=	D
0–35	=	F

PART 5

Error tolerance: 5 or fewer

WPM		*Grade*
52+	=	A
48–51	=	B
44–47	=	C
40–43	=	D
0–39	=	F

PART 6

Error tolerance: 5 or fewer

WPM		*Grade*
55+	=	A
51–54	=	B
48–50	=	C
44–47	=	D
0–43	=	F

Document processing jobs in the part tests should be completed in the order in which they are presented. Only completed jobs should be graded. Students should be allowed to edit copy and make any corrections before a job is complete. When grading document processing jobs, consider the speed with which a student completes a job. Also consider imposing a penalty for uncorrected errors in the job. The GDP software will compute the time for each job, and the results are available in the Portfolio.

The last document in most units is a Progress Check/ Proofreading Check. Documents designated as Progress Check/ Proofreading Checks serve as a check of your students' proofreading skill. Their goal is to have zero typographical errors when the GDP software first scores their document. If they have typographical errors when their document is first scored, you might want to recommend that they re-create the document and try again for zero scoring errors. Clicking the **Create** button allows them to begin again with a blank document. You may also want to include proofreading as a grading component. The GDP software will identify the number of scored attempts in the Portfolio. The following document processing standards are suggested; however, you may wish to alter the standards to meet your students' abilities and course requirements.

END-OF-SEMESTER GRADES

Grading has always been a challenging task for the keyboarding instructor. The instructor must develop procedures that reflect the conditions of the learning environment. It is necessary to identify the factors to be considered in giving a grade and then to decide what weight should be assigned to each factor. These decisions must be based on the objectives for the course and the relative degree of importance of the various factors in the course. Three important factors are typing technique, straight-copy skill (as measured by timed writings), and document processing performance.

Typing technique may appropriately be given a heavier weight during the first weeks of the beginning course as an inducement to develop habits that will contribute to later document processing skill. However, relatively little weight should be given to typing technique when the course grade is determined (probably no more than 10 percent of the final course grade should be based on technique).

Although straight-copy skill should be considered throughout the keyboarding program, the assigned weight should decrease at each stage of instruction. The timed writing grade from the last part in each book can be used to determine the final course grade.

Since skilled document processing performance is the real goal of keyboarding, the weight assigned to document processing should be higher at each stage of instruction.

The following suggested weights for computing the single final grade at the end of two semesters of typing instruction reflect this philosophy.

LESSONS 1–60

Typing Technique	10%
Timed Writings	30%
Document Processing	60%

LESSONS 61–120

Typing Technique	5%
Timed Writings	25%
Document Processing	70%

DEFAULT WEIGHTS

Activity	*Weight*
Technique	10%
Timed Writings	25%
Progress Checks	15%
Production Tests	50%

GRADING SUGGESTIONS FOR PROGRESS CHECKS AND PART TESTS

Part 2

Progress Check

PART 2 TIMED WRITINGS

WPM		*Grade*
41+	=	A
37–40	=	B
32–36	=	C
28–31	=	D
0–27	=	F

Error tolerance: 4 or less

Progress Check

REPORT 30–10

Errors	*Total Elapsed Time (Minutes)* <22	≥22 &<25	≥25 &<28	≥28
0–1	A	B	C	D
2	B	C	D	F
3	C	D	F	F
4	D	F	F	F

Progress Check

CORRESPONDENCE 35-19

Errors	*Total Elapsed Time (Minutes)* <12	≥12 &<15	≥15 &<18	≥18
0–1	A	B	C	D
2	B	C	D	F
3	C	D	F	F
4	D	F	F	F

Progress Check

TABLE 40-15

Errors	*Total Elapsed Time (Minutes)* <8	≥8 &<11	≥11 &<14	≥14
0–1	A	B	C	D
2	B	C	D	F
3	C	D	F	F
4	D	F	F	F

Test 2

CORRESPONDENCE TEST 2-21

Errors	*Total Elapsed Time (Minutes)* <12	≥12 &<15	≥15 &<18	≥18
0–1	A	B	C	D
2	B	C	D	F
3	C	D	F	F
4	D	F	F	F

Test 2

TABLE TEST 2-16

Errors	*Total Elapsed Time (Minutes)* <8	≥8 &<11	≥11 &<14	≥14
0–1	A	B	C	D
2	B	C	D	F
3	C	D	F	F
4	D	F	F	F

Test 2

REPORT TEST 2-12

Errors	*Total Elapsed Time (Minutes)* <20	≥20 &<23	≥23 &<26	≥26
0–1	A	B	C	D
2	B	C	D	F
3	C	D	F	F
4	D	F	F	F

Part 3

Progress Check

PART 3 TIMED WRITINGS

WPM		*Grade*
45+	=	A
41–44	=	B
37–40	=	C
33–36	=	D
0–32	=	F

Error tolerance: 5 or less

Progress Check

REPORT 45-24 THROUGH REPORT 45-26

Errors	*Total Elapsed Time (Minutes)* <45	≥45 &<48	≥48 &<51	≥51
0–1	A	B	C	D
2	B	C	D	F
3	C	D	F	F
4	D	F	F	F

Progress Check

CORRESPONDENCE 50-35

Errors	*Total Elapsed Time (Minutes)* <14	≥14 &<17	≥17 &<20	≥20
0–1	A	B	C	D
2	B	C	D	F
3	C	D	F	F
4	D	F	F	F

Progress Check

CORRESPONDENCE 55-44

Errors	*Total Elapsed Time (Minutes)* <18	≥18 &<21	≥21 &<24	≥24
0–1	A	B	C	D
2	B	C	D	F
3	C	D	F	F
4	D	F	F	F

Progress Check

TABLE 60-22

Errors	*Total Elapsed Time (Minutes)* <10	≥10 &<13	≥13 &<16	≥16
0–1	A	B	C	D
2	B	C	D	F
3	C	D	F	F
4	D	F	F	F

Test 3

CORRESPONDENCE 3-53

	Total Elapsed Time (Minutes)			
Errors	*<9*	*≥9 &<12*	*≥12 &<15*	*≥15*
0–1	A	B	C	D
2	B	C	D	F
3	C	D	F	F
4	D	F	F	F

Test 3

CORRESPONDENCE 3-54

	Total Elapsed Time (Minutes)			
Errors	*<10*	*≥10 &<13*	*≥13 &<16*	*≥16*
0–1	A	B	C	D
2	B	C	D	F
3	C	D	F	F
4	D	F	F	F

Test 3

REPORT 3-34

	Total Elapsed Time (Minutes)			
Errors	*<20*	*≥20 &<23*	*≥23 &<26*	*≥26*
0–1	A	B	C	D
2	B	C	D	F
3	C	D	F	F
4	D	F	F	F

Part 4

Progress Check

PART 4 TIMED WRITINGS

WPM		*Grade*
48+	=	A
44–47	=	B
40–43	=	C
36–39	=	D
0–35	=	F

Error tolerance: 5 or less

Progress Check

CORRESPONDENCE 65-63

	Total Elapsed Time (Minutes)			
Errors	*<10*	*≥10 &<13*	*≥13 &<16*	*≥16*
0–1	A	B	C	D
2	B	C	D	F
3	C	D	F	F
4	D	F	F	F

Progress Check

REPORT 70-54

	Total Elapsed Time (Minutes)			
Errors	*<22*	*≥22 &<25*	*≥25 &<28*	*≥28*
0–1	A	B	C	D
2	B	C	D	F
3	C	D	F	F
4	D	F	F	F

Progress Check

REPORT 75-57

	Total Elapsed Time (Minutes)			
Errors	*<20*	*≥20 &<23*	*≥23 &<26*	*≥26*
0–1	A	B	C	D
2	B	C	D	F
3	C	D	F	F
4	D	F	F	F

Progress Check

TABLE 80-40

	Total Elapsed Time (Minutes)			
Errors	*<18*	*≥18 &<21*	*≥21 &<24*	*≥24*
0–1	A	B	C	D
2	B	C	D	F
3	C	D	F	F
4	D	F	F	F

Test 4

CORRESPONDENCE TEST 4-76

	Total Elapsed Time (Minutes)			
Errors	*<12*	*≥12 &<15*	*≥15 &<18*	*≥18*
0–1	A	B	C	D
2	B	C	D	F
3	C	D	F	F
4	D	F	F	F

Test 4

CORRESPONDENCE TEST 4-77

	Total Elapsed Time (Minutes)			
Errors	*<8*	*≥8 &<11*	*≥11 &<14*	*≥14*
0–1	A	B	C	D
2	B	C	D	F
3	C	D	F	F
4	D	F	F	F

Test 4

TABLE 4-41

	Total Elapsed Time (Minutes)			
Errors	*<10*	*≥10 &<13*	*≥13 &<16*	*≥16*
0–1	A	B	C	D
2	B	C	D	F
3	C	D	F	F
4	D	F	F	F

Part 5

Progress Check

PART 5 TIMED WRITINGS

WPM		*Grade*
52+	=	A
48–51	=	B
44–47	=	C
40–43	=	D
0–39	=	F

Error tolerance: 5 or less

Progress Check

REPORT 85-61

	Total Elapsed Time (Minutes)			
Errors	*<8*	*≥8 &<11*	*≥11 &<14*	*≥14*
0–1	A	B	C	D
2	B	C	D	F
3	C	D	F	F
4	D	F	F	F

Progress Check

CORRESPONDENCE 90-87

Errors	Total Elapsed Time (Minutes)			
	<11	≥11 &<14	≥14 &<17	≥17
0–1	A	B	C	D
2	B	C	D	F
3	C	D	F	F
4	D	F	F	F

Progress Check

CORRESPONDENCE 95-93

Errors	Total Elapsed Time (Minutes)			
	<12	≥12 &<15	≥15 &<18	≥18
0–1	A	B	C	D
2	B	C	D	F
3	C	D	F	F
4	D	F	F	F

Progress Check

REPORT 100-73

Errors	Total Elapsed Time (Minutes)			
	<10	≥10 &<13	≥13 &<16	≥16
0–1	A	B	C	D
2	B	C	D	F
3	C	D	F	F
4	D	F	F	F

Test 5

CORRESPONDENCE 5-98

Errors	Total Elapsed Time (Minutes)			
	<10	≥10 &<13	≥13 &<16	≥16
0–1	A	B	C	D
2	B	C	D	F
3	C	D	F	F
4	D	F	F	F

Test 5

TABLE 5-54

Errors	Total Elapsed Time (Minutes)			
	<15	≥15 &<18	≥18 &<21	≥21
0–1	A	B	C	D
2	B	C	D	F
3	C	D	F	F
4	D	F	F	F

Test 5

REPORT 5-74

Errors	Total Elapsed Time (Minutes)			
	<15	≥15 &<18	≥18 &<21	≥21
0–1	A	B	C	D
2	B	C	D	F
3	C	D	F	F
4	D	F	F	F

Part 6

Progress Check

PART 6 TIMED WRITINGS

WPM		Grade
55+	=	A
51–54	=	B
48–50	=	C
44–47	=	D
0–43	=	F

Error tolerance: 5 or less

Progress Check

FORM 105-14

Errors	Total Elapsed Time (Minutes)			
	<10	≥10 &<13	≥13 &<16	≥16
0–1	A	B	C	D
2	B	C	D	F
3	C	D	F	F
4	D	F	F	F

Progress Check

REPORT 110-86

Errors	Total Elapsed Time (Minutes)			
	<15	≥15 &<18	≥18 &<21	≥21
0–1	A	B	C	D
2	B	C	D	F
3	C	D	F	F
4	D	F	F	F

Progress Check

REPORT 115-100

Errors	Total Elapsed Time (Minutes)			
	<15	≥18 &<21	≥21 &<24	≥24
0–1	A	B	C	D
2	B	C	D	F
3	C	D	F	F
4	D	F	F	F

Progress Check

CORRESPONDENCE 120-102

Errors	Total Elapsed Time (Minutes)			
	<18	≥18 &<21	≥21 &<24	≥24
0–1	A	B	C	D
2	B	C	D	F
3	C	D	F	F
4	D	F	F	F

Test 6

FORM 6-18

Errors	Total Elapsed Time (Minutes)			
	<12	≥12 &<15	≥15 &<18	≥18
0–1	A	B	C	D
2	B	C	D	F
3	C	D	F	F
4	D	F	F	F

Test 6

REPORT 6-106

Errors	Total Elapsed Time (Minutes)			
	<25	≥25 &<28	≥28 &<31	≥31
0–1	A	B	C	D
2	B	C	D	F
3	C	D	F	F
4	D	F	F	F

Test 6

REPORT 6-107

Errors	Total Elapsed Time (Minutes)			
	<15	≥15 &<18	≥18 &<21	≥21
0–1	A	B	C	D
2	B	C	D	F
3	C	D	F	F
4	D	F	F	F

Helping the Adult Student

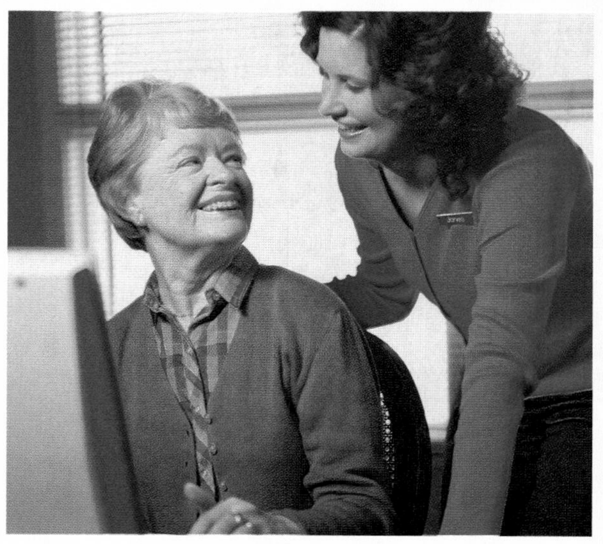

If you teach adult students, you've no doubt noticed that they differ in many ways from middle school and high school students. There are strategies and approaches you can employ to make the adult student's experience in your class a successful one.

HELP THEM LEARN TO CONCENTRATE

It may have been quite a long time since your adult students had to devote full attention to learning a new topic. They may be accustomed to reading the newspaper while surrounded by family tumult and television noise, but studying requires a different environment. Encourage them to find a quiet, well-lit area and to arrange times when they can expect to be uninterrupted. Have them schedule periods of concentration, using a timer if necessary—starting with 5 minutes of concentration followed by a 1-minute break, and working up to 20 or 30 minutes of concentration followed by a 5- or 10-minute break.

ACCEPT THAT ADULT STUDENTS ARE THEIR OWN PERSONS

A teacher of grade school students may meet with a student's parent or guardian to brainstorm ways to help a student improve performance. With an adult student, you can meet with the student personally. You and the adult student can discuss coping strategies, time constraints, transportation problems, and anything else that is interfering with the student's learning.

REALIZE THAT AN ADULT STUDENT DEVOTES TIME AND ENERGY TO CLASSWORK AT THE EXPENSE OF OTHER PRIORITIES

Your class, no matter how essential its subject matter, competes for the adult student's attention with family, work, and other personal activities. This is particularly true in the development of a skill such as keyboarding. Most adult students have lives crammed full of obligations even without a college class and its attendant homework. To become a student again means trimming other activities without compromising vital roles such as parent, partner, employee, and community member.

DON'T PUSH ADULT STUDENTS TOO HARD

Returning to school after an absence of some years is difficult. Be clear about assignments and expectations. Look for puzzled expressions, and when you see them, offer extra examples or invite questions. Offer your office hours for adult students who may need help adjusting to school life.

DON'T WASTE THEIR TIME

Adult students have shoehorned you and your class into their lives. Make good use of every minute of class time. Complete your attendance taking and other clerical tasks during the initial warmups or other spare moments, but never make the class wait for your attention. Try to engage everyone in discussions to give all students a sense of participation.

BUILD A CLASSROOM COMMUNITY

Often an adult learner returning to the classroom is burdened by the memory of negative experiences in school. This anxiety combines with the pressures of a crowded schedule to add stress to an already challenging activity, going back to school as an adult. Help your adult students overcome stress by forming the class into a peer support group. Let them share experiences and sustain one another by example and encouragement. The students in your class already know they have similar goals; help them see that their pressures and anxieties are shared, as well, in a collective social environment.

RESPECT THE ADULT STUDENT'S PRIOR LEARNING, NOT ONLY IN SCHOOL BUT ALSO IN THE WORKPLACE

Not all of the knowledge that your students will carry away from your class needs to come from you. In discussing work-related problems, let students offer solutions they have either observed or devised in their own lives. Doing so will help them feel like contributors instead of recipients and will afford the whole group, yourself included, a wider set of experiences from which to draw.

RECOGNIZE THAT ADULT STUDENTS ARE SELF-MOTIVATED

Fear of a poor grade or a wish to please the instructor is not a strong motivator for adult learners. Rather, they can be expected to learn what they themselves perceive they need to learn. This does not mean they cannot be reached; in fact, quite the contrary: when convinced that mastering the material is important to their future, adult students can demonstrate far more determination to succeed than an instructor could ever impart. Accordingly, adult students should participate fully in setting their own learning goals.

PROVIDE ACTIVE, NOT PASSIVE, LEARNING EXPERIENCES

A many-to-many discussion rather than a one-to-many lecture is a good tactic. Have students experiment with new techniques for the workplace rather than merely parroting your lectures. Welcome the adult learner's passionate involvement in discussions. Adult students who experience a high level of intellectual stimulation in your class will grow faster and develop further, making them better suited for the workplace.

SCHEDULE REGULAR FEEDBACK SESSIONS

Adult students can modify their own behavior, as we know. But they can also modify yours, to the benefit of the program and all participants, if you are open to their feedback. Encourage your adult students to tell you what works best for them and what needs to change in the classroom. If you have only one or two adult learners in a class full of younger students, the adults can act as extra eyes for you. You can take advantage of their viewpoints to adjust your program.

LET YOUR ADULT STUDENTS DESIGN THEIR OWN LEARNING PROGRAMS

If it is feasible at your institution, help adult learners design individual learning programs tailored around their particular needs and situations. If at present such innovation is not feasible, consider discussing a feasibility study in your next faculty meeting. In a self-directed learning environment, students take responsibility for their own learning. What could be better?

REWARD INTELLECTUAL CREATIVITY

Treat your adult students as peers. Listen to their opinions and ask them for their suggestions when problem solving. When an adult learner facilitates the education of others, the classroom community is strengthened, and everyone wins.

BE SURE EVERYTHING THEY LEARN HAS PRACTICAL VALUE

To facilitate the learning of adult students, you'll have to contextualize the information you teach so that they can integrate it into their own lives. Minimize theory; maximize practice. Link anything abstract to concrete examples, and let them learn by doing whenever possible.

LET YOUR ADULT STUDENTS SHARE WITH THE CLASS WHAT THEY KNOW

As designers of 12-step programs recognized long ago, an excellent way to foster learning is to have people teach what you want them to know. The process of imparting information maximizes retention and moreover provides the rest of the class with welcome variety in teaching methods and styles. Cooperative learning bolsters the classroom community and prepares students particularly well for the world of work.

BE A MENTOR

Adult learners are hungry for support, challenge, and vision. A mentor can provide all these, along with acceptance. To be recognized by a competent and well-educated stranger as valuable persons in their own right, regardless of any success or failure in the other roles they perform, is vital for adult students. Let your adult students advance your own development and become the best mentor you can be with their help.

HELP THEM ACHIEVE EMPOWERMENT

Adults return to school because they perceive needs that education can fill. Let their experiences in your class strengthen their feeling of accomplishment. Help them visualize graduating and taking their place as valued citizens and members of the larger community. Let them know, for example, that you expect to see letters to the editor from them in the local newspaper. Completing your class can help them be emancipated from social and cultural forces that control their lives and limit their futures. The self-esteem of adult learners can be nourished by successful class experiences to the point where they see new opportunities to express themselves and to make their voices heard.

ENCOURAGE CRITICAL REFLECTION

In metacognitive terms, students—especially adult students—can teach themselves by paying attention to what they are thinking. Incorporate into your classroom such reflective tools as diaries, autobiographical stories, and action learning groups. Allow students time and mental room to examine the changes they are going through. Critical reflection consists of analyzing one's assumptions and becoming aware of their context, speculating on how things could be different, and examining each possibility skeptically. It is one of the ways adults learn how to interpret their experiences in order to create new knowledge. Learning how to learn is essential for the changing face of work in this century.

INVITE YOUR ADULT LEARNERS TO TAKE RESPONSIBILITY FOR THEIR CHOICES

If your students are self-directed and have actively participated in setting their own learning goals, then you are a resource person facilitating their journey—but it is still their journey, not yours. Give them respect and demand respect in return. Require them to be accountable and be accountable yourself. Make it clear that learning is an interactive process constructed by the learner rather than passively received from the surrounding environment.

As the table below illustrates, the number of adults participating in adult education since 1995 is steadily increasing. Most adults (30 percent) participate in work-related adult education programs, and the greater number of participants are female (49 percent). Adult learners are diverse, and they bring a wealth of life experiences to the learning environment. Active forms of learning help connect the content to the students' own meaning structures. Students want to be able to relate subject matter to specific contexts in their lives; they prefer to have some degree of control over their learning. If a student perceives that class sessions are meaningful and productive, outside distractions are less likely to prevent them from attending. Adult learners indicate that they continue in a program because they know the instructor cares about them and their success. Build commitment from students to achieve their goals. When short-term goals are realistic, students are more likely to persist and increase their commitment toward the achievement of long-term goals.

PARTICIPATION IN ADULT EDUCATION: 2000–2001

Characteristic	*Total Adults (number)*	*Overall Participation (percent)*	*Work-Related Courses (percent)*	*Personal Interest Courses (percent)*	*Basic Skills Education (percent)*	*Vocational or Technical Programs (percent)*
Total	198,803*	46	30	21	1	1
Age						
16 to 30 years old	46,905	53	28	24	3	2
31 to 40 years old	41,778	53	39	20	1	1
41 to 50 years old	41,255	55	42	21	1	1
51 to 65 years old	39,523	41	28	21	—	1
66 years and older	29,342	22	4	19	—	—
Gender						
Female	103,848	49	30	26	1	1
Male	94,955	43	29	16	1	2

Source: U.S. Department of Education, National Center for Education Statistics, *2001 National Household Education Surveys.*
*Participation in 1995 was 189,543; participation in 1999 was 194,434.

Helping the Special-Needs Student

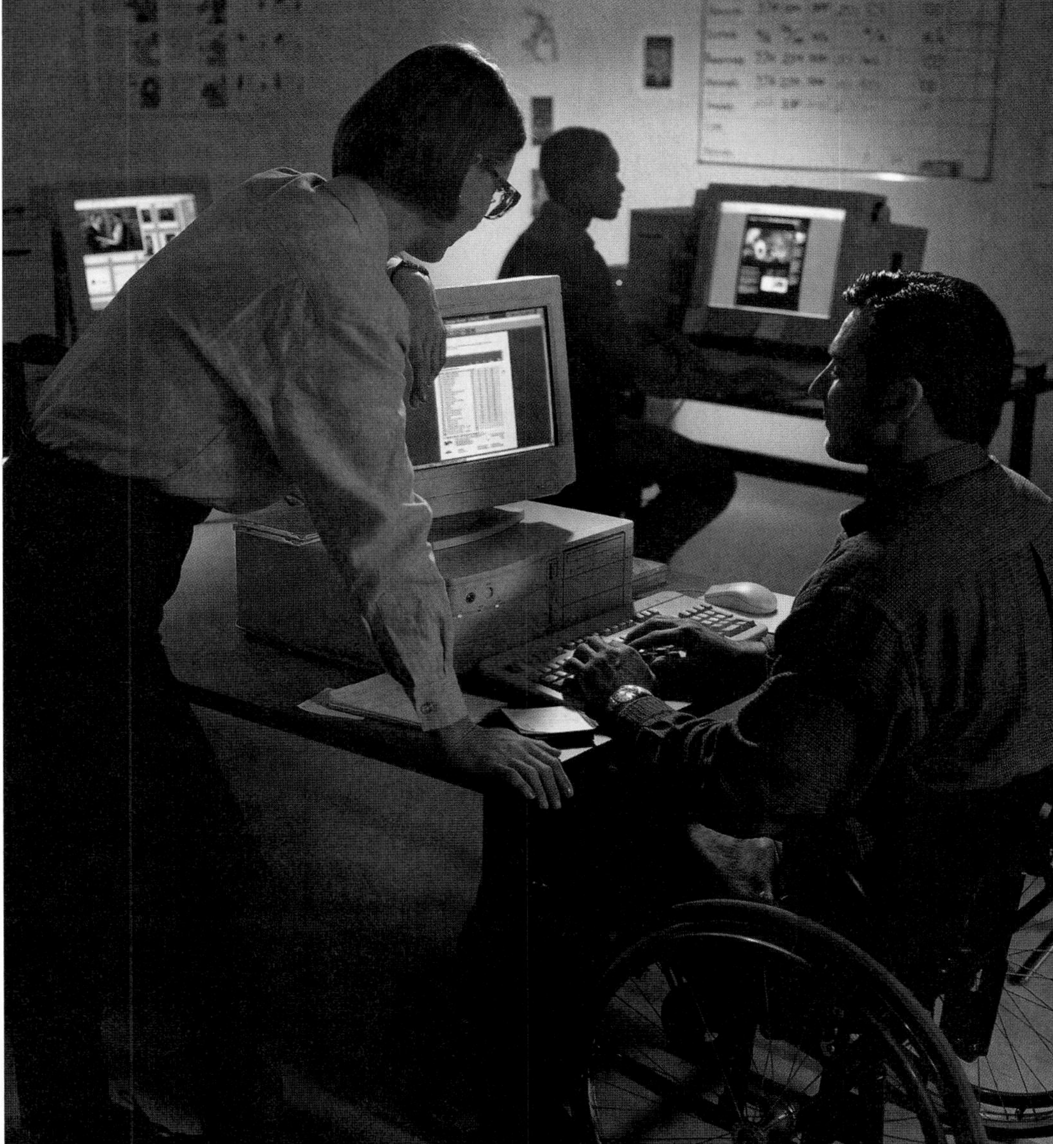

MEETING INDIVIDUAL NEEDS AND LEARNING STYLES

One of your greatest challenges as an instructor is to provide a positive learning environment for all students in your classroom. Because each student has his or her own unique set of abilities, perceptions, and needs, the learning styles and the physical abilities of your students may vary widely.

ASSISTING STUDENTS WITH INDIVIDUAL NEEDS

In order to help you provide all your students with a positive learning experience, this program offers a variety of activities. This diversity will stimulate student interest, motivate learning, and facilitate understanding. The Instructor Wraparound Edition also provides individualized practice activities. These activities reinforce lesson learning by allowing students to progress at their own pace.

TEACHING STUDENTS WITH SPECIAL NEEDS

Students in your classroom may have orthopedic impairments. They may have hearing or vision impairments, learning disabilities, or behavioral disorders—all of which may interfere with their ability to learn. The learning styles of your students may also vary. Some students may be visual learners; others may learn more effectively through hands-on activities. Some students may work well independently, whereas others need the interaction of others. Students may come from a variety of cultural backgrounds, and some may be second-language learners.

Once you determine the special needs of your students, you can identify the areas in the curriculum that may present barriers to them. In order to remove those barriers, you may need to modify your teaching methods.

On the following pages are two tables. Table 5, Meeting Special Needs, describes some of the special needs the students in your classroom may have. It also identifies sources of information. Also provided are tips for modifying your teaching style to accommodate the special needs of your students.

Table 6, Eight Ways of Learning, will help you identify your students' learning styles. The table gives a description of each type of learner; describes the likes of each type, what each type is good at, and how each learns best; and names some famous learners. Once you have identified each student's learning style, you can modify your teaching strategies to best suit his or her needs.

Table 5. MEETING

Subject	*Description*	*Sources of Information**
Second-Language Learners	Certain students speak English as a second language, or not at all. The customs and behavior of people in the majority culture may be confusing for some of these students. Cultural values may inhibit some of these students from full participation in the classroom.	• *Teaching English as a Second Language* • *Mainstreaming and the Minority Child*
Behavioral Disorders	Students with behavioral disorders deviate from standards or expectations of behavior. Their behavior may negatively affect the functioning of others and themselves. These students may also be gifted or have learning disabilities.	• *Exceptional Children* • *Journal of Special Education*
Visual Impairments	Students with visual impairments have partial or total loss of sight. Individuals with visual impairments are not significantly different from their sighted peers in ability range or personality. However, blindness may affect cognitive, motor, and social development.	• *Journal of Visual Impairment and Blindness* • *Education of Visually Handicapped* • American Foundation for the Blind
Hearing Impairments	Students with hearing impairments have partial or total loss of hearing. Individuals with hearing impairments are not significantly different from their peers in ability range or personality. However, deafness may affect cognitive, motor, social, and speech development.	• *American Annals of the Deaf* • *Journal of Speech and Hearing Research* • *Sign Language Studies*
Physical Impairments	Students with physical impairments fall into two categories—those with orthopedic impairments (use of one or more limbs severely restricted) and those with other physical impairments.	• *The Source Book for the Disabled* • *Teaching Exceptional Children*
Gifted Students	Although no formal definition of "gifted" exists, these students can be described as having above average ability, task commitment, and creativity. They rank in the top 5 percent of their classes. They usually finish work more quickly than other students.	• *Journal for the Education of the Gifted* • *Gifted Child Quarterly* • *Gifted Creative/Talented*
Learning Disabilities	Students with learning disabilities have a problem in one or more areas, such as academic learning, language, perception, social-emotional adjustment, memory, or ability to pay attention.	• *Journal of Learning Disabilities* • *Learning Disability Quarterly*

*An Internet search using a search engine such as Google.com or a Web site such as Amazon.com will provide many sources for each of these titles.

SPECIAL NEEDS

Tips for Instruction

- Remember that students' difficulties in speaking English do not reflect their academic ability.
- Try to incorporate students' cultural experiences into your instruction. The help of a bilingual aide may be effective.
- Include information about different cultures in your curriculum to help build students' self-image.
- Avoid cultural stereotypes.
- Encourage students to share information about their cultures in the classroom.

- Work for long-term improvement; do not expect immediate success.
- Talk with students about their strengths and weaknesses and clearly outline objectives.
- Structure schedules, rules, room arrangement, and safety practices for an environment conducive to learning.
- Model appropriate behavior for students and reinforce proper behavior.

- Modify assignments as needed to help students be independent.
- Teach classmates how to serve as guides for the visually impaired.
- Tape lectures and reading assignments for the visually impaired.
- Encourage students to use their sense of touch; provide tactile models whenever possible.
- Verbally describe people and events as they occur in the classroom.

- Limit unnecessary noise in the classroom.
- Provide appropriate seating arrangements so that students can see speakers and read their lips (or interpreters can assist); avoid visual distractions.
- Write out all instructions on paper or on the board; overhead projectors enable you to maintain eye contact while writing.
- Avoid standing with your back to a window or light source.

- With the student, determine when you should offer aid.
- Help other students and adults learn about students with physical impairments.
- Learn about special devices or procedures and find out whether any special safety precautions are needed.
- Allow students to participate in all activities, including field trips, special events, and projects.

- Emphasize concepts, theories, relationships, ideas, and generalizations.
- Let students express themselves in a variety of ways, including drawing, creative writing, and acting.
- Make arrangements for students to work on independent projects.
- Make arrangements for students to take selected subjects early.

- Provide assistance and direction; clearly define rules, assignments, and duties.
- Allow for pair interaction during class time; utilize peer helpers.
- Practice skills frequently.
- Distribute outlines of material presented to the class.
- Allow extra time to complete tests and assignments.

Table 6. EIGHT WAYS

Type of Learner	*Description*	*Likes to . . .*
Verbal/Linguistic	Intelligence is related to words and language, both written and spoken.	read, write, tell stories, play word games, and tell jokes and riddles.
Logical/Mathematical	Intelligence deals with inductive and deductive thinking and reasoning, numbers, and abstractions.	perform experiments, solve puzzles, work with numbers, ask questions, and explore patterns and relationships.
Visual/Spatial	Intelligence relies on the sense of sight and being able to visualize an object, including the ability to create mental images.	draw, build, design, and create things; daydream; do jigsaw puzzles and solve mazes; watch videos; look at photos; and draw maps and charts.
Naturalistic	Intelligence has to do with observing, understanding, and seeing patterns in the natural environment.	spend time outdoors and work with plants, animals, and other parts of the natural environment; identify plants and animals, and hear and see connections to nature.
Musical/Rhythmic	Intelligence is based on recognition of tonal patterns, including various environmental sounds, and on sensitivity to rhythm and beats.	sing and hum, listen to music, play an instrument, move body when music is playing, and make up songs.
Bodily/Kinesthetic	Intelligence is related to physical movement and the brain's motor cortex, which controls bodily motion.	learn by hands-on methods, demonstrate skill in crafts, tinker, perform, display physical endurance, and be challenged physically.
Interpersonal	Intelligence operates primarily through person-to-person relationships and communication.	have lots of friends, talk to people, join groups, play cooperative games, solve problems as part of a group, and volunteer help when others need it.
Intrapersonal	Intelligence is related to inner states of being, self-reflection, metacognition, and awareness of spiritual realities.	work alone, pursue own interests, daydream, keep a personal diary or journal, and think about starting own business.

OF LEARNING

Is Good at . . .	*Learns Best by . . .*	*Famous Learners*
memorizing names, dates, places, and trivia; spelling; using descriptive language; and creating imaginary worlds.	saying, hearing, and seeing words.	Maya Angelou—poet Abraham Lincoln—U.S. President and statesman Jerry Seinfeld—comedian Mary Hatwood Futrell—international instructor, leader, orator
math, reasoning, logic, problem solving, computing numbers, moving from the concrete to the abstract, and thinking conceptually.	categorizing, classifying, and working with abstract patterns and relationships.	Stephen Hawking—physicist Albert Einstein—theoretical physicist Marilyn Burns—math educator Alexa Canady—neurosurgeon
understanding the use of space and how to get around in it, thinking in three-dimensional terms, and imagining things in clear visual images.	visualizing, dreaming, using the mind's eye, and working with colors and pictures.	Pablo Picasso—artist Maria Martinez—Pueblo Indian famous for black pottery Faith Ringgold—painter, quilter, and writer I. M. Pei—architect
measuring, charting, mapping, observing plants and animals, keeping journals, collecting, classifying, and participating in outdoor activities.	visualizing, hands-on activities, bringing outdoors into the classroom, relating the home and the classroom to the natural world.	George Washington Carver—agricultural chemist Rachel Carson—scientific writer Charles Darwin—naturalist and evolutionist John James Audubon—ornithologist
remembering melodies; keeping time; mimicking beat and rhythm; noticing pitches, rhythms, and background and environmental sounds.	rhythm, melody, and music.	Henry Mancini—composer Marian Anderson—contralto Midori—violinist Paul McCartney—singer, songwriter, musician
physical activities such as sports, dancing, acting, and crafts.	touching, moving, interacting with space, and processing knowledge through bodily sensations.	Marcel Marceau—mime Jackie Joyner-Kersey—Olympic gold medalist in track and field Katherine Dunham—modern dancer Christian Bernard—cardiac surgeon
understanding people and their feelings, leading others, organizing, communicating, manipulating, and mediating conflicts.	sharing, comparing, relating, cooperating, and interviewing.	Jimmy Carter—U.S. President and statesman Eleanor Roosevelt—former first lady Lee Iacocca—former president of Chrysler Corporation Mother Teresa—winner of Nobel Peace Prize
understanding self, focusing inwardly on feelings or dreams, following instincts, pursuing interests, and being original.	working alone, doing individualized projects, engaging in self-paced instruction.	Marva Collins—educator Maria Montessori—educator and physician Sigmund Freud—neurologist Anne Sexton—poet

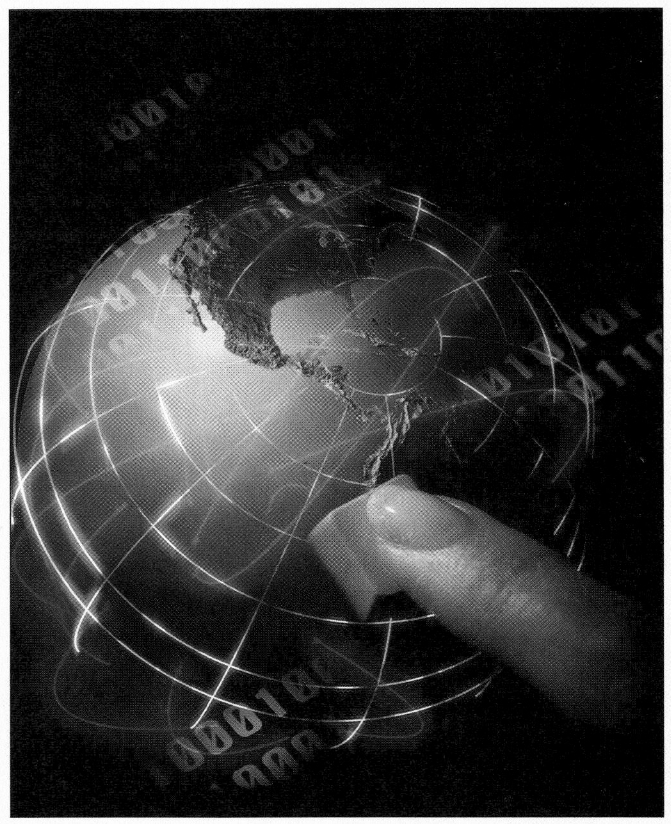

Teaching in a Distance-Learning Environment

INTRODUCTION

Today's classroom is no longer defined by four walls, a chalkboard, and scheduled meeting times. Today's classroom knows no geographical boundaries, nor are the classes restricted by schedules arranged at the convenience of people or institutions.

The computer and access to the World Wide Web have transformed today's classroom into an "any time, any place, anywhere" environment. Virtual classrooms are available around the world to those who have the basic hardware and software capabilities to access the Internet. Because of this availability, educational institutions are able to create a good match between a learner's needs and his or her teaching environment.

The term that has been coined for this dramatic transformation in the learning environment is *distance learning*. In a 1999 *NBEA Yearbook* chapter, Johnson describes distance learning as "a medium used to provide instructional programs to students separated by physical location from the instructor."* For the purposes of this discussion, the abbreviation *DL* will be used when reference is made to distance learning.

DEFINITION OF TERMS

DL instruction has been available for many years, but only recently have advancements in computer technology brought this delivery system to the forefront. As with many technology-based systems, DL uses a few special terms that need definition. The following is a list of some of the more common terms used in DL:

DL Mode. Teaching in a DL environment may take place in an audio, a video, or a data-exchange mode. The first two modes involve sound and graphics. The data-exchange mode is most frequently encountered in online chat rooms, e-mail, and discussion groups. The three modes can be used singly or in any combination.

DL Transmission. Information can be transmitted from one site to another or from one instructor to a student or to several students in a DL environment. Transmission takes place through such media as telephone lines, cable, networks, DSL, T-1 or T-3 lines, ISDN lines, fiber optic, wireless, or satellites. The information is then broadcast over the Internet, through a cable television station, or through some other transmission system.

DL Learning Environments. The two most common learning environments associated with DL are synchronous and asynchronous. A *synchronous* learning environment allows participants to interact immediately and simultaneously with their classmates and/or the instructor. With an *asynchronous* learning environment, the interaction between students and the instructor or other students is delayed.

An example of a synchronous environment would be a classroom in which a teacher is interacting with students in a chat room conversation or a classroom in which the instructor is linked via a two-way audio and video connection that allows for immediate communication about classroom activities.

*Jack E. Johnson, "Distance Education: Learning for the 21st Century," *NBEA 1999 Yearbook,* National Business Education Association, p. 90.

LEARNING PLATFORMS

If a course is going to be transmitted over the Internet, several media may be used. Three of the most common platforms used to carry this transmission are WebCT, FirstClass, and Blackboard. These platforms are designed to assist the instructor in designing and teaching his or her class on the Internet. They come with templates through which the most common teaching tools—such as syllabus, tests, and lectures—are provided on the screen. The teacher merely uploads his or her syllabus, lectures, and tests to the icon that represents each of these teaching activities. Students can then view what the teacher has uploaded to the screen by clicking on the appropriate icon.

WebCT. WebCT is one of the most popular DL platforms used by educational institutions in this country. Students can click on one of several links on the WebCT home page to access different aspects of the course, such as Course Information or Course Calendar. They can also communicate with the instructor or with other students by clicking on the Communications icon. The instructor creates the links on the home page to direct the students to specific sites where they can access information for completing assignments or for communicating with other students or with the instructor.

FirstClass. In FirstClass, the opening screen consists of a toolbar at the top and a folder group in the left column. The toolbar provides links to messaging, chat rooms, and other desktop shortcuts. The folder group contains a student's mailbox and a group of conferences in which students can send and receive messages.

Blackboard.com. In this platform, students click on one of several buttons at the left of the screen that allow them to retrieve information about the course, get assignments from the instructor, send messages to the instructor or other students, receive messages from the instructor or other students, and perform other tasks required in the course.

CREATING A DL CLASS

Once you decide on the platform to use for your DL course, you must create a class site for the students to use to access the home page. From the home page, students will link to other screens in your site to complete assignments, send and receive messages, and obtain other information for the course.

Some general guidelines should be followed as you build your home page. Keep in mind that you may not have any face-to-face contact with your students. Therefore, it is critical that all the information you would typically share with your class on a day-to-day basis is readily available on the home page or through a link that you have placed on that page. The general formatting guidelines for a class home page are as follows:

1. Do not crowd the home page with excessive text and graphics. This is the first screen students will see as they log on to the site. It should be well organized and contain considerable white space.
2. Use a consistent layout and format on the home page and throughout all of the linked pages. For example, in a keyboarding course, you might want to have four or five links that appear on every page because of their frequent use in the course. The illustration below displays a home page with the most frequent activities linked at the top of the page. These icons should also appear on all of the linked pages.

3. Detailed instructions must be provided to assist students when they first log on to the course. These instructions should be sent by e-mail to all students who registered for the course. Included in the instructions should be information on both the hardware and the software needed to participate in the course as an online student.

   For example, hardware information might include the following specifications:
   - PC, Pentium II or higher
   - Hard disk with 1 Gbyte of free space
   - SVGA color monitor, 640 × 480 resolution
   - High-density 3.5″ floppy disk drive
   - CD-ROM drive (8X or faster)
   - Modem
   - Mouse and standard keyboard

Other requirements for enrolling in an online course might be as follows:

- An Internet provider
- Web browser
- E-mail account
- Microsoft Windows 2000, ME, or XP
- Microsoft Word 2003
- Virus program
- Textbook for the course

4. Tell your online students what your expectations are. Not all students are good candidates for an online course. To be successful, online students should:
    - Have the necessary hardware and software to participate in the class.
    - Be good readers. Much of what students get out of an online course is directly related to their ability to read directions and follow instructions that appear daily on various screens used in the course.
    - Be able to follow directions and know how to resolve a problem by accessing the various screens you have provided for the course.
    - Be self-disciplined. The instructor is not in the classroom with them to provide encouragement or to motivate them to move from assignment to assignment through the course. Students must be disciplined enough to do this on their own.
    - Know how to install software and how to use a Web browser, an e-mail program, and a computer.

USING DL IN A KEYBOARDING CLASS

Using DL in a keyboarding class requires some unique skills on the part of the instructor.

Course content can be introduced conventionally, but keyboarding is a psychomotor skill that requires detailed attention to student performance on a continuing basis, sometimes several times per class period. Skills must be measured using several different assessment techniques. For example, timed writings must be assessed using both speed and accuracy measures; skillbuilding must be measured in a pretest and posttest environment to determine how much improvement has taken place; production must be assessed to determine how accurately a document has been typed, how long it took to produce that document, and how many attempts were needed to complete a mailable copy. A significant degree of detail must appear on the Web page to provide information for students so that they can determine how much progress they are making, what work must be accomplished, and how that work is to be transmitted to the instructor.

Once the decision has been made to offer a keyboarding course online, one of the first actions you must take is to build a Web site for the students. Many of the students will be located a considerable distance from the school and may not be able to attend a face-to-face meeting during the first days of the course.

The home page in an online keyboarding course should have sufficient items on it to allow students to observe the details of the course, such as the course name; instructor's name, address, e-mail address, and telephone numbers; an overview of the course; supplies required; grading policies; and assignment due dates. Examples of a home page for a DL keyboarding course appear below. These sample screens are taken from a site (http://caot.lacitycollege.edu/001/) that Arlene Zimmerly, of Los Angeles City College and coauthor of this textbook, created for her online course.

Ms. Zimmerly's home page displays links that are frequently used by students to access various pages on the keyboarding Web site, such as Course Outline, Getting Started, and Assignments.

When students click on the Course Outline link, they gain access to additional Web pages that, in turn, can be accessed by clicking on one of the links at the bottom of the screen such as Course Overview, Supplies, and Class and Grading Policies.

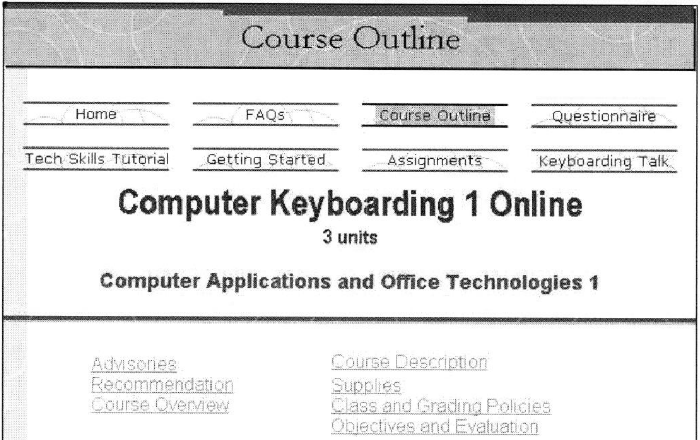

A Web page exists for each of these links. The Course Overview Web page describes how this course differs from a traditional course and emphasizes to the students that everything they do will be transmitted via the Internet to the instructor. Students get a pretty clear picture of what this course consists of and how testing sessions will be administered when they review the Course Overview Web page.

Course Overview

Computer Keyboarding 1 Online is a full-semester, 3-unit course delivered online via the Internet, e-mail, and special course software. You will learn to type by touch and will also learn the basic features of Word 2003 in order to produce mailable documents such as letters, tables, reports, and memos.

Mandatory testing sessions will take place at LA City College (unless you have made other arrangements with me) about three times during the semester. Dates and times for testing will be arranged by me.

The Supplies link provides students with information on the books and software they will need for the course. At Ms. Zimmerly's Web site, supplies consist of a textbook, a software manual, a CD-ROM, and other items:

Supplies

Book 1 (Lessons 1-60), Gregg College Keyboarding & Document Processing for Windows, 10th Edition; Ober, Johnson, Rice, and Hanson; 2006; McGraw-Hill/Higher Education. This book comes bundled with the Word Manual, GDP CD-ROM software, and easel included.

- **Word Manual**
- ***CD ROM Home Version Software Package for Gregg College Keyboarding & Document Processing for Windows***, 10th Edition, Lessons 1-120, For Home Use; and easel.
- **Headset:** If you work in our campus labs, you will need to bring your own headset to listen to any audio or video instruction so that you don't disturb students around you.

The Class and Grading Policies link informs students of the grading and assessment policy for the course. You might like to start by informing students how their document processing tests and timed writings are going to be evaluated, as Ms. Zimmerly has done on the following screen:

Class and Grading Policies

1. **Drop Policy, LACC Schedule of Classes**: It is the student's responsibility to drop a class no longer being attended. Failure to drop a class in a timely manner may result in a "W" or an "F" on your academic record. The student agrees to be familiar with the information in the college catalog and schedule of classes, and know and observe all policies and procedures related to the program of study being pursued.
2. **Skillbuilding and Production Jobs**. All work assigned for a particular week, including practice tests and regular tests, is due no later than Sunday evening at the end of the week in which the work is assigned. A document assigned a D or F may be resubmitted one time by editing the document.

   ✔Up to 1 percent per week will be deducted from your final average any late or missing skillbuilding or production jobs. for

Additional information on grading and evaluation should be provided on screen for the students, such as speed and accuracy requirements for students, how techniques will be assessed, and the weight of each of the grading criteria.

1. Type a minimum of 30 wpm on a 3-minute timed writing with 3 or fewer errors.
2. Demonstrate good work habits, acceptable typing technique, and skill in using the computer and printer.
3. Recognize, evaluate, and correct errors in content and format of documents.
4. Demonstrate skill in language arts, including word division, proofreading, punctuation, grammar, spelling, and keyboard composing.
5. Produce mailable business documents including letters, tables, reports, and memos using Microsoft Word 2003.

50% 3-Minute Timing, 3-Error Limit, by Touch

- A = 40+ wpm
- B = 35–39
- C = 30–34
- D = 25–29
- F = 24 or below

30% Document Processing Tests

10% each Practice Document Processing Tests and Document Processing Jobs

Grade	Formatting Errors
A	0 errors
B	1 error
C	2 errors
D	3 errors
F	4+ errors

Up to +10% **Extra Credit:** (Keyboarding Talk; extra Proofreading Checks, documents, and skillbuilding)

Up to −10% each **Deductions:** Proofreading Checks; Technique Check; missing assignments; late assignments; Keyboarding Talk (up to minus −5%)

STUDENT RESPONSIBILITIES

Students must assume responsibility for gaining access to the Internet; for purchasing necessary books, supplies, and other materials; for completing their assignments on time; and for uploading their work to you so that it can be evaluated.

If this is the first course they have taken online, they will need specific and accurate instructions on the steps necessary for them to get started in the class. All this information must be provided online for students to access as they wish. The screen below shows selected information that should be provided to online keyboarding students:

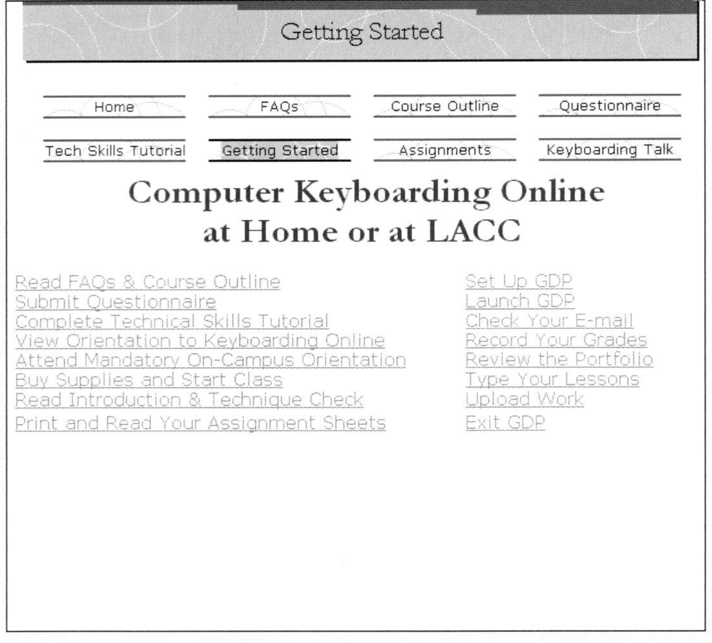

CHECKING TECHNIQUE ONLINE

Unlike students in a traditional class setting, online students are not physically present to have their keyboarding techniques checked. This does not minimize the necessity to check techniques, and many online instructors schedule one or two class periods during which online students are required to go to the classroom so that their keyboarding techniques can be checked. A link for technique checking should be placed on the keyboarding Web site to let students know how their keyboarding technique will be checked.

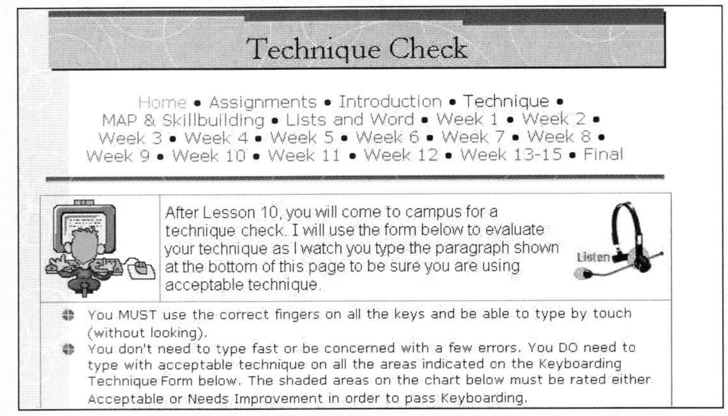

A form similar to the one below can be used to check technique when the students come to the classroom. This form is available at the College Keyboarding Web site at www.mhhe.com/gdp.

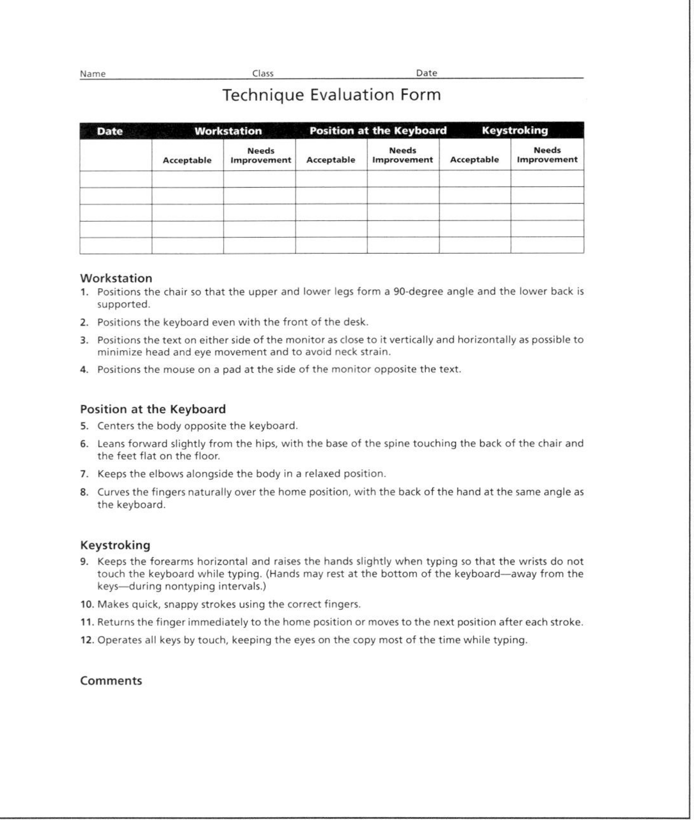

Name Class Date

Technique Evaluation Form

Date	Workstation		Position at the Keyboard		Keystroking	
	Acceptable	Needs Improvement	Acceptable	Needs Improvement	Acceptable	Needs Improvement

Workstation

1. Positions the chair so that the upper and lower legs form a 90-degree angle and the lower back is supported.
2. Positions the keyboard even with the front of the desk.
3. Positions the text on either side of the monitor as close to it vertically and horizontally as possible to minimize head and eye movement and to avoid neck strain.
4. Positions the mouse on a pad at the side of the monitor opposite the text.

Position at the Keyboard

5. Centers the body opposite the keyboard.
6. Leans forward slightly from the hips, with the base of the spine touching the back of the chair and the feet flat on the floor.
7. Keeps the elbows alongside the body in a relaxed position.
8. Curves the fingers naturally over the home position, with the back of the hand at the same angle as the keyboard.

Keystroking

9. Keeps the forearms horizontal and raises the hands slightly when typing so that the wrists do not touch the keyboard while typing. (Hands may rest at the bottom of the keyboard—away from the keys—during nontyping intervals.)
10. Makes quick, snappy strokes using the correct fingers.
11. Returns the finger immediately to the home position or moves to the next position after each stroke.
12. Operates all keys by touch, keeping the eyes on the copy most of the time while typing.

Comments

Students should be aware that keyboarding technique continues to be an essential component in learning how to keyboard successfully, even if they are not in the classroom with the instructor every day to have their techniques observed.

MOTIVATING STUDENTS ONLINE

Motivating students is a critical aspect of any keyboarding class and even more so when students are online because they are not physically present so that you can work with them on an individual basis every day.

Special techniques for motivation must be employed with online students. For example, you can motivate students through the feedback you give them on assignments they complete. These annotations are an integral component of an online keyboarding class and should be used frequently to motivate students as well as to provide them with comments on the quality of the work they submit.

Annotations can be used as shown in the illustration below to communicate with your students and to motivate them periodically.

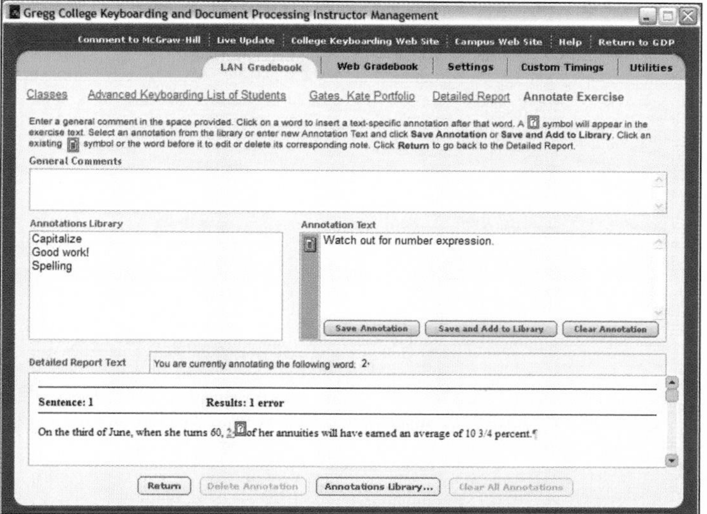

SUMMARY

Online keyboarding courses will grow in popularity as access to the Internet grows. They will also grow because of a changing student profile in which we find an abundance of nontraditional students who are seeking to upgrade their skills and cannot gain access to traditional classroom courses because of a work schedule that does not permit them to attend classes at a location that is a considerable distance from their work site.

We must adjust our teaching styles to accommodate these students, thereby ensuring that they will have access to the skills training that will enhance their opportunities to succeed in the new millennium's workforce.

Understanding the Lesson

The textbook organization provides a structure that is easy for students to follow. Warmup and skillbuilding drills precede word processing, formatting, and document processing. The text instruction follows an organized sequence of skill development.

The **Part Opener** helps students focus on the four units to come. The objectives list and describe the variety of skill areas within which students learn to apply their knowledge through keyboarding, language arts, word processing, document processing, and technical skill development.

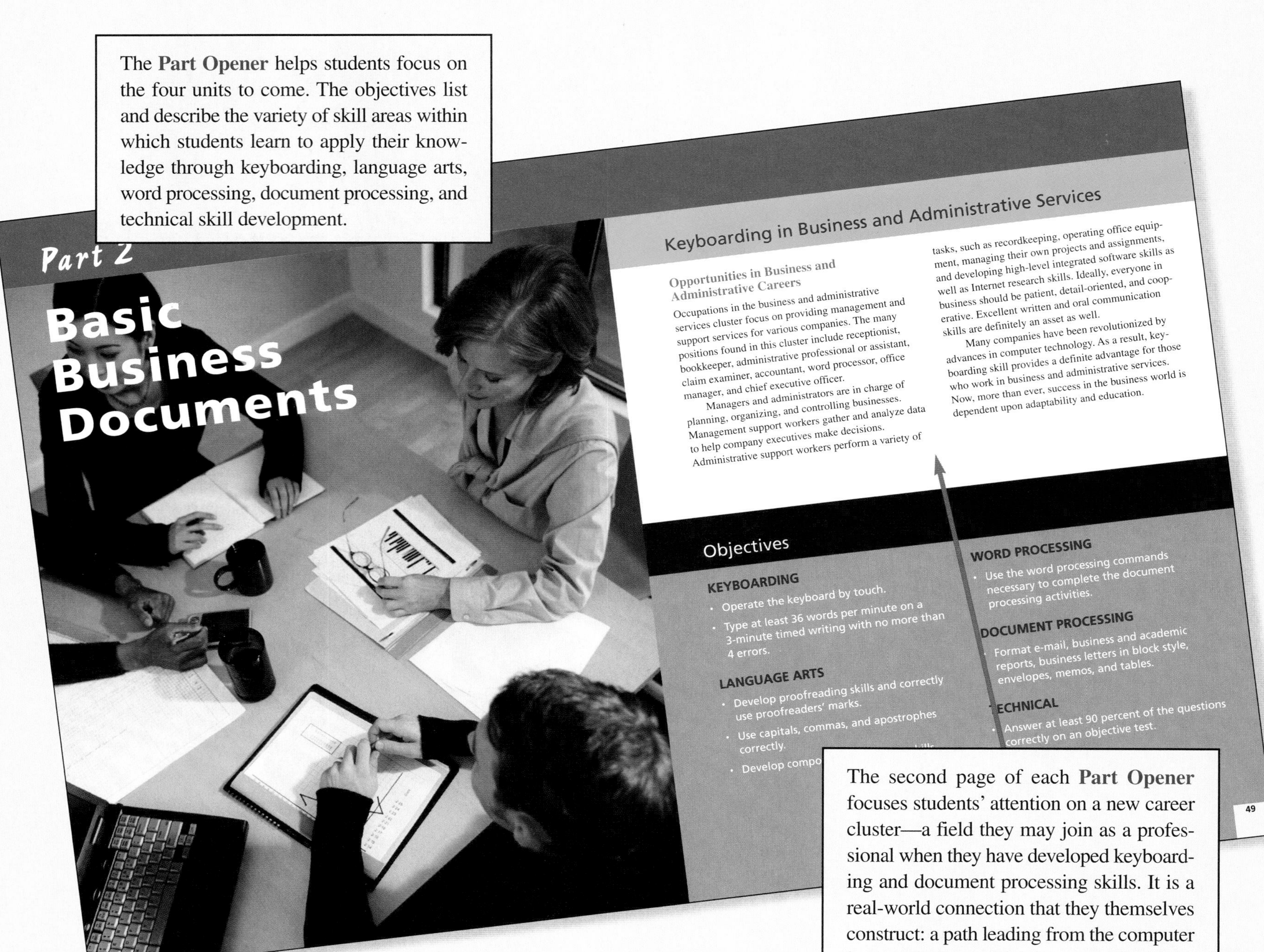

Part 2

Basic Business Documents

Keyboarding in Business and Administrative Services

Opportunities in Business and Administrative Careers

Occupations in the business and administrative services cluster focus on providing management and support services for various companies. The many positions found in this cluster include receptionist, bookkeeper, administrative professional or assistant, claim examiner, accountant, word processor, office manager, and chief executive officer.

Managers and administrators are in charge of planning, organizing, and controlling businesses. Management support workers gather and analyze data to help company executives make decisions. Administrative support workers perform a variety of tasks, such as recordkeeping, operating office equipment, managing their own projects and assignments, and developing high-level integrated software skills as well as Internet research skills. Ideally, everyone in business should be patient, detail-oriented, and cooperative. Excellent written and oral communication skills are definitely an asset as well.

Many companies have been revolutionized by advances in computer technology. As a result, keyboarding skill provides a definite advantage for those who work in business and administrative services. Now, more than ever, success in the business world is dependent upon adaptability and education.

Objectives

KEYBOARDING

- Operate the keyboard by touch.
- Type at least 36 words per minute on a 3-minute timed writing with no more than 4 errors.

LANGUAGE ARTS

- Develop proofreading skills and correctly use proofreaders' marks.
- Use capitals, commas, and apostrophes correctly.
- Develop compo

WORD PROCESSING

- Use the word processing commands necessary to complete the document processing activities.

DOCUMENT PROCESSING

- Format e-mail, business and academic reports, business letters in block style, envelopes, memos, and tables.

TECHNICAL

- Answer at least 90 percent of the questions correctly on an objective test.

49

The second page of each **Part Opener** focuses students' attention on a new career cluster—a field they may join as a professional when they have developed keyboarding and document processing skills. It is a real-world connection that they themselves construct: a path leading from the computer keyboard to a good job in a rewarding field.

Understanding the Lesson

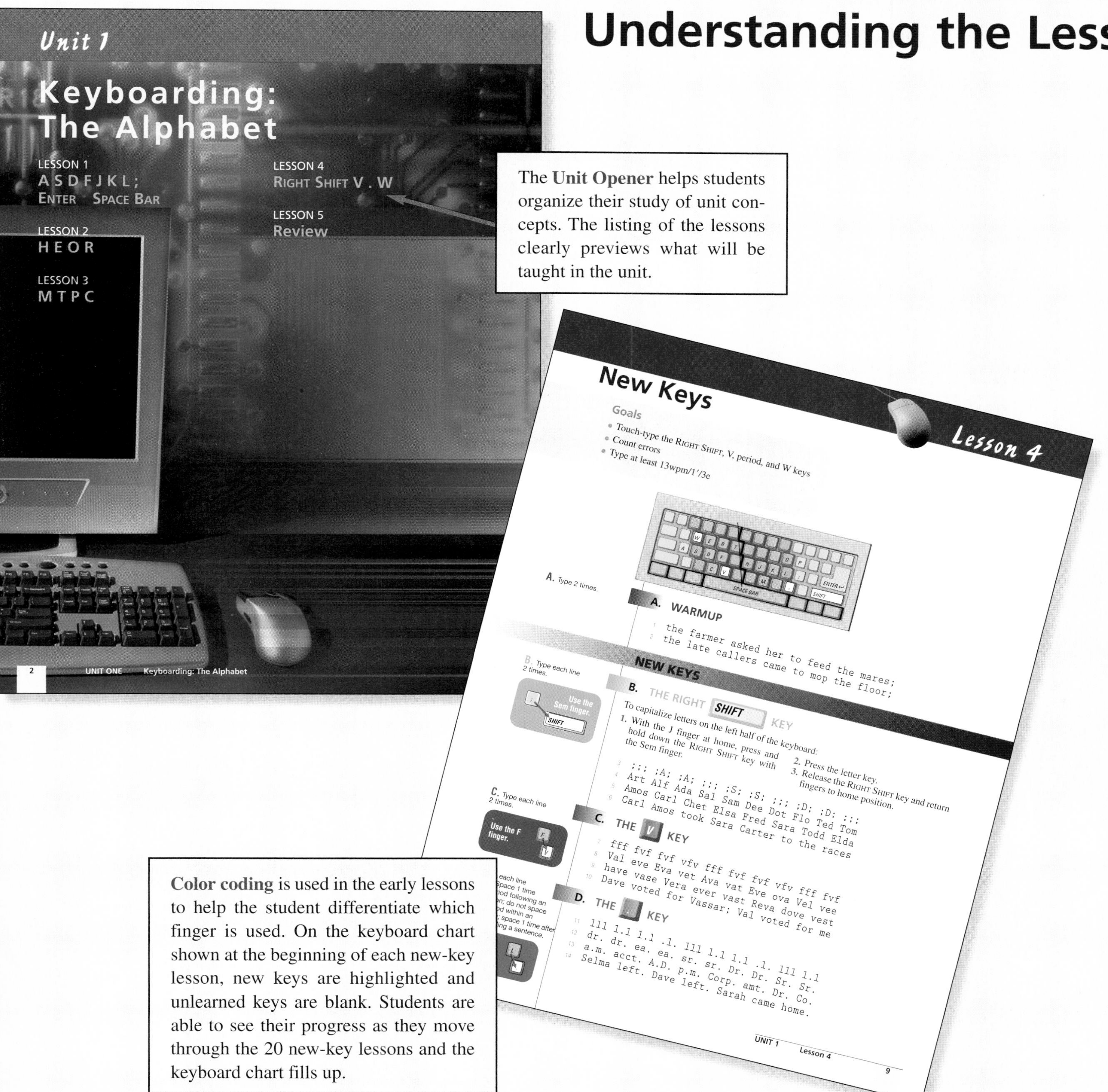

Unit 1
Keyboarding: The Alphabet
LESSON 1
A S D F J K L ;
ENTER SPACE BAR
LESSON 2
H E O R
LESSON 3
M T P C
LESSON 4
RIGHT SHIFT V . W
LESSON 5
Review
2 UNIT ONE Keyboarding: The Alphabet
New Keys
Lesson 4
Goals
Touch-type the RIGHT SHIFT, V, period, and W keys
Count errors
Type at least 13wpm/1'/3e
A. WARMUP
the farmer asked her to feed the mares;
the late callers came to mop the floor;
NEW KEYS
B. THE RIGHT SHIFT KEY
To capitalize letters on the left half of the keyboard:
1. With the J finger at home, press and hold down the RIGHT SHIFT key with the Sem finger.
2. Press the letter key.
3. Release the RIGHT SHIFT key and return fingers to home position.
;;; ;A; ;A; ;;; ;S; ;S; ;;; ;D; ;D; ;;;
Art Alf Ada Sal Sam Dee Dot Flo Ted Tom
Amos Carl Chet Elsa Fred Sara Todd Elda
Carl Amos took Sara Carter to the races
C. THE V KEY
fff fvf fvf vfv fff fvf fvf vfv fff fvf
Val eve Eva vet Ava vat Eve ova Vel vee
have vase Vera ever vast Reva dove vest
Dave voted for Vassar; Val voted for me
D. THE . KEY
lll l.l l.l .l. lll l.l l.l .l. lll l.l
dr. dr. ea. ea. sr. sr. Dr. Dr. Sr. Sr.
a.m. acct. A.D. p.m. Corp. amt. Dr. Co.
Selma left. Dave left. Sarah came home.
UNIT 1 Lesson 4 9

The **Unit Opener** helps students organize their study of unit concepts. The listing of the lessons clearly previews what will be taught in the unit.

Color coding is used in the early lessons to help the student differentiate which finger is used. On the keyboard chart shown at the beginning of each new-key lesson, new keys are highlighted and unlearned keys are blank. Students are able to see their progress as they move through the 20 new-key lessons and the keyboard chart fills up.

Understanding the Lesson

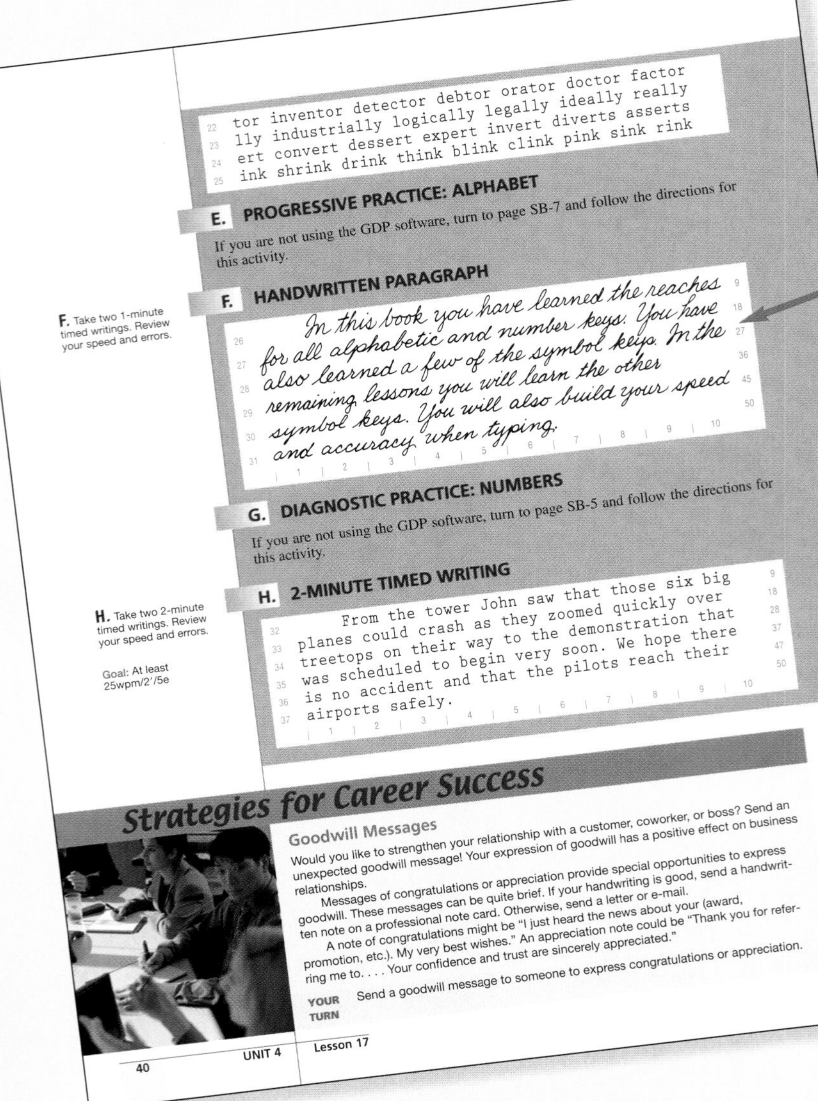

22 tor inventor detector debtor orator doctor factor
23 lly industrially logically legally ideally really
24 ert convert dessert expert invert diverts asserts
25 ink shrink drink think blink clink pink sink rink

E. PROGRESSIVE PRACTICE: ALPHABET

If you are not using the GDP software, turn to page SB-7 and follow the directions for this activity.

F. HANDWRITTEN PARAGRAPH

F. Take two 1-minute timed writings. Review your speed and errors.

In this book you have learned the reaches for all alphabetic and number keys. You have also learned a few of the symbol keys. In the remaining lessons you will learn the other symbol keys. You will also build your speed and accuracy when typing.

G. DIAGNOSTIC PRACTICE: NUMBERS

If you are not using the GDP software, turn to page SB-5 and follow the directions for this activity.

H. 2-MINUTE TIMED WRITING

H. Take two 2-minute timed writings. Review your speed and errors.

Goal: At least 25wpm/2'/5e

From the tower John saw that those six big planes could crash as they zoomed quickly over treetops on their way to the demonstration that was scheduled to begin very soon. We hope there is no accident and that the pilots reach their airports safely.

Strategies for Career Success

Goodwill Messages

Would you like to strengthen your relationship with a customer, coworker, or boss? Send an unexpected goodwill message! Your expression of goodwill has a positive effect on business relationships.

Messages of congratulations or appreciation provide special opportunities to express goodwill. These messages can be quite brief. If your handwriting is good, send a handwritten note on a professional note card. Otherwise, send a letter or e-mail.

A note of congratulations might be "I just heard the news about your (award, promotion, etc.). My very best wishes." An appreciation note could be "Thank you for referring me to. . . . Your confidence and trust are sincerely appreciated."

YOUR TURN Send a goodwill message to someone to express congratulations or appreciation.

40 UNIT 4 Lesson 17

Handwritten examples are used to make lessons more realistic since many memos, letters, reports, and so on, are originally prepared by writers using pen and paper. Including handwritten manuscript also enhances students' ability to read and type accurately at the same time.

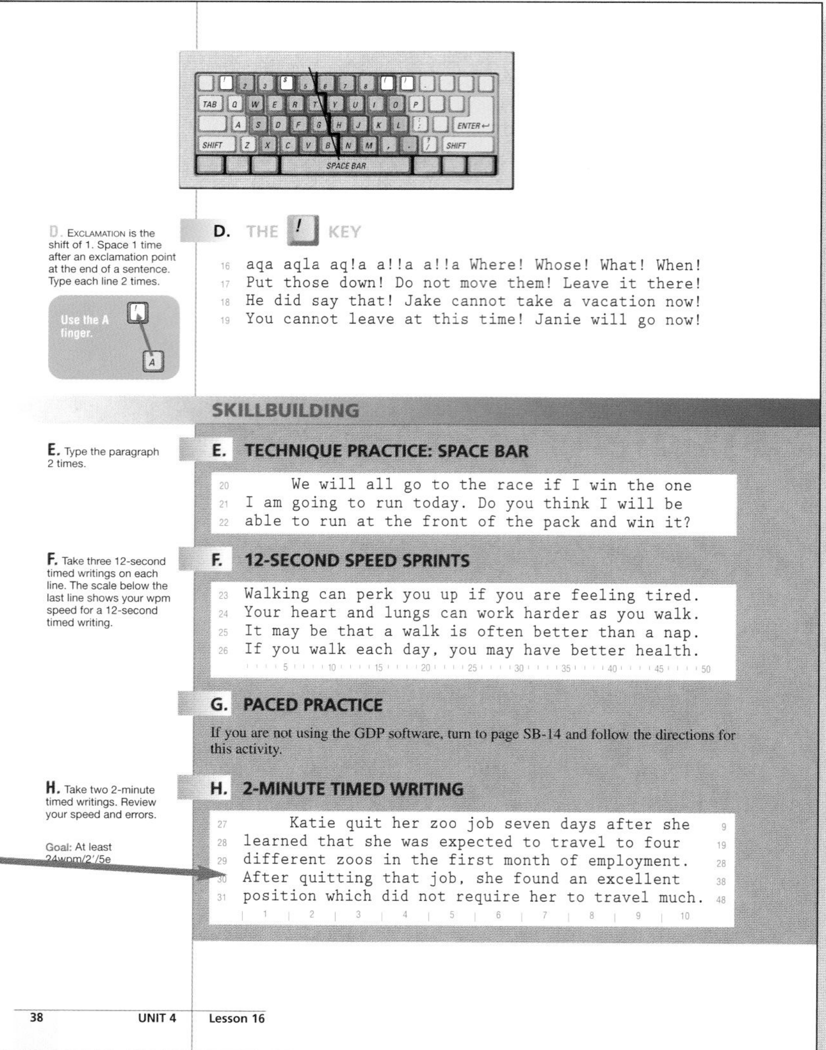

D. THE ! KEY

D. EXCLAMATION is the shift of 1. Space 1 time after an exclamation point at the end of a sentence. Type each line 2 times.

Use the A finger.

16 aqa aqla aq!a a!!a a!!a Where! Whose! What! When!
17 Put those down! Do not move them! Leave it there!
18 He did say that! Jake cannot take a vacation now!
19 You cannot leave at this time! Janie will go now!

SKILLBUILDING

E. TECHNIQUE PRACTICE: SPACE BAR

E. Type the paragraph 2 times.

We will all go to the race if I win the one I am going to run today. Do you think I will be able to run at the front of the pack and win it?

F. 12-SECOND SPEED SPRINTS

F. Take three 12-second timed writings on each line. The scale below the last line shows your wpm speed for a 12-second timed writing.

23 Walking can perk you up if you are feeling tired.
24 Your heart and lungs can work harder as you walk.
25 It may be that a walk is often better than a nap.
26 If you walk each day, you may have better health.

G. PACED PRACTICE

If you are not using the GDP software, turn to page SB-14 and follow the directions for this activity.

H. 2-MINUTE TIMED WRITING

H. Take two 2-minute timed writings. Review your speed and errors.

Goal: At least 24wpm/2'/5e

Katie quit her zoo job seven days after she learned that she was expected to travel to four different zoos in the first month of employment. After quitting that job, she found an excellent position which did not require her to travel much.

38 UNIT 4 Lesson 16

Timed Writings are used to improve both accuracy and speed. Timed writings measure how well students are progressing in keyboarding skill development. In addition, students find that making measurable progress on the timed writing results adds to their self-esteem and confidence level.

Understanding the Lesson

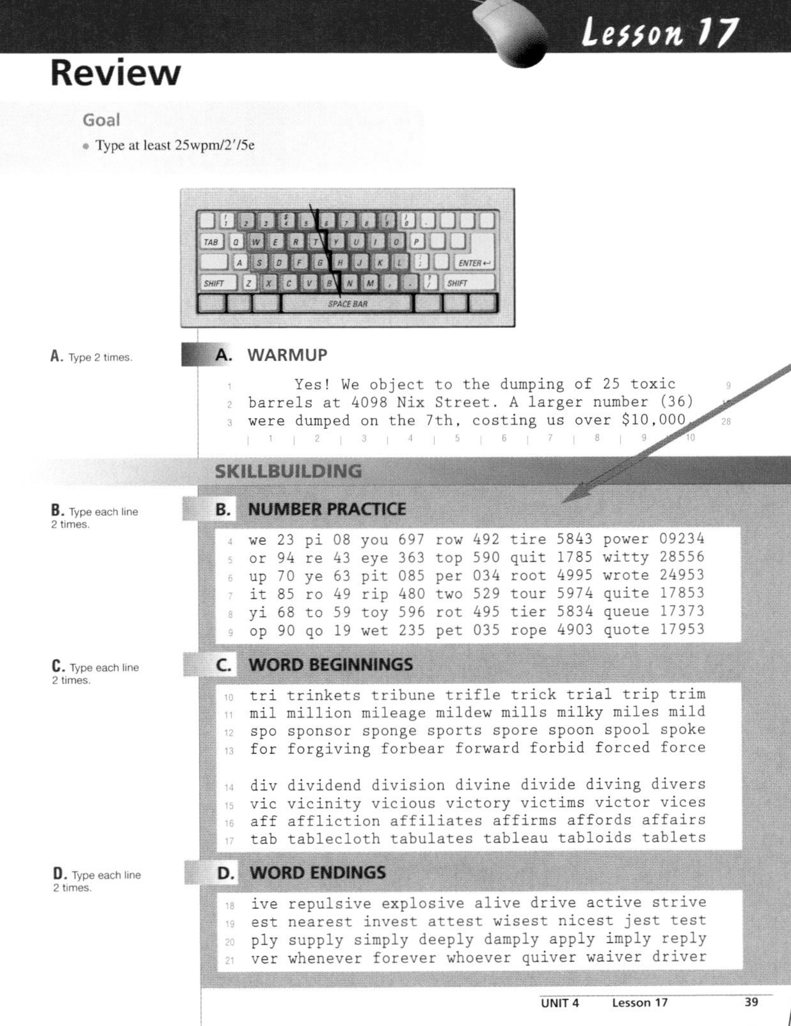

Lesson 17

Review

Goal

- Type at least 25wpm/2'/5e

A. Type 2 times.

A. WARMUP

```
     Yes! We object to the dumping of 25 toxic        9
barrels at 4098 Nix Street. A larger number (36)     19
were dumped on the 7th, costing us over $10,000.     28
 | 1 | 2 | 3 | 4 | 5 | 6 | 7 | 8 | 9 | 10
```

SKILLBUILDING

B. Type each line 2 times.

B. NUMBER PRACTICE

```
we 23 pi 08 you 697 row 492 tire 5843 power 09234
or 94 re 43 eye 363 top 590 quit 1785 witty 28556
up 70 ye 63 pit 085 per 034 root 4995 wrote 24953
it 85 ro 49 rip 480 two 529 tour 5974 quite 17853
yi 68 to 59 toy 596 rot 495 tier 5834 queue 17373
op 90 qo 19 wet 235 pet 035 rope 4903 quote 17953
```

C. Type each line 2 times.

C. WORD BEGINNINGS

```
tri trinkets tribune trifle trick trial trip trim
mil million mileage mildew mills milky miles mild
spo sponsor sponge sports spore spoon spool spoke
for forgiving forbear forward forbid forced force

div dividend division divine divide diving divers
vic vicinity vicious victory victims victor vices
aff affliction affiliates affirms affords affairs
tab tablecloth tabulates tableau tabloids tablets
```

D. Type each line 2 times.

D. WORD ENDINGS

```
ive repulsive explosive alive drive active strive
est nearest invest attest wisest nicest jest test
ply supply simply deeply damply apply imply reply
ver whenever forever whoever quiver waiver driver
```

UNIT 4 Lesson 17 39

Skillbuilding practice in every lesson offers an individualized plan for students to develop speed and accuracy. A variety of skillbuilding exercises—including. Technique Practice, Pretest/Practice/Posttest, Sustained Practice, 12-Second Speed Sprints, Diagnostic Practice, Progressive Practice, Paced Practice, and Number Practice—provide the foundation for progress in students' skill development.

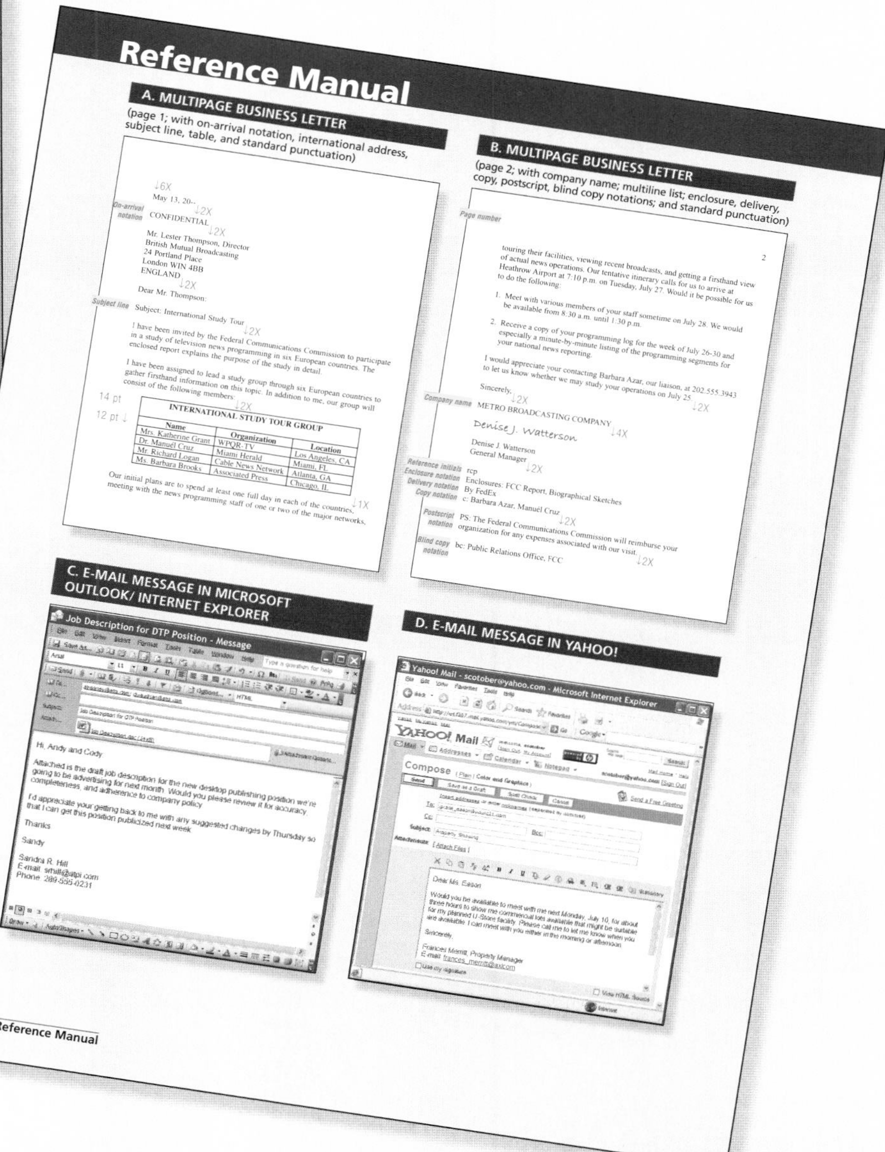

Reference Manual

A. MULTIPAGE BUSINESS LETTER (page 1; with on-arrival notation, international address, subject line, table, and standard punctuation)

B. MULTIPAGE BUSINESS LETTER (page 2; with company name; multiline list; enclosure, delivery, copy, postscript, blind copy notations; and standard punctuation)

C. E-MAIL MESSAGE IN MICROSOFT OUTLOOK/ INTERNET EXPLORER

D. E-MAIL MESSAGE IN YAHOO!

R-5 Reference Manual

The **Reference Manual** located in the front of the book and in the Word Processing Manual enables students to rapidly and easily locate information regarding the proper way to format business letters, reports, e-mail messages, memos, and other forms of written communication. Elements such as line spacing and the placement of letterhead and body text are all illustrated in detail to give students visual reinforcement to support the instruction. In addition, 50 essential rules for language arts in business contexts are included, with examples, in the Reference Manual to help improve students' writing skills.

Understanding the Lesson

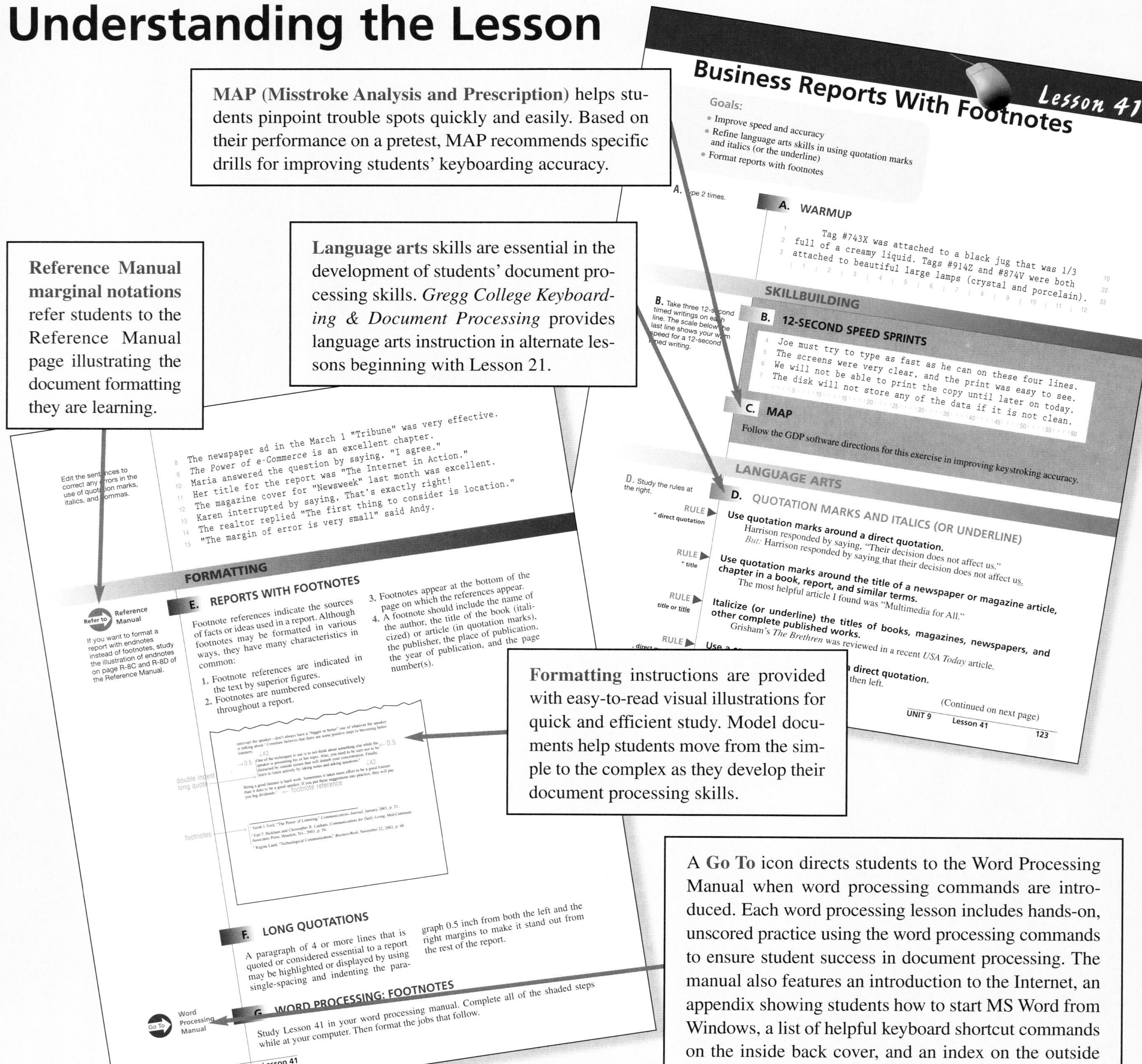

Lesson 41
Business Reports With Footnotes
Goals:
Improve speed and accuracy
Refine language arts skills in using quotation marks and italics (or the underline)
Format reports with footnotes
A. WARMUP
SKILLBUILDING
B. 12-SECOND SPEED SPRINTS
C. MAP
Follow the GDP software directions for this exercise in improving keystroking accuracy.
LANGUAGE ARTS
D. QUOTATION MARKS AND ITALICS (OR UNDERLINE)
FORMATTING
E. REPORTS WITH FOOTNOTES
F. LONG QUOTATIONS
G. WORD PROCESSING: FOOTNOTES
Refer to Reference Manual
Go To Word Processing Manual

MAP (Misstroke Analysis and Prescription) helps students pinpoint trouble spots quickly and easily. Based on their performance on a pretest, MAP recommends specific drills for improving students' keyboarding accuracy.

Reference Manual marginal notations refer students to the Reference Manual page illustrating the document formatting they are learning.

Language arts skills are essential in the development of students' document processing skills. *Gregg College Keyboarding & Document Processing* provides language arts instruction in alternate lessons beginning with Lesson 21.

Formatting instructions are provided with easy-to-read visual illustrations for quick and efficient study. Model documents help students move from the simple to the complex as they develop their document processing skills.

A **Go To** icon directs students to the Word Processing Manual when word processing commands are introduced. Each word processing lesson includes hands-on, unscored practice using the word processing commands to ensure student success in document processing. The manual also features an introduction to the Internet, an appendix showing students how to start MS Word from Windows, a list of helpful keyboard shortcut commands on the inside back cover, and an index on the outside back cover—all for students' convenience.

Understanding the Lesson

The last document processing exercise in most units is designated as a Progress Check/Proofreading Check. Students should aim for the goal of zero typographical errors when the GDP software first scores the document in order to earn a satisfactory proofreading grade. If students need a second chance, they should click the **Create** button in the GDP software to retype the document and try again to have zero typos on the first scored attempt. The GDP Portfolio notes how many scored attempts were made when a document was created or re-created to help you track proofreading scores.

Correspondence 55-44

Personal-Business Letter in Modified-Block Style

Assume that you have interviewed for the position mentioned in the previous letter and that you would now like to send a follow-up letter dated June 15, 20--, to Mr. Blair N. Scarborough, thanking him for the interview. Use the inside address, salutation, and closing lines shown in Correspondence 55-43 to create the follow-up letter below:

Progress and Proofreading Check

Documents designated as Proofreading Checks serve as a check of your proofreading skill. Your goal is to have zero typographical errors when the GDP software first scores the document.

¶ Thank you for the time you spent with me, yesterday telling me about the Computer Specialist position with Wyatt. My interview with you reafirmed my interest in working for Wyatt.

¶ I was very impresed with work done in your Information Processing department. The hardware and software you use for writing computer code and the people working in that department are very apealing to me.

¶ I believe my particular background and skills blend perfectly with the this position. I hope to hear from you by the end of next week for a positive decision on my employment. Thank you again for bringing me in for the interview.

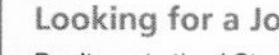

Strategies for Career Success

Looking for a Job

Don't waste time! Start your job search early. Scan the Help Wanted section in major Sunday newspapers for job descriptions and salaries. The Internet provides electronic access to worldwide job listings. If you are interested in a particular company, access its home page.

Ask a reference librarian for handbooks (for example, *Occupational Outlook Handbook*), government publications (for example, *Federal Career Opportunities*), and journals or magazines in your field. Visit your college placement office. Sign up for interviews with companies that visit your campus.

Talk with people in your field to get advice. Look for an internship or join a professional organization in your field. Attend local chapter meetings to network with people in your chosen profession.

Taking the initiative in your job search will pay off!

YOUR TURN Visit the Internet site for the *National Business Employment Weekly* at http://www.employmentguide.com, which provides more than 45,000 national and international job listings online.

Special features are designed to enhance students' study of keyboarding. The Keyboarding Connection features illustrate the importance of keyboarding skills in the real world. The Strategies for Career Success features offer an employment-related narrative including useful hints for succeeding in any career.

Appendix

Ten-Key Numeric Keypad

Goal

- To control the ten-key numeric keypad keys.

Some computer keyboards have a separate ten-key numeric keypad located to the right of the alphanumeric keyboard. The arrangement of the keypad enables you to type numbers more rapidly than you can when using the top row of the alphanumeric keyboard.

To input numbers using the ten-key numeric keypad, you must activate the Num Lock (Numeric Lock) key. Usually, an indicator light signals that the Num Lock is activated.

On the keypad, 4, 5, and 6 are the home keys. Place your fingers on the keypad home row as follows:

- First finger (J finger) on 4
- Second finger (K finger) on 5
- Third finger (L finger) on 6

The keypad keys are controlled as follows:

- First finger controls 1, 4, and 7
- Second finger controls 2, 5, and 8
- Third finger controls 3, 6, 9, and decimal point
- Right thumb controls 0
- Fourth finger controls ENTER

Since different computers have different arrangements of ten-key numeric keypads, study the arrangement of your keypad. The illustration shows the most common arrangement. If your keypad is arranged differently from the one shown in the illustration, check with your instructor for the correct placement of your fingers on the keypad.

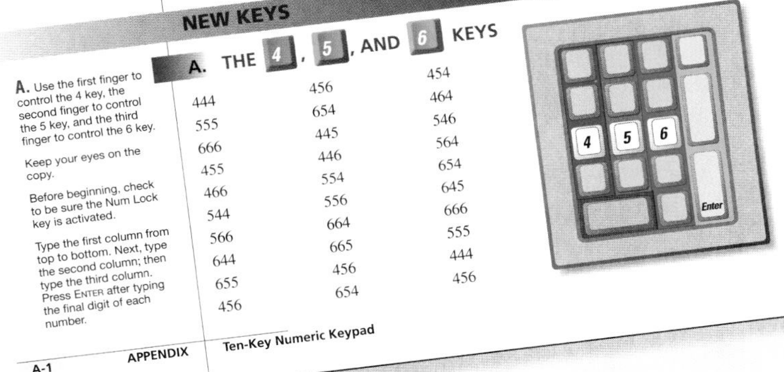

NEW KEYS

A. THE 4, 5, AND 6 KEYS

A. Use the first finger to control the 4 key, the second finger to control the 5 key, and the third finger to control the 6 key.

Keep your eyes on the copy.

Before beginning, check to be sure the Num Lock key is activated.

Type the first column from top to bottom. Next, type the second column; then type the third column. Press ENTER after typing the final digit of each number.

444	456	454
555	654	464
666	445	546
455	446	564
466	554	654
544	556	645
566	664	666
644	665	555
655	456	444
456	654	456

A-1 APPENDIX Ten-Key Numeric Keypad

The **Appendix** contains instructions for the ten-key numeric keypad. Students practice entering numerical data using touch-typing techniques on the keypad instead of using the number keys on the top row of the keyboard.

Understanding the Lesson

Back-of-the-book **Skillbuilding** content is designed with students in mind. The Paced Practice skill-building paragraphs use an upbeat, motivational story line containing guidance in career choices. The Supplementary Timed Writings relate critical thinking skills to careers.

SKILLBUILDING

42wpm

temporary job within a chosen field. You will become more familiar with a specific job while developing your skills. You'll gain valuable experience, whether you choose that career or not.

Whichever path you choose, strive for a high level of pride in yourself and your work. Your image is affected by what you believe other people think of you as well as by how you view yourself. Evaluate your level of confidence in yourself. If you have self-doubts, begin to build up your self-confidence and self-esteem.

44wpm

Self-esteem is essential for a positive attitude, and a positive attitude is essential for success in the world of work. While you cannot control everything that happens at work, you can control how you react. Your attitude matters. Becoming more confident and cultivating positive thoughts can bring you power in your life and on the job.

46wpm

Several factors lead to success on the job. People who have studied the factors say that it is the personal traits that often determine who is promoted or who is not. One of the finest traits a person can possess is the trait of being likable. Being likable means a person is honest, courteous, loyal, thoughtful, pleasant, kind, and most assuredly, positive.

48wpm

If you are likable, probably you relate well with others. Your kindness serves you well in the workplace. Developing good interpersonal relationships with coworkers will make work more enjoyable. After all, think of all the hours you will spend together. By showing that you are willing to collaborate with your coworkers, most likely you will receive their cooperation in return.

Cooperation begins on the first day of your new job.

SB-17 SKILLBUILDING Paced Practice

SKILLBUILDING

Supplementary Timed Writing 3

Office employees perform a variety of tasks during 10
their workday. These tasks vary from handling telephone 21
calls to forwarding personal messages, from sending short 33
e-mail messages to compiling complex office reports, and 44
from writing simple letters to assembling detailed letters 56
with tables, graphics, and imported data. Office workers 67
are a fundamental part of a company's structure. 77
The office worker uses critical thinking in order to 88
accomplish a wide array of daily tasks. Some of the tasks 100
are more urgent than other tasks and should be completed 111
first. Some tasks take only a short time, while others take 123
a lot more time. Some tasks demand a quick response, while 135
others may be taken up as time permits or even postponed 147
until the future. Some of the tasks require input from 158
coworkers or managers. Whether a job is simple or complex, 170
big or small, the office worker must decide what is to be 182
tackled first by determining the priority of each task. 193
When setting priorities, critical thinking skills are 204
essential. The office worker evaluates each aspect of the 216
task. It is a good idea to identify the size of the task, 228
determine its complexity, estimate its effort, judge its 239
importance, and set its deadline. Once the office worker 250
assesses each task that is to be finished within a certain 262
period of time, then the priority for completing all tasks 274
can be set. Critical thinking skills, if applied well, 285
can save the employer money or, if executed poorly, can 296
cost the employer. 300

| 1 | 2 | 3 | 4 | 5 | 6 | 7 | 8 | 9 | 10 | 11 | 12

SKILLBUILDING Supplementary Timed Writings SB-30

Understanding the Lesson

Test 2

Skills Assessment on Part 2

3-Minute Timed Writing

```
     From the first day of class, you have continuously   10
worked to improve your typing skill. You have worked hard   22
to increase your typing speed and accuracy. You have also   34
learned to format letters, memos, reports, and tables. All   46
of this work is quite an amazing accomplishment.   56
     In your lessons, you have worked on learning a wide   66
range of word processing skills. You can expect to make   78
even more progress if you practice your skills regularly.   90
Learn as much as you can each day. Ask questions, and then   102
move toward a new goal each day.   108
| 1 | 2 | 3 | 4 | 5 | 6 | 7 | 8 | 9 | 10 | 11 | 12
```

Correspondence Test 2-21 Business Letter in Block Style

Note: Omit the return address on the envelope.

March 17 , 20-- | Ms. ~~Arlene~~ Dorothy Turner | Global Moving and Storage | 6830 Via Del Monte | San Jose, CA 95119 | Dear Ms. Turner:

¶ Thank you ~~you~~ for registering your pc Graphics software so promptly. As a registered user, you are entitled to free technical support 24 hours a day. The brochure enclosed will explain in detail how you can reach us ~~either~~ by fax, e-mail or phone whenever you need help. Also, help is always available on our website at www.pcgraphics.com. All our PC Graphics users will receive our monthly newsletter, which is filled with tips on using your new software and other material we know you will be interested in ~~seeing~~ reading. You can also access our newest graphics online at our Web site. Please call me or send me an e-mail message if you have any questions or would like to receive any additional information. Your satisfaction is our number 1 priority. Sincerely | Roy Phillips | Support Technician | urs | enclosure

Report Test 2-12 Academic Report

TELECOMMUTERS
Visibility at Work
Roy Phillips

¶ Have you ever wondered how to remain "visible" at work when you aren't there for most of the work week? This is a problem many telecommuters are struggling to overcome as

(Continued on next page)

Each part ends with a **Skills Assessment** to measure straight-copy and document processing skill development. An alternate form of the test is available in the Tests and Solution Keys booklet.

POSSIBLE SOLUTIONS ↓2X

Flexible scheduling is one creative way in which employers can respond to the needs of employees. If workers are given the opportunity for a flexible working schedule, stress levels should go down and personal needs can be handled during the time they are off. Another solution might be to give employees a fixed number of days off each year for reasons other than illness. This gives workers a legitimate reason for a planned absence and gives employers some advance notice so that absences do not hurt productivity.

Report 26-2 Business Report

Open the file for Report 26-1 and make the following changes:

1. Delete the subtitle, and change the byline to `Amy Ho`.
2. Change the date to `October 23`.
3. Change the second side heading to `EMPLOYER RESPONSIVENESS`.
4. Delete the last two sentences in the last paragraph at the end of the report. Add the following sentences to the end of the last paragraph:

```
Employees will not feel the
need to invent elaborate
reasons for their absences.
They will feel as if they are
in control of their schedule
outside of work so that they
can determine the best way to
schedule their time off. When
they return to work, they will
feel relaxed and ready to work.
```

The real-world **photographs** in the student text can spark discussions about the need for keyboarding skills in the workplace of the future. Students can understand how their keyboarding skills will be valuable in many careers, and how important the keyboard is, and will remain, in technological development.

INTRODUCTION

The Instructor Wraparound Edition (IWE) highlights several contemporary issues facing keyboarding educators in this century, such as using technology, the increasing number of adjunct instructors, changing classroom configurations, and addressing shifting student demographics.

THE FOUR-STEP TEACHING PLAN

1. **FOCUS** The first step in the teaching plan is to establish a schedule for the keyboarding or document processing lesson. The suggested guidelines are for a 50-minute time period. Adjust as necessary.

2. **TEACH** This section is the central part of the teaching plan. Teaching suggestions employing a variety of approaches, strategies, and activities appear in the margins of the IWE. These suggestions will help the experienced or the novice and/or adjunct keyboarding instructor. The suggestions for the use of textbook pictures, comments on the use of technology, information that can be used to hold students' interest, and real-world connections for keyboarding skills are invaluable.

3. **ASSESS** The third step in the teaching plan is to evaluate students' skills in keyboarding and document processing. Most units end with a Progress Check/Proofreading Check that can be used to assess progress in the unit. Skills Assessments should be used to evaluate straight-copy and document processing skills at the end of Parts 2 through 6. Objective tests are also available. Proper technique is so important in keyboarding classes that it should be continuously assessed.

4. **CLOSE** The final step in the teaching plan is to determine whether students have mastered the goals of each lesson. Students practice and apply what they have learned. Providing students with a variety of ways to demonstrate what they have learned also gives you opportunities to evaluate the level of their skills and to identify students who need additional reinforcement and practice.

PART RESOURCE MANAGER

To provide the best possible learning experience for your students, you need to know the variety of materials that are available to supplement your teaching. You cannot plan your lessons effectively unless you know what materials are available and the appropriate time to utilize them.

The **Part Resource Manager** gives you a comprehensive reference to the teaching resources in each part. It provides a quick overview of the content of the part and the resources available to the student and the instructor.

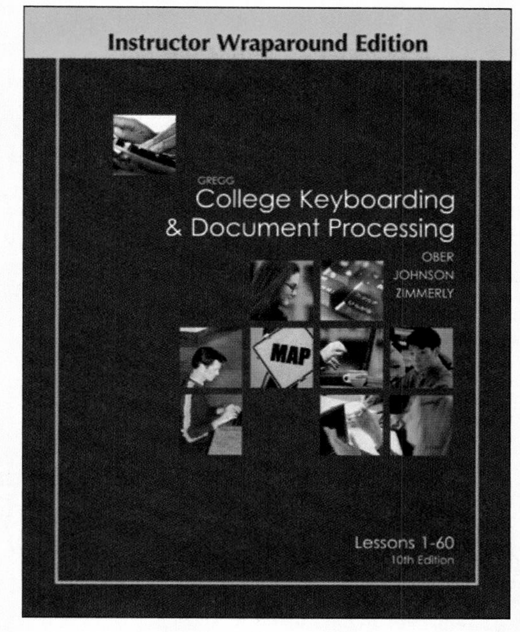

Part Resources provide a quick reference to the part objectives covered, including the goals for timed writings. You will find a list of the content covered in each unit, language arts skills taught, formatting and word processing skills presented, and illustrations provided.

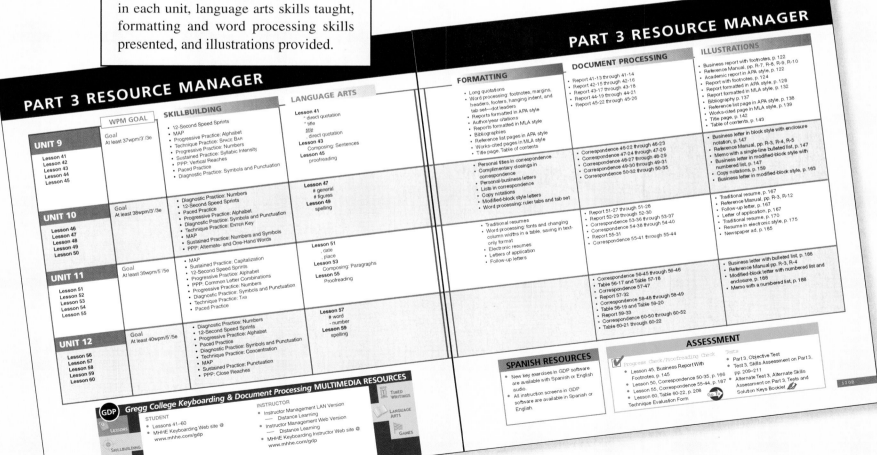

Teaching Resources at a Glance provides an overview of the resources such as the Reference Manual, Microsoft Word Manual, Skills Assessments, and the GDP software.

The **MOS Correlation Chart** illustrates the many word processing skills presented in *Gregg College Keyboarding & Document Processing* that are competencies tested in the Microsoft Office Specialist (MOS) exam.

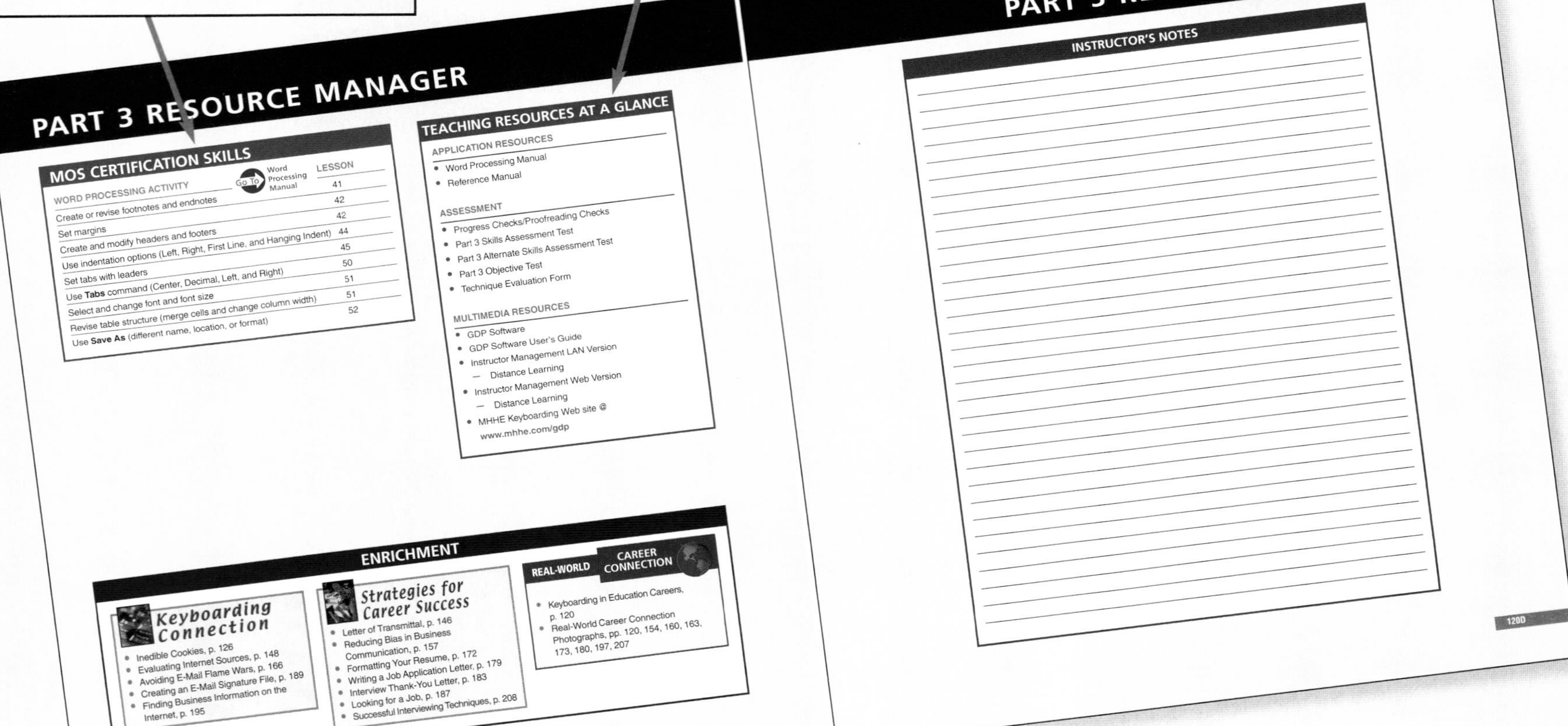

PART 3 RESOURCE MANAGER

MOS CERTIFICATION SKILLS

WORD PROCESSING ACTIVITY	LESSON
Create or revise footnotes and endnotes	41
Set margins	42
Create and modify headers and footers	42
Use indentation options (Left, Right, First Line, and Hanging Indent)	44
Set tabs with leaders	45
Use **Tabs** command (Center, Decimal, Left, and Right)	50
Select and change font and font size	51
Revise table structure (merge cells and change column width)	51
Use **Save As** (different name, location, or format)	52

Go To Word Processing Manual

TEACHING RESOURCES AT A GLANCE

APPLICATION RESOURCES
- Word Processing Manual
- Reference Manual

ASSESSMENT
- Progress Checks/Proofreading Checks
- Part 3 Skills Assessment Test
- Part 3 Alternate Skills Assessment Test
- Part 3 Objective Test
- Technique Evaluation Form

MULTIMEDIA RESOURCES
- GDP Software
- GDP Software User's Guide
- Instructor Management LAN Version
  — Distance Learning
- Instructor Management Web Version
  — Distance Learning
- MHHE Keyboarding Web site @ www.mhhe.com/gdp

ENRICHMENT

Keyboarding Connection
- Inedible Cookies, p. 126
- Evaluating Internet Sources, p. 148
- Avoiding E-Mail Flame Wars, p. 166
- Creating an E-Mail Signature File, p. 189
- Finding Business Information on the Internet, p. 195

Strategies for Career Success
- Letter of Transmittal, p. 146
- Reducing Bias in Business Communication, p. 157
- Formatting Your Resume, p. 172
- Writing a Job Application Letter, p. 179
- Interview Thank-You Letter, p. 183
- Looking for a Job, p. 187
- Successful Interviewing Techniques, p. 208

REAL-WORLD CAREER CONNECTION
- Keyboarding in Education Careers, p. 120
- Real-World Career Connection Photographs, pp. 120, 154, 160, 163, 173, 180, 197, 207

120C

PART 3 RESOURCE MANAGER

INSTRUCTOR'S NOTES

120D

Enrichment activities include the special features, Keyboarding Connection and Strategies for Career Success, that are designed to motivate and challenge students while building skills and expanding understanding. Real-World Career Connections are listed for the part.

UNIT AND LESSON OPENERS

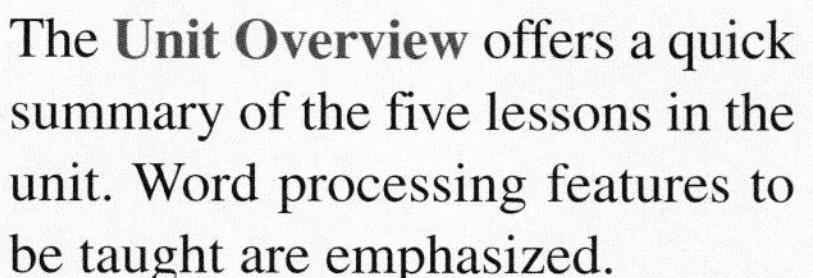
The **Unit Overview** offers a quick summary of the five lessons in the unit. Word processing features to be taught are emphasized.

The lesson **Focus** helps instructors plan the time schedule for the lesson.

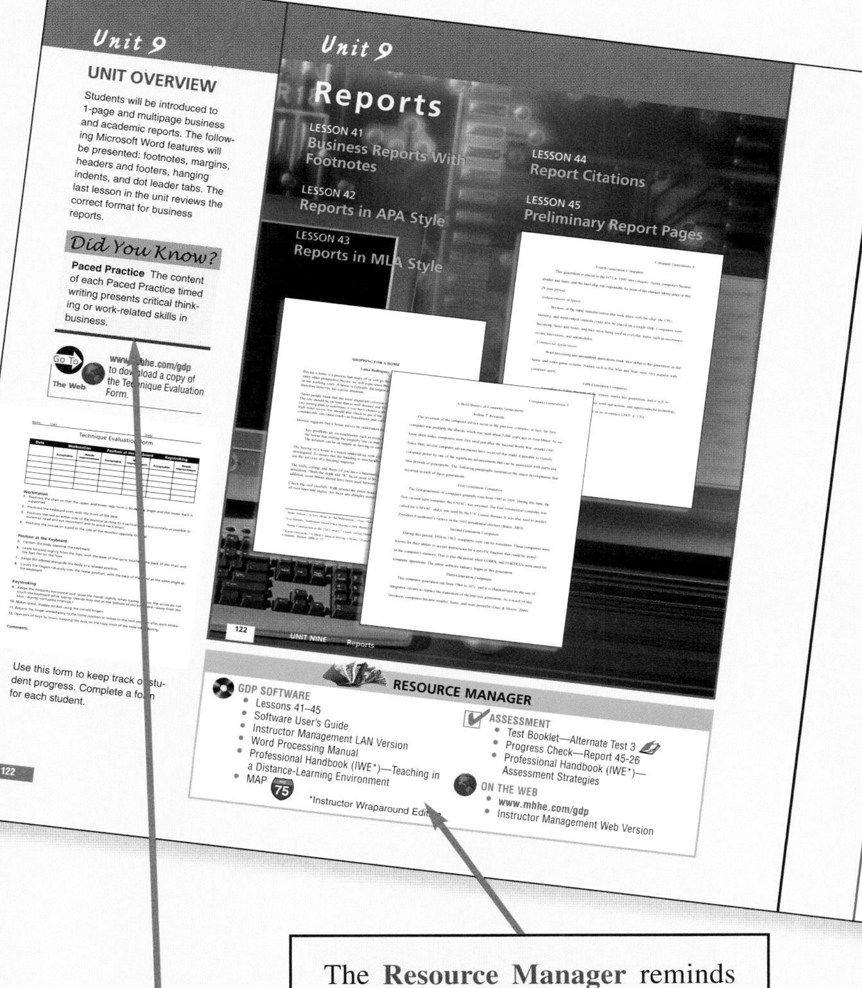
Unit 9

UNIT OVERVIEW

Students will be introduced to 1-page and multipage business and academic reports. The following Microsoft Word features will be presented: footnotes, margins, headers and footers, hanging indents, and dot leader tabs. The last lesson in the unit reviews the correct format for business reports.

Did You Know?

Paced Practice The content of each Paced Practice timed writing presents critical thinking or work-related skills in business.

Go To The Web www.mhhe.com/gdp to download a copy of the Technique Evaluation Form.

Technique Evaluation Form

Use this form to keep track of student progress. Complete a form for each student.

122

Unit 9

Reports

LESSON 41 Business Reports With Footnotes

LESSON 42 Reports in APA Style

LESSON 43 Reports in MLA Style

LESSON 44 Report Citations

LESSON 45 Preliminary Report Pages

122 UNIT NINE Reports

RESOURCE MANAGER

GDP SOFTWARE
- Lessons 41–45
- Software User's Guide
- Instructor Management LAN Version
- Word Processing Manual
- Professional Handbook (IWE*)—Teaching in a Distance-Learning Environment
- MAP 75

ASSESSMENT
- Test Booklet—Alternate Test 3
- Progress Check—Report 45-26
- Professional Handbook (IWE*)—Assessment Strategies

ON THE WEB
- www.mhhe.com/gdp
- Instructor Management Web Version

*Instructor Wraparound Edition

Lesson 41

Business Reports With Footnotes

Goals:

Improve speed and accuracy
Refine language arts skills in using quotation marks and italics (or the underline)
Format reports with footnotes

A. Type 2 times.

A. WARMUP

```
1      Tag #743X was attached to a black jug that was 1/3     10
2 full of a creamy liquid. Tags #914Z and #874V were both    22
3 attached to beautiful large lamps (crystal and porcelain).  33
  | 1 | 2 | 3 | 4 | 5 | 6 | 7 | 8 | 9 | 10 | 11 | 12
```

SKILLBUILDING

B. Take three 12-second timed writings on each line. The scale below the last line shows your wpm speed for a 12-second timed writing.

B. 12-SECOND SPEED SPRINTS

```
4 Joe must try to type as fast as he can on these four lines.
5 The screens were very clear, and the print was easy to see.
6 We will not be able to print the copy until later on today.
7 The disk will not store any of the data if it is not clean.
  5 | 10 | 15 | 20 | 25 | 30 | 35 | 40 | 45 | 50 | 55 | 60
```

C. MAP

Follow the GDP software directions for this exercise in improving keystroking accuracy.

LANGUAGE ARTS

D. Study the rules at the right.

D. QUOTATION MARKS AND ITALICS (OR UNDERLINE)

RULE " direct quotation

Use quotation marks around a direct quotation.
Harrison responded by saying, "Their decision does not affect us."
But: Harrison responded by saying that their decision does not affect us.

RULE " title

Use quotation marks around the title of a newspaper or magazine article, chapter in a book, report, and similar terms.
The most helpful article I found was "Multimedia for All."

RULE title or title

Italicize (or underline) the titles of books, magazines, newspapers, and other complete published works.
Grisham's *The Brethren* was reviewed in a recent *USA Today* article.

RULE , direct quotation

Use a comma before and after a direct quotation.
James said, "I shall return," and then left.

(Continued on next page)

EXTENDING LANGUAGE ARTS

Quotation Marks Use quotation marks to enclose someone's exact words. Example: The principal said, "There will be no school tomorrow."

Quotation Marks Quotation marks are also used for the titles of magazine articles, chapters in books, essays, newspaper columns, reports, and songs. Example: I read "Domestic Policy" in that magazine.

Italics or Underlining Explain that italics (or, if you are writing by hand or on a typewriter, underlining) can be used to identify the names of books, magazines, newspapers, operas, movies, or plays. Example: The couple saw *Saving Private Ryan* (or Saving Private Ryan) last week.

Lesson 41

FOCUS

TIME MANAGEMENT
Suggested Schedule:

Warmup	2′
Skillbuilding	17′
Language Arts	6′
Formatting	6′
Document Processing	19′
Total	50′

TEACH

SKILLBUILDING

LESSON 41B Speed sprints are very motivational. Have students push hard for speed on these easy sentences.

LESSON 41C MAP 75 When keyboarding was done on typewriters, there was only a weak correlation between production typing speed and accuracy and straight-copy speed and accuracy. This was because, in production typing, the planning, decision making, and machine manipulation were more important than simple keystroking speed. With word processing, the software takes care of most of the decision making. (Compare, for instance, the way footnotes are done on the typewriter and on the computer.) Today, production typing is very similar to straight-copy typing, so straight-copy speed and accuracy have never been more important than they are today.

LANGUAGE ARTS

Review the language arts rules for using quotation marks and italics or underline.

123

The **Resource Manager** reminds instructors of the complete range of resources available in the program.

Did You Know? provides informative tips for instructors about the many features included in the *Gregg College Keyboarding & Document Processing* program.

Features such as GDP Software Tips, Teaching the Adult Learner, Meeting Special Needs, Extending Language Arts, and Ergonomically Speaking provide instructors with ideas to enhance instruction.

Teach helps instructors with step-by-step suggestions for teaching the Skillbuilding, Formatting, and Document Processing sections of the lesson.

FEATURES AND TEACHING STRATEGIES

SOFTWARE TIPS

TIMED WRITINGS

LANGUAGE ARTS

GAMES

Log-On Information

Encourage students to press the TAB key to move from one text box to another—new students may need help in locating the TAB key. Remind students to select a password that is easy to remember, and caution students not to share the password.

Instructor Options

You can prevent students from correcting errors in timed writings, in drill lines, or in both. From the GDP Menu bar, choose **Options**, **Instructor Options**, **Settings**, **Class Settings**. Deselect the boxes for timed writings and drills under **Full Editing**.

GDP Software Tips introduces instructors to the fine points of our GDP software, which is designed to maximize the effectiveness of every minute students spend at their keyboards.

Technology Tips

LINE SPACING

Remind students that line spacing is a paragraph format. All lines of the paragraph will be formatted. To change the line spacing for a single paragraph, students can position the insertion point in the paragraph and change the line spacing. It is not necessary to select the entire paragraph.

To format multiple paragraphs, select the paragraphs prior to applying the line spacing format.

Technology Tips offers detailed advice for using computers and their peripherals in the keyboarding classroom.

Windows Wizard

TWO WAYS TO RENAME FILES OR FOLDERS

One way to rename files or folders in Windows 2000, Me, and XP:

- Open **My Computer** or **Windows Explorer**.
- Select the file or folder you want to rename.
- Choose **Rename** from the **File** menu.
- Type the name and press ENTER.

Another way:

- In the **Open** dialog box, select the file or folder you want to rename.
- Click the right mouse button.
- Choose **Rename**.
- Type the name and press ENTER.

Windows Wizard gives step-by-step instructions for using Windows to enhance instructor competencies in Windows.

ERGONOMICALLY SPEAKING

POSITION Check that each student's work surface or keyboarding tray is at elbow height; feet should be flat on the floor, with knees slightly bent below the hips. The backrest should support the lower part, or lumbar curve, of the back. Chair arms should not prevent moving the chair close to the work surface.

The following Web site contains ergonomic guidelines for workstation health and safety: **http://www.lib.utexas.edu/ergonomics/general.html**.

Ergonomically Speaking shows instructors how to keep students (and themselves) healthy and unstressed as they work on the computer.

MHHE Champions provides successful teaching tips from instructors around the country.

MHHE CHAMPIONS

Early Assessment Technique

Paul Neatrour
Cambria County Area Community College
Johnstown, Pennsylvania

PENNSYLVANIA

Students need to feel a sense of accomplishment and feel good about what they have learned. After Lesson 10, give an objective test covering the following topics:

- Name the five components of your computer system.
- Identify all menus and name all buttons.
- Describe proper technique at the keyboard.
- Indicate correct spacing following punctuation marks.
- Count words per minute in a short paragraph.

This test is quick and easy, and it provides feedback to the students and to the instructor.

Instructors Helping One Another

Teaching the Adult Learner shows instructors how to understand the needs, motivations, and special abilities of the returning student who may have been in the workplace for many years.

TEACHING THE ADULT LEARNER

LISTENING SKILLS Provide the adult learner with some guidelines on how to be an active listener in the classroom. Tell your students to follow these guidelines:

- Ask for clarification if instructions or procedures are not clear.
- Highlight important rules or explanations.
- Record due dates on a calendar.
- Answer questions raised in class.
- Share experiences relative to the lesson.

Keyboarding is not a lecture class, but students must learn to listen to verbal instructions. This skill is necessary in classes as well as in real-world business and social interaction.

Meeting Special Needs provides appropriate guidelines for the special needs, abilities, and learning styles of your students.

Meeting Special Needs

ACCESSIBILITY FEATURES Windows 2000, Me, and XP includes several Accessibility Options that enhance the display, sound, mouse, and keyboarding settings. For example, if it is difficult for a student to use a mouse, change the MouseKeys settings to use the numeric keypad for moving the mouse pointer.

To locate Accessibility Options:

- Click the **Start** button.
- Point to **Settings**, and click **Control Panel**.
- Double-click **Accessibility Options**.
- Select the appropriate tab, and change settings.

Visit **www.mhhe.com/gdp**.

Extending Language Arts provides instructors with additional strategies to teach and reinforce the language arts rules presented in the lesson.

EXTENDING LANGUAGE ARTS

Direct Address Comma Explain that direct address means speaking to someone directly. Example: "I congratulate you, Bill."

Sentence Fragment A sentence fragment is a sentence that does not express a complete thought. Example: "Needs more time." The fragment does not say who or what needs more time. To correct this fragment, add a subject. Example: "Jaime needs more time."

Run-On Sentence Go over the definition of a run-on sentence on p. 52 with students. Discuss the two examples and the two corrections shown.

GDP KEYBOARDING SOFTWARE

Gregg College Keyboarding & Document Processing (GDP) software is an engaging and compelling program for instructors and students alike. The Web-based look and feel interface is designed to meet the expectations of the technologically savvy marketplace.

INSTRUCTOR MANAGEMENT

Sophisticated Instructor Management Web and Instructor Management LAN versions are available to monitor students' performance and generate reports on their progress. A powerful and time-saving feature of both Instructor Management versions is grade computation.

GDP supports 26 unique installation configurations for maximum flexibility.

- Students can use GDP on a campus LAN with Instructor Management, on a campus stand-alone system with Web Instructor Management, on their home system, or in the Lessons 1–20 Web site.
- Each configuration supports four or five types of data storage options, ranging from the network file server to floppy disks and removable media.
- Students can combine their exercise data generated on campus, at home, and on the Web.

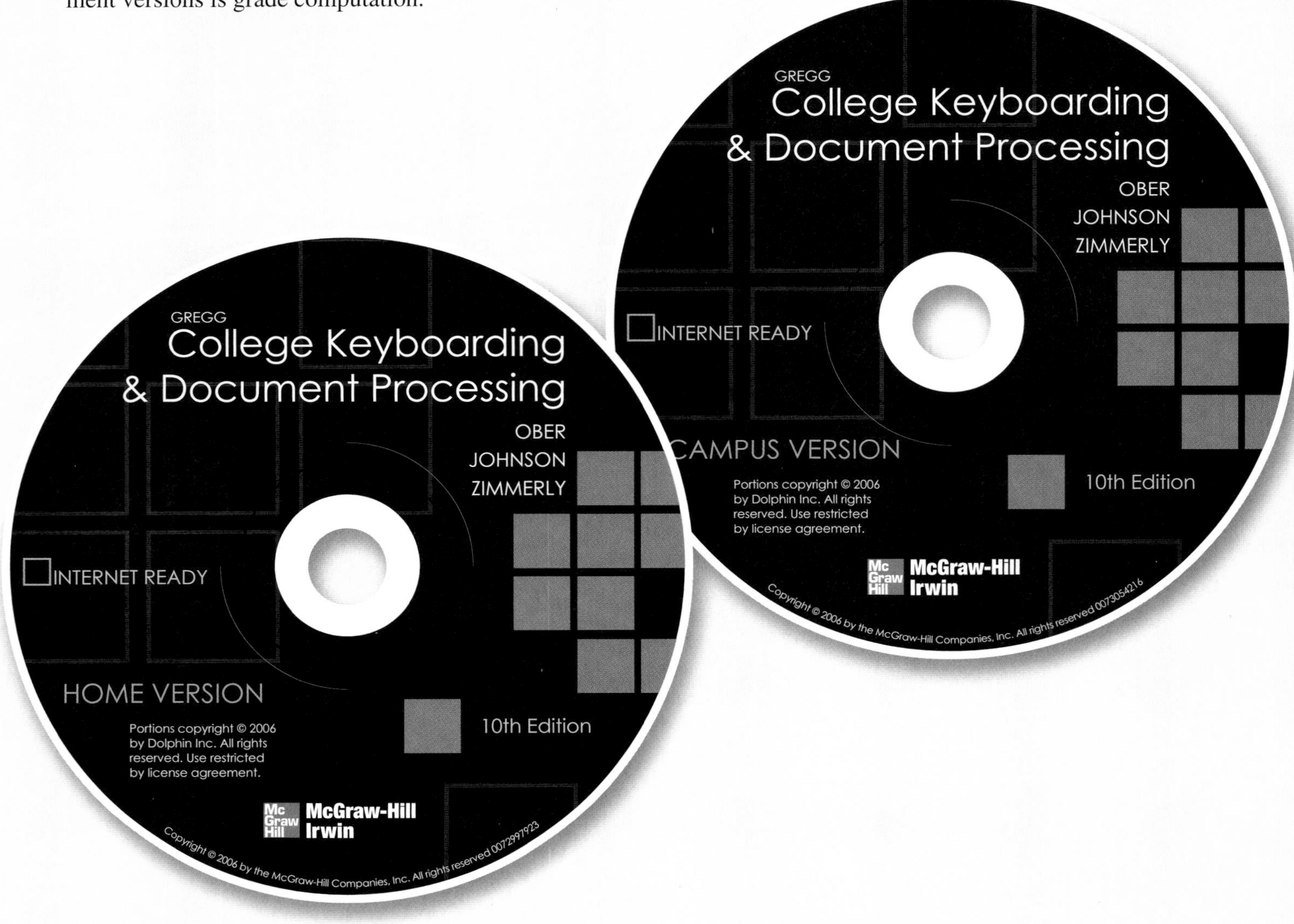

GDP contains a variety of user features that make it easy to learn and easy to teach.

- One-click navigation
- Data storage flexibility
- Distance-learning flexibility
- Misstroke Analysis and Prescription (MAP) individualized skillbuilding
- Dynamically created practice documents
- Grading parameters options
- Full range of timed writings, including custom timed writings and open timed writings
- Class announcements and annotations feature
- Bilingual (English/Spanish) instructions
- Multimedia welcome tutorial
- Interactive language arts tutorials
- Animated technique tips
- Pace Car game and Tennis game

ENRICHMENT AND EXTENSION

COLLEGE KEYBOARDING WEB SITE

The College Keyboarding Web site provides students and instructors with information on careers, technology advancements, supplementary activities, teaching tips, and much, much more.

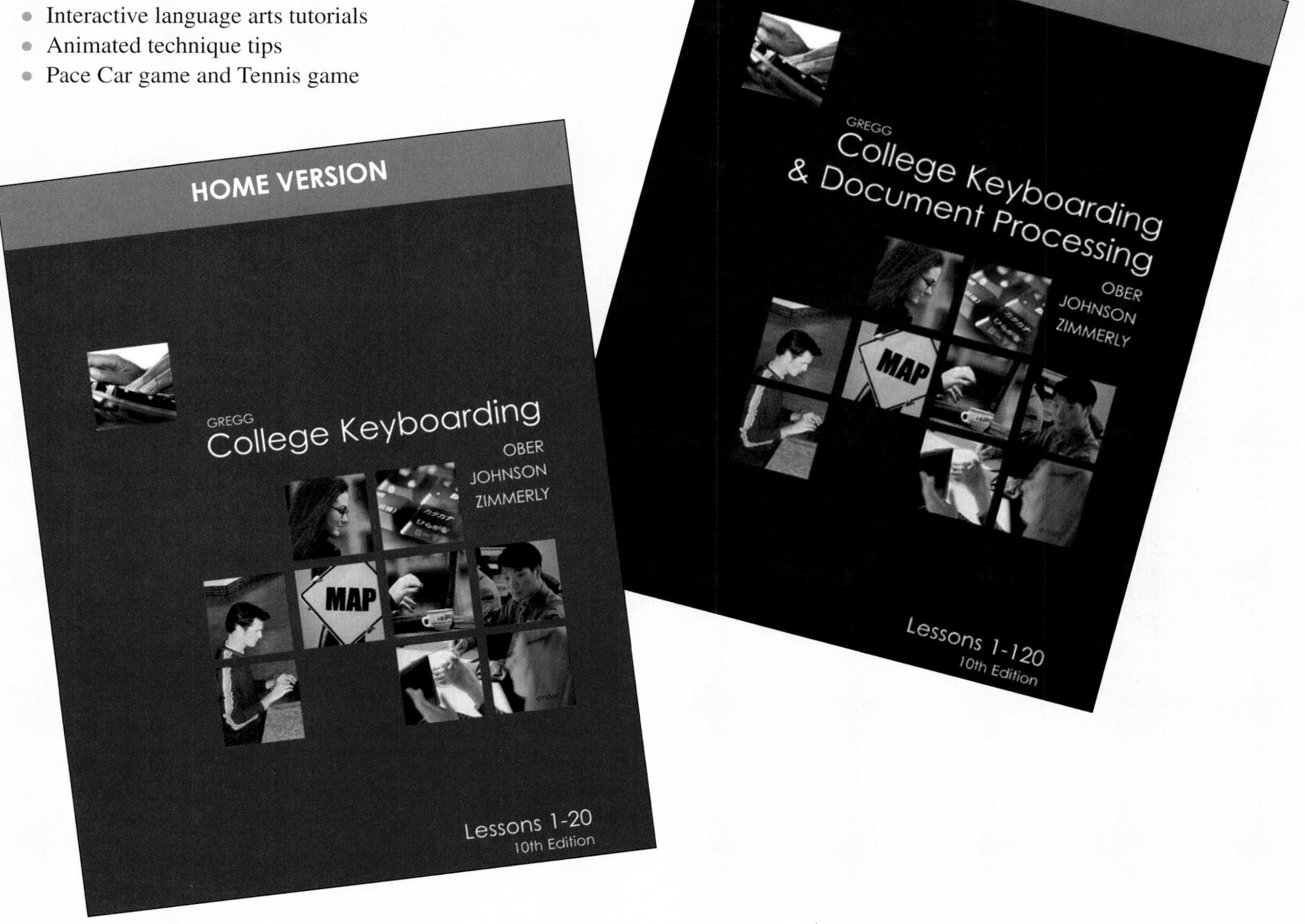

ASSESSMENT

Assessment and evaluation materials help you measure the progress of students through a large selection of testing and assessment resources.

Skills Assessments for each part measure student progress in straight-copy and document processing development. An alternate form of the Skills Assessment test is available in the Tests and Solutions Manual, as is an objective test for each part. The last document in most units is designated as a Progress Check/Proofreading Check that can be used as a quiz, midterm test, or review test.

Proper technique is critical in keyboarding skill development. Evaluate individual student technique throughout the keyboarding course to ensure that students develop, improve, and refine technique.

Name Class Date

Technique Evaluation Form

Date	Workstation		Position at the Keyboard		Keystroking	
	Acceptable	Needs Improvement	Acceptable	Needs Improvement	Acceptable	Needs Improvement

Workstation

1. Positions the chair so that the upper and lower legs form a 90-degree angle and the lower back is supported.
2. Positions the keyboard even with the front of the desk.
3. Positions the text on either side of the monitor as close to it vertically and horizontally as possible to minimize head and eye movement and to avoid neck strain.
4. Positions the mouse on a pad at the side of the monitor opposite the text.

Position at the Keyboard

5. Centers the body opposite the keyboard.
6. Leans forward slightly from the hips, with the base of the spine touching the back of the chair and the feet flat on the floor.
7. Keeps the elbows alongside the body in a relaxed position.
8. Curves the fingers naturally over the home position, with the back of the hand at the same angle as the keyboard.

Keystroking

9. Keeps the forearms horizontal and raises the hands slightly when typing so that the wrists do not touch the keyboard while typing. (Hands may rest at the bottom of the keyboard—away from the keys—during nontyping intervals.)
10. Makes quick, snappy strokes using the correct fingers.
11. Returns the finger immediately to the home position or moves to the next position after each stroke.
12. Operates all keys by touch, keeping the eyes on the copy most of the time while typing.

Comments

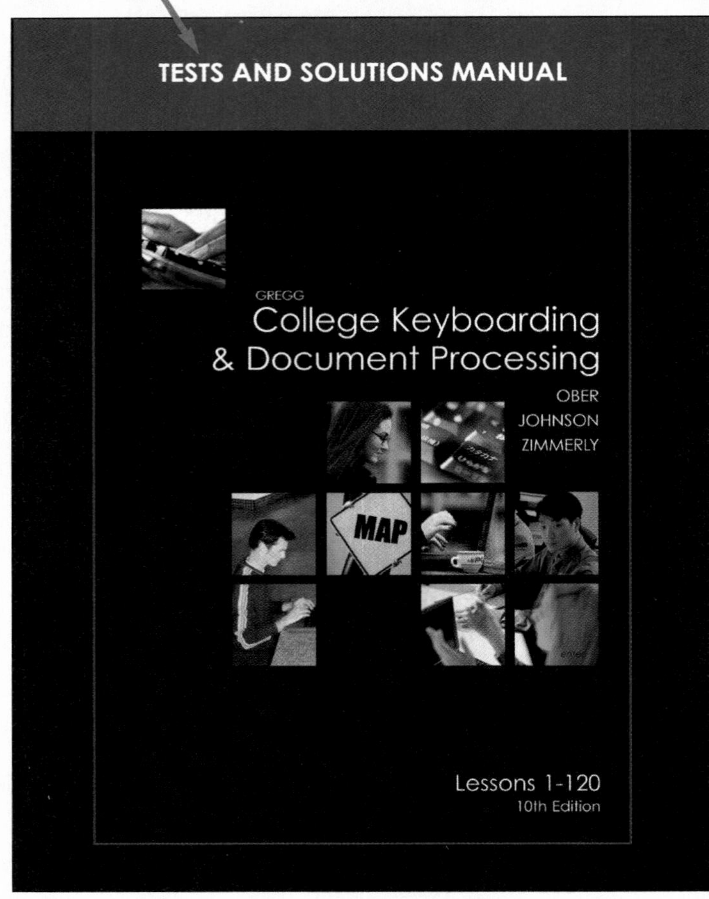

Solutions for document processing exercises (except those created by students) are provided in an easy-to-use format if you wish to grade papers manually. GDP software scores student documents and calculates student grades (never grade another student paper!) with Instructor Management LAN and Instructor Management Web components.

STUDENT AND INSTRUCTOR SUPPORT

The Instructor Software User's Guide provides instructors with complete information on how to use GDP software effectively. The information provided by the software developer includes system requirements, installation guidelines, GDP user tips, Instructor Management procedures and hints, and troubleshooting information.

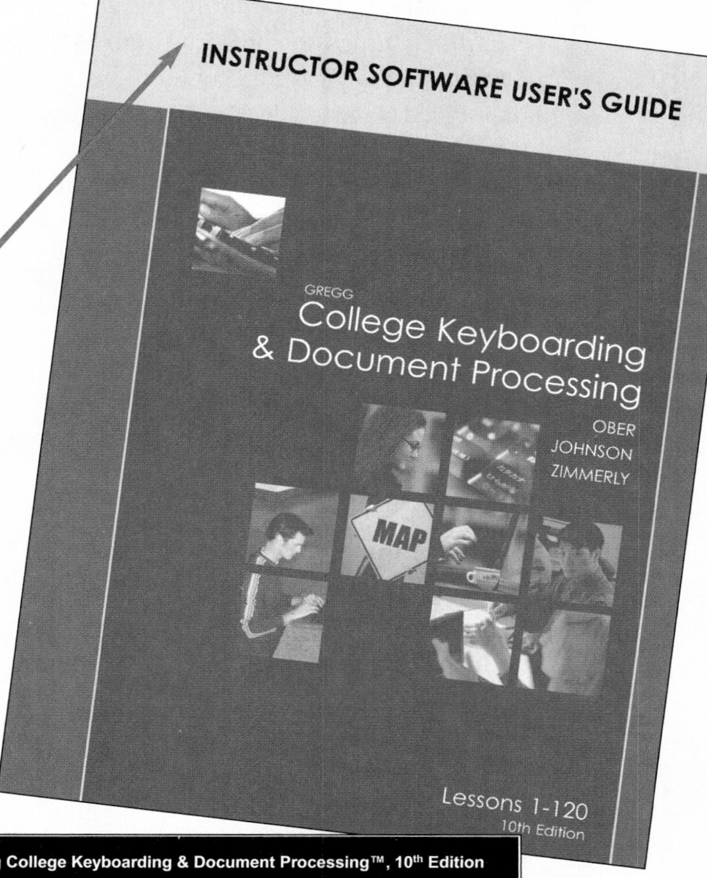

The Student Software User's Guide provides a complete description of all program functions so that students can use GDP at home.

Instructor and student packages include a Quick Reference Guide for an easy-to-use GDP start-up.

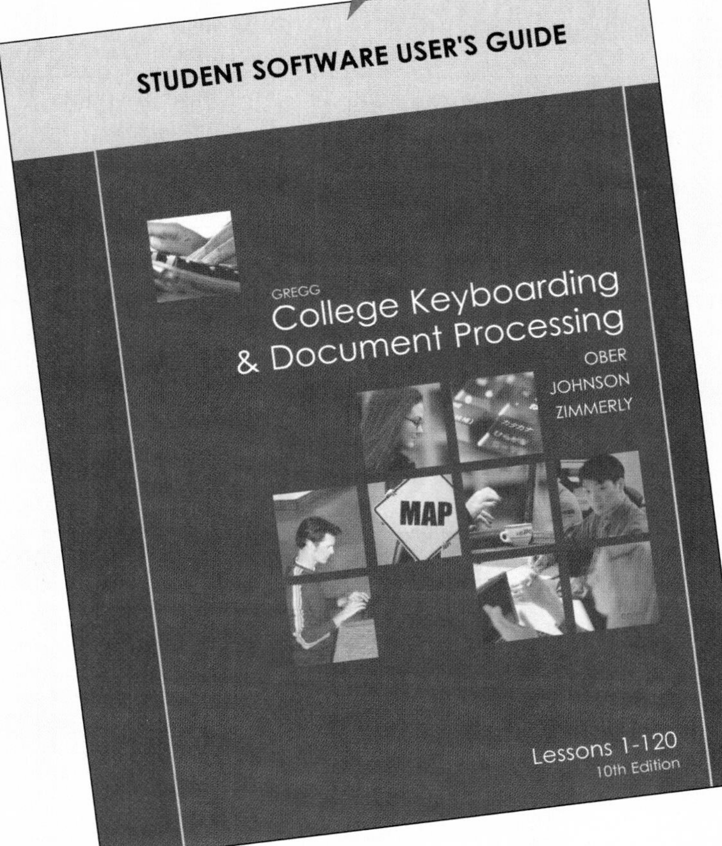

Gregg College Keyboarding & Document Processing™, 10th Edition

Quick Reference Guide

Before You Begin. . .

If you are not familiar with Windows™, work through the HELP feature in your Windows™ version.

Running the Program

1. If you are storing your work on a floppy disk, insert a blank floppy disk into the floppy drive.
2. Locate the McGraw-Hill Keyboarding program group.
3. Select the appropriate program icon:

- *GDP Classes* if you are on a Campus LAN,
- *GDP Distance Learning* if you are a distance-learning student, or
- *GDP Standalone* if you are in a standalone configuration.

4. The title screen displays for several seconds, followed by the log-on screen. (To advance to the log-on screen immediately, click anywhere on the title screen.)

- If you are working on a campus LAN, choose your class from the course/selection list, then choose your name from the student list and click **OK**. If your name is not listed, click **New Student**, complete the logon registration form, and click **Save**.
- If you are using GDP as a standalone or distance-learning student, complete the logon registration and click **Save**.

5. Go through the "How to Use. . ." tutorial, which provides first-time users an overview of how GDP works.
6. If your instructor has posted a class announcement, it will appear next: read it and click **OK** to continue.
7. The Lessons menu appears next, with Lesson 1 selected. Double-click the first exercise to begin working on it.
8. Read the introductory or instruction screen(s) and turn to the appropriate page in the textbook. Type the text for the exercise.

- *Timings:* Type until time is up, at which point the software scores your work and allows you to review your scored text.
- *Document processing exercises:* Type and proofread the document, print a copy of it or check your results in the Portfolio, and then exit Word by selecting *Return to GDP* on the Word toolbar.
- *All other exercises:* Type the exercise to completion, following on-screen instruction.

9. The program automatically sequences through the exercises in the lesson. At the end of the last exercise for a lesson, the program returns to the Lessons menu. (A ■ precedes completed exercises, and a ◩ precedes started but not completed exercises.) To start the next lesson, select the lesson number on the menu, then double-click the first exercise in the lesson.
10. If you are a distance-learning student, be sure to update your data at the end of each GDP session. To do so, click **Update** on the GDP toolbar and follow on-screen instructions.
11. When you are finished with your work for the session, select *Exit GDP* on the File drop-down menu or press *Ctrl+X*.

Drop-Down Menus

Use the menu bar at the top of screen to access drop-down menus. Either click on an item on the menu bar to display its drop-down menu or press the Alt key and type the underlined letter of the desired menu.

File Menu

Portfolio. . . Displays a report showing your scores on completed GDP exercises and gives you access to your scored text for any exercise.

This document has been prepared with the assistance of Dolphin Inc., Gibbsboro, NJ.

NEW DIRECTIONS

Gregg College Keyboarding & Document Processing, 10th Edition, brings keyboarding into the twenty-first century with state-of-the-art technology and print components designed with today's learner in mind. From the engaging and compelling software, with a host of distance-learning features, to the visually appealing and user-friendly textbooks and manuals, the program will bring a whole new keyboarding experience to you and your students.

Features	***Content***	***Revised Design***	***Software***
Real-world content connections	Enhanced language arts emphasis	Visually appealing	Intuitive, dynamic, and innovative Web-based look and feel design
Exclusive instructor wraparound editions	Supplementary timed writings focus on critical thinking in careers	Improved labeling	Enhanced Misstroke Analysis and Prescription (MAP)—diagnostic/prescriptive skillbuilding
Instructor lesson plan models	Motivational Paced Practice timed writings on soft skills relevant to career success	Two-page part openers featuring real-world career connection using keyboarding skills	Misstroke Analysis and Prescription (MAP) slideshow
Tips on teaching adult and special-needs learners	Simplified formatting	Unit Openers offer visual outline	Multimedia welcome tutorial
Instructor strategies	E-mail formatting	Lessons always begin at top of page	Instructor Management LAN and Web versions
Software tips	Web speech recognition units	Improved color coding for lesson parts	Lessons 1–20 Web version
Career tips feature, Strategies for Career Success	International formatting	Larger model documents	Distance learning with or without the Internet
Keyboarding Connection feature	Web page design	Reference Manual review notations	Enhanced student portfolio
MOS competencies correlation	Medical and legal office applications	Word processing review notations	Live software updates
Real-world career connection photos	Electronic resumes	Language arts callouts	Bilingual instruction and new-key demonstration screens

CONTENTS Student Edition

PART ONE: The Alphabet, Number, and Symbol Keys

CONTENTS Student Edition

PART TWO
Basic Business Documents

PART THREE: Reports, Correspondence, and Employment Documents

CONTENTS Student Edition

Each day the world becomes more and more technologically advanced. As a result, learning new skills for the world of work is even more important.

One such skill that can prepare you for virtually any job in the world is keyboarding. From accountants to zoologists and every occupation in between, the ability to quickly and accurately type information is an essential skill that can increase your chances of being hired (or getting your dream job).

Formerly referred to as "typing," keyboarding is the act of entering data by means of designated computer keys. Today, as we rely more and more on computers to handle everyday work and leisure activities, the ability to accurately convey information is a necessity. So, whether you are e-mailing a relative, developing a class presentation, or downloading map directions, keyboarding knowledge can make the job easier.

PREFACE Student Edition

Gregg College Keyboarding & Document Processing Lessons 1–120, 10th Edition, is a multicomponent instructional program designed to give the student and the instructor a high degree of both flexibility and success in meeting their respective goals. For student and instructor convenience, the core components of this instructional system are available in either a kit format or a book format. *Gregg College Keyboarding Lessons 1–20, 6th Edition,* is also available for the development of touch-typing skills in shorter computer keyboarding classes.

The Kit Format

Gregg College Keyboarding & Document Processing Lessons 1–120, 10th Edition, provides a complete kit of materials for both courses in the keyboarding curriculum generally offered by colleges. Each kit, which is briefly described below, contains a softcover textbook and a student word processing manual.

Kit 1: Lessons 1–60. This kit provides the text and word processing manual for the first course. Since this kit is designed for the beginning student, its major objectives are to develop touch control of the keyboard and proper typing techniques, to build basic speed and accuracy, and to provide practice in applying those basic skills to the formatting of reports, letters, memos, tables, and other kinds of personal and business communications.

Kit 2: Lessons 61–120. This kit provides the text and word processing manual for the second course. This course continues developing basic typing skills and emphasizes the formatting of various kinds of business correspondence, reports, tables, electronic forms, and desktop publishing projects from arranged, unarranged, and rough-draft sources.

The Book Format

For the convenience of those who wish to obtain the core instructional materials in separate volumes, *Gregg College Keyboarding & Document Processing Lessons 1–120, 10th Edition,* offers textbooks for the first course: *Gregg College Keyboarding & Document Processing Lessons 1–60, 10th Edition,* or *Gregg College Keyboarding Lessons 1–20, 6th Edition.* For the second course, *Gregg College Document Processing Lessons 61–120* is offered, and for the two-semester course, *Gregg College Keyboarding & Document Processing Lessons 1–120* is available. In each instance, the content of the textbooks is identical to that of the corresponding textbooks in kit format. Third semester instruction is available in *Gregg College Document Processing Lessons 121–180.*

Supporting Materials

Gregg College Keyboarding & Document Processing Lessons 1–120, 10th Edition, includes the following additional components:

Instructional Materials. Supporting materials are provided for instructor use with either the kits or the textbooks. The special Instructor Wraparound Edition (IWE) offers lesson plans and reduced-size student pages to enhance classroom instruction. Distance-learning tips, instructional methodology, adult learner strategies, and special needs features are also included in this wraparound edition. Solution keys for all of the formatting exercises in Lessons 1–180 are contained in separate booklets used with this program. Finally, test booklets are available with the objective tests and alternative document processing tests for each part.

Computer Software. PC-compatible computer software is available for the entire program. The computer software provides complete lesson-by-lesson instruction for the entire 120 lessons.

Structure

Gregg College Keyboarding & Document Processing, 10th Edition, opens with a two-page part opener that introduces students to the focus of the instruction. Objectives are presented, and opportunities within career clusters are highlighted. The unit opener familiarizes students with the lesson content to be presented in the five lessons in the unit.

Every lesson begins with a Warmup that should be typed as soon as students are settled at the keyboard. Drill lines in this section provide the practice necessary to achieve keyboarding skills.

An easily identifiable Skillbuilding section can be found in every lesson. Each drill presents to the student a variety of different activities designed to improve speed and accuracy. Skillbuilding exercises include Technique Timings, Diagnostic Practices, Paced Practices, MAP (Misstroke Analysis and Prescription), and Timed Writings, which progress from 1 to 5 minutes in length.

Many of the skillbuilding sections also include a Pretest/Practice/Posttest routine. This routine is designed to build speed and accuracy skills as well as confidence. The Pretest helps identify speed and accuracy needs. The Practice activities consist of a variety of intensive enrichment drills. Finally, the Posttest measures improvement.

Part 1

The Alphabet, Number, and Symbol Keys

Keyboarding in Arts, Audio, Video Technology, and Communications Services

Occupations in this cluster deal with organizing and communicating information to the public in various forms and media. This cluster includes jobs in radio and television broadcasting, journalism, motion pictures, the recording industry, the performing arts, multimedia publishing, and the entertainment services. Book editors, computer artists, technical writers, radio announcers, news correspondents, and camera operators are just a few jobs within this cluster.

Qualifications and Skills

Strong oral and written communication skills and technical skills are necessary for anyone in communications and media. Without a doubt, competent keyboarding skill is extremely advantageous.

Working in the media requires creativity, talent, and accurate use of language. In journalism, being observant, thinking clearly, and seeing the significance of events are all of utmost importance. Announcers must have exceptional voices, excellent speaking skills, and a unique style. The ability to work under pressure is important in all areas of media.

Objectives

KEYBOARDING

- Operate by touch the letter, number, and symbol keys.
- Demonstrate proper typing technique.
- Use the correct spacing with punctuation.
- Type at least 28 words per minute on a 2-minute timed writing with no more than 5 errors.

TECHNICAL

- Answer correctly at least 90 percent of the questions on an objective test.

1

Goals

- Type at least 30 wpm/3'/5e
- Format one-page business reports

Starting a Lesson

Each lesson begins with the goals for that lesson. Read the goals carefully so that you understand the purpose of your practice. In the example at the left, the goals for the lesson are to type 30 wpm (words per minute) on a 3-minute timed writing with no more than 5 errors and to format one-page business reports.

Building Straight-Copy Skill

Warmups. Each lesson begins with a Warmup that reinforces learned alphabet, number, and/or symbol keys.

Skillbuilding. The skillbuilding portion of each lesson includes a variety of drills to individualize your keyboarding speed and accuracy development. Instructions for completing the drills are always provided beside each activity.

Additional skillbuilding drills are included in the back of the textbook. These drills are intended to help you meet your individual goals.

Measuring Straight-Copy Skill

Straight-copy skill is measured in wpm (words per minute). All timed writings are the exact length needed to meet the speed goal for the lesson. If you finish a timed writing before time is up, you have automatically reached your speed goal for the lesson.

Counting Errors. Specific criteria are used for counting errors. Count an error when:

1. Any stroke is incorrect.
2. Any punctuation after a word is incorrect or omitted. Count the word before the punctuation as incorrect.
3. The spacing after a word or after its punctuation is incorrect. Count the word as incorrect.
4. A letter or word is omitted.
5. A letter or word is repeated.
6. A direction about spacing, indenting, and so on, is violated.
7. Words are transposed.

(**Note:** Only one error is counted for each word, no matter how many errors it may contain.)

Determining Speed. Typing speed is measured in words per minute (wpm). To compute wpm, count every 5 strokes, including spaces, as 1 "word." Horizontal word scales below an activity divide lines into 5-stroke words. Vertical word scales beside an activity show the number of words in each line cumulatively totaled. For example, in the illustration below, if you complete a line, you have typed 8 words. If you complete 2 lines, you have typed 16 words. Use the bottom word scale to determine the word count of a partial line. Add that number to the cumulative total for the last complete line.

```
Ada lost her letter; Dee lost her card.          8
Dave sold some of the food to a market.         16
Alva asked Walt for three more matches.         24
Dale asked Seth to watch the last show.         32
| 1 | 2 | 3 | 4 | 5 | 6 | 7 | 8 |
```

Correcting Errors

As you learn to type, you will probably make some errors. To correct an error, press **BACKSPACE** (shown as ← on some keyboards) to delete the incorrect character. Then type the correct character.

If you notice an error on a different line, use the up, down, left, or right arrows to move the insertion point immediately to the left or right of the error. Press **BACKSPACE** to delete a character to the left of the insertion point, or **DELETE** to delete a character to the right of the insertion point. Error-correction settings in the GDP software determine whether you can correct errors in timed writings and drills. Consult your instructor for error-correction guidelines.

Typing Technique

Correct position at the keyboard enables you to type with greater speed and accuracy and with less fatigue. When typing for a long period, rest your eyes occasionally by looking away from the screen. Change position, walk around, or stretch when your muscles feel tired. Making such movements and adjustments may help prevent your body from becoming too tired. Additionally, long-term bodily damage, such as carpal tunnel syndrome, can be prevented.

If possible, adjust your workstation as follows:

Chair. Adjust the height so that your upper and lower legs form a 90-degree angle and your lower back is supported by the back of the chair.
Keyboard. Center your body opposite the J key and lean forward slightly. Keep your forearms horizontal to the keyboard.
Screen. Position the monitor so that the top of the screen is just below eye level and about 18 to 26 inches away.
Text. Position your textbook or other copy on either side of the monitor as close to it as vertically and horizontally possible to minimize head and eye movement and to avoid neck strain.

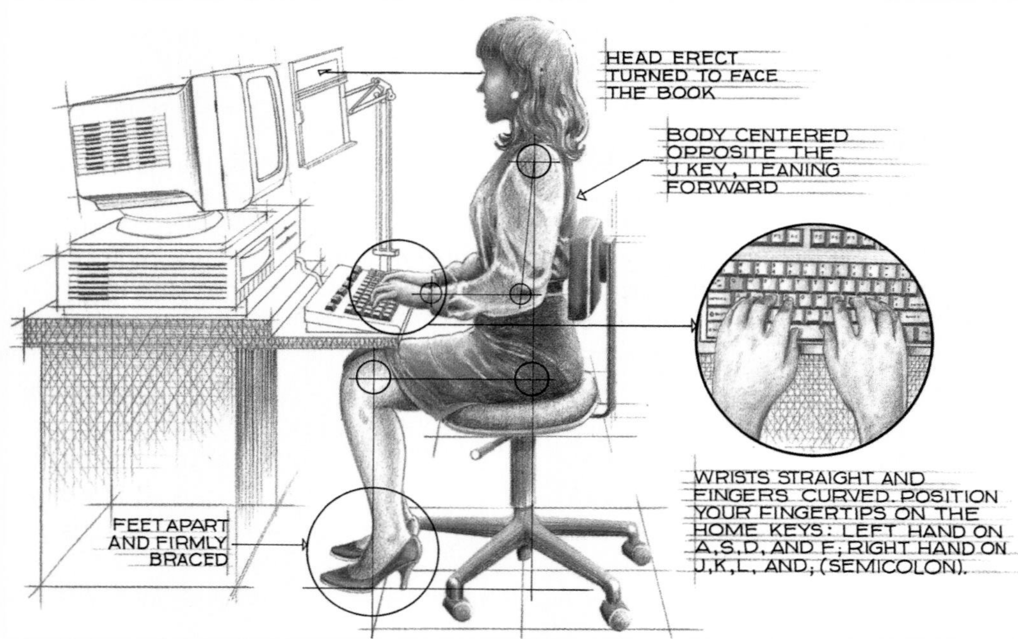
HEAD ERECT TURNED TO FACE THE BOOK
BODY CENTERED OPPOSITE THE J KEY, LEANING FORWARD
WRISTS STRAIGHT AND FINGERS CURVED. POSITION YOUR FINGERTIPS ON THE HOME KEYS: LEFT HAND ON A,S,D, AND F; RIGHT HAND ON J,K,L, AND ; (SEMICOLON).
FEET APART AND FIRMLY BRACED

BEFORE YOU BEGIN
Student Edition

Using Microsoft Windows

If you are using *Gregg College Keyboarding & Document Processing Lessons 1–120, 10th Edition,* you must know how to use a mouse, and you must know some basic information about Microsoft Windows.

Before you begin Lesson 1, turn to the *Getting Started* section in your word processing manual and read the information presented there. **Note:** If you are using the book for Lessons 1–20, use the Help feature in Windows to familiarize yourself with Windows.

Starting Your Program

Once you have completed the *Getting Started* section in your Word Processing Manual, you are ready to begin Lesson 1. If you are using the *Gregg College Keyboarding & Document Processing Lessons 1–120, 10th Edition* software (hereafter referred to as GDP), begin by starting Windows.

Next, start GDP by locating and clicking the Irwin Keyboarding group icon in your Windows program list to open the program group. (**Note:** If you are saving data to a data disk, you should insert it now.) If you are working at your school on a network, click the GDP Classes icon, click your class and then your name from the class list. If you are a new student, follow the directions on the screen to add yourself as a new student. Then follow the directions to log on and begin using GDP.

If you see any other icons or are working on a different installation of GDP, consult your instructor for help in logging on.

Reference Manual

COMPUTER SYSTEM

CORRESPONDENCE

EMPLOYMENT DOCUMENTS

FORMS

LANGUAGE ARTS

PROOFREADERS' MARKS

REPORTS

TABLES

U.S. POSTAL SERVICE STATE ABBREVIATIONS

Reference Manual

A. MAJOR PARTS OF A MICROCOMPUTER SYSTEM

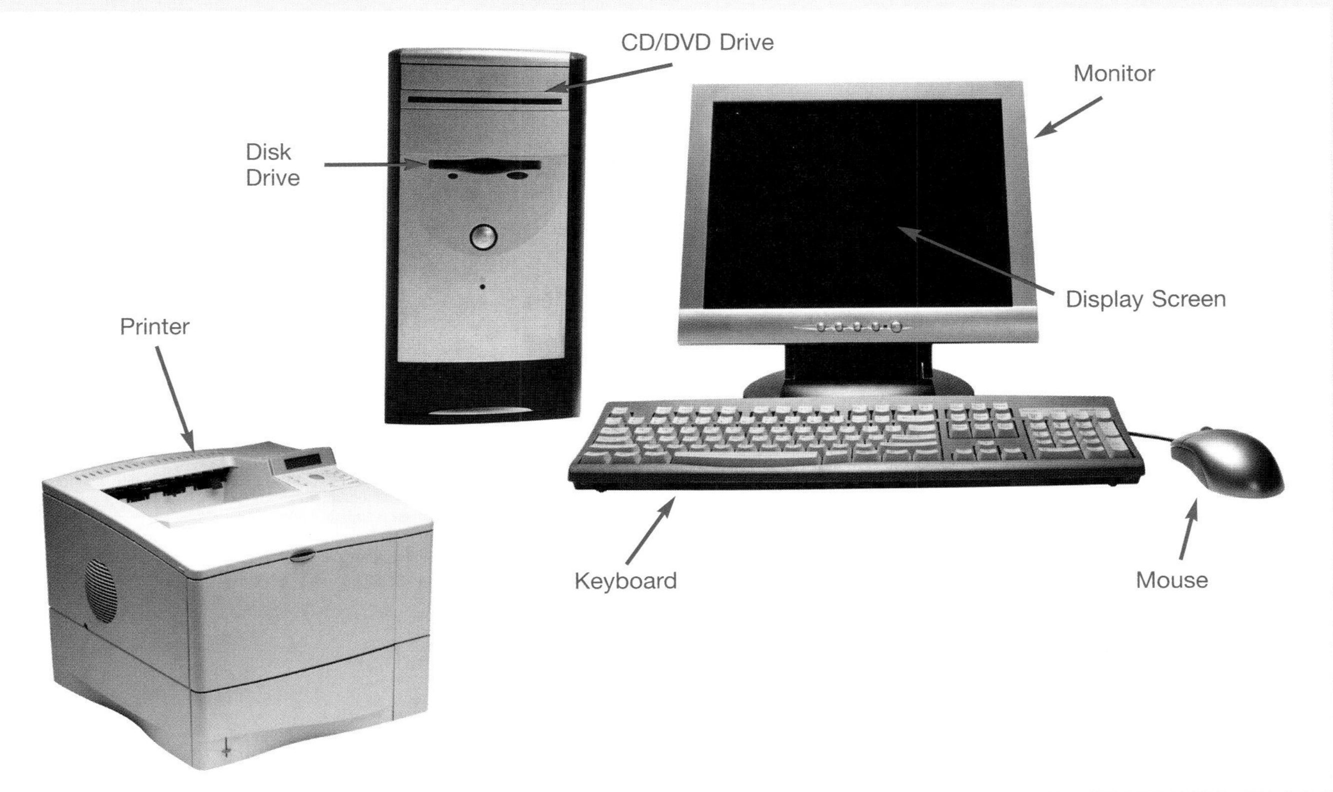

B. THE COMPUTER KEYBOARD

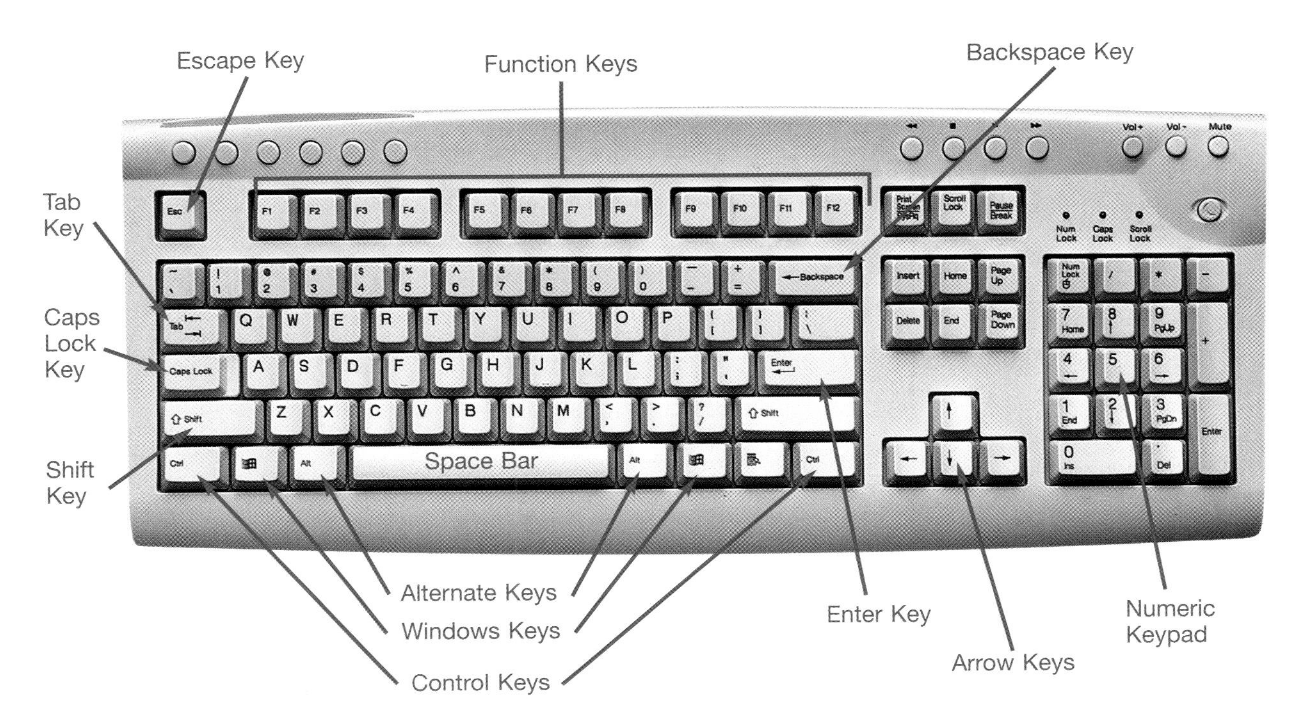

Reference Manual

A. BUSINESS LETTER IN BLOCK STYLE

(with standard punctuation)

↓6X

Date line — September 5, 20-- ↓4X

Inside address — Ms. Joan R. Hunter
Bolwater Associates
One Parklands Drive
Darien, CT 06820 ↓2X

Salutation — Dear Ms. Hunter: ↓2X

You will soon receive the signed contract to have your organization conduct a one-day workshop for our employees on eliminating repetitive-motion injuries in the workplace. As we agreed, this workshop will apply to both our office and factory workers and you will conduct separate sessions for each group.

Body

We revised Paragraph 4b to require the instructor of this workshop to be a full-time employee of Bolwater Associates. In addition, we made changes to Paragraph 10-c to require our prior approval of the agenda for the workshop.

If these revisions are satisfactory, please sign and return one copy of the contract for our files. We look forward to this opportunity to enhance the health of our employees. I know that all of us will enjoy this workshop. ↓2X

Complimentary closing — Sincerely, ↓4X

John L. Merritt

Writer's identification — John L. Merritt, Director ↓2X

Reference initials — fej

B. BUSINESS LETTER IN MODIFIED-BLOCK STYLE

(with open punctuation, multiline list, and enclosure notation)

Left tab: 3"

↓6X

→tab to centerpoint May 15, 20-- ↓4X

Mr. Ichiro Xie
Bolwater Associates
One Parklands Drive
Darien, CT 06820 ↓2X

Dear Mr. Xie ↓2X

I am returning a signed contract to have your organization conduct a one-day workshop for our employees on eliminating repetitive-motion injuries in the workplace. We have made the following changes to the contract:

Multiline list

1. We revised Paragraph 4b to require the instructor of this workshop to be a full-time employee of Bolwater Associates.
2. We made changes to Paragraph 10-c to require our prior approval of the agenda for the workshop.

If these revisions are satisfactory, please sign and return one copy of the contract for our files. We look forward to this opportunity to enhance the health of our employees. I know that all of us will enjoy this workshop. ↓2X

→tab to centerpoint Sincerely ↓4X

Reinalda Guerrero

Reinalda Guerrero, Director ↓2X

pec

Enclosure notation — Enclosure

C. BUSINESS LETTER IN SIMPLIFIED STYLE

(with single-line list, enclosure notation, and copy notation)

↓6X

October 5, 20-- ↓4X

Mr. Dale P. Griffin
Bolwater Associates
One Parklands Drive
Darien, CT 06820 ↓3X

Subject line — WORKSHOP CONTRACT ↓3X

I am returning the signed contract, Ms. Hunter, to have your organization conduct a one-day workshop for our employees on eliminating repetitive-motion injuries in the workplace. We have amended the following sections of the contract:

Single-line list

- Paragraph 4b
- Table 3
- Attachment 2

If these revisions are satisfactory, please sign and return one copy of the contract for our files. We look forward to this opportunity to enhance the health of our employees. I know that all of us will enjoy this workshop. ↓4X

Kachina Haddad

KACHINA HADDAD, DIRECTOR ↓2X

iww
Enclosure

Copy notation — c: Legal Department

D. PERSONAL-BUSINESS LETTER IN MODIFIED-BLOCK STYLE

(with international address and standard punctuation)

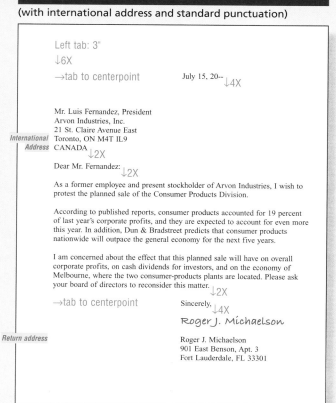

Left tab: 3"

↓6X

→tab to centerpoint July 15, 20-- ↓4X

Mr. Luis Fernandez, President
Arvon Industries, Inc.
21 St. Claire Avenue East

International Address — Toronto, ON M4T IL9
CANADA ↓2X

Dear Mr. Fernandez: ↓2X

As a former employee and present stockholder of Arvon Industries, I wish to protest the planned sale of the Consumer Products Division.

According to published reports, consumer products accounted for 19 percent of last year's corporate profits, and they are expected to account for even more this year. In addition, Dun & Bradstreet predicts that consumer products nationwide will outpace the general economy for the next five years.

I am concerned about the effect that this planned sale will have on overall corporate profits, on cash dividends for investors, and on the economy of Melbourne, where the two consumer-products plants are located. Please ask your board of directors to reconsider this matter. ↓2X

→tab to centerpoint Sincerely, ↓4X

Roger J. Michaelson

Return address — Roger J. Michaelson
901 East Benson, Apt. 3
Fort Lauderdale, FL 33301

A. BUSINESS LETTER ON EXECUTIVE STATIONERY

(7.25" x 10.5"; 1" side margins; with delivery notation and standard punctuation.)

↓6X

July 18, 20-- ↓4X

Mr. Rodney Eastwood
BBL Resources
52A Northern Ridge
Fayetteville, PA 17222 ↓2X

Dear Rodney: ↓2X

I see no reason why we should continue to consider the locality around Geraldton for our new plant. Even though the desirability of this site from an economic view is undeniable, there is insufficient housing readily available for our workers.

In trying to control urban growth, the city has been turning down the building permits for new housing or placing so many restrictions on foreign investment as to make it too expensive.

Please continue to seek out other areas of exploration where we might form a joint partnership. ↓2X

Sincerely, ↓4X

Dalit Chande

Dalit Chande
Vice President for Operations ↓2X

mme
Delivery notation By Fax

B. BUSINESS LETTER ON HALF-PAGE STATIONERY

(5.5" x 8.5"; 0.75" side margins and standard punctuation)

↓4X

July 18, 20-- ↓4X

Mr. Aristeo Olivas
BBL Resources
52A Northern Ridge
Fayetteville, PA 17222 ↓2X

Dear Aristeo: ↓2X

We should continue considering Geraldton for our new plant. Even though the desirability of this site from an economic view is undeniable, there is insufficient housing readily available.

Please continue to search out other areas of new exploration where we might someday form a joint partnership. ↓2X

Sincerely, ↓4X

Mieko Nakamura

Mieko Nakamura
Vice President for Operations ↓2X

adk

C. BUSINESS LETTER FORMATTED FOR A WINDOW ENVELOPE

(with standard punctuation)

↓6X

July 18, 20-- ↓3X

Ms. Reinalda Guerrero
BBL Resources
52A Northern Ridge
Fayetteville, PA 17222 ↓3X

Dear Ms. Guerrero: ↓2X

I see no reason why we should continue to consider the locality around Geraldton for our new plant. Even though the desirability of this site from an economic view is undeniable, there is insufficient housing readily available for our workers.

In trying to control urban growth, the city has been turning down the building permits for new housing or placing so many restrictions on foreign investment as to make it too expensive.

Please continue to seek out other areas of exploration where we might form a joint partnership. ↓2X

Sincerely, ↓4X

Arlyn J. Bunch

Arlyn J. Bunch
Vice President for Operations ↓2X

woc

D. MEMO

(with table and attachment notation)

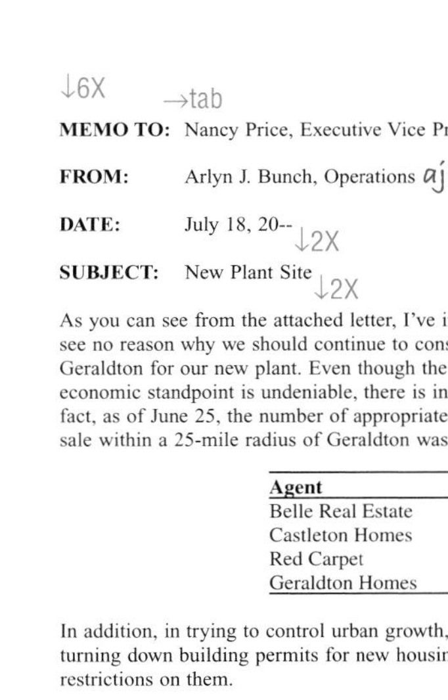

↓6X →tab

MEMO TO: Nancy Price, Executive Vice President ↓2X

FROM: Arlyn J. Bunch, Operations *ajb* ↓2X

DATE: July 18, 20-- ↓2X

SUBJECT: New Plant Site ↓2X

As you can see from the attached letter, I've informed BBL Resources that I see no reason why we should continue to consider the locality around Geraldton for our new plant. Even though the desirability of this site from an economic standpoint is undeniable, there is insufficient housing available. In fact, as of June 25, the number of appropriate single-family houses listed for sale within a 25-mile radius of Geraldton was as follows: ↓2X

Agent	Units
Belle Real Estate	123
Castleton Homes	11
Red Carpet	9
Geraldton Homes	5

↓1X

In addition, in trying to control urban growth, Geraldton has been either turning down building permits for new housing or placing excessive restrictions on them.

Because of this deficiency of housing for our employees, we have no choice but to look elsewhere. ↓2X

woc
Attachment notation Attachment

A. MULTIPAGE BUSINESS LETTER

(page 1; with on-arrival notation, international address, subject line, table, and standard punctuation)

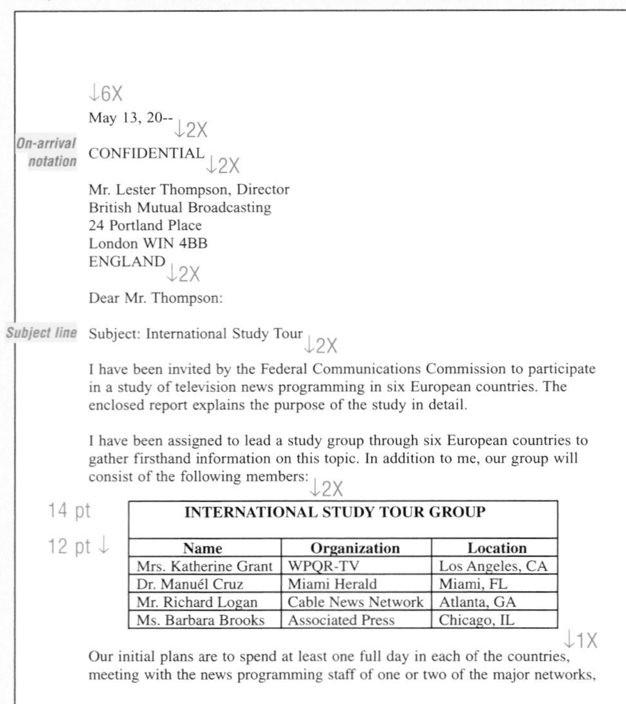

↓6X

May 13, 20-- ↓2X

On-arrival notation — CONFIDENTIAL ↓2X

Mr. Lester Thompson, Director
British Mutual Broadcasting
24 Portland Place
London WIN 4BB
ENGLAND ↓2X

Dear Mr. Thompson:

Subject line — Subject: International Study Tour ↓2X

I have been invited by the Federal Communications Commission to participate in a study of television news programming in six European countries. The enclosed report explains the purpose of the study in detail.

I have been assigned to lead a study group through six European countries to gather firsthand information on this topic. In addition to me, our group will consist of the following members: ↓2X

14 pt

INTERNATIONAL STUDY TOUR GROUP		
Name	**Organization**	**Location**
Mrs. Katherine Grant	WPQR-TV	Los Angeles, CA
Dr. Manuél Cruz	Miami Herald	Miami, FL
Mr. Richard Logan	Cable News Network	Atlanta, GA
Ms. Barbara Brooks	Associated Press	Chicago, IL

12 pt ↓

↓1X

Our initial plans are to spend at least one full day in each of the countries, meeting with the news programming staff of one or two of the major networks,

B. MULTIPAGE BUSINESS LETTER

(page 2; with company name; multiline list; enclosure, delivery, copy, postscript, blind copy notations; and standard punctuation)

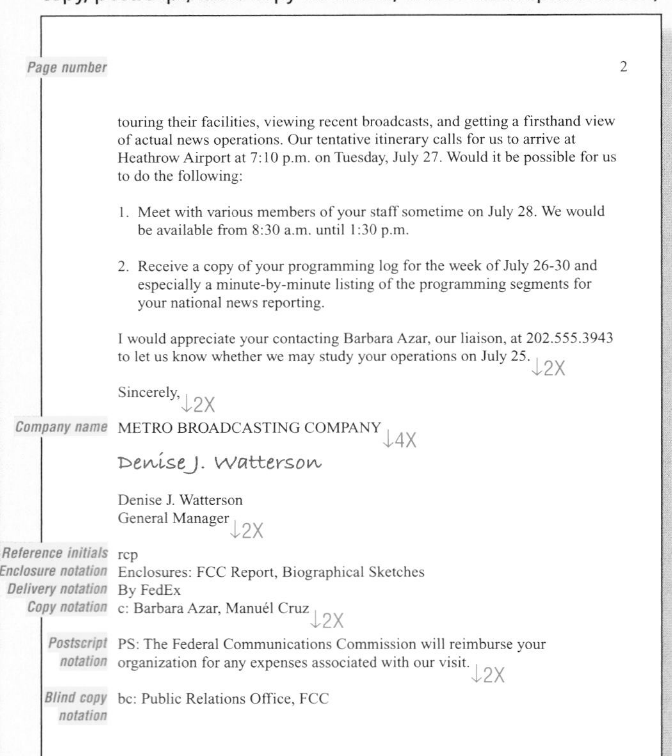

Page number — 2

touring their facilities, viewing recent broadcasts, and getting a firsthand view of actual news operations. Our tentative itinerary calls for us to arrive at Heathrow Airport at 7:10 p.m. on Tuesday, July 27. Would it be possible for us to do the following:

1. Meet with various members of your staff sometime on July 28. We would be available from 8:30 a.m. until 1:30 p.m.

2. Receive a copy of your programming log for the week of July 26-30 and especially a minute-by-minute listing of the programming segments for your national news reporting.

I would appreciate your contacting Barbara Azar, our liaison, at 202.555.3943 to let us know whether we may study your operations on July 25. ↓2X

Sincerely, ↓2X

Company name — METRO BROADCASTING COMPANY ↓4X

Denise J. Watterson

Denise J. Watterson
General Manager ↓2X

Reference initials — rcp
Enclosure notation — Enclosures: FCC Report, Biographical Sketches
Delivery notation — By FedEx
Copy notation — c: Barbara Azar, Manuél Cruz ↓2X

Postscript notation — PS: The Federal Communications Commission will reimburse your organization for any expenses associated with our visit. ↓2X

Blind copy notation — bc: Public Relations Office, FCC

C. E-MAIL MESSAGE IN MICROSOFT OUTLOOK/ INTERNET EXPLORER

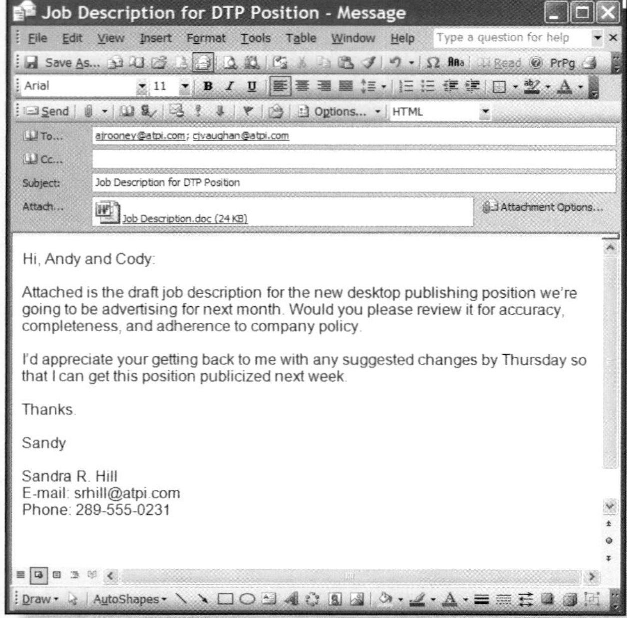

Job Description for DTP Position - Message

File Edit View Insert Format Tools Table Window Help

To... airooney@atpi.com; ctvaughan@atpi.com
Cc...
Subject: Job Description for DTP Position
Attach... Job Description.doc (24 KB)

Hi, Andy and Cody:

Attached is the draft job description for the new desktop publishing position we're going to be advertising for next month. Would you please review it for accuracy, completeness, and adherence to company policy.

I'd appreciate your getting back to me with any suggested changes by Thursday so that I can get this position publicized next week.

Thanks.

Sandy

Sandra R. Hill
E-mail: srhill@atpi.com
Phone: 289-555-0231

D. E-MAIL MESSAGE IN YAHOO!

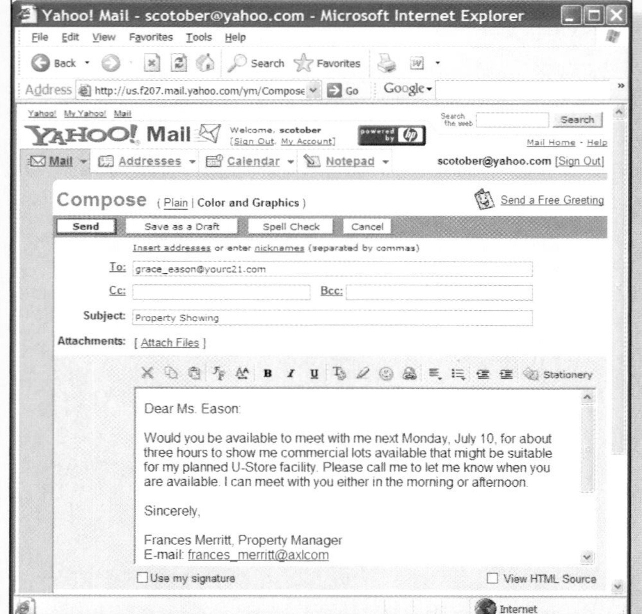

Yahoo! Mail - scotober@yahoo.com - Microsoft Internet Explorer

File Edit View Favorites Tools Help

Address http://us.f207.mail.yahoo.com/ym/Compose

YAHOO! Mail — Welcome, scotober

Mail | Addresses | Calendar | Notepad — scotober@yahoo.com [Sign Out]

Compose (Plain | Color and Graphics) — Send a Free Greeting

Send | Save as a Draft | Spell Check | Cancel

To: grace_eason@yourc21.com
Cc: Bcc:
Subject: Property Showing
Attachments: [Attach Files]

Dear Ms. Eason:

Would you be available to meet with me next Monday, July 10, for about three hours to show me commercial lots available that might be suitable for my planned U-Store facility. Please call me to let me know when you are available. I can meet with you either in the morning or afternoon.

Sincerely,

Frances Merritt, Property Manager
E-mail: frances_merritt@axlcom

Use my signature — View HTML Source

A. FORMATTING ENVELOPES

A standard large (No. 10) envelope is 9.5 by 4.125 inches. A standard small (No. 6¼) envelope is 6.5 by 3.625 inches. Although either address format shown below is acceptable, the format shown for the large envelope (all caps and no punctuation) is recommended by the U.S. Postal Service for mail that will be sorted by an electronic scanning device.

Window envelopes are often used in a word processing environment because of the difficulty of aligning envelopes correctly in some printers. A window envelope requires no formatting, since the letter is formatted and folded so that the inside address is visible through the window.

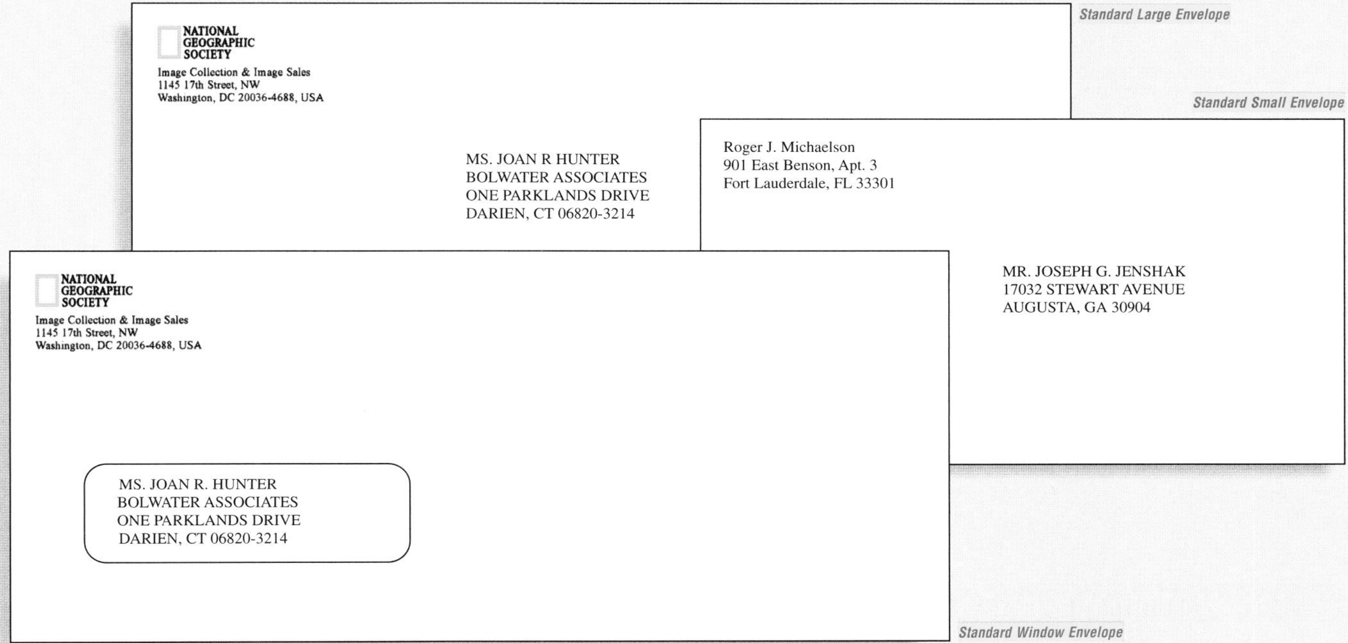

B. FOLDING LETTERS

To fold a letter for a large envelope:

1. Place the letter *face up* and fold up the bottom third.
2. Fold the top third down to 0.5 inch from the bottom edge.
3. Insert the last crease into the envelope first, with the flap facing up.

To fold a letter for a small envelope:

1. Place the letter *face up* and fold up the bottom half to 0.5 inch from the top.
2. Fold the right third over to the left.
3. Fold the left third over to 0.5 inch from the right edge.
4. Insert the last crease into the envelope first, with the flap facing up.

To fold a letter for a window envelope:

1. Place the letter *face down* with the letterhead at the top and fold the bottom third of the letter up.
2. Fold the top third down so that the address shows.
3. Insert the letter into the envelope so that the address shows through the window.

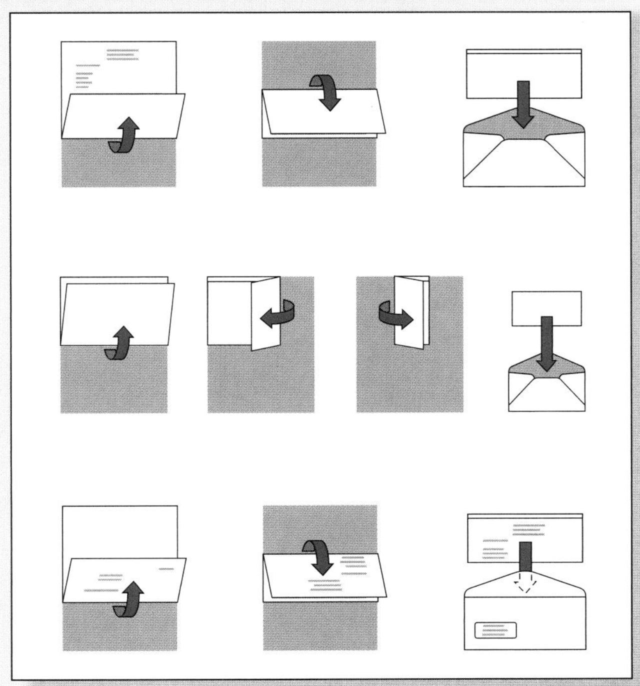

Reference Manual

A. OUTLINE

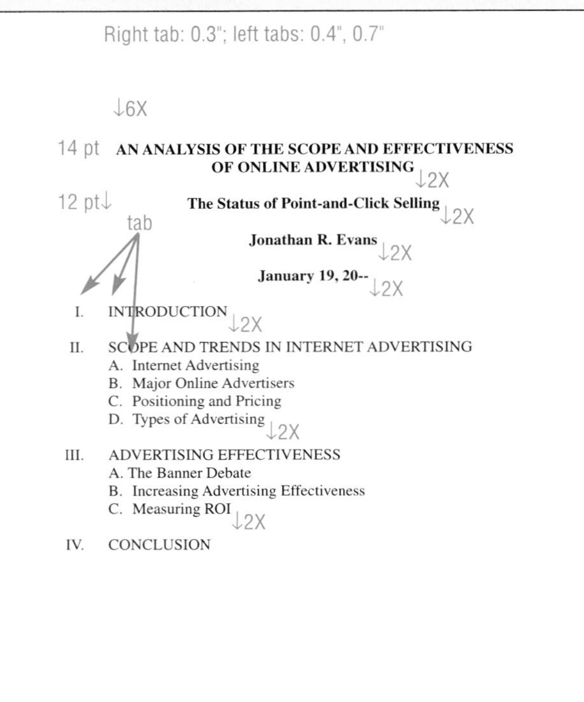

Right tab: 0.3"; left tabs: 0.4", 0.7"

↓6X

14 pt **AN ANALYSIS OF THE SCOPE AND EFFECTIVENESS OF ONLINE ADVERTISING** ↓2X

12 pt↓ **The Status of Point-and-Click Selling** ↓2X

tab

Jonathan R. Evans ↓2X

January 19, 20-- ↓2X

I. INTRODUCTION ↓2X

II. SCOPE AND TRENDS IN INTERNET ADVERTISING
- A. Internet Advertising
- B. Major Online Advertisers
- C. Positioning and Pricing
- D. Types of Advertising ↓2X

III. ADVERTISING EFFECTIVENESS
- A. The Banner Debate
- B. Increasing Advertising Effectiveness
- C. Measuring ROI ↓2X

IV. CONCLUSION

B. TITLE PAGE

center page↓

14 pt **AN ANALYSIS OF THE SCOPE AND EFFECTIVENESS OF ONLINE ADVERTISING** ↓2X

12 pt↓ **The Status of Point-and-Click Selling** ↓12X

Submitted to ↓2X

Luis Torres
General Manager
ViaWorld, International ↓12X

Prepared by ↓2X

Jonathan R. Evans
Assistant Marketing Manager
ViaWorld, International ↓2X

January 19, 20--

C. TRANSMITTAL MEMO

(with 2-line subject line and attachment notation)

↓6X

→ tab

MEMO TO: Luis Torres, General Manager ↓2X

FROM: Jonathan R. Evans, Assistant Marketing Manager *jre* ↓2X

DATE: January 19, 20-- ↓2X

SUBJECT: An Analysis of the Scope and Effectiveness of Online Advertising ↓2X

Here is the report analyzing the scope and effectiveness of Internet advertising that you requested on January 5, 20--.

The report predicts that the total value of the business-to-business e-commerce market will reach $1.3 trillion by 2003, up from $190 billion in 1999. New technologies aimed at increasing Internet ad interactivity and the adoption of standards for advertising response measurement and tracking will contribute to this increase. Unfortunately, as discussed in this report, the use of "rich media" and interactivity in Web advertising will create its own set of problems.

I enjoyed working on this assignment, Luis, and learned quite a bit from my analysis of the situation. Please let me know if you have any questions about the report. ↓2X

plw
Attachment

D. TABLE OF CONTENTS

Left tab: 0.5"; right dot-leader tab: 6".

↓6X

14 pt **CONTENTS** ↓2X

12 pt↓ INTRODUCTION .... 1 ↓2X

SCOPE AND TRENDS IN ONLINE ADVERTISING .... 3 ↓2X

→tab Internet Advertising Spending 4
Major Online Advertisers 5
Positioning and Pricing 7
Types of Advertising .... 8 ↓2X

ADVERTISING EFFECTIVENESS .... 9 ↓2X

The Banner Debate 9
Increasing Advertising Effectiveness 11
Measuring ROI .... 12 ↓2X

CONCLUSION .... 13 ↓2X

APPENDIX ↓2X

Sample Internet Advertising 15
Proposed WEFA Standards .... 18 ↓2X

BIBLIOGRAPHY 19

A. BUSINESS REPORT

(page 1; with footnotes and multiline list)

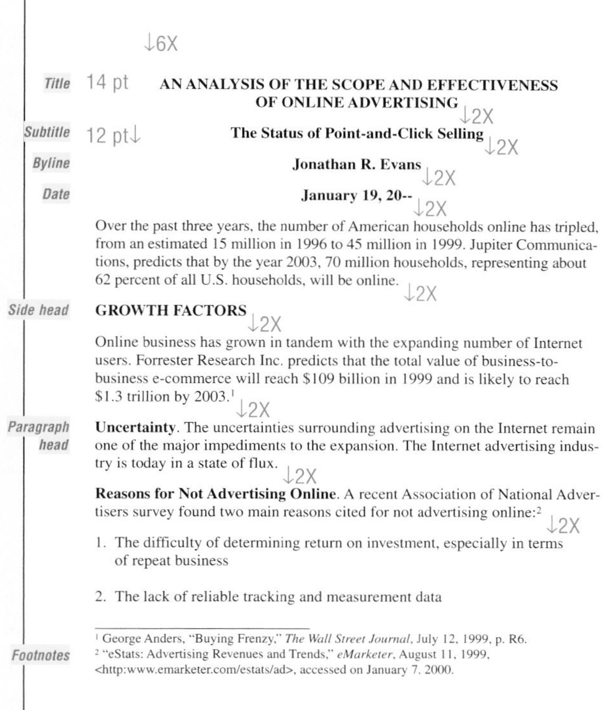

↓6X

Title 14 pt **AN ANALYSIS OF THE SCOPE AND EFFECTIVENESS OF ONLINE ADVERTISING** ↓2X

Subtitle 12 pt↓ **The Status of Point-and-Click Selling** ↓2X

Byline **Jonathan R. Evans** ↓2X

Date **January 19, 20--** ↓2X

Over the past three years, the number of American households online has tripled, from an estimated 15 million in 1996 to 45 million in 1999. Jupiter Communications, predicts that by the year 2003, 70 million households, representing about 62 percent of all U.S. households, will be online. ↓2X

Side head **GROWTH FACTORS** ↓2X

Online business has grown in tandem with the expanding number of Internet users. Forrester Research Inc. predicts that the total value of business-to-business e-commerce will reach $109 billion in 1999 and is likely to reach $1.3 trillion by 2003.[1] ↓2X

Paragraph head **Uncertainty**. The uncertainties surrounding advertising on the Internet remain one of the major impediments to the expansion. The Internet advertising industry is today in a state of flux. ↓2X

Reasons for Not Advertising Online. A recent Association of National Advertisers survey found two main reasons cited for not advertising online:[2] ↓2X

1. The difficulty of determining return on investment, especially in terms of repeat business
2. The lack of reliable tracking and measurement data

Footnotes

[1] George Anders, "Buying Frenzy," *The Wall Street Journal*, July 12, 1999, p. R6.
[2] "eStats: Advertising Revenues and Trends," *eMarketer*, August 11, 1999, <http:www.emarketer.com/estats/ad>, accessed on January 7, 2000.

B. BUSINESS REPORT

(page 3; with long quotation and table)

3

who argue that banners have a strong potential for advertising effectiveness point out that it is not the banner format itself which presents a problem to advertising effectiveness, but rather the quality of the banner and the attention to its placement. According to Mike Windsor, president of Ogilvy Interactive: ↓2X

indent 0.5″→ ← indent 0.5″

Long quotation

> It's more a case of bad banner ads, just like there are bad TV ads. The space itself has huge potential. As important as using the space within the banner creatively is to aim it effectively. Unlike broadcast media, the Web offers advertisers the opportunity to reach a specific audience based on data gathered about who is surfing at a site and what their interests are[1]

Thus, while some analysts continue to argue that the banner advertisement is passé, there is little evidence of its abandonment. Instead, ad agencies are focusing on increasing the banner's effectiveness. ↓2X

SCOPE AND TRENDS IN ONLINE ADVERTISING ↓2X

Starting from zero in 1994, analysts agree that the volume of Internet advertising spending has risen rapidly. However, as indicated in Table 3, analysts provide a wide range of the exact amount of such advertising. ↓2X

14 pt **TABLE 3. INTERNET ADVERTISING**

12 pt ↓ **1998 Estimates**

Source	**Estimate**
Internet Advertising Board	$1.92 billion
Forester	1.30 billion
IDC	1.20 billion
Burst! Media	560 million

Table source Source: "Advertising Age Teams with eMarketer for Research Report," *Advertising Age*, May 3, 1999, p. 24. ↓1X

The differences in estimates of total Web advertising spending is generally attributed to the different methodologies used by the research agencies to

[1] Lisa Napoli, "Banner Ads Are Under the Gun—And On the Move," *The New York Times*, June 17, 1999, p. D1.

C. ACADEMIC REPORT

(page 1; with endnotes and multiline list)

↓3DS

14 pt **AN ANALYSIS OF THE SCOPE AND EFFECTIVENESS OF ONLINE ADVERTISING** ↓1DS

12 pt↓ **The Status of Point-and-Click Selling** ↓1DS

Jonathan R. Evans ↓1DS

January 19, 20-- ↓1DS

Over the past three years, the number of American households online has tripled, from an estimated 15 million in 1996 to 45 million in 1999. Jupiter Communications, predicts that by the year 2003, 70 million households, representing about 62 percent of all U.S. households, will be online. ↓1DS

GROWTH FACTORS ↓1DS

Online business has grown in tandem with the expanding number of Internet users. Forrester Research Inc. predicts that the total value of business-to-business e-commerce will reach $109 billion in 1999.[i]

Reasons for Not Advertising Online. A recent Association of National Advertisers survey found two main reasons cited for not advertising online:[ii]

1. The difficulty of determining return on investment, especially in terms of repeat business.
2. The lack of reliable tracking and measurement data.

Some analysts argue that advertising on the Internet can and should follow the same principles as advertising on television.[iii] Other visual media

D. ACADEMIC REPORT

(last page; with long quotation and endnotes)

14

advertising effectiveness, but rather the quality of the banner and the attention to its placement. According to Mike Windsor, president of Ogilvy Interactive: ↓1DS

indent 0.5″→ ← indent 0.5″

Long quotation

> It's more a case of bad banner ads, just like there are bad TV ads. The space itself has huge potential. As important as using the space within the banner creatively is to aim it effectively. Unlike broadcast media, the Web offers advertisers the opportunity to reach a specific audience based on data gathered about who is surfing at a site and what their interests are.[vii] ↓1SS

From the advertiser's perspective, the most effective Internet ads do more than just deliver information to the consumer and grab the consumer's attention—they also gather information about consumers (e.g., through "cookies" and other methodologies). From the consumer's perspective, this type of interactivity may represent an intrusion and an invasion of privacy. There appears to be a shift away from the ad-supported model and toward the transaction model, wherein users pay for the content they want and the specific transactions they perform.

Endnotes

i George Anders, "Buying Frenzy," *The Wall Street Journal*, July 12, 1999, p. R6.
ii "eStats: Advertising Revenues and Trends," *eMarketer*, August 11, 1999, <http:www.emarketer.com/estats/ad>, accessed on August 11, 1999.
iii Bradley Johnson, "Nielsen/NetRatings Index Shows 4% Rise in Web Ads," *Advertising Age*, July 19, 2003, p. 18.
iv Tom Hyland, "Web Advertising: A Year of Growth," *Internet Advertising Board*, November 13, 1999, <http:www.iab.net/advertise>, accessed on January 8, 2000.
v Adrian Mand, "Click Here: Free Ride Doles Out Freebies to Ad Surfers," *Brandweek*, March 8, 1999, p. 30.
vi Andrea Petersen, "High Price of Internet Banner Ads Slips Amid Increase in Web Sites," *The Wall Street Journal*, March 2, 1999, p. B20.
vii Lisa Napoli, "Banner Ads Are Under the Gun—And On the Move," *The New York Times*, June 17, 1999, p. D1.

Reference Manual

A. LEFT-BOUND BUSINESS REPORT

(page 1; with endnotes and single-line list)

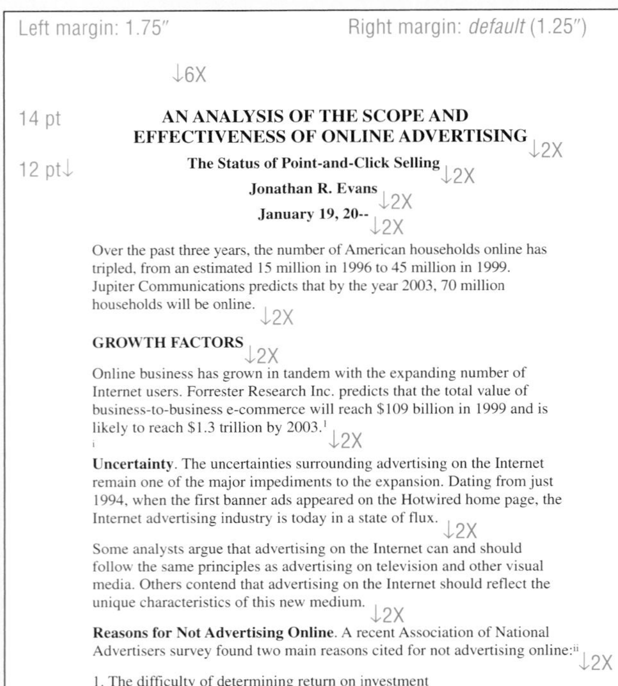

Left margin: 1.75″ Right margin: *default* (1.25″)

↓6X

14 pt **AN ANALYSIS OF THE SCOPE AND EFFECTIVENESS OF ONLINE ADVERTISING** ↓2X

12 pt↓ **The Status of Point-and-Click Selling** ↓2X

Jonathan R. Evans ↓2X

January 19, 20-- ↓2X

Over the past three years, the number of American households online has tripled, from an estimated 15 million in 1996 to 45 million in 1999. Jupiter Communications predicts that by the year 2003, 70 million households will be online. ↓2X

GROWTH FACTORS ↓2X

Online business has grown in tandem with the expanding number of Internet users. Forrester Research Inc. predicts that the total value of business-to-business e-commerce will reach $109 billion in 1999 and is likely to reach $1.3 trillion by 2003.[i] ↓2X

Uncertainty. The uncertainties surrounding advertising on the Internet remain one of the major impediments to the expansion. Dating from just 1994, when the first banner ads appeared on the Hotwired home page, the Internet advertising industry is today in a state of flux. ↓2X

Some analysts argue that advertising on the Internet can and should follow the same principles as advertising on television and other visual media. Others contend that advertising on the Internet should reflect the unique characteristics of this new medium. ↓2X

Reasons for Not Advertising Online. A recent Association of National Advertisers survey found two main reasons cited for not advertising online:[ii] ↓2X

1. The difficulty of determining return on investment
2. The lack of reliable tracking and measurement data

B. BIBLIOGRAPHY

(for business or academic style using either endnotes or footnotes)

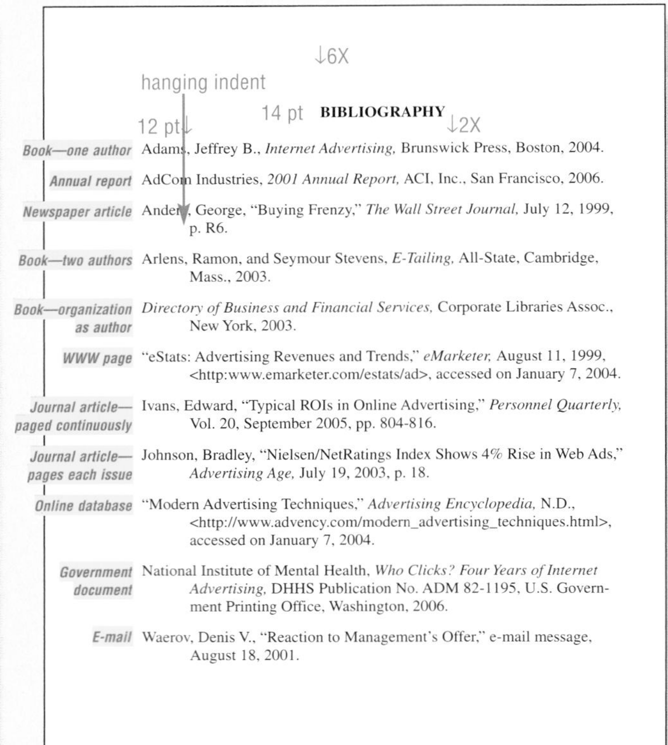

↓6X

hanging indent

14 pt **BIBLIOGRAPHY** ↓2X

12 pt↓

Book—one author: Adams, Jeffrey B., *Internet Advertising*, Brunswick Press, Boston, 2004.

Annual report: AdCom Industries, *2001 Annual Report*, ACI, Inc., San Francisco, 2006.

Newspaper article: Anders, George, "Buying Frenzy," *The Wall Street Journal*, July 12, 1999, p. R6.

Book—two authors: Arlens, Ramon, and Seymour Stevens, *E-Tailing*, All-State, Cambridge, Mass., 2003.

Book—organization as author: *Directory of Business and Financial Services*, Corporate Libraries Assoc., New York, 2003.

WWW page: "eStats: Advertising Revenues and Trends," *eMarketer*, August 11, 1999, <http:www.emarketer.com/estats/ad>, accessed on January 7, 2004.

Journal article—paged continuously: Ivans, Edward, "Typical ROIs in Online Advertising," *Personnel Quarterly*, Vol. 20, September 2005, pp. 804-816.

Journal article—pages each issue: Johnson, Bradley, "Nielsen/NetRatings Index Shows 4% Rise in Web Ads," *Advertising Age*, July 19, 2003, p. 18.

Online database: "Modern Advertising Techniques," *Advertising Encyclopedia*, N.D., <http://www.advency.com/modern_advertising_techniques.html>, accessed on January 7, 2004.

Government document: National Institute of Mental Health, *Who Clicks? Four Years of Internet Advertising*, DHHS Publication No. ADM 82-1195, U.S. Government Printing Office, Washington, 2006.

E-mail: Waerov, Denis V., "Reaction to Management's Offer," e-mail message, August 18, 2001.

C. MEMO REPORT

(page 1, with single-line list)

↓6X

→tab

MEMO TO: Luis Torres, General Manager ↓2X

FROM: Jonathan R. Evans, Assistant Marketing Manager *jre* ↓2X

DATE: January 19, 20-- ↓2X

SUBJECT: An Analysis of the Scope and Effectiveness of Online Advertising ↓2X

According to a July 12, 1999, Wall Street Journal article, over the past three years, the number of American households online has tripled, from an estimated 15 million in 1996 to 45 million in 1999. Jupiter Communications, predicts that by the year 2003, 70 million households, representing 62 percent of all U.S. households, will be online. Online business has grown in tandem with the expanding number of Internet users. Forrester Research Inc. predicts that the total value of business-to-business e-commerce will reach $109 billion in 1999 and is likely to reach $1.3 trillion by 2003. ↓2X

UNCERTAINTY ↓2X

The uncertainties surrounding advertising on the Internet remain one of the major impediments to the expansion. Dating from just 1994, when the first banner ads appeared on the Hotwired home page, the Internet advertising industry is today in a state of flux.

Some analysts argue that advertising on the Internet can and should follow the same principles as advertising on television and other visual media. Others contend that all of the advertising on the Internet should reflect the unique characteristics of this new medium.

A recent Association of National Advertisers survey found two main reasons cited for not advertising online:

1. The difficulty of determining return on investment
2. The lack of reliable tracking and measurement data

D. REPORTS: SPECIAL FEATURES

Margins and Spacing. Use a 2-inch top margin for the first page of each section of a report (for example, the table of contents, first page of the body, and bibliography page) and a 1-inch top margin for other pages. Use default side margins (1.25 inches) and bottom margins (1 inch) for all pages. If the report is going to be bound on the left, add 0.5 inch to the left margin. Single-space business reports and double-space academic reports.

Headings. Center the report title in 14-point font (press ENTER to space down before switching to 12-point font). Single-space multiline report titles in a single-spaced report and double-space multiline titles in a double-spaced report. Insert 1 blank line before and after all parts of a heading block (consisting of the title, subtitle, author, and/or date) and format all lines in bold.

Insert 1 blank line before and after side headings and format in bold, beginning at the left margin. Format paragraph headings in bold; begin at the left margin for single-spaced reports and indent for double-spaced reports. The text follows on the same line, preceded by a period and 1 space.

Citations. For business and academic reports, format citations using your word processor's footnote (or endnote) feature. For reports formatted in APA or MLA style, use the format shown on page R-10.

A. REPORT IN APA STYLE

(page 1; with author/year citations)

Top, bottom, and side margins: 1″

Online Advertising 3 *header*

An Analysis of the Scope and Effectiveness
of Online Advertising
Jonathan R. Evans

Over the past three years, the number of American households online has tripled, from an estimated 15 million in 1996 to 45 million in 1999. Jupiter Communications predicts that by the year 2003, 70 million households, which represent 62 percent of all U.S. households, will be online (Napoli, 2003).

main head Growth Factors

Online business has grown in tandem with the expanding number of Internet users. Forrester Research Inc. predicts that the total value of business-to-business e-commerce will reach $109 billion in 2003 (Arlens & Stevens, 2003).

subhead *Uncertainty*

The uncertainties surrounding advertising on the Internet remain one of the major impediments to the expansion. Dating from just 1994. when the first banner ads appeared on the Hotwired home page, the Internet advertising industry is today in a state of flux.

Some analysts argue that advertising on the Internet can and should follow the same principles as advertising on television and other visual media ("eStats," 2004). Others contend that advertising on the Internet should reflect

B. REFERENCES IN APA STYLE

Top, bottom, and side margins: 1″
Double-space throughout.

Online Advertising 14 *header*

hanging indent

References

Book—one author Adams, J. B. (2004). *Internet advertising.* Boston: Brunswick Press.

Annual report AdCom Industries. (2006). 2005 *annual report.* San Francisco: ACI, Inc.

Newspaper article Anders, G. (2003, July 12). Buying frenzy. *The Wall Street Journal,* p. R6.

Book—two authors Arlens, R., & Stevens, S. (2003). *E-tailing.* Cambridge, MA: All-State.

Book—organization as author *Directory of business and financial services.* (2003). New York: Corporate Libraries Association.

WWW page eStats: Advertising revenues and trends. (n.d.). New York: eMarketer. Retrieved August 11, 2004, from the World Wide Web: http://www.emarketer.com/estats/ad

Journal article—paged continuously Ivans, E. (2005). Typical ROIs in online advertising. *Personnel Quarterly,* 20, 804-816.

Journal article—paged each issue Johnson, B. (2003, July 19). Nielsen/NetRatings Index shows 4% rise in Web ads. Advertising Age, 39, 18.

Online database *Modern advertising techniques.* (1998, January). *Advertising Encyclopedia.* Retrieved January 7, 2004, from http://www.advency.com/ads.html

Government document National Institute of Mental Health *Who clicks? Four years of Internet advertising* (DHHS Publication No. ADM 82-1195). Washington, DC. (2006).

C. REPORT IN MLA STYLE

(page 1; with author/page citations)

Top, bottom, and side margins: 1″
Double-space throughout.

Evans 1 *header*

Jonathan R. Evans
Professor Inman
Management 302
19 January 20--

An Analysis of the Scope and Effectiveness
of Online Advertising

Over the past three years, the number of American households online has tripled, from an estimated 15 million in 1996 to 45 million in 1999. Jupiter Communications predicts that by the year 2003, 70 million households, representing about 62% of all U.S. households, will be online (Napoli D1). Online business has grown in tandem with the expanding number of Internet users. Forrester Research Inc. predicts that the total value of business-to-business e-commerce will reach $109 billion in 1999 and is likely to reach $1.3 trillion by 2003 (Arlens & Stevens 376-379).

The uncertainties surrounding advertising on the Internet remain one of the major impediments to the expansion. Dating from just 1994, when the first banner ads appeared on the Hotwired home page, the Internet advertising industry is today in a state of flux.

Some analysts argue that advertising on the Internet can and should follow the same principles as advertising on television and other visual media ("eStats"). Others contend that advertising on the Internet should reflect the

D. WORKS CITED IN MLA STYLE

Top, bottom, and side margins: 1″
Double-space throughout.

Evans 13 *header*

hanging indent

Works Cited

Book—one author Adams, Jeffrey B. *Internet Advertising.* Boston: Brunswick Press, 2004.

Annual report AdCom Industries. *2006 Annual Report.* San Francisco: ACI, Inc., 2005.

Newspaper article Anders, George. "Buying Frenzy," *Wall Street Journal,* July 12, 2003, p. R6.

Book—two authors Arlens, Ramon, and Seymour Stevens. *E-Tailing.* Cambridge, MA: All-State, 2003.

Book—organization as author Corporate Libraries Association. *Directory of Business and Financial Services.* New York: Corporate Libraries Association, 2003.

WWW page "eStats: Advertising Revenues and Trends." *eMarketer,* 11 Aug. 1999. 7 Jan. 2004. <http:www.emarketer.com/estats/ad>.

Journal article—paged continuously Ivans, Edward. "Typical ROIs in Online Advertising." *Personnel Quarterly* Sep. 2005: 804-816.

Journal article—paged each issue Johnson, Bradley. "Nielsen/NetRatings Index Shows 4% Rise in Web Ads." *Advertising Age* 19 July 2003: 18.

Online database *Modern Advertising Techniques.* 2003. Advertising Encyclopedia. 7 Jan. 2004 <http://www.advency.com/modern_advertising_techniques.html>.

Government document National Institute of Mental Health. *Who Clicks? Four Years of Internet Advertising.* DHHS Publication No. ADM 82-1195. Washington, DC: GPO, 2006.

E-mail Richards, Denis V. E-mail to the author. 18 Dec. 2005.

A. MEETING AGENDA

↓6X

14 pt **MILES HARDWARE EXECUTIVE COMMITTEE** ↓2X

12 pt↓ **Meeting Agenda** ↓2X

June 7, 20--, 3 p.m. ↓2X

1. Call to order ↓2X
2. Approval of minutes of May 5 meeting
3. Progress report on building addition and parking lot restrictions (Norman Hodges and Anthony Pascarelli)
4. May 15 draft of Five-Year Plan
5. Review of National Hardware Association annual convention
6. Employee grievance filed by Ellen Burrows (John Landstrom)
7. New expense-report forms (Anne Richards)
8. Announcements
9. Adjournment

B. MINUTES OF A MEETING

↓6X

14 pt **RESOURCE COMMITTEE** ↓2X

12 pt↓ **Minutes of the Meeting** ↓2X

March 13, 20-- ↓1X

ATTENDANCE	The Resource Committee met on March 13, 20--, at the Airport Sheraton in Portland, Oregon, with all members present. Michael Davis, chairperson, called the meeting to order at 2:30 p.m. ↓1X
APPROVAL OF MINUTES	The minutes of the January 27 meeting were read and approved. ↓1X
OLD BUSINESS	The members of the committee reviewed the sales brochure on electronic copyboards and agreed to purchase one for the conference room. Cynthia Giovanni will secure quotations from at least two suppliers. ↓1X
NEW BUSINESS	The committee reviewed a request from the Purchasing Department for three new computers. After extensive discussion regarding the appropriate use of the computers and software to be purchased, the committee approved the request. ↓1X
ADJOURNMENT	The meeting was adjourned at 4:45 p.m. ↓2X Respectfully submitted, ↓4X *D. S. Madsen* D. S. Madsen, Secretary

(Note: Table shown with "Show Gridlines" active.)

C. ITINERARY

↓6X

14 pt **ITINERARY** ↓2X

12 pt↓ **For Arlene Gilsdorf** ↓2X

March 12-15, 20-- ↓1X

THURSDAY, MARCH 12	↓1X
5:10 p.m.-7:06 p.m.	Flight from Detroit to Portland; Northwest 83 (Phone: 800-555-1212); e-ticket; Seat 8D; nonstop; dinner ↓2X Jack Weatherford (Home: 503-555-8029; Office: 503-555-7631) will meet your flight on Thursday, provide transportation during your visit, and return you to the airport on Saturday morning. ↓2X Airport Sheraton (503-555-4032) King-sized bed, nonsmoking room; late arrival guaranteed (Reservation No. 30ZM6-02) ↓1X
FRIDAY, MARCH 13	
9 a.m.-5:30 p.m.	Portland Sales Meeting 1931 Executive Way, Suite 10 Portland (503-555-7631)
Evening	On your own
SATURDAY, MARCH 14	
7:30 a.m.-2:47 p.m.	Flight from Portland to Detroit; Northwest 360; e-ticket; Seat 9a; nonstop; breakfast

(Note: Table shown with "Show Gridlines" active.)

D. LEGAL DOCUMENT

Left tabs: 1", 3"

↓6X

12 pt↓ POWER OF ATTORNEY ↓2X

KNOW ALL MEN BY THESE PRESENTS that I, ATTORNEY LEE FERNANDEZ, of the City of Tulia, County of Swisher, State of Texas, do hereby appoint my son, Robert Fernandez, of this City, County, and State as my attorney-in-fact to act in my name, place, and stead as my agent in the management of my business operating transactions.

I give and grant unto my said attorney full power and authority to do and perform every act and thing requisite and necessary to be done in the said management as fully, to all intents and purposes, as I might or could do if personally present, with full power of revocation, hereby ratifying all that my said attorney shall lawfully do.

IN WITNESS WHEREOF, I have hereunto set my hand and seal this _____ day of ____________________, 20--. ↓2X

5 underscores ↑ 20 underscores ↑

→tab to centerpoint ______________________ ↓2X

SIGNED and affirmed in the presence of: ↓4X

______________________ ↓4X

____

A. RESUME

↓6X

14 pt **TERRY M. MARTINA** ↓2X 12 pt ↓ **250 Maxwell Avenue, Boulder, CO 80305** **Phone: 303-555-9311; e-mail: tmartina@ecc.edu** ↓1X	
OBJECTIVE	Position in resort management anywhere in Colorado or the Southwest. ↓1X
EDUCATION	A.A. in hotel management to be awarded May 2005 Edgewood Community College, Boulder, Colorado. ↓1X
EXPERIENCE	*Assistant Manager, Burger King Restaurant* Boulder, Colorado: 2003-Present • Achieved grade point average of 3.1 (on 4.0 scale). • Received Board of Regents tuition scholarship. • Financed all college expenses. ↓2X *Student Intern, Ski Valley Haven* Aspen, Colorado: September-December 2004 • Worked as an assistant to the night manager. • Gained experience in operating First-Guest software. • Was in charge of producing daily occupancy reports. • Received Employee-of-the-Month award. ↓1X
PERSONAL	• Speak and write fluent Spanish. • Competent in Microsoft Office 2003. • Secretary of ECC Hospitality Services Association. • Special Olympics volunteer: Summer 2004. ↓1X
REFERENCES	Available upon request

↓1X

(Note: Table shown with "Show Gridlines" active.)

B. APPLICATION LETTER IN BLOCK STYLE

(with standard punctuation)

↓6X

March 1, 20-- ↓4X

Mr. Lou Mansfield, Director
Human Resources Department
Rocky Resorts International
P.O. Box 1412
Denver, CO 80214 ↓2X

Dear Mr. Mansfield: ↓2X

Please consider me an applicant for the position of concierge for Suite Retreat, as advertised in last Sunday's *Denver Times.*

I will receive my A.A. degree in hotel administration from Edgewood Community College in May and will be available for full-time employment immediately. In addition to my extensive coursework in hospitality services and business, I've had experience in working for a ski lodge similar to Suite Retreats in Aspen. As a lifelong resident of Colorado and an avid skier, I would be able to provide your guests with any information they request.

After you've reviewed my enclosed resume, I would appreciate having an opportunity to discuss with you why I believe I have the right qualifications and personality to serve as your concierge. I can be reached at 303-555-9311. ↓2X

Sincerely, ↓4X

Terry M. Martina

Terry M. Martina
250 Maxwell Avenue, Apt. 8
Boulder, CO 80305 ↓2X

Enclosure

C. FORMATTING LISTS

Numbers or bullets may be used in letters, memos, and reports to call attention to items in a list. If the sequence of the items is important, use numbers rather than bullets.

- ❑ Begin the number or bullet at the paragraph point, that is, at the left margin for blocked paragraphs and indented 0.5 inch for indented paragraphs.
- ❑ Insert 1 blank line before and after the list.
- ❑ Within the list, use the same spacing (single or double) as is used in the rest of the document.
- ❑ For single-spaced documents, if all items require no more than 1 line, single-space the items in the list. If any item requires more than 1 line, single-space each item and insert 1 blank line between each item.

To format a list:

1. Type the list unformatted.
2. Select the items in the list.
3. Apply the number or bullet feature.
4. If necessary, use the Decrease Indent or Increase Indent button in Microsoft Word to adjust the position of the list.

The three bulleted and numbered lists shown at the right are all formatted correctly.

D. EXAMPLES OF DIFFERENT TYPES OF LISTS

According to PricewaterhouseCoopers and the Internet Advertising Bureau, the following are the most common types of advertising on the Internet:

- Banner ads that feature some type of animation to attract the viewer's attention.

- Sponsorship, in which an advertiser sponsors a content-based Web site.

- Interstitials, ads that flash up while a page downloads.

There is now considerable controversy about the effectiveness of banner ads. As previously noted, a central goal of banner advertisements is to increase the

***

According to PricewaterhouseCoopers, the following are the most common types of advertising on the Internet, shown in order of popularity:

1. Banner ads
2. Sponsorship
3. Interstitials

There is now considerable controversy about the effectiveness of banner ads. As previously noted, a central goal of banner advertisements is to increase the

***

According to PricewaterhouseCoopers, the following are the most common types of advertising on the Internet:

- Banner ads that feature some type of animation to attract the viewer's attention.
- Sponsorship, in which an advertiser sponsors a Web site.
- Interstitials, ads that flash up while a page downloads.

There is now considerable controversy about the effectiveness of banner advertising. As previously noted, a central goal of banner advertisements is to

A. BOXED TABLE (DEFAULT STYLE)

(with subtitle, braced headings, total line, and table note.)

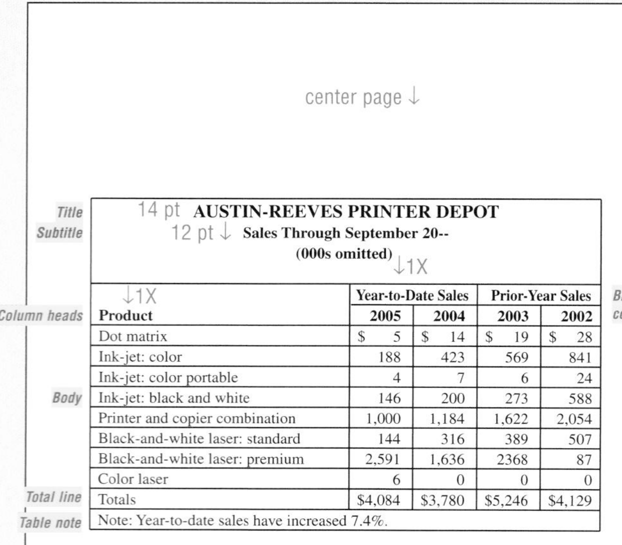

center page ↓

Title: 14 pt **AUSTIN-REEVES PRINTER DEPOT**

Subtitle: 12 pt ↓ **Sales Through September 20--**

(000s omitted) ↓1X

Product	Year-to-Date Sales 2005	Year-to-Date Sales 2004	Prior-Year Sales 2003	Prior-Year Sales 2002
Dot matrix	$ 5	$ 14	$ 19	$ 28
Ink-jet: color	188	423	569	841
Ink-jet: color portable	4	7	6	24
Ink-jet: black and white	146	200	273	588
Printer and copier combination	1,000	1,184	1,622	2,054
Black-and-white laser: standard	144	316	389	507
Black-and-white laser: premium	2,591	1,636	2368	87
Color laser	6	0	0	0
Totals	$4,084	$3,780	$5,246	$4,129

Note: Year-to-date sales have increased 7.4%.

B. OPEN TABLE

(with subtitle, blocked column headings, and 2-line heading)

center page ↓

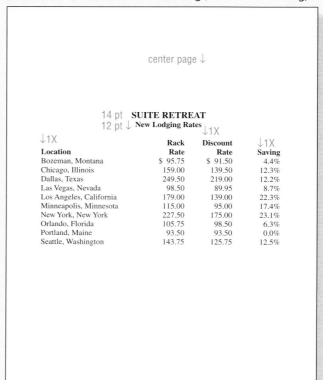

14 pt **SUITE RETREAT**

12 pt ↓ **New Lodging Rates** ↓1X

Location	Rack Rate	Discount Rate	Saving
Bozeman, Montana	$ 95.75	$ 91.50	4.4%
Chicago, Illinois	159.00	139.50	12.3%
Dallas, Texas	249.50	219.00	12.2%
Las Vegas, Nevada	98.50	89.95	8.7%
Los Angeles, California	179.00	139.00	22.3%
Minneapolis, Minnesota	115.00	95.00	17.4%
New York, New York	227.50	175.00	23.1%
Orlando, Florida	105.75	98.50	6.3%
Portland, Maine	93.50	93.50	0.0%
Seattle, Washington	143.75	125.75	12.5%

C. RULED TABLE

(with table number and centered column headings)

2

an effort to reduce errors and provide increased customer support, we have recently added numerous additional telephone support services, some of which are available 24 hours a day and others available during the workday. These are shown in Table 2. ↓2X

14 pt **Table 2. COMPUTER SUPPLIES SUPPORT SERVICES** ↓1X

12 pt↓

Support Service	Telephone	Hours
Product literature	800-555-3867	6 a.m. to 5 p.m.
Replacement parts	303-555-3388	24 hours a day
Technical documentation	408-555-3309	24 hours a day
Troubleshooting	800-555-8277	10 a.m. to 5 p.m.
Printer drivers	800-555-2377	6 a.m. to 5 p.m.
Software notes	800-555-3496	24 hours a day
Technical support	800-555-1205	24 hours a day
Hardware information	303-555-4289	6 a.m. to 5 p.m.

↓1X

We hope you will take advantage of these additional services to ensure that the computer hardware and software you purchase from Computer Supplies continues to provide you the quality and service you have come to expect from our company.

Sincerely,

Douglas Pullis

Douglas Pullis
General Manager

cds

D. TABLES: SPECIAL FEATURES

Vertical Placement. Vertically center a table that appears on a page by itself. Insert 1 blank line before and after a table appearing with other text.

Heading Block. Center and bold all lines of the heading, typing the title in all caps and 14-point font and the subtitle in upper- and lowercase and in 12-point font. If a table has a number, type the word *Table* in upper- and lowercase. Follow the table number with a period and 1 space.

Column Headings. If *all* columns in the table consist of text (such as words, phone numbers, or years), center all column headings and left-align all column entries. In all other situations, left-align all text column headings and text column entries and right-align all quantity column headings and quantity column entries. Regardless of the type of column, center braced headings. Use bold upper- and lowercase.

Column Capitalization. Capitalize only the first word and proper nouns in column entries.

Percentages and Dollars. Repeat the % sign for each number in a column (unless the heading identifies the data as percentages). Insert the $ sign only before the first amount and before a total amount. Align the $ sign with the longest amount in the column, inserting spaces after the $ sign as needed (leaving 2 spaces for each digit and 1 space for each comma).

Total Line. Add a border above a total line. Use the word *Total* or *Totals* as appropriate.

Reference Manual

A. FORMATTING BUSINESS FORMS

Many business forms can be created and filled in by using templates that are provided within commercial word processing software. Template forms can be used "as is" or they can be edited. Templates can also be used to create customized forms for any business.

When a template is opened, the form is displayed on screen. The user can then fill in the necessary information, including personalized company information. Data are entered into cells or fields, and you can move quickly from field to field with a single keystroke—usually by pressing TAB or ENTER.

Masco Shipping
1335 Dublin Road
Columbus, OH 43215
614-555-3971

PURCHASE ORDER

The following number must appear on all related correspondence, shipping papers, and invoices:
P.O. NUMBER: 1074

To:
Reliable Office Supply
Great Lakes Distribution Center
1001 West Van Buren Street
Chicago, IL 60607

Ship To:

P.O. DATE	REQUISITIONER	SHIP VIA	F.O.B. POINT	TERMS
10/22/--	DV	FedEx		

QTY	UNIT	DESCRIPTION	UNIT PRICE	TOTAL
120	H0 2048	Perforated ruled pads	$ 0.48	$ 57.60
20	564LQ4	Correction fluid	$ 1.09	$ 21.80
2	22Z398	Paper punch	$ 58.67	$ 117.34
1	B48560	Hi-style tackboard, 24" x 36", burgundy frame/blue fabric	$ 31.98	$ 31.98
20	J22502	Fax rolls	$ 11.33	$ 226.60
1	NS2314	Kraft catalog envelopes, 10" x 13", clasp with gummed flap, box of 500	$ 104.86	$ 104.86
36	AC7861	Recyclable storage boxes, legal size	$ 3.69	$ 132.84
			SUBTOTAL	$ 693.02
			SALES TAX	$ 69.30
			SHIPPING & HANDLING	
			OTHER	
			TOTAL	$ 762.32

1. Please send two copies of your invoice.
2. Enter this order in accordance with the prices, terms, delivery method, and specifications listed above.
3. Please notify us immediately if you are unable to ship as specified.
4. Send all correspondence to:
   Masco Shipping Lines
   1335 Dublin Road
   Columbus, OH 43215
   614-555-3971

Authorized by Date

B. U.S. POSTAL SERVICE ABBREVIATIONS

(for States, Territories, and Canadian Provinces)

States and Territories

Alabama .... AL
Alaska .... AK
Arizona .... AZ
Arkansas .... AR
California .... CA
Colorado .... CO
Connecticut .... CT
Delaware .... DE
District of Columbia .... DC
Florida .... FL
Georgia .... GA
Guam .... GU
Hawaii .... HI
Idaho .... ID
Illinois IL
Indiana .... IN
Iowa .... IA
Kansas .... KS
Kentucky .... KY
Louisiana .... LA
Maine .... ME
Maryland .... MD
Massachusetts .... MA
Michigan .... MI
Minnesota .... MN
Mississippi .... MS
Missouri .... MO
Montana .... MT
Nebraska .... NE
Nevada .... NV
New Hampshire .... NH
New Jersey .... NJ
New Mexico .... NM
New York .... NY
North Carolina .... NC
North Dakota .... ND
Ohio .... OH
Oklahoma .... OK
Oregon .... OR
Pennsylvania .... PA
Puerto Rico .... PR
Rhode Island .... RI
South Carolina .... SC
South Dakota .... SD
Tennessee .... TN
Texas .... TX
Utah .... UT
Vermont .... VT
Virgin Islands VI
Virginia .... VA
Washington .... WA
West Virginia .... WV
Wisconsin .... WI
Wyoming .... WY

Canadian Provinces

Alberta .... AB
British Columbia .... BC
Labrador .... LB
Manitoba .... MB
New Brunswick .... NB
Newfoundland .... NF
Northwest Territories .... NT
Nova Scotia .... NS
Ontario .... ON
Prince Edward Island .... PE
Quebec .... PQ
Saskatchewan .... SK
Yukon Territory .... YT

C. PROOFREADERS' MARKS

Proofreaders' Marks		Draft	Final Copy
⁀	Omit space	data base	database
∨ or ∧	Insert	if he's going (not)	if he's not going,
≡	Capitalize	Maple street	Maple Street
⌿	Delete	a final draft	a draft
#	Insert space	allready to	all ready to
when / if	Change word	and if you (when)	and when you
/	Use lowercase letter	our President	our president
¶	Paragraph	… to use it.¶We can	… to use it. We can
•••	Don't delete	a true story	a true story
○	Spell out	the only (1)	the only one
∽	Transpose	they all see	they see all

Proofreaders' Marks		Draft	Final Copy
SS	Single-space	first line second line	first line second line
ds	Double-space	first line second line	first line second line
⊐	Move right	Please send	Please send
⊏	Move left	May I	May I
∿∿	Bold	Column Heading	**Column Heading**
ital	Italic	Time magazine	*Time* magazine
u/l	Underline	Time magazine	<u>Time</u> magazine
♂	Move as shown	readers will see	will see readers

Language Arts for Business

(50 "must-know" rules)

PUNCTUATION

COMMAS

RULE 1 , direct address (L. 21)

Use commas before and after a name used in direct address.

Thank you, John, for responding to my e-mail so quickly.

Ladies and gentlemen, the program has been canceled.

RULE 2 , independent clause (L. 27)

Use a comma between independent clauses joined by a coordinate conjunction (unless both clauses are short).

Ellen left her job with IBM, and she and her sister went to Paris.

But: Ellen left her job with IBM and went to Paris with her sister.

But: John drove and I navigated.

Note: An independent clause is one that can stand alone as a complete sentence. The most common coordinate conjunctions are *and, but, or,* and *nor.*

RULE 3 , introductory expression (L. 27)

Use a comma after an introductory expression (unless it is a short prepositional phrase).

Before we can make a decision, we must have all the facts.

But: In 2004 our nation elected a new president.

Note: An introductory expression is a group of words that come before the subject and verb of the independent clause. Common prepositions are *to, in, on, of, at, by, for,* and *with.*

RULE 4 , direct quotation (L. 41)

Use a comma before and after a direct quotation.

James said, "I shall return," and then left.

RULE 5 , date (L. 57)

Use a comma before and after the year in a complete date.

We will arrive on June 2, 2006, for the conference.

But: We will arrive on June 2 for the conference.

RULE 6 , place (L. 57)

Use a comma before and after a state or country that follows a city (but not before a ZIP Code).

Joan moved to Vancouver, British Columbia, in May.

Send the package to Douglasville, GA 30135, by Express Mail.

But: Send the package to Georgia by Express Mail.

RULE 7 ▶
, series
(L. 61)

Use a comma between each item in a series of three or more.

We need to order paper, toner, and font cartridges_for the printer.

They saved their work, exited their program, and turned off their computers_when they finished.

Note: Do not use a comma after the last item in a series.

RULE 8 ▶
, transitional expression
(L. 61)

Use a comma before and after a transitional expression or independent comment.

It is critical, therefore, that we finish the project on time.

Our present projections, you must admit, are inadequate.

But: You must admit_our present projections are inadequate.

Note: Examples of transitional expressions and independent comments are *in addition to, therefore, however, on the other hand, as a matter of fact,* and *unfortunately.*

RULE 9 ▶
, nonessential expression
(L. 71)

Use a comma before and after a nonessential expression.

Andre, who was there, can verify the statement.

But: Anyone_who was there_can verify the statement.

Van's first book, *Crisis of Management,* was not discussed.

Van's book_*Crisis of Management*_was not discussed.

Note: A nonessential expression is a group of words that may be omitted without changing the basic meaning of the sentence. Always examine the noun or pronoun that comes before the expression to determine whether the noun needs the expression to complete its meaning. If it does, the expression is *essential* and does *not* take a comma.

RULE 10 ▶
, adjacent adjectives
(L. 71)

Use a comma between two adjacent adjectives that modify the same noun.

We need an intelligent, enthusiastic_individual for this job.

But: Please order a new_bulletin board for our main_conference room.

Note: Do not use a comma after the second adjective. Also, do not use a comma if the first adjective modifies the combined idea of the second adjective and the noun (for example, *bulletin board* and *conference room* in the second example above).

SEMICOLONS

RULE 11 ▶
; no conjunction
(L. 97)

Use a semicolon to separate two closely related independent clauses that are *not* joined by a conjunction (such as *and, but, or,* or *nor*).

Management favored the vote; stockholders did not.

But: Management favored the vote, but stockholders did not.

RULE 12 ▶
; series
(L. 97)

Use a semicolon to separate three or more items in a series if any of the items already contain commas.

Staff meetings were held on Thursday, May 7; Monday, June 7; and Friday, June 12.

Note: Be sure to insert the semicolon *between* (not within) the items in a series.

HYPHENS

RULE 13 - number (L. 57)

Hyphenate compound numbers between twenty-one and ninety-nine and fractions that are expressed as words.

Twenty-nine recommendations were approved by at least three-fourths of the members.

RULE 14 - compound adjective (L. 67)

Hyphenate compound adjectives that come before a noun (unless the first word is an adverb ending in *-ly).*

We reviewed an up-to-date report on Wednesday.

But: The report was up to date.

But: We reviewed the highly rated report.

Note: A compound adjective is two or more words that function as a unit to describe a noun.

APOSTROPHES

RULE 15 ' singular noun (L. 37)

Use *'s* to form the possessive of singular nouns.

The hurricane's force caused major damage to North Carolina's coastline.

RULE 16 ' plural noun (L. 37)

Use only an apostrophe to form the possessive of plural nouns that end in *s.*

The investors' goals were outlined in the stockholders' report.

But: The investors outlined their goals in the report to the stockholders.

But: The women's and children's clothing was on sale.

RULE 17 ' pronoun (L. 37)

Use *'s* to form the possessive of indefinite pronouns (such as *someone's* or *anybody's*); do not use an apostrophe with personal pronouns (such as *hers, his, its, ours, theirs,* and *yours*).

She could select anybody's paper for a sample.

It's time to put the file back into its cabinet.

COLONS

RULE 18 ▶
: explanatory material
(L. 91)

Use a colon to introduce explanatory material that follows an independent clause.

The computer satisfies three criteria: speed, cost, and power.

But: The computer satisfies the three criteria of speed, cost, and power.

Remember this: only one coupon is allowed per customer.

Note: An independent clause can stand alone as a complete sentence. Do not capitalize the word following the colon.

PERIODS

RULE 19 ▶
. polite request
(L. 91)

Use a period to end a sentence that is a polite request.

Will you please call me if I can be of further assistance.

Note: Consider a sentence a polite request if you expect the reader to respond by doing as you ask rather than by giving a yes-or-no answer.

QUOTATION MARKS

RULE 20 ▶
" quotation
(L. 41)

Use quotation marks around a direct quotation.

Harrison responded by saying, "Their decision does not affect us."

But: Harrison responded by saying that their decision does not affect us.

RULE 21 ▶
" title
(L. 41)

Use quotation marks around the title of a newspaper or magazine article, chapter in a book, report, and similar terms.

The most helpful article I found was "Multimedia for All."

ITALICS (OR UNDERLINE)

RULE 22 ▶
title
(L. 41)

Italicize (or underline) the titles of books, magazines, newspapers, and other complete published works.

Grisham's *The Brethren* was reviewed in a recent *USA Today* article.

GRAMMAR

SENTENCES

RULE 23 ▶ fragment (L. 21)

Avoid sentence fragments.

Not: She had always wanted to be a financial manager. But had not had the needed education.

But: She had always wanted to be a financial manager but had not had the needed education.

Note: A fragment is a part of a sentence that is incorrectly punctuated as a complete sentence. In the first example above, "but had not had the needed education" is not a complete sentence because it does not contain a subject.

RULE 24 ▶ run-on (L. 21)

Avoid run-on sentences.

Not: Mohamed is a competent worker he has even passed the MOS exam.

Not: Mohamed is a competent worker, he has even passed the MOS exam.

But: Mohamed is a competent worker; he has even passed the MOS exam.

Or: Mohamed is a competent worker. He has even passed the MOS exam.

Note: A run-on sentence is two independent clauses that run together without any punctuation between them or with only a comma between them.

AGREEMENT

RULE 25 ▶ agreement singular, agreement plural (L. 67)

Use singular verbs and pronouns with singular subjects; use plural verbs and pronouns with plural subjects.

<u>I</u> <u>was</u> happy with <u>my</u> performance.

<u>Janet and Phoenix</u> <u>were</u> happy with <u>their</u> performance.

Among the items discussed <u>were</u> our <u>raises and benefits</u>.

RULE 26 ▶ agreement pronoun (L. 81)

Some pronouns *(anybody, each, either, everybody, everyone, much, neither, no one, nobody,* and *one)* are always singular and take a singular verb. Other pronouns *(all, any, more, most, none,* and *some)* may be singular or plural, depending on the noun to which they refer.

<u>Each</u> of the employees <u>has</u> finished <u>his or her</u> task.

<u>Much</u> <u>remains</u> to be done.

<u>Most</u> of the pie <u>was</u> eaten, but <u>most</u> of the cookies <u>were</u> left.

RULE 27 ▶ agreement intervening words (L. 81)

Disregard any intervening words that come between the subject and verb when establishing agreement.

The <u>box</u> containing the books and pencils <u>has</u> not been found.

<u>Alex</u>, accompanied by Tricia, <u>is</u> attending the conference and taking <u>his</u> computer.

RULE 28 ▶ agreement nearer noun (L. 101)

If two subjects are joined by *or, either/or, neither/nor,* or *not only/but also,* make the verb agree with the subject nearer to the verb.

Neither the coach nor the <u>players</u> <u>are</u> at home.

Not only the coach but also the <u>referee</u> <u>is</u> at home.

But: <u>Both</u> the coach and the referee <u>are</u> at home.

PRONOUNS

RULE 29 ▶ nominative pronoun (L. 107)

Use nominative pronouns (such as *I, he, she, we, they,* and *who)* as subjects of a sentence or clause.

The programmer and he are reviewing the code.

Barb is a person who can do the job.

RULE 30 ▶ objective pronoun (L. 107)

Use objective pronouns (such as *me, him, her, us, them,* and *whom)* as objects of a verb, preposition, or infinitive.

The code was reviewed by the programmer and him.

Barb is the type of person whom we can trust.

ADJECTIVES AND ADVERBS

RULE 31 ▶ adjective/adverb (L. 101)

Use comparative adjectives and adverbs (*-er, more,* and *less)* when referring to two nouns or pronouns; use superlative adjectives and adverbs *(-est, most,* and *least)* when referring to more than two.

The shorter of the two training sessions is the more helpful one.

The longest of the three training sessions is the least helpful one.

WORD USAGE

RULE 32 ▶ accept/except (L. 117)

***Accept* means "to agree to"; *except* means "to leave out."**

All employees except the maintenance staff should accept the agreement.

RULE 33 ▶ affect/effect (L. 117)

***Affect* is most often used as a verb meaning "to influence"; *effect* is most often used as a noun meaning "result."**

The ruling will affect our domestic operations but will have no effect on our Asian operations.

RULE 34 ▶ farther/further (L. 117)

***Farther* refers to distance; *further* refers to extent or degree.**

The farther we drove, the further agitated he became.

RULE 35 ▶ personal/personnel (L. 117)

***Personal* means "private"; *personnel* means "employees."**

All personnel agreed not to use e-mail for personal business.

RULE 36 ▶ principal/principle (L. 117)

***Principal* means "primary"; *principle* means "rule."**

The principle of fairness is our principal means of dealing with customers.

MECHANICS

CAPITALIZATION

RULE 37 ▶ ≡ sentence (L. 31)

Capitalize the first word of a sentence.

Please prepare a summary of your activities.

RULE 38 ▶ ≡ proper noun (L. 31)

Capitalize proper nouns and adjectives derived from proper nouns.

Judy Hendrix drove to Albuquerque in her new Pontiac convertible.

Note: A proper noun is the official name of a particular person, place, or thing.

RULE 39 ▶ ≡ time (L. 31)

Capitalize the names of the days of the week, months, holidays, and religious days (but do not capitalize the names of the seasons).

On Thursday, November 25, we will celebrate Thanksgiving, the most popular holiday in the fall.

RULE 40 ▶ ≡ noun # (L. 77)

Capitalize nouns followed by a number or letter (except for the nouns *line, note, page, paragraph,* and *size).*

Please read Chapter 5, which begins on page 94.

RULE 41 ▶ ≡ compass point (L. 77)

Capitalize compass points (such as *north, south,* or *northeast)* only when they designate definite regions.

From Montana we drove south to reach the Southwest.

RULE 42 ▶ ≡ organization (L. 111)

Capitalize common organizational terms (such as *advertising department* and *finance committee)* only when they are the actual names of the units in the writer's own organization and when they are preceded by the word *the.*

The report from the Advertising Department is due today.

But: Our advertising department will submit its report today.

RULE 43 ▶ ≡ course (L. 111)

Capitalize the names of specific course titles but not the names of subjects or areas of study.

I have enrolled in Accounting 201 and will also take a marketing course.

NUMBER EXPRESSION

RULE 44 ▶ # general (L. 41)

In general, spell out numbers zero through ten, and use figures for numbers above ten.

We rented two movies for tonight.

The decision was reached after 27 precincts sent in their results.

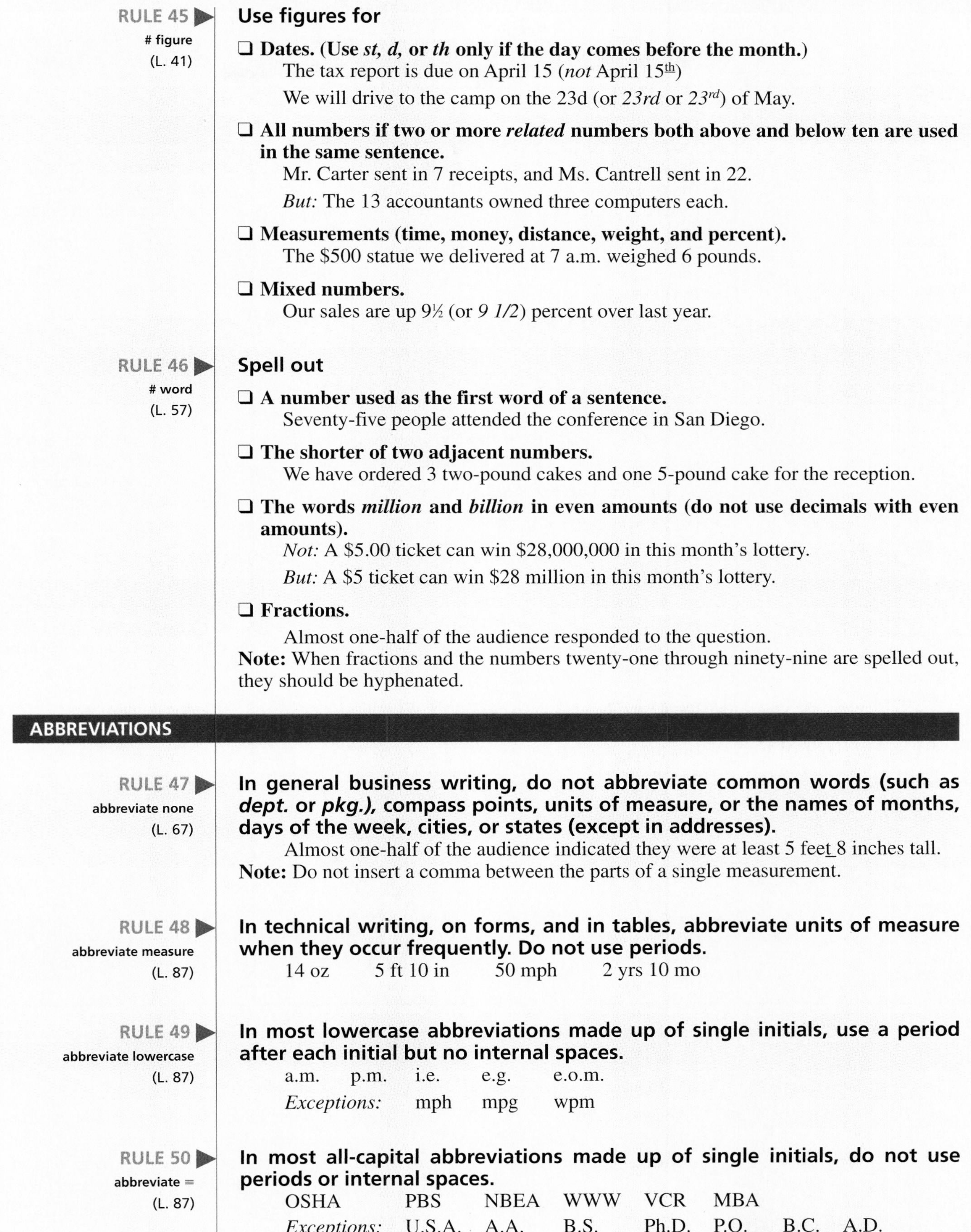

RULE 45 ▶ # figure (L. 41)

Use figures for

❑ **Dates. (Use *st, d,* or *th* only if the day comes before the month.)**
The tax report is due on April 15 (*not* April 15$^{\underline{\text{th}}}$)
We will drive to the camp on the 23d (or *23rd* or *23rd*) of May.

❑ **All numbers if two or more *related* numbers both above and below ten are used in the same sentence.**
Mr. Carter sent in 7 receipts, and Ms. Cantrell sent in 22.
But: The 13 accountants owned three computers each.

❑ **Measurements (time, money, distance, weight, and percent).**
The $500 statue we delivered at 7 a.m. weighed 6 pounds.

❑ **Mixed numbers.**
Our sales are up 9½ (or *9 1/2*) percent over last year.

RULE 46 ▶ # word (L. 57)

Spell out

❑ **A number used as the first word of a sentence.**
Seventy-five people attended the conference in San Diego.

❑ **The shorter of two adjacent numbers.**
We have ordered 3 two-pound cakes and one 5-pound cake for the reception.

❑ **The words *million* and *billion* in even amounts (do not use decimals with even amounts).**
Not: A $5.00 ticket can win $28,000,000 in this month's lottery.
But: A $5 ticket can win $28 million in this month's lottery.

❑ **Fractions.**
Almost one-half of the audience responded to the question.

Note: When fractions and the numbers twenty-one through ninety-nine are spelled out, they should be hyphenated.

ABBREVIATIONS

RULE 47 ▶ abbreviate none (L. 67)

In general business writing, do not abbreviate common words (such as *dept.* or *pkg.*), compass points, units of measure, or the names of months, days of the week, cities, or states (except in addresses).

Almost one-half of the audience indicated they were at least 5 feet 8 inches tall.

Note: Do not insert a comma between the parts of a single measurement.

RULE 48 ▶ abbreviate measure (L. 87)

In technical writing, on forms, and in tables, abbreviate units of measure when they occur frequently. Do not use periods.

14 oz   5 ft 10 in   50 mph   2 yrs 10 mo

RULE 49 ▶ abbreviate lowercase (L. 87)

In most lowercase abbreviations made up of single initials, use a period after each initial but no internal spaces.

a.m.   p.m.   i.e.   e.g.   e.o.m.
Exceptions: mph   mpg   wpm

RULE 50 ▶ abbreviate ≡ (L. 87)

In most all-capital abbreviations made up of single initials, do not use periods or internal spaces.

OSHA   PBS   NBEA   WWW   VCR   MBA
Exceptions: U.S.A.   A.A.   B.S.   Ph.D.   P.O.   B.C.   A.D.

	NEW KEYS	SKILLBUILDING
UNIT 1 **Lesson 1** **Lesson 2** **Lesson 3** **Lesson 4** **Lesson 5** Goal At least 14wpm/1′/3e	• The Home Keys • The Space Bar • The Enter Key • The F and J Keys • The D and K Keys • The S and L Keys • The A and ; Keys • The H Key • The E Key • The O Key • The R Key • The M Key • The T Key • The P Key • The C Key • The Right Shift Key • The V Key • The . Key • The W Key	• Word Building • Phrases • Word Patterns • Short Phrases • Build Skill on Sentences • Counting Errors in Sentences • Sentences • Paragraph
UNIT 2 **Lesson 6** **Lesson 7** **Lesson 8** **Lesson 9** **Lesson 10** Goal At least 19wpm/1′/3e	• The I Key • The Left Shift Key • The – Key • The G Key • The U Key • The B Key • The : Key • The X Key • The Y Key • The , Key • The Q Key • The / Key • The N Key • The Z Key • The ? Key • The Tab Key • Practice the Tab Key	• Technique Practice: Space Bar • Technique Practice: Hyphen Key • Technique Practice: Colon Key • Word Practice • Phrases • Technique Practice: Shift Key • Technique Practice: Question Mark • Punctuation Practice • Short Paragraphs
UNIT 3 **Lesson 11** **Lesson 12** **Lesson 13** **Lesson 14** **Lesson 15** Goal At least 23wpm/2′/5e	• The 5 Key • The 7 Key • The 3 Key • The 9 Key • The 8 Key • The 2 Key • The 0 Key • The 4 Key • The 6 Key • The 1 Key	• Number Practice: 5, 7, 3, and 9 • Technique Practice: Shift Key • Progressive Practice: Alphabet • 12-Second Speed Sprints • Sustained Practice: Syllabic Intensity • Alphabet Practice • Number Practice • Technique Practice: Enter Key • Technique Practice: Space Bar
UNIT 4 **Lesson 16** **Lesson 17** **Lesson 18** **Lesson 19** **Lesson 20** Goal At least 28wpm/2′/5e	• The $ Key • The (and) Keys • The ! Key • The * Key • The # Key • The ' Key • The & Key • The % Key • The " Key • The @ Key	• Technique Practice: Space Bar • 12-Second Speed Sprints • Paced Practice • Number Practice • Word Beginnings • Word Endings • Progressive Practice: Alphabet • Handwritten Paragraph • Diagnostic Practice: Numbers

GDP *Gregg College Keyboarding & Document Processing* MULTIMEDIA RESOURCES

Lessons

Skillbuilding

Map

STUDENT

- Lessons 1–20
- MHHE Keyboarding Web site @ **www.mhhe.com/gdp**

INSTRUCTOR

- Instructor Management LAN Version
  — Distance Learning
- Instructor Management Web Version
  — Distance Learning
- MHHE Keyboarding Instructor Web site @ **www.mhhe.com/gdp**

Timed Writings

Language Arts

Games

SKILLBUILDING *(CONTINUED)*	ILLUSTRATIONS
	Keyboard illustrations for all lessons.
• Word Patterns • Alphabet Review	Keyboard illustrations for all lessons.
• Technique Practice: TAB Key • Paced Practice • Diagnostic Practice: Symbols and Punctuation • Progressive Practice: Numbers • Handwritten Paragraph • Diagnostic Practice: Symbols and Punctuation • Technique Practice: TAB Key • Punctuation Practice • PPP: Vertical Reaches	Keyboard illustrations for all lessons.
• Diagnostic Practice: Symbols and Punctuation • Alphabet and Symbol Practice • Sustained Practice: Numbers and Symbols • Punctuation Practice • PPP: Alternate- and One-Hand Words • MAP	Keyboard illustrations for all lessons.

SPANISH RESOURCES

- New key exercises in GDP software are available with Spanish or English audio.
- All instruction screens in GDP software are available in Spanish or English.

ASSESSMENT

Tests

- Part 1 Objective Test
- Technique Evaluation Form

TEACHING RESOURCES AT A GLANCE

APPLICATION RESOURCES

- MHHE Keyboarding Web site @ **www.mhhe.com/gdp**
- Word Processing Manual
- Reference Manual

ASSESSMENT

- Part 1 Objective Test
- Technique Evaluation Form

MULTIMEDIA RESOURCES

- GDP Software
- GDP Software User's Guide
- Instructor Management LAN Version —Distance Learning
- Instructor Management Web Version —Distance Learning
- MHHE Keyboarding Web site @ **www.mhhe.com/gdp**

ENRICHMENT

Keyboarding Connection

- What Is the Internet? p. 6
- Using Search Engines, p. 12

Strategies for Career Success

- Being a Good Listener, p. 8
- Preparing a Job Interview Portfolio, p. 22
- Goodwill Messages, p. 40

REAL-WORLD CAREER CONNECTION

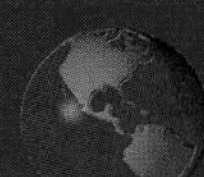

- Arts, Audio, Video Technology, and Communication Services, pp. 1-2
- Real-World Career Connection Photograph, pp. 1-2

INSTRUCTOR'S NOTES

PART 1

INTRODUCING THE PART

PART 1 teaches the keyboard including alphabet, number, and symbol keys. **Unit 1** and **Unit 2** introduce the alphabetic keys. **Unit 3** presents numbers, and **Unit 4** teaches symbols.

Discussion

Survey your students to determine their reasons for taking a keyboarding class and to ascertain their keyboarding experience.

WPM GOAL

Encourage students to type using the touch method and to use correct technique. Challenge students to reach the goal of typing **at least 28 words per minute for 2 minutes with 5 or fewer errors.** Provide positive reinforcement to all students for improving speed and accuracy.

Part 1

The Alphabet, Number, and Symbol Keys

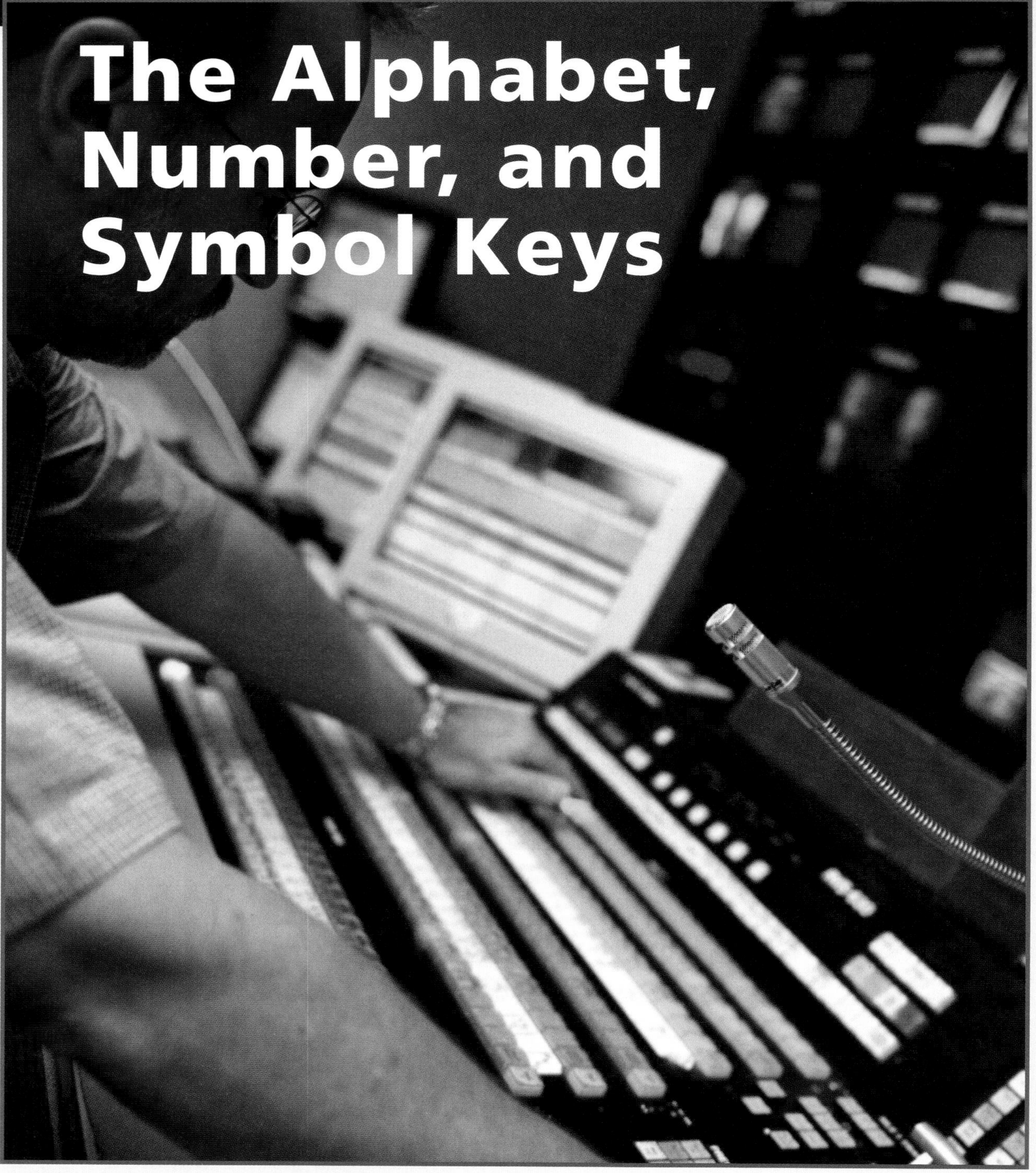

Software Overview

Gregg College Keyboarding & Document Processing (GDP) is more versatile, dynamic, and intuitive than ever before. Review carefully in the Software User's Guide all the options you have for class management and data storage. With both an Instructor Management LAN Version and an Instructor Management Web Version, GDP will meet your individual needs.

A multimedia tutorial within the software will help students understand the GDP software quickly, whether they are enrolled in traditional or open-entry lab classes.

PART 1

Keyboarding in Arts, Audio, Video Technology, and Communications Services

Occupations in this cluster deal with organizing and communicating information to the public in various forms and media. This cluster includes jobs in radio and television broadcasting, journalism, motion pictures, the recording industry, the performing arts, multimedia publishing, and the entertainment services. Book editors, computer artists, technical writers, radio announcers, news correspondents, and camera operators are just a few jobs within this cluster.

Qualifications and Skills

Strong oral and written communication skills and technical skills are necessary for anyone in communications and media. Without a doubt, competent keyboarding skill is extremely advantageous.

Working in the media requires creativity, talent, and accurate use of language. In journalism, being observant, thinking clearly, and seeing the significance of events are all of utmost importance. Announcers must have exceptional voices, excellent speaking skills, and a unique style. The ability to work under pressure is important in all areas of media.

Objectives

KEYBOARDING

- Operate by touch the letter, number, and symbol keys.
- Demonstrate proper typing technique.
- Use the correct spacing with punctuation.
- Type at least 28 words per minute on a 2-minute timed writing with no more than 5 errors.

TECHNICAL

- Answer correctly at least 90 percent of the questions on an objective test.

CAREER CONNECTION

Arts, Audio, Video Technology, and Communication Services Encourage students to read the information on arts, audio, video technology, and communications services. Ask students why oral and written communication skills are necessary for this field of technology. Why is keyboarding skill an important skill for these careers?

Encourage students to investigate opportunities for employment in arts and communications services careers in their community. What are the job requirements and where can they receive training? Are internships available?

Remind students to visit the college keyboarding Web site at **www.mhhe.com/gdp** to learn more about careers in arts and communications services.

INSTRUCTOR'S NOTES/INTERNET BOOKMARKS

Visit us on the Web at www.mhhe.com/gdp.

Unit 1

UNIT OVERVIEW

Students learn the alphabetic keys using the touch method and correct technique. Students build skill by typing word patterns, phrases, and sentences.

Did You Know?

Students who have previous keyboarding experience may be given the Placement Test found in the Tests and Solution Keys booklet. The test includes multiple-choice questions, a timed writing, unarranged copy, and rough-draft copy.

www.mhhe.com/gdp to download a copy of the Technique Evaluation Form.

TECHNIQUE EVALUATION FORM

Walk around the room to observe the students' technique. Complete a Technique Evaluation Form for each student.

Name ____________ Class ____________ Date ____________

Technique Evaluation Form

Date	Workstation		Position at the Keyboard		Keystroking	
	Acceptable	Needs Improvement	Acceptable	Needs Improvement	Acceptable	Needs Improvement

Workstation

1. Positions the chair so that the upper and lower legs form a 90-degree angle and the lower back is supported.
2. Positions the keyboard even with the front of the desk.
3. Positions the text on either side of the monitor as close to it vertically and horizontally as possible to minimize head and eye movement and to avoid neck strain.
4. Positions the mouse on a pad at the side of the monitor opposite the text.

Position at the Keyboard

5. Centers the body opposite the keyboard.
6. Leans forward slightly from the hips, with the base of the spine touching the back of the chair and the feet flat on the floor.
7. Keeps the elbows alongside the body in a relaxed position.
8. Curves the fingers naturally over the home position, with the back of the hand at the same angle as the keyboard.

Keystroking

9. Keeps the forearms horizontal and raises the hands slightly when typing so that the wrists do not touch the keyboard while typing. (Hands may rest at the bottom of the keyboard—away from the keys—during nontyping intervals.)
10. Makes quick, snappy strokes using the correct fingers.
11. Returns the finger immediately to the home position or moves to the next position after each stroke.
12. Operates all keys by touch, keeping the eyes on the copy most of the time while typing.

Comments

Unit 1

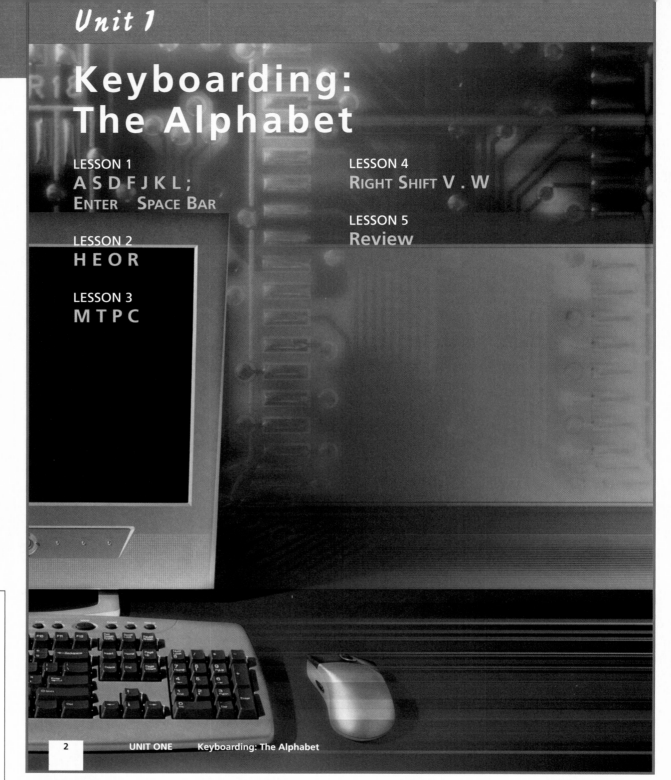

Keyboarding: The Alphabet

LESSON 1
A S D F J K L ;
ENTER SPACE BAR

LESSON 2
H E O R

LESSON 3
M T P C

LESSON 4
RIGHT SHIFT V . W

LESSON 5
Review

RESOURCE MANAGER

GDP SOFTWARE

- Lessons 1–5
- Software User's Guide
- Instructor Management LAN Version
- Professional Handbook (IWE*)—Teaching Strategies; Teaching in a Distance-Learning Environment

ASSESSMENT

- Technique Evaluation Form
- Professional Handbook (IWE*)—Assessment Strategies

ON THE WEB

- **www.mhhe.com/gdp**
- Instructor Management Web Version

*Instructor Wraparound Edition

Home Keys

Goals

- Touch-type the home keys (A S D F J K L ;)
- Touch-type the SPACE BAR
- Touch-type the ENTER key
- Type at least 10wpm/1′/3e

LEFT HAND
First Finger F
Second Finger D
Third Finger S
Fourth Finger A

RIGHT HAND
J First Finger
K Second Finger
L Third Finger
; Fourth Finger
SPACE BAR Thumb

NEW KEYS

A. Follow the directions to become familiar with the home keys.

The semicolon (;) is commonly called the sem key.

A. THE HOME KEYS

The **A S D F J K L ;** keys are known as the home keys.

1. Place the fingers of your left hand on the home keys as follows: first finger on **F**; second finger on **D**; third finger on **S**; fourth finger on **A**.
2. Place the fingers of your right hand on the home keys as follows: first finger on **J**; second finger on **K**; third finger on **L**; and fourth finger on **;**.
3. Curve your fingers.
4. Using the correct fingers, type each character as you say it to yourself: `a s d f j k l ;`.
5. Remove your fingers from the keyboard and replace them on the home keys.
6. Press each home key again as you say each character: `a s d f j k l ;`.

B. THE SPACE BAR

The SPACE BAR, located beneath the letter keys, is used to space between words and after marks of punctuation.

1. With fingers held motionless on the home keys, poise your right thumb about a half inch above the SPACE BAR.
2. Type the characters and then press the SPACE BAR 1 time. Bounce your thumb off.

C. Type each line 1 time, pressing the SPACE BAR where you see a space and pressing the ENTER key at the end of a line.

C. THE ENTER↵ KEY

The ENTER key moves the insertion point to the beginning of a new line. Reach to the ENTER key with the fourth finger of your right hand. Keep your J finger at home. Lightly press the ENTER key. Practice using the ENTER key until you can do so with confidence and without looking at your hands.

```
asdf jkl; asdf jkl; ↵
asdf jkl; asdf jkl; ↵
```


INSTRUCTOR STRATEGIES

The First Day of Class
To eliminate confusion and possible surprises:

- Check with lab technician to determine whether software is installed and where it is installed (network or workstation).
- Check procedure to access the GDP software—shortcut on the desktop, **Start** button, and so on.
- Set Instructor Options.
- Turn on all computers and ready the classroom.
- Bring blank diskettes and markers for boards.

New students may need assistance with inserting, caring for, or storing a diskette.

To make sure that all students can participate on the first day of class, make a few photocopies of Lesson 1 for any students who do not have books. All students must type on the first day of class.

Lesson 1

FOCUS

TIME MANAGEMENT

Suggested Schedule:

New Keys	30′
Skillbuilding	20′
Total	**50′**

TEACH

NEW KEYS

Discuss the importance of correct posture at the keyboard for speed and accuracy. Observe every student's posture.

VISUAL INSTRUCTION

Keyboard Illustration. Review the purpose of the keyboard illustration.

- Keys are color-coded according to which fingers are used.
- Keys being introduced are highlighted, and unlearned keys are blank.

LESSON 1-A Stress the importance of the home keys in learning to touch-type.

The home keys are in the middle of the keyboard so that each row can easily be reached.

Each finger operates one alphabetic key in each row except for the first finger, which operates two keys in each row.

LESSON 1-B AND 1-C Fingers must return at once to the home keys. Demonstrate the correct use of the ENTER key, and explain the consequences of holding it down too long.

Lesson 1

TEACH

Explain to students that they should not try to correct errors at this point.

LESSON 1-D Other fingers should be in home position while the reaches to F and J are made.

LESSON 1-G The F and J fingers are the anchors when the A and sem keys are typed.

SKILLBUILDING

LESSON 1-H Check students fingering techniques and posture.

LESSON 1-I If time permits, have students type the drill again. Emphasize the importance of keeping eyes on the copy.

LESSON 1-J Remind students to start again if they finish before time is up.

ASSESS

www.mhhe.com/gdp to download a copy of the Technique Evaluation Form.

TECHNIQUE EVALUATION FORM Walk around the room to observe the students' technique.

LESSON 1-J Review students' timed writings as they are completed. Comment on speed and accuracy.

Extending the Lesson

Encourage students to practice the lesson at a computer in the computer lab or in a library.

CLOSE

Remind students to remove their data diskettes and to organize their materials and workstation.

LEFT HAND			RIGHT HAND
First Finger	F	J	First Finger
Second Finger	D	K	Second Finger
Third Finger	S	L	Third Finger
Fourth Finger	A	;	Fourth Finger
		SPACE BAR	Thumb

D. THE F AND J KEYS

D. Press the SPACE BAR with your right thumb. Type each line 2 times.

```
1  fff fff jjj jjj fff jjj ff jj ff jj f j
2  fff fff jjj jjj fff jjj ff jj ff jj f j
```

E. THE D AND K KEYS

E. The A and Sem fingers remain on the home keys. Type each line 2 times.

```
3  ddd ddd kkk kkk ddd kkk dd kk dd kk d k
4  ddd ddd kkk kkk ddd kkk dd kk dd kk d k
```

F. THE S AND L KEYS

F. The A and Sem fingers remain on the home keys. Type each line 2 times.

```
5  sss sss lll lll sss lll ss ll ss ll s l
6  sss sss lll lll sss lll ss ll ss ll s l
```

G. THE A AND ; KEYS

G. The F and J fingers remain on the home keys. Type each line 2 times.

```
7  aaa aaa ;;; ;;; aaa ;;; aa ;; aa ;; a ;
8  aaa aaa ;;; ;;; aaa ;;; aa ;; aa ;; a ;
```

SKILLBUILDING

H. WORD BUILDING

H. Type lines 9–15 two times. Press ENTER 2 times to leave a blank line after each pair. Note the word patterns.

```
9   aaa ddd ddd add aaa lll lll all add all
10  aaa sss kkk ask ddd aaa ddd dad ask dad
11  lll aaa ddd lad fff aaa ddd fad lad fad
12  aaa ddd ;;; ad; aaa sss ;;; as; ad; as;
13  f fa fad fads; a as ask asks; d da dad;
14  l la las lass; f fa fal fall; s sa sad;
15  a ad add adds; l la lad lads; a ad ads;
```

I. PHRASES

I. Type lines 16–17 two times. Space 1 time after a semicolon. Leave a blank line after each pair. Note the phrase patterns.

```
16  dad ask; ask a lad; dad ask a lad; as a
17  a fall; a lass; ask a lass; a lad asks;
```

J. 1-MINUTE TIMED WRITING

J. Take two 1-minute timed writings. Try to complete both lines each time.

```
18  ask a sad lad; a fall fad; add a salad;
19  ask a dad;
    | 1 | 2 | 3 | 4 | 5 | 6 | 7 | 8 |
```

Goal: At least 10wpm/1'/3e

GDP SOFTWARE TIPS

LESSONS
SKILLBUILDING
MAP

Log-On Information

Encourage students to press the TAB key to move from one text box to another—new students may need help in locating the TAB key. Remind students to select a password that is easy to remember, and caution students not to share the password.

Instructor Options

You can prevent students from correcting errors in timed writings, in drill lines, or in both. From the GDP Menu bar, choose **Options**, **Instructor Options**, **Settings**, **Class Settings**. Deselect the boxes for timed writings and drills under **Full Editing**.

New Keys

Goals

- Touch-type the H, E, O, and R keys
- Type at least 11wpm/1′/3e

Fingers are named for home keys. (Example: The middle finger of the left hand is the D finger.)

A. Type 2 times.

A. WARMUP

```
1 fff jjj ddd kkk sss lll aaa ;;; fff jjj
2 a salad; a lad; alas a fad; ask a lass;
```

NEW KEYS

B. Type each line 2 times. Space 1 time after a semicolon.

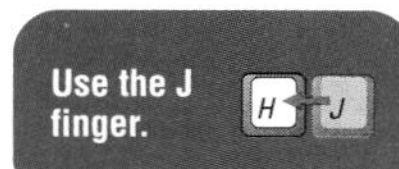

Use the J finger.
H J

B. THE H KEY

```
3 jjj jhj jhj hjh jjj jhj jhj hjh jjj jhj
4 has has hah hah had had aha aha ash ash
5 hash half sash lash dash hall shad shah
6 as dad had; a lass has half; add a dash
```

C. Type each line 2 times. Keep your eyes on the copy as you type.

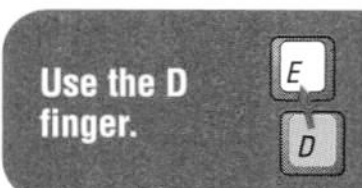

Use the D finger.
E
D

C. THE E KEY

```
7 ddd ded ded ede ddd ded ded ede ddd ded
8 lea led he; he see; eke fed sea lee fee
9 feed keel ease heal held seal lead fake
10 he fed a seal; she held a lease; a keel
```

D. Type each line 2 times. Keep fingers curved.

Use the L finger.

D. THE O KEY

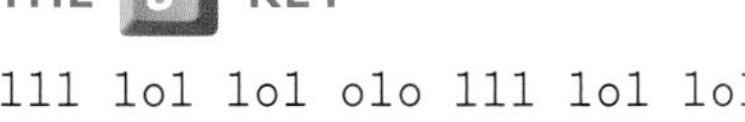

```
11 lll lol lol olo lll lol lol olo lll lol
12 doe off foe hod oh; oak odd ode old sod
13 shoe look kook joke odes does solo oleo
14 he held a hook; a lass solos; old foes;
```


Windows Wizard

FORMATTING A DISK To format a disk in Windows 2000, Me, or XP:

- Insert the disk in the appropriate drive.
- Open **My Computer**, and click the icon for the disk you want to format.
- From the Menu bar, click **File/Format**.
- In the **Format** dialog box, click **Start**. You cannot format a disk if it has any open files.

MHHE CHAMPIONS

NORTH CAROLINA

Improve Typing Skill

Students should key Lessons 1–20 at least twice in order to log enough practice time in learning these new keystrokes.

Rebecca Jones
Bladen Community College
Dublin, North Carolina

Instructors Helping One Another

FOCUS

TIME MANAGEMENT

Suggested Schedule:

Warmup	5′
New Keys	32′
Skillbuilding	13′
Total	**50′**

TEACH

NEW KEYS

Remind students to have correct position at the keyboard.

- Center the body opposite the keyboard.
- Lean forward slightly from the hips.
- Keep feet flat on the floor.
- Keep elbows alongside the body.
- Curve fingers naturally over the home position.

Remind students to keep other fingers at home as they reach to the new keys.

Walk around the room to observe students and correct problems immediately.

Encourage students to spell the words letter by letter to build confidence in their reaches.

LESSON 3-C Practice the reach to the letter E with the students. This is the first time students will reach to the top row.

Lesson 2

TEACH

SKILLBUILDING

LESSON 2-F Explain that students should not pause at the vertical lines. The lines are used to separate word patterns.

To move from typing individual letters to words, have students silently pronounce each word.

Encourage students to keep their eyes on the copy.

LESSON 2-G Remind students to start again if they finish before time is up.

ASSESS

www.mhhe.com/gdp to download a copy of the Technique Evaluation Form.

TECHNIQUE EVALUATION FORM Walk around the room to observe the students' technique.

Print the lesson or review the practice lines on the monitor.

A printout of the lesson will provide immediate feedback to the student.

Review results of timed writings.

Extending the Lesson

Encourage students to practice the lesson. Remind students that daily practice improves typing skills.

CLOSE

Remind students to remove their student data diskette and to organize their workstation.

E. Type each line 2 times. Keep the A finger at home.

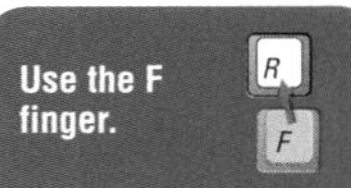

E. THE R KEY

```
15 fff frf frf rfr fff frf frf rfr fff frf
16 red ark ore err rah era rod oar her are
17 oars soar dear fare read role rare door
18 a dark red door; he read a rare reader;
```

SKILLBUILDING

F. Type each line 2 times. Do not type the red vertical lines.

F. WORD PATTERNS

```
19 dale kale sale hale|fold sold hold old;
20 feed deed heed seed|dash sash lash ash;
21 lake rake sake fake|dear sear rear ear;
```

G. Take two 1-minute timed writings. Try to complete both lines each time. Press ENTER only at the end of line 23.

Goal: At least 11wpm/1'/3e

G. 1-MINUTE TIMED WRITING

```
22 she asked for a rare old deed; he held
23 a red door ajar;
   | 1 | 2 | 3 | 4 | 5 | 6 | 7 | 8 |
```

Keyboarding Connection

What Is the Internet?

What is the easiest way to go to the library? Try using your fingertips! The Internet creates a "virtual library"—a library with no walls. Nothing can match the Internet as a research device. It is not just one computer but an immense connection of computers talking to one another and organizing and exchanging information.

The Internet is synonymous with cyberspace, a word describing the power and control of information. The Internet has been called "a network of networks" linked together to deliver information to users. The Internet connects more than 200 million people to over 3 million computer networks.

The Internet is considered a wide area network (WAN) because the computers on it span the entire world. Each day the Net increases at about 1000 new users every hour.

YOUR TURN List some ways the Internet, as a virtual library, enhances your research activities.

Windows Wizard

COPYING A DISK To copy a disk in Windows 2000, Me, and XP:

- Open **My Computer**, and click the icon for the disk you want to copy.
- Choose **Copy Disk** from the **File** menu.
- Click the drive you want to **Copy** from.
- Click the drive you want to **Copy** to.
- Click **Start**.

INSTRUCTOR STRATEGIES

Printing
Show students the procedure for printing a lesson.

Prepare a handout or use a projector to show the procedures for students to follow if the printer is out of paper, not printing, displaying error messages, and so on. Lesson printouts can be included as part of a daily grade.

New Keys

Goals

- Touch-type the M, T, P, and C keys
- Type at least 12wpm/1′/3e

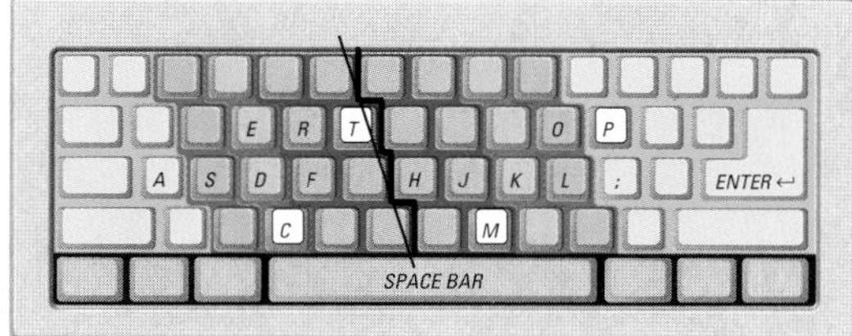

A. Type 2 times.

A. WARMUP

```
1  aa ;; ss ll dd kk ff jj hh ee oo rr aa;
2  he held a sale for her as she had asked
```

NEW KEYS

B. Type each line 2 times.

Use the J finger.

B. THE  KEY

```
3  jjj jmj jmj mjm jjj jmj jmj mjm jjj jmj
4  mad mom me; am jam; ram dam ham mar ma;
5  arms loam lame roam make fame room same
6  she made more room for some of her ham;
```

C. Type each line 2 times.

Use the F finger.

C. THE  KEY

```
7  fff ftf ftf tft fff ftf ftf tft fff ftf
8  tar tam mat hot jot rat eat lot art sat
9  told take date late mart mate tool fate
10 he told her to set a later date to eat;
```

D. Type each line 2 times.

Use the Sem finger.

D. THE  KEY

```
11 ;;; ;p; ;p; p;p ;;; ;p; ;p; p;p ;;; ;p;
12 pat pal sap rap pet par spa lap pad mop
13 pale palm stop drop pelt plea slap trap
14 please park the red jeep past the pool;
```


GDP SOFTWARE TIPS

Navigating in the Software

Remind students to select the appropriate lesson and to complete the exercises in sequential order. Students should check the Status bar and the header below the Toolbar frequently to be sure that they are on the correct lesson. If necessary, review the process to navigate from one screen to another, using the Forward and Back arrows.

FOCUS

TIME MANAGEMENT

Suggested Schedule:

Warmup	5′
New Keys	32′
Skillbuilding	13′
Total	**50′**

TEACH

NEW KEYS

LESSON 3-B Practice the reach to the letter M with students. This is the first time students will reach to the bottom row. Encourage them to keep the K, L, and Sem fingers anchored to the home position.

LESSON 3-C Help students distinguish between the reach to R and the reach to T—the index finger is used for typing both keys.

LESSON 3-D Observe that students keep elbows alongside the body as they reach for the letter P. Fingers should be curved.

Explain the importance of maintaining an even rhythm when learning to type and of keeping eyes on the copy.

INSTRUCTOR STRATEGIES

Technique Evaluation Form

Print copies of the Technique Evaluation Form.

Review the Technique Evaluation Form with students—both before you observe their technique and after you have completed the Technique Evaluation Form.

Lesson 3

TEACH

LESSON 3-E Remind students that they must reach down and slightly to the right for the letter C.

SKILLBUILDING

LESSON 3-F Urge students to keep their eyes on the copy and to maintain an even pace.

ASSESS

www.mhhe.com/gdp to download a copy of the Technique Evaluation Form.

TECHNIQUE EVALUATION FORM Complete a Technique Evaluation Form for each student.

Extending the Lesson

Encourage students to practice the lesson outside of class.

CLOSE

Remind students to remove their data diskette and to organize their materials and workstation.

E. Type each line 2 times.

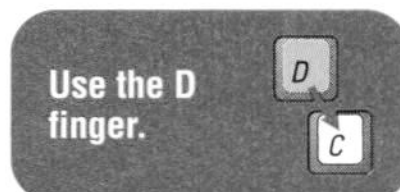

E. THE C KEY

```
15 ddd dcd dcd cdc ddd dcd dcd cdc ddd dcd
16 cot cod sac act car coo arc ace cop cat
17 pack tack chat coat face aces deck cost
18 call her to race cool cars at the track
```

SKILLBUILDING

F. Sit in the correct position as you type these drills. Refer to the illustration in the Introduction. Type each line 2 times. Do not type the red vertical lines.

F. SHORT PHRASES

```
19 as so|she had|has met|let her|fast pace
20 to do|ask her|for the|had pop|look past
21 do as|lap top|her pad|let pat|halt them
22 as he|had for|red cap|she let|fast plot
```

G. Take two 1-minute timed writings. Try to complete both lines each time. Use word wrap. Press ENTER only at the end of line 24.

Goal: At least 12wpm/1'/3e

G. 1-MINUTE TIMED WRITING

```
23 the old store at home had lots of cheap
24 stools for the sale;
   | 1 | 2 | 3 | 4 | 5 | 6 | 7 | 8 |
```

Strategies for Career Success

Being a Good Listener

Silence is golden! Listening is essential for learning, getting along, and forming relationships.

Do you tend to forget people's names after being introduced? Do you look away from the speaker instead of making eye contact? Do you interrupt the speaker before he or she finishes talking? Do you misunderstand people? Answering yes can indicate poor listening skills.

To improve your listening skills, follow these steps. *Hear the speaker clearly.* Do not interrupt; let the speaker develop his or her ideas before you speak. *Focus on the message.* At the end of a conversation, identify major items discussed. Mentally ask questions to help you assess the points the speaker is making. *Keep an open mind.* Do not judge. Developing your listening skills benefits everyone.

YOUR TURN Assess your listening behavior. What techniques can you use to improve your listening skills? Practice them the next time you have a conversation with someone.

TEACHING THE ADULT LEARNER

LISTENING SKILLS Provide the adult learner with some guidelines on how to be an active listener in the classroom. Tell your students to follow these guidelines:

- Ask for clarification if instructions or procedures are not clear.
- Highlight important rules or explanations.
- Record due dates on a calendar.
- Answer questions raised in class.
- Share experiences relative to the lesson.

Keyboarding is not a lecture class, but students must learn to listen to verbal instructions. This skill is necessary in classes as well as in real-world business and social interaction.

New Keys

Goals

- Touch-type the RIGHT SHIFT, V, period, and W keys
- Count errors
- Type at least 13wpm/1′/3e

A. Type 2 times.

A. WARMUP

```
1 the farmer asked her to feed the mares;
2 the late callers came to mop the floor;
```

NEW KEYS

B. Type each line 2 times.

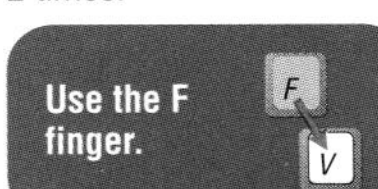

B. THE RIGHT SHIFT KEY

To capitalize letters on the left half of the keyboard:

1. With the J finger at home, press and hold down the RIGHT SHIFT key with the Sem finger.
2. Press the letter key.
3. Release the RIGHT SHIFT key and return fingers to home position.

```
3 ;;; ;A; ;A; ;;; ;S; ;S; ;;; ;D; ;D; ;;;
4 Art Alf Ada Sal Sam Dee Dot Flo Ted Tom
5 Amos Carl Chet Elsa Fred Sara Todd Elda
6 Carl Amos took Sara Carter to the races
```

C. Type each line 2 times.

C. THE V KEY

```
7 fff fvf fvf vfv fff fvf fvf vfv fff fvf
8 Val eve Eva vet Ava vat Eve ova Vel vee
9 have vase Vera ever vast Reva dove vest
10 Dave voted for Vassar; Val voted for me
```

D. Type each line 2 times. Space 1 time after a period following an abbreviation; do not space after a period within an abbreviation; space 1 time after a period ending a sentence.

Use the L finger.

D. THE . KEY

```
11 111 1.1 1.1 .1. 111 1.1 1.1 .1. 111 1.1
12 dr. dr. ea. ea. sr. sr. Dr. Dr. Sr. Sr.
13 a.m. acct. A.D. p.m. Corp. amt. Dr. Co.
14 Selma left. Dave left. Sarah came home.
```


GDP SOFTWARE TIPS

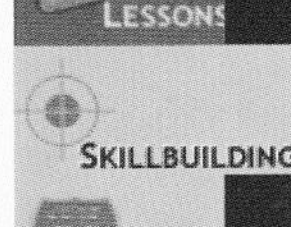

Bookmarking

Explain to students how lessons and individual exercises within lessons are marked when they are completed.

Summary Report

Show students the procedure to display their Summary Reports:

- Choose **Portfolio** from the **File** menu.
- Select the appropriate Start and End dates.
- Select the lesson(s).
- Select the exercise type(s).
- Click **OK**.
- Review the Summary Report.
- Print the Summary Report, if desired.

Lesson 4

FOCUS

TIME MANAGEMENT

Suggested Schedule:

Warmup	5′
New Keys	32′
Skillbuilding	13′
Total	**50′**

TEACH

VISUAL INSTRUCTION

Keyboard Illustration. Review the purpose of the keyboard illustration.

- Keys are color-coded according to which fingers are used.
- New keys are highlighted, previously learned keys are labeled, and unlearned keys are blank.
- Ask students what keys are being introduced.

NEW KEYS

LESSON 4-B Before students type the drill lines, pace them through the three steps of making a capital letter: SHIFT A release, SHIFT S release, and so on.

Be sure students are correctly using the RIGHT SHIFT key.

Students must hold down the SHIFT key until the letter reach is completed.

LESSON 4-D Explain the spacing rules for the period.

Lesson 4

TEACH

NEW KEYS

LESSON 4-E Remind students that the left hand should not move from the home position as they reach for the W.

SKILLBUILDING

LESSON 4-F Remind students to space 1 time after punctuation within a sentence.

Consider assigning more practice to experienced students.

- Students typing 15wpm or fewer type each line 2 times.
- Students typing 16–25wpm type each line 3 times.

LESSON 4-H The timed writing contains 13 words.

ASSESS

www.mhhe.com/gdp to download a copy of the Technique Evaluation Form.

TECHNIQUE EVALUATION FORM Walk around the room to assess the students' technique.

Encourage students to compete with themselves and to practice using correct technique.

Extending the Lesson

Encourage students to practice the lesson if they have access to a computer.

CLOSE

Remind students to remove their data diskette and to organize their materials and workstation.

E. Type each line 2 times.

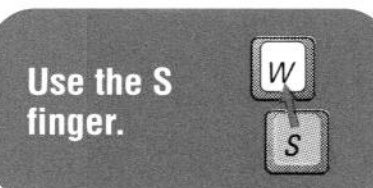

E. THE W KEY

```
sss sws sws wsw sss sws sws wsw sss sws
wow sow war owe was mow woe few wee row
wake ward wart wave wham whom walk what
Wade watched Walt Shaw walk for a week.
```

SKILLBUILDING

F. Type each line 2 times.

F. BUILD SKILL ON SENTENCES

```
Amos Ford saw Emma Dale feed the mares.
Dr. Drake called Sam; he asked for Ted.
Vera told a tale to her old classmates.
Todd asked Cale to move some old rakes.
```

G. Type each line 1 time. After typing all the lines, count your errors. Refer to the Introduction if you need help.

G. COUNTING ERRORS IN SENTENCES

```
Ada lost her letter; Dee lost her card.
Dave sold some of the food to a market.
Alva asked Walt for three more matches.
Dale asked Seth to watch the last show.
```

H. Take two 1-minute timed writings. Try to complete both lines each time.

Goal: At least 13wpm/1'/3e

H. 1-MINUTE TIMED WRITING

```
Val asked them to tell the major to see
Carla at that local farm.
| 1 | 2 | 3 | 4 | 5 | 6 | 7 | 8 |
```


INSTRUCTOR STRATEGIES

Typing Sentences If students are experiencing problems typing sentences, have them break the sentence into manageable parts:

- Practice difficult reaches.
- Practice words and phrases containing difficult reaches.
- Practice sentences containing the phrases.

Meeting Special Needs

WINDOWS MODIFICATIONS You can adjust the performance of Windows, your mouse, and your keyboard to suit varying vision and motor abilities, without adding any hardware or software. Microsoft Windows application notes describe specific methods that can be downloaded from **http://www.microsoft.com/enable**.

Review

Goals

- Reinforce new-key reaches
- Type at least 14wpm/1′/3e

A. Type 2 times.

A. WARMUP

```
Dave called Drew to ask for a road map.
Elsa took three old jars to her mother.
```

SKILLBUILDING

B. Type each line 2 times. Do not type the red vertical lines.

B. WORD PATTERNS

```
feed seed deed heed|fold cold mold told
fame tame lame same|mate late date fate
lace face mace race|vast last cast fast
park dark hark mark|rare dare fare ware
```

C. Type each line 2 times.

C. PHRASES

```
at the|he has|her hat|for the|come home
or the|he had|her top|ask the|late date
to the|he met|her mop|ask her|made more
of the|he was|her pop|ask too|fast pace
```

D. Type each line 2 times.

D. BUILD SKILL ON SENTENCES

```
She asked Dale to share the jar of jam.
Cal took the tools from store to store.
Darel held a sale to sell some clothes.
Seth watched the old cat chase the car.
```


FOCUS

TIME MANAGEMENT

Suggested Schedule:

Warmup	5′
Skillbuilding	45′
Total	**50′**

TEACH

SKILLBUILDING

Remind students to make quick, snappy strokes using the correct fingers.

Continue to emphasize the importance of operating all keys by touch-typing and of keeping eyes on the copy.

Consider assigning additional practice for students who have had previous typing experience.

- Students typing 15wpm or fewer type each line 2 times.
- Students typing 16–25wpm type each line 3 times.
- Students typing over 25wpm type each line 4 times.

INSTRUCTOR STRATEGIES

Confidence Review

If time permits, this is the ideal lesson for a comprehensive review to eliminate student frustration. Before your students type the exercises in this lesson, you may want to have them practice these familiar exercises: 1-H, 1-I, 2-F, 3-F, and 4-F.

GDP SOFTWARE TIPS

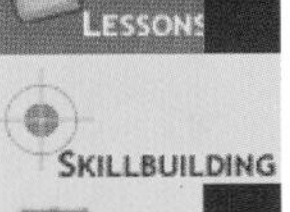

Timed Writings and Performance Chart

Remind students that they can click the **Restart** button within the first 15 seconds of a timed writing.

Encourage students to monitor their progress frequently by accessing the Performance Chart, which graphs the performance on timed writings. The chart is a very motivational tool.

Lesson 5

TEACH

SKILLBUILDING

LESSON 5-G The timed writing contains 14 words.

ASSESS

www.mhhe.com/gdp to download a copy of the Technique Evaluation Form.

TECHNIQUE EVALUATION FORM Complete a Technique Evaluation Form for each student.

Name ____ Class ____ Date ____

Technique Evaluation Form

Date	Workstation		Position at the Keyboard		Keystroking	
	Acceptable	Needs Improvement	Acceptable	Needs Improvement	Acceptable	Needs Improvement

Workstation

1. Positions the chair so that the upper and lower legs form a 90-degree angle and the lower back is supported.
2. Positions the keyboard even with the front of the desk.
3. Positions the text on either side of the monitor as close to it vertically and horizontally as possible to minimize head and eye movement and to avoid neck strain.
4. Positions the mouse on a pad at the side of the monitor opposite the text.

Position at the Keyboard

5. Centers the body opposite the keyboard.
6. Leans forward slightly from the hips, with the base of the spine touching the back of the chair and the feet flat on the floor.
7. Keeps the elbows alongside the body in a relaxed position.
8. Curves the fingers naturally over the home position, with the back of the hand at the same angle as the keyboard.

Keystroking

9. Keeps the forearms horizontal and raises the hands slightly when typing so that the wrists do not touch the keyboard while typing. (Hands may rest at the bottom of the keyboard—away from the keys—during nontyping intervals.)
10. Makes quick, snappy strokes using the correct fingers.
11. Returns the finger immediately to the home position or moves to the next position after each stroke.
12. Operates all keys by touch, keeping the eyes on the copy most of the time while typing.

Comments

Review timed writings and print skillbuilding exercises for Lessons 2–5.

Extending the Lesson

Encourage students to repeat exercises introducing new keys from previous lessons.

CLOSE

Remind students to remove their data diskettes and to organize their materials and workstation.

E. Take a 1-minute timed writing on each line. Review your speed and errors.

E. SENTENCES

```
Carl loved to talk to the tall teacher.
She dashed to take the jet to her home.
Walt asked her to deed the farm to Ted.
 | 1 | 2 | 3 | 4 | 5 | 6 | 7 | 8 | = Number of 5-stroke words
```

F. Take two 1-minute timed writings on the paragraph. Press ENTER only at the end of the paragraph. Review your speed and errors.

F. PARAGRAPH

```
                                               CUMULATIVE WORDS
Rachael asked Sal to take her to school               8
for two weeks. She had to meet Freda or              16
Walt at the school to work on the maps.              24
 | 1 | 2 | 3 | 4 | 5 | 6 | 7 | 8 |
```

G. Take two 1-minute timed writings. Review your speed and errors.

Goal: At least 14wpm/1′/3e

G. 1-MINUTE TIMED WRITINGS

```
Dot Crews asked Al Roper to meet her at               8
the tree to look for a jacket.                       14
 | 1 | 2 | 3 | 4 | 5 | 6 | 7 | 8 |
```

Keyboarding Connection

Using Search Engines

How can you most efficiently find information on the Web? Use a search engine! A search engine guides you to the Web's resources. It analyzes the information you request, navigates the Web's many networks, and retrieves a list of relevant documents. Popular search engines include Google, Excite, Alta Vista, and Yahoo.

A search engine examines electronic databases, wire services, journals, article summaries, articles, home pages, and user group lists. It can access material found in millions of Web sites. When you request a specific keyword search, a search engine scans its large database and searches the introductory lines of text, as well as the title, headings, and subheadings of a Web page. The search engine displays the information that most closely matches your request.

YOUR TURN Try different search engines and see which ones you like best. Choose three of your favorite search engines. Then conduct a search using the keywords "touch typing." (Don't forget the quotation marks.) Compare the results for each search engine.

ERGONOMICALLY SPEAKING

POSITION Check that each student's work surface or keyboarding tray is at elbow height; feet should be flat on the floor, with knees slightly bent below the hips. The backrest should support the lower part, or lumbar curve, of the back. Chair arms should not prevent moving the chair close to the work surface.

The following Web site contains ergonomic guidelines for workstation health and safety: **http://www.lib.utexas.edu/ergonomics/general.html**.

Keyboarding: The Alphabet

LESSON 6
I LEFT SHIFT - G

LESSON 7
U B : X

LESSON 8
Y , Q /

LESSON 9
N Z ? TAB

LESSON 10
Review

Unit 2

UNIT OVERVIEW

Students complete the presentation of the alphabetic keys using the touch method and correct technique. Students learn to operate the TAB key. Students take a 1-minute timed writing on paragraph text. The last lesson in the unit reviews and reinforces the alphabetic keys taught.

Did You Know?

All timed writings consist of the precise number of words for the speed goal for that lesson.

www.mhhe.com/gdp to download a copy of the Technique Evaluation Form.

TECHNIQUE EVALUATION FORM

Walk around the room to observe the students' technique. Complete a Technique Evaluation Form for each student.

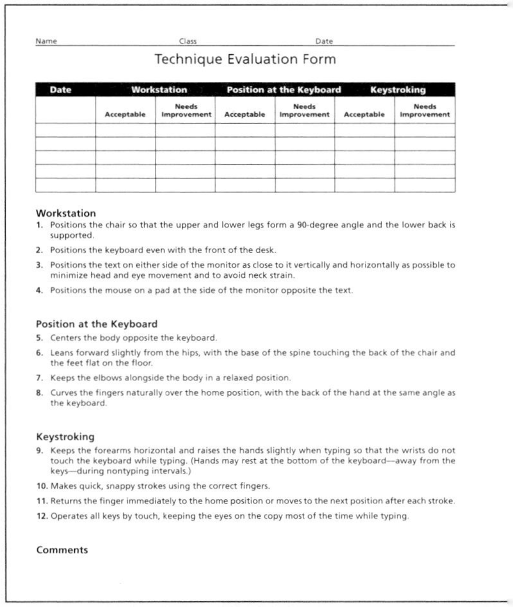

Name ____ Class ____ Date ____

Technique Evaluation Form

Date	Workstation		Position at the Keyboard		Keystroking	
	Acceptable	Needs Improvement	Acceptable	Needs Improvement	Acceptable	Needs Improvement

Workstation

1. Positions the chair so that the upper and lower legs form a 90-degree angle and the lower back is supported.
2. Positions the keyboard even with the front of the desk.
3. Positions the text on either side of the monitor as close to it vertically and horizontally as possible to minimize head and eye movement and to avoid neck strain.
4. Positions the mouse on a pad at the side of the monitor opposite the text.

Position at the Keyboard

5. Centers the body opposite the keyboard.
6. Leans forward slightly from the hips, with the base of the spine touching the back of the chair and the feet flat on the floor.
7. Keeps the elbows alongside the body in a relaxed position.
8. Curves the fingers naturally over the home position, with the back of the hand at the same angle as the keyboard.

Keystroking

9. Keeps the forearms horizontal and raises the hands slightly when typing so that the wrists do not touch the keyboard while typing. (Hands may rest at the bottom of the keyboard—away from the keys—during nontyping intervals.)
10. Makes quick, snappy strokes using the correct fingers.
11. Returns the finger immediately to the home position or moves to the next position after each stroke.
12. Operates all keys by touch, keeping the eyes on the copy most of the time while typing.

Comments

RESOURCE MANAGER

GDP SOFTWARE

- Lessons 6–10
- Software User's Guide
- Instructor Management LAN Version
- Professional Handbook (IWE*)—Teaching Strategies; Teaching in a Distance-Learning Environment

ASSESSMENT

- Technique Evaluation Form
- Professional Handbook (IWE*)—Assessment Strategies

ON THE WEB

- **www.mhhe.com/gdp**
- Instructor Management Web Version

*Instructor Wraparound Edition

Lesson 6

FOCUS

TIME MANAGEMENT 

Suggested Schedule:

Warmup	5′
New Keys	25′
Skillbuilding	20′
Total	**50′**

TEACH

NEW KEYS

Review correct posture at the keyboard with students.

Walk around the room to observe students' techniques.

Remind students to refer to the keyboard chart to find the location of a key rather than look at their keyboards.

LESSON 6-C Pace students through the three steps of capitalizing a letter before they type the drill lines.

- Shift J release
- Shift K release
- Shift L release
- Shift H release
- Shift I release
- Shift O release
- Shift P release
- Shift M release

Watch students carefully to be sure they are correctly using the Left Shift key.

Students must hold down the Shift key until the letter reach is completed.

LESSON 6-D Remind students to keep the J finger in the home position as they reach to the hyphen key.

New Keys

Goals

- Touch-type the I, Left Shift, hyphen, and G keys
- Type at least 15wpm/1′/3e

A. Type 2 times.

A. WARMUP

```
The major sold three wool hats at cost.
Dale took her cats to the vet at three.
```

NEW KEYS

B. Type each line 2 times.

Use the K finger.

B. THE   KEY

```
kkk kik kik iki kkk kik kik iki kkk kik
aid did fir him kid lid mid pit sip tip
chip dice itch film hide iris kite milk
This time he left his tie at the store.
```

C. Type each line 2 times.

Use the A finger.

C. THE LEFT  KEY

To capitalize letters on the right half of the keyboard:

1. With the F finger at home, press and hold down the Left Shift key with the A finger.
2. Press the letter key.
3. Release the Left Shift key and return fingers to the home position.

```
aaa Jaa Jaa aaa Kaa Kaa aaa Laa Laa aaa
Joe Kip Lee Hal Mat Pat Jim Kim Les Pam
Jake Karl Lake Hope Mark Jack Kate Hale
Les Lee rode with Pat Mace to the park.
```

D. Type each line 2 times. Do not space before or after a hyphen; keep the J finger in home position.

Use the Sem finger.

D. THE  KEY

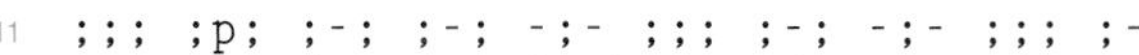

```
;;; ;p; ;-; ;-; -;- ;;; ;-; -;- ;;; ;-;
two-thirds two-fifths trade-off tip-off
look-alike jack-of-all-trades free-fall
I heard that Ms. Lee-Som is well-to-do.
```


Windows Wizard

FOLDERS To create a new folder from My Computer or Windows Explorer in Windows:

- Select the folder or drive where you want to create the new folder.
- Select **New** from the **File** menu.
- Click **Folder**. The new folder appears with a temporary name.
- Type a new folder name and press Enter.

MHHE CHAMPIONS

RHODE ISLAND

Improve Accuracy

To help students who are making numerous errors, tell them to say each letter as they strike it. This procedure reduces errors and improves student concentration.

Elizabeth C. Hoch
New England Institute of Technology
Warwick, Rhode Island

E. Type each line 2 times. Keep wrists low but not resting on the keyboard.

E. THE G KEY

```
fff fgf fgf gfg fff fgf fgf gfg fff fgf
age cog dig fig hog jog lag peg rag sag
gold rage sage grow page cage gate wage
Gail G. Grove greeted the great golfer.
```

SKILLBUILDING

F. Type each line 2 times.

F. TECHNIQUE PRACTICE: SPACE BAR

```
Vic will meet. Ed is here. Ava is here.
See them. Do it. Make these. Hold this.
See Lester. See Kate. See Dad. See Mom.
Take this car. Make the cakes. Hide it.
```

G. Type each line 2 times.

G. TECHNIQUE PRACTICE: HYPHEN KEY

```
Two-thirds were well-to-do look-alikes.
Jo Hames-Smith is a jack-of-all-trades.
Phil saw the trade-offs at the tip-off.
Two-fifths are packed for Jo Mill-Ross.
```

H. Take two 1-minute timed writings. Review your speed and errors.

Goal: At least 15wpm/1′/3e

H. 1-MINUTE TIMED WRITING

	WORDS
Al Hall left the firm two weeks ago. I	8
will see him at the office at three.	15
1 | 2 | 3 | 4 | 5 | 6 | 7 | 8	

Lesson 6

TEACH

NEW KEYS

LESSON 6-G Review the purpose of the hyphen key. To:

- Connect compound words
- Show word division
- Create a dash

LESSON 6-H The timed writing contains 15 words.

SKILLBUILDING

Review the proper technique for the SPACE BAR.

ASSESS

Walk around the room to observe student technique.

Extending the Lesson

Ask students to list additional compound words requiring the use of the hyphen.

CLOSE

Review the keyboard illustration and remind students to practice all learned keys.

INSTRUCTOR STRATEGIES

Additional Practice
If students finish early, have them repeat skillbuilding exercises in this lesson and earlier lessons.

GDP SOFTWARE TIPS

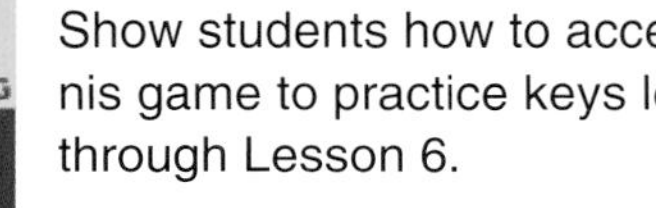

LESSONS · SKILLBUILDING · MAP · TIMED WRITINGS · LANGUAGE ARTS · GAMES

Tennis Game

Show students how to access the tennis game to practice keys learned through Lesson 6.

W E R T	I O P -
A S D F G	H J K L ;
C V	M .
LEFT SHIFT	RIGHT SHIFT

FOCUS

TIME MANAGEMENT

Suggested Schedule:

Warmup	5′
New Keys	25′
Skillbuilding	20′
Total	**50′**

TEACH

NEW KEYS

Check students' posture:

- Feet—apart, flat on floor
- Back—erect, leaning slightly forward

LESSON 7-B Remind students to keep the Sem finger in home position as they reach to the U key.

LESSON 7-C Check students' technique to be sure they are using the correct finger to type the B key.

LESSON 7-D Remind students to space 1 time after punctuation.

New Keys

Goals

- Touch-type the U, B, colon, and X keys
- Type at least 16wpm/1′/3e

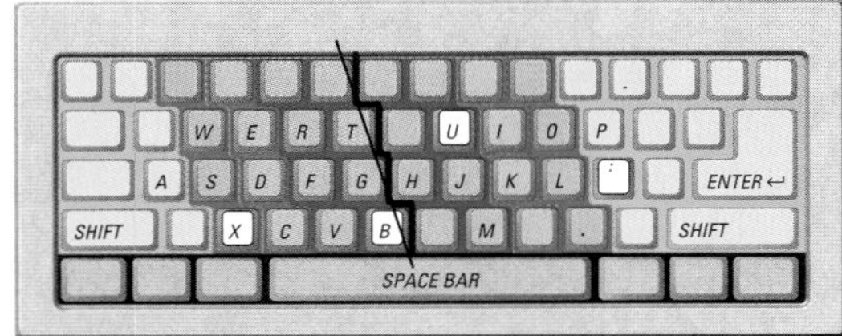

A. Type 2 times.

A. WARMUP

```
1 Evette jogged eight miles with Christi.
2 Philip gave Shari the award for spirit.
```

NEW KEYS

B. Type each line 2 times. Keep your other fingers at home as you reach to U.

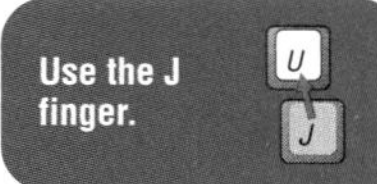

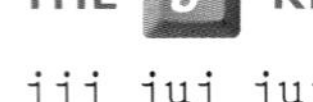

B. THE U KEY

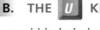

```
3 jjj juj juj uju jjj juj juj uju jjj juj
4 cue due hue put rut cut dug hut pup rum
5 cult duet fuel hulk just lump mule pull
6 Hugh urged us to put out the hot fires.
```

C. Type each line 2 times.

Use the F finger.

C. THE B KEY

```
7 fff fbf fbf bfb fff fbf fbf bfb fff fbf
8 bag cab bad lab bat rib bar tab beg web
9 bake back bead beef bath bail beam both
10 Bart backed Bill for a big blue bumper.
```

D. The colon is the shift of the semicolon key. Type each line 2 times. Space 1 time after a period following an abbreviation and 1 time after a colon.

Use the Sem finger.

D. THE : KEY

```
11 ;:; ;:; ;:; ;:; ;:; ;:; ;:; ;:; ;:; ;:;
12 Dr. Poole: Ms. Shu: Mr. Rose: Mrs. Tam:
13 Dear Ed: Dear Flo: Dear James: Dear Di:
14 Date: To: From: Subject: for the dates:
```


Windows Wizard

TWO WAYS TO RENAME FILES OR FOLDERS

One way to rename files or folders in Windows 2000, Me, and XP:

- Open **My Computer** or **Windows Explorer**.
- Select the file or folder you want to rename.
- Choose **Rename** from the **File** menu.
- Type the name and press ENTER.

Another way:

- In the **Open** dialog box, select the file or folder you want to rename.
- Click the right mouse button.
- Choose **Rename**.
- Type the name and press ENTER.

E. THE X KEY

E. Type each line 2 times.

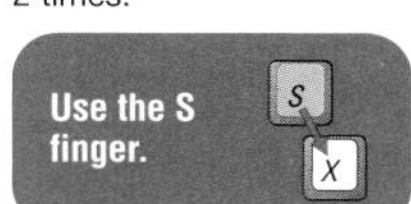


```
15 sss sxs sxs xsx sss sxs sxs xsx sss sxs
16 box fox hex lax lux mix six tax vex wax
17 apex axle exam flax flex flux taxi text
18 Max asked six pals to fix a sixth taxi.
```

SKILLBUILDING

F. TECHNIQUE PRACTICE: COLON KEY

F. Type each line 2 times.

```
19 as follows: these people: this example:
20 Dear Sirs: Dear Madam: Dear Mrs. Smith:
21 Dear Di: Dear Bo: Dear Peter: Dear Mom:
22 for this part: as listed: the projects:
```

G. WORD PRACTICE

G. Type each line 2 times.

Top row

```
23 We were told to take our truck to Hugo.
24 There were two tired people at the hut.
25 Please write to their home to tell Tom.
```

Home row

```
26 Jake asked his dad for small red flags.
27 Sara added a dash of salt to the salad.
28 Dale said she had a fall sale at Drake.
```

Bottom row

```
29 He came to the mall at five to meet me.
30 Victoria came to vote with ample vigor.
31 Mable Baxter visited via the Marta bus.
```

H. 1-MINUTE TIMED WRITING

H. Take two 1-minute timed writings. Review your speed and errors.

Goal: At least 16wpm/1'/3e

```
                                              WORDS
32 Dear Jack: Fred would like to take Jill        8
33 Wells to the home game at five tomorrow.      16
   | 1 | 2 | 3 | 4 | 5 | 6 | 7 | 8 |
```


Lesson 7

TEACH

NEW KEYS

LESSON 7-E Caution students to keep fingers on home position when reaching for the letter X.

SKILLBUILDING

LESSON 7-G Ask students to note problem reaches and to determine whether they have more problems with the top or the bottom row.

Remind students to press ENTER at the end of each line.

LESSON 7-H Administer additional timed writings if time permits.

ASSESS

www.mhhe.com/gdp to download a copy of the Technique Evaluation Form.

TECHNIQUE EVALUATION FORM Walk around the room to observe the students' technique. Complete a Technique Evaluation Form for each student.

Review results of timed writings.

Extending the Lesson

Encourage students to practice the skillbuilding exercises outside of class for the more difficult reaches.

CLOSE

Review the use of the colon key:

- Follows a salutation in a letter.
- Introduces a series or emphasizes important information.

The words before the colon should make up a complete sentence.

GDP SOFTWARE TIPS

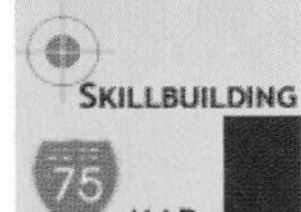

Portfolio

Explain how to manage students' files electronically with the GDP Portfolio. The feature is useful for viewing errors without printing. Be sure students understand that the Portfolio can be accessed through the **File** menu or with the **Portfolio** button on the toolbar.

FOCUS

TIME MANAGEMENT

Suggested Schedule:

Warmup	3′
New Keys	20′
Skillbuilding	27′
Total	**50′**

TEACH

NEW KEYS

LESSON 8-B Demonstrate the reach to the Y key. This is the farthest reach students will make with the index finger on the right hand.

LESSON 8-C Check students' technique to be sure they are using the correct finger to type the comma.

LESSON 8-D Demonstrate the reach to the Q key. This is a difficult reach because it is made with the fourth finger on the left hand.

New Keys

Goals

- Touch-type the Y, comma, Q, and slash keys
- Type at least 17wpm/1′/3e

A. Type 2 times.

A. WARMUP

```
Jack asked Philip if Charlie came home.
Kim had a short meal with Victor Baker.
```

NEW KEYS

B. Type each line 2 times.

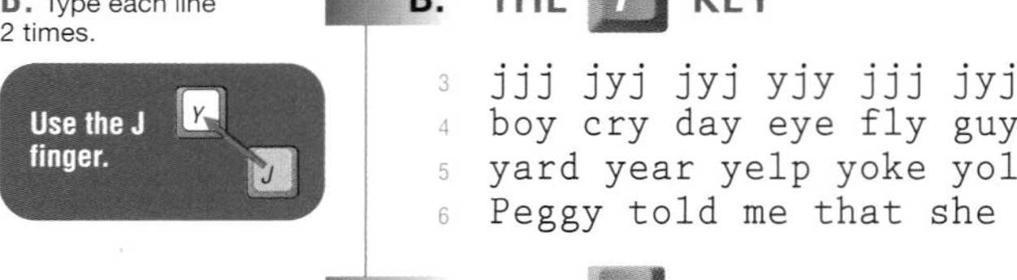

Use the J finger.

B. THE Y KEY

```
jjj jyj jyj yjy jjj jyj jyj yjy jjj jyj
boy cry day eye fly guy hay joy key may
yard year yelp yoke yolk your yule play
Peggy told me that she may try to stay.
```

C. Type each line 2 times.

Use the K finger.

C. THE , KEY

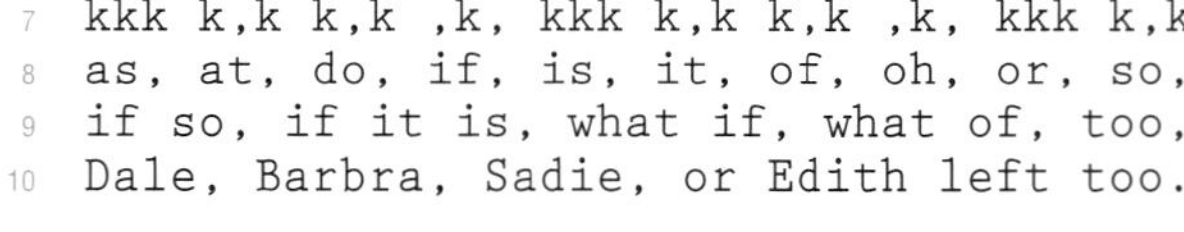

```
kkk k,k k,k ,k, kkk k,k k,k ,k, kkk k,k
as, at, do, if, is, it, of, oh, or, so,
if so, if it is, what if, what of, too,
Dale, Barbra, Sadie, or Edith left too.
```

D. Type each line 2 times.

Use the A finger.

D. THE Q KEY

```
aaa aqa aqa qaq aaa aqa aqa qaq aaa aqa
quip quit quack quail quake quart quash
quest quick quilts quotes quaver queasy
Four quiet squires quilted aqua quilts.
```


Windows Wizard

DELETING FILES OR FOLDERS To delete files or folders in Windows 2000, Me, and XP:

- Open **My Computer** or **Windows Explorer**.
- Select the file(s) or folder(s) to be deleted.
- Choose **Delete** from the **File** menu, or right-click; then select **Delete** from the **Shortcut** menu.
- Click **Yes** in the **Confirm File Delete** dialog box.

E. Type each line 2 times. Do not space before or after a slash.

Use the Sem finger.

E. THE / KEY

```
15 ;;; ;/; ;/; /;/ ;;; ;/; ;/; /;/ ;;; ;/;
16 his/her him/her he/she either/or ad/add
17 do/due/dew hale/hail fir/fur heard/herd
18 Ask him/her if he/she chose true/false.
```

SKILLBUILDING

F. Type each line 2 times.

F. PHRASES

```
19 if it is|she will do|will he come|he is
20 he said so|who left them|will she drive
21 after all|he voted|just wait|to ask her
22 some said it|for that firm|did she seem
```

G. Type each line 2 times.

G. TECHNIQUE PRACTICE: SHIFT KEY

```
23 Ada, Idaho; Kodiak, Alaska; Lima, Ohio;
24 Lula, Georgia; Sully, Iowa; Alta, Utah;
25 Mr. Ray Tims; Mr. Ed Chu; Mr. Cal York;
26 Ms. Vi Close; Ms. Di Ray; Ms. Sue Ames;
```

H. Take two 1-minute timed writings. Review your speed and errors.

Goal: At least 17wpm/1'/3e

H. 1-MINUTE TIMED WRITING

```
27 George predicted that Lu will have five     8
28 boxed quilts. David Quayle was to pack     16
29 a mug.                                     17
   | 1 | 2 | 3 | 4 | 5 | 6 | 7 | 8 |
```


INSTRUCTOR STRATEGIES

Motivation

Watch for students who may be frustrated or not interested in the class. Determine why they are frustrated or not interested and encourage them not to quit. It is important to motivate students every day—especially if typing is not easy for them.

Lesson 8

TEACH

NEW KEYS

LESSON 8-E Remind students to keep their wrists straight when reaching to the slash key.

SKILLBUILDING

LESSON 8-G Review the steps for typing capitals before this drill.

Consider assigning additional practice for experienced students.

- Students typing 15wpm or fewer type each line 2 times.
- Students typing 16–25wpm type each line 3 times.

LESSON 8-H The timed writing contains 17 words.

ASSESS

www.mhhe.com/gdp to download a copy of the Technique Evaluation Form.

TECHNIQUE EVALUATION FORM Walk around the room to observe the students' technique.

Review results of timed writings.

Extending the Lesson

Review punctuation learned: comma, period, semicolon, colon, and slash.

CLOSE

Remind students that they should practice letters that are difficult to reach or to remember.

FOCUS

TIME MANAGEMENT

Suggested Schedule:

Warmup	3′
New Keys	20′
Skillbuilding	27′
Total	**50′**

TEACH

NEW KEYS

Remind students that correct posture and periodic rest breaks during intensive typing will help avoid repetitive strain injuries such as carpal tunnel syndrome.

LESSON 9-C Demonstrate the reach to the Z key. This is a difficult reach, and students tend to remove their hand from the home position. Encouragement is helpful.

LESSON 9-D Demonstrate the reach to the question mark and remind students to press SHIFT with the left hand.

New Keys

Goals

- Touch-type the N, Z, question mark, and TAB keys
- Type at least 18wpm/1′/3e

A. Type 2 times.

A. WARMUP

```
I quit the sales job at Huber, Georgia.
Alice packed two boxes of silver disks.
```

NEW KEYS

B. Type each line 2 times.

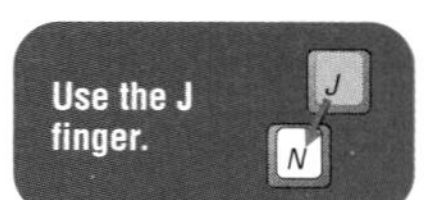

B. THE N KEY

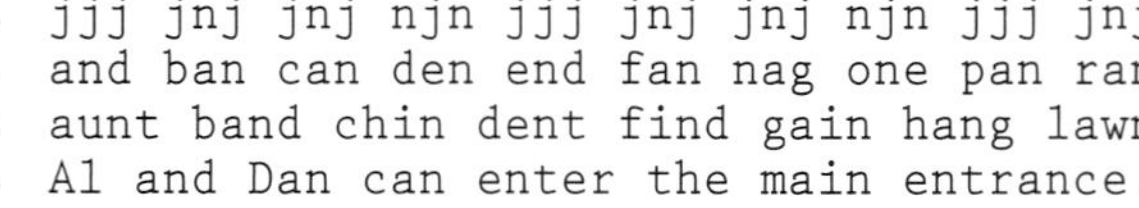

```
jjj jnj jnj njn jjj jnj jnj njn jjj jnj
and ban can den end fan nag one pan ran
aunt band chin dent find gain hang lawn
Al and Dan can enter the main entrance.
```

C. Type each line 2 times. Keep the F finger at home as you reach to the Z.

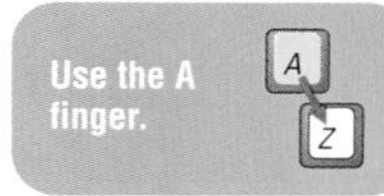

C. THE Z KEY

```
aaa aza aza zaz aaa aza aza zaz aaa aza
zap zig buzz gaze haze jazz mazes oozes
zip zoo zinc zing zone zoom blaze craze
The size of the prized pizza amazed us.
```

D. The question mark is the shift of the slash. Space 1 time after a question mark at the end of a sentence. Type each line 2 times.

D. THE ? KEY

```
;;; ;?; ;?; ?;? ;;; ;?; ;?; ?;? ;;; ;?;
Can John go? If not Jane, who? Can Ken?
Who will see? Can this be? Is that you?
Why not quilt? Can they go? Did he ask?
```


Meeting Special Needs

ACCESSIBILITY FEATURES Windows 2000, Me, and XP includes several Accessibility Options that enhance the display, sound, mouse, and keyboarding settings. For example, if it is difficult for a student to use a mouse, change the MouseKeys settings to use the numeric keypad for moving the mouse pointer.

To locate Accessibility Options:

- Click the **Start** button.
- Point to **Settings**, and click **Control Panel**.
- Double-click **Accessibility Options**.
- Select the appropriate tab, and change settings.

Visit **www.mhhe.com/gdp**.

TEACH

NEW KEYS

LESSON 9-E Have students use default tab settings. Setting tabs is presented later in Lesson 50.

LESSON 9-F Observe that students are not removing their right hand from the home position to press the TAB key.

LESSON 9-G Observe students' technique as they reach for the question mark key.

SKILLBUILDING

LESSON 9-H Urge students to keep their eyes on the copy and maintain an even pace.

E. The word counts in this book credit you with 1 stroke for each paragraph indention in a timed writing. Press the TAB key after the timing starts.

E. THE TAB KEY

The TAB key is used to indent paragraphs. Reach to the TAB key with the A finger. Keep your other fingers on the home keys as you quickly press the TAB key. Pressing the TAB key moves the insertion point 0.5 inch (the default setting) to the right.

F. Type each paragraph 2 times. Press ENTER only at the end of the paragraph.

F. PRACTICE THE TAB KEY

```
15 Each  Tab→ day   Tab→ set   Tab→ your  Tab→ goal
16 to         type       with       more       speed.

17 You        will       soon       reach      your
18 goal       if         you        work       hard.
```

SKILLBUILDING

G. Type each line 2 times.

G. TECHNIQUE PRACTICE: QUESTION MARK

```
19 Who? Why? How? When? What? True? False?
20 Is it Mo? Why not? What for? Which one?
21 Did Mary go? Is Clinton ready? Why not?
22 Who competed with me? Dana? James? Kay?
```

H. Type each line 2 times.

H. PHRASES

```
23 and the| for the| she is able| can they go
24 for him| ask him| they still| did they fly
25 of them| with us| can he send| ought to be
26 has been able| they need it| he will call
```


INSTRUCTOR STRATEGIES

The Familiar Alphabet Keys

Observe students and determine their confidence level with the keyboard. Numeric keys will be introduced in Lesson 11, and you do not want students to feel overwhelmed.

- Lesson 10 provides a review, but you may want to develop additional exercises to make sure students know the alphabetic reaches.
- You may want to create an illustration of a blank keyboard and ask students to write the alphabet and punctuation learned on the appropriate keys.

Lesson 9

TEACH

SKILLBUILDING

LESSON 9-I Instruct students to type the first paragraph (lines 27–30) 2 times before typing the second paragraph (lines 31–33).

Explain and show the difference between a hyphen and a dash.

LESSON 9-K The timed writing contains 18 words.

This is the first alphabetic paragraph and may be more difficult than the previous timed writings.

ASSESS

www.mhhe.com/gdp to download a copy of the Technique Evaluation Form.

TECHNIQUE EVALUATION FORM Walk around the room and observe the students' technique.

Review timed writings. Check speed and accuracy levels.

Extending the Lesson

Explain that word processing programs include special symbol keys to create a dash.

CLOSE

Encourage students to practice typing every day.

I. Type each paragraph 2 times.

I. TECHNIQUE PRACTICE: HYPHEN

Hyphens are used:

- To show that a word is divided (lines 27 and 31).
- To make a dash using two hyphens with no space before or after (lines 28 and 31).
- To join words in a compound word (lines 29, 30, and 32).

```
     Can Larry go to the next tennis tourna-
ment? I am positive he--like Lane--will find
the event to be a first-class sports event.
If he can go, I will get first-rate seats.
     Larry--like Ella--enjoys going to tourna-
ments that are always first-rate, first-class
sporting events.
```

J. Space 1 time after a semicolon, colon, and comma and 1 time after a period and question mark at the end of a sentence. Type each line 2 times.

J. PUNCTUATION PRACTICE

```
Kate writes; John sings. Are they good?
Send these items: pens, pencils, clips.
Hal left; she stayed. Will they attend?
Wes made these stops: Rome, Bern, Kiev.
```

K. Take two 1-minute timed writings. Review your speed and errors.

Goal: At least 18wpm/1'/3e

K. 1-MINUTE TIMED WRITING

```
     Zelda judged six typing contests          7
that a local firm held in Piqua. Vick         14
Bass was a winner.                            18
  | 1 | 2 | 3 | 4 | 5 | 6 | 7 | 8 |
```

Strategies for Career Success

Preparing a Job Interview Portfolio

Don't go empty-handed to that job interview! Take a portfolio of items with you. Definitely include copies of your resume and your list of references, with at least three professional references. Your academic transcript is useful, especially if you are asked to complete a company application form. Appropriate work samples and copies of certificates and licenses are also helpful portfolio items.

The interview process provides you the opportunity to interview the organization. Include a list of questions you want to ask during the interview.

A comprehensive portfolio of materials will benefit you by giving you a measure of control during the interview process.

YOUR TURN Start today to compile items for your interview portfolio. Include copies of your resume, your reference list, and copies of certificates and licenses. Begin developing a list of interview questions. Think about appropriate work samples to include in your portfolio.

Strategies for Career Success

GDP ELECTRONIC PORTFOLIO Help your students become very comfortable with the many ways to use the GDP Portfolio. Students learn electronic management of files. Later they will be able to access document processing exercises that could be included in a job interview portfolio.

Review

Goals

- Reinforce new key reaches
- Type at least 19wpm/1′/3e

A. Type 2 times.

A. WARMUP

1 She expects to work hard at her job.
2 Keith had a very quiet, lazy afternoon.

SKILLBUILDING

B. Take a 1-minute timed writing on each paragraph. Review your speed and errors.

B. SHORT PARAGRAPHS

3 You can utilize your office skills 7
4 to complete tasks. Some types of jobs 15
5 require more skills. 19

6 You will be amazed at how easily 7
7 and quickly you complete your task when 15
8 you can concentrate. 19

| 1 | 2 | 3 | 4 | 5 | 6 | 7 | 8 |

C. Type each line 2 times.

C. WORD PATTERNS

9 banister minister adapter filter master
10 disable disband discern discord discuss
11 embargo emerge embody empty employ emit
12 enforce endure energy engage engine end
13 precept precise predict preside premier
14 subtract subject subsist sublime subdue
15 teamster tearful teaches teak team tear
16 theater theirs theory thefts therm them
17 treason crimson season prison bison son
18 tribune tribute tripod trial tribe trim

ERGONOMICALLY SPEAKING

REPETITIVE STRAIN INJURY Inappropriate and extended use of keyboards and input devices has been associated with repetitive strain injury (RSI) to soft tissues in the hands and arms. Encourage students to maintain good posture and position when working on the computer, to help them avoid RSI and also considerably improve their comfort. Visit us on the Web at **www.mhhe.com/gdp** for more information.

Lesson 10

FOCUS

TIME MANAGEMENT

Suggested Schedule:

Warmup	3′
Skillbuilding	47′
Total	**50′**

TEACH

SKILLBUILDING

Remind students to have correct position at the keyboard.

- Center the body opposite the keyboard.
- Lean forward slightly from the hips.
- Keep feet flat on the floor.
- Keep elbows alongside the body.
- Curve fingers naturally over the home position.

LESSON 10-B Remind students to press TAB to indent each paragraph.

LESSON 10-C Remind students to keep eyes on the copy and to make quick, snappy strokes using the correct fingers.

Lesson 10

TEACH

SKILLBUILDING

LESSON 10-E The timed writing contains 19 words.

ASSESS

www.mhhe.com/gdp to download a copy of the Technique Evaluation Form.

TECHNIQUE EVALUATION FORM

Walk around the room to observe the students' technique. Complete a Technique Evaluation Form for each student.

Print the lesson or review the practice lines on the monitor.

Review results of timed writings.

Print a report for all skillbuilding exercises for Lessons 6–10.

Extending the Lesson

Encourage students to use Exercise 10-D for selective practice. Students can choose the drill lines containing the letters that cause them difficulty in typing.

CLOSE

Remind students that all alphabetic letters have been presented. Encourage students to repeat exercises in previous lessons to develop confidence in their typing.

D. Type each line 2 times. Keep fingers curved and wrists low but not resting on the keyboard as you practice these lines.

D. ALPHABET REVIEW

Alda asked Alma Adams to fly to Alaska.
Both Barbara and Bill liked basketball.
Carl can accept a classic car in Cairo.
David dined in a dark diner in Detroit.
Elmo said Eddie edited the entire text.
Five friars focused on the four fables.
Guy gave a bag of green grapes to Gina.
Haughty Hugh hoped Hal had helped Seth.
Irene liked to pickle pickles in brine.
Jon Jones joined a junior jogging team.
Kenny kept a kayak for a trek to Akron.
Lowell played a well-planned ball game.
Monica made more money on many markups.
Ned knew ten men in a main dining room.
Opal Orem opened four boxes of oranges.
Pat paid to park the plane at the pump.
Quincy quickly quit his quarterly quiz.
Robin read rare books in their library.
Sam signed, sealed, and sent the lease.
Todd caught trout in the little stream.
Uncle Rubin urged Julie to go to Utica.
Viva Vista vetoed the five voice votes.
Walt waited while Wilma went to Weston.
Xu mixed extra extract exactly as told.
Yes, your young sister played a cymbal.
Zesty zebras zigzagged in the Ohio zoo.

E. Take two 1-minute timed writings. Review your speed and errors.

Goal: At least 19wpm/1′/3e

E. 1-MINUTE TIMED WRITING

Zoe expected a quiet morning to do 7
all of her work. Jean Day was to bring 15
five of the tablets. 19

| 1 | 2 | 3 | 4 | 5 | 6 | 7 | 8 |

MHHE CHAMPIONS

Paul Neatrour
Cambria County Area Community College
Johnstown, Pennsylvania

PENNSYLVANIA

Early Assessment Technique

Instructors Helping One Another

Students need to feel a sense of accomplishment and feel good about what they have learned. After Lesson 10, give an objective test covering the following topics:

- Name the five components of your computer system.
- Identify all menus and name all buttons.
- Describe proper technique at the keyboard.
- Indicate correct spacing following punctuation marks.
- Count words per minute in a short paragraph.

This test is quick and easy, and it provides feedback to the students and to the instructor.

Unit 3

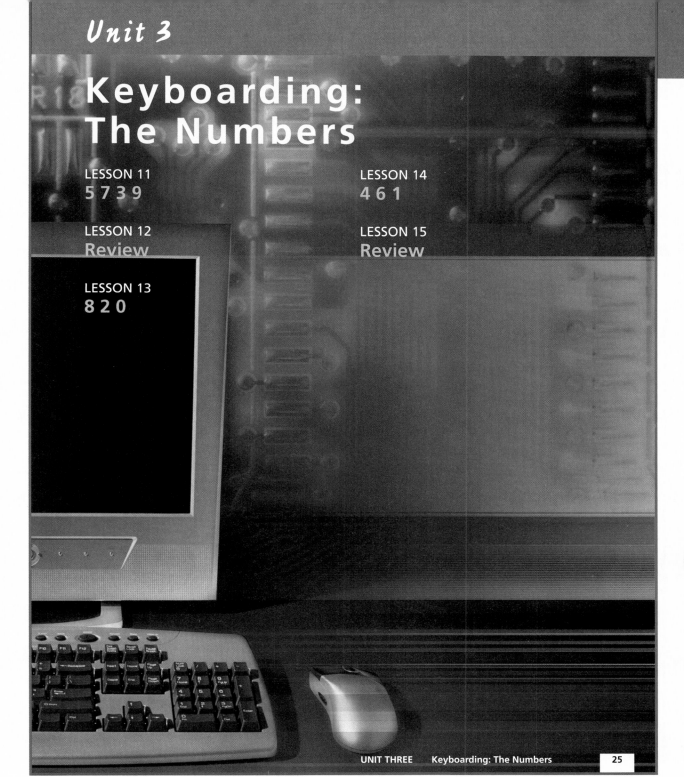

Keyboarding: The Numbers

LESSON 11
5 7 3 9

LESSON 12
Review

LESSON 13
8 2 0

LESSON 14
4 6 1

LESSON 15
Review

UNIT OVERVIEW

Students learn to touch-type number keys. Skillbuilding exercises include practice on numbers, technique, and alphabetic keys. Diagnostic typing and 2-minute timed writings provide evaluation of students' typing skill. The last lesson in the unit reviews and reinforces the number keys taught in the unit.

Did You Know?

PPP A Pretest/Practice/Posttest (PPP) routine appears in each unit and provides individualized guidance to the student on whether to work on speed or to work on accuracy—based on the number of errors made on the pretest.

INSTRUCTOR STRATEGIES

Zero or Oh?
Ask students to point out times when the symbols for zero and capital O can be mistaken for each other. When is it best to say *zero* rather than *oh*? (For instance, say *zero* when pronouncing the catalog number of a book to a librarian or when pronouncing the item number of a catalog purchase to a company representative.)

RESOURCE MANAGER

GDP SOFTWARE

- Lessons 11–15
- Software User's Guide
- Instructor Management LAN Version
- Professional Handbook (IWE*)—Teaching Strategies; Teaching in a Distance-Learning Environment

ASSESSMENT

- Technique Evaluation Form
- Professional Handbook (IWE*)—Assessment Strategies

ON THE WEB

- **www.mhhe.com/gdp**
- Instructor Management Web Version

*Instructor Wraparound Edition

FOCUS

TIME MANAGEMENT 

Suggested Schedule:

Warmup	3′
New Keys	27′
Skillbuilding	20′
Total	**50′**

TEACH

LESSON 11-A Warmups from now on are paragraphs with word counts and may be used for additional timed writings.

NEW KEYS

Stress the importance of good position:

- Center the body opposite the keyboard.
- Lean forward slightly from the hips.
- Keep feet flat on the floor.
- Keep elbows alongside the body.
- Curve fingers naturally over the home position.

LESSON 11-B Emphasize keeping eyes on the copy when typing numbers.

Check to be sure students use correct fingers when typing numbers.

Also, check that students keep both hands in the home row position. Students tend to remove both hands from the home row position as they key line 4.

Remind students that their fingers should not straighten as they reach for the number keys. The fingers must remain curved.

LESSON 11-C Remind students to keep the Sem finger in the home position as they reach for the number 7.

Number Keys

Goals

- Touch-type the 5, 7, 3, and 9 keys
- Type at least 19wpm/2′/5e

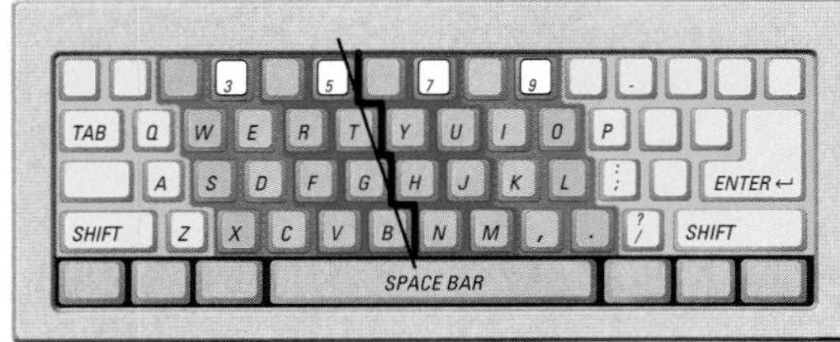

A. Type 2 times.

A. WARMUP

1 The law firm of Quayle, Buster, Given, and 9
2 Rizzo processed all the cases last June and July; 19
3 however, we will seek a new law firm next summer. 29

| 1 | 2 | 3 | 4 | 5 | 6 | 7 | 8 | 9 | 10 |

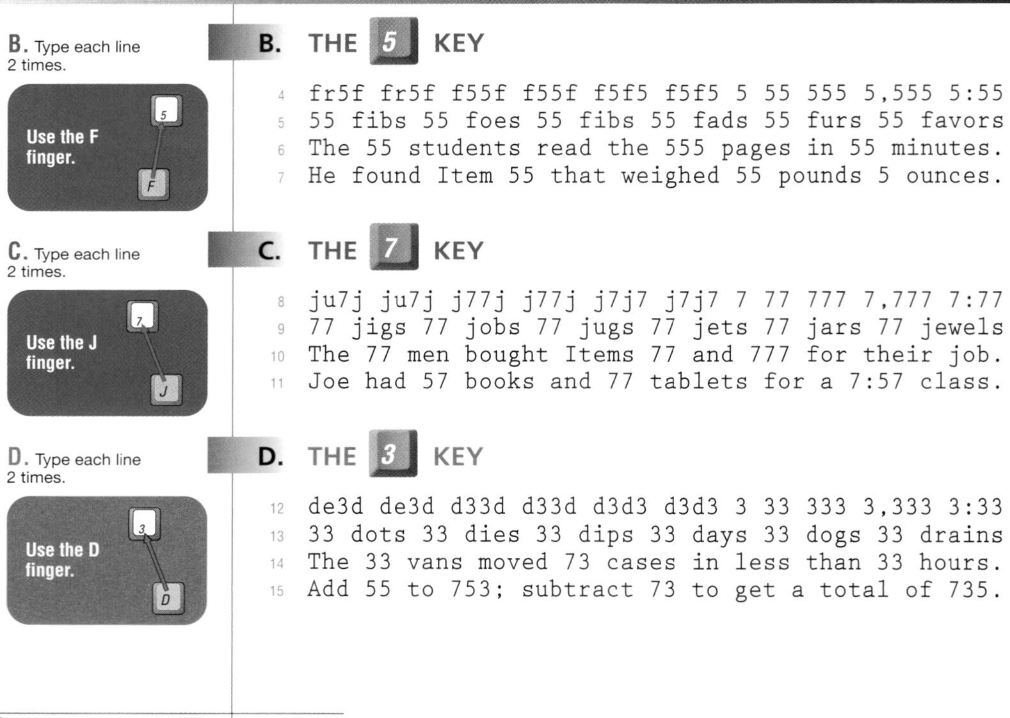

NEW KEYS

B. Type each line 2 times.

Use the F finger.

B. THE 5 KEY

4 fr5f fr5f f55f f55f f5f5 f5f5 5 55 555 5,555 5:55
5 55 fibs 55 foes 55 fibs 55 fads 55 furs 55 favors
6 The 55 students read the 555 pages in 55 minutes.
7 He found Item 55 that weighed 55 pounds 5 ounces.

C. Type each line 2 times.

Use the J finger.

C. THE 7 KEY

8 ju7j ju7j j77j j77j j7j7 j7j7 7 77 777 7,777 7:77
9 77 jigs 77 jobs 77 jugs 77 jets 77 jars 77 jewels
10 The 77 men bought Items 77 and 777 for their job.
11 Joe had 57 books and 77 tablets for a 7:57 class.

D. Type each line 2 times.

Use the D finger.

D. THE 3 KEY

12 de3d de3d d33d d33d d3d3 d3d3 3 33 333 3,333 3:33
13 33 dots 33 dies 33 dips 33 days 33 dogs 33 drains
14 The 33 vans moved 73 cases in less than 33 hours.
15 Add 55 to 753; subtract 73 to get a total of 735.

Windows Wizard 

SEARCH To search for files or folders in Windows 2000 or Me:

- Click the **Start** button and then click **Search**.
- Choose **For Files or Folders**.
- Type the name of the file or folder in the **Search for files or folders named:** text box.
- Choose the appropriate drive from the **Look in** drop-down arrow list, then click **Search Now**.

SEARCH To search for files or folders in Windows XP:

- Click the **Start** button and then click **Search**.
- Choose **For Files or Folders**.
- Choose **All files and folders**.
- Type the name of the file or folder in the **All or part of the file name** text box.
- Click **Search**.

E. Type each line 2 times.

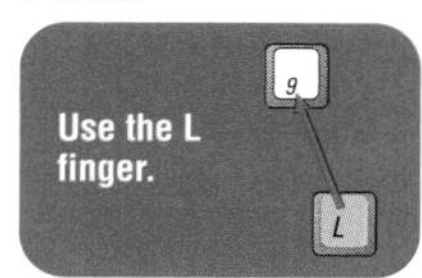

E. THE 9 KEY

```
lo9l lo9l 1991 1991 1919 1919 9 99 999 9,999 9:99
99 lads 99 lights 99 labs 99 legs 99 lips 99 logs
Their 99 cans of No. 99 were sold to 99 managers.
He had 39 pens, 59 pads, 97 pencils, and 9 clips.
```

SKILLBUILDING

F. Type each line 2 times.

F. NUMBER PRACTICE: 5, 7, 3, AND 9

```
The 57 tickets were for the April 3 show at 9:59.
Mary was to read pages 33, 57, 95, and 97 to him.
Kate planted 53 tulips, 39 mums, and 97 petunias.
Only 397 of the 573 coeds could register at 5:39.
```

G. Type each line 2 times. Keep other fingers at home as you reach to the SHIFT keys.

G. TECHNIQUE PRACTICE: SHIFT KEY

```
Vera Rosa Tao Fay Jae Tab Pat Yuk Sue Ann Sal Joe
Andre Fidel Pedro Chong Alice Mike Juan Fern Dick
Carlos Caesar Karen Ojars Julie Marta Scott Maria
Marge Jerry Joan Mary Bill Ken Bob Ray Ted Mel Al
```

H. PROGRESSIVE PRACTICE: ALPHABET

If you are not using the GDP software, turn to page SB-7 and follow the directions for this activity.

I. Take two 2-minute timed writings. Review your speed and errors.

Goal: At least 19wpm/2'/5e

I. 2-MINUTE TIMED WRITING

```
     Zach paid for six seats and quit because he      9
could not get the views he wanted near the middle    19
of the field. In August he is thinking of going      29
to the ticket office early to purchase tickets.      38
| 1 | 2 | 3 | 4 | 5 | 6 | 7 | 8 | 9 | 10
```


GDP SOFTWARE TIPS

Progressive Practice: Alphabet

Students type a 1-minute timed writing to determine their beginning speeds. Encourage students to type with control during the entry timed writing. Students then take six 30-second timed writings. The goal is to complete the passage within 30 seconds and with no errors.

Show students the procedure to restart a timed writing. Inform them that a restart counts as one try, and six attempts per day are allowed. Students should be encouraged to reset the speed goal if they are having difficulty completing the 30-second timed writing with no errors.

TEACH

NEW KEYS

LESSON 11-E Remind students that the first character in the sequence lo9l is the letter l; not the number 1.

SKILLBUILDING

Tell students not to worry if typing numbers affects their typing speed. Once they develop confidence in the number reaches, their typing speed will improve.

LESSON 11-H Students take repeated timed writings on a passage containing the exact number of words for their speed goal until they can complete it with no errors. Then they move to the next-higher passage and start again.

LESSON 11-I The length of the timed writing is 2 minutes.

ASSESS

www.mhhe.com/gdp to download a copy of the Technique Evaluation Form.

TECHNIQUE EVALUATION FORM Walk around the room to observe the students' technique.

Review results of timed writings especially since this is the first 2-minute timed writing.

Extending the Lesson

Ask students if they have experienced a problem with a bill because of a typographical error.

CLOSE

Remind students to practice typing each day—even if time is limited to 10 minutes.

Lesson 12

FOCUS

TIME MANAGEMENT 

Suggested Schedule:

Warmup	3′
Skillbuilding	47′
Total	**50′**

TEACH

SKILLBUILDING

LESSON 12-B Speed sprints are very motivational. Have students push moderately for speed on these easy sentences.

Students love this exercise and will want to repeat it. Encourage them to finish the other skillbuilding exercises before they repeat the speed sprints.

LESSON 12-C Each paragraph is more difficult than the preceding one—based on syllabic intensity (SI = average number of syllables per word):

Paragraph 1: SI = 1.38
Paragraph 2: SI = 1.46
Paragraph 3: SI = 1.58
Paragraph 4: SI = 1.68

Review

Goal

- Type at least 20wpm/2′/5e

A. Type 2 times.

A. WARMUP

```
     Rex played a very quiet game of bridge with      9
Zeke. In March they played in competition with        18
39 players; in January they played with 57 more.      28
| 1 | 2 | 3 | 4 | 5 | 6 | 7 | 8 | 9 | 10
```

SKILLBUILDING

B. Take three 12-second timed writings on each line. The scale below the last line shows your wpm speed for a 12-second timed writing.

B. 12-SECOND SPEED SPRINTS

```
A good neighbor paid for these ancient ornaments.
Today I sit by the big lake and count huge rocks.
The four chapels sit by the end of the old field.
The signal means help is on its way to the child.
5 10 15 20 25 30 35 40 45 50
```

C. Take a 1-minute timed writing on the first paragraph to establish your base speed. Then take four 1-minute timed writings on the remaining paragraphs. As soon as you equal or exceed your base speed on one paragraph, advance to the next, more difficult paragraph.

C. SUSTAINED PRACTICE: SYLLABIC INTENSITY

```
     People continue to rent autos for personal         9
use and for their work, and car rental businesses      19
just keep growing. You may want to try one soon.       29

     It is likely that a great deal of insurance        9
protection is part of the standard rental cost to      19
you. You may, however, make many other choices.        28

     Perhaps this is not necessary, as you might        9
already have the kind of protection you want in a      19
policy that you currently have on the automobile.      29

     Paying separate mileage charges could evolve       9
into a very large bill. This will undoubtedly be       19
true if your trip involves distant destinations.       29
```


Windows Wizard

MOVE/COPY FILES OR FOLDERS: To move or copy files or folders in Windows:

- Open **My Computer** or **Windows Explorer**.
- Select the file or folder.
- Click **Edit** on the **Menu** bar.
- Choose **Copy** to copy the file or **Cut** to move it.
- Click the destination folder.
- Choose **Paste** from the **Edit** menu.

INSTRUCTOR STRATEGIES

Punctuation Practice

You may want to develop a practice exercise for students on spacing before and after punctuation. Include the semicolon, period, hyphen, colon, comma, slash, and the question mark keys.

D. Type each line 2 times.

D. ALPHABET PRACTICE

Packing jam for the dozen boxes was quite lively.
Fay quickly jumped over the two dozen huge boxes.
We vexed Jack by quietly helping a dozen farmers.
The quick lynx from the zoo just waved a big paw.
Lazy brown dogs do not jump over the quick foxes.

E. Type each line 2 times.

E. NUMBER PRACTICE

Mary was to read pages 37, 59, 75, and 93 to Zoe.
He invited 53 boys and 59 girls to the 7:35 show.
The 9:37 bus did not come to our stop until 9:55.
Purchase Order 53 listed Items 35, 77, 93, and 9.
Flight 375 will be departing Gate 37 at 9:59 p.m.

F. Type each sentence on a separate line. Type 2 times.

F. TECHNIQUE PRACTICE: ENTER KEY

Can he go? If so, what? We are lost. Jose is ill.
Did she type the memos? Tina is going. Jane lost.
Max will drive. Xenia is in Ohio. She is tallest.
Nate is fine. Ty is not. Who won? Where is Nancy?
No, she cannot go. Was he here? Where is Roberta?

G. Type each line 2 times. Space without pausing.

G. TECHNIQUE PRACTICE: SPACE BAR

a b c d e f g h i j k l m n o p q r s t u v w x y
an as be by go in is it me no of or to we but for
Do you go to Ada or Ida for work every day or so?
I am sure he can go with you if he has some time.
He is to be at the car by the time you get there.

H. Take two 2-minute timed writings. Review your speed and errors.

Goal: At least 20wpm/2'/5e

H. 2-MINUTE TIMED WRITING

Jack and Alex ordered six pizzas at a price 9
that was quite a bit lower than was the one they 19
ordered yesterday. They will order from the same 29
place tomorrow for the parties they are planning 38
to have. 40

| 1 | 2 | 3 | 4 | 5 | 6 | 7 | 8 | 9 | 10

Lesson 12

TEACH

SKILLBUILDING

LESSON 12-E Check to see if students are keeping their eyes on the copy when typing numbers.

LESSON 12-F Check that students do not move the entire hand from home position to press the ENTER key.

Check to be sure students type each sentence on a separate line.

LESSON 12-G Press and release the SPACE BAR quickly.

ASSESS

www.mhhe.com/gdp to download a copy of the Technique Evaluation Form.

TECHNIQUE EVALUATION FORM Walk around the room to observe the students' technique. Complete a Technique Evaluation Form for each student.

Print the lesson or review the practice lines on the monitor.

Review results of timed writings.

Extending the Lesson

If time permits, have students repeat the following exercises for additional practice: 11-B, 11-C, 11-D, 11-E, and 11-F.

CLOSE

Review the importance of practicing each element of keyboarding: alphabetic letters, technique (SPACE BAR, ENTER, TAB), punctuation (, . ; : / ?), and numbers.

GDP SOFTWARE TIPS

LESSONS
SKILLBUILDING
MAP

Sustained Practice

Explain the Sustained Practice exercise to students. Students may not understand base speed and how it affects the paragraph timed writings. Remind students that they must equal or exceed the base speed (first paragraph timed writing) before they can continue to the next paragraph.

FOCUS

TIME MANAGEMENT

Suggested Schedule:

Warmup	3′
New Keys	27′
Skillbuilding	20′
Total	**50′**

TEACH

NEW KEYS

LESSON 13-B Encourage students to learn the number reaches the same way they learned the reaches for alphabetic keys. Students should:

- Maintain good posture.
- Maintain home key position.
- Return fingers to home keys without hesitaion.
- Use a quick, staccato reach when pressing the SPACE BAR.
- Practice new keys until they are confident with the reach and can type without looking at their hands.

INSTRUCTOR STRATEGIES

The Number 8 Key Introduce the number 8 key as follows:

- Have students reach for the number 8 key and return to the home row while looking at the key-board, but without typing.
- Dictate "*ki8k, space, ki8k, space,*" and so on as students type from dicta-tion without looking at their keyboard.
- Have students check their work, then practice dictat-ing until students are com-fortable with the reach.

Number Keys

Goals

- Touch-type the 8, 2, and 0 keys
- Type at least 21wpm/2′/5e

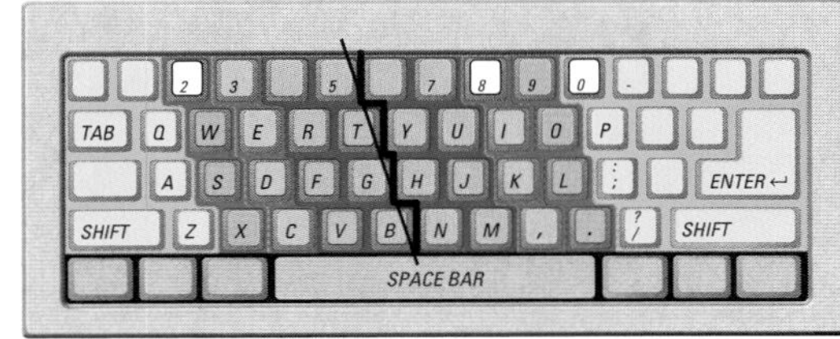

A. Type 2 times.

A. WARMUP

```
     Mary, Jenny, and Quinn packed 79 prizes in        9
53 large boxes for the party. They will take all      19
of the boxes to 3579 North Capitol Avenue today.      29
| 1 | 2 | 3 | 4 | 5 | 6 | 7 | 8 | 9 | 10
```

NEW KEYS

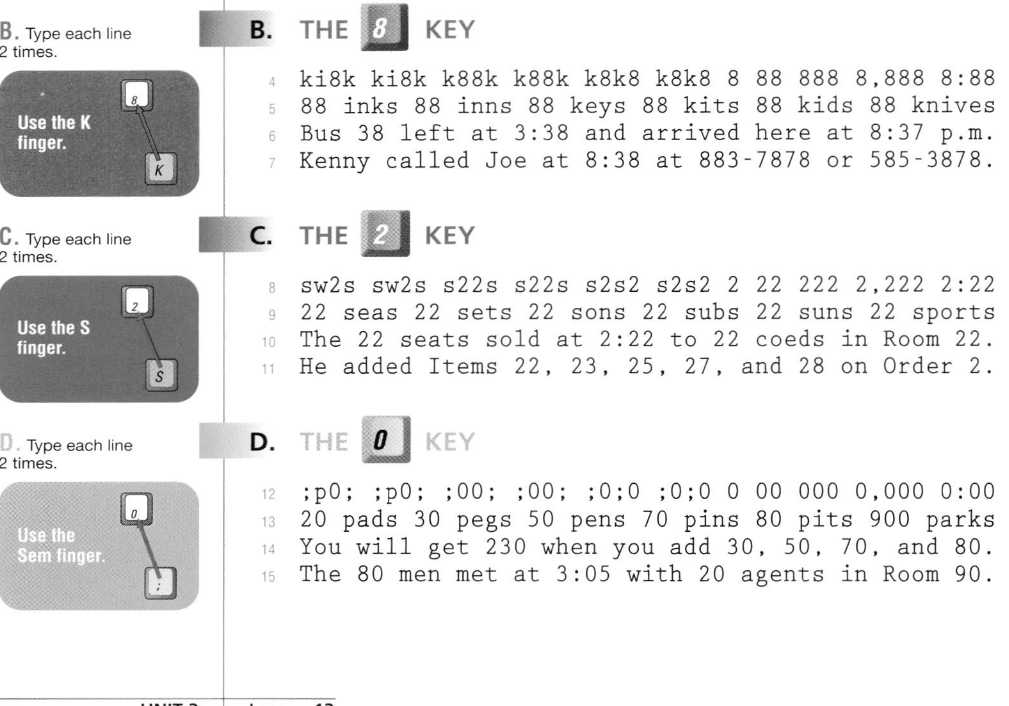

B. Type each line 2 times.

Use the K finger.

B. THE 8 KEY

```
ki8k ki8k k88k k88k k8k8 k8k8 8 88 888 8,888 8:88
88 inks 88 inns 88 keys 88 kits 88 kids 88 knives
Bus 38 left at 3:38 and arrived here at 8:37 p.m.
Kenny called Joe at 8:38 at 883-7878 or 585-3878.
```

C. Type each line 2 times.

Use the S finger.

C. THE 2 KEY

```
sw2s sw2s s22s s22s s2s2 s2s2 2 22 222 2,222 2:22
22 seas 22 sets 22 sons 22 subs 22 suns 22 sports
The 22 seats sold at 2:22 to 22 coeds in Room 22.
He added Items 22, 23, 25, 27, and 28 on Order 2.
```

D. Type each line 2 times.

Use the Sem finger.

D. THE 0 KEY

```
;p0; ;p0; ;00; ;00; ;0;0 ;0;0 0 00 000 0,000 0:00
20 pads 30 pegs 50 pens 70 pins 80 pits 900 parks
You will get 230 when you add 30, 50, 70, and 80.
The 80 men met at 3:05 with 20 agents in Room 90.
```


TEACHING THE ADULT LEARNER

THEY CAN BE LED BUT NOT DRIVEN Today's adult learners may be highly challenging as class-room consumers. They often feel that they are enti-tled to choose what they will and will not do, since they are paying for their own educations.

Remember that they are altogether unlike younger college students in the rest of their life activities. Rather than living in a dormitory and hav-ing few responsibilities, adult learners often main-tain full-time jobs and participate in family activities.

Assure them that they have not been wasting their time in class. Remind adult students of the progress they have made since they were intro-duced to the home keys in Lesson 1.

E. Type each line 2 times.

E. NUMBER PRACTICE

Jill bought 55 tickets for the 5:50 or 7:50 show.
Maxine called from 777-7370 or 777-7570 for Mary.
Sally had 23 cats, 23 dogs, and 22 birds at home.
Items 35, 37, 38, and 39 were sent on October 30.
Did Flight 2992 leave from Gate 39 at 9:39 today?
Sue went from 852 28th Street to 858 28th Street.
He sold 20 tires, 30 air filters, and 200 wipers.

F. Type each sentence on a separate line. For each sentence, press TAB, type the sentence, and then press ENTER. After you have typed all 11 sentences, insert a blank line and type them all a second time.

F. TECHNIQUE PRACTICE: TAB KEY

Casey left to go home. Where is John? Did Susan go home with them?

Isaiah drove my car to work. Sandy parked the car in the lot. They rode together.

Pat sold new cars for a new dealer. Dana sold vans for the same dealer.

Nick bought the nails to finish the job. Chris has the bolts. Dave has the wood.

G. PACED PRACTICE

If you are not using the GDP software, turn to page SB-14 and follow the directions for this activity.

H. PROGRESSIVE PRACTICE: ALPHABET

If you are not using the GDP software, turn to page SB-7 and follow the directions for this activity.

I. Take two 2-minute timed writings. Review your speed and errors.

Goal: At least 21wpm/2'/5e

I. 2-MINUTE TIMED WRITING

Jim told Bev that they must keep the liquid 9
oxygen frozen so that it could be used by the new 19
plant managers tomorrow. The oxygen will then be 29
moved quickly to its new location by transport or 39
rail on Tuesday. 42

| 1 | 2 | 3 | 4 | 5 | 6 | 7 | 8 | 9 | 10

TEACH

SKILLBUILDING

LESSON 13-G Paced Practice helps students reach individual speed and accuracy goals in 2-wpm increments by pacing them as they strive for a slightly faster rate.

LESSON 13-H Students take repeated timed writings on a passage containing the exact number of words for their speed goal until they can complete it with no errors. Then they move to the next-higher passage and start again.

ASSESS

www.mhhe.com/gdp to download a copy of the Technique Evaluation Form.

TECHNIQUE EVALUATION FORM Walk around the room to observe the students' technique.

Print the lesson or review the practice lines on the monitor.

Review results of timed writings—especially the number of errors.

Extending the Lesson

Provide additional practice for students by repeating the New Key exercises 13-B through 13-E.

CLOSE

Remind students that

- The letter O and the number 0 are not interchangeable.
- The letter I and the number 1 are not interchangeable.

GDP SOFTWARE TIPS

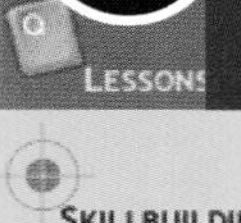

Paced Practice

Students will complete a 1-minute timed writing to determine beginning speed for the Paced Practice exercise. Encourage students to type with control—2 or fewer errors. Students should not do more than six total timed writings—three for speed and three for accuracy. Be sure to explain the purpose of the pacing markers.

Paced Practice is available through the lesson structure, or students can practice pacing using the Pace Car Game: Paced Practice.

FOCUS

TIME MANAGEMENT

Suggested Schedule:

Warmup	3′
New Keys	20′
Skillbuilding	27′
Total	**50′**

TEACH

NEW KEYS

Stress the importance of good position:

- Center the body opposite the keyboard.
- Lean forward slightly from the hips.
- Keep feet flat on the floor.
- Curve fingers naturally over the home position.

LESSON 14-C Be sure students use the right hand for the number 6 key.

LESSON 14-D Remind students that the character represented in the sequence "aq1a" is the number 1; not the letter l.

INSTRUCTOR STRATEGIES

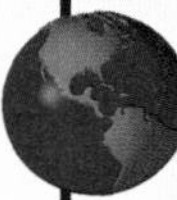

The Number 4 Key Introduce the number 4 key as follows:

- Have students reach for the number 4 key and return to the home row while looking at the keyboard, but without typing.
- Dictate "*fr4f, space, fr4f, space*," and so on as students type from dictation without looking at their keyboard.
- Have students check their work, then practice dictating until students are comfortable with the reach.

Number Keys

Goals

- Touch-type the 4, 6, and 1 keys
- Type at least 22wpm/2′/5e

A. Type 2 times.

A. WARMUP

```
     We quickly made 30 jars of jam and won a big       9
prize for our efforts on March 29. Six of the jam      19
jars were taken to 578 Culver Drive on April 28.       29
|  1  |  2  |  3  |  4  |  5  |  6  |  7  |  8  |  9  |  10
```

NEW KEYS

B. Type each line 2 times.

Use the F finger.
4
F

B. THE 4 KEY

```
fr4f fr4f f44f f44f f4f4 f4f4 4 44 444 4,444 4:44
44 fans 44 feet 44 figs 44 fins 44 fish 44 flakes
The 44 boys had 44 tickets for the games at 4:44.
Matthew read 4 books, 54 articles, and 434 lines.
```

C. Type each line 2 times.

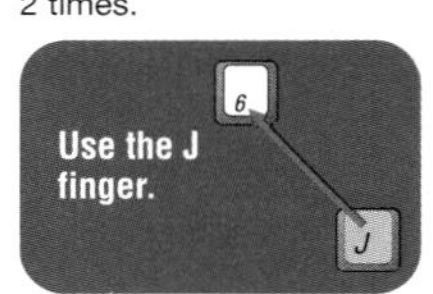

Use the J finger.
6
J

C. THE 6 KEY

```
jy6j jy6j j66j j66j j6j6 j6j6 6 66 666 6,666 6:66
66 jabs 66 jams 66 jobs 66 jars 66 jots 66 jewels
Tom Lux left at 6:26 on Train 66 to go 600 miles.
There were 56,640 people in Bath; 26,269 in Hale.
```

D. Type each line 2 times.

Use the A finger.

D. THE 1 KEY

```
aq1a aq1a a11a a11a a1a1 a1a1 1 11 111 1,111 1:11
11 aces 11 arms 11 aims 11 arts 11 axes 11 arenas
Sam left here at 1:11, Sue at 6:11, Don at 11:11.
Eric moved from 1661 Main Street to 1116 in 1995.
```


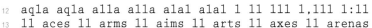

GDP SOFTWARE TIPS

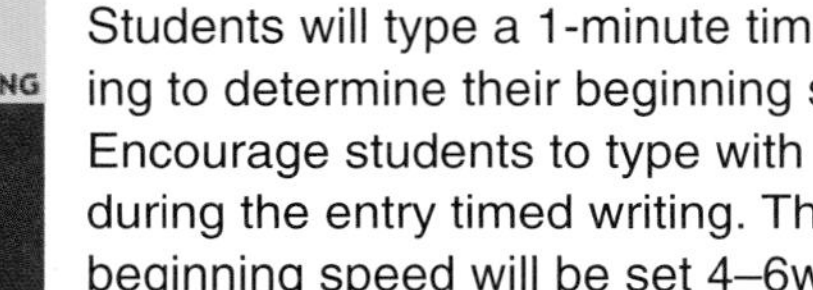

Progressive Practice: Numbers

Students will type a 1-minute timed writing to determine their beginning speed. Encourage students to type with control during the entry timed writing. The beginning speed will be set 4–6wpm slower than the speed on the timed writing. Students will then take six 30-second timed writings. The goal is to complete the passage within 30 seconds and with no errors.

SKILLBUILDING

E. Type each line 2 times. Focus on accuracy rather than speed as you practice the number drills.

E. NUMBER PRACTICE

Adding 10 and 20 and 30 and 40 and 70 totals 170.
Al selected Nos. 15, 16, 17, 18, and 19 to study.
The test took Sam 10 hours, 8 minutes, 3 seconds.
Did the 39 men drive 567 miles on Route 23 or 27?
The 18 shows were sold out by 8:37 on October 18.
On April 29-30 we will be open from 7:45 to 9:30.

F. PROGRESSIVE PRACTICE: NUMBERS

If you are not using the GDP software, turn to page SB-11 and follow the directions for this activity.

G. Take two 1-minute timed writings. Review your speed and errors.

G. HANDWRITTEN PARAGRAPH

Good writing skills are critical for success 9
in business. Numerous studies have shown 18
that these skills are essential for job advancement. 27

1 | 2 | 3 | 4 | 5 | 6 | 7 | 8 | 9 | 10

H. PACED PRACTICE

If you are not using the GDP software, turn to page SB-14 and follow the directions for this activity.

I. Take two 2-minute timed writings. Review your speed and errors.

Goal: At least 22wpm/2'/5e

I. 2-MINUTE TIMED WRITING

James scheduled a science quiz next week for 9
George, but he did not let him know what time the 19
exam was to be taken. George must score well on 29
this exam in order to be admitted to the class 38
at the Mount Garland Academy. 44

1 | 2 | 3 | 4 | 5 | 6 | 7 | 8 | 9 | 10

Meeting Special Needs

LEARNING STYLES The Index of Learning Styles, developed at North Carolina State University, is an online instrument that assesses learning preferences on four dimensions (active/reflective, sensing/intuitive, visual/verbal, and sequential/global). The student's learning style profile provides an indication of strengths and tendencies in academic settings. This is especially true in a keyboarding class. Some students may prefer written instructions, whereas others may prefer verbal instructions.

Locate the Web page at **http://www.ncsu.edu/FELDER.Public/ILSdir/styles.htm**.

Lesson 14

TEACH

SKILLBUILDING

LESSON 14-E Check that students complete all lines of this exercise and that they are using correct technique.

LESSON 14-F Students take repeated timings on a passage containing the exact number of words for their speed goal until they can complete it with no errors. Then they move to the next-higher passage and start again.

LESSON 14-H Paced Practice helps students reach individual speed and accuracy goals in 2-wpm increments by pacing them as they strive for a slightly faster rate.

ASSESS

www.mhhe.com/gdp to download a copy of the Technique Evaluation Form.

TECHNIQUE EVALUATION FORM Walk around the room to observe the students' technique.

Print the lesson or review the practice lines on the monitor.

Review results of timed writings.

Extending the Lesson

If time permits, have students repeat the following exercises for additional practice: 14-B, 14-C, 14-D, and 14-E.

CLOSE

Encourage students not to get frustrated or overwhelmed. The next lesson is a review lesson.

FOCUS

TIME MANAGEMENT 

Suggested Schedule:

Warmup	3′
Skillbuilding	47′
Total	**50′**

TEACH

SKILLBUILDING

LESSON 15-B Speed sprints are very motivational. Have students push moderately for speed on these easy sentences.

LESSON 15-C Observe students to be sure they are not removing their entire hand from the home position to reach the TAB key.

LESSON 15-D Observe to see that students are using correct technique for the SHIFT key.

Review

Goal

- Type at least 23wpm/2′/5e

A. Type 2 times.

A. WARMUP

```
     Jeffrey Mendoza quickly plowed six fields so     9
that he could plant 19 rows of beets, 28 rows of     19
corn, 37 rows of grapes, and 45 rows of olives.      28
 | 1 | 2 | 3 | 4 | 5 | 6 | 7 | 8 | 9 | 10
```

SKILLBUILDING

B. Take three 12-second timed writings on each line. The scale below the last line shows your wpm speed for a 12-second timed writing.

B. 12-SECOND SPEED SPRINTS

```
The lane to the lake might make the auto go away.
They go to the lake by bus when they work for me.
He just won and lost, won and lost, won and lost.
The man and the girl rush down the paths to town.
    5    10    15    20    25    30    35    40    45    50
```

C. Press TAB 1 time between columns. Type 2 times.

C. TECHNIQUE PRACTICE: TAB KEY

aisle Tab→	break Tab→	crank Tab→	draft Tab→	earth
Frank	Guinn	Henry	Ivan	Jacob
knack	learn	mason	night	ocean
print	quest	rinse	slide	title
Umberto	Victor	Wally	Xavier	Zenger

D. Type each line 2 times. Try not to slow down for the capital letters.

D. TECHNIQUE PRACTICE: SHIFT KEY

```
Sue, Pat, Ann, and Gail left for Rome on June 10.
The St. Louis Cardinals and New York Mets played.
Dave Herr took Flight 481 for Memphis and Toledo.
An address for Karen Cook is 5 Bar Street, Provo.
Harry Truman was born in Missouri on May 8, 1884.
```


ERGONOMICALLY SPEAKING

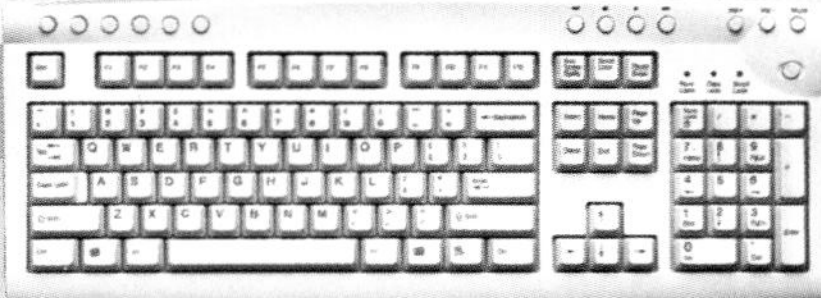

KEYBOARD TRAY An adjustable keyboard tray may be useful if a student cannot adjust the chair or work surface to an appropriate height for typing. The tray should adjust in height from 25 to 30 inches (64 to 76 centimeters) above the floor and tilt forward and backward to help locate the most comfortable position. Visit us on the Web at **www.mhhe.com/gdp** for more information.

E. Type each line 2 times.

E. PUNCTUATION PRACTICE: HYPHEN

```
Jan Brooks-Smith was a go-between for the author.
The off-the-record comment led to a free-for-all.
Louis was a jack-of-all-trades as a clerk-typist.
Ask Barbara--who is in Central Data--to find out.
Joanne is too old-fashioned to be that outspoken.
```

PPP PRETEST → PRACTICE → POSTTEST

PRETEST
Take a 1-minute timed writing. Review your speed and errors.

F. PRETEST: Vertical Reaches

```
     A few of our business managers attribute the    9
success of the bank to a judicious and scientific   19
reserve program. The bank cannot drop its guard.    29
|  1  |  2  |  3  |  4  |  5  |  6  |  7  |  8  |  9  |  10
```

PRACTICE
Speed Emphasis:
If you made 2 or fewer errors on the Pretest, type each *individual line* 2 times.
Accuracy Emphasis:
If you made 3 or more errors, type each *group* of lines (as though it were a paragraph) 2 times.

G. PRACTICE: Up Reaches

```
at atlas plate water later batch fatal match late
dr draft drift drums drawn drain drama dress drab
ju jumpy juror junky jumbo julep judge juice just
```

H. PRACTICE: Down Reaches

```
ca cable cabin cadet camel cameo candy carve cash
nk trunk drink prank rinks brink drank crank sink
ba batch badge bagel baked banjo barge basis bank
```

POSTTEST
Repeat the Pretest timed writing and compare performance.

I. POSTTEST: Vertical Reaches

J. PROGRESSIVE PRACTICE: ALPHABET

If you are not using the GDP software, turn to page SB-7 and follow the directions for this activity.

K. Take two 2-minute timed writings. Review your speed and errors.

Goal: At least 23wpm/2′/5e

K. 2-MINUTE TIMED WRITING

```
     Jeff Malvey was quite busy fixing all of the    9
frozen pipes so that his water supply would not     19
be stopped. Last winter Jeff kept the pipes from    29
freezing by wrapping them with an insulated tape    38
that protected them from snow and ice.              46
|  1  |  2  |  3  |  4  |  5  |  6  |  7  |  8  |  9  |  10
```


Lesson 15

TEACH

SKILLBUILDING

LESSON 15-E Remind students to differentiate between a hyphen and a dash.

PRETEST → PRACTICE → POSTTEST

PPP The Pretest/Practice/Posttest (PPP) routine is designed to build speed and accuracy through a three-step program:

15-F The Pretest is the preliminary effort to determine the learner's initial skill level. Vertical reaches include up and down reaches. Up reaches go from the home row to the upper row and back to the home row. Down reaches go from the home row to the lower row and back to the home row.

15-G AND 15-H The Practice section consists of intensive drills to improve the reaches focused on in the Pretest.

15-I The Posttest measures the effect of the Practice.

LESSON 15-J Students take repeated timed writings to reach a speed goal with no errors.

ASSESS

TECHNIQUE EVALUATION FORM Observe the students' technique.

CLOSE

It is important for students to do additional practice if they are not confident with reaches.

INSTRUCTOR STRATEGIES

Skillbuilding: PPP Explain the purpose of the Pretest—to evaluate speed and accuracy for vertical reaches. Exercises 15-G and 15-H provide practice on up and down reaches. Review, if necessary, correct technique for typing difficult reaches—q, z, w, x, t, b, y, n, p, comma, and period. A Posttest follows to check progress on typing vertical reaches.

MHHE CHAMPIONS

MINNESOTA

Feedback

Give students immediate feedback by checking their work at the computer screen with them.

Darlinda Alexander
Hennepin Technical College
Brooklyn Park, Minnesota

Instructors Helping One Another

UNIT OVERVIEW

Students learn to touch-type symbol keys. Diagnostic practices and skillbuilding exercises reinforce touch-typing alphabetic, number, and symbol keys. The last lesson in the unit reviews and reinforces the alphabetic, number, and symbol keys taught in the unit.

Did You Know?

All timed writing passages in Lessons 1–60 have a syllabic intensity (SI) of 1.30 to 1.40. Syllabic intensity is determined by dividing the number of syllables in a passage by the number of actual words in that passage.

www.mhhe.com/gdp to download a copy of the Technique Evaluation Form.

TECHNIQUE EVALUATION FORM

Walk around the room to observe the students' technique.

Name ______ Class ______ Date ______

Technique Evaluation Form

Date	Workstation		Position at the Keyboard		Keystroking	
	Acceptable	Needs Improvement	Acceptable	Needs Improvement	Acceptable	Needs Improvement

Workstation

1. Positions the chair so that the upper and lower legs form a 90-degree angle and the lower back is supported.
2. Positions the keyboard even with the front of the desk.
3. Positions the text on either side of the monitor as close to it vertically and horizontally as possible to minimize head and eye movement and to avoid neck strain.
4. Positions the mouse on a pad at the side of the monitor opposite the text.

Position at the Keyboard

5. Centers the body opposite the keyboard.
6. Leans forward slightly from the hips, with the base of the spine touching the back of the chair and the feet flat on the floor.
7. Keeps the elbows alongside the body in a relaxed position.
8. Curves the fingers naturally over the home position, with the back of the hand at the same angle as the keyboard.

Keystroking

9. Keeps the forearms horizontal and raises the hands slightly when typing so that the wrists do not touch the keyboard while typing. (Hands may rest at the bottom of the keyboard—away from the keys—during nontyping intervals.)
10. Makes quick, snappy strokes using the correct fingers.
11. Returns the finger immediately to the home position or moves to the next position after each stroke.
12. Operates all keys by touch, keeping the eyes on the copy most of the time while typing.

Comments

Unit 4

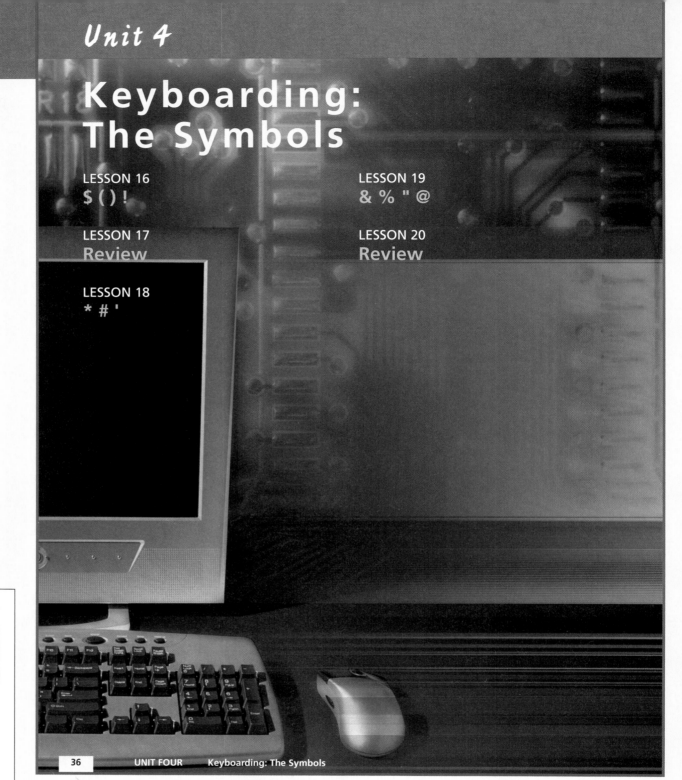

Keyboarding: The Symbols

RESOURCE MANAGER

GDP SOFTWARE

- Lessons 16–20
- Software User's Guide
- Instructor Management LAN Version
- Professional Handbook (IWE*)—Teaching in a Distance-Learning Environment
- MAP

ASSESSMENT

- Test and Solution Keys—Objective Test Part 1 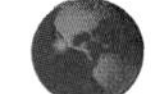
- Professional Handbook (IWE*)—Assessment Strategies

ON THE WEB

- **www.mhhe.com/gdp**
- Instructor Management Web Version

*Instructor Wraparound Edition

Symbol Keys

Goals

- Touch-type the $ ( ) and ! keys
- Type at least 24wpm/2′/5e

A. Type 2 times.

A. WARMUP

```
1      Gill was quite vexed by that musician who      9
2  played 5 jazz songs and 13 country songs at the   18
3  fair. He wanted 8 rock songs and 4 blues songs.   28
   | 1 | 2 | 3 | 4 | 5 | 6 | 7 | 8 | 9 | 10
```

NEW KEYS

B. DOLLAR is the shift of 4. Do not space between the dollar sign and the number. Type each line 2 times.

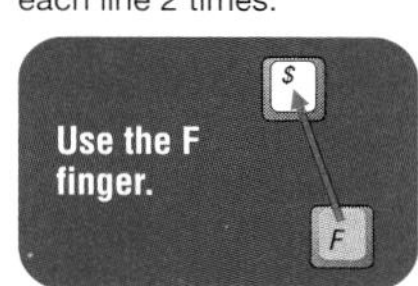

B. THE $ KEY

```
4  frf fr4f f4f f4$f f$$f f$$f $44 $444 $4,444 $4.44
5  I quoted $48, $64, and $94 for the set of chairs.
6  Her insurance paid $150; our insurance paid $175.
7  Season concert seats were $25, $30, $55, and $75.
```

C. PARENTHESES are the shifts of 9 and 0. Do not space between the parentheses and the text within them. Type each line 2 times.

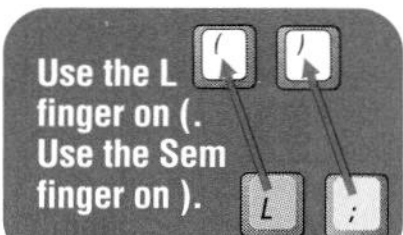

Use the L finger on (.
Use the Sem finger on).

C. THE (AND) KEYS

```
8  lo91 lo91 lo(1 lo(1 l((1 ;p0; ;p0; ;p); ;p); ;));
9  Please ask (1) Al, (2) Pat, (3) Ted, and (4) Dee.
10 Sue has some (1) skis, (2) sleds, and (3) skates.
11 Mary is (1) prompt, (2) speedy, and (3) accurate.

12 Our workers (Lewis, Jerry, and Ty) were rewarded.
13 The owner (Ms. Parks) went on Friday (August 18).
14 The Roxie (a cafe) had fish (salmon) on the menu.
15 The clerk (Ms. Fay Green) will vote yes (not no).
```


Windows Wizard

SELECTING MULTIPLE FILES You can select multiple files or folders to copy, move, or delete in Windows 2000, Me, or XP.

- To select nonadjacent files or folders: Press and hold CTRL and click each file or folder.
- To select adjacent files or folders: Click to select the first file.

  Press and hold SHIFT and click the last file.
- To select all files or folders: Press CTRL + A or choose **Select All** from the **Edit** menu.

FOCUS

TIME MANAGEMENT

Suggested Schedule:

Warmup	3′
New Keys	22′
Skillbuilding	25′
Total	**50′**

TEACH

NEW KEYS

Stress the importance of good position:

- Center the body opposite the keyboard.
- Lean forward slightly from the hips.
- Keep feet flat on the floor.
- Keep elbows alongside the body.
- Curve fingers naturally over the home position.

LESSON 16-B Emphasize keeping eyes on the copy when typing symbols.

LESSON 16-C Remind students to keep the J finger in the home position as they reach for the (and) keys. Also, remind students to keep elbows alongside the body and to curve the fingers.

Lesson 16

TEACH

NEW KEYS

LESSON 16-D Remind students to keep the F finger in the home position as they reach for the ! key.

SKILLBUILDING

LESSON 16-E Press and release the SPACE BAR quickly.

LESSON 16-F Speed sprints are very motivational. Have students push moderately for speed on these easy sentences.

LESSON 16-G Paced Practice helps students reach individual skill goals in 2-wpm increments by pacing them as they strive for a slightly faster rate.

ASSESS

www.mhhe.com/gdp to download a copy of the Technique Evaluation Form.

TECHNIQUE EVALUATION FORM Walk around the room to observe the students' technique.

Print the lesson or review the practice lines on the monitor.

Review results of timed writings.

Extending the Lesson

If time permits, have students repeat the following exercises for additional practice.

Exercise 16-B (Dollar)
Exercise 16-C (Parentheses)

CLOSE

Continue to praise students for their hard work, and encourage them to continue practicing.

D. THE ! KEY

D. EXCLAMATION is the shift of 1. Space 1 time after an exclamation point at the end of a sentence. Type each line 2 times.

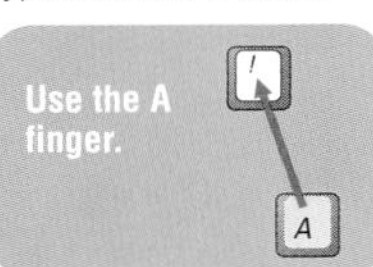


```
aqa aqla aq!a a!!a a!!a Where! Whose! What! When!
Put those down! Do not move them! Leave it there!
He did say that! Jake cannot take a vacation now!
You cannot leave at this time! Janie will go now!
```

SKILLBUILDING

E. TECHNIQUE PRACTICE: SPACE BAR

E. Type the paragraph 2 times.

```
     We will all go to the race if I win the one
I am going to run today. Do you think I will be
able to run at the front of the pack and win it?
```

F. 12-SECOND SPEED SPRINTS

F. Take three 12-second timed writings on each line. The scale below the last line shows your wpm speed for a 12-second timed writing.

```
Walking can perk you up if you are feeling tired.
Your heart and lungs can work harder as you walk.
It may be that a walk is often better than a nap.
If you walk each day, you may have better health.
    5    10    15    20    25    30    35    40    45    50
```

G. PACED PRACTICE

If you are not using the GDP software, turn to page SB-14 and follow the directions for this activity.

H. 2-MINUTE TIMED WRITING

H. Take two 2-minute timed writings. Review your speed and errors.

Goal: At least 24wpm/2'/5e

```
     Katie quit her zoo job seven days after she       9
learned that she was expected to travel to four       19
different zoos in the first month of employment.      28
After quitting that job, she found an excellent       38
position which did not require her to travel much.    48
  1    2    3    4    5    6    7    8    9    10
```

GDP SOFTWARE TIPS

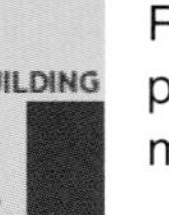

Paced Practice

Review the strategy to achieve good pacing by discussing how to use pacing markers.

Technique Tips

The animated technique tips appear every 15 minutes in GDP or when students reach a new instruction screen.

Encourage a quick discussion emphasizing good technique by asking students to see how many of the techniques they can recall accessing in GDP.

Review

Goal

- Type at least 25wpm/2′/5e

A. Type 2 times.

A. WARMUP

1 Yes! We object to the dumping of 25 toxic 9
2 barrels at 4098 Nix Street. A larger number (36) 19
3 were dumped on the 7th, costing us over $10,000. 28

| 1 | 2 | 3 | 4 | 5 | 6 | 7 | 8 | 9 | 10

SKILLBUILDING

B. Type each line 2 times.

B. NUMBER PRACTICE

4 we 23 pi 08 you 697 row 492 tire 5843 power 09234
5 or 94 re 43 eye 363 top 590 quit 1785 witty 28556
6 up 70 ye 63 pit 085 per 034 root 4995 wrote 24953
7 it 85 ro 49 rip 480 two 529 tour 5974 quite 17853
8 yi 68 to 59 toy 596 rot 495 tier 5834 queue 17373
9 op 90 qo 19 wet 235 pet 035 rope 4903 quote 17953

C. Type each line 2 times.

C. WORD BEGINNINGS

10 tri trinkets tribune trifle trick trial trip trim
11 mil million mileage mildew mills milky miles mild
12 spo sponsor sponge sports spore spoon spool spoke
13 for forgiving forbear forward forbid forced force

14 div dividend division divine divide diving divers
15 vic vicinity vicious victory victims victor vices
16 aff affliction affiliates affirms affords affairs
17 tab tablecloth tabulates tableau tabloids tablets

D. Type each line 2 times.

D. WORD ENDINGS

18 ive repulsive explosive alive drive active strive
19 est nearest invest attest wisest nicest jest test
20 ply supply simply deeply damply apply imply reply
21 ver whenever forever whoever quiver waiver driver

Lesson 17

FOCUS

TIME MANAGEMENT

Suggested Schedule:

Warmup	3′
Skillbuilding	47′
Total	**50′**

TEACH

SKILLBUILDING

LESSON 17-B Tell students that the reaches they make to the top row of letters are the same reaches they will make to the number row as they type the combinations of letters and numbers. For example, the same fingers are used to type the letters w and e and the numbers 2 and 3.

Remind students to keep eyes on copy.

Consider assigning additional practice for students who have had previous typing experience.

- Students typing 15wpm or fewer type each line 2 times.
- Students typing 16–25wpm type each line 3 times.
- Students typing over 25wpm type each line 4 times.

INSTRUCTOR STRATEGIES

Progressive Practice Students will begin at the point where they finished in Lesson 15. Each passage contains the exact number of words required to meet the speed goal. Remind students that the 30-second timed writing must be completed without errors.

Diagnostic Practice: Numbers This skillbuilding exercise will identify number keys causing difficulty. Students will type a paragraph that will be scored, and misstrokes will be identified.

- For each number with 2 or more errors, type the drill line 2 times.
- For each number with 1 error, type the drill line 1 time.
- If no errors were made, type one group of drill lines that includes all numbers.

Lesson 17

TEACH

SKILLBUILDING

LESSON 17-E Students take repeated timings on a passage containing the exact number of words for their speed goal until they can complete it with no errors. Then they move to the next-higher passage and start again.

LESSON 17-G Encourage students to push moderately for speed on the Pretest. Remind students to press the Forward arrow—this is not a timed exercise.

ASSESS

www.mhhe.com/gdp to download a copy of the Technique Evaluation Form.

TECHNIQUE EVALUATION FORM Walk around the room to observe the students technique. Complete a Technique Evaluation Form for each student.

Print the lesson or review the practice lines on the monitor.

Review results of timed writings.

Extending the Lesson

Ask students to compare skillbuilding in keyboarding with football practice, basketball practice, or other activities requiring hard work to be successful.

CLOSE

Encourage students to practice skillbuilding every day.

```
tor inventor detector debtor orator doctor factor
lly industrially logically legally ideally really
ert convert dessert expert invert diverts asserts
ink shrink drink think blink clink pink sink rink
```

E. PROGRESSIVE PRACTICE: ALPHABET

If you are not using the GDP software, turn to page SB-7 and follow the directions for this activity.

F. HANDWRITTEN PARAGRAPH

F. Take two 1-minute timed writings. Review your speed and errors.

In this book you have learned the reaches 9
for all alphabetic and number keys. You have 18
also learned a few of the symbol keys. In the 27
remaining lessons you will learn the other 36
symbol keys. You will also build your speed 45
and accuracy when typing. 50

| 1 | 2 | 3 | 4 | 5 | 6 | 7 | 8 | 9 | 10

G. DIAGNOSTIC PRACTICE: NUMBERS

If you are not using the GDP software, turn to page SB-5 and follow the directions for this activity.

H. 2-MINUTE TIMED WRITING

H. Take two 2-minute timed writings. Review your speed and errors.

Goal: At least 25wpm/2'/5e

```
     From the tower John saw that those six big     9
planes could crash as they zoomed quickly over     18
treetops on their way to the demonstration that    28
was scheduled to begin very soon. We hope there    37
is no accident and that the pilots reach their     47
airports safely.                                   50
  | 1 | 2 | 3 | 4 | 5 | 6 | 7 | 8 | 9 | 10
```

Strategies for Career Success

Goodwill Messages

Would you like to strengthen your relationship with a customer, coworker, or boss? Send an unexpected goodwill message! Your expression of goodwill has a positive effect on business relationships.

Messages of congratulations or appreciation provide special opportunities to express goodwill. These messages can be quite brief. If your handwriting is good, send a handwritten note on a professional note card. Otherwise, send a letter or e-mail.

A note of congratulations might be "I just heard the news about your (award, promotion, etc.). My very best wishes." An appreciation note could be "Thank you for referring me to. . . . Your confidence and trust are sincerely appreciated."

YOUR TURN Send a goodwill message to someone to express congratulations or appreciation.

Strategies for Career Success

GOODWILL MESSAGES A letter or note expressing praise or thanks can help an employee take on an active part in the workplace community. Supporting one another is what friends and teammates do; it demonstrates membership. At the least, reading a goodwill message will make the recipient associate the sender's name with a positive feeling. At best, who knows—sending a sincere goodwill message at the right time may mean being suggested for a plum assignment. Ask your students for examples of goodwill messages they have received or written.

Symbol Keys

Goals

- Touch-type * # and ' keys
- Type at least 26wpm/2′/5e

A. Type 2 times.

A. WARMUP

1 Bill Waxmann quickly moved all 35 packs of 9
2 gear for the Amazon trip (worth $987) 26 miles 18
3 into the jungle. The move took 14 days in all. 27

| 1 | 2 | 3 | 4 | 5 | 6 | 7 | 8 | 9 | 10

NEW KEYS

B. Asterisk is the shift of 8. Type each line 2 times.

Use the K finger.
K

B. THE * KEY

4 kik ki8k k8*k k8*k k**k k**k This book* is great.
5 Use an * to show that a table source is included.
6 Asterisks keyed in a row (*******) make a border.
7 The article quoted Hanson,* Pyle,* and Peterson.*

C. Number (if before a figure) or Pounds (if after a figure) is the shift of 3. Type each line 2 times.

Use the D finger.
D

C. THE # KEY

8 de3d de3#d d3#d d3#d d##d d##d #3 #33 #333 #3,333
9 Al wants 33# of #200 and 38# of #400 by Saturday.
10 My favorite seats are #2, #34, #56, #65, and #66.
11 Please order 45# of #245 and 13# of #24 tomorrow.

INSTRUCTOR STRATEGIES

Asterisks
When students reach the screen for practicing lines 4–7, you may want to first practice the asterisk * key reach with them:

- Have students reach for the asterisk and return to the home row while looking at the keyboard but without typing.
- Dictate "*k8*k, space, k8*k, space*," and so on as students type from dictation without looking at their keyboard.
- Have students check their work, then practice dictating until students are comfortable with the reach.
- You might also want to do practice reaches for Exercise C.

Lesson 18

FOCUS

TIME MANAGEMENT
Suggested Schedule:

Warmup	3′
New Keys	15′
Skillbuilding	32′
Total	**50′**

TEACH

NEW KEYS

Continue to emphasize the importance of operating all keys by touch-typing and of keeping eyes on the copy.

LESSON 18-B Asterisks are used to do the following:

- Refer the reader to a footnote at the bottom of a page or table.
- Replace words that are considered unprintable.

Students must hold down the Shift key until the symbol reach is completed.

LESSON 18-C Explain that there is no space between the figure and the symbol.

Lesson 18

TEACH

NEW KEYS

LESSON 18-D The apostrophe is used in contractions and to show possession. There is no space before or after an apostrophe unless it is at the end of a word within a sentence; for example, *ladies*' coats.

SKILLBUILDING

LESSON 18-E Paced Practice helps students reach individual speed and accuracy goals in 2-wpm increments by pacing them as they strive for a slightly faster rate.

LESSON 18-F Students should select a different paragraph for the Pretest. Encourage students to push moderately for speed on the Pretest.

ASSESS

www.mhhe.com/gdp to download a copy of the Technique Evaluation Form.

TECHNIQUE EVALUATION FORM Walk around the room to observe the students' technique.

Review results of timed writings.

Extending the Lesson

Ask students if they have used the asterisk, number sign, or apostrophe in their writing. List examples.

CLOSE

If time permits, have students repeat the following exercises for additional practice: 18-B, 18-C, and 18-D.

D. APOSTROPHE is to the right of the semicolon. Type each line 2 times.

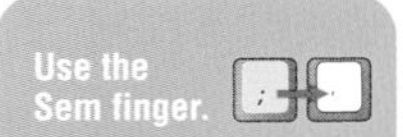

D. THE ' KEY

```
;'; ';' ;'; ';' Can't we go in Sue's or Al's car?
It's Bob's job to cover Ted's work when he's out.
What's in Joann's lunch box for Sandra's dessert?
He's gone to Ty's banquet, which is held at Al's.
```

SKILLBUILDING

E. PACED PRACTICE

If you are not using the GDP software, turn to page SB-14 and follow the directions for this activity.

F. PROGRESSIVE PRACTICE: NUMBERS

If you are not using the GDP software, turn to page SB-11 and follow the directions for this activity.

G. HANDWRITTEN PARAGRAPH

G. Take two 1-minute timed writings. Review your speed and errors.

You have completed the first segment of 8
your class. You have learned to type all of 17
the alphabetic keys, the number keys, and some 26
of the symbol keys. Next you will learn the 35
remaining symbol keys on the top row. 42

| 1 | 2 | 3 | 4 | 5 | 6 | 7 | 8 | 9 | 10

H. 2-MINUTE TIMED WRITING

H. Take two 2-minute timed writings. Review your speed and errors.

Goal: At least 26wpm/2'/5e

```
     Max had to make one quick adjustment to his        9
television set before the football game began.         18
The picture during the last game was fuzzy and          28
hard to see. If he cannot fix the picture, he may       38
have to purchase a new television set; and that         47
may be difficult to do.                                 52
  | 1 | 2 | 3 | 4 | 5 | 6 | 7 | 8 | 9 | 10
```

SOFTWARE TIPS

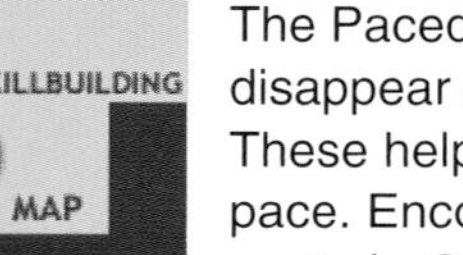

Paced Practice

The Paced Practice pacing markers disappear at 15-second increments. These help students type at the proper pace. Encourage students to type with control—2 or fewer errors.

Progressive Practice: Numbers

The Numbers Progressive Practice activities are used to evaluate students' weaknesses on numeric keys. GDP then provides exercises to help students maintain an expected words per minute goal with no errors.

Symbol Keys

Goals

- Touch-type & % " and @ keys
- Type at least 27wpm/2′/5e

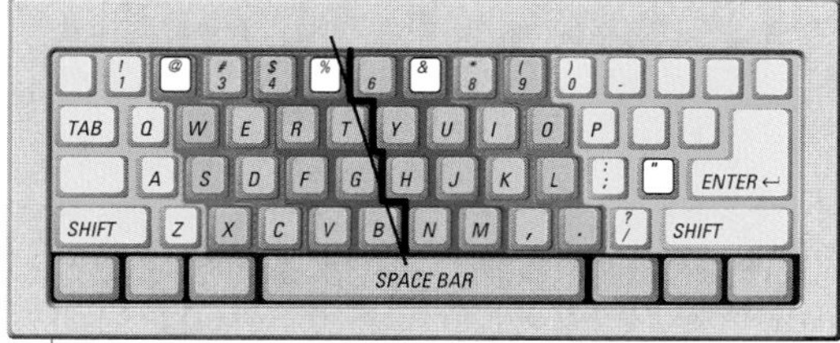

A. Type 2 times.

A. WARMUP

```
     The teacher (James Quayle) gave us some work    9
to do for homework for 11-28-05. Chapters 3 and 4   19
from our text* are to be read for a hard quiz.      28
|  1  |  2  |  3  |  4  |  5  |  6  |  7  |  8  |  9  |  10
```

NEW KEYS

B. Ampersand (sign for *and*) is the shift of 7. Space before and after the ampersand. Type each line 2 times.

B. THE & KEY

```
juj ju7j j7j j7&j j&&j j&&j Max & Dee & Sue & Ken
Brown & Sons shipped goods to Crum & Lee Company.
Johnson & Loo brought a case against May & Green.
Ball & Trump vs. Vens & See is being decided now.
```

C. Percent is the shift of 5. Do not space between the number and the percent sign. Type each line 2 times.

C. THE % KEY

```
ft5f ft5%f f5%f f5%f f%%f f%%f 5% 55% 555% 5,555%
Robert quoted rates of 8%, 9%, 10%, 11%, and 12%.
Pat scored 82%, Jan 89%, and Ken 90% on the test.
Only 55% of the students passed 75% of the exams.
```


INSTRUCTOR STRATEGIES

Symbols To provide additional practice on the symbols presented in this lesson, have students repeat the following exercises: 19-B, 19-C, 19-D, and 19-E.

Lesson 19

FOCUS

TIME MANAGEMENT

Suggested Schedule:

Warmup	3′
New Keys	15′
Formatting	5′
Skillbuilding	27′
Total	**50′**

TEACH

NEW KEYS

Stress the importance of good position:

- Center the body opposite the keyboard.
- Lean forward slightly from the hips.
- Keep feet flat on the floor.
- Keep elbows alongside the body.
- Curve fingers naturally over the home position.

LESSON 19-B Remind students to keep the Sem finger in the home position as they reach for the ampersand. Also remind students to keep the F finger in the home position as they reach for the Shift.

LESSON 19-C Remind students to keep the A finger in the home position as they reach for the percent symbol. Also remind students to keep the J finger in the home position as they reach for the Shift.

Lesson 19

TEACH

NEW KEYS

LESSON 19-D Remind students not to remove their hands from the home position to reach for the SHIFT and the quotation symbol.

LESSON 19-E Observe that students use correct technique as they reach for the At symbol (@).

FORMATTING

LESSON 19-F Review the application of these rules in lines 20–23 for placing quotation marks before students begin typing.

D. QUOTATION is the shift of the apostrophe. Do not space between quotation marks and the text they enclose. Type each line 2 times.

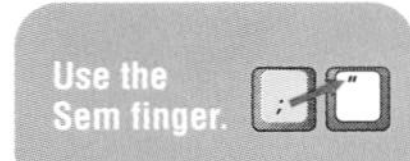

D. THE " KEY

```
12 ;'; ";" ;"; ";" "That's a super job," said Mabel.
13 The theme of the meeting is "Improving Your Job."
14 John said, "Those were good." Sharon said, "Yes."
15 Allison said, "I'll take Janice and Ed to Flint."
```

E. AT is the shift of 2. Space before and after @ except when used in an e-mail address. Type each line 2 times.

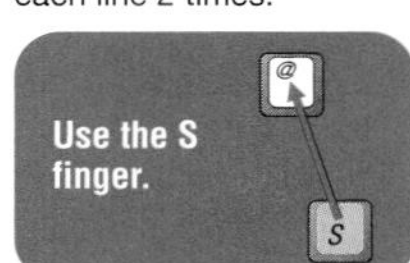

E. THE @ KEY

```
16 sws sw2s s2@s s2@s s@@s s@@s Buy 15 @ $5 in June.
17 He can e-mail us at this address: projec@edu.com.
18 Order 12 items @ $14 and another 185 items @ $16.
19 Lee said, "I'll buy 8 shares @ $6 and 5 @ $7.55."
```

FORMATTING

F. Read these rules about the placement of quotation marks. Then type lines 20-23 two times.

F. PLACEMENT OF QUOTATION MARKS

1. The closing quotation mark is always typed *after* a period or comma but *before* a colon or semicolon.
2. The closing quotation mark is typed *after* a question mark or exclamation point if the quoted material itself is a question or an exclamation; otherwise, the quotation mark is typed *before* the question mark or exclamation point.

```
20 "Hello," I said. "My name is Hal; I am new here."
21 Zack read the article "Can She Succeed Tomorrow?"
22 James said, "I'll mail the check"; but he didn't.
23 Did Amy say, "We lost"? She said, "I don't know."
```


Meeting Special Needs

LEARNING-DISABLED STUDENTS Learning-disabled (LD) students often have difficulty completing tests in a specified time limit, accurately reading test questions, and writing test answers. Try alternatives when working with LD students. Extend time limits for test taking. Permit test questions and answers in different formats (audiotapes, orally, and so on). Allow take-home tests. Visit us on the Web at **www.mhhe.com/gdp** for more information.

G. Type each line 2 times.

G. ALPHABET AND SYMBOL PRACTICE

```
Gaze at views of my jonquil or red phlox in back.
Jan quickly moved the six dozen big pink flowers.
Joe quietly picked six razors from the woven bag.
Packing jam for the dozen boxes was quite lively.

Mail these "Rush": #38, #45, and #67 (software).
No! Joe's note did not carry a rate of under 9%.
Lee read "The Computer Today." It's here Monday.
The book* cost us $48.10, 12% higher than yours.
```

H. Take a 1-minute timed writing on the first paragraph to establish your base speed. Then take four 1-minute timed writings on the remaining paragraphs. As soon as you equal or exceed your base speed on one paragraph, advance to the next, more difficult paragraph.

H. SUSTAINED PRACTICE: NUMBERS AND SYMBOLS

```
     We purchased several pieces of new computer      9
equipment for our new store in Boston. We were       19
amazed at all the extra work we could get done.      28

     For our department, we received 5 printers,      9
12 computers, and 3 fax machines. We heard that      19
the equipment cost us several thousand dollars.      28

     Next week 6 computers (Model ZS86), 4 old        9
copiers (drums are broken), and 9 shredders will     18
need to be replaced. Total cost will be high.        28

     Last year $150,890 was spent on equipment        9
for Iowa's offices. Breaman & Sims predicted a       18
17% to 20% increase (*over '99); that's amazing.     28
| 1 | 2 | 3 | 4 | 5 | 6 | 7 | 8 | 9 | 10
```

I. Take two 2-minute timed writings. Review your speed and errors.

Goal: At least 27wpm/2′/5e

I. 2-MINUTE TIMED WRITING

```
     Topaz and onyx rings were for sale at a very     9
reasonable price last week. When Jeanette saw the    19
rings with these stones, she quickly bought them     29
both for her sons. These jewels were difficult to    39
find, and Jeanette was pleased she could purchase    49
those rings when she did.                            54
| 1 | 2 | 3 | 4 | 5 | 6 | 7 | 8 | 9 | 10
```


Lesson 19

TEACH

SKILLBUILDING

LESSON 19-H Each paragraph is more difficult than the preceding one—based on the number of figures and symbols in each paragraph.

Paragraph 1: 0
Paragraph 2: 4
Paragraph 3: 7
Paragraph 4: 19

LESSON 19-I Review student timed writings, and check accuracy and speed levels.

ASSESS

www.mhhe.com/gdp to download a copy of the Technique Evaluation Form.

TECHNIQUE EVALUATION FORM Walk around the room to observe the students' technique. Complete a Technique Evaluation Form for each student.

Print the lesson or review the practice lines on the monitor.

Review results of timed writings.

Extending the Lesson

Ask students to list the names of some companies that use the ampersand in their name. Type the company names for additional practice.

CLOSE

This lesson concludes learning the keyboard.

GDP SOFTWARE TIPS

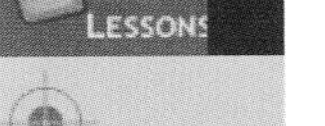

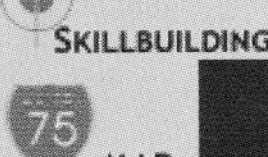

MAP

Sustained Practice

Explain the Sustained Practice exercise to students. The students will be expected to complete a 1-minute timed writing on the first of four paragraphs with three or fewer errors to establish a base speed. Remind students that they must equal or exceed the base speed (first paragraph timed writing) before they can continue to the next paragraph. If students do not meet their base score after three tries, a dialog box is displayed, indicating that the exercise is over.

GAMES

Lesson 20

FOCUS

TIME MANAGEMENT 

Suggested Schedule:

Warmup	3′
Skillbuilding	47′
Total	**50′**

TEACH

SKILLBUILDING

LESSON 20-B Review the required spacing before and after punctuation marks before students type this exercise.

PRETEST→PRACTICE→POSTTEST

PPP The Pretest/ Practice/Posttest (PPP) routine is designed to build speed and accuracy through a three-step program:

20-C The Pretest is the preliminary effort to determine the learner's initial skill level. This Pretest evaluates speed and accuracy for alternate- and one-hand words.

20-D AND 20-E The Practice section consists of intensive drills to improve the reaches focused on in the Pretest.

20-F The Posttest measures the effect of the Practice.

Review

Goal

- Type at least 28wpm/2′/5e

A. Type 2 times.

A. WARMUP

```
     Vin went to see Exhibits #794 and #860. He        9
had quickly judged these zany projects that cost      19
$321 (parts & labor)--a 5% markup from last year.     29
  | 1 | 2 | 3 | 4 | 5 | 6 | 7 | 8 | 9 | 10
```

SKILLBUILDING

B. Type each line 2 times.

B. PUNCTUATION PRACTICE

```
period             Go to Reno. Drive to Yuma. Call Mary. Get Samuel.
comma              We saw Nice, Paris, Bern, Rome, Munich, and Bonn.
semicolon          Type the memo; read reports. Get pens; get paper.
colon, hyphen      Read the following pages: 1-10, 12-22, and 34-58.
exclamation point  No! Stop! Don't look! Watch out! Move over! Jump!

question mark      Can you wait? Why not? Can he drive? Where is it?
colon, apostrophe  I have these reports: Susan's, Bill's, and Lou's.
dash               It's the best--and cheapest! Don't lose it--ever.
quotation marks    "I can," she said, "right now." Val said, "Wait!"
parentheses        Quint called Rome (GA), Rome (NY), and Rome (WI).
```

PPP PRETEST → PRACTICE → POSTTEST

PRETEST
Take a 1-minute timed writing. Review your speed and errors.

C. PRETEST: Alternate- and One-Hand Words

```
     The chairman should handle the tax problem        9
downtown. If they are reversed, pressure tactics      19
might have changed the case as it was discussed.      28
  | 1 | 2 | 3 | 4 | 5 | 6 | 7 | 8 | 9 | 10
```


TEACHING THE ADULT LEARNER

EXPECTATION Adult learners today are likely to view themselves as consumers of a product rather than seekers of knowledge. They tend to expect well-planned and well-prepared course goals and objectives. They are likely to be more self-directed than younger students. They generally know what they want and where they want to go.

Prepare a course syllabus that includes an outline of the course requirements. Give a syllabus to each student. Review your expectations with the students.

PRACTICE
Speed Emphasis: If you made 2 or fewer errors on the Pretest, type each *individual* line 2 times.
Accuracy Emphasis: If you made 3 or fewer errors, type each *group* of lines (as though it were a paragraph) 2 times.

D. PRACTICE: Alternate-Hand Words

```
the with girl right blame handle antique chairman
for wish town their panel formal problem downtown
pan busy they flair signs thrown signals problems
```

E. PRACTICE: One-Hand Words

```
lip fact yolk poplin yummy affect reverse pumpkin
you cast kill uphill jumpy grease wagered opinion
tea cage lump limply hilly served bravest minimum
```

POSTTEST
Repeat the Pretest timed writing and compare performance.

F. POSTTEST: Alternate- and One-Hand Words

G. Take three 12-second timed writings on each line. The scale below the last line shows your wpm speed for a 12-second timed writing.

G. 12-SECOND SPEED SPRINTS

```
Paul likes to work for the bank while in college.
They will make a nice profit if the work is done.
The group of friends went to a movie at the mall.
The man sent the forms after she called for them.
    5    10    15    20    25    30    35    40    45    50
```

H. Take two 1-minute timed writings. Review your speed and errors.

H. HANDWRITTEN PARAGRAPH

In your career, you will use the 7
skills you are learning in this course. 15
However, you will soon discover that you 23
must also possess human relations skills. 31

I. MAP

Follow the GDP software directions for this exercise in improving keystroking accuracy.

J. DIAGNOSTIC PRACTICE: NUMBERS

If you are not using the GDP software, turn to page SB-5 and follow the directions for this activity.

K. Take two 2-minute timed writings. Review your speed and errors.

Goal: At least 28wpm/2'/5e

K. 2-MINUTE TIMED WRITING

```
     Jake or Peggy Zale must quickly fix the fax      9
machine so that we can have access to regional       18
reports that we think might be sent within the       28
next few days. Without the fax, we will not be       37
able to complete all our monthly reports by the      47
deadlines. Please let me know of any problems.       56
|  1  |  2  |  3  |  4  |  5  |  6  |  7  |  8  |  9  |  10
```


TEACH

SKILLBUILDING

LESSON 20-I MAP is a simple, comprehensive, and individualized software program for improving keystroking accuracy.

ASSESS

www.mhhe.com/gdp to download a copy of the Technique Evaluation Form.

TECHNIQUE EVALUATION FORM

Walk around the room to observe the students' technique. Complete a Technique Evaluation Form for each student.

Print a report for all skillbuilding exercises for Lessons 16–20.

Extending the Lesson

Provide time for students to play the tennis game available from the GDP software to reinforce their knowledge of the keyboard.

CLOSE

Remind students that all keys have been presented. Encourage students to repeat exercises in previous lessons to develop confidence in their typing.

MAP 75

Map

In this lesson, an exciting feature, Misstroke Analysis and Prescription (MAP), is introduced. Quite simply put, the material typed by each student is analyzed, and specific drills are prescribed to help the student correct errors. More than 75 different kinds of typed errors are included in the analysis. (Read more about this feature in the instructor material that precedes the text material in this book.)

	WPM GOAL	SKILLBUILDING	LANGUAGE ARTS
UNIT 5 Lesson 21 Lesson 22 Lesson 23 Lesson 24 Lesson 25	Goal At least 29wpm/3′/5e	• Progressive Practice: Numbers • Paced Practice • Hyphen Practice • Progressive Practice: Alphabet • Sustained Practice: Capitals • Diagnostic Practice: Symbols and Punctuation • 12-Second Speed Sprints • PPP: Common Letter Combinations • Technique Practice: Tab Key	**Lesson 21** , direct address fragment run-on **Lesson 23** Composing: Sentences **Lesson 25** Proofreading
UNIT 6 Lesson 26 Lesson 27 Lesson 28 Lesson 29 Lesson 30	Goal At least 32wpm/3′/5e	• 12-Second Speed Sprints • Diagnostic Practice: Symbols and Punctuation • Sustained Practice: Punctuation • Progressive Practice: Alphabet • 12-Second Speed Sprints • PPP: Close Reaches • Technique Practice: Concentration • Paced Practice • MAP • Diagnostic Practice: Numbers	**Lesson 27** , independent clause , introductory expression **Lesson 29** spelling
UNIT 7 Lesson 31 Lesson 32 Lesson 33 Lesson 34 Lesson 35	Goal At least 34wpm/3′/5e	• 12-Second Speed Sprints • Progressive Practice: Alphabet • Progressive Practice: Numbers • Technique Practice: Backspace Key • PPP: Discrimination Practice • 12-Second Speed Sprints • Paced Practice • Diagnostic Practice: Symbols and Punctuation • MAP • Sustained Practice: Alternate-Hand Words	**Lesson 31** ≡ sentence ≡ proper ≡ time **Lesson 33** Composing: Sentences **Lesson 35** Proofreading
UNIT 8 Lesson 36 Lesson 37 Lesson 38 Lesson 39 Lesson 40	Goal At least 36wpm/3′/4e	• 12-Second Speed Sprints • Diagnostic Practice: Symbols and Punctuation • Sustained Practice: Rough Draft • Paced Practice • 12-Second Speed Sprints • Progressive Practice: Alphabet • Technique Practice: Shift and Caps Lock Keys • PPP: Horizontal Reaches • MAP • Diagnostic Practice: Numbers	**Lesson 37** 'singular 'plural 'pronoun **Lesson 39** spelling

GDP
Gregg College Keyboarding & Document Processing MULTIMEDIA RESOURCES

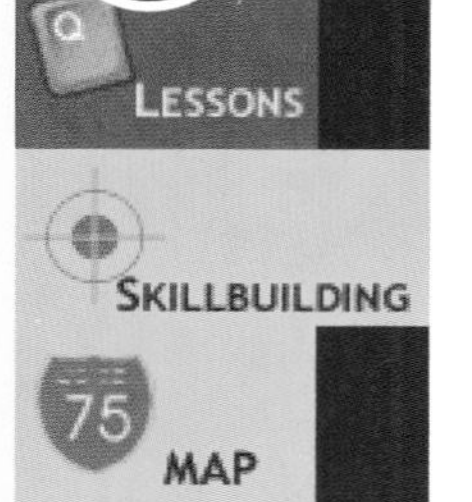

STUDENT

- Lessons 21-40
- MHHE Keyboarding Web site @ **www.mhhe.com/gdp**

INSTRUCTOR

- Instructor Management LAN Version
  — Distance Learning
- Instructor Management Web Version
  — Distance Learning
- MHHE Keyboarding Instructor Web site @ **www.mhhe.com/gdp**

FORMATTING	DOCUMENT PROCESSING	ILLUSTRATIONS
• Orientation to word processing • E-mail	• Correspondence 25-1 through 25-2	• E-mail message, p. 50 • Reference Manual, p. R-5 • E-mail message, p. 60 • Word Processing Manual, Lessons 21–25
• Business reports • Business reports with side headings • Basic proofreaders' marks • Multipage business reports • Business reports with paragraph headings • Business reports with lists • More proofreaders' marks • Academic reports • Academic reports with lists • Academic reports with indented displays	• Report 26-1 through 26-2 • Report 26-3 through 26-4 • Report 28-5 through 28-6 • Report 29-7 through 29-8 • Report 30-9 through 30-10	• Business report, p. 62 • Reference Manual, p. R-8, R-14 • Multipage academic report with displayed paragraph, p. 62 • Basic parts of a report, p. 64 • Multipage business report, p. 69 • Word Processing Manual, Lessons 26–30
• Business letters in block style • Enclosure notation • Envelopes • Labels • Folding letters • Memos • Attachment notation	• Correspondence 31-3 through 31-5 • Correspondence 32-6 through 32-8 • Correspondence 33-9 through 33-13 • Correspondence 34-14 through 34-16 • Correspondence 35-17 through 35-19	• Block-style letter, p. 83 • Reference Manual, p. R-3, R-4, R-6 • Memo, p. 83 • Envelope, p. 83 • Basic parts of a business letter, p. 85 • Envelope, p. 93 • Folding letters, p. 93 • Word Processing Manual, Lessons 31, 33, and 35
• Boxed tables • Table heading block (title and subtitle) • Open tables • Column headings • Ruled tables with number columns	• Table 36-1 through 36-4 • Table 37-5 through 37-7 • Table 38-8 through 38-11 • Table 39-12 through 39-14 • Report 40-11 • Correspondence 40-20 • Table 40-15	• Three-column ruled table with number columns, p. 102 • Reference Manual, p. R-13 • Three-column boxed table with number columns, p. 102 • Two-column open table with column headings, p. 102 • Basic parts of a table, p. 104 • Word Processing Manual, Lessons 36–39

SPANISH RESOURCES

- New key exercises in GDP software are available with Spanish or English audio.
- All instruction screens in GDP software are available in Spanish or English.

ASSESSMENT

Progress Check/Proofreading Check

- Lesson 30, Report 30-10, p. 82
- Lesson 35, Correspondence 35-19, p. 101
- Lesson 40, Table 40-15, p. 117

Tests

- Part 2 Objective Test
- Test 2, Skills Assessment on Part 2, pp. 118–119
- Alternate Test 2, Alternate Skills Assessment on Part 2, Tests and Solution Keys Booklet

Technique Evaluation Form

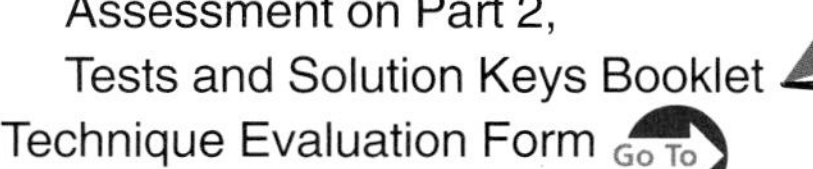

PART 2 RESOURCE MANAGER

MOS* CERTIFICATION SKILLS

WORD PROCESSING ACTIVITY (Go To Word Processing Manual)	LESSON
Locate and open an existing document	21
Use **Save**	22
Use **Save As**	22
Navigate through a document	22
Use the Office Assistant	23
Apply font formats (bold, italic, and underline)	23, 35
Use the **Undo**, **Redo** commands	24
Use the Spelling feature	24
Use the Grammar feature	24
Print a document	24
Use **Print Preview**	24
Send a Word document via e-mail	25
Select and change font and font size	26
Align text in paragraphs	26
Insert page breaks	27
Insert page numbers	27
Create and modify page numbers	27
Add bullets and numbering	28
Set line and paragraph spacing options	29
Insert and move text	30
Cut, **Copy**, **Paste** commands	30
Use indentation options	30
Insert date and time	31
Prepare and print envelopes and labels	33

*MOS: Microsoft Office Specialist

TEACHING RESOURCES AT A GLANCE

APPLICATION RESOURCES

- Word Processing Manual
- Reference Manual

ASSESSMENT

- Progress Checks/Proofreading Checks
- Part 2 Skills Assessment Test
- Part 2 Alternate Skills Assessment Test
- Part 2 Objective Test
- Technique Evaluation Form

MULTIMEDIA RESOURCES

- GDP Software
- GDP Software User's Guide
- Instructor Management LAN Version
  — Distance Learning
- Instructor Management Web Version
  — Distance Learning
- MHHE Keyboarding Web site @ **www.mhhe.com/gdp**

ENRICHMENT

Keyboarding Connection

- Defining the E-Mail Address, p. 52
- Business E-Mail Style Guide, p. 58
- Searching the Web, p. 98

Strategies for Career Success

- Preparing to Conduct a Meeting, p. 54
- Turning Negative Messages Positive, p. 75
- Nonverbal Communication, p. 105

REAL-WORLD CAREER CONNECTION

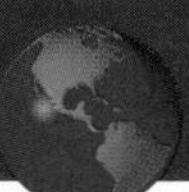

- Business and Administrative Services, p. 49
- Real-World Career Connection Photographs, pp. 48, 56, 66, 91, 95, 117

INSTRUCTOR'S NOTES

PART 2

INTRODUCING THE PART

PART 2 provides an introduction to typing basic business documents. **Unit 5** is an orientation to word processing and formatting e-mail. **Unit 6** covers business and academic reports as well as bulleted and numbered lists. **Unit 7** introduces correspondence, including business letters, envelopes, and memos. **Unit 8** builds skill in formatting boxed and open tables.

Discussion

Ask students if they are experienced in using e-mail and Microsoft Word. Ask students if their experiences with e-mail and Microsoft Word have been just for personal use or if they use e-mail and Microsoft Word in business situations.

Students will develop proofreading skills and reinforce language arts skills.

WPM GOAL

Encourage students to type using the touch method and to use correct technique. Challenge students to reach the goal of typing **at least 36 wpm for 3 minutes with 4 or fewer errors.** Provide positive reinforcement to all students for speed and accuracy improvements.

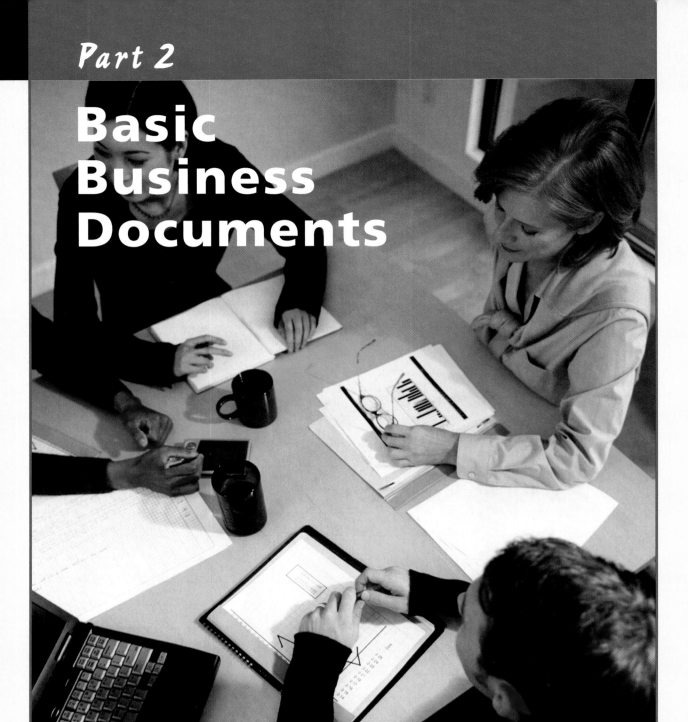

Part 2

Basic Business Documents

Software Overview

The GDP software creates unscored practice documents as students learn about word processing features in their manuals. When students are ready to complete document processing exercises, Microsoft Word is launched, and the software opens a specific document to be typed or edited. Students should not open Microsoft Word outside the GDP program. Document processing exercises are scored automatically by the GDP software, and the student's work can be viewed or printed.

A template has been created that resets a number of Microsoft Word options including automatic hyphenation, AutoCorrect, and AutoFormat options. Review the Software User's Guide for a complete list of the default settings within the GDP program.

Remind students to use the **GDP, Return to GDP** command when exiting from Microsoft Word.

PART 2

Keyboarding in Business and Administrative Services

Opportunities in Business and Administrative Careers

Occupations in the business and administrative services cluster focus on providing management and support services for various companies. The many positions found in this cluster include receptionist, bookkeeper, administrative professional or assistant, claim examiner, accountant, word processor, office manager, and chief executive officer.

Managers and administrators are in charge of planning, organizing, and controlling businesses. Management support workers gather and analyze data to help company executives make decisions. Administrative support workers perform a variety of tasks, such as recordkeeping, operating office equipment, managing their own projects and assignments, and developing high-level integrated software skills as well as Internet research skills. Ideally, everyone in business should be patient, detail-oriented, and cooperative. Excellent written and oral communication skills are definitely an asset as well.

Many companies have been revolutionized by advances in computer technology. As a result, keyboarding skill provides a definite advantage for those who work in business and administrative services. Now, more than ever, success in the business world is dependent upon adaptability and education.

Objectives

KEYBOARDING

- Operate the keyboard by touch.
- Type at least 36 words per minute on a 3-minute timed writing with no more than 4 errors.

LANGUAGE ARTS

- Develop proofreading skills and correctly use proofreaders' marks.
- Use capitals, commas, and apostrophes correctly.
- Develop composing and spelling skills.

WORD PROCESSING

- Use the word processing commands necessary to complete the document processing activities.

DOCUMENT PROCESSING

- Format e-mail, business and academic reports, business letters in block style, envelopes, memos, and tables.

TECHNICAL

- Answer at least 90 percent of the questions correctly on an objective test.

CAREER CONNECTION

Business and Administrative Services. Review the feature information on careers in Business and Administrative Services Career Cluster. Ask how many students plan to major in a business-related course of study.

Encourage students to check local newspaper advertisements and the school placement office for opportunities in Business and Administrative Services Careers.

Remind students to visit the College Keyboarding Web site at **www.mhhe.com/gdp** to learn more about career choices.

INSTRUCTOR'S NOTES/INTERNET BOOKMARKS

Visit us on the Web at www.mhhe.com/gdp.

Unit 5

UNIT OVERVIEW

Students will be introduced to Microsoft Word and will learn how to navigate in a document, select text, edit text, and print documents. Students will also learn to use Help and to check spelling and grammar. The basics of using e-mail will also be presented.

Did You Know?

If a student makes more than 1 error on the language arts pretest in the software, a language arts tutorial automatically appears when the student clicks the Forward arrow.

In order to conform to industry standards, only 1 space is used after punctuation in this program.

www.mhhe.com/gdp to download a copy of the Technique Evaluation Form.

TECHNIQUE EVALUATION FORM

Use this form to keep track of student progress. Complete a form for each student.

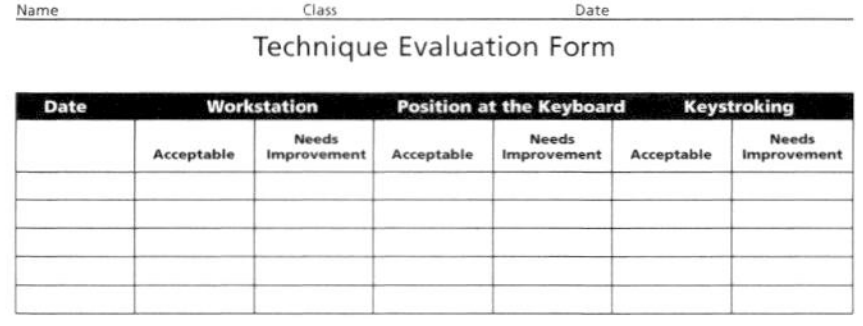

Name Class Date

Technique Evaluation Form

Date	Workstation		Position at the Keyboard		Keystroking	
	Acceptable	Needs Improvement	Acceptable	Needs Improvement	Acceptable	Needs Improvement

Workstation

1. Positions the chair so that the upper and lower legs form a 90-degree angle and the lower back is supported.
2. Positions the keyboard even with the front of the desk.
3. Positions the text on either side of the monitor as close to it vertically and horizontally as possible to minimize head and eye movement and to avoid neck strain.
4. Positions the mouse on a pad at the side of the monitor opposite the text.

Position at the Keyboard

5. Centers the body opposite the keyboard.
6. Leans forward slightly from the hips, with the base of the spine touching the back of the chair and the feet flat on the floor.
7. Keeps the elbows alongside the body in a relaxed position.
8. Curves the fingers naturally over the home position, with the back of the hand at the same angle as the keyboard.

Keystroking

9. Keeps the forearms horizontal and raises the hands slightly when typing so that the wrists do not touch the keyboard while typing. (Hands may rest at the bottom of the keyboard—away from the keys—during nontyping intervals.)
10. Makes quick, snappy strokes using the correct fingers.
11. Returns the finger immediately to the home position or moves to the next position after each stroke.
12. Operates all keys by touch, keeping the eyes on the copy most of the time while typing.

Comments

Unit 5

E-Mail and Word Processing

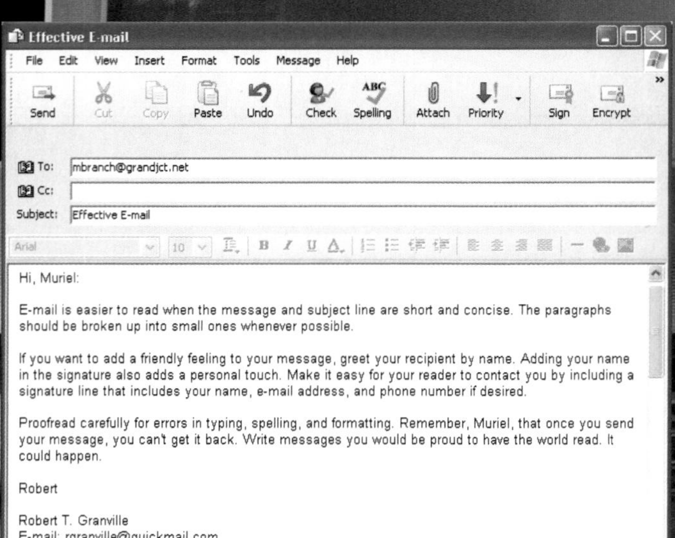

RESOURCE MANAGER

GDP SOFTWARE

- Lessons 21–25
- Software User's Guide
- Instructor Management LAN Version
- Word Processing Manual
- Professional Handbook (IWE*)—Teaching in a Distance Learning Environment
- MAP 

ASSESSMENT

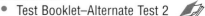

- Test Booklet–Alternate Test 2
- Professional Handbook (IWE*)—Assessment Strategies

ON THE WEB

- **www.mhhe.com/gdp**
- Instructor Management Web Version

*Instructor Wraparound Edition

Orientation to Word Processing: A

Goals

- Improve speed and accuracy
- Refine language arts skills in punctuation and grammar
- Practice basic word processing commands

A. Type 2 times.

A. WARMUP

```
     Juan Valdez will lead 10 managers during this sales       10
period; his expert input has always been valuable. Will        22
Quentin earn 8% commission ($534) after order #K76 arrives?    34
|  1  |  2  |  3  |  4  |  5  |  6  |  7  |  8  |  9  |  10  |  11  |  12
```

SKILLBUILDING

B. PROGRESSIVE PRACTICE: NUMBERS

If you are not using the GDP software, turn to page SB-11 and follow the directions for this activity.

C. PACED PRACTICE

If you are not using the GDP software, turn to page SB-14 and follow the directions for this activity.

LANGUAGE ARTS

D. Study the rules at the right.

D. COMMAS AND SENTENCES

Note: The callout signals in the left margin indicate which language arts rule from this lesson has been applied.

RULE ▶ , direct address

Use commas before and after a name used in direct address.

Thank you, John, for responding to my e-mail so quickly.

Ladies and gentlemen, the program has been canceled.

RULE ▶ fragment

Avoid sentence fragments.

Not: She had always wanted to be a financial manager. But had not had the needed education.

But: She had always wanted to be a financial manager but had not had the needed education.

Note: A fragment is a part of a sentence that is incorrectly punctuated as a complete sentence. In the first sentence above, "but had not had the needed education" is not a complete sentence because it does not contain a subject.

EXTENDING LANGUAGE ARTS

Direct Address Comma Explain that direct address means speaking to someone directly. Example: "I congratulate you, Bill."

Sentence Fragment A sentence fragment is a sentence that does not express a complete thought. Example: "Needs more time." The fragment does not say who or what needs more time. To correct this fragment, add a subject. Example: "Jaime needs more time."

Run-On Sentence Go over the definition of a run-on sentence on p. 52 with students. Discuss the two examples and the two corrections shown.

Lesson 21

FOCUS

TIME MANAGEMENT

Suggested Schedule:

Warmup	2′
Skillbuilding	14′
Language Arts	6′
Word Processing	28′
Total	**50′**

TEACH

LANGUAGE ARTS

LESSON 21-D Remind your students that the call-out signals in the left margin indicate which language arts rule has been applied. If your students are not using the GDP software, have them type a correct version of the paragraph.

INSTRUCTOR STRATEGIES

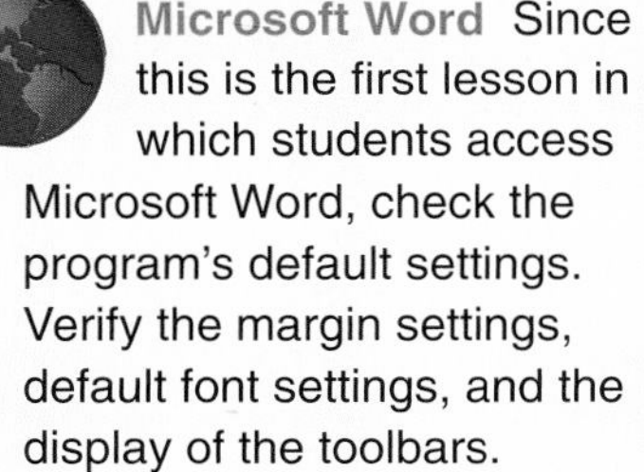

Microsoft Word Since this is the first lesson in which students access Microsoft Word, check the program's default settings. Verify the margin settings, default font settings, and the display of the toolbars.

You may want to show students how to open a menu using the keyboard. Example: Press and hold ALT and type the underlined letter of the menu option ALT + F to open the **File** menu.

Emphasize that the CTRL and ALT keys are combination keys and are used with other keys to execute commands.

Lesson 21

TEACH

LANGUAGE ARTS

SOLUTION: Lines 4–12

4. Sean,
5. concise and
6. line. The
8. writing. Use
10. message than
11. techniques that
12. do, Sean, is closing. Your

FORMATTING

LESSON 21-E Help students become familiar with the Word Processing Manual.

ASSESS

Go To The Web

www.mhhe.com/gdp to download a copy of the Technique Evaluation Form.

TECHNIQUE EVALUATION FORM
Walk around the classroom to observe students' technique.

Use ALT + PRINT SCREEN to make a copy of the Microsoft Word window. Paste your copy into a new document and print it out for students. They can identify the following parts: Title bar, Menu bar, Standard toolbar, Formatting toolbar, Ruler, Scroll bars, Status bar, Insertion point, and Task bar.

Extending the Lesson

Have students make up 10 sentences that illustrate the language arts rules presented in this lesson.

CLOSE

Stress the correct procedure to exit Microsoft Word and the GDP program.

RULE ▶ run-on

Avoid run-on sentences.

Not: Mohamed is a competent worker he has even passed the MCSE exam.
Not: Mohamed is a competent worker, he has even passed the MCSE exam.
But: Mohamed is a competent worker; he has even passed the MCSE exam.
Or: Mohamed is a competent worker. He has even passed the MCSE exam.

Note: A run-on sentence is two independent clauses that run together without any punctuation between them or with only a comma between them.

Edit the paragraph to insert any needed punctuation and to correct any errors in grammar.

You must be certain, Sean that every e-mail message is concise. And also complete. In addition, Sean, use a clear subject line the subject line describes briefly the principal content of the e-mail message. You should use a direct style of writing, use short lines and paragraphs. The recipient of your e-mail message will be more likely to read and respond to a short message. Than a long one. Your reader will be grateful for any writing techniques. That save time. Another thing you should do Sean is to include an appropriate closing, your reader should know immediately who wrote the message.

FORMATTING

Word Processing Manual

E. WORD PROCESSING

Study Lesson 21 in your word processing manual. Complete all of the shaded steps while at your computer.

Keyboarding Connection

Defining the E-Mail Address

With most e-mail software, a header at the top of each e-mail message contains the sender's address. What is the meaning of the strange configuration of an e-mail address?

An e-mail address contains three parts: anyname@server.com. First is the e-mail user's name (before the @ symbol). Next is the name of the host computer the person uses (before the period). The third part is the zone, or domain, for the type of organization or institution to which the host belongs (e.g., *edu* = education; *gov* = government; *com* = company).

Be careful to include each part of an e-mail address and punctuate the address completely and correctly. Even a small error will prevent your message from reaching the recipient.

YOUR TURN Have you ever sent an e-mail that did not reach its recipient because of an address error? What type of error did you make?

Keyboarding Connection

E-Mail Address

Discuss the importance of checking an e-mail address for accuracy. Encourage students to share personal experiences regarding errors made in typing an e-mail address.

Ask students to list additional examples of domains.

YOUR TURN If time permits, ask students to complete the Your Turn activity.

Orientation to Word Processing: B

Goals

- Practice hyphenation
- Type at least 28wpm/3′/5e
- Practice basic word processing commands

A. Type 2 times.

A. WARMUP

```
1      Zenobia bought 987 reams of 16# bond paper from V & J   11
2 Co. @ $5/ream. Part of this week's order is usable. About   23
3 24 percent is excellent quality; the rest cannot be used.   34
  | 1 | 2 | 3 | 4 | 5 | 6 | 7 | 8 | 9 | 10 | 11 | 12
```

SKILLBUILDING

B. Type each line 2 times.

B. HYPHEN PRACTICE

Hyphens are used:

1. To show that a word is divided (lines 4 and 8).
2. To make a dash by typing two hyphens with no space before or after (lines 5 and 8).
3. To join words in a compound (lines 6, 7, and 9).

```
4 Can Larry possibly go with us next week to the golf tourna-
5 ment? I am positive that he--like you--would enjoy the game
6 and realize that it is a first-class sporting event. If you
7 think he can go, I will get first-class reservations on the
8 next plane. Larry--just like Tom and me--always likes every-
9 thing to be first-class and first-rate. Money is no object.
```

Note: In your word processing program, when you type text followed by two hyphens (--) followed by more text and then a space, an em dash (—) will automatically be inserted.

C. PROGRESSIVE PRACTICE: ALPHABET

If you are not using the GDP software, turn to page SB-7 and follow the directions for this activity.

Windows Wizard

CREATE SHORTCUTS To create a shortcut to a program or document in Windows 2000, Me, or XP:

- Click the **Start** button.
- Click **Programs** and choose **Windows Explorer**.
- Locate the program or document. If necessary, click the **Restore** button so that you can see your desktop.
- Point to the icon for the program or document for which you wish to create a shortcut. Hold down the right mouse button, and drag the pointer to your desktop.
- Click **Create Shortcut(s) Here** from the menu.
- Close **Windows Explorer**.

Lesson 22

FOCUS

TIME MANAGEMENT

Suggested Schedule:

Warmup	2′
Skillbuilding	18′
Word Processing	30′
Total	**50′**

TEACH

SKILLBUILDING

LESSON 22-B Use the material given to explain and demonstrate the difference between a hyphen and a dash. Have students explain the usage of the hyphens in each line before they practice typing the lines.

LESSON 22-C Students take repeated timed writings on a passage containing the exact number of words for their speed goal until they can complete the passage with no errors. Then they move to the next, more difficult passage and start again.

INSTRUCTOR STRATEGIES

Navigating Practice the ways to navigate in a document, using the mouse as well as keyboard commands. Stress that using the scroll bar does not move the insertion point.

Lesson 22

TEACH

FORMATTING

LESSON 22-E Help students to navigate in a file, save a file, close a file, and create a new blank document.

ASSESS

www.mhhe.com/gdp to download a copy of the Technique Evaluation Form.

TECHNIQUE EVALUATION FORM Check the **Save As** dialog box on everyone's monitor to be sure the documents will be saved in the correct location.

Review results of timed writings.

Extending the Lesson

Discuss the importance of naming a file in a way that is relevant to its content and assigning names that meet Windows requirements. Tell students that file names cannot contain the following symbols: \ / : * ? " < > |

You may also want to discuss file management guidelines for organizing files—creating and naming folders.

CLOSE

Stress the correct procedure to exit Microsoft Word and the GDP program.

D. Take two 3-minute timed writings. Review your speed and errors.

Goal: At least 28wpm/3'/5e

D. 3-MINUTE TIMED WRITING

Once you learn to use a variety of software programs, 11
you will feel confident and comfortable as you are using a 23
computer. All you have to do is take that first step and 34
decide to strive for excellence. 41
Initially, you might have several questions as you 52
gaze up at a screen that is filled with icons. If you try 62
to learn to use just one or two commands each day, you may 75
soon find that using software is very exciting. 84

| 1 | 2 | 3 | 4 | 5 | 6 | 7 | 8 | 9 | 10 | 11 | 12

FORMATTING

Word Processing Manual

E. WORD PROCESSING

Study Lesson 22 in your word processing manual. Complete all of the shaded steps while at your computer.

Strategies for Career Success

Preparing to Conduct a Meeting

Do you want to conduct a successful meeting? Meetings tend to fail because they last too long and attendees do not stay focused. First, determine the meeting's purpose (e.g., to make a decision or obtain/provide information).

Decide who needs to attend the meeting. Include those who can significantly contribute, as well as decision makers. Prepare an agenda, that is, a list of items to be discussed. Distribute it to attendees a few days before the meeting.

Choose where you will conduct the meeting and schedule the room. Determine if you will be teleconferencing, videoconferencing, or needing audiovisual equipment. If appropriate, arrange for refreshments. Check the room temperature, acoustics, and lighting. Attention to these details will increase your chances for a successful outcome.

YOUR TURN Think about a meeting you attended that was a failure. What could the meeting leader have done to better prepare for the meeting?

Strategies for Career Success

PREPARING TO CONDUCT A MEETING Discuss with students the importance of planning carefully for conducting a meeting. Have students create a checklist to help organize a meeting. Discuss items that should be added to or deleted from the checklist.

YOUR TURN If time permits, ask students to complete the Your Turn activity.

Orientation to Word Processing: C

Goals

- Improve speed and accuracy
- Refine language arts skills in composing
- Practice basic word processing commands

A. Type 2 times.

A. WARMUP

We expect the following sizes to be mailed promptly 11
on January 8: 5, 7, and 9. Send your payment quickly so 22
that the items will be sure to arrive before 2:35* (*p.m.)! 33

| 1 | 2 | 3 | 4 | 5 | 6 | 7 | 8 | 9 | 10 | 11 | 12

SKILLBUILDING

B. Take a 1-minute timed writing on the first paragraph to establish your base speed. Then take four 1-minute timed writings on the remaining paragraphs. As soon as you equal or exceed your base speed on one paragraph, advance to the next, more difficult paragraph.

B. SUSTAINED PRACTICE: CAPITALS

The insurance industry will see some changes because 11
of the many natural disasters the United States has seen in 23
the last few years in places like California and Florida. 34

The major earthquakes in San Francisco, Northridge, 11
and Loma Prieta cost thousands of dollars. Faults like 22
the San Andreas are being watched carefully for activity. 33

Some tropical storms are spawned in the West Indies 11
and move from the Caribbean Sea into the Atlantic Ocean. 22
They could affect Georgia, Florida, Alabama, and Texas. 33

Some U.S. cities have VHF-FM radio weather stations. 11
NASA and NOAA are agencies that launch weather satellites 23
to predict the locations, times, and severity of storms. 34

C. DIAGNOSTIC PRACTICE: SYMBOLS AND PUNCTUATION

If you are not using the GDP software, turn to page SB-2 and follow the directions for this activity.

TEACHING THE ADULT LEARNER

INDIVIDUAL DIFFERENCES The diversity of today's adult learners is noteworthy: each student has a preferred mode of learning. Address students' differences by giving individual help, knowing students' names and how to pronounce them, and being aware of differing backgrounds and experiences. Also, use different types of classroom activities. Try new ideas. Some experts suggest varying activities every 20 minutes.

Many adult learners have full-time jobs, as well, which may make it hard for them to attend class. You may want to offer an adult student the option of attending another section on certain days rather than miss the class session altogether.

Lesson 23

FOCUS

TIME MANAGEMENT

Suggested Schedule:

Warmup	2′
Skillbuilding	12′
Language Arts	6′
Word Processing	30′
Total	**50′**

TEACH

SKILLBUILDING

LESSON 23-B Each paragraph is more difficult than the preceding one—based on the number of capital letters in each paragraph:

Paragraph 1: 5
Paragraph 2: 9
Paragraph 3: 12
Paragraph 4: 16

LESSON 23-C Encourage students to push moderately for speed on the Pretest.

INSTRUCTOR STRATEGIES

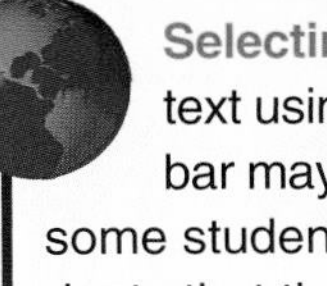

Selecting Text Selecting text using the selection bar may be difficult for some students. Remind students that the mouse pointer shape in the selection bar will be a white arrow pointing to the right.

Emphasize the importance of accessing the Microsoft Word Help system. Demonstrate using the Office Assistant, the question mark button in dialog boxes, and the online index.

Lesson 23

LANGUAGE ARTS

LESSON 23-D The ability to compose at the keyboard is essential. Encourage students to think and type in one motion. Remind students to compose complete sentences.

Walk around the room and assist students with their sentence composition.

FORMATTING

LESSON 23-E Help students to select text, bold, undo and redo a command, and use Help.

ASSESS

www.mhhe.com/gdp to download a copy of the Technique Evaluation Form.

TECHNIQUE EVALUATION FORM
Walk around the room to observe student technique. Complete a Technique Evaluation Form for each student.

Extending the Lesson

Practice using the Help system by having students look up various topics. Examples: bold, undo, and select text.

CLOSE

Stress the correct procedure to use to exit Microsoft Word and the GDP program.

LANGUAGE ARTS

D. Answer each question with a complete sentence.

D. COMPOSING SENTENCES

Do you prefer Word as a word processing software, or do you prefer something else?
What search engine do you prefer when you search for information on the Web?
Do you like Internet Explorer, or do you prefer Netscape Navigator as a Web browser?
What class are you now taking that is best preparing you for the workplace?
If you could work in any foreign country, which one would you choose?
What documents do you type most frequently as a student: letters, reports, or tables?

FORMATTING

Word Processing Manual

E. WORD PROCESSING

Study Lesson 23 in your word processing manual. Complete all of the shaded steps while at your computer.

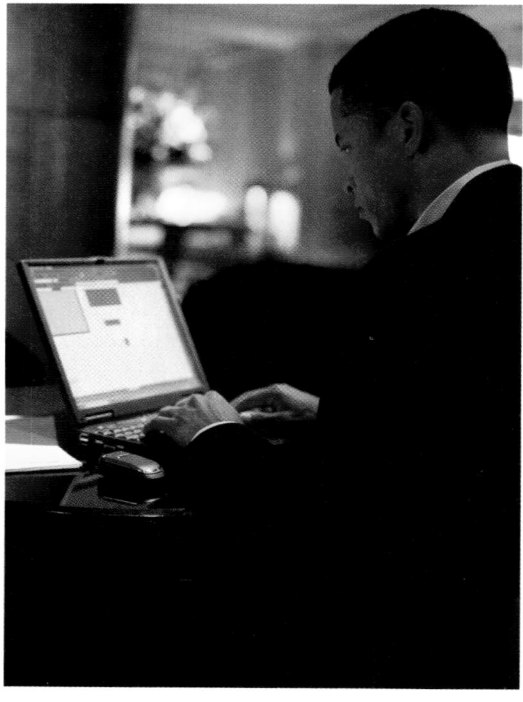

EXTENDING LANGUAGE ARTS

Composing Sentences The widely accepted use of personal computers for both personal and business activities has made composing at the keyboard an essential skill. Encourage students to think and type simultaneously; the better they can do this, the better their efficiency. Occasionally, students will want to write the sentences on paper prior to typing them. Tell these students that the purpose of composing at the keyboard is to process thoughts faster.

As you walk around the room, observe closely to determine that each student has both a subject and a verb in each sentence. This is an excellent review of the rules learned in Lesson 21 on sentence fragments and run-ons. You might ask several students to read their sentences aloud. Have other students verbally indicate how to punctuate or add a conjunction to these clauses to correct run-ons.

Orientation to Word Processing: D

Goals

- Type at least 29wpm/3′/5e
- Practice basic word processing commands

A. Type 2 times.

A. WARMUP

```
     The experts quickly realized that repairs could cost    11
"$985 million" and might exceed 60% of their budget. Will    22
Valdez & Co. begin work before 12 or just wait until 4:30?   34
| 1 | 2 | 3 | 4 | 5 | 6 | 7 | 8 | 9 | 10 | 11 | 12
```

SKILLBUILDING

B. Take three 12-second timed writings on each line. The scale below the last line shows your wpm speed for a 12-second timed writing.

B. 12-SECOND SPEED SPRINTS

```
Mary will be able to go home when she can run fast and far.
Sam can come to the store if he is able to stop for a soda.
Suzy knows that she must send the mail out by noon or else.
Only a few good desks will be made by the end of this week.
5 10 15 20 25 30 35 40 45 50 55 60
```

PRETEST → PRACTICE → POSTTEST

PRETEST
Take a 1-minute timed writing. Review your speed and errors.

C. PRETEST: Common Letter Combinations

```
     He tried to explain the delay in a logical way. The     11
man finally agreed to insure the package and demanded to     22
know why the postal worker did not record the total amount.  34
| 1 | 2 | 3 | 4 | 5 | 6 | 7 | 8 | 9 | 10 | 11 | 12
```

PRACTICE
Speed Emphasis:
If you made 2 or fewer errors on the Pretest, type each *individual* line 2 times.
Accuracy Emphasis:
If you made 3 or more errors, type each *group* of lines (as though it were a paragraph) 2 times.

D. PRACTICE: Word Beginnings

```
re reuse react relay reply return reason record results red
in inset inept incur index indeed intend inning insured ink
de dents dealt death delay detest devote derive depicts den
```

E. PRACTICE: Word Endings

```
ly lowly dimly apply daily barely unruly deeply finally sly
ed cured tamed tried moved amused tasted billed creamed fed
al canal total equal local postal plural rental logical pal
```

POSTTEST
Repeat the Pretest timed writing and compare performance.

F. POSTTEST: Common Letter Combinations

Meeting Special Needs

ATTENTION DEFICIT DISORDER Consider these tips on classroom management when a student has attention deficit disorder (ADD).

Use instructional methods that provide structure, such as the following:

- Lists to summarize
- Previews to preorganize
- Repetition to reinforce
- Frequent eye contact
- Frequent feedback
- Small, manageable tasks.

Visit us on the Web at **www.mhhe.com/gdp** for more information.

Lesson 24

FOCUS

TIME MANAGEMENT
Suggested Schedule:

Warmup	2′
Skillbuilding	21′
Word Processing	27′
Total	**50′**

TEACH

SKILLBUILDING

PRETEST → PRACTICE → POSTTEST

PPP **LESSON 24-C** Some letter combinations occur so frequently that students eventually learn to type them automatically without having to "spell out" each letter. These drills help develop this fast typing response.

LESSON 24-D These are some of the most frequently used two-letter word beginnings.

LESSON 24-E These are some of the most frequently used two-letter word endings.

INSTRUCTOR STRATEGIES

Print Preview When students access Print Preview, you may want to discuss the following:

- Displaying 1 page of a document.
- Displaying multiple pages of a document.
- Changing the zoom level.
- Editing a document using the magnifier button.

Lesson 24

FORMATTING

LESSON 24-H Remind students that clicking the **Print** button on the Standard toolbar will not open the **Print** dialog box. To control default print options, access the **Print** dialog box using the **File** menu or CTRL + P.

Students may want to hide non-printing characters in a document. However, explain that the nonprinting characters are used to troubleshoot document formatting.

Help students to preview pages before printing, check spelling and grammar, show formatting codes, and print.

ASSESS

www.mhhe.com/gdp to download a copy of the Technique Evaluation Form.

TECHNIQUE EVALUATION FORM Walk around the classroom to observe students' technique.

Review results of timed writings.

Extending the Lesson

Ask students to list examples of document errors that the Spelling and Grammar feature will not identify.

If time allows, you may want to elaborate on the AutoCorrect feature.

CLOSE

Stress the correct procedure to use to exit Microsoft Word and the GDP program.

G. Take two 3-minute timed writings. Review your speed and errors.

Goal: At least 29wpm/3'/5e

G. 3-MINUTE TIMED WRITING

```
     If you ever feel tired as you are typing, you should   11
take a rest. Question what you are doing that is causing    22
your muscles to be fatigued. You will realize that you      33
can change the fundamental source of your anxiety.          43
     Take a deep breath and enjoy the relaxing feeling as   54
you exhale slowly. Check your posture to be sure that       65
you are sitting up straight with your back against the      76
chair. Stretch your neck and back for total relaxation.     87
| 1 | 2 | 3 | 4 | 5 | 6 | 7 | 8 | 9 | 10 | 11 | 12
```

FORMATTING

Word Processing Manual

H. WORD PROCESSING

Study Lesson 24 in your word processing manual. Complete all of the shaded steps while at your computer.

Keyboarding Connection

Business E-Mail Style Guide

Watch those e-mail p's and q's! Even though e-mail is relatively informal, you need to be succinct and clear. Greet your reader with a formal "Dear . . . ," or an informal "Hi . . . ," etc. Put the most important part of your message first. Watch the length of your paragraphs; four to five lines per paragraph won't put off your reader.

Use asterisks, caps, dashes, etc., for emphasis. Avoid unfamiliar abbreviations, slang, or jargon. Not everyone who receives your business e-mail may know a particular catchword or phrase. Proofread your e-mail. Be concerned about grammar, punctuation, and word choice. Use your e-mail's spell checker.

End your business e-mail politely. Expressions of appreciation (e.g., "Thanks") or goodwill (e.g., "Best wishes") let your reader know you are finishing your message.

YOUR TURN In Lesson 25 you will learn how to format and compose e-mail messages. Create an e-mail message to send to a coworker, colleague, or friend. Review the e-mail for adherence to the guidelines listed above.

Keyboarding Connection

E-Mail Etiquette

Discuss with students the importance of e-mail etiquette. Read examples of appropriate and inappropriate e-mail messages to the class. Ask students to share personal experiences related to offensive or poorly communicated messages.

YOUR TURN If time permits, ask students to complete the Your Turn activity.

E-Mail Basics

Goals

- Improve speed and accuracy
- Refine language arts skills in proofreading
- Format and compose a basic e-mail message

A. Type 2 times.

A. WARMUP

```
     Exactly 610 employees have quit smoking! About half      11
of them just quit recently. They realized why they can't      22
continue to smoke inside the buildings and decided to stop.   34
|  1  |  2  |  3  |  4  |  5  |  6  |  7  |  8  |  9  |  10  |  11  |  12
```

SKILLBUILDING

B. Tab 1 time between columns. Type 2 times.

B. TECHNIQUE PRACTICE: TAB KEY

A. Uyeki	B. Vorton	C. Wetzel	D. Xenios	E. Young
F. Zeller	G. Ambrose	H. Brown	I. Carter	J. Denney
K. Elmer	L. Fraser	M. Greene	N. Hawkins	O. Irvin
P. Jarvis	Q. Krueger	R. Larkin	S. Majors	T. Norris
U. Vassar	V. Hagelin	W. Wesley	X. Bernet	Y. Robins

C. MAP

Follow the GDP software directions for this exercise in improving keystroking accuracy.

LANGUAGE ARTS

D. Study the proofreading techniques at the right.

D. PROOFREADING YOUR DOCUMENTS

Proofreading and correcting errors are essential parts of document processing. To become an expert proofreader:

1. Use the spelling feature of your word processing software to check for spelling errors; then read the copy aloud to see if it makes sense.
2. Proofread for all kinds of errors, especially repeated, missing, or transposed words; grammar and punctuation; and numbers and names.
3. Check for formatting errors such as line spacing, tabs, margins, and use of bold.

E. Compare these lines with lines 4–7 in the 12-second speed sprints on page 57. Edit the lines to correct any errors.

E. PROOFREADING

```
Mary will be able to go when she can run fast and far.
Sam can come to the store if she is able to stop for soda.
Suzy know that she must send the mail out by noon or else.
Only a few good disks will be made by the end of this week.
```


MAP 75

MAP
ENSURING ACCURACY IMPROVEMENT

Unless practice is specific for the individual student's errors, it will not aid the student. Each student has individual keystroking weaknesses, which cause lack of accuracy. The analysis and prescription provided in MAP (Misstroke Analysis and Prescription) enable the instructor to assist each individual student in achieving accuracy.

Lesson 25

FOCUS

TIME MANAGEMENT

Suggested Schedule:

Warmup	2′
Skillbuilding	18′
Language Arts	6′
Formatting	10′
Document Processing	14′
Total	**50′**

TEACH

SKILLBUILDING

LESSON 25-B Check students' technique as they reach for the TAB key.

LESSON 25-C MAP is a simple, comprehensive, and individualized software program for improving keystroking accuracy.

LANGUAGE ARTS

LESSON 25-D Demonstrate how to use the bottom of the document window as a visual ruler to help students focus on one line at a time. Ask if any students have used this technique.

Ask students to share which proofreading techniques they have used successfully.

Lesson 25

LANGUAGE ARTS

LESSON 25-E If your students are not using the GDP software, have them type a correct version of the lines.

SOLUTION: Lines 9–12

9. home
10. he
11. knows
12. desks

FORMATTING

Refer to Reference Manual

Ask students to review the basic parts of an e-mail message in the **Reference Manual, R-5C** and **R-5D,** before they begin typing.

VISUAL INSTRUCTION

E-Mail message.
Discuss the basic parts of an e-mail message:

- To field
- Copy field
- Subject field
- Greeting
- Body
- Closing
- Signature
- Attachment

You may also want to discuss additional features, such as creating groups to send a message to multiple recipients and creating an address book for frequently used e-mail addresses.

FORMATTING

F. BASIC PARTS OF AN E-MAIL MESSAGE

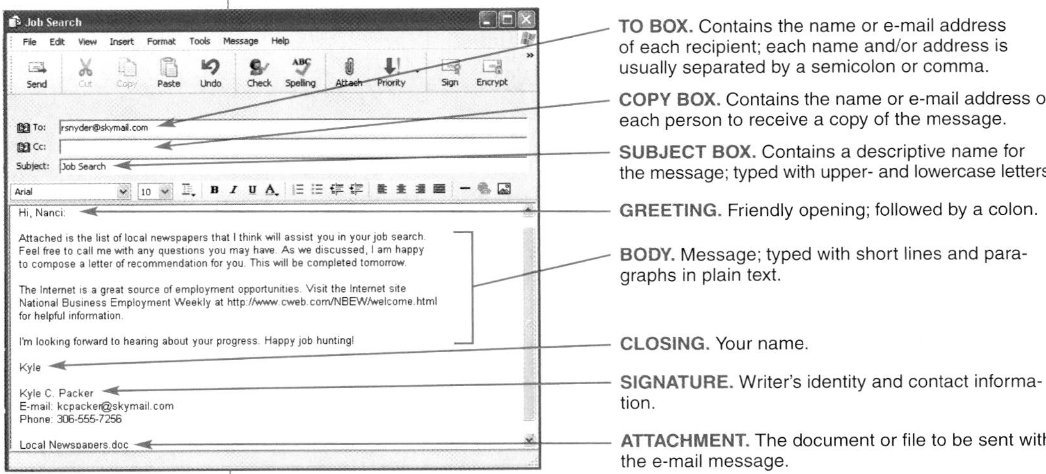

G. FORMATTING AND COMPOSING AN E-MAIL MESSAGE

(!) E-mail formats will vary, depending on your e-mail provider. Most e-mail message screens will allow space for the *To*, *Cc*, and *Subject* entries as well as a separate area for the e-mail message. The attachment feature is often displayed on the toolbar as a paper clip icon.

1. Use the address book feature or type the e-mail address of each recipient in the *To*, *Cc*, or *Bcc* boxes. A semicolon or comma is usually automatically inserted to separate several names.
2. If you use the reply feature, include the original message if it helps the reader remember the topic(s) more easily.
3. Use a descriptive, concise subject line with upper- and lowercase letters.
   Example: Items for Meeting Agenda
4. Use the attachment feature if you need to attach a file or document.
5. Use a friendly greeting. Follow the greeting with a colon. Use the recipient's first name or a courtesy title and last name for a more businesslike greeting.
   Example: Hi, Jim: or Dear Jim:
   Example: Jim: or Mr. Andrews:
6. Use short lines (about 60 characters) with plain text, or let the lines word wrap if your e-mail program supports word wrap.
7. Keep paragraphs short and type them with normal capitalization and punctuation in plain text. Typing in all-caps is considered shouting.
8. Type paragraphs single-spaced and blocked at the left with 1 blank line between them.
9. A closing is optional. Type your name in the closing, and leave 1 blank line above and below the closing.
   Example: Sandy Hill or Sandy
10. Use a signature line so the recipient clearly knows your identity and contact information.
    Example:
    Sandra R. Hill
    E-mail: srhill@server.com
    Phone: 661-555-1223
11. Revise and proofread your message carefully before sending it. You can't get it back!

EXTENDING LANGUAGE ARTS

Proofreading An essential component of proofreading is comparing what you were given to type with the material that you actually typed. Put this example on the board for your students:

Typed	Given to Type
Mr. Wong	Mrs. Wong
April of 2002	April of 2003
This is an examples.	This is an example.
Maria was flying	Maria went flying.

Have students identify any discrepancies between what was given to type and what was typed. Explain to them that they should type exactly what is given to them. If they have a question about the accuracy of a word or statement, they should question the person who originated the material.

Word Processing Manual

H. WORD PROCESSING: E-MAIL A DOCUMENT

Study Lesson 25 in your word processing manual. Complete all of the shaded steps while at your computer. Then format the jobs that follow.

DOCUMENT PROCESSING

Correspondence 25-1

E-Mail Message

1. Type the greeting and body for the e-mail message below.
2. Type the sender's name 1 blank line below the final line of the e-mail message.
3. Type the sender's signature line, including the e-mail address, 1 blank line below the sender's name
4. Type the phone number below the signature line.
5. Proofread your e-mail message for typing, spelling, and formatting errors.

Hi, Muriel: ↓2X

E-mail is easier to read when the message and subject line are short and concise. The paragraphs should be broken up into small ones whenever possible. ↓2X

If you want to add a friendly feeling to your message, greet your recipient by name. Adding your name in the signature also adds a personal touch. Make it easy for your reader to contact you by including a signature line that includes your name, e-mail address, and phone number if desired. ↓2X

Proofread carefully for errors in typing, spelling, and formatting. Remember, Muriel, that once you send your message, you can't get it back. Write messages you would be proud to have the world read. It could happen. ↓2X

Robert ↓2X

Robert T. Granville
E-mail: rgranville@quickmail.com
Phone: 701-555-4832

Correspondence 25-2

E-Mail Message

1. Type an e-mail message to `Ernesto Sanchez`.
2. Type the greeting as: `Hi, Ernesto:`
3. Type the following message: `I now have e-mail access using my new cable modem. You can now send me the photos you took at our annual meeting, because I will be able to access them at a much faster rate.`

   `Thank you, Ernesto, for bringing your digital camera to the meeting so that we could all enjoy the photos you took.`
4. Type the closing as `Karen` and the signature line as `Karen Drake`.
5. Type Karen Drake's e-mail address as `kdrake@brightway.net` and her phone number as `404-555-6823`.
6. Proofread your e-mail message for typing, spelling, and formatting errors.

Lesson 25

DOCUMENT PROCESSING

CORRESPONDENCE 25-1

Guide students step by step through completing this first e-mail message. Be sure they know how to open their e-mail program.

CORRESPONDENCE 25-2

Optional. Students should feel free to look back at the display e-mail message to review any details. Remind students to keep lines short (about 60 characters), and to press ENTER between lines if necessary.

ASSESS

www.mhhe.com/gdp to download a copy of the Technique Evaluation Form.

TECHNIQUE EVALUATION FORM

Print a report for all skillbuilding exercises for Lessons 21–25.

Walk around the classroom and check e-mail formatting.

Extending the Lesson

Discuss the address book feature and how to add names and addresses. Also discuss the importance of having a hard copy of address book information.

CLOSE

Stress the correct procedure to use to exit Microsoft Word and the GDP program.

MHHE CHAMPIONS

Keyboard Shortcuts

Remind students to use keyboard shortcuts. Example: CTRL + B for bold, CTRL + U for underline, and CTRL + I for italic.

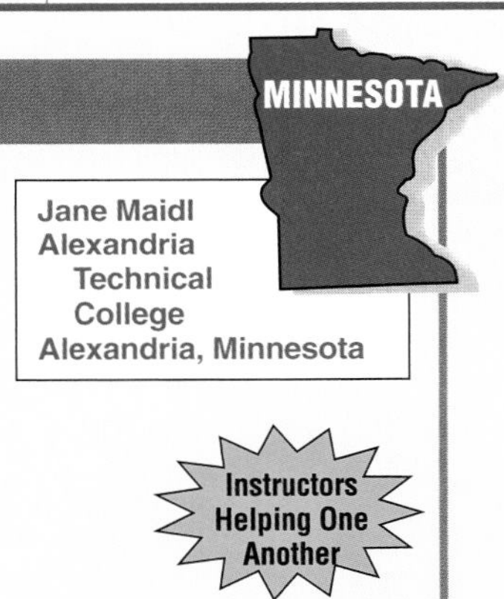

MINNESOTA
Jane Maidl
Alexandria Technical College
Alexandria, Minnesota
Instructors Helping One Another

Unit 6

UNIT OVERVIEW

Students will be introduced to reports, including business reports and academic reports. Several features of Microsoft Word will be used to format the reports—numbered and bulleted lists, page numbering, indents, and line spacing.

Did You Know?

Simplified formatting is taught throughout the program, thus increasing productivity as well as taking advantage of word processing features and defaults.

www.mhhe.com/gdp to download a copy of the Technique Evaluation Form.

TECHNIQUE EVALUATION FORM

Use this form to keep track of student progress. Complete a form for each student.

Name ______ Class ______ Date ______

Technique Evaluation Form

Date	Workstation		Position at the Keyboard		Keystroking	
	Acceptable	Needs Improvement	Acceptable	Needs Improvement	Acceptable	Needs Improvement

Workstation

1. Positions the chair so that the upper and lower legs form a 90-degree angle and the lower back is supported.
2. Positions the keyboard even with the front of the desk.
3. Positions the text on either side of the monitor as close to it vertically and horizontally as possible to minimize head and eye movement and to avoid neck strain.
4. Positions the mouse on a pad at the side of the monitor opposite the text.

Position at the Keyboard

5. Centers the body opposite the keyboard.
6. Leans forward slightly from the hips, with the base of the spine touching the back of the chair and the feet flat on the floor.
7. Keeps the elbows alongside the body in a relaxed position.
8. Curves the fingers naturally over the home position, with the back of the hand at the same angle as the keyboard.

Keystroking

9. Keeps the forearms horizontal and raises the hands slightly when typing so that the wrists do not touch the keyboard while typing. (Hands may rest at the bottom of the keyboard—away from the keys—during nontyping intervals.)
10. Makes quick, snappy strokes using the correct fingers.
11. Returns the finger immediately to the home position or moves to the next position after each stroke.
12. Operates all keys by touch, keeping the eyes on the copy most of the time while typing.

Comments

Unit 6

Reports

LESSON 26
One-Page Business Reports

LESSON 27
Multipage Rough-Draft Business Reports

LESSON 28
Business Reports With Lists

LESSON 29
Academic Reports

LESSON 30
Academic Reports With Displays

AN ANALYSIS OF CORPORATE SICK-LEAVE POLICIES

Recent Trends in the Business World

Linda C. Motonaga

April 5, 20--

Corporate sick-leave policies must be studied carefully in order to maximize employee productivity and minimize excessive absenteeism. The reasons for absences and the responsiveness of employers to the needs of the employees must be examined in order to determine some practical alternatives to current policies.

REASONS FOR ABSENCE

There are many reasons employees are absent from work. Illness and personal emergency are common reasons for absenteeism. However, recent surveys have shown that about 28% of reported sick time isn't due to illness. This percentage is on the rise. Recent studies have also shown that absences due to personal needs and stress are increasing. Also, many workers believe that they are "entitled" to a day off now and then. Perhaps it is time for employers to revamp their sick-leave policies and make these policies more responsive to the needs of the employees.

RESPONSIVENESS OF EMPLOYERS

If employees are finding it necessary to take sick days when they are not ill, it makes sense to conclude that possibly employers are either not aware of why absenteeism exists or have chosen not to respond to their employees' needs. One thing is certain—ignoring the problem will not make it go away.

POSSIBLE SOLUTIONS

Flexible scheduling is one creative way in which employers can respond to the needs of employees. If workers are given the opportunity for a flexible working schedule, stress levels should go down, and personal needs can be handled during the time they are off. Another solution might be to give employees a fixed number of days off each year for reasons other than illness. This gives workers a legitimate reason for a planned absence and gives employers some advance notice so that absences do not hurt productivity.

ENDING PROCRASTINATION

Judy Baca

Everyone at one time or another has put off some task, goal, or important plan at work for any number of reasons. Perhaps you think time is too short or the task isn't really that important. Either way, procrastination can lead to a stalled life and career.

EVALUATE YOUR SITUATION

Joyce Winfrey of Time Management Incorporated has some very good advice that will help you begin to move forward. She says that you should ask yourself two very basic questions about why you are procrastinating:

1. Am I procrastinating because the task at hand is not really what I want?
2. Is there a valid reason for my procrastination?

After you have asked yourself these questions, Ms. Winfrey suggests that you do the following:

> Look deep within yourself. If you are looking for excuses, then the process of asking these questions will be a waste of your time. However, if you answer these questions honestly, you might find answers that surprise you and that will help clarify your situation.

She also recommends several techniques that can help you get back on task and put an end to procrastination.

PRACTICE NEW TECHNIQUES

Identifying and understanding the techniques that follow is the first step. Once you know what to do, you can begin to practice these steps daily.

2

Take Baby Steps. Don't make any task bigger than it really is by looking at the whole thing at once. Break it down into baby steps that are manageable.

Don't Strive for Perfectionism. If you are waiting for the perfect solution or the perfect opportunity, you will be immobilized. Accept the fact that no one and nothing is perfect. Then accept your mistakes and move on.

Enjoy the Task. Enjoy the task at hand and find something in it that is positive and rewarding. Confront your fears with a plan of action.

Remind yourself of all these techniques daily. Post them by your telephone, by your desk, or in your car. You will find that your personal life and career will gain momentum, and success will soon be yours.

RESOURCE MANAGER

GDP SOFTWARE

- Lessons 26–30
- Software User's Guide
- Instructor Management LAN Version
- Word Processing Manual
- Professional Handbook (IWE*)—Teaching in a Distance-Learning Environment
- MAP 

ASSESSMENT

- Test Booklet–Alternate Test 2
- Progress Check–Report 30-10
- Professional Handbook (IWE*)—Assessment Strategies

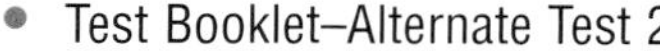
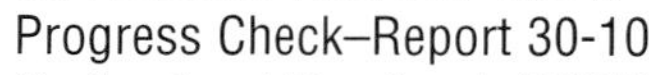

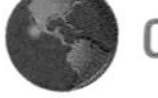

ON THE WEB

- www.mhhe.com/gdp
- Instructor Management Web Version

*Instructor Wraparound Edition

One-Page Business Reports

Goals

- Type at least 30wpm/3′/5e
- Format one-page business reports

A. Type 2 times.

A. WARMUP

Mr. G. Yoneji ordered scanners* (*800 dots per inch) 11
in vibrant 24-bit color! He quickly realized that exactly 22
31% of the work could be scanned in order to save money. 34
| 1 | 2 | 3 | 4 | 5 | 6 | 7 | 8 | 9 | 10 | 11 | 12

SKILLBUILDING

B. Take three 12-second timed writings on each line. The scale below the last line shows your wpm speed for a 12-second timed writing.

B. 12-SECOND SPEED SPRINTS

She went to the same store to find some good books to read.
Frank will coach eight games for his team when he has time.
Laura sent all the mail out today when she left to go home.
These pages can be very hard to read when the light is dim.
5 10 15 20 25 30 35 40 45 50 55 60

C. DIAGNOSTIC PRACTICE: SYMBOLS AND PUNCTUATION

If you are not using the GDP software, turn to page SB-2 and follow the directions for this activity.

D. Take two 3-minute timed writings. Review your speed and errors.

Goal: At least 30wpm/3′/5e

D. 3-MINUTE TIMED WRITING

Holding a good business meeting may require a great 11
deal of thought and planning. The meeting must be well 22
organized, and an agenda must be prepared. It may be hard 33
to judge how long a meeting will take or how many people 45
will discuss important issues. 51
A good leader is required to execute the agenda. He or 62
she must know when to move on to the next topic or when to 73
continue debate on a topic. After a productive meeting, a 85
leader should be pleased. 90
| 1 | 2 | 3 | 4 | 5 | 6 | 7 | 8 | 9 | 10 | 11 | 12

Lesson 26

FOCUS

TIME MANAGEMENT

Suggested Schedule:

Warmup	2′
Skillbuilding	18′
Formatting	8′
Document Processing	22′
Total	**50′**

TEACH

SKILLBUILDING

LESSON 26-B Speed sprints are very motivational. Have students push moderately for speed on these easy sentences.

LESSON 26-C Encourage students to push moderately for speed on the Pretest.

LESSON 26-D Encourage students to type with control.

Windows Wizard

CUSTOMIZE THE TASK BAR To move, hide, or resize the **Task Bar** in Windows 2000, Me, and XP:

- To move the **Task Bar**, click an empty area of the **Task Bar** and drag the **Task Bar** to the right, top, or left.
- To hide the **Task Bar**, right-click an empty area of the **Task Bar** and choose **Properties**. Select the **Auto hide** check box and click **Apply**. Click **OK** to close the dialog box. To display the **Task Bar** and the **Start** menu, press CTRL + ESC.
- To resize the **Task Bar**, point to the top edge of the **Task Bar** and drag the edge of the **Task Bar** up when a double-headed arrow appears.

Lesson 26

FORMATTING

LESSON 26-E Explain the differences between the two basic styles of reports: business and academic. If possible, share examples of each type. Show a company report and an academic report, such as a term paper. Direct students to the Reference Manual in their textbook and in the GDP software. Encourage them to find their own answers using the index and contents. Review all the callouts in the report illustration.

VISUAL INSTRUCTION

Parts of a Business Report. Review the basic parts of a business report and help students apply correct spacing and identify the formatting differences between side headings and paragraph headings.

- Title
- Subtitle
- Byline
- Date
- Body
- Side Heading
- Paragraph Heading
- List

LESSON 26-F Software defaults are used as much as possible to simplify formatting. You may want to explain default software settings to students.

Help students resolve any questions they may have regarding the formatting of business reports.

FORMATTING

Reference Manual

Refer to page R-8C of the Reference Manual for an illustration of a report in academic style.

E. BASIC PARTS OF A REPORT

There are two basic styles of reports: business and academic. The illustration that follows is for a business report.

↓6X

14 pt **AN ANALYSIS OF CORPORATE SICK-LEAVE POLICIES** ↓2X

12 pt↓ **Recent Trends in the Business World**

Linda C. Motonaga ↓2X

April 5, 2003 ↓2X

Corporate sick-leave policies must be studied carefully in order to maximize employee productivity and minimize excessive absenteeism. The reasons for absences and the responsiveness of employers to the needs of the employees must be examined in order to determine some practical alternatives to current policies. ↓2X

REASONS FOR ABSENCE ↓2X

There are many reasons employees are absent from work. Illness and personal emergency are common reasons for absenteeism. ↓2X

Illness. Illness is often caused by all the stress in the workplace. Employees may have to care for parents and children. ↓2X

Personal Needs. Recent studies have also shown that absences due to personal needs are increasing. Two important questions must be addressed. ↓2X

1. Should employers rethink their sick-leave policies? ↓2X

2. How can a newly instituted sick-leave policy be more responsive to the needs of the employee? ↓2X

POSSIBLE SOLUTIONS ↓2X

Flexible scheduling is one creative way in which employers can respond to the needs of employees. If workers are given the opportunity for a flexible working schedule, stress levels should go down and personal needs can be handled during the time they are off. Another solution might be to give employees a fixed number of days off each year for reasons other than illness. This gives workers a legitimate reason for a planned absence and gives employers some advance notice so that absences do not hurt productivity.

TITLE. Subject of the report; centered; typed about 2 inches from the top of the page in bold and all-caps, with a 14-point font size; 2-line titles are single-spaced.

SUBTITLE. Secondary or explanatory title; centered; typed 1 blank line below the title, in bold, with upper- and lowercase letters.

BYLINE. Name of the writer; centered; typed 1 blank line below the previous line, in bold.

DATE. Date of the report; centered; typed 1 blank line below the previous line, in bold.

BODY. Text of the report; typed 1 blank line below the previous line, single-spaced and positioned at the left margin, with 1 blank line between paragraphs.

SIDE HEADING. Major subdivision of the report; typed 1 blank line below the previous line and beginning at the left margin, in bold and all-caps.

PARAGRAPH HEADING. Minor subdivision of the report; typed 1 blank line below the previous line at the left margin, in bold, with upper- and lowercase letters; followed by a period (also in bold).

LIST. Numbered or bulleted items in a report; typed at the left margin, single-spaced, with 1 blank line above and below the list. If the list includes multiline items, insert 1 blank line between the individual items.

F. BUSINESS REPORTS

To format a business report:

- Single-space business reports.
- Press ENTER 6 times to begin the first line of the report approximately 2 inches from the top of the page.
- Change the font size to 14 point, and type the title in all-caps, centered, in bold. Single-space a 2-line title.
- Press ENTER 2 times and change the font size to 12 point.
- If the report includes a subtitle, byline, or date, type each item centered and in bold upper- and lowercase letters.
- Press ENTER 2 times after each line in the heading block.
- Insert 1 blank line after all paragraphs.
- Do not number the first page of a report.

INSTRUCTOR STRATEGIES

Alignment Show students the difference between paragraphs that are left-aligned and paragraphs that are justified. Which is easier to read? Which format do business reports use?

Fonts Help students understand that fonts are measured in points and that there are 72 points in 1 inch. Standard font size is 12 points.

G. REPORTS WITH SIDE HEADINGS

To format side headings:

- Insert 1 blank line before and after side headings.
- Type side headings at the left margin, in bold, and in all-caps.

Word Processing Manual

H. WORD PROCESSING: ALIGNMENT AND FONT SIZE

Study Lesson 26 in your word processing manual. Complete all of the shaded steps while at your computer. Then format the jobs that follow.

DOCUMENT PROCESSING

Report 26-1

Business Report

Type this report in standard format for a business report with side headings.

Type the actual current year in place of 20--.

↓6X

14 pt. **AN ANALYSIS OF CORPORATE SICK-LEAVE POLICIES** ↓1X ↓2X

14 pt.↓ **Recent Trends in the Business World** ↓2X

Linda C. Motonaga ↓2X

April 5, 20-- ↓2X

Corporate sick-leave policies must be studied carefully in order to maximize employee productivity and minimize excessive absenteeism. The reasons for absences and the responsiveness of employers to the needs of the employees must be examined in order to determine some practical alternatives to current policies. ↓2X

REASONS FOR ABSENCE ↓2X

There are many reasons employees are absent from work. Illness and personal emergency are common reasons for absenteeism. However, recent surveys have shown that about 28 percent of reported sick time isn't due to illness. This percentage is on the rise. Recent studies have also shown that absences due to personal needs and stress are increasing. Also, many workers believe that they are "entitled" to a day off now and then. Perhaps it is time for employers to revamp their sick-leave policies and make these policies more responsive to the needs of the employees. ↓2X

RESPONSIVENESS OF EMPLOYERS ↓2X

If employees are finding it necessary to take sick days when they are not ill, it makes sense to conclude that possibly employers either are not aware of why absenteeism exists or have chosen not to respond to their employees' needs. One thing is certain—ignoring the problem will not make it go away. ↓2X

(!) In your word processor, when you type text followed by two hyphens (--), followed by more text and then a space, an em dash (—) will automatically be inserted.

(Continued on next page)

FORMATTING

Reference Manual

Ask students to review the business report format in the **Reference Manual, R-8A, R-8B,** and **R-9A,** before they begin typing.

LESSON 26-H Help students use the alignment and font size commands.

DOCUMENT PROCESSING

REPORT 26-1 Guide students step by step through this first business report. Encourage them to use the electronic Reference Manual in the GDP software as they create the document in the word processor.

Remind students that word wrap is on and that their line endings may differ from those shown here. Point out the em dash in the document.

Remind students that, in their word processor, when they type text followed by two hyphens (--) followed by more text and then a space, an em dash (—) will automatically be inserted.

Tell students to spell-check, proofread, and preview their documents before printing. This procedure should be standard for all documents.

GDP SOFTWARE TIPS

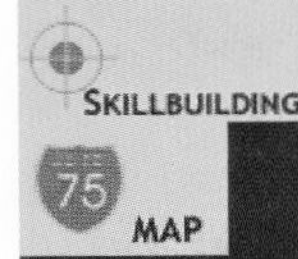

Document Processing

Assist students with the correct procedure to use to access Microsoft Word within GDP when completing Report 26-1. Remind them to spell-check the document and also to proofread it to locate errors the spell checker missed.

You may need to help students locate Report 26-1, which will be edited to create Report 26-2.

If time permits, ask students to display a Summary Report. Notice that the report includes the time spent in Microsoft Word.

Remind students that they must use the **GDP, Return to GDP** commands rather than closing the document through Microsoft Word.

Lesson 26

DOCUMENT PROCESSING

Stress the importance of good technique while formatting documents.

REPORT 26-2 Optional. If time is short, you may have students skip the optional job. No new features are presented.

ASSESS

www.mhhe.com/gdp to download a copy of the Technique Evaluation Form.

TECHNIQUE EVALUATION FORM Review results of timed writings.

Walk around the room to observe report formatting.

Evaluate Report 26-1.

Extending the Lesson

Display examples of different font sizes. (Examples would be pages from magazines, newspaper articles, telephone book pages, and letters.)

CLOSE

Stress the correct procedure to use to exit Microsoft Word and the GDP program.

Ask students to bring examples of alignment and font size to class.

POSSIBLE SOLUTIONS ↓2X

Flexible scheduling is one creative way in which employers can respond to the needs of employees. If workers are given the opportunity for a flexible working schedule, stress levels should go down and personal needs can be handled during the time they are off. Another solution might be to give employees a fixed number of days off each year for reasons other than illness. This gives workers a legitimate reason for a planned absence and gives employers some advance notice so that absences do not hurt productivity.

Report 26-2
Business Report

Open the file for Report 26-1 and make the following changes:

1. Delete the subtitle, and change the byline to `Amy Ho`.
2. Change the date to `October 23`.
3. Change the second side heading to `EMPLOYER RESPONSIVENESS`.
4. Delete the last two sentences in the last paragraph at the end of the report. Add the following sentences to the end of the last paragraph:

`Employees will not feel the need to invent elaborate reasons for their absences. They will feel as if they are in control of their schedule outside of work so that they can determine the best way to schedule their time off. When they return to work, they will feel relaxed and ready to work.`

INSTRUCTOR STRATEGIES

Sick-Leave Policies Stimulate a class discussion on sick-leave policies. Have any students had experience with sick-leave policies they found fair? Unfair? Do students believe that most people use their sick-leave days responsibly or irresponsibly? How could corporate sick-leave policies be improved?

Multipage Rough-Draft Business Reports

Goals

- Improve speed and accuracy
- Refine language arts skills in punctuation
- Identify and apply basic proofreaders' marks
- Format multipage rough-draft business reports

A. Type 2 times.

A. WARMUP

```
     On 7/23 the office will convert to a new phone system.   11
A freeze on all toll calls is requested for July. Account     23
#GK95 has a balance of $68 and isn't expected to "pay up."    35
| 1 | 2 | 3 | 4 | 5 | 6 | 7 | 8 | 9 | 10 | 11 | 12
```

SKILLBUILDING

B. Take a 1-minute timed writing on the first paragraph to establish your base speed. Then take four 1-minute timed writings on the remaining paragraphs. As soon as you equal or exceed your base speed on one paragraph, advance to the next, more difficult paragraph.

B. SUSTAINED PRACTICE: PUNCTUATION

```
     Anyone who is successful in business realizes that the   11
needs of the customer must always come first. A satisfied     23
consumer is one who will come back to buy again and again.    34

     Consumers must learn to lodge a complaint in a manner    11
that is fair, effective, and efficient. Don't waste time      22
talking to the wrong person. Go to the person in charge.      34

     State your case clearly; be prepared with facts and      11
figures to back up any claim--warranties, receipts, bills,    22
and checks are all very effective. Don't be intimidated.      34

     If the company agrees to work with you, you're on the    11
right track. Be specific: "I'll expect a check Tuesday,"      22
or "I'll expect a replacement in the mail by Saturday."       33
```

C. PROGRESSIVE PRACTICE: ALPHABET

If you are not using the GDP software, turn to page SB-7 and follow the directions for this activity.

Lesson 27

FOCUS

TIME MANAGEMENT

Suggested Schedule:

Warmup	2′
Skillbuilding	12′
Language Arts	6′
Formatting	8′
Document Processing	22′
Total	**50′**

TEACH

SKILLBUILDING

LESSON 27-B Each paragraph is more difficult than the preceding one—based on the number of internal, not end, punctuation marks.

Paragraph 1: none
Paragraph 2: 3
Paragraph 3: 6
Paragraph 4: 10

LESSON 27-C Students take repeated timed writings on a passage containing the exact number of words for their speed goal until they can complete it with no errors. Then they move to the next, more difficult passage and start again.

Windows Wizard

CUSTOMIZE THE MOUSE To adjust the mouse pointer speed, create a left-handed mouse, or add mouse trails in Windows 2000, Me, and XP:

- Click the **Start** button.
- Select **Settings** and choose **Control Panel**.
- Double-click **Mouse** to display the **Mouse Properties** dialog box.
- Select the **Buttons** tab to select the **Left-handed** mouse option or to control the **Double click speed**.
- Select the **Pointer Options** tab (in Windows XP) or the **Motion** tab (in Windows 2000 and Me) to control the **Pointer speed** and to select **Pointer trail**.

Lesson 27

LANGUAGE ARTS

LESSON 27-D Review the most commonly used coordinate conjunctions: *and, but, or,* and *nor.* If your students are not using the GDP software, have them type a correct version of the paragraph.

SOLUTION: Lines 16–23

16. single-spaced,
17. *Correct*
18. lines,
19. title, [optional]
20. title,
22. date, [optional]
23. heading,

FORMATTING

Reference Manual

Ask students to review basic proofreaders' marks in the **Reference Manual, R-14C,** before they begin typing.

LESSON 27-E Review the basic proofreaders' marks, especially the ones to capitalize, insert a space, and use a lowercase letter.

LANGUAGE ARTS

D. Study the rules at the right.

D. COMMAS AND SENTENCES

Note: The callout signals in the left margin indicate which language arts rule from this lesson has been applied.

RULE ▶ , independent

Use a comma between independent clauses joined by a coordinate conjunction (unless both clauses are short).

Ellen left her job with IBM, and she and her sister went to Paris.

But: Ellen left her job with IBM and went to Paris with her sister.

But: John drove and I navigated.

The underline calls attention to a point in the sentence where a comma might mistakenly be inserted.

Note: An independent clause is one that can stand alone as a complete sentence. The most common coordinate conjunctions are *and, but, or,* and *nor.*

RULE ▶ , introductory

Use a comma after an introductory expression (unless it is a short prepositional phrase).

Before we can make a decision, we must have all the facts.

But: In 2000 our nation elected a new president.

Note: An introductory expression is a group of words that come before the subject and verb of the independent clause. Common prepositions are *to, in, on, of, at, by, for,* and *with.*

Edit the paragraph to insert any needed punctuation and to correct any errors in grammar.

Business reports should be single-spaced and all lines in the heading block should be typed in bold. If the report title has two lines it should be single-spaced and in all caps. Include a subtitle below the title. You should type the subtitle 1 blank line below the title and it should be typed in both upper- and lowercase letters. Most reports include a byline and a date. After the date begin typing the report body. If there is a side heading type it in all caps and bold.

FORMATTING

E. BASIC PROOFREADERS' MARKS

Proofreaders' marks are used to indicate changes or corrections to be made in a document (called a *rough draft*) that is being revised for final copy. Study the chart to learn what each proofreaders' mark means.

Proofreaders' Marks	Draft	Final copy
⁀ Omit space	data base	database
∨ or ∧ Insert	if hes going, (not)	if he's not going,
≡ Capitalize	Maple street	Maple Street
Delete	a final draft	a draft
# Insert space	allready to	all ready to

(Continued on next page)

EXTENDING LANGUAGE ARTS

Independent Clause Comma To make reading more interesting, we often join independent clauses with a coordinating conjunction and a comma. List the most common coordinating conjunctions: *and, but, or* and *nor.* Then, write two sentences on the board. Example: **Jim likes to walk. He walks five miles each day.** Illustrate how changing the period in the first sentence to a comma and adding the conjunction *and* coordinates the sentence.

Introductory Comma Explain that some introductory expressions are followed by a comma. Write these common introductory expressions on the board: **Yes, No, Look, Well, In fact, For example,** and **Therefore.** Ask students to provide examples of introductory expressions used in sentences. Example: **Yes, I can do this.**

Proofreaders' Marks	Draft	Final Copy
when / ~~if~~ ^ Change word	and ~~if~~ ^ you (when)	and when you
/ Use lowercase letter	our ~~P~~resident	our president
∿ Transpose	they all see (transposed)	they see all
ss Single-space	ss [first line / second line	first line second line
¶ New paragraph	. . . to use it. ¶ We can	. . . to use it. We can

Note that a new paragraph may be formatted either by inserting a blank line before it in a single-spaced document or by indenting the first line 0.5 inch ( ) in a double-spaced document.

F. MULTIPAGE BUSINESS REPORTS

To format a multipage report:

- Use the same side margins for all pages of the report.
- Leave an approximate 2-inch top margin on page 1.
- Leave an approximate 1-inch bottom margin on all pages.

Note: When you reach the end of a page, your word processing software will automatically insert a soft page break. If a soft page break separates a side heading from the paragraph that follows it, insert a hard page break just above the side heading to keep them together.

- Leave a 1-inch top margin on continuing pages.
- Do not number the first page. However, number all continuing pages at the top right margin.

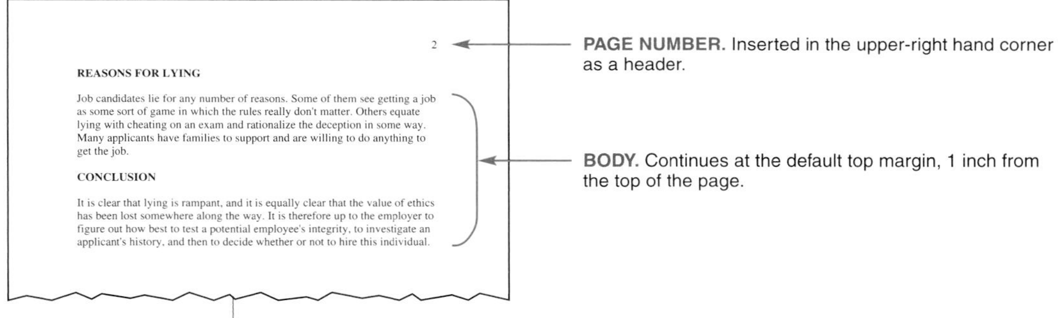

2

REASONS FOR LYING

Job candidates lie for any number of reasons. Some of them see getting a job as some sort of game in which the rules really don't matter. Others equate lying with cheating on an exam and rationalize the deception in some way. Many applicants have families to support and are willing to do anything to get the job.

CONCLUSION

It is clear that lying is rampant, and it is equally clear that the value of ethics has been lost somewhere along the way. It is therefore up to the employer to figure out how best to test a potential employee's integrity, to investigate an applicant's history, and then to decide whether or not to hire this individual.

PAGE NUMBER. Inserted in the upper-right hand corner as a header.

BODY. Continues at the default top margin, 1 inch from the top of the page.

G. BUSINESS REPORTS WITH PARAGRAPH HEADINGS

To format paragraph headings:

- Type paragraph headings at the left margin in bold and in upper- and lowercase letters.
- Follow the paragraph heading by a bold period and 1 space.

Word Processing Manual

H. WORD PROCESSING: PAGE NUMBERING AND PAGE BREAK

Study Lesson 27 in your word processing manual. Complete all of the shaded steps while at your computer. Then format the jobs that follow.

INSTRUCTOR STRATEGIES

Page Numbering Have students open a 2-page document in Microsoft Word. Demonstrate suppressing the page number on the first page of a document.

Lesson 27

FORMATTING

Reference Manual

Ask students to review multipage business reports and business reports with paragraph headings in the **Reference Manual, R-8A** and **R-8B,** before they begin typing.

VISUAL INSTRUCTION

Multipage Business Reports. Remind students that the format of the first page of a business report is different from succeeding pages—the top margin is approximately 2 inches. Continuing pages have a 1-inch top margin and page numbers at the top right.

LESSON 27-F Explain how to format a multipage business report. Distinguish a soft page break from a hard page break. Illustrate how a 1-line paragraph or a heading at the bottom of a page is not acceptable. Show students how to insert a hard page break to avoid leaving a 1-line paragraph. Explain suppressed page numbering on the first page.

LESSON 27-G Emphasize that the period following a paragraph heading is also in bold.

LESSON 27-H Help students use the page-numbering and page break commands.

Demonstrate the procedures to use to switch between Normal view and Print Layout view.

Lesson 27

DOCUMENT PROCESSING

REPORT 27-3 Guide students step by step through this first multipage rough-draft business report. Explain the extra spacing in the report that is needed to accommodate the proofreaders' marks.

Encourage them to use the electronic Reference Manual in the GDP software as they create the document in the word processor.

Remind students that word wrap is on and that their line endings may differ from those shown here.

Explain that the ¶ symbol indicates the start of a new blocked paragraph.

Explain the language arts callout signals in the margin.

Remind students to spell-check, proofread, and preview their documents before printing. This procedure should be standard for all documents.

DOCUMENT PROCESSING

Report 27-3

Business Report

Note: The report lines are shown with extra spacing to accommodate the proofreaders' marks. Use standard business report spacing when you type the report.

1. Type the report using standard business report format.
2. Type side headings at the left margin in bold and all-caps.
3. Type any paragraph headings at the left margin in bold and in upper- and lowercase letters, followed by a bold period and 1 space.
4. Insert a page number at the top right, and suppress the page number on the first page.
5. Spell-check, preview, and proofread your document for spelling and formatting errors before printing it.

The ¶ symbol indicates the start of a new paragraph. In a business report, paragraphs are blocked (not indented).

THE INTEGRITY AND ~~MORALS~~ ETHICS

OFJOB APPLICANTS

~~By~~ Elizabeth Reddix

April 5, 20--

INTRODUCTION

¶ Some studies have found that about ~~9 out of 10~~ 90 percent of job applicants have lied in someway in order to land a job. The lies range from small exaggerations to blatant and completely fraudulent information such as lying about a degree or perhaps about ones history of earnings. After tallying the results of a survey of a large group of College students, one psychologist found that ~~approximately~~ about 90 out of 100 of them were willing to lie ~~in order~~ to land a job that they really wanted. (, introductory)

¶ One way to help screen out the deceptions from the truth is to identify the most common deceptions. A nother way is to try to understand why applicants feel the need to lie. After these factors are identified and understood it will be easier tomake some judgment calls on the ethical integrity of an applicant. (, introductory)

COMMON DECEPTIONS

¶ There are ~~a great~~ many areas in which job applicants are willing to make false statements in order to get a job. These could include verbal statements or written ones.

School activities. Many ~~job~~ applicants are willing to exaggerate or totally falsify ~~totally~~ their participation in school activities. In order to prove leader ship ability, an applicant might be willing to say that he or she was president of a nonexistent club or perhaps organized some type of fund-raising fictional activity. (, introductory)

(Continued on next page)

INSTRUCTOR STRATEGIES

Unethical Employees Discuss the following unethical behaviors by employees. Ask students to contribute to the list. How do unethical behaviors cost all employees, not just the employer?

- Calling in "sick" to take an unauthorized day off
- Being tardy
- Leaving work early
- Taking home office supplies and other company property
- Having employees punch in or out for them
- Shrinkage
- Fraud

Former Job titles. Another area rampant with deception is the list of previous Job Titles. In order to make a ~~previous~~ former job sound more impressive, a job contender might add a word or two to the title or perhaps rename the title al together.

, introductory

Computer Experience. Since we live in an age of computer technology, most employers are looking for people with computer experience. Usually the more computer experience a ~~person~~ candidate has, the better off he or she willbe in terms of competing with others for the same position.

, introductory

REASONS FOR LYING

¶ Job Candidates lie for any number of reasons. Some of them see getting a job as some sort of game in which the rules don't really matter. Others equate lying with cheating on an exam and rationalize the deception in some way. Many applicants have families to support and are willing to do any thing to get the job.

Conclusion

, independent

¶ It is clear that lying is ~~quite~~ rampant, and it is equally clear that the value of ethics has been lost some where along the way. It is therefore up to the employer to figure out how best to test a potential employee's integrity, to investigate an applicant's history, and then to decide whether or not to hire this individual.

Report 27-4
Business Report

Open the file for Report 27-3 and make the following changes:

1. Change the byline to `Diane Jackson`.
2. Change the date to `July 7`.
3. Change the third side heading to `COMMON REASONS FOR LYING`.
4. Add this sentence to the end of the last paragraph:

```
The importance of ethics in
a future employee should
never be underestimated.
```


DOCUMENT PROCESSING

REPORT 27-4 Optional. If time is short, you may have students skip the optional job. No new features are presented.

ASSESS

www.mhhe.com/gdp to download a copy of the Technique Evaluation Form.

TECHNIQUE EVALUATION FORM
Walk around the room to observe report formatting.

Evaluate Report 27-3.

Create a quiz to practice the proofreaders' marks—five sentences in which students have to identify proofreaders' marks and five sentences in which they have to insert proofreaders' marks.

Extending the Lesson

Create a list of ten sentences to reinforce the language arts rules presented—comma, independent, and comma, introductory.

Ask students if they have observed proofreaders' marks being used in office documents.

CLOSE

Stress the correct procedure to use to exit Microsoft Word and the GDP program.

GDP SOFTWARE TIPS

LESSONS
SKILLBUILDING

MAP
TIMED WRITINGS
LANGUAGE ARTS
GAMES

Template

GDP software has been developed to launch Microsoft Word with special template default settings. This template was developed to ensure that students' screens look similar, avoid the problems caused by changes previous users made to the software, avoid having Microsoft Word automatically correct *some* typos but not others, and avoid most automatic changes Microsoft Word makes. The reset Microsoft Word options include the following settings:

- Automatic hyphenation
- Print layout view
- Standard and Formatting toolbars in two rows
- Inactive AutoCorrect options

FOCUS

TIME MANAGEMENT 

Suggested Schedule:

Warmup	2′
Skillbuilding	21′
Formatting	6′
Document Processing	21′
Total	**50′**

TEACH

SKILLBUILDING

LESSON 28-B Speed sprints are very motivational. Have students push moderately for speed on these easy sentences.

LESSON 28-C Close reaches include adjacent keys and consecutive-finger reaches.

LESSON 28-D Adjacent keys are side by side on the same row. Ensure that students are typing their practice lines in the correct pattern for either speed or accuracy.

LESSON 28-E Consecutive-finger reaches are two consecutive keys that are typed with the same finger.

Lesson 28

Business Reports With Lists

Goals

- Type at least 31wpm/3′/5e
- Format business reports with bulleted and numbered lists

A. Type 2 times.

A. WARMUP

```
     At 8:30, Horowitz & Co. will fax Order #V546 to us for  11
immediate processing! Just how many additional orders they  23
will request isn't known. About 7% of the orders are here.  35
 | 1 | 2 | 3 | 4 | 5 | 6 | 7 | 8 | 9 | 10 | 11 | 12
```

SKILLBUILDING

B. Take three 12-second timed writings on each line. The scale below the last line shows your wpm speed for a 12-second timed writing.

B. 12-SECOND SPEED SPRINTS

```
Mary will not be able to meet them at the game later today.
The class is not going to be able to meet if they are gone.
They could not open that old door when the chair fell over.
This very nice piece of paper may be used to print the job.
    5    10    15    20    25    30    35    40    45    50    55    60
```

PRETEST → PRACTICE → POSTTEST

PRETEST
Take a 1-minute timed writing. Review your speed and errors.

C. PRETEST: Close Reaches

```
     The growth in the volume of company assets is due to  11
the astute group of twenty older employees. Their answers  23
were undoubtedly the reason for the increase in net worth.  35
 | 1 | 2 | 3 | 4 | 5 | 6 | 7 | 8 | 9 | 10 | 11 | 12
```

PRACTICE
Speed Emphasis:
If you made 2 or fewer errors on the Pretest, type each *individual* line 2 times.
Accuracy Emphasis:
If you made 3 or more errors, type each *group* of lines (as though it were a paragraph) 2 times.

D. PRACTICE: Adjacent Keys

```
as ashes cases class asset astute passes chased creased ask
we weave tweed towed weigh wealth twenty fewest answers wet
rt worth alert party smart artist sorted charts turtles art
```

E. PRACTICE: Consecutive Fingers

```
un undue bunch stung begun united punish outrun untie funny
gr grand agree angry grade growth egress hungry group graph
ol older solid tools spool volume evolve uphold olive scold
```

POSTTEST
Repeat the Pretest timed writing and compare performance.

F. POSTTEST: Close Reaches

TEACHING THE ADULT LEARNER

STUDENT SUCCESS To help adult learners process information more accurately in the classroom, try to maintain a moderate pace of speaking during lectures. Provide an introduction or preorganizer to the material being presented to the class. Also, provide a summary of the major concepts or points covered.

Encourage adult learners to schedule study sessions together to review their notes. They can meet in an unoccupied space on campus before class.

G. Take two 3-minute timed writings. Review your speed and errors.

Goal: At least 31wpm/3′/5e

G. 3-MINUTE TIMED WRITING

```
     Credit cards can make shopping very convenient, and       11
they frequently help you record and track your spending.       22
However, many card companies charge high fees for using        33
their credit cards.                                            37
     You must realize that it may be better to pay in cash     48
and not use a credit card. Look at all your options. Some      60
card companies do not charge yearly fees. Some may give        71
you extended warranties on goods you buy with their credit     83
cards. Judge all the details; you may be surprised.            93
| 1 | 2 | 3 | 4 | 5 | 6 | 7 | 8 | 9 | 10 | 11 | 12
```

FORMATTING

H. BULLETED AND NUMBERED LISTS

- Numbers or bullets call attention to items in a list. If the sequence of the items is important, use numbers rather than bullets.
- Numbers and bullets either appear at the left margin or are indented to the same point as the paragraphs in the document.
- The numbers and bullets themselves are followed by an indent, and carry-over lines are indented automatically to align with the text in the previous line, not the bullet or number.

I. BUSINESS REPORTS WITH LISTS

To format a list in a business report:

- Press ENTER 2 times to insert 1 blank line above the list.
- Type the list *unformatted* (without the bullets or numbers) at the left margin.
- If all the items in the list are 1 line long, single-space the entire list.
- If any items in the list are multiline, single-space each item in the list but insert a blank line between the items for readability.
- Press ENTER 2 times to insert 1 blank line below the list.
- Select all lines of the list and apply the number or bullet feature to the selected lines of the list only.

Word Processing Manual

J. WORD PROCESSING: BULLETS AND NUMBERING

Study Lesson 28 in your word processing manual. Complete all of the shaded steps while at your computer. Then format the jobs that follow.

ERGONOMICALLY SPEAKING

KEYBOARD POSITION When students use the keyboard or mouse, their arms should be relaxed and loose, with the elbows close to the sides and forearms and hands approximately parallel to the floor. The wrists should be as straight as possible. They should not be curved sideways or more than 10 degrees up or down.

Visit us on the Web at **www.mhhe.com/gdp** for more information.

Lesson 28

FORMATTING

Reference Manual

Ask students to review bulleted and numbered lists and business reports with lists in the **Reference Manual, R-8A** and **R-9A,** before they begin typing.

LESSON 28-H Explain how to format bullets and numbers, and point out examples in the Reference Manual and illustrations.

LESSON 28-I Explain the steps for formatting a list in a business report. Emphasize how critical it is to type the list unformatted first and then go back and apply the number or bullet feature to the selected lines of the list only.

LESSON 28-J Help students use the bullets and numbering commands.

Remind students to select the correct tab in the **Bullets and Numbering** dialog box.

INSTRUCTOR STRATEGIES

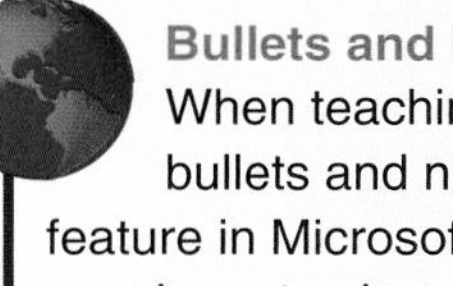

Bullets and Numbering When teaching the bullets and numbering feature in Microsoft Word, you may have to change the settings for format, style, and position. To change settings:

- Choose **Bullets and Numbering** from the **Format** menu.
- Choose the **Bulleted** or **Numbered** tab.
- Select a bullet or number option.
- Click **Customize**.
- Edit the settings and click **OK**.

Lesson 28

DOCUMENT PROCESSING

REPORT 28-5 Guide students step by step through this first business report with a list.

Remind them that the list should appear at the left margin.

Remind them that, in a list, any items that have multiple lines are typed single-spaced with a blank line between items. It is critical that students type the list unformatted first and then go back to apply the bullet or number command.

Remind students that the basic parts of a report appear in the **Reference Manual, R8-A** and **R8-B.**

REPORT 28-6 Optional. If time is short, you may have students skip the optional job. No new features are presented.

ASSESS

www.mhhe.com/gdp to download a copy of the Technique Evaluation Form.

TECHNIQUE EVALUATION FORM Review results of timed writings.

Walk around the room to observe report formatting.

Evaluate Report 26-5.

Extending the Lesson

Discuss the difference between using bullets and numbers in a list. Which one would be used to indicate priorities?

CLOSE

Review report formatting.

DOCUMENT PROCESSING

Report 28-5
Business Report

1. Type the report using standard business report format.
2. Use the bullet and numbering feature to add bullets or numbers to the list after typing the list unformatted.

INCREASING YOUR ENERGY
Shannon Wahlberg
August 21, 20--

When your energy level is running high, you are more creative, happier, and more relaxed. Some people believe that we are born with a personality that is innately energetic, lethargic, or somewhere in between. However, we are all capable of generating more energy in our lives at home or at work.

CREATING MORE ENERGY

There are many ways in which you can generate more energy before you leave for work. These two methods are simple and can be practiced without a great deal of planning:

1. Wake up to natural light by opening your curtains before you go to bed. The light coming in signals your body to stop releasing melatonin, a hormone that tells your body to continue sleeping.
2. Play music that is lively and upbeat. This will set the tone for the day.

MAINTAINING MORE ENERGY

Once you have raised your energy level at home, you can also learn to maintain your energy level at work.

- Remain positive throughout the day.
- Avoid people who are negative and have low energy. Instead, seek out those who are cheerful and positive. They will boost your energy level.
- Avoid high-fat foods, sweets, and heavy meals during the working day.
- Accept your periods of low energy as natural rhythms, knowing that they will pass. This will help you relax.

If you practice these methods to create and maintain your energy levels, you will find that these techniques will become a natural part of your daily life. Enjoy the change and experiment with your own techniques!

Report 28-6
Business Report

Open the file for Report 28-5 and make the following changes:

1. Change the first side heading to `HOW TO CREATE MORE ENERGY.`
2. Change the second side heading to `HOW TO MAINTAIN MORE ENERGY.`
3. Change the third bulleted item to this: `Avoid foods with caffeine, such as sodas and coffee.`
4. Change the fourth bulleted item to this: `Monitor your sleep. Sleeping too long can make you just as tired as sleeping too little.`

Windows Wizard

RECOVER FILES To recover deleted files in Windows 2000, Me, and XP:

- Double-click the **Recycle Bin** icon on the desktop.
- Click the file to be recovered.
- Choose **Restore** from the **File** menu.

To recover several files at once, press CTRL and click each file.

Note: Point out to students the vital fact that files deleted from network locations and floppy disks are **not** moved to the **Recycle Bin**. **They are deleted permanently.**

Academic Reports

Goals

- Improve speed and accuracy
- Refine language arts skills in proofreading
- Format academic reports

A. Type 2 times.

A. WARMUP

```
1      Will the package arrive at 9:45 or 11:29? The exact      11
2  answer to this question could mean the difference between    23
3  losing or saving their account; Joyce also realizes this.    34
   | 1 | 2 | 3 | 4 | 5 | 6 | 7 | 8 | 9 | 10 | 11 | 12
```

SKILLBUILDING

B. Type each paragraph 1 time. Change every masculine pronoun to a feminine pronoun. Change every feminine pronoun to a masculine pronoun.

B. TECHNIQUE PRACTICE: CONCENTRATION

```
4      She will finish composing the report as soon as he has
5  given her all the research. Her final draft will be turned in
6  to her boss; he will submit it to the company president.
7      His new job with her company was fascinating. When the
8  chance to join her firm came up, he jumped at it immediately.
9  I wonder if she will give him a promotion anytime soon.
```

C. PACED PRACTICE

If you are not using the GDP software, turn to page SB-14 and follow the directions for this activity.

Strategies for Career Success

Turning Negative Messages Positive

Accentuate the positive. When communicating bad news (e.g., layoffs, product recalls, price increases, personnel problems), find the positive.

People respond better to positive rather than negative language, and they are more likely to cooperate if treated fairly and with respect. Avoid insults, accusations, criticism, or words with negative connotations (e.g., *failed*, *delinquent*, *bad*). Focus on what the reader can do rather than on what you won't or can't let the reader do. Instead of "You will not qualify unless . . . ," state "You will qualify if you are . . . ."

Assuage your audience's response by providing an explanation to support your decision and examples of how they might benefit. Analyze your audience and decide whether to give the negative news in the beginning, middle, or end of your message. Regardless of your approach, always maintain goodwill.

YOUR TURN Review some of your written documents and observe if they have a positive tone.

Strategies for Career Success

POSITIVE MESSAGES

Discuss positive and negative sentences. Ask students to rewrite negative sentences to have a positive tone.

YOUR TURN If time permits, ask students to complete the Your Turn activity.

Lesson 29

FOCUS

TIME MANAGEMENT

Suggested Schedule:

Warmup	2′
Skillbuilding	14′
Language Arts	6′
Formatting	6′
Document Processing	22′
Total	**50′**

TEACH

SKILLBUILDING

LESSON 29-B Students should emphasize accuracy rather than speed.

SOLUTION: Lines 4–9

4. He, she
5. him, His
6. his, she
7. Her, his
8. his, she
9. he, her

LESSON 29-C Paced Practice helps students reach individual speed and accuracy goals in 2-wpm increments by pacing them as they strive for a slightly higher rate.

Lesson 29

LANGUAGE ARTS

LESSON 29-D Alternative routine: Dictate each word and have students type the word once. For each word mistyped, have students study the spelling and type the word correctly 3 times. Discuss the meaning or use of selected words.

SOLUTION: Lines 15–20

15. personnel
16. Our, their
17. Their committee
18. employee, opportunity
19. further, its
20. appropriate, procedures

FORMATTING

Reference Manual

Ask students to review basic proofreaders' marks in the **Reference Manual, R-14C,** before they begin typing.

LESSON 29-E Review the additional proofreaders' marks, especially the ones to move right, to move left, and to indicate a new paragraph.

LANGUAGE ARTS

D. SPELLING

D. Type these frequently misspelled words, paying special attention to any spelling problems in each word.

```
10 personnel information its procedures their committee system
11 receive employees which education services opportunity area
12 financial appropriate interest received production contract
13 important through necessary customer employee further there
14 property account approximately general control division our
```

Edit the sentences to correct any misspellings.

```
15 All company personel will receive important information.
16 Are division has some control over there financial account.
17 There comittee has received approximately three contracts.
18 The employe and the customer have an oportunity to attend.
19 We have no farther interest in the property or it's owner.
20 When it is necessary, apropriate proceedures are followed.
```

FORMATTING

E. MORE PROOFREADERS' MARKS

1. Review the most frequently used proofreaders' marks introduced in Lesson 27.
2. Study the additional proofreaders' marks presented here.

Proofreaders' Marks	Draft	Final Copy
ds Double-space	ds first line second line	first line second line
...... Don't delete	a ~~true~~ story	a true story
○ Spell out	the only ①	the only one
⊐ Move right	Please send	Please send
⊏ Move left	May 1	May 1
~~ Bold	Column Heading	**Column Heading**
ital Italic	ital Time magazine	*Time* magazine
u/l Underline	u/l Time magazine	Time magazine readers
Move as shown	(readers) will see	will see

Note that a new paragraph may be formatted either by inserting a blank line before it in a single-spaced document or by indenting the first line 0.5 inch (⊐) in a double-spaced document.

EXTENDING LANGUAGE ARTS

Spelling Unfamiliar words are an additional challenge to the typist. Before your students begin typing these words, take time to give them a brief definition of each word. Once you have discussed the definitions of the words, dictate them to the students. Ask the students to look at you while they are typing the words. Then ask them to check their typed words against the copy in the textbook. Have students type each word they missed 3 times.

For homework, ask the students to prepare a list of the definitions of these words. By looking up the words in a dictionary, students will reinforce their own understanding of the meaning of each word.

F. ACADEMIC REPORTS

To format an academic report:

1. Double-space academic reports.
2. After you have set the line spacing to double, press ENTER 3 times to begin the first line of the academic report about 2 inches from the top of the page.
3. Type the title in all-caps, centered, in bold, and change the font size to 14 point. Double-space a 2-line title.
4. Press ENTER 1 time and change the font size to 12 point.
5. If the report includes a subtitle, byline, or date, type each item centered, in bold and upper- and lowercase letters; press ENTER 1 time after each line in the heading block.
6. Type side headings at the left margin, in bold and all-caps.
7. Press TAB 1 time at the start of paragraphs and paragraph headings to indent them 0.5 inch.
8. Type paragraph headings in bold and in upper- and lowercase letters, and follow the paragraph heading with a bold period and 1 space.
9. Insert an approximate 1-inch bottom margin on all pages, and insert a 1-inch top margin on continuation pages.
10. Do not number the first page. However, number all continuation pages at the top right margin.

Go To Word Processing Manual

G. WORD PROCESSING: LINE SPACING

Study Lesson 29 in your word processing manual. Complete all of the shaded steps while at your computer. Then format the jobs that follow.

DOCUMENT PROCESSING

Report 29-7
Academic Report

1. Type this report in standard format for an academic report.
2. Type the 2-line title double-spaced, and use standard format for the rest of the heading block.
3. Insert a page number at the top right, and suppress the page number on the first page.
4. Spell-check, preview, and proofread your document for spelling and formatting errors before printing it.

Refer to Reference Manual

See page R-8C and R-8D of the Reference Manual for an illustration of a multipage report in academic style.

Indent paragraphs in an academic report.

Highlighted words are spelling words from the language arts activities.

ELECTRONIC SAFEGUARDS IN THE DIGITAL WORLD

Trends in Technology

Kevin Nguyen

July 13, 20--

More and more people are using computers and the Internet for a wide variety of reasons, both personal and professional. Most of the technology requires the use of passwords, user names, pin numbers, and miscellaneous other important codes for users to access their accounts. Unfortunately, at times it seems as if the number of codes that are necessary is increasing in geometric proportions. The problem is how to maintain accurate records of these various security codes and still preserve a secure environment, technologically speaking.

(Continued on next page)

FORMATTING

Refer to Reference Manual

Ask students to review academic reports in the **Reference Manual, R-8C** and **R-8D,** before they begin typing.

LESSON 29-F Explain how to format an academic report. Give an example of an academic report, such as a term paper.

LESSON 29-G Help students use the line spacing command.

DOCUMENT PROCESSING

REPORT 29-7 Guide students step by step through this first multipage academic report with rough-draft scripting.

Encourage them to use the electronic Reference Manual in the GDP software as they create the document in the word processor.

Remind students that word wrap is on and that their line endings may differ from those shown here.

Explain that shaded words indicate spelling words introduced in the lesson.

Meeting Special Needs

LECTURE NOTES Learning-disabled (LD) students may have difficulty taking notes in class. A tape recorder can be a valuable auxiliary aid for them. It reduces demands on their auditory memory, language processing, and writing skills. Some students request independent note takers, who are other students in the class. A copy of the notes is provided to the learning-disabled student.

Visit us on the Web at **www.mhhe.com/gdp** for more information.

Lesson 29

DOCUMENT PROCESSING

REPORT 29-8 Optional. If time is short, you may have students skip the optional job. No new features are presented.

ASSESS

www.mhhe.com/gdp to download a copy of the Technique Evaluation Form.

TECHNIQUE EVALUATION FORM Walk around the classroom to observe students' technique. Complete a Technique Evaluation Form for each student.

Review report formatting.

Extending the Lesson

Create a list of sentences requiring students to insert proofreaders' marks to edit the document.

CLOSE

Review the differences between business reports and academic reports.

SECURITY CODE OVERLOAD

People need 1 or sometimes 2 security codes just to log on to their computers. Several more are needed to access web sites, trade stocks, and shop and bank online, just to name a few activities. In addition most people need to remember codes for their home phones, work phones, cell phones, and voice mail. Banks require codes to withdraw money and use credit cards and ATMs. With so many security codes proliferating on a daily basis, its no wonder that we are often frustrated and frazzled as we move through our daily lives going about our personal and professional business. To add insult to injury we are often being asked to change our passwords and codes on a regular basis.

MANAGING SECURITY CODES

Several things can be done to help manage this ever-growing list of security codes. Try to choose passwords that are in some way meaningful to you but that cannot be guessed at by an intruder. Use a combination of letters and numbers. An article in the magazine Technology Bytes suggests using using street addresses or names of pets that can be easily remembered but that have no logical association with anything else.

If you decide to keep a list of security codes, make sure to protect the file in an appropriate way. If you must write down your passwords, physically lock them up. You must control and manage these important and necessary security codes to protect your personal and financial information.

Report 29-8

Academic Report

Open the file for Report 29-7 and make the following changes:

1. Change the byline to Nancy Dodson.
2. Add this paragraph below the last paragraph at the end of the report:

   A number of Web sites are available to help you remember your passwords and user names. However, these sites can help you do much more than simply manage your security codes. Some sites can provide instant registration at new sites with just one click. They also offer price comparisons while you shop anywhere on the Web, and they bring together the best search engines all in one place for easier searching. They can also filter e-mail to help you eliminate cluttered e-mail boxes full of junk.

Technology Tips

LINE SPACING

Remind students that line spacing is a paragraph format. All lines of the paragraph will be formatted. To change the line spacing for a single paragraph, students can position the insertion point in the paragraph and change the line spacing. It is not necessary to select the entire paragraph.

To format multiple paragraphs, select the paragraphs prior to applying the line spacing format.

Academic Reports With Displays

Goals

- Type at least 32wpm/3′/5e
- Format rough-draft academic reports with indented lists and displays

A. Type 2 times.

A. WARMUP

```
     Did Zagorsky & Sons charge $876 for the renovation?     11
An invoice wasn't quite right; the exact amount charged in   22
July can be found in an e-mail message to zagsons@post.com.  34
| 1 | 2 | 3 | 4 | 5 | 6 | 7 | 8 | 9 | 10 | 11 | 12
```

SKILLBUILDING

B. MAP

Follow the GDP software directions for this exercise in improving keystroking accuracy.

C. DIAGNOSTIC PRACTICE: NUMBERS

If you are not using the GDP software, turn to page SB-5 and follow the directions for this activity.

D. Take two 3-minute timed writings. Review your speed and errors.

Goal: At least 32wpm/3′/5e

D. 3-MINUTE TIMED WRITING

```
     If you want to work in information processing, you     10
may realize that there are steps that you must take to      21
plan for such an exciting career. First, you must decide    33
whether or not you have the right personality traits.       44
     Then you must be trained in the technical skills you   54
need in such an important field. The technology is changing 66
each day. You must stay focused on keeping up with these    78
changes. Also, you must never quit wanting to learn new     89
skills each day you are on the job.                         96
| 1 | 2 | 3 | 4 | 5 | 6 | 7 | 8 | 9 | 10 | 11 | 12
```


MAP 75

MAP

TRUE OR FALSE? The more your students practice, the more accurately they will type.

False.

The statement should read: "The more students practice **prescriptive drills**, the more accurately they will type." This is the philosophy behind Mis-stroke Analysis and Prescription (MAP), and it is the very reason it is so important for your students.

Lesson 30

FOCUS

TIME MANAGEMENT

Suggested Schedule:

Warmup	2′
Skillbuilding	21′
Formatting	4′
Document Processing	23′
Total	**50′**

TEACH

SKILLBUILDING

LESSON 30-B MAP is a simple, comprehensive, and individualized software program for improving keystroking accuracy.

LESSON 30-C Encourage students to push moderately for speed on the Pretest.

Lesson 30

FORMATTING

Reference Manual

Ask students to review academic reports with lists and indented displays in the **Reference Manual, R-8C** and **R-8D,** before they begin typing.

LESSON 30-E Explain how to format an academic report with a list.

LESSON 30-F Explain how to format an academic report with an indented display.

LESSON 30-G Help students use the **Cut**, **Copy**, **Paste**, and **Indent** commands.

DOCUMENT PROCESSING

REPORT 30-9 Guide students step by step through this first multipage academic report with a displayed paragraph.

Encourage them to use the electronic Reference Manual in the GDP software as they create the document in the word processor.

Remind students that word wrap is on and that their line endings may differ from those shown here.

FORMATTING

E. ACADEMIC REPORTS WITH LISTS

To format a list in an academic report:

- Press ENTER 1 time to begin the list.
- Type the list *unformatted* at the left margin, double-spaced.
- Press ENTER 1 time after the last line in the list.
- Select all lines of the list and apply the number or bullet feature to the selected lines of the list only. Do not include the blank lines above and below the list in your selection.
- Increase or decrease the indent of the list as needed so that the list begins at the same point of indention as the paragraphs in the report.

F. ACADEMIC REPORTS WITH INDENTED DISPLAYS

A paragraph having 4 lines or more that are quoted or having lines that need special emphasis should be formatted so that the paragraph stands out from the rest of the report. To format academic reports with indented displays:

- Type the paragraph single-spaced and indented 0.5 inch from both the left and the right margins (instead of enclosing it in quotation marks).
- Use the indent command in your word processing software to format a displayed paragraph.

Word Processing Manual

G. WORD PROCESSING: INCREASE INDENT AND CUT, COPY, AND PASTE

Study Lesson 30 in your word processing manual. Complete all of the shaded steps while at your computer. Then format the jobs that follow.

DOCUMENT PROCESSING

Report 30-9
Academic Report

1. Type the report using standard academic report format.
2. Type the list using standard format for lists in an academic report. Use the number feature to add numbers to the list after you have typed the list unformatted. Use the cut-and-paste feature to move the second numbered item.
3. Type the display using standard format for indented displays in an academic report.
4. Type paragraph headings indented 0.5 inch, in bold, and in upper- and lowercase letters, and follow the paragraph heading with a bold period and 1 space.
5. Insert a page number at the top right margin, and suppress the page number on the first page.

Reference Manual

See page R-8D of the Reference Manual for an illustration of a multipage report in academic style with a displayed paragraph.

ENDING PROCRASTINATION

Judy Baca

Every one at one time or another has put of some task, goal or important plan at work for any number of reasons. perhaps you think time is too short or the task isn't really that important. Either way, procrastination can lead to a stalled life and career.

(Continued on next page)

INSTRUCTOR STRATEGIES

Gender Differences Researchers have found that American women are more likely than American men to be supportive, tentative, and emotionally expressive when communicating. Males are found to be more direct, fact-oriented, and assertive. It is probable that in every culture or country men and women differ somewhat in their communication styles.

Lesson 30

DOCUMENT PROCESSING

EVALUATE YOUR SITUATION

Joyce Winfrey of Time Management Incorporated has some very good advice that will help you to begin to move forward. She says that you should ask yourself 2 very basic questions about why you are procrastinating:

1. Is there a valid reason for my procrastination?
2. Am I procrastinating because the task at hand is not really what I want?

After you have asked yourself these questions, ms. Winfrey suggests that you do the following:

Look deep within yourself. If you are looking for excuses, then the process of asking these questions will be a waste of your time. However, if you answer these questions honestly, you might find answers that surprise you and that will help clarify your situation.

She also recommends several techniques can help your get back on task and put an end to procrastination.

PRACTICE NEW TECHNIQUES

Identifying and understanding the techniques which follow is the first step. Once you know what to do you can begin to practice these steps daily.

Take Baby Steps. Don't make any task bigger than it really is by looking at the whole thing at once. Break it down into babysteps that are manageable.

Dont Strive for Perfectionism. If you are waiting for the perfect solution or the perfect opportunity, you will immobilized. Accept the fact that no one and nothing is perfect. Then accept your mistakes and move on.

Enjoy the Task. Enjoy the task at hand and find something in it that is positive and rewarding. Confront your fears with a plan of action.

Remind yourself of all these techniques daily. Post them by your telephone, your desk, or your car. You will find that your personal life and career will gain momentum, and success will soon be yours.

INSTRUCTOR STRATEGIES

Rough Drafts Remind students that a good technique for typing rough-draft copy is to first read the entire document for comprehension before they begin typing.

Technology Tips

DRAG AND DROP

You may want to demonstrate the procedure to drag and drop text as an alternative to the **Cut** and **Copy** commands. Remind students that when text is moved using drag and drop, it does not appear on the clipboard.

Lesson 30

DOCUMENT PROCESSING

Reference Manual

Ask students to review the academic report format in the **Reference Manual, R-8C** and **R-8D,** before they begin typing.

Progress Check and Proofreading Check

REPORT 30-10 All major formatting features presented in this unit are included in this document. You may want to use this as a short document processing test. In addition, you may want to inform students that this document also serves as a check of their proofreading skill and that they may have only one opportunity to have the GDP software check the document in order for them to receive a satisfactory proofreading grade.

ASSESS

www.mhhe.com/gdp to download a copy of the Technique Evaluation Form.

TECHNIQUE EVALUATION FORM

Review results of timed writings.

Print a report for all skillbuilding exercises for Lessons 26–30.

Extending the Lesson

Ask students if they have to create a report for any of their other classes. Discuss content and formatting requirements.

CLOSE

Remind students to check their documents for correct format.

Report 30-10

Academic Report

Progress and Proofreading Check

Documents designated as Proofreading Checks serve as a check of your proofreading skill. Your goal is to have zero typographical errors when the GDP software first scores the document.

1. Type the report using standard academic report format for a multipage academic report with a list.
2. Make all changes as indicated by the proofreaders' marks.

TIPS FOR HELPING YOU
PREPARE FOR YOUR EXAM
Betty Goldberg
June 8, 20--

in school you have taken ~~some~~ many exams. Whether you are an excellent exam taker or a novice at the task, you probably have experienced a degree of stress related to your performance on an exam. There are some steps you can take to reduce the stress of taking an exam, and these suggestions will likely help you throughout your life.

PREPARING FOR THE EXAM

Of course, it's always easier to take an exam from an Instructor whom you have had in previous classes, because you know what to expect. From past experience, you know whether the Instructor likes to use objective questions or subjective questions, whether the Instructor focuses on the textbook or on class notes, and the difficulty of the questions the Instructor asks.

If you (don't) know what to expect, however, you need to prepare for all possibilities. Be sure that you review ~~all~~ pertinent materials for the exam—whether they come from classnotes, the textbook, field trips, or class room presentations.

SURVIVING THE DAY BEFORE THE EXAM

Be sure you know where and at what time the exam will be administered. Organize the materials you need to bring with you to the exam. You may need pencils, pens, calculators, disks, or paper. Try to get a good night's sleep the night before the exam, and don't upset your usual routine.

Taking The Exam

Now that the day of the exam has arrived, there are several actions you should take to ensure that you perform well:

1. Arrive at the test ~~sight~~ site early so that you are ready to take the exam when the instructor announces the beginning time. That means that (before) you have to be sure to get up early enough to have a light breakfast leaving for the exam.
2. Read very carefully the instructions provided on the exam to be sure you answer the questions correctly.
3. Keep track of time so that you don't get stuck and spend too much of your time on any one part of the exam.
4. Try to keep a positive attitude.
5. Relax as best you can—a relaxed performance is ~~much~~ more productive than a stressed performance.

GDP SOFTWARE TIPS

Progress Check/ Proofreading Check

From this point on, the last document in each unit is labeled a Progress Check/ Proofreading Check.

MHHE CHAMPIONS

Skills Test

A midsemester skills test is helpful to identify where students' weaknesses lie.

Use the Progress Checks to customize a midsemester test.

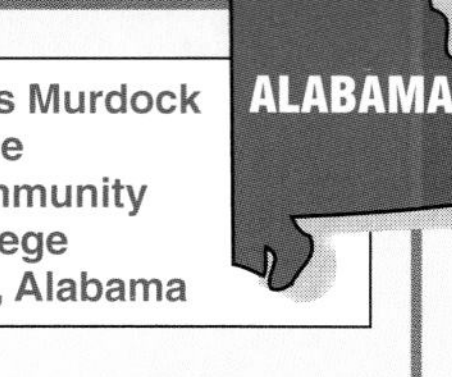

Phyliss Murdock
Wallace Community College
Selma, Alabama

Correspondence

April 3, 20--

Ms. Linda Lopez
Account Manager
The Internet Connection
7625 Maple Avenue
Pomona, CA 91765

Dear Ms. Lopez:

Our company is interested in hosting an educational seminar this spring that will focus on meeting the growing need for information industry professionals to keep abreast of emerging new technologies and trends. We are specifically interested in information on high-speed Internet connections.

I understand that The Internet Connection specializes in these seminars and will also help businesses analyze their needs and choose an appropriate solution. I am in the process of contacting several companies similar to yours who might be interested in conducting these seminars. Please contact me by Thursday or Friday at the latest so that we can discuss this matter further.

I appreciate the fine service we have always received from you in the past, Ms. Lopez, and I look forward to hearing from you.

Sincerely,

Ruzanna Petroska
Technology Specialist

urs

MEMO TO: All Salaried Employees

FROM: Amy Vigil, Human Resources

DATE: November 2, 20--

SUBJECT: Health Care Benefit Plan

Effective January 1, Allied Aerospace Industries will contract with MedNet to begin a new health benefits program for all eligible salaried personnel. A brochure outlining important program information will be mailed to you soon.

An open enrollment period will be in effect during the entire month of January. If you and your family are interested in one of the MedNet health plan options, you may transfer yourself and your dependents into any appropriate plan. All applications must be received no later than midnight, January 31. You may also access your plan over the Internet at www.mednet.com if it is more convenient.

If you have any questions or need any help understanding your options, please call me at Ext. 134. I will be happy to help you select the plan that is best for you.

urs

Trend Electronics
2206 31st Street
Minneapolis, MN 55407-1911

Mr. Charles Goldstein
Software Solutions
2981 Canwood Street
Roselle, IL 60172

RESOURCE MANAGER

GDP SOFTWARE

- Lessons 31–35
- Software User's Guide
- Instructor Management LAN Version
- Word Processing Manual
- Professional Handbook (IWE*)—Teaching in a Distance-Learning Environment
- MAP 

*Instructor Wraparound Edition

ASSESSMENT

- Test Booklet—Alternate Test 2
- Progress Check—Correspondence 35-19
- Professional Handbook (IWE*)—Assessment Strategies

ON THE WEB

- **www.mhhe.com/gdp**
- Instructor Management Web Version

Unit 7

UNIT OVERVIEW

Students will be introduced to business letters using the block style as well as the use of enclosure notations in letters. The envelope feature of Microsoft Word will be used to create envelopes. Students will also learn how to write interoffice memos.

Did You Know?

Reference Manual

The front of the student text contains a Reference Manual which shows the correct formatting of all documents students will learn in this course plus additional formats for their reference.

www.mhhe.com/gdp to download a copy of the Technique Evaluation Form.

TECHNIQUE EVALUATION FORM

Use this form to keep track of student progress. Complete a form for each student.

Name Class Date

Technique Evaluation Form

Date	Workstation		Position at the Keyboard		Keystroking	
	Acceptable	Needs Improvement	Acceptable	Needs Improvement	Acceptable	Needs Improvement

Workstation

1. Positions the chair so that the upper and lower legs form a 90-degree angle and the lower back is supported.
2. Positions the keyboard even with the front of the desk.
3. Positions the text on either side of the monitor as close to it vertically and horizontally as possible to minimize head and eye movement and to avoid neck strain.
4. Positions the mouse on a pad at the side of the monitor opposite the text.

Position at the Keyboard

5. Centers the body opposite the keyboard.
6. Leans forward slightly from the hips, with the base of the spine touching the back of the chair and the feet flat on the floor.
7. Keeps the elbows alongside the body in a relaxed position.
8. Curves the fingers naturally over the home position, with the back of the hand at the same angle as the keyboard.

Keystroking

9. Keeps the forearms horizontal and raises the hands slightly when typing so that the wrists do not touch the keyboard while typing. (Hands may rest at the bottom of the keyboard—away from the keys—during nontyping intervals.)
10. Makes quick, snappy strokes using the correct fingers.
11. Returns the finger immediately to the home position or moves to the next position after each stroke.
12. Operates all keys by touch, keeping the eyes on the copy most of the time while typing.

Comments

FOCUS

TIME MANAGEMENT

Suggested Schedule:

Warmup	2′
Skillbuilding	15′
Language Arts	6′
Formatting	8′
Document Processing	19′
Total	**50′**

TEACH

SKILLBUILDING

LESSON 31-B Speed sprints are very motivational. Have students push moderately for speed on these easy sentences.

LESSON 31-C Students take repeated timed writings on a passage containing the exact number of words for their speed goal until they can complete the passage with no errors. Then they move to the next, more difficult passage and start again.

LESSON 31-D Students take repeated timed writings on a passage containing the exact number of words for their speed goal until they can complete the passage with no errors. Then they move to the next longer passage and start again.

Lesson 31

Business Letters

Goals

- Improve speed and accuracy
- Refine language arts skills in capitalization
- Format a business letter in block style

A. Type 2 times.

A. WARMUP

```
     You can save $1,698 when you buy the 20-part video         10
series! Just ask for Series #MX5265 in the next 7 days;         22
ordering early qualifies you for a sizable discount of 5%.      33
| 1 | 2 | 3 | 4 | 5 | 6 | 7 | 8 | 9 | 10 | 11 | 12
```

SKILLBUILDING

B. Take three 12-second timed writings on each line. The scale below the last line shows your wpm speed for a 12-second timed writing.

B. 12-SECOND SPEED SPRINTS

```
Mary will be able to go home when she can run fast and far.
Sam can come to the store if he is able to stop for a soda.
Suzy knows that she must send the mail out by noon or else.
Only a few good desks will be made by the end of this week.
    5    10    15    20    25    30    35    40    45    50    55    60
```

C. PROGRESSIVE PRACTICE: ALPHABET

If you are not using the GDP software, turn to page SB-7 and follow the directions for this activity.

D. PROGRESSIVE PRACTICE: NUMBERS

If you are not using the GDP software, turn to page SB-11 and follow the directions for this activity.

LANGUAGE ARTS

E. Study the rules at the right.

E. CAPITALIZATION

Note: The callout signals in the left margin indicate which language arts rule from this lesson has been applied.

RULE ▶ = sentence

Capitalize the first word of a sentence.

Please prepare a summary of your activities.

RULE ▶ = proper

Capitalize proper nouns and adjectives derived from proper nouns.

Judy Hendrix drove to Albuquerque in her new Pontiac convertible.

Note: A proper noun is the official name of a particular person, place, or thing.

(Continued on next page)

Windows Wizard

WINDOWS EXPLORER VIEWS To change the view in Windows Explorer in Windows 2000, Me, or XP:

- Right-click the **Start** button and choose **Explore**.
- Click the Down arrow to the right of the **Views** button.
- Choose **Thumbnails, Tiles, Icons, List**, or **Details** (in Windows XP) or **Large Icons, Small Icons, List**, or **Details** (in Windows 2000 or Me).

You can also choose an option from the **View** menu.

RULE ▶ = time

Capitalize the names of the days of the week, months, holidays, and religious days (but do not capitalize the names of the seasons).

On Thursday, November 25, we will celebrate Thanksgiving, the most popular holiday in the fall.

Edit the paragraph to insert or delete capitalization.

The american flag can be seen flying over the White House in Washington. Our Country's flag is often seen flying over Government buildings on holidays like July 4, independence day. Memorial Day signals the end of spring and the start of Summer. Most Americans consider Labor day the beginning of the fall season. In december many people observe christmas and Hanukkah. most government holidays are scheduled to fall on either a Monday or a friday. Sometimes the birthdays of Historical figures are also celebrated.

FORMATTING

F. BASIC PARTS OF A BUSINESS LETTER

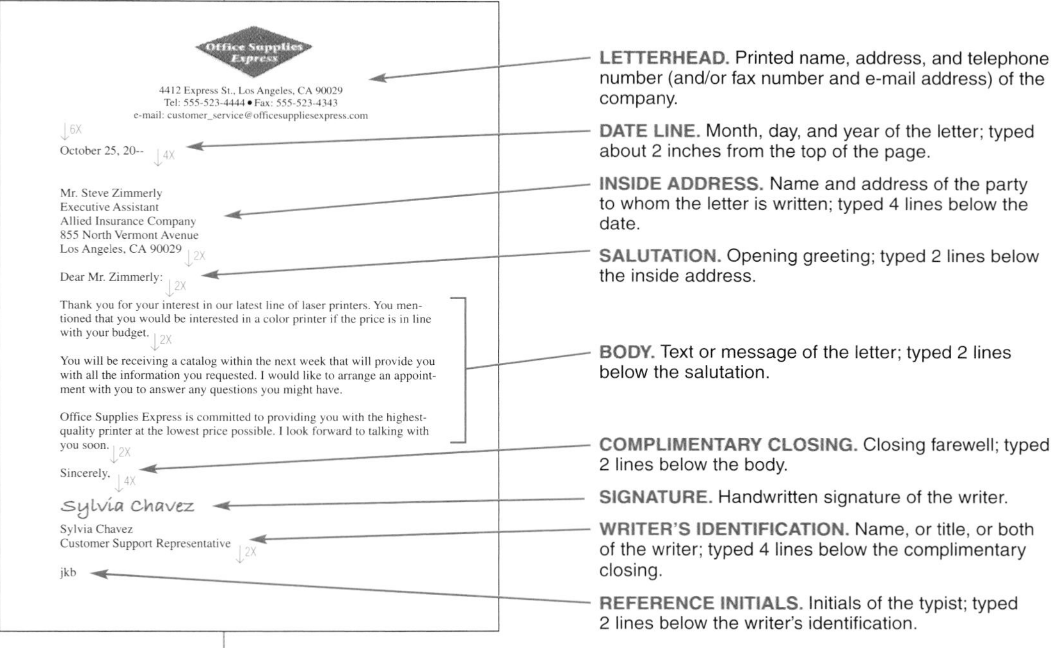

Office Supplies Express
4412 Express St., Los Angeles, CA 90029
Tel: 555-523-4444 • Fax: 555-523-4343
e-mail: customer_service@officesuppliesexpress.com

↓6X

October 25, 20-- ↓4X

Mr. Steve Zimmerly
Executive Assistant
Allied Insurance Company
855 North Vermont Avenue
Los Angeles, CA 90029 ↓2X

Dear Mr. Zimmerly: ↓2X

Thank you for your interest in our latest line of laser printers. You mentioned that you would be interested in a color printer if the price is in line with your budget. ↓2X

You will be receiving a catalog within the next week that will provide you with all the information you requested. I would like to arrange an appointment with you to answer any questions you might have.

Office Supplies Express is committed to providing you with the highest-quality printer at the lowest price possible. I look forward to talking with you soon. ↓2X

Sincerely, ↓4X

Sylvia Chavez

Sylvia Chavez
Customer Support Representative ↓2X

jkb

LETTERHEAD. Printed name, address, and telephone number (and/or fax number and e-mail address) of the company.
DATE LINE. Month, day, and year of the letter; typed about 2 inches from the top of the page.
INSIDE ADDRESS. Name and address of the party to whom the letter is written; typed 4 lines below the date.
SALUTATION. Opening greeting; typed 2 lines below the inside address.
BODY. Text or message of the letter; typed 2 lines below the salutation.
COMPLIMENTARY CLOSING. Closing farewell; typed 2 lines below the body.
SIGNATURE. Handwritten signature of the writer.
WRITER'S IDENTIFICATION. Name, or title, or both of the writer; typed 4 lines below the complimentary closing.
REFERENCE INITIALS. Initials of the typist; typed 2 lines below the writer's identification.

G. BUSINESS LETTERS IN BLOCK STYLE

1. Type all lines beginning at the left margin.
2. Press ENTER 6 times to begin the first line of the letter about 2 inches from the top of the page, and then type the date.
3. After the date, press ENTER 4 times and type the inside address. Leave 1 space between the state and the ZIP Code.

(Continued on next page)

EXTENDING LANGUAGE ARTS

Capitalization Most students know that a sentence always begins with a capital letter, but they often neglect to look for capital letters in proper nouns within a sentence.

Write these examples on your board:

They traveled to Florida, where they visited Florida State University, Sea World, and Key West.

This spring, Easter is on Sunday, April 7.

Explain that Florida is a specific state, Florida State University is a specific university, Sea World is a specific place, and Key West is a specific island off the coast of Florida.

Remind the students that the season, spring, is not capitalized, but a religious holiday, a day of the week, and a month are capitalized.

Lesson 31

LANGUAGE ARTS

LESSON 31-E If your students are not using the GDP software, have them type a correct version of the paragraph.

SOLUTION: Lines 8–16

8. American
9. country's
10. government
11. Independence Day
12. summer, Day
13. December
14. Christmas, Most
15. Friday
16. historical

FORMATTING

Reference Manual

Ask students to review the basic parts of a business letter in the **Reference Manual, R-3A,** before they begin typing.

VISUAL INSTRUCTION

Basic Parts of a Business Letter.

- Letterhead
- Date line
- Inside address
- Salutation
- Body
- Complimentary closing
- Signature
- Writer's identification
- Reference initials

LESSON 31-F Discuss all major parts of the letter in the illustration and their sequence.

LESSON 31-G An alternative to starting the letter about 2 inches from the top of the page is to vertically center the letter or start the letter at least 0.5 inch below the letterhead.

Lesson 31

FORMATTING

LESSON 31-H Help students become familiar with the automatic date insert feature in their software. Explain that the date may be typed manually or may be inserted by using a software command.

DOCUMENT PROCESSING

CORRESPONDENCE 31-3 Guide students step by step through this first business letter; note especially starting the letter 2 inches from the top of the page and inserting their own reference initials. Emphasize the overall letter format.

Remind students to use word wrap for the paragraphs, and remind them that their line endings might be different from the ones in the model letter. Open punctuation (no colon after the salutation and no comma after the complimentary closing) is an acceptable alternative in the business world to standard punctuation.

Explain that the block style is most efficient because all lines begin at the left margin; therefore, no changes in default settings are required.

Ask students to bring sample business letters to class. Discuss the various letterhead styles and letter formatting used in the samples.

4. After the inside address, press ENTER 2 times and type the salutation. For standard punctuation, type a colon after the salutation. Press ENTER 2 times after the salutation.
5. Single-space the body of the letter, but press ENTER 2 times between paragraphs. Do not indent paragraphs.
6. Press ENTER 2 times after the last paragraph and type the complimentary closing. For standard punctuation, type a comma after the complimentary closing.
7. Press ENTER 4 times after the complimentary closing and type the writer's identification.
8. Press ENTER 2 times after the writer's identification and type your reference initials in lowercase letters with no periods or spaces.

Word Processing Manual

H. WORD PROCESSING: INSERT DATE

Study Lesson 31 in your word processing manual. Complete all of the shaded steps while at your computer. Then format the jobs that follow.

DOCUMENT PROCESSING

Correspondence 31-3

Business Letter in Block Style

1. Type the letter using standard block style.
2. Use standard punctuation: a colon after the salutation and a comma after the complimentary closing.
3. Use word wrap for the paragraphs. Press ENTER only at the end of each paragraph. Your lines may end differently from those shown in the illustration.
4. Type your initials for the reference initials.
5. Spell-check, preview, and proofread your letter for typing, spelling, and formatting errors.

↓6X
March 27, 20-- ↓4X

(= proper) Ms. Linda Lopez
Account Manager
The Internet Connection
7625 Maple Avenue
Pomona, CA 91765 ↓2X

(= proper) Dear Ms. Lopez: ↓2X

(= sentence, = time; = proper) Our company is interested in hosting an educational seminar this spring that will focus on meeting the growing need for information industry professionals to keep abreast of emerging new technologies and trends. We are specifically interested in information on high-speed Internet connections. ↓2X

(= sentence; = time) I understand that The Internet Connection specializes in these seminars and will also help businesses analyze their needs and choose an appropriate solution. I am in the process of contacting several companies similar to yours who might be interested in conducting these seminars. Please contact me by Thursday or Friday at the latest so that we can discuss this further. ↓2X

(Continued on next page)

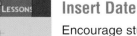

GDP SOFTWARE TIPS

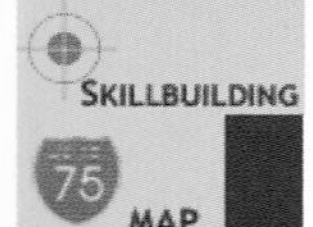

Insert Date

Encourage students to practice inserting the various date and time formats in the **Date and Time** dialog box. Remind students that the keyboard shortcut (ALT + SHIFT + D) style is MM/DD/YY unless the default format is changed.

= sentence I appreciate the fine service we have always received from you in the past,
= proper Ms. Lopez, and look forward to hearing from you. ↓2X

Sincerely, ↓4X

= proper Ruzanna Petroska
= proper Technology Specialist ↓2X

urs

(!) Remember to type your initials in place of urs.

Correspondence 31-4

Business Letter in Block Style

Open the file for Correspondence 31-3 and make the following changes:

1. Change the date to `May 8`.
2. Change the writer's identification to: `Gail Madison` and her job title to `Technology Engineer`.

Correspondence 31-5

Business Letter in Block Style

Note: The | symbol indicates the end of a line. The ¶ symbol indicates the start of a new paragraph.

1. Type the letter using standard block style.
2. Spell-check, preview, and proofread your letter for typing, spelling, and formatting errors.

= time May 25, 20-- | Ms. Linda Lopez | Account Manager |
= proper The Internet Connection | 7625 Maple Avenue | Pomona, CA 91765 | Dear Ms. Lopez:

¶ Thank you so much for hosting the educational seminar last Tuesday that focused on the topic of high-speed
= proper Internet connections. Our company and our employees are now well prepared to make a decision about the best type of
= proper Internet connection for their particular needs.

¶ Because this seminar was so successful, I have been authorized to contract with The Internet Connection for a continuing series of seminars on any topics related to emerging new technologies and trends as they apply to the needs of our company and our employees. I will
= time call you on Monday so that we can arrange for a meeting to finalize some contractual issues.

¶ Once again, thank you for a very successful and productive seminar!

Sincerely, | Ruzanna Petroska | Technology Specialist |

urs

(!) The ¶ symbol indicates the start of a new paragraph. In a business letter, paragraphs are blocked (not indented).

Lesson 31

DOCUMENT PROCESSING

Reference Manual

Ask students to review the letter in block style in the **Reference Manual, R-3A,** before they begin typing.

CORRESPONDENCE 31-4

Explain to students that the file for Correspondence 31-3 is opened by clicking on a button in the GDP software designed to do this automatically after Correspondence 31-3 has been finished. They do not need to go backward in the **Lesson** menu to open Correspondence 31-3 in order to type Correspondence 31-4.

CORRESPONDENCE 31-5

Optional. Encourage students to review the letter illustrated on page 85.

ASSESS

The Web

www.mhhe.com/gdp to download a copy of the Technique Evaluation Form.

TECHNIQUE EVALUATION FORM

Walk around the room to observe business letter formatting.

Evaluate Correspondence 31-3.

Extending the Lesson

Refer students to the **Reference Manual, R-14,** for a list of the two-letter state abbreviations. Explain the purpose of using the state abbreviation rather than typing the state name.

CLOSE

Stress the correct procedure to use to exit Microsoft Word and the GDP program.

EXTENDING LANGUAGE ARTS

Reinforcing the Rules Create a list of ten sentences to reinforce the language arts rules presented—capitalize the first word of a sentence; capitalize proper nouns and adjectives derived from proper nouns; and capitalize the names of the days of the week, months, holidays, and religious days.

INSTRUCTOR STRATEGIES

The Pipe and the ¶ Explain the | (pipe) symbol in Correspondence 31-5, which signals students to start a new line by pressing ENTER. Explain the ¶ (paragraph) symbol at the start of a new paragraph, which signals students to press ENTER 2 times to start a new paragraph.

FOCUS

TIME MANAGEMENT 

Suggested Schedule:

Warmup	2′
Skillbuilding	21′
Formatting	4′
Document Processing	23′
Total	**50′**

TEACH

SKILLBUILDING

LESSON 32-B Explain the directions for this drill so that the students are clear about what they should do. Observe technique on the BACKSPACE key and correct as needed.

LESSON 32-C Discrimination Practice concentrates on common substitution errors—that is, keys that are commonly confused.

LESSON 32-D Make sure that students are typing their practice lines in the correct pattern for either speed or accuracy.

Business Letters With Enclosure Notations

Goals

- Type at least 33wpm/3′/5e
- Format a business letter with an enclosure notation

A. Type 2 times.

A. WARMUP

```
     Sales by two travel agencies (Quill, Virgil, & Johnson  11
and Keef & Zane) exceeded all prior amounts. Total sales     23
for that year were as follows: $1,540,830 and $976,233.      34
  | 1 | 2 | 3 | 4 | 5 | 6 | 7 | 8 | 9 | 10 | 11 | 12
```

SKILLBUILDING

B. Type each line 2 times.

Technique Tip: Press the BACKSPACE key with the Sem finger without looking at your keyboard.

B. TECHNIQUE PRACTICE: BACKSPACE KEY

1. Type each letter (or group of letters) as shown.
2. When you reach the backspace sign (←), backspace 1 time to delete the last keystroke.
3. Type the next group of letters. The result will be a new word. For example, if you see "hi← at," you would type "hi," backspace 1 time, and then type "at," resulting in the new word "hat" instead of the original word "hit."

```
p←cat c←tab b←peg p←but p←tie t←pop m←pat f←sit m←but t←cub
t←mop b←fib r←fat w←fin p←tin c←top p←ban f←can y←get m←let
di←ye be←ag ge←um ri←ob mu←ad la←id fi←an bi←ad to←ip ro←id
pa←it ti←on fi←un ra←un pi←an ge←ot ba←it fa←it ma←it sa←it
bin←t any←t new←t was←r sea←t tap←n fan←t lap←d for←x fin←x
pin←t ham←d sod←n rid←p rap←n tap←n dip←n sin←p lip←d put←n
```

PPP PRETEST → PRACTICE → POSTTEST

PRETEST
Take a 1-minute timed writing. Review your speed and errors.

PRACTICE
Speed Emphasis: If you made 2 or fewer errors on the Pretest, type each *individual* line 2 times.
Accuracy Emphasis: If you made 3 or more errors, type each *group* of lines (as though it were a paragraph) 2 times.

C. PRETEST: Discrimination Practice

```
     Steven saw the younger, unruly boy take flight as he    11
threw the coin at the jury. The brave judge stopped the      22
fight. He called out to the youth, who recoiled in fear.     33
  | 1 | 2 | 3 | 4 | 5 | 6 | 7 | 8 | 9 | 10 | 11 | 12
```

D. PRACTICE: Left Hand

```
vbv verb bevy vibes bevel brave above verbal bovine behaves
wew west weep threw wedge weave fewer weight sewing dewdrop
fgf gulf gift fight fudge fugue flags flight golfer feigned
```


Windows Wizard

SORT FILES AND FOLDERS IN WINDOWS EXPLORER To change the sort order in Windows Explorer in Windows 2000, Me, and XP:

- Right-click the **Start** button and choose **Explore**.
- Click the **Views** tab and choose **Details**.
- Click the column title (**Name, Size, Type,** or **Modified**) to sort the files in ascending order.
- Click the column title again to sort in descending order.

You can also sort files and folders by selecting the **View** menu and choosing an option from the **Arrange Icon by** submenu.

Lesson 32

E. PRACTICE: Right Hand

```
uyu buys your usury unity youth buoys unruly untidy younger
oio coin lion oiled foils foist prior recoil iodine rejoice
jhj jury huge enjoy three judge habit adjust slight jasmine
```

POSTTEST
Repeat the Pretest timed writing and compare performance.

F. POSTTEST: Discrimination Practice

G. Take two 3-minute timed writings. Review your speed and errors.

Goal: At least 33wpm/3′/5e

G. 3-MINUTE TIMED WRITING

```
     Be zealous in your efforts when you write business      10
letters. Your business writing must convey clearly what      22
it is you want people to read. All of your letters should    33
be formatted neatly in proper business letter format.        44
     Before sending your letters, read them quickly just to  55
make sure that they explain clearly what you want to say.    67
Proofread the letters you write for correct grammar and      78
spelling. Use all of your writing skills to display the      89
best image. Your readers will welcome the effort.            99
| 1 | 2 | 3 | 4 | 5 | 6 | 7 | 8 | 9 | 10 | 11 | 12
```

FORMATTING

H. ENCLOSURE NOTATION

- To indicate that an item is enclosed with a letter, type the word *Enclosure* on the line below the reference initials.

Example: urs
Enclosure

- If more than one item is being enclosed, type the word *Enclosures*.

DOCUMENT PROCESSING

Correspondence 32-6

Business Letter in Block Style

Refer to Reference Manual

See page R-3B and R-3C of the Reference Manual for an illustration of a business letter with an enclosure notation.

The | symbol indicates the end of a line.

1. Type the letter using standard business letter format.
2. Spell-check, preview, and proofread your document for spelling and formatting errors.

October 10, 20-- | Ms. Denise Bradford | Worldwide Travel, Inc. | 1180 Alvarado, SE | Albuquerque, NM 87108 | Dear Ms. Bradford:
¶ Our company has decided to hold its regional sales meeting in Scottsdale, Arizona, during the second week of January. I need information on a suitable conference site.

(Continued on next page)

FORMATTING

Refer to Reference Manual

Ask students to review enclosure notations in the **Reference Manual, R-3B, R-3C, R-5B,** and **R-12B,** before they begin typing.

LESSON 32-H Encourage students to read the correspondence so that they understand what is being enclosed with the letter and why. Remind them that an enclosure notation is a reminder to the sender and the recipient that something should be included with the letter.

DOCUMENT PROCESSING

CORRESPONDENCE 32-6
Review the purpose of the ¶ symbol and the | symbol to indicate the end of a line. Remind students to press ENTER 1 time to move from the reference initials to the enclosure notation.

GDP SOFTWARE TIPS

LESSONS · SKILLBUILDING · MAP

Timed Writings

Instructor Management (LAN and Web Versions) timed writing grades are computed using the following rules:

- A student's three best timed writings for each part and the best of all completed timed writing tests are selected, and an average grade is computed.
- Only completed timed writings within a prescribed error tolerance are included in the grade.
- If the student has no timed writings within the error tolerance, the timed writings grade is an F.

Lesson 32

DOCUMENT PROCESSING

CORRESPONDENCE 32-7

Review the procedure to open an existing file.

If necessary, remind students to select text to be deleted and press DELETE. This is much more efficient than pressing the DELETE key or the BACKSPACE key to delete several words or lines.

Remind students to refer to the **Reference Manual, R-3A,** for guidelines on correct business letter formatting.

CORRESPONDENCE 32-8

Optional. If time is short, you may have students skip the optional job. No new features are presented.

The ¶ symbol indicates the start of a new paragraph.

¶ We will need a meeting room with the following items: 30 computer workstations with an Internet connection, copy stands, mouse pads, and adjustable chairs; an LCD projector with a large screen; and a microphone and podium. The hotel should have a fax machine and on-site secretarial services. We might also need a messenger service.
¶ A final decision on the conference site must be made within the next two weeks. Please send me any information you have available for a suitable location in Scottsdale immediately. I have enclosed a list of conference attendees and their room preferences. Thank you for your help.
Sincerely yours, | Bill McKay | Marketing Manager | urs | Enclosure

Correspondence 32-7

Business Letter in Block Style

1. Open the file for Correspondence 32-6.
2. Change the inside address to `1032 San Pedro, SE.`
3. Change the first sentence as follows:
   `Our company has decided to hold its annual national sales meeting during the first week of February in Scottsdale, Arizona.`
4. In the first sentence of the second paragraph, change the information after the colon as follows:
   `30 computer workstations, an LCD projector with a large screen, and a microphone and podium.`

Correspondence 32-8

Business Letter in Block Style

October 20, 20-- | Mr. Bill McKay | Marketing Manager | Viatech Communications | 9835 Osuna Road, NE | Albuquerque, NM 87111 | Dear Mr. McKay:
¶ Thank you for your inquiry, regarding a conference site in Scottsdale, Arizona, for 35 people during the second week of January.
¶ I have enclosed the following brochures with detailed information on some properties in Scottsdale that provide exclusive service to businesses like yours: Camelback Resorts, Shadow Pines Suites, and Desert Inn Resorts and Golf Club. All these properties have meeting rooms that will accommodate your needs and also offer additional services you might be interested in using.

(Continued on next page)

Meeting Special Needs

HEARING-IMPAIRED STUDENTS When you talk to a hearing-impaired student, be sure to look directly at the student and enunciate clearly. Remember to avoid talking when you are writing on the board, when your back is turned to the class, or when looking at the textbook. To further assist hearing-impaired students, you may want to repeat questions that other students have asked. Also try to repeat answers you provide to the class.

Visit us on the Web at **www.mhhe.com/gdp** for more information.

¶ Please call me when you have reached a decision. I will be happy to make the final arrangements as well as issue any airline tickets you may need. Yours truly, | Ms. Denise Bradford | Travel Agent | urs | Enclosures

Lesson 32

ASSESS

www.mhhe.com/gdp to download a copy of the Technique Evaluation Form.

TECHNIQUE EVALUATION FORM

Walk around the classroom to observe students' technique.

Review results of timed writings.

Review business letter formatting.

Extending the Lesson

Discuss the importance of producing a quality document in a limited time. Remind students that the Portfolio's Summary Report records how much time they have spent in Microsoft Word for each activity, and tell them you review that information when you evaluate their work. As students become more familiar with business letters, they should see improvement in the number of minutes it takes to complete a letter.

Review the importance of proofreading the letter.

CLOSE

Stress the correct procedure to use to exit Microsoft Word and the GDP program.

Technology Tips

DISCUSSING THE ILLUSTRATION

The marvels of PDAs (personal data assistants) have been with us since 1996 when the original Palm Pilot was introduced. PDAs have been a hit with consumers because they are easy to use and can store thousands of contacts and telephone numbers.

Students who own PDAs are also likely to use them to download and play games or music from the Internet, play movies, and send and receive e-mails.

Students will be eager to share the multitude of ways that PDAs have impacted their lives.

FOCUS

TIME MANAGEMENT 

Suggested Schedule:

Warmup	2′
Skillbuilding	14′
Language Arts	6′
Formatting	8′
Document Processing	20′
Total	**50′**

TEACH

SKILLBUILDING

LESSON 33-B Speed sprints are very motivational. Have students push moderately for speed on these easy sentences.

LESSON 33-C Paced Practice helps students reach individual speed and accuracy goals in 2-wpm increments by pacing them as they strive for a slightly higher rate.

LANGUAGE ARTS

LESSON 33-D The ability to compose at the keyboard is becoming essential. Encourage students to think and type in one step. Check students' work to be sure they are composing complete sentences.

Lesson 33

Envelopes and Labels

Goals

- Improve speed and accuracy
- Refine language arts skills in composing sentences
- Format envelopes and labels and fold letters

A. Type 2 times.

A. WARMUP

```
     Does Quentin know if half of the January order will be  11
ready on 1/7/05? At 4:20 only 36% of the orders had been      23
mailed! Mr. Gray expects a very sizable loss this month.      34
|  1  |  2  |  3  |  4  |  5  |  6  |  7  |  8  |  9  |  10  |  11  |  12
```

SKILLBUILDING

B. Take three 12-second timed writings on each line. The scale below the last line shows your wpm speed for a 12-second timed writing.

B. 12-SECOND SPEED SPRINTS

```
Today we want to find out if our work will be done on time.
Doug will be able to drive to the store if the car is here.
Jan will sign this paper when she has done all of the work.
This time she will be sure to spend two days with her sons.
    5    10    15    20    25    30    35    40    45    50    55    60
```

C. PACED PRACTICE

If you are not using the GDP software, turn to page SB-14 and follow the directions for this activity.

LANGUAGE ARTS

D. Answer each question with a complete sentence.

D. COMPOSING: SENTENCES

What are your best traits that you will bring to your job when you graduate?
What are the best traits that you will want to see in your new boss?
Would you rather work for a large or a small company?
How much money do you expect to earn on your first job?
Would you like your first job to be in a small town or a large city?
What do you see yourself doing in ten years?
What types of benefits do you think you would like to have?

TEACHING THE ADULT LEARNER

PARTICIPATION Select classroom materials for adult learners that will promote interaction between you and the students as well as interaction among the students. Stimulate or initiate discussions and encourage participation from the adult learners in your classroom. Provide positive reinforcement for those who contribute to classroom discussions.

Online discussion groups and e-mail are wonderful ways for students to increase their participation. Electronic communication can be spontaneous and fun.

FORMATTING

E. ENVELOPES

The envelope feature of your word processor simplifies your task of addressing a No. 10 envelope. The standard size for business envelopes is 9½ by 4⅛ inches. A business envelope should include the following:

- **Return Address.** If necessary, type the sender's name and address in upper- and lowercase style in the upper left corner. Business stationery usually has a printed return address. Use the default placement and the default font of your word processor for the return address.
- **Mailing Address.** Type the recipient's name and address in upper- and lowercase style (or in all-capital letters without any punctuation) toward the center of the envelope. Use the default placement and the default font of your word processor for the mailing address.

Note: Postal scanners read addresses more efficiently if they are typed in all-capital letters without any punctuation.

Trend Electronics
2206 31st Street
Minneapolis, MN 55407-1911

Mr. Charles R. Harrison
Reliable Software, Inc.
5613 Brunswick Avenue
Minneapolis, MN 55406

Standard large envelope, No. 10, is 9½ 3 4⅛ inches.

F. FOLDING LETTERS

To fold a letter for a No. 10 envelope:

1. Place the letter face up, and fold up the bottom third of the page.
2. Fold the top third of the page down to about 0.5 inch from the bottom edge of the page.
3. Insert the last crease into the envelope first with the flap facing up.

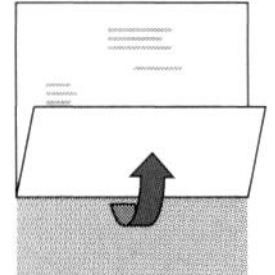
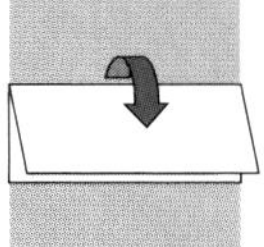
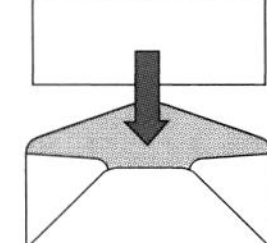

Lesson 33

FORMATTING

Reference Manual

Ask students to review envelopes, labels, and folding letters in the **Reference Manual, R-6A,** before they begin typing.

VISUAL INSTRUCTION

Envelopes. Help students differentiate between the return address and the mailing address.

- Return address
- Mailing address

Show samples of a variety of envelopes. Include different sizes of envelopes and envelopes with and without a preprinted return address.

LESSON 33-E Explain OCR format to students. Also provide them with postal instructions for using two-letter state abbreviations and ZIP Codes. Printing envelopes is a very common task in business. If necessary, students can print the envelopes on plain paper instead of envelopes.

LESSON 33-F Demonstrate folding a letter for a No. 10 envelope.

ERGONOMICALLY SPEAKING

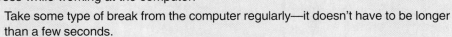

GOOD WORK HABITS Discuss the following suggestions to maintain good work habits and reduce soreness, fatigue, and stress while working at the computer:

- Take some type of break from the computer regularly—it doesn't have to be longer than a few seconds.
- Alternate working at the computer with noncomputer tasks, such as phone calls, filing, and meetings.
- Change your posture frequently. Even readjusting the chair slightly changes posture.

Lesson 33

FORMATTING

LESSON 33-G Printing mailing labels is a very common task in business. If necessary, students can print the labels on plain paper instead of label forms. The Instructor's Manual contains a master label form for you to duplicate for student use.

LESSON 33-H Help students create envelopes and labels using their software. Explain that label definitions will vary in their software depending on the type of printer they are using.

DOCUMENT PROCESSING

CORRESPONDENCE 33-9
Make sure that your students' printers are set up to print envelopes easily. Remind them that most printers use a manual feed to print envelopes.

CORRESPONDENCE 33-10
Review the procedure to use to open an existing file.

CORRESPONDENCE 33-11
Make sure that your students' printers are set up to print labels easily. Remind them that most printers use a manual feed to print labels.

G. LABELS

The label feature of your word processor simplifies the task of preparing various labels. You can use different label settings to print a full sheet of labels or to print a single label. You may want to use a mailing label as an alternative to printing an envelope.

When preparing labels, test the label settings by printing your labels on a blank page before you print them on the actual label form.

Word Processing Manual

H. WORD PROCESSING: ENVELOPES AND LABELS

Study Lesson 33 in your word processing manual. Complete all of the shaded steps while at your computer. Then format the jobs that follow.

DOCUMENT PROCESSING

Correspondence 33-9
Envelope

1. Prepare an envelope with the following mailing address:

   Mr. Charles Goldstein| Software Solutions| 2981 Canwood Street| Roselle, IL 60172

2. Insert the following return address.

   Shannon Stone| Data Systems, Inc.| 2201 South Street| Racine, WI 53404

3. Add the envelope to a blank document.

Correspondence 33-10
Envelope

1. Open the file for Correspondence 32-8 and prepare an envelope for the letter.
2. Do not insert a return address.
3. Add the envelope to the letter.

Correspondence 33-11
Mailing Labels

1. Select an address label product about 1 inch deep, large enough to fit a 4-line address. Label choices will vary; however, Avery standard, 5160, Address is a good choice for laser and ink jet printers.
2. Prepare address labels for the names and addresses that follow.
3. Type the addresses in order from left to right as you see them displayed below in the first group.
4. Move to the second group of labels and type them again from left to right.

Purchasing Dept. Abbott Laboratories Abbott Park Chicago, IL 60064	Frank Zimmerly Cartridges, Etc. 1220 Charleston Road Oso Park, CA 90621	John Sanchez Adobe Systems 1585 Charleston Road Los Angeles, CA 90029
Mike Rashid Internet Services 901 Thompson Place Sunnyvale, CA 94088	Jennifer Reagan Aetna Life 151 Farmington Avenue Hartford, CT 06156	Bob Patterson Affiliated Publishing 135 Morrisey Boulevard Boston, MA 02107

INSTRUCTOR STRATEGIES

Folding Letters Demonstrate the correct procedure to use to fold letters for a No. 10 envelope, a small envelope, and a window envelope; students should practice the procedure along with you. Provide students with an envelope of each type so they can practice inserting the folded letters into the envelopes.

Correspondence 33-12

Mailing Labels

1. Select an address label product about 1 inch deep, large enough to fit a 4-line address. Label choices will vary; however, Avery standard, 5160, Address is a good choice for laser and ink jet printers.
2. Prepare a full page of the same label with the following address:

   Shipping and Receiving|E-Office Outlet|1122 North Highland Street|Arlington, VA 22201

Correspondence 33-13

Envelope

1. Open the file for Correspondence 32-6 and prepare an envelope for the letter.
2. Insert the following return address:

   Bill McKay|Viatech Communications|9835 Osana Road, NE|Albuquerque, NM 87111
3. Add the envelope to the letter.

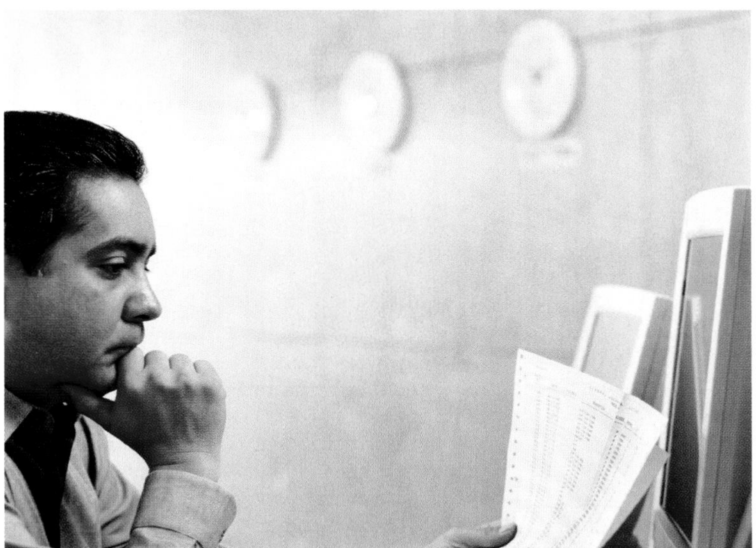

Lesson 33

DOCUMENT PROCESSING

CORRESPONDENCE 33-13

Optional. If time is short, you may have students skip the optional job. No new features are presented.

ASSESS

www.mhhe.com/gdp to download a copy of the Technique Evaluation Form.

TECHNIQUE EVALUATION FORM

Have students practice folding letters for insertion into a No. 10 envelope.

Review envelope and label formatting.

Extending the Lesson

Remind students that the letterhead and envelope for a company are designed to match in appearance and in weight and color of paper.

Show students various label formats that can be printed with a laser or inkjet printer.

CLOSE

Stress the correct procedure to use to exit Microsoft Word and the GDP program.

INSTRUCTOR STRATEGIES

Discussing the Illustration Help students select correct label products using the following activities.

- List various sizes of labels on the board or on a transparency—for example, 2″ × 2.75″.
- Using the **Envelopes and Labels** dialog box, see how quickly students can identify the label product number and its general usage.

FOCUS

TIME MANAGEMENT 

Suggested Schedule:

Warmup	2′
Skillbuilding	18′
Formatting	4′
Document Processing	26′
Total	**50′**

TEACH

SKILLBUILDING

LESSON 34-B Encourage students to push moderately for speed on the Pretest.

LESSON 34-C Students take repeated timed writings on a passage containing the exact number of words for their speed goal until they can complete it with no errors. Then they move to the next longer passage and start again.

Memos

Goals

- Type at least 34wpm/3′/5e
- Format interoffice memos

A. Type 2 times.

A. WARMUP

```
     The series* (*6 films, 28 minutes) by J. Zeller goes       11
beyond the "basics" of computers. Viewers keep requesting       22
an extension on the following due dates: 3/2, 5/5, and 8/9.    34
| 1 | 2 | 3 | 4 | 5 | 6 | 7 | 8 | 9 | 10 | 11 | 12
```

SKILLBUILDING

B. DIAGNOSTIC PRACTICE: SYMBOLS AND PUNCTUATION

If you are not using the GDP software, turn to page SB-2 and follow the directions for this activity.

C. PROGRESSIVE PRACTICE: ALPHABET

If you are not using the GDP software, turn to page SB-7 and follow the directions for this activity.

D. Take two 3-minute timed writings. Review your speed and errors.

Goal: At least 34wpm/3′/5e

D. 3-MINUTE TIMED WRITING

```
     Companies that place their ads on the Internet use a       11
process called data mining. They look for patterns in the       22
quantities of data they get from those who visit Web sites.     34
     Data mining tracks buying habits of customers and then     46
decides to send ads to them based on their current and past     58
buying patterns. Data mining can also be used to explain        69
buyer behavior and to look at trends. First, a survey is        80
filled out, and then the results are gathered and stored in     92
a file to be analyzed in detail at a later time.               102
| 1 | 2 | 3 | 4 | 5 | 6 | 7 | 8 | 9 | 10 | 11 | 12
```


Meeting Special Needs

DYSLEXIA Consider these tips on instructional strategies when students in the class have dyslexia:

- Use instructional methods that provide structure, such as lists to summarize, previews to preorganize, and repetition to reinforce.
- Provide frequent feedback.
- Provide activities to enable students to put concepts and theory into practice.

Visit us on the Web at **www.mhhe.com/gdp** for more information.

FORMATTING

E. MEMOS

A memo is usually sent from one person to another in the same organization. To format a memo on plain paper or on letterhead stationery:

1. Press ENTER 6 times for a top margin of about 2 inches.
2. Type the headings (including the colons) in all-caps and bold: `MEMO TO:`, `FROM:`, `DATE:`, and `SUBJECT:`.
3. Press TAB 1 time after typing the colon to reach the point where the heading entries begin.
4. Insert 1 blank line between the heading lines and between the heading lines and the memo body.
5. Insert 1 blank line between paragraphs. Most memos are typed with blocked paragraphs (no indentions).
6. Insert 1 blank line between the body and the reference initials.

DOCUMENT PROCESSING

Correspondence 34-14

Memo

Refer to Reference Manual

Refer to page R-7C of the Reference Manual for an illustration of a memo.

1. Type the memo using standard memo format.
2. Spell-check, preview, and proofread your document for spelling and formatting errors before printing it.

↓6X

MEMO TO: All Salaried Employees ↓2X

FROM: Amy Vigil, Human Resources ↓2X

DATE: November 2, 20-- ↓2X

SUBJECT: Health Care Benefit Plan ↓2X

Effective January 1, Allied Aerospace Industries will contract with MedNet to begin a new health benefits program for all eligible salaried personnel. A brochure outlining important program information will be mailed to you soon. ↓2X

An open enrollment period will be in effect during the entire month of January. If you and your family are interested in one of the MedNet health plan options, you may transfer yourself and your dependents into any appropriate plan. All applications must be received no later than midnight, January 31. You may also access your plan over the Internet at www.mednet.com if it is more convenient. ↓2X

If you have any questions or need any help understanding your options, please call me at Ext. 134. I will be happy to help you select the plan that is best for you. ↓2X

urs

TEACHING THE ADULT LEARNER

HEALTH CARE AND SOCIAL SECURITY Politically and socially, everyone seems to have an opinion on how health care for the aging population should be handled. Ask students to conduct a Web search on proposed legislation regarding health care and Social Security benefits. Discuss students' findings.

FORMATTING

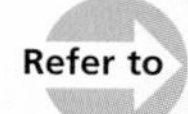

Refer to Reference Manual

Ask students to review memos in the **Reference Manual, R-4D** and **R-7C,** before they begin typing.

VISUAL INSTRUCTION

Memos—Headings. Review the four parts of a memo heading. Mention that companies may choose to vary the order and formatting of their memos.

- Memo to:
- From:
- Date:
- Subject:

Show samples of memos. Include different sizes (full page and half page) and memos with preprinted guide words.

LESSON 34-E Review all steps to use to format memos. Point out the memo in the Reference Manual, R-4D.

DOCUMENT PROCESSING

CORRESPONDENCE 34-14
Guide students through each step in this first memo. Remind them to bold the colons after the guide words and to press TAB after each heading to align the information that follows.

Lesson 34

DOCUMENT PROCESSING

CORRESPONDENCE 34-16

Optional. If time is short, you may have students skip the optional job. No new features are presented.

ASSESS

www.mhhe.com/gdp to download a copy of the Technique Evaluation Form.

TECHNIQUE EVALUATION FORM

Review results of timed writings.

Review memo formatting.

Extending the Lesson

Discuss the difference in the appearance of stationery used for letters and envelopes and stationery used for a memo. Remind students that memo stationery should match letterhead stationery in weight and color.

CLOSE

Stress the correct procedure to use to exit Microsoft Word and the GDP program.

Correspondence 34-15
Memo

The ¶ symbol indicates the start of a new paragraph. In a memo, paragraphs are blocked (not indented).

MEMO TO: Amy Vigil, Human Resources | **FROM:** Dan Westphal | **DATE:** November 23, 20-- | **SUBJECT:** MedNet Benefit Plan
¶ Thank you for the brochure detailing the various options for employees under the MedNet plan. I would like clarification on some of the services included in the plan.
¶ Because both my wife and I are employees of Allied Aerospace Industries, do we have the choice of enrolling separately under different options? In our present plan, I know that this is possible.
¶ We have two dependents. Is it possible to enroll both dependents under different options of the plan, or do they both fall under either one option or the other? I know that in the past you have asked for evidence of dependent status and dates of birth.
¶ If you need any further information, please let me know. Thank you very much for your help.
urs

Correspondence 34-16
Memo

Open the file for Correspondence 34-14 and make the following changes:

1. Send the memo to `All Allied Aerospace Industries Employees.`
2. Change the date to `December 2.`
3. Change the subject line to `Health Care Open Enrollment Period.`

Keyboarding Connection

Searching the Web

Research projects on the World Wide Web! Access up-to-date information from all over the world.

To conduct a search, specify keywords and certain relationships among them. Many search engines use arithmetic operators to symbolize Boolean relationships. A plus sign (+) is used instead of AND, a minus sign (−) instead of NOT, and no sign instead of OR.

Simple document searches match a single keyword (e.g., *cherry*). Advanced searches might match any of the words (e.g., *cherry pie*); all words (e.g., +*cherry* +*pie*); a phrase (e.g., "*cherry pie*"); or some words and not others (e.g., +*cherry* +*pie* −*tree*). There is no space between the plus or minus sign and its word.

YOUR TURN From your Web browser, open a Web search engine site. Type various searches in the entry box of the search engine and start the search. Compare the results.

Keyboarding Connection

Searching the Web

Have students use three different search engines to conduct an advanced search. Compare the results.

YOUR TURN If time permits, ask students to complete the Your Turn activity.

Correspondence Review

Goals

- Improve speed and accuracy
- Refine language arts skills in proofreading
- Format various types of correspondence with an attachment notation
- Practice italicizing and underlining

A. Type 2 times.

A. WARMUP

```
     Item #876 won't be ordered until 9/10. Did you gather   11
all requests and input them exactly as they appeared? Zack   23
will never be satisfied until he contacts jack@orders.com.   34
  | 1 | 2 | 3 | 4 | 5 | 6 | 7 | 8 | 9 | 10 | 11 | 12
```

SKILLBUILDING

B. MAP

Follow the GDP software directions for this exercise in improving keystroking accuracy.

C. Take a 1-minute timed writing on the first paragraph to establish your base speed. Then take four 1-minute timed writings on the remaining paragraphs. As soon as you equal or exceed your base speed on one paragraph, advance to the next, more difficult paragraph.

C. SUSTAINED PRACTICE: ALTERNATE-HAND WORDS

```
     When eight of them began a formal discussion on some     11
of the major issues, the need for a chair was very evident.  23
A chair would be sure to handle the usual work with ease.     35

     The eight people in that group decided that the work     11
would be done only if they selected one person to be chair    23
of their group. They began to debate all the major issues.    35

     One issue that needed to be settled right up front was   11
the question of how to handle proxy votes. It seemed for a    23
short time that a fight over this very issue would result.    35

     The group worked diligently in attempting to solve the   11
issues that were being discussed. All of the concerns that    23
were brought to the group were reviewed in depth by them.     34
  | 1 | 2 | 3 | 4 | 5 | 6 | 7 | 8 | 9 | 10 | 11 | 12
```


MAP

Why should students use Misstroke Analysis and Prescription? There are six clear and concise reasons for students to use MAP. It is:

- Simple to use.
- Comprehensive.
- Individualized.
- Fast and efficient.
- Motivational.
- Research-based.

Misstroke Analysis and Prescription will greatly benefit your students' keyboarding accuracy.

Lesson 35

FOCUS

TIME MANAGEMENT

Suggested Schedule:

Warmup	2′
Skillbuilding	17′
Language Arts	6′
Formatting	3′
Document Processing	22′
Total	**50′**

TEACH

SKILLBUILDING

LESSON 35-B MAP is a simple, comprehensive, and individualized software program for improving keystroking accuracy.

LESSON 35-C Each paragraph is more difficult than the preceding one—based on the number of alternate-hand words of four letters or more.

Paragraph 1: 10
Paragraph 2: 6
Paragraph 3: 4
Paragraph 4: 1

Lesson 35

LANGUAGE ARTS

LESSON 35-D If your students are not using the GDP software, have them type a correct version of the paragraph.

SOLUTION: Lines 16–23

16. doesn't, can type
17. know, that
18. *Correct*
19. spelling,
20. sentences. Make
21. Sometimes
22. just above
23. *Correct*

FORMATTING

Reference Manual

Ask students to review attachment notations in the **Reference Manual, R-4D** and **R-7C,** before they begin typing.

LESSON 35-E Encourage students to read the correspondence so that they understand what is being attached to the document and why.

Remind them that an attachment notation is a reminder to the sender and the recipient that something should be physically attached to the correspondence.

LESSON 35-F Help students use the italic and underline commands.

DOCUMENT PROCESSING

CORRESPONDENCE 35-17
Remind students to underline and italicize words as indicated in the document.

LANGUAGE ARTS

D. Edit this paragraph to correct any typing or formatting errors.

D. PROOFREADING

It doesnt matter how fast you can type or how well you now a software program if you produce documents taht are filled with errors. You must learn to watch for errors in spelling punctuation, and formatting. Look carefully between words and sentences.Make sure that after a period at the end of a sentence, you see one space. Sometime it helps to look at the characters in the sentence justabove the one you are proofreading to ensure accuracy.

FORMATTING

E. ATTACHMENT NOTATION

The word *Attachment* (rather than *Enclosure*) is typed below the reference initials when material is physically attached (stapled or clipped) to a memo.

Example: urs
Attachment

Word Processing Manual

F. WORD PROCESSING: ITALIC AND UNDERLINE

Study Lesson 35 in your word processing manual. Complete all of the shaded steps while at your computer. Then format the jobs that follow.

DOCUMENT PROCESSING

Correspondence 35-17
Memo

MEMO TO: All Executive Assistants | **FROM:** Barbara Azar, Staff Development Coordinator | **DATE:** March 25, 20-- | **SUBJECT:** Standardizing Document Formats

¶ Last month we received our final shipment of new laser printers. The installation of these printers in your offices marked the final phase-out of all ink-jet printers.

¶ Because all of us can now use a variety of standardized fonts in our correspondence, please note the following change: <u>From now on, all book and journal titles should be set in Arial Narrow.</u> This new formatting change will help us to standardize our correspondence.

¶ The latest edition of the book *Quick Reference for the Automated Office* has two pages of helpful information on laser printers, which I have attached. Please read these pages carefully, and we will discuss them at our next meeting.

urs | Attachment

EXTENDING LANGUAGE ARTS

Editing Explain that editing skill is more complex than proofreading. Editing is the revision of a sentence, a paragraph, or a document to make it more effective. When you edit, check for the six C's:

Is the material correct? complete? clear? courteous? concise? consistent?

Write the following phrases on the board and ask students to provide a more concise way to express them: At the present moment (Now); In the event that (If); Due to the fact that (Because); In the near future (Soon); During the time (While).

Ask students to bring to class any examples of materials they have received that used more words than necessary to explain a situation. These are always fun and add realism to the classroom discussion.

Correspondence 35-18

Memo

MEMO TO: Barbara Azar, Staff Development Coordinator | **FROM:** Sharon Hearshen, Executive Assistant | **DATE:** April 3, 20-- | **SUBJECT:** Laser Printer Workshop

¶ The new laser printers we received are fabulous! I know that you worked very hard to get these printers for us, and all of us in the Sales and Marketing Department certainly appreciate your effort.

¶ Several of us would be very interested in seeing the printers demonstrated. Would it be possible to have a workshop with some hands-on training? We are particularly interested in learning about font selection, paper selection, and envelopes and labels.

¶ I have attached an article on laser printers from the latest issue of *Office Technology*. It is very informative, and you might like to include it as a part of the workshop. Please let me know if I can help you in any way.

urs | Attachment

Correspondence 35-19

Business Letter in Block Style

1. Type the following business letter, and then prepare an envelope for the document.
2. Do not include a return address.
3. Add the envelope to the letter.

Progress and Proofreading Check

Documents designated as Proofreading Checks serve as a check of your proofreading skill. Your goal is to have zero typographical errors when the GDP software first scores the document.

October 1, 20-- | Mrs. Elizabeth McGraw | 844 Lincoln Boulevard | Santa Monica, CA 90403 | Dear Mrs. McGraw:

¶ The League of Women Voters is looking for volunteers to work at the various polling places during the upcoming elections. If you think you will be able to volunteer your time, please fill out and mail the following enclosed items: registration form, schedule of availability, and insurance waiver form.

¶ After I receive these items, I will contact you to confirm a location, time, and date.

¶ Your efforts are greatly appreciated, Mrs. McGraw. Concerned citizens like you make it possible for the public to have a convenient place to vote. Thank you for your interest in this very worthy cause!

Sincerely yours, | Ashley Abbott | Public Relations Volunteer | urs | Enclosures

Lesson 35

DOCUMENT PROCESSING

Progress Check/ Proofreading Check

CORRESPONDENCE 35-19

All major formatting features presented in this unit are included in this document. You may want to use this as a short document processing test. In addition, you may want to inform students that this document also serves as a check of their proofreading skill and that they may have only one opportunity to have the GDP software check the document in order for them to receive a satisfactory proofreading grade.

ASSESS

www.mhhe.com/gdp to download a copy of the Technique Evaluation Form.

TECHNIQUE EVALUATION FORM

Walk around the room to observe student technique. Complete a Technique Evaluation Form for each student.

Print a report for all skillbuilding exercises for Lessons 31–35.

Review memo formatting.

Review letter formatting.

Extending the Lesson

Ask students to bring in newspaper articles containing proofreading errors.

CLOSE

Stress the correct procedure to use to exit Microsoft Word and the GDP program.

MHHE CHAMPIONS

Envelopes

The United States Postal Service (USPS) prefers that envelope addresses be keyed in all-caps with no punctuation.

Donna Snyder
Fairmont State College
Fairmont, West Virginia

WEST VIRGINIA

An excellent Web site for students to get to know is **www.usps.com**. Changes to envelope style will always be published there.

Instructors Helping One Another

Unit 8

UNIT OVERVIEW

Students will be introduced to tables. They will learn to create boxed, open, and ruled tables. The last lesson in the unit provides a formatting review.

Did You Know?

In the simplified formatting used in this text, table titles are typed in the first row rather than outside the table. This format ensures that if the table is moved, the title will move with the table.

www.mhhe.com/gdp to download a copy of the Technique Evaluation Form.

TECHNIQUE EVALUATION FORM

Use this form to keep track of student progress. Complete a form for each student.

Name ______ Class ______ Date ______

Technique Evaluation Form

Date	Workstation		Position at the Keyboard		Keystroking	
	Acceptable	Needs Improvement	Acceptable	Needs Improvement	Acceptable	Needs Improvement

Workstation
1. Positions the chair so that the upper and lower legs form a 90-degree angle and the lower back is supported.
2. Positions the keyboard even with the front of the desk.
3. Positions the text on either side of the monitor as close to it vertically and horizontally as possible to minimize head and eye movement and to avoid neck strain.
4. Positions the mouse on a pad at the side of the monitor opposite the text.

Position at the Keyboard
5. Centers the body opposite the keyboard.
6. Leans forward slightly from the hips, with the base of the spine touching the back of the chair and the feet flat on the floor.
7. Keeps the elbows alongside the body in a relaxed position.
8. Curves the fingers naturally over the home position, with the back of the hand at the same angle as the keyboard.

Keystroking
9. Keeps the forearms horizontal and raises the hands slightly when typing so that the wrists do not touch the keyboard while typing. (Hands may rest at the bottom of the keyboard—away from the keys—during nontyping intervals.)
10. Makes quick, snappy strokes using the correct fingers.
11. Returns the finger immediately to the home position or moves to the next position after each stroke.
12. Operates all keys by touch, keeping the eyes on the copy most of the time while typing.

Comments

Unit 8

Tables

LESSON 36
Boxed Tables

LESSON 37
Open Tables With Titles

LESSON 38
Open Tables With Column Headings

LESSON 39
Ruled Tables With Number Columns

LESSON 40
Formatting Review

GENERAL EQUITY MUTUAL FUNDS

Fund	Current Y
Duncan Insurance	16.3%
Strident Nova	9.3%
First Value	10.7%
Safeguard Policy	11.1%
Vanguard Life	8.5%

PERSONAL ASSET ACCOUNTS Wanda Nelson		
Account	**Amount**	**Interest Rate**
Interest Checking	$ 972.55	3.10%
Money Market	4,500.35	4.90%
	3,250.76	5.07%
sit	550.00	7.41%

CABLE SERVICES AVAILABILITY

Type of Service	Currently Available
Basic	Phoenix
Lifeline	Scottsdale
Expanded	Glendale
Expanded (per channel)	Camelback City

RESOURCE MANAGER

GDP SOFTWARE
- Lessons 36–40
- Software User's Guide
- Instructor Management LAN Version
- Word Processing Manual
- Professional Handbook (IWE*)—Teaching in a Distance-Learning Environment
- MAP 

ASSESSMENT

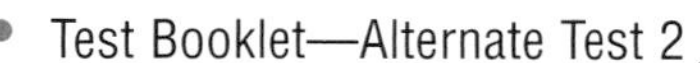

- Test Booklet—Alternate Test 2
- Progress Check—Table 40-15

- Professional Handbook (IWE*)—Assessment Strategies

ON THE WEB
- **www.mhhe.com/gdp**
- Instructor Management Web Version

* Instructor Wraparound Edition

Boxed Tables

Goals

- Type at least 35wpm/3′/4e
- Format boxed tables

A. Type 2 times.

A. WARMUP

```
     A plain paper reader/printer must be ordered; it must   11
accept jackets and have a footprint of 15 x 27* (*inches).   23
Please ask Gary to request Model Z-340 whenever he arrives.  35
| 1 | 2 | 3 | 4 | 5 | 6 | 7 | 8 | 9 | 10 | 11 | 12
```

SKILLBUILDING

B. Take three 12-second timed writings on each line. The scale below the last line shows your wpm speed for a 12-second timed writing.

B. 12-SECOND SPEED SPRINTS

```
The book that is on top of the big desk will be given away.
Bill must pay for the tape or he will have to give it back.
They left the meeting after all of the group had gone away.
The third person to finish all of the work today may leave.
5 10 15 20 25 30 35 40 45 50 55 60
```

C. DIAGNOSTIC PRACTICE: SYMBOLS AND PUNCTUATION

If you are not using the GDP software, turn to page SB-2 and follow the directions for this activity.

D. Take two 3-minute timed writings. Review your speed and errors.

Goal: At least 35wpm/3′/4e

D. 3-MINUTE TIMED WRITING

```
     Technology that tracks eye movements is used by Web        11
designers to judge how people interact with Web pages. It       22
must find out which zone of the page is viewed first, which     34
feature is viewed most often, and how quickly a page comes      46
to the screen.                                                   49
     Eye movements are tracked by use of hardware and data      60
analysis software. A camera is employed to find out the eye     72
movements of people who watch a screen. Pupil dilations and     84
scanning patterns of the eyes are measured to document the      96
amount of mental strain that has been exerted.                  105
| 1 | 2 | 3 | 4 | 5 | 6 | 7 | 8 | 9 | 10 | 11 | 12
```


Lesson 36

FOCUS

TIME MANAGEMENT

Suggested Schedule:

Warmup	2′
Skillbuilding	18′
Formatting	8′
Document Processing	22′
Total	**50′**

TEACH

SKILLBUILDING

LESSON 36-B Speed sprints are very motivational. Have students push moderately for speed on these easy sentences.

LESSON 36-C Encourage students to push moderately for speed on the Pretest.

ERGONOMICALLY SPEAKING

CHAIR A chair can contribute to well-being and productivity when a student is working with the computer. The chair should provide a comfortable sitting position and have a stable base, such as five legs with casters. Chair height should be from about 16 to 21 inches, measured from the top of the seat to the floor. Visit us on the Web at **www.mhhe.com/gdp** for more information.

Lesson 36

FORMATTING

Reference Manual

Ask students to review the basic parts of a table in the **Reference Manual, R-13A,** before they begin typing.

LESSON 36-E Discuss all parts of a table. Explain the difference between a column (vertical and identified with a letter) and a row (horizontal and identified with a number). Tell students that, to simplify column heading and column entry format, the alignment has been standardized. Review the alignments in the illustration.

VISUAL INSTRUCTION

Parts of a Table.

- Title
- Subtitle
- Heading block
- Column headings
- Column entries

LESSON 36-F Help students become familiar with creating tables and automatically adjusting column widths with their software.

DOCUMENT PROCESSING

TABLE 36-1 Guide students step by step through this first table. Remind them that in Lesson 38 they will learn to center tables horizontally and vertically. Emphasize that they should use the undo feature of their word processing software when they make any type of error.

3 columns
3 rows

Column entries:

Left-align column entries

FORMATTING

E. BASIC PARTS OF A TABLE

- Tables have vertical columns (identified by a letter in the illustration) and horizontal rows (identified by a number in the illustration).
- A cell, or "box," is created where a column and a row intersect.
- Tables formatted with borders all around (as shown in the illustration) are called boxed tables.
- Tables formatted with no borders are called open tables.
- Center a table vertically when it appears alone on the page.
- Center a table horizontally if the cell widths have been adjusted automatically to fit the contents.

Note: You will learn to center tables vertically and horizontally in Lesson 38.

↓ center page

14 pt **ALASKAN VACATIONS**
12 pt ↓ **Sailing Dates and Prices**
↓1X

↓1X Northern Departures	Interior Stateroom	Ocean View Stateroom	↓1X Guest	
January 12	$599	$699	$ 99	Row 3
February 14	599	699	99	Row 4
March 11	699	799	199	Row 5
April 2	699	799	199	Row 6
May 11	699	799	299	Row 7
June 6	799	899	399	Row 8
July 1	799	899	399	Row 9
August 21	799	899	399	Row 10
Column A	Column B	Column C	Column D	

Row 1 (title and subtitle); Row 2 (column headings)

TITLE. Center and type in all-caps and bold, with a 14-point font. If there is no subtitle, insert 1 blank line after the title.

SUBTITLE. Center on the line below the title, and type in upper- and lowercase letters and bold. Press Enter 1 time to insert a blank line below the subtitle.

HEADING BLOCK. Title and subtitle.

COLUMN HEADINGS. Center or left-align (for text) or right-align (for numbers). Press ENTER to split a 2-line column heading or to move a 1-line column heading down 1 line.

COLUMN ENTRIES. Align text entries at the left; align number entries at the right. Capitalize only the first word and proper nouns. Add spaces after the dollar sign to align with the widest column entry below (add 2 spaces for each digit and 1 space for each comma).

Word Processing Manual

F. WORD PROCESSING: TABLE—INSERT AND AUTOFIT TO CONTENTS

Study Lesson 36 in your word processing manual. Complete all of the shaded steps while at your computer. Then format the jobs that follow.

DOCUMENT PROCESSING

Table 36-1

Boxed Table

Simple tables often do not have titles, subtitles, or column headings.

1. Insert a boxed table with 3 columns and 3 rows.
2. Left-align all column entries.
3. Automatically adjust the column widths for all columns.

Mary Spangler	President	Administration
Joyce Moore	Dean	Jefferson Hall
Thelma Day	Chairperson	Da Vinci Hall

GDP SOFTWARE TIPS

Creating Tables

Demonstrate how quick and easy it is to create tables in Microsoft Word by working with the students to produce tables of various sizes. Use both the **Insert Table** button and the **Table, Insert Table** menu for the demonstration. Practice navigational techniques with the students—such as using the mouse, arrow keys, and TAB key.

Table 36-2
Boxed Table

1. Insert a boxed table with 2 columns and 4 rows.
2. Left-align all column entries.
3. Automatically adjust the column widths for all columns.

Marie Covey, Executive Editor	Santa Clarita, California
Albert Russell, Associate Editor	Newport, Rhode Island
Bob Harris, Contributing Writer	St. Louis, Missouri
Sylvestra Zimmerly, Art Director	Albuquerque, New Mexico

Table 36-3
Boxed Table

1. Open the file for Table 36-2.
2. Change the name and title in Row 4, Column A, to `Theodore Easton, Film Editor`.
3. Change the city in Row 4, Column B, to `Socorro`.

Table 36-4
Boxed Table

Barbara Azar	Professor	Computer Technologies
Ken Kennedy	Professor	Foreign Languages
Bonnie Marquette	Instructor	Computer Technologies
Kevin Nguyen	Assistant	Social Sciences

Strategies for Career Success

Nonverbal Communication

"It's not what he said, but how he said it." More than 90 percent of your spoken message contains nonverbal communication that expresses your feelings and desires. People respond to this nonverbal language.

Posture can convey your mood. For example, leaning toward a speaker indicates interest. Leaning backward suggests dislike or indifference. Your handshake, an important nonverbal communicator, should be firm but not overpowering.

Your head position provides many nonverbal signals. A lowered head usually expresses shyness or withdrawal. An upright head conveys confidence and interest. A tilted head signifies curiosity or suspicion. Nodding your head shows positive feeling, while left-right head shakes signify negative feeling. Your face strongly expresses your emotions. Narrow, squinting eyes signify caution, reflection, or uncertainty. Wide-open eyes convey interest and attention.

YOUR TURN Turn off the sound on a television program. How much of the plot can you understand just from the nonverbal communication signals?

Strategies for Career Success

NONVERBAL COMMUNICATION Discuss with students the importance of positive nonverbal communication. Ask students to describe examples of positive and negative nonverbal communication they have experienced at school or at work.

YOUR TURN If time permits, ask students to complete the Your Turn activity.

DOCUMENT PROCESSING

TABLE 36-2

2 columns
4 rows

Column entries: Left-align column entries

TABLE 36-3 Explain that students should open the file for Table 36-2 by clicking on the button in the GDP software that is designed to do this automatically. They do not need to go backward in the lesson menu to Table 36-2 to open it in order to type Table 36-3.

TABLE 36-4 Optional. Students should feel free to look back at the table illustration on page 104 to review any details.

3 columns
4 rows

Column entries:

Left-align column entries

ASSESS

www.mhhe.com/gdp to download a copy of the Technique Evaluation Form.

TECHNIQUE EVALUATION FORM
Review results of timed writings.

Review table formatting.

Extending the Lesson

Ask students to bring sample tables to class. Discuss formatting and layout for the tables.

CLOSE

Stress the correct procedure to use to exit Microsoft Word and the GDP program.

FOCUS

TIME MANAGEMENT 

Suggested Schedule:

Warmup	2′
Skillbuilding	14′
Language Arts	6′
Formatting	8′
Document Processing	20′
Total	**50′**

TEACH

SKILLBUILDING

LESSON 37-B Each paragraph is more difficult than the preceding one—based on the number of proofreaders' marks.

Paragraph 1: 0
Paragraph 2: 4
Paragraph 3: 8
Paragraph 4: 9

LESSON 37-C Students take repeated timed writings on a passage containing the exact number of words for their speed goal until they can complete it with no errors. Then they move to the next longer passage and start again.

Lesson 37

Open Tables With Titles

Goals

- Improve speed and accuracy
- Refine language arts skills in punctuation
- Format open tables with titles

A. Type 2 times.

A. WARMUP

```
     The check for $432.65 wasn't mailed on time! Late       10
charges of up to 10% can be expected. To avoid a sizable     22
penalty, just send an e-mail message to quickpay@epay.com.   33
  | 1 | 2 | 3 | 4 | 5 | 6 | 7 | 8 | 9 | 10 | 11 | 12
```

SKILLBUILDING

B. Take a 1-minute timed writing on the first paragraph to establish your base speed. Then take four 1-minute timed writings on the remaining paragraphs. As soon as you equal or exceed your base speed on one paragraph, advance to the next, more difficult paragraph.

B. SUSTAINED PRACTICE: ROUGH DRAFT

```
     Various human responses are asymmetrical. This means       11
that we ask more from one side of the body than the other       23
each time we wave, wink, clap our hands, or cross our legs.     35

     Each one of these actions demands a clear desision,        11
usually unconscious and instantaneous, to start the course      23
of moving parts of the body in different directions.            34

All children go though remarkably involved steps as they        12
develop their preferried. As children grows she or he may       23
favor the right hand, the left, or both the same at times.      35

When most kids are eihgt or seven, stability ocurrs,            11
and one hand is permanently domenent over the other. Fore       22
some unnown reason, choose the right hand.                      34
  | 1 | 2 | 3 | 4 | 5 | 6 | 7 | 8 | 9 | 10 | 11 | 12
```

C. PACED PRACTICE

If you are not using the GDP software, turn to page SB-14 and follow the directions for this activity.

ERGONOMICALLY SPEAKING

FLAT-PANEL MONITORS Eyestrain is a concern for computer users who spend the majority of their days looking at a monitor. Flat-panel displays sharply reduce reflection and virtually eliminate glare. Thus, they also reduce eyestrain. Because the screen contains liquid crystals, these monitors can be placed facing a window and still provide comfortable viewing. The difference between flat panels and CRTs is amazing—especially if your work area is by a window.

Lesson 37

LANGUAGE ARTS

D. Study the rules at the right.

D. APOSTROPHE

Note: The callout signals in the left margin indicate which language arts rule from this lesson has been applied.

RULE ▶ ' singular

Use *'s* to form the possessive of singular nouns.
The hurricane's force caused major damage to North Carolina's coastline.

RULE ▶ ' plural

Use only an apostrophe to form the possessive of plural nouns that end in *s*.
The investors' goals were outlined in the stockholders' report.
But: The investors outlined their goals in the report to the stockholders.
But: The women's and children's clothing was on sale.

RULE ▶ ' pronoun

Use *'s* to form the possessive of indefinite pronouns (such as *someone's* or *anybody's*); do not use an apostrophe with personal pronouns (such as *hers, his, its, ours, their,* and *yours*).
She could select anybody's paper for a sample.
It's time to put the file back into its cabinet.

Edit the sentences to insert any needed punctuation.

```
16 The womans purse was stolen as she held her childs hand.
17 If the book is yours, please return it to the library now.
18 The girls decided to send both parents donations to school.
19 The childs toy was forgotten by his mothers good friend.
20 The universities presidents submitted the joint statement.
21 The four secretaries salaries were raised just like yours.
22 One boys presents were forgotten when he left the party.
23 If these blue notebooks are not ours, they must be theirs.
24 The plant was designed to recycle its own waste products.
```

FORMATTING

E. TABLE HEADING BLOCK

Note: The title and subtitle (if any) make up the table heading block.

To format a table heading block:

- Type the title centered in all-caps and bold, with a 14-point font in Row 1 of the table. If the table does not have a subtitle, insert 1 blank line after the title.
- Type the subtitle (if any) with a 12-point font centered on the line below the title in upper- and lowercase letters in bold.
- Insert 1 blank line after the subtitle.

Word Processing Manual

F. WORD PROCESSING: TABLE—MERGE CELLS AND BORDERS

Study Lesson 37 in your word processing manual. Complete all of the shaded steps while at your computer. Then format the jobs that follow.

LANGUAGE ARTS

LESSON 37-D If students are not using the GDP software, have them type a correct version of the sentences.

SOLUTION: Lines 16–24

16. woman's, child's
17. *Correct*
18. parents'
19. child's, mother's
20. universities'
21. secretaries'
22. boy's
23. *Correct*
24. *Correct*

FORMATTING

Reference Manual

Ask students to review the table heading block in the **Reference Manual, R-13A, R-13B,** and **R-13D,** before they begin typing.

LESSON 37-E Discuss the parts and formatting of a table heading block.

LESSON 37-F Help students learn the merge cells and borders features of their word processing software.

EXTENDING LANGUAGE ARTS

Apostrophe Explain that you form the possessive of a singular noun by adding an apostrophe (') and *s*.

editor's notes	driver's tire
boy's bicycle	clerk's file

Circle the second noun in each item to show that a noun always follows a word or phrase indicating possession or ownership.

Simply add an apostrophe to a plural noun to show possession or ownership.

boys' bicycles	the mothers' walk
babies' toys	the fathers' game

To form the possessive of an indefinite pronoun (*someone, anybody*), add an apostrophe (') and *s*. Possessive forms of personal pronouns do not use an apostrophe (*hers, his, ours, theirs, its, yours*). The use of an apostrophe at the end of these words is a common mistake among novice writers.

Lesson 37

DOCUMENT PROCESSING

TABLE 37-5 Guide students step by step through this first open table with a table heading block. Remind them to insert 1 blank line below the title and to remove the borders.

2 columns
5 rows

Column entries:

Left-align column entries

TABLE 37-6 Remind students to bold both the title and the subtitle in the table heading block and to insert 1 blank line below the subtitle.

3 columns
5 rows

Column entries:

Left-align column entries

TABLE 37-7 Optional. Refer students to basic table parts on page 104.

2 columns
6 rows

Column entries:

Left-align column entries

ASSESS

www.mhhe.com/gdp to download a copy of the Technique Evaluation Form.

TECHNIQUE EVALUATION FORM
Review table formatting.

Extending the Lesson

Create a list of ten sentences to reinforce the language arts rules on the use of the apostrophe.

CLOSE

Review the difference between an open table and a boxed table.

DOCUMENT PROCESSING

Table 37-5
Open Table

1. Insert a table with 2 columns and 5 rows.
2. Merge the cells in Row 1; then center and type the title in bold and all-caps, with a 14-point font.
3. Press ENTER once to insert 1 blank line after the title.
4. Left-align all column entries.
5. Automatically adjust the column widths for all columns.
6. Remove the table borders.

' singular

PC CONNECTION'S LOCATIONS

Valencia Mall	Santa Clarita, California
Town Center Square	Stevenson Ranch, California
Northridge Mall	Northridge, California
Granary Square	Valencia, California

Table 37-6
Open Table

1. Insert a table with 3 columns and 5 rows.
2. Merge the cells in Row 1; then center and type the title in bold and all-caps, with a 14-point font.
3. Press ENTER 1 time, change to a 12-point font, and type the subtitle centered in bold.
4. Press ENTER 1 time to insert 1 blank line after the subtitle.
5. Left-align all column entries.
6. Automatically adjust the column widths for all columns.
7. Remove the table borders.

' singular
' plural

NEWHALL DISTRICT'S REGISTRATION
Seniors' Schedule

Meadows	Monday, February 14	11 a.m.
Stevenson Ranch	Monday, February 21	10 a.m.
Old Orchard	Monday, February 28	11 a.m.
Wiley Canyon	Monday, March 7	10 a.m.

Table 37-7
Open Table
' singular

1. Insert a table with 2 columns and 6 rows.
2. Use standard table format for an open table with a title and subtitle.

MAR VISTA REALTY'S TOP SELLERS
First Quarter

James Kinkaid	Santa Clarita
Deborah Springer	Northbridge
Patricia Morelli	Woodland Hills
Jan McKay	Malibu
Daniel Aboud	San Luis Obispo

INSTRUCTOR STRATEGIES

Tables and Borders Highlight the following buttons on the Tables and Borders toolbar.

- Line style
- Line weight
- Border color
- Shading color
- Merge cells

Open Tables With Column Headings

Goals

- Type at least 35wpm/3′/4e
- Format open tables with column headings

A. Type 2 times.

A. WARMUP

Jerry wrote a great article entitled "Interviewing 10
Techniques" on pp. 23 and 78! A&B@bookstore.com expected a 22
sizable number of requests; thus far, 65% have been sold. 33

| 1 | 2 | 3 | 4 | 5 | 6 | 7 | 8 | 9 | 10 | 11 | 12

SKILLBUILDING

B. Take three 12-second timed writings on each line. The scale below the last line shows your wpm speed for a 12-second timed writing.

B. 12-SECOND SPEED SPRINTS

Blake was paid to fix the handle on the bowls that he made.
Alan led the panel of four men until the work was all done.
Jan will sign this paper when she has done all of the work.
They will focus on their main theme for the last six weeks.

5 10 15 20 25 30 35 40 45 50 55 60

C. PROGRESSIVE PRACTICE: ALPHABET

If you are not using the GDP software, turn to page SB-7 and follow the directions for this activity.

D. Take two 3-minute timed writings. Review your speed and errors.

Goal: At least 35wpm/3′/4e

D. 3-MINUTE TIMED WRITING

Telecommuting is a word you may have heard before but 11
do not quite understand. Very simply, it means working at 23
home instead of driving in to work. Many people like the 34
convenience of working at home. They realize they can save 46
money on expenses like gas, food, and child care. 56
Most home office workers use a computer in their job. 67
When their work is done, they can just fax or e-mail it to 79
the office. If they must communicate with other workers, 90
they can use the phone, fax, or computer and never have to 102
leave your home. 105

| 1 | 2 | 3 | 4 | 5 | 6 | 7 | 8 | 9 | 10 | 11 | 12

TEACHING THE ADULT LEARNER

NOTETAKING Adult learners may not be aware that taking notes helps them be active listeners. Offer suggestions such as the following:

- Don't write every spoken word.
- Listen for keywords such as *most important* or *remember*.
- Listen for lists, such as *point one is . . .*
- Note what the instructor writes on the board or projects on a screen.

Lesson 38

FOCUS

TIME MANAGEMENT
Suggested Schedule:

Warmup	2′
Skillbuilding	20′
Formatting	6′
Document Processing	22′
Total	**50′**

TEACH

SKILLBUILDING

LESSON 38-B Speed sprints are very motivational. Have students push moderately for speed on these easy sentences.

LESSON 38-C Students take repeated timed writings on a passage containing the exact number of words for their speed goal until they can complete the passage with no errors. Then they move to the next longer passage and start again.

Lesson 38

FORMATTING

Ask students to review column headings in the **Reference Manual, R-13A, R-13B, R-13C,** and **R-13D,** before they begin typing.

LESSON 38-E Discuss the formatting of table column headings and their various alignments. Explain the vertical alignment of 1-line column headings in the same table with 2-line column headings.

LESSON 38-F Help students learn to center tables vertically and horizontally using their word processing software.

DOCUMENT PROCESSING

TABLE 38-8

2 columns
6 rows

Column headings and entries:

Center column headings
Left-align column entries

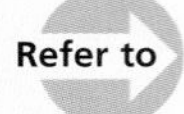

Ask students to review table format in the **Reference Manual, R-13,** before they begin typing.

FORMATTING

E. COLUMN HEADINGS

Column headings describe the information contained in the column entries. Refer to page R-13A in the Reference Manual for an illustration of column headings.

To format column headings:

- Type the column headings in upper- and lowercase letters and bold.
- If a table has a combination of 1- and 2-line column headings, press ENTER 1 time before typing the 1-line column heading to push the heading down so that it aligns vertically at the bottom of the cell.
- Center column headings in tables with all-text columns.
- Left-align column headings in a column with all text.
- Right-align column headings in a column with all numbers.

F. WORD PROCESSING: TABLE—CENTER HORIZONTALLY AND CENTER PAGE

Study Lesson 38 in your word processing manual. Complete all of the shaded steps while at your computer. Then format the jobs that follow.

DOCUMENT PROCESSING

Table 38-8
Open Table

Note: Center all tables horizontally and vertically from now on.

1. Insert a table with 2 columns and 6 rows.
2. Type the title block in standard table title block format.
3. Type the column headings centered in upper- and lowercase letters and bold.
4. Left-align the column entries.
5. Automatically adjust the column widths for all columns.
6. Remove all table borders.

↓center page

VENDOR LIST
July 1, 20-- ↓1X

Product	Vendor
Laser printers	Office Supplies Unlimited
Workstations	PC Junction, Inc.
Cell phones	Satellite Communications
Scanners	Atlantic-Pacific Digital

INSTRUCTOR STRATEGIES

Centering Help students understand the difference between centering paragraph text using the Standard toolbar and centering tables using the Table Properties dialog box. You may want to demonstrate the align button on the Tables and Borders toolbar.

Table 38-9 ▶

Open Table

1. Insert a table with 2 columns and 6 rows.
2. Type the title block in standard table title block format.
3. Type the column headings centered in upper- and lowercase letters and bold.
4. In Column A, press ENTER 1 time to split the column heading into two lines as shown.
5. In Column B, press ENTER 1 time before typing the 1-line column heading to push the heading down so that it aligns vertically at the bottom of the cell.
6. Left-align the column entries.
7. Automatically adjust the column widths for all columns.
8. Remove all table borders.

(!) Press ENTER to create a column heading of 2 lines or to move a single-line heading down 1 line.

COMMITTEE ASSIGNMENTS

Academic Committee Assignments	**Professor**
Institutional Integrity	Anne McCarthy
Educational Programs	Bill Zimmerman
Student Services	John Yeh
Financial Resources	Steve Williams

Table 38-10 ▶

Open Table

1. Open the file for Table 38-8.
2. Change the date to `September 30`.
3. Change the 4 products in Column A as follows:

```
Copiers
Processors
Controller cards
Modems
```

Table 38-11 ▶

Open Table

CABLE SERVICES AVAILABILITY ↓1X

Type of Service	**Currently Available**
Basic	Phoenix
Lifeline	Scottsdale
Expanded	Glendale
Expanded (per channel)	Camelback City

Meeting Special Needs

PHYSICALLY CHALLENGED STUDENTS Never assume that physically challenged students can't do something, but make sure that they have the opportunity to fully participate in class. They must have access to the classroom. A barrier can be a stair, a curb, a narrow hallway, a heavy door, or an elevator door that does not allow sufficient time for a wheelchair to exit. Classroom tables must have at least 27½ inches of clearance for wheelchair access.

Lesson 38

DOCUMENT PROCESSING

TABLE 38-9 Remind students to press ENTER before typing the column heading in Column B.

2 columns
6 rows

Columns headings and entries:

Center column headings
Left-align column entries

TABLE 38-10

2 columns
6 rows

Column headings and entries:

Center column headings

Left-align column entries

TABLE 38-11 Optional. Remind students to press ENTER before typing the column heading in Column A.

2 columns
6 rows

Column headings and entries:

Center column headings
Left-align column entries

ASSESS

www.mhhe.com/gdp to download a copy of the Technique Evaluation Form.

TECHNIQUE EVALUATION FORM Review results of timed writings.

Extending the Lesson

Show examples of tables centered horizontally and vertically and tables not centered. Which are easier to read? Which look more professional?

CLOSE

Remind students to refer to their Word Processing Manual to review table formatting.

FOCUS

TIME MANAGEMENT

Suggested Schedule:

Warmup	2′
Skillbuilding	13′
Language Arts	6′
Formatting	6′
Document Processing	23′
Total	**50′**

TEACH

SKILLBUILDING

LESSON 39-B Observe technique on the SHIFT key and CAPS LOCK, and correct as needed.

LESSON 39-C Horizontal reaches include in and out reaches.

LESSON 39-D In reaches go from the outside of the keyboard to the center of the keyboard. Make sure that students are typing their practice lines in the correct pattern for either speed or accuracy.

LESSON 39-E Out reaches go from the center of the keyboard to the outside of the keyboard.

Lesson 39

Ruled Tables With Number Columns

Goals

- Improve speed and accuracy
- Refine language arts skills in spelling
- Format ruled tables with number columns

A. Type 2 times.

A. WARMUP

```
     Does Xavier know that around 8:04 a.m. his July sales  11
quota was realized? Invoice #671 indicates a 9% increase!   23
Several of the employees weren't able to regain their lead. 34
| 1 | 2 | 3 | 4 | 5 | 6 | 7 | 8 | 9 | 10 | 11 | 12
```

SKILLBUILDING

B. Type the paragraph 2 times. Use the CAPS LOCK key to type a word or series of words in all-caps. Tap the CAPS LOCK key with the A finger.

B. TECHNIQUE PRACTICE: SHIFT KEY AND CAPS LOCK

```
     The new computer has CD-ROM, PCI IDE HDD controller,
and an SVGA card. Mr. J. L. Jones will order one from PC
EXPRESS out of Orem, Utah. IT ARRIVES NO LATER THAN JULY.
```

PPP PRETEST → PRACTICE → POSTTEST

PRETEST
Take a 1-minute timed writing. Review your speed and errors.

C. PRETEST: Horizontal Reaches

```
     The chief thinks the alarm was a decoy for the armed  11
agent who coyly dashed away. She was dazed as she dodged   22
a blue sedan. He lured her to the edge of the high bluff.  33
| 1 | 2 | 3 | 4 | 5 | 6 | 7 | 8 | 9 | 10 | 11 | 12
```

PRACTICE
Speed Emphasis: If you made 2 or fewer errors on the Pretest, type each *individual* line 2 times.
Accuracy Emphasis: If you made 3 or more errors, type each *group* of lines (as though it were a paragraph) 2 times.

D. PRACTICE: In Reaches

```
oy foyer loyal buoys enjoy decoy coyly royal cloy ploy toys
ar argue armed cared alarm cedar sugar radar area earn hear
lu lucid lunch lured bluff value blunt fluid luck lush blue
```

E. PRACTICE: Out Reaches

```
ge geese genes germs agent edges dodge hinge gear ages page
da daily dazed dance adapt sedan adage panda dash date soda
hi hints hiked hired chief think ethic aphid high ship chip
```

POSTTEST
Repeat the Pretest timed writing and compare performance.

F. POSTTEST: Horizontal Reaches

Meeting Special Needs

COGNITIVE OR LANGUAGE IMPAIRMENTS
Cognitive or language impairments may range from dyslexia or memory problems to problems understanding and using language. For students who have these disabilities, inconsistent visual displays or word choices can make using computers more difficult. Keyboard filters, including word prediction utilities and add-on spell checkers, can help these students.

Visit us on the Web at **www.mhhe.com/gdp** for more information.

LANGUAGE ARTS

G. Type these frequently misspelled words, paying special attention to any spelling problems in each word.

G. SPELLING

```
16 prior activities additional than faculty whether first with
17 subject material equipment receiving completed during basis
18 available please required decision established policy audit
19 section schedule installation insurance possible appreciate
20 benefits requirements business scheduled office immediately
```

Edit the sentences to correct any misspellings.

```
21 We requierd the office to schedule all prior activities.
22 The business scheduled the instalation of the equipment.
23 The decision established the basis of the insurance policy.
24 Please audit any additionl material available to faculty.
25 If possible, they would appreciate recieving them soon.
26 Section requirements to receive benefits were completed.
```

FORMATTING

Review the use of borders in Lesson 37 or in your word processing manual as needed.

H. RULED TABLES WITH NUMBER COLUMNS

To format a ruled table with number columns:

1. Remove all table borders.
2. Apply borders to the top and bottom of Row 2 and to the bottom of the last row.
3. Right-align column headings and column entries with numbers.
4. If the column entry includes a dollar sign, add spaces after the dollar sign to align the dollar sign just to the left of the widest column entry below it as follows: add 2 spaces for each number and 1 space for each comma. In the example below, 3 spaces were added after the dollar sign.

Example:

$ 375
2,150
49

Word Processing Manual

I. WORD PROCESSING: TABLE—ALIGN TEXT IN A COLUMN

Study Lesson 39 in your word processing manual. Complete all of the shaded steps while at your computer. Then format the jobs that follow.

EXTENDING LANGUAGE ARTS

Spelling Many students are not aware of how to pronounce the words in Lesson 39-G. Begin this exercise by pronouncing each word. Then, have the students pronounce the words in unison. After this, ask individual students to pronounce a line at a time. When they have completed these steps, they should do far better in typing the words in the exercise. For homework, have the students prepare a list of definitions of these words. Knowing the definitions and knowing how to pronounce the words will make their spelling more accurate.

LANGUAGE ARTS

LESSON 39-G Alternative routine: Dictate each word, and have students type the word once. For each word mistyped, have students study its spelling and type it correctly 3 times. Discuss the meaning or usage of selected words.

Solution: Lines 21–26

21. required
22. installation
23. *Correct*
24. additional
25. receiving
26. *Correct*

FORMATTING

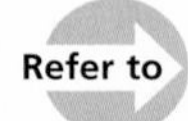

Reference Manual

Ask students to review ruled tables with number columns in the Reference **Manual, R-13A, R-13B,** and **R-13D,** before they begin typing.

LESSON 39-H Explain the steps to use to format ruled tables with number columns. Point out that numbers that could be used as numeric data (in a calculation, for example) are always aligned at the right, as opposed to numbers that are used like text (such as a phone number). Illustrate adding 2 spaces for each number and 1 space for each comma to align the dollar sign in the first line of a column entry.

LESSON 39-I Help students practice aligning text in their tables using their word processing software.

Lesson 39

DOCUMENT PROCESSING

Refer to Reference Manual

Ask students to review table format in the **Reference Manual, R-13C,** before they begin typing.

TABLE 39-12 Guide students step by step through this first ruled table with number columns.

3 columns
5 rows

Column headings and entries:

Center column headings
Left-align Column A,
Right-align Columns B and C

TABLE 39-13

4 columns
7 rows

Column headings and entries:

Left-align Column A
Right-align Columns B, C, and D

TABLE 39-14 Optional.

3 columns
7 rows

Column headings and entries:

Left-align Column A
Right-align Columns B and C

ASSESS

TECHNIQUE EVALUATION FORM
Complete a Technique Evaluation Form for each student.

Extending the Lesson

Remind students that text is usually left-aligned and numbers are usually right-aligned.

CLOSE

Stress the correct procedure to use to exit Microsoft Word and the GDP program.

DOCUMENT PROCESSING

Table 39-12
Ruled Table

1. Insert a ruled table with 3 columns and 5 rows.
2. Type the heading block and table in standard table format.
3. Add spaces after the dollar sign as needed to align the dollar sign just to the left of the widest column entry below it.
4. Remove all table borders and apply borders to the top and bottom of Row 2 and to the bottom of the last row.

Highlighted words are spelling words from the language arts activity.

↓center page

NORTHERN BELL PHONES
Inside Wire Repair Service ↓1X

Per-Month Plan	Today's Rates	1995 Rates
Residence	$ .60	$1.00
Business	1.30	1.30
Private Line	3.50	4.50

Table 39-13
Ruled Table

1. Insert a ruled table with 4 columns and 7 rows.
2. Type the heading block and table in standard table format.
3. Add spaces after the dollar sign to align the dollar sign just to the left of the widest column entry below it.
4. Remove all table borders; then apply borders to the top and bottom of Row 2 and to the bottom of the last row.

To align the dollar sign correctly, add 2 spaces for each digit.

↓center page

HOLIDAY RESORT SUITES
Available Rates ↓1X

Hotel	Rack Rate	Club Rate	3-Night Savings
Porter Ranch Inn	$ 92.00	$36.00	$ 68.00
Jamaican Inn	119.00	59.50	178.50
Casitas Suites	120.00	60.00	180.00
The Desert Inn Resort	135.00	75.50	178.50
Sannibel Courtyard	150.00	75.00	225.00

Table 39-14
Ruled Table

GENERAL EQUITY MUTUAL FUNDS

Fund	Current Year	Previous Year
Duncan Insurance	16.3%	2.0%
Strident Nova	9.3%	3.5%
First Value	10.7%	12.1%
Safeguard Policy	11.1%	9.7%
Vanguard Life	8.5%	10.1%

TEACHING THE ADULT LEARNER

EXPERIENCE COUNTS IN THE CLASSROOM
Instructors of the adult learner should assume that each person comes to the education process with his or her own life's story and experiences. Therefore, everything that instructors say is not automatically accepted by the adult learner (as it might be by a child) but is interpreted according to the adult learner's perception of the situation and background. Try to find out quickly what each adult learner knows and build from there. Implement various teaching strategies—written, oral, hands-on. The adult learner probably can grasp the concept presented and apply it to the task or topic at hand.

Formatting Review

Goals

- Type at least 36wpm/3′/4e
- Format tables with a variety of features
- Format documents with a variety of features

A. Type 2 times.

A. WARMUP

```
     On July 15, a check for exactly $329.86 was mailed to   11
Zak & Quinn, Inc.; they never received Check #104. Does      22
Gary know if the check cleared the company's bank account?   34
|  1  |  2  |  3  |  4  |  5  |  6  |  7  |  8  |  9  |  10  |  11  |  12
```

SKILLBUILDING

B. MAP

Follow the GDP software directions for this exercise in improving keystroking accuracy.

C. DIAGNOSTIC PRACTICE: NUMBERS

If you are not using the GDP software, turn to page SB-5 and follow the directions for this activity.

D. Take two 3-minute timed writings. Review your speed and errors.

Goal: At least 36wpm/3′/4e

D. 3-MINUTE TIMED WRITING

```
     Employee complaints are often viewed as a negative       10
force in a workplace. In fact, these complaints should be     22
viewed as a chance to communicate with the employee and to    34
improve morale. To ignore the complaint does not make it go   46
away. If you just listen to complaints, you may help to       57
solve small problems before they turn into bigger ones.       68
     Often workers expect a chance to be heard by a person    79
who is willing to listen to them quite openly. That person    90
should recognize that the employee has concerns that need    102
to be addressed at this time.                                108
|  1  |  2  |  3  |  4  |  5  |  6  |  7  |  8  |  9  |  10  |  11  |  12
```


Lesson 40

FOCUS

TIME MANAGEMENT

Suggested Schedule:

Warmup	2′
Skillbuilding	21′
Document Processing	27′
Total	**50′**

TEACH

SKILLBUILDING

LESSON 40-B  **MAP**

MAP (Misstroke Analysis and Prescription) is a simple, comprehensive, and individualized software program designed to improve keystroking accuracy.

In an effort to improve each student's accuracy, the instructor must have a way to call out these errors to the individual student. Practice, in and of itself, is not the solution. Prescribed practice for specific errors is the solution. Providing the prescribed practice is made easy and accurate through the use of MAP, which is included in the software for this program.

LESSON 40-C Encourage students to push moderately for speed on the Pretest.

MHHE CHAMPIONS

Proofreading

Remind students that in the real world it is not wise to rely solely on spell check and grammar check.

You may want to have students discuss the following poem, which has circulated on the Internet in many variations. Students may want to write their own verses.

Sue Krissler
Orange County Community College
Middletown, New York

NEW YORK

Aye have a spelling checker.
It came with my pea sea.
It plane lea marks four my revue
Miss steaks eye can knot sea.
Eye ran this poem threw it.
I'm shore your please too no
Its vary polished in it's weigh:
My checker tolled me sew.

Lesson 40

DOCUMENT PROCESSING

Reference Manual

Ask students to review the academic report format in the **Reference Manual, R-8C** and **R-8D,** before they begin typing.

This lesson reviews Units 6, 7, and 8. Have students type each document without detailed instructions from you.

Encourage them to use the Reference Manual and the Word Processing Manual. Help them identify areas needing improvement.

CORRESPONDENCE 40-20

Remind students to add the envelope to the letter.

DOCUMENT PROCESSING

Report 40-11

Academic Report

RELATIONSHIPS AT WORK

Jensen Zhao

¶ Do you believe that as long as you get your work done at the end of the day, you have had a successful day on the job? If so, you are badly mistaken. Doing the work is only half the job. The other half is relating to and working with the people around you.

TAKE A TEAM APPROACH

¶ Everything you do and every action you take affects those around you in a close working relationship. Operating as a team means thinking about others and taking actions that will help them reach their goals and achieve the goals of the company.

MAINTAIN A SPIRIT OF COOPERATION

¶ When you work in a spirit of cooperation, those around you will reflect that spirit. Your job will be easier because you will minimize resistance. It takes much more energy to resist one another than it does to cooperate and work together.

VALIDATE THE OPINIONS OF OTHERS

¶ You will find that this simple act of validation will go a long way in helping the spirit of your coworkers. Here are two simple ways to validate the opinions of others:

1. Take time to listen to the issues and accomplishments of those around you.
2. Reflect their opinions in your own words in a spirit of genuine interest.

There is a saying that states, "Your success is my success." Adopt this as your motto, and you will find a great deal of satisfaction at the end of each day.

Correspondence 40-20

Business Letter in Block Style

Note: Omit the return address on the envelope.

December 1, 20--| Mrs. Yvonne Spillotro | 105 North Field Avenue | Edison NJ 08837 | Dear mrs. Spillotro:

¶ Thank you for choosing Insurance Alliance Of America. Open enrollment for your insurance medical plan is scheduled to begin the first day of January. I hope it was possible for you to review the materials you received last week. ¶ Selecting the right benefit plan for you and your family can be an over whelming task. To make ~~this~~ your decision a little easier, I have enclosed a brochure ~~with this letter~~ that summarizing es the key features of each policy.

(Continued on next page)

TEACHING THE ADULT LEARNER

TEAMWORK Today, the team concept is what makes businesses successful. Ideas and decisions are generated within teams and not from the top down as in the past. Ask students what successful strategies they have experienced as members of teams—whether at work, on a playing field, or at home with family members. What makes a team effective and successful?

Please call me if I can help in any way.

You might want to browse through our website at www.IAA.com for further details.

Sincerely, | Denise Broers | Customer Support | urs | enclosure

Table 40-15

Three-Column Boxed Table

PERSONAL ASSET ACCOUNTS Wanda Nelson		
Account	**Amount**	**Interest Rate**
Interest Checking	$ 972.55	3.10%
Money Market	4,500.35	4.90%
Smart Saver	3,250.76	5.07%
Certificate of Deposit	550.00	7.41%

Progress and Proofreading Check

Documents designated as Proofreading Checks serve as a check of your proofreading skill. Your goal is to have zero typographical errors when the GDP software first scores the document.

INSTRUCTOR STRATEGIES

Discussing the Illustration Ask for creative ideas for using tables to present information. Start the class discussion with an idea to create a family cookbook.

- Create a table with 2 columns and 2 rows.
- Select the first row; merge the cells for a single block to use for the heading and recipe instructions.
- Type the ingredients below the merged row in both columns.

DOCUMENT PROCESSING

Progress Check/ Proofreading Check

TABLE 40-15 All major formatting features presented in this unit are included in this document. You may want to use this as a small document processing test. In addition, you may want to inform students that this document also serves as a check of their proofreading skill and that they may have only one opportunity to have the GDP software check the document in order for them to receive a satisfactory proofreading grade.

3 columns
6 rows

Column headings and entries:

Left-align Column A
Right-align Columns B and C

ASSESS

www.mhhe.com/gdp to download a copy of the Technique Evaluation Form.

TECHNIQUE EVALUATION FORM Review results of timed writings.

Print a report for all skillbuilding exercises for Lessons 36–40.

Extending the Lesson

Remind students to refer to their Word Processing Manual to review formatting commands learned in this unit.

CLOSE

Remind students to proofread their document and to check its format.

ASSESS

An alternate Progress Test (similar to this one) is included in the Tests and Solution Keys booklet.

Because of time constraints, you may want to give Test 2-A the day before the production jobs (Tests 2-B, 2-C, and 2-D).

See the Instructor's Manual for suggested grading standards for Test 2.

CORRESPONDENCE TEST 2-21 Review proofreaders' marks on page R-14C in the Reference Manual Focus on the marks for capitalize, insert space, underline, spell out, and don't delete.

Review the format for a business letter in block style in Lesson 31-F, Basic Parts of a Business Letter, on page 85. Also review the business letter on page R-3A in the Reference Manual. Review the format of an enclosure notation in Lesson 32-H, Enclosure Notation, on page 89.

Review the steps for preparing an envelope for a letter in the Word Processing Manual. Lesson 33, Envelopes, on pages 68–69.

REPORT TEST 2-12 Review the format for a multipage academic report with side headings and paragraph headings in Lesson 29-F, Academic Reports, on page 77 and pages R-8C and R-8D in the Reference Manual.

Review the format for an academic report with a list in Lesson 30-E, Academic Reports With Lists, on page 80.

Skills Assessment on Part 2

3-Minute Timed Writing

From the first day of class, you have continuously 10
worked to improve your typing skill. You have worked hard 22
to increase your typing speed and accuracy. You have also 34
learned to format letters, memos, reports, and tables. All 46
of this work is quite an amazing accomplishment. 56
In your lessons, you have worked on learning a wide 66
range of word processing skills. You can expect to make 78
even more progress if you practice your skills regularly. 90
Learn as much as you can each day. Ask questions, and then 102
move toward a new goal each day. 108

| 1 | 2 | 3 | 4 | 5 | 6 | 7 | 8 | 9 | 10 | 11 | 12

Correspondence Test 2-21

Business Letter in Block Style

Note: Omit the return address on the envelope.

March 17 , 20-- | Ms. ~~Arlene~~ Dorothy Turner | Global Moving and Storage | 6830 Via Del Monte | San Jose, CA 95119 | Dear Ms. Turner:

¶ Thank you ~~you~~ for registering your pc Graphics software so promptly. As a registered user, you are entitled to free technical support 24 hours a day. The brochure enclosed will explain in detail how you can reach us ~~either~~ by fax, e-mail, or phone whenever you need help. Also, help is always available on our website at www.pcgraphics.com. All our PC Graphics users will receive our monthly newsletter, which is filled with tips on using your new software and other material we know you will be interested in ~~seeing~~ reading. You can also access our newest graphics online at our Web site. Please call me or send me an e-mail message if you have any questions or would like to receive any additional information. Your satisfaction is our number 1 priority.

Sincerely, | Roy Phillips | Support Technician | urs | enclosure

Report Test 2-12

Academic Report

TELECOMMUTERS
Visibility at Work
Roy Phillips

¶ Have you ever wondered how to remain "visible" at work when you aren't there for most of the work week? This is a problem many telecommuters are struggling to overcome as

(Continued on next page)

INSTRUCTOR'S NOTES/INTERNET BOOKMARKS

Visit us on the Web at www.mhhe.com/gdp.

more and more people do their work from home. We all know the advantages of working at home, but it may come with a heavy price unless you work smart. Here are some ways for telecommuters to increase visibility at work.

ATTEND KEY MEETINGS

¶ Make sure that you are notified by e-mail of all key meetings so that you can be sure to be there and make your opinions and your presence known. If meeting agendas or schedules normally are distributed through office mail, make sure there is a procedure in place that distributes these important documents electronically.

COMMUNICATE WITH YOUR SUPERVISOR

¶ Don't think that there is any virtue in keeping quiet about your accomplishments. Make your accomplishments known in an assertive, regular manner. This can be done easily in several different ways.

¶ E-Mail. Use e-mail messages or attachments to e-mail messages to summarize your accomplishments on a project. It would also be a good idea to send your list of work objectives for the week to your supervisor. When a project is finished, send the final documents related to the project. If a picture could help, invest in a digital camera or a scanner and attach a picture.

¶ Answering Machines and Pagers. Make it easy for your boss to contact you. Check your pager and answering machine frequently and return calls promptly. All of these techniques will help ensure your visibility when you aren't there.

Table Test 2-16
Boxed Table

SIENNA VILLA CONDOMINIUMS Association Fees		
Category	**Average Monthly Bill**	**Proposed Increase**
Insurance	$150	$25
Earthquake rider	75	32
Water	65	20
Landscaping	30	5

ASSESS

Review the steps for changing line spacing in the Word Processing Manual, Lesson 29, Academic Reports, Line Spacing, on pages 56–57.

Review the steps for suppressing page numbers on the first page of a report and adding page numbers on the second page in the Word Processing Manual, Lesson 27, Multipage Business Reports, Page Numbering, on page 47.

TABLE TEST 2-16 Review the format for a table with 2-line column headings and number columns in Lesson 36-E, Basic Parts of a Table, on page 104.

Review the steps for creating a table in the Word Processing Manual, Lesson 36, Boxed Tables, Table—Insert, on pages 75–76. Then review the steps under Table—AutoFit to Contents, on pages 77–78.

Review the steps for merging cells in a table in the Word Processing Manual, Lesson 37, Open Tables with Titles, Table—Merge Cells, on pages 79–80.

INSTRUCTOR'S NOTES/INTERNET BOOKMARKS

Visit us on the Web at www.mhhe.com/gdp.

	WPM GOAL	SKILLBUILDING	LANGUAGE ARTS
UNIT 9 **Lesson 41** **Lesson 42** **Lesson 43** **Lesson 44** **Lesson 45**	Goal At least 37wpm/3′/3e	• 12-Second Speed Sprints • MAP • Progressive Practice: Alphabet • Technique Practice: SPACE BAR • Progressive Practice: Numbers • Sustained Practice: Syllabic Intensity • PPP: Vertical Reaches • Paced Practice • Diagnostic Practice: Symbols and Punctuation	**Lesson 41** “ direct quotation ” title _title_ , direct quotation **Lesson 43** Composing: Sentences **Lesson 45** proofreading
UNIT 10 **Lesson 46** **Lesson 47** **Lesson 48** **Lesson 49** **Lesson 50**	Goal At least 38wpm/3′/3e	• Diagnostic Practice: Numbers • 12-Second Speed Sprints • Paced Practice • Progressive Practice: Alphabet • Diagnostic Practice: Symbols and Punctuation • Technique Practice: ENTER Key • MAP • Sustained Practice: Numbers and Symbols • PPP: Alternate- and One-Hand Words	**Lesson 47** # general # figures **Lesson 49** spelling
UNIT 11 **Lesson 51** **Lesson 52** **Lesson 53** **Lesson 54** **Lesson 55**	Goal At least 39wpm/5′/5e	• MAP • Sustained Practice: Capitalization • 12-Second Speed Sprints • Progressive Practice: Alphabet • PPP: Common Letter Combinations • Progressive Practice: Numbers • Diagnostic Practice: Symbols and Punctuation • Technique Practice: TAB • Paced Practice	**Lesson 51** , date , place **Lesson 53** Composing: Paragraphs **Lesson 55** Proofreading
UNIT 12 **Lesson 56** **Lesson 57** **Lesson 58** **Lesson 59** **Lesson 60**	Goal At least 40wpm/5′/5e	• Diagnostic Practice: Numbers • 12-Second Speed Sprints • Progressive Practice: Alphabet • Paced Practice • Diagnostic Practice: Symbols and Punctuation • Technique Practice: Concentration • MAP • Sustained Practice: Punctuation • PPP: Close Reaches	**Lesson 57** # word - number **Lesson 59** spelling

GDP
Gregg College Keyboarding & Document Processing MULTIMEDIA RESOURCES

SKILLBUILDING

MAP

STUDENT

- Lessons 41–60
- MHHE Keyboarding Web site @ **www.mhhe.com/gdp**

INSTRUCTOR

- Instructor Management LAN Version
  — Distance Learning
- Instructor Management Web Version
  — Distance Learning
- MHHE Keyboarding Instructor Web site @ **www.mhhe.com/gdp**

FORMATTING	DOCUMENT PROCESSING	ILLUSTRATIONS
• Long quotations • Word processing: footnotes, margins, headers, footers, hanging indent, and tab set—dot leaders • Reports formatted in APA style • Author/year citations • Reports formatted in MLA style • Bibliographies • Reference list pages in APA style • Works-cited pages in MLA style • Title page, Table of contents	• Report 41-13 through 41-14 • Report 42-15 through 42-16 • Report 43-17 through 43-18 • Report 44-19 through 44-21 • Report 45-22 through 45-26	• Business report with footnotes, p. 122 • Reference Manual, pp. R-7, R-8, R-9, R-10 • Academic report in APA style, p. 122 • Report with footnotes, p. 124 • Report formatted in APA style, p. 128 • Report formatted in MLA style, p. 132 • Bibliography p. 137 • Reference list page in APA style, p. 138 • Works-cited page in MLA style, p. 139 • Title page, p. 142 • Table of contents, p. 143
• Personal titles in correspondence • Complimentary closings in correspondence • Personal-business letters • Lists in correspondence • Copy notations • Modified-block style letters • Word processing: ruler tabs and tab set	• Correspondence 46-22 through 46-23 • Correspondence 47-24 through 47-26 • Correspondence 48-27 through 48-29 • Correspondence 49-30 through 49-31 • Correspondence 50-32 through 50-35	• Business letter in block style with enclosure notation, p. 147 • Reference Manual, pp. R-3, R-4, R-5 • Memo with a single-line bulleted list, p. 147 • Business letter in modified-block style with numbered list, p. 147 • Copy notations, p. 159 • Business letter in modified-block style, p. 163
• Traditional resumes • Word processing: fonts and changing column widths in a table, saving in text-only format • Electronic resumes • Letters of application • Follow-up letters	• Report 51-27 through 51-28 • Report 52-29 through 52-30 • Correspondence 53-36 through 53-37 • Correspondence 54-38 through 54-40 • Report 55-31 • Correspondence 55-41 through 55-44	• Traditional resume, p. 167 • Reference Manual, pp. R-3, R-12 • Follow-up letter, p. 167 • Letter of application, p. 167 • Traditional resume, p. 170 • Resume in electronic style, p. 175 • Newspaper ad, p. 185
	• Correspondence 56-45 through 56-46 • Table 56-17 and Table 57-18 • Correspondence 57-47 • Report 57-32 • Correspondence 58-48 through 58-49 • Table 58-19 and Table 59-20 • Report 59-33 • Correspondence 60-50 through 60-52 • Table 60-21 through 60-22	• Business letter with bulleted list, p. 188 • Reference Manual pp. R-3, R-4 • Modified-block letter with numbered list and enclosure, p. 188 • Memo with a numbered list, p. 188

SPANISH RESOURCES

- New key exercises in GDP software are available with Spanish or English audio.
- All instruction screens in GDP software are available in Spanish or English.

ASSESSMENT

Progress Check/Proofreading Check

- Lesson 45, Business Report With Footnotes, p. 145
- Lesson 50, Correspondence 50-35, p. 166
- Lesson 55, Correspondence 55-44, p. 187
- Lesson 60, Table 60-22, p. 208

Technique Evaluation Form Go To

Tests

- Part 3, Objective Test
- Test 3, Skills Assessment on Part 3, pp. 209–211
- Alternate Test 3, Alternate Skills Assessment on Part 3, Tests and Solution Keys Booklet 

MOS CERTIFICATION SKILLS

WORD PROCESSING ACTIVITY	Go To Word Processing Manual LESSON
Create or revise footnotes and endnotes	41
Set margins	42
Create and modify headers and footers	42
Use indentation options (Left, Right, First Line, and Hanging Indent)	44
Set tabs with leaders	45
Use **Tabs** command (Center, Decimal, Left, and Right)	50
Select and change font and font size	51
Revise table structure (merge cells and change column width)	51
Use **Save As** (different name, location, or format)	52

TEACHING RESOURCES AT A GLANCE

APPLICATION RESOURCES

- Word Processing Manual
- Reference Manual

ASSESSMENT

- Progress Checks/Proofreading Checks
- Part 3 Skills Assessment Test
- Part 3 Alternate Skills Assessment Test
- Part 3 Objective Test
- Technique Evaluation Form

MULTIMEDIA RESOURCES

- GDP Software
- GDP Software User's Guide
- Instructor Management LAN Version
  - Distance Learning
- Instructor Management Web Version
  - Distance Learning
- MHHE Keyboarding Web site @ **www.mhhe.com/gdp**

ENRICHMENT

Keyboarding Connection

- Inedible Cookies, p. 126
- Evaluating Internet Sources, p. 148
- Avoiding E-Mail Flame Wars, p. 166
- Creating an E-Mail Signature File, p. 189
- Finding Business Information on the Internet, p. 195

Strategies for Career Success

- Letter of Transmittal, p. 146
- Reducing Bias in Business Communication, p. 157
- Formatting Your Resume, p. 172
- Writing a Job Application Letter, p. 179
- Interview Thank-You Letter, p. 183
- Looking for a Job, p. 187
- Successful Interviewing Techniques, p. 208

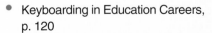

REAL-WORLD CAREER CONNECTION

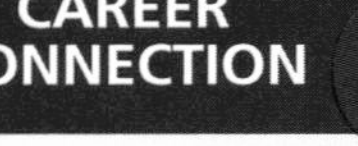

- Keyboarding in Education Careers, p. 120
- Real-World Career Connection Photographs, pp. 120, 154, 160, 163, 173, 180, 197, 207

INSTRUCTOR'S NOTES

PART 3

INTRODUCING THE PART

PART 3 provides an introduction to typing correspondence, reports, and employment documents. **Unit 9** introduces reports with footnotes, academic reports, report citations, and preliminary report pages. **Unit 10** presents additional formatting for correspondence, including personal-business letters, memos with lists, and letters in modified-block style. **Unit 11** introduces employment documents, such as electronic resumes and letters of application. **Unit 12** emphasizes skillbuilding and a comprehensive review.

Discussion

Ask students if they have written academic reports using APA (American Psychological Association) or MLA (Modern Language Association) style. Make a list on the board which illustrates the main differences between the two styles.

Students will develop proofreading skills and reinforce language arts skills.

WPM Goal

Encourage students to continue to set individual typing goals. Students will move from 3-minute timed writings to 5-minute timed writings in this part. Challenge students to reach the goal of typing **at least 40 words per minute for 5 minutes with 5 or fewer errors.** Provide positive reinforcement to all students for improvements in speed and accuracy.

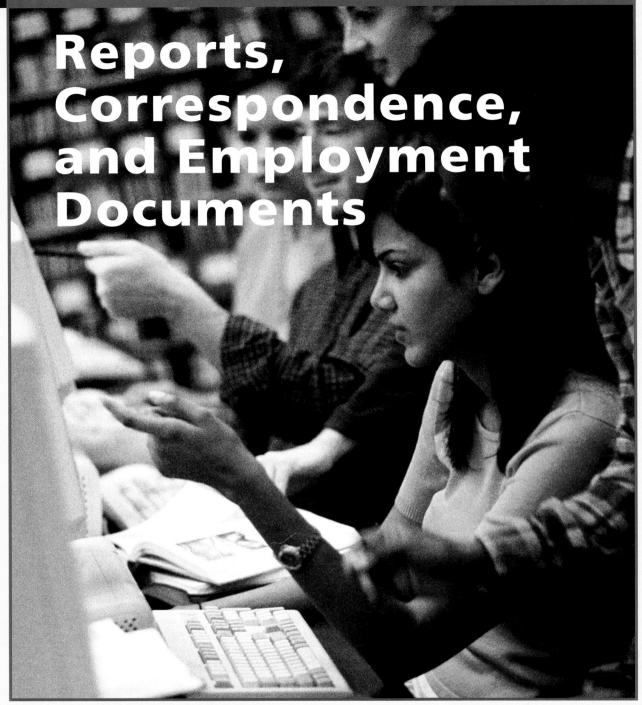

Part 3

Reports, Correspondence, and Employment Documents

Technology Overview

Reference Manual

GDP software makes it easy for your students to study and review document processing formatting techniques through the use of a Reference Manual, an electronic guide to sample document processing applications. The Reference Manual is available from the GDP main screen as well as from within a document when the word processor is active.

Personal Information

Certain lessons (for example, those needing reference initials for business letters) require students to enter personal information into the document to be typed. Before starting an exercise that requires personal information, GDP will prompt students to enter the necessary information. GDP will store the information so that it has to be entered just once.

PART 3

Keyboarding in Education Careers

The education field has many career opportunities, including positions such as teacher, counselor, teacher assistant, administrator, and curriculum designer. Although two of three workers in educational services have professional and related occupations, the education field employs many administrative support, managerial, and service workers.

Teacher assistants provide support for classroom teachers in many ways, allowing instructors more time for lesson planning and actual teaching. Teacher assistants also grade assignments and tests, check homework, keep attendance records, and perform typing, data entry, and filing. Office administration staff perform similar functions for the heads of departments in colleges and universities and for the principals and education boards of elementary and secondary schools.

The use of computer technology in the educational setting is constantly growing. Being proficient with a computer, including keyboarding and formatting skills, is essential for success in the field. The use of the Internet in classrooms has expanded greatly, helping instructors and students to communicate with each other, as well as to perform research for class assignments. Distance learning is growing, too. Increasing numbers of higher education institutions use Internet-based technology to post lessons and coursework electronically. *The Gregg College Keyboarding & Document Processing* text and software are good examples of this development.

Objectives

KEYBOARDING

- Type at least 40 words per minute on a 5-minute timed writing with no more than 5 errors.

LANGUAGE ARTS

- Refine proofreading skills and correctly use proofreaders' marks.
- Use punctuation and grammar correctly.
- Improve composing and spelling skills.

WORD PROCESSING

- Use the word processing commands necessary to complete the document processing activities.

DOCUMENT PROCESSING

- Format business and academic reports, personal-business letters, memos, business letters in modified-block style, and resumes.

TECHNICAL

- Answer at least 90 percent of the questions correctly on an objective test.

CAREER CONNECTION

Education. Review with students the variety of career opportunities in education. Discuss the prominent role technology plays in an education career.

Encourage students to talk to other teachers about the preparation needed to become a teacher, what they like about teaching careers, and the opportunities available to those who pursue careers in education.

Remind students to visit the College Keyboarding Web site at **www.mhhe.com/gdp** to learn more about career choices.

INSTRUCTOR STRATEGIES

Classroom Visuals Create three handouts from the Web to illustrate correct formatting for business reports with footnotes, reports in APA style, and reports in MLA format. Students may use the visuals to compare the different report styles and the different formatting required for each. Visit **www.mla.org/** and **www.apa.org/**.

INSTRUCTOR'S NOTES/INTERNET BOOKMARKS

Visit us on the Web at www.mhhe.com/gdp.

Unit 9

UNIT OVERVIEW

Students will be introduced to 1-page and multipage business and academic reports. The following Microsoft Word features will be presented: footnotes, margins, headers and footers, hanging indents, and dot leader tabs. The last lesson in the unit reviews the correct format for business reports.

Did You Know?

Paced Practice The content of each Paced Practice timed writing presents critical thinking or work-related skills in business.

www.mhhe.com/gdp to download a copy of the Technique Evaluation Form.

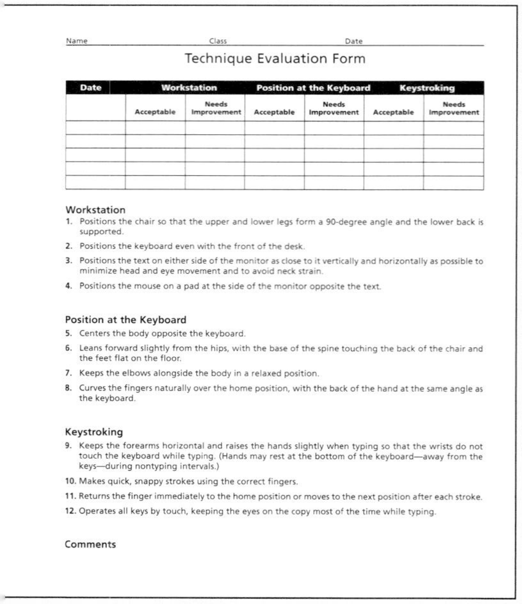

Name ____ Class ____ Date ____

Technique Evaluation Form

Date	Workstation		Position at the Keyboard		Keystroking	
	Acceptable	Needs Improvement	Acceptable	Needs Improvement	Acceptable	Needs Improvement

Workstation

1. Positions the chair so that the upper and lower legs form a 90-degree angle and the lower back is supported.
2. Positions the keyboard even with the front of the desk.
3. Positions the text on either side of the monitor as close to it vertically and horizontally as possible to minimize head and eye movement and to avoid neck strain.
4. Positions the mouse on a pad at the side of the monitor opposite the text.

Position at the Keyboard

5. Centers the body opposite the keyboard.
6. Leans forward slightly from the hips, with the base of the spine touching the back of the chair and the feet flat on the floor.
7. Keeps the elbows alongside the body in a relaxed position.
8. Curves the fingers naturally over the home position, with the back of the hand at the same angle as the keyboard.

Keystroking

9. Keeps the forearms horizontal and raises the hands slightly when typing so that the wrists do not touch the keyboard while typing. (Hands may rest at the bottom of the keyboard—away from the keys—during nontyping intervals.)
10. Makes quick, snappy strokes using the correct fingers.
11. Returns the finger immediately to the home position or moves to the next position after each stroke.
12. Operates all keys by touch, keeping the eyes on the copy most of the time while typing.

Comments

Use this form to keep track of student progress. Complete a form for each student.

Unit 9

Reports

Computer Generations 4

Fourth-Generation Computers

This generation is placed in the 1971 to 1999 time category. Again, computers became smaller and faster, and the Intel chip was responsible for most of the changes taking place in this 29-year period.

Enhancements in Speed

Because of the rapid miniaturization that took place with the chip, the CPU, memory, and input/output controls could now be placed on a single chip. Computers were becoming faster and faster, and they were being used in everyday items such as microwave ovens, televisions, and automobiles.

Commercial Applications

Word processing and spreadsheet applications made their debut in this generation, as did home and video game systems. Names such as Pac Man and Atari were very popular with computer users.

Fifth-Generation Computers

Computer Generations 3

A Brief History of Computer Generations

Joshua T. Reynolds

The invention of the computer did not occur in the past two centuries; in fact, the first computer was probably the abacus, which was used about 5,000 years ago in Asia Minor. As we know them today, computers were first used just after the Second World War, around 1945. Since then, several computer advancements have occurred that make it possible to classify computer power by one of the significant advancements that can be associated with particular time periods or generations. The following paragraphs summarize the major developments that occurred in each of these generations.

First-Generation Computers

The first generation of computers generally runs from 1945 to 1956. During this time, the first vacuum tube computer, the ENIAC, was invented. The first commercial computer was called the UNIVAC, and it was used by the U.S. Census Bureau. It was also used to predict President Eisenhower's victory in the 1952 presidential election (Baker, 2003).

Second-Generation Computers

During this period, 1956 to 1963, computers were run by transistors. These computers were known for their ability to accept instructions for a specific function that could be stored in the computer's memory. This is also the period when COBOL and FORTRAN were used for computer operations. The entire software industry began in this generation.

Third-Generation Computers

This computer generation ran from 1964 to 1971, and it is characterized by the use of integrated circuits to replace the transistors of the previous generation. As a result of this invention, computers became smaller, faster, and more powerful (Diaz & Moore, 2004).

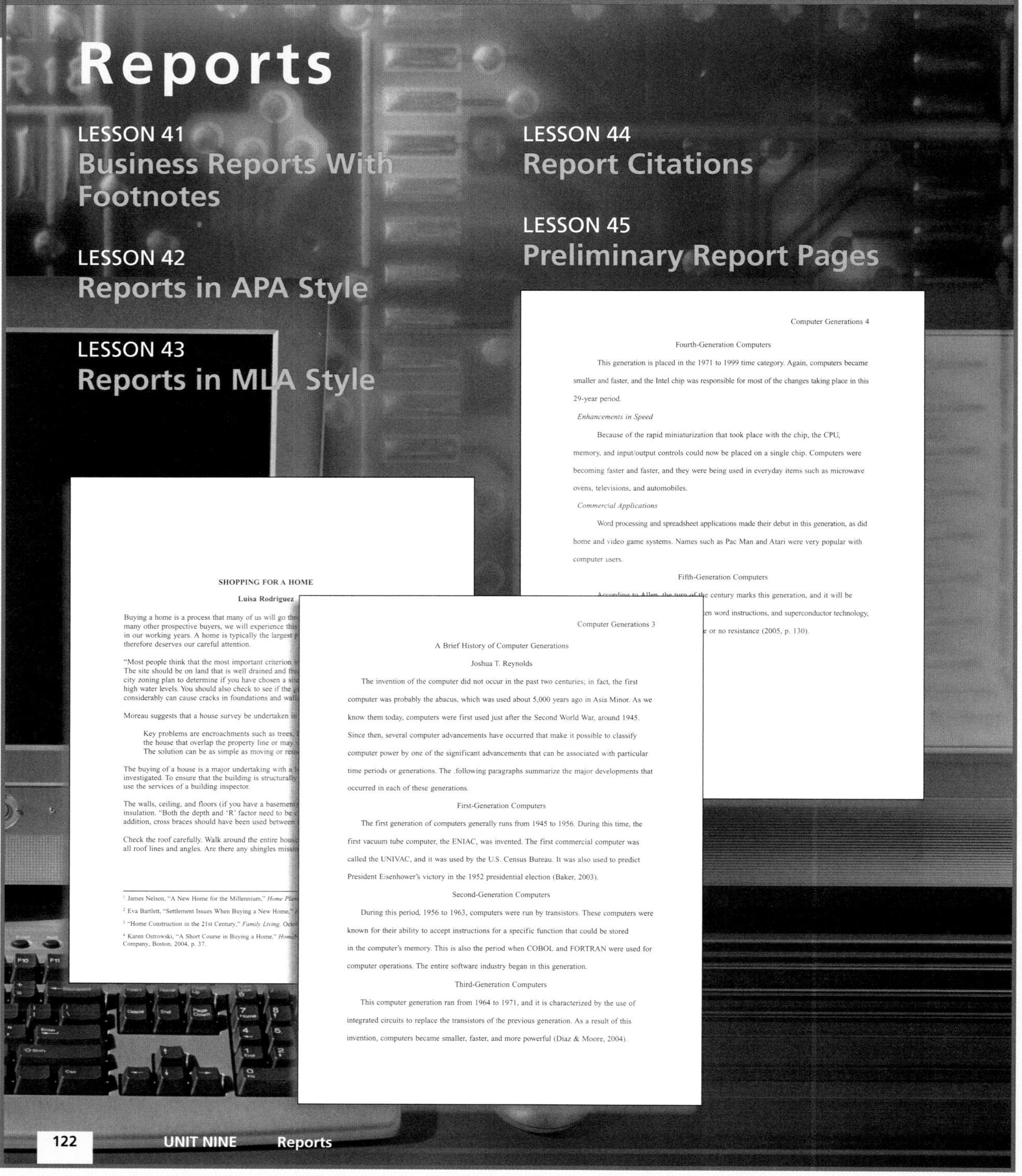

RESOURCE MANAGER

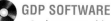

GDP SOFTWARE

- Lessons 41–45
- Software User's Guide
- Instructor Management LAN Version
- Word Processing Manual
- Professional Handbook (IWE*)—Teaching in a Distance-Learning Environment
- MAP 

ASSESSMENT

- Test Booklet—Alternate Test 3
- Progress Check—Report 45-26
- Professional Handbook (IWE*)—Assessment Strategies

ON THE WEB

- **www.mhhe.com/gdp**
- Instructor Management Web Version

*Instructor Wraparound Edition

Business Reports With Footnotes

Goals:
- Improve speed and accuracy
- Refine language arts skills in using quotation marks and italics (or the underline)
- Format reports with footnotes

A. Type 2 times.

A. WARMUP

```
     Tag #743X was attached to a black jug that was 1/3     10
full of a creamy liquid. Tags #914Z and #874V were both     22
attached to beautiful large lamps (crystal and porcelain).  33
|  1  |  2  |  3  |  4  |  5  |  6  |  7  |  8  |  9  |  10  |  11  |  12
```

SKILLBUILDING

B. Take three 12-second timed writings on each line. The scale below the last line shows your wpm speed for a 12-second timed writing.

B. 12-SECOND SPEED SPRINTS

```
Joe must try to type as fast as he can on these four lines.
The screens were very clear, and the print was easy to see.
We will not be able to print the copy until later on today.
The disk will not store any of the data if it is not clean.
''''5''''10''''15''''20''''25''''30''''35''''40''''45''''50''''55''''60
```

C. MAP

Follow the GDP software directions for this exercise in improving keystroking accuracy.

LANGUAGE ARTS

D. Study the rules at the right.

D. QUOTATION MARKS AND ITALICS (OR UNDERLINE)

RULE ▶ " direct quotation

Use quotation marks around a direct quotation.

Harrison responded by saying, "Their decision does not affect us."

But: Harrison responded by saying that their decision does not affect us.

RULE ▶ " title

Use quotation marks around the title of a newspaper or magazine article, chapter in a book, report, and similar terms.

The most helpful article I found was "Multimedia for All."

RULE ▶ *title* or <u>title</u>

Italicize (or underline) the titles of books, magazines, newspapers, and other complete published works.

Grisham's *The Brethren* was reviewed in a recent *USA Today* article.

RULE ▶ , direct quotation

Use a comma before and after a direct quotation.

James said, "I shall return," and then left.

(Continued on next page)

EXTENDING LANGUAGE ARTS

Quotation Marks Use quotation marks to enclose someone's exact words. Example: The principal said, "There will be no school tomorrow."

Quotation Marks Quotation marks are also used for the titles of magazine articles, chapters in books, essays, newspaper columns, reports, and songs. Example: I read "Domestic Policy" in that magazine.

Italics or Underlining Explain that italics (or, if you are writing by hand or on a typewriter, underlining) can be used to identify the names of books, magazines, newspapers, operas, movies, or plays. Example: The couple saw *Saving Private Ryan* (or <u>Saving Private Ryan</u>) last week.

FOCUS

TIME MANAGEMENT

Suggested Schedule:

Warmup	2′
Skillbuilding	17′
Language Arts	6′
Formatting	6′
Document Processing	19′
Total	**50′**

TEACH

SKILLBUILDING

LESSON 41-B Speed sprints are very motivational. Have students push hard for speed on these easy sentences.

LESSON 41-C 

MAP

When keyboarding was done on typewriters, there was only a weak correlation between production typing speed and accuracy and straight-copy speed and accuracy. This was because, in production typing, the planning, decision making, and machine manipulation were more important than simple keystroking speed. With word processing, the software takes care of most of the decision making. (Compare, for instance, the way footnotes are done on the typewriter and on the computer.) Today, production typing is very similar to straight-copy typing, so straight-copy speed and accuracy have never been more important than they are today.

LANGUAGE ARTS

Review the language arts rules for using quotation marks and italics or underline.

Lesson 41

LANGUAGE ARTS

LESSON 41-D If students are not using the GDP software, have them type a correct version of the sentences.

SOLUTION: Lines 4-11

4. *Tribune*.
5. "The Power of eCommerce"
6. *Correct*
7. *Correct*
8. *Newsweek*
9. "That's exactly right!"
10. replied,
11. small,"

FORMATTING

LESSON 41-E Use copies of actual reports with footnotes and explain why footnotes are necessary.

As a special project, a volunteer might research and report on the status of copyright-protection regarding books, films, photographs, musical compositions, and computer software.

VISUAL INSTRUCTION

Footnotes. Review footnote formatting:

- Consecutive numbering
- Placement
- Footnote text

Refer to Reference Manual

Ask students to review the report in business style format in the **Reference Manual, R-8A** and **R-8B,** before they begin typing.

LESSON 41-F Remind students to refer to Lesson 30 in their Word Processing Manual to review the steps for indenting a displayed paragraph.

Edit the sentences to correct any errors in the use of quotation marks, italics, and commas.

```
8  The newspaper ad in the March 1 "Tribune" was very effective.
9  The Power of e-Commerce is an excellent chapter.
10 Maria answered the question by saying, "I agree."
11 Her title for the report was "The Internet in Action."
12 The magazine cover for "Newsweek" last month was excellent.
13 Karen interrupted by saying, That's exactly right!
14 The realtor replied "The first thing to consider is location."
15 "The margin of error is very small" said Andy.
```

FORMATTING

Refer to Reference Manual

If you want to format a report with endnotes instead of footnotes, study the illustration of endnotes on page R-8C and R-8D of the Reference Manual.

E. REPORTS WITH FOOTNOTES

Footnote references indicate the sources of facts or ideas used in a report. Although footnotes may be formatted in various ways, they have many characteristics in common:

1. Footnote references are indicated in the text by superior figures.
2. Footnotes are numbered consecutively throughout a report.
3. Footnotes appear at the bottom of the page on which the references appear.
4. A footnote should include the name of the author, the title of the book (italicized) or article (in quotation marks), the publisher, the place of publication, the year of publication, and the page number(s).

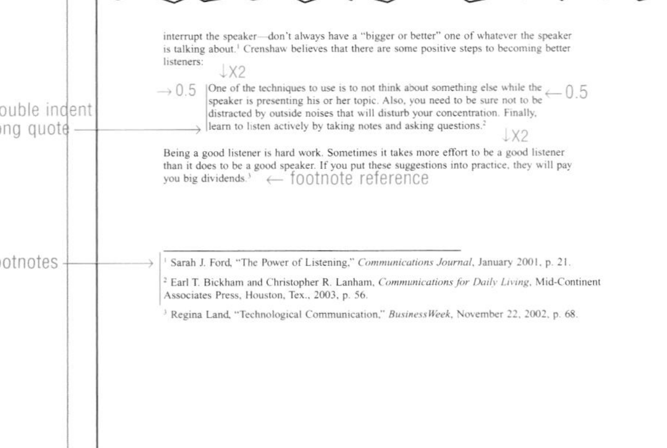

interrupt the speaker—don't always have a "bigger or better" one of whatever the speaker is talking about.[1] Crenshaw believes that there are some positive steps to becoming better listeners:

One of the techniques to use is to not think about something else while the speaker is presenting his or her topic. Also, you need to be sure not to be distracted by outside noises that will disturb your concentration. Finally, learn to listen actively by taking notes and asking questions.[2]

Being a good listener is hard work. Sometimes it takes more effort to be a good listener than it does to be a good speaker. If you put these suggestions into practice, they will pay you big dividends.[3]

[1] Sarah J. Ford, "The Power of Listening," *Communications Journal*, January 2001, p. 21.

[2] Earl T. Bickham and Christopher R. Lanham, *Communications for Daily Living*, Mid-Continent Associates Press, Houston, Tex., 2003, p. 56.

[3] Regina Land, "Technological Communication," *BusinessWeek*, November 22, 2002, p. 68.

F. LONG QUOTATIONS

A paragraph of 4 or more lines that is quoted or considered essential to a report may be highlighted or displayed by using single-spacing and indenting the paragraph 0.5 inch from both the left and the right margins to make it stand out from the rest of the report.

Go To Word Processing Manual

G. WORD PROCESSING: FOOTNOTES

Study Lesson 41 in your word processing manual. Complete all of the shaded steps while at your computer. Then format the jobs that follow.

Windows Wizard

START MENU To change the **Start** menu in Windows XP:

- Right-click a blank space in the **Taskbar**.
- Click **Properties, Start Menu, Customize**.
- Click the **Add** button to add a program.
- Click the **Remove** button to delete a program.
- Click the **Clear** button to remove the list of documents from the **Documents** menu.

START MENU To change the **Start** menu in Windows 2000 or Me:

- Right-click a blank space in the **Taskbar**.
- Click **Properties, Start Menu Properties**.
- Click the **Add** button to add a program.
- Click the **Remove** button to delete a program.
- Click the **Clear** button to remove the list of documents from the **Documents** menu.

DOCUMENT PROCESSING

Report 41-13
Business Report

SHOPPING FOR A HOME

Luisa Rodriguez

¶ Buying a home is a proces that many of us will go through in our life time. If we are like many prospective buyers, we will experience this decision three or four major times in our working years. A home is typically the largest purchase we will make, and it deserves therefore our careful attention. We must be certain to look carefully at all the information available to us.

" direct quotation

¶ "Most people think that the important criteria in shopping for a home is its site,"[1] says John Calendar. The site should be on land that is well drained and free from from flooding that can cause extensive damage. Check the area city zoning plan to determine if you have choosen a site that is free from flooding and highwater levels that can cause extensive damage. You should also check to see if the ground is stable. Ground that shifts can cause cracks in foundations and walls.

¶ Moreau suggests that a home survey be undertaken in the early stages:

> Key problems are encroachments such as tees, buildings, or additions to the house that overlap the property line or may violate zoning regulations. The solution can be as simple as moving or removing trees or bushes from the front or back of your house.[2]

¶ The buying of a house is a major under taking with a long list of items that must be investigated. To ensure that the building is structurally sound, many prospective buyers use the services of a building inspector.

¶ The walls, ceiling, and floors need to be checked for proper insulation. "Both depth and 'r' factor need to be checked for proper levels."[3] In addition, crossbraces should have been used between the beams supporting a floor.

(Continued on next page)

DOCUMENT PROCESSING

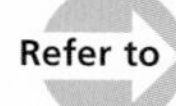

Reference Manual

Ask students to review the report format in the **Reference Manual, R-8A** and **R-8B,** before they begin typing.

REPORT 41-13 Preview with students the proofreaders' marks used in this report.

Check for the following:

- Correct top margin setting
- Left and right indents for the long quotation
- Correct formatting of footnotes

Encourage students to review the language arts rules as they type the report and apply the rules.

Technology Tips

CHANGING FOOTNOTE DEFAULTS

You may want to show students how to change the footnote default settings.

Click the **Options** button in the **Footnote and Endnote** dialog box.

- Change the placement from bottom of page to beneath the text.
- Change the number format from Arabic to letters, Roman numerals, or symbols.
- Change the start number from 1 to another number.
- Change numbering from continuous to restarting on each page or section.

Lesson 41

DOCUMENT PROCESSING

REPORT 41-14 Review the procedure to open a document and to save a document with a new name.

ASSESS

www.mhhe.com/gdp to download a copy of the Technique Evaluation Form.

TECHNIQUE EVALUATION FORM Walk around the classroom to observe student technique.

Groups can prepare copies of the sentences in 41-D that have been turned into quizzes and exchange them with other groups—for example, fill-in-the-blank, short answer, or multiple-choice quiz items.

Review the formatting for Report 41-13.

Extending the Lesson

Ask students to describe the effect and the look of italics compared to quotation marks. Which treatment would make a business report look more impressive? Ask students how a title that is quoted can be a part of a title that is in italics. Example: "Bali Hai" is a song in *South Pacific*.

CLOSE

Have students compose and share sentences in which titles need italics or quotation marks in order to make sense. Example: We have two seats for Rent next weekend. (*Rent*)

¶ Carefully check the roof. Walk around the entire house so that you have a clear view of all roof lines and angles. Are there any shingles missing or is there water damage?[4]

" title — [1] James Nelson, "A New Home for the Millennium," *home planning magazine*, April 27, 2003, pp. 19-24.

title — [2] Eva Bartlett, "Settlement Issues when Buying a New Home," *Home Finances*, 2002 July, p. 68.

" title — [3] "Home Construction in the 21st Century," *Family Living*, October 9, 2002, p. 75

title — [4] Karen Ostrowski, "A Short Course in Buying a Home," *Homebuilders' Guide*, Kramer Publishing Company, Boston, 2004, p. 37.

Report 41-14
Business Report

Open the file for Report 41-13 and make the following changes:

1. Add these lines to the end of the final paragraph in the report:

```
Finally, a thorough check
should be made of the
heating, cooling, and
electrical systems in the
home. "These features are
as critical as any others
to be examined."5
```

```
5 Maria Gonzalez, Home
Facilities Planning, Bradshaw
Publishing, Salt Lake City,
Utah, 2003, p. 64.
```

2. Insert the footnote as indicated.
3. Remember to italicize book and magazine titles.

Keyboarding Connection

Inedible Cookies

Is that cookie good for you? A cookie is a short text entry stored on your computer that identifies your preferences to the server of the Web site you are viewing.

Certain Web sites use cookies to customize pages for return visitors. Only the information you provide or the selections you make while visiting a Web site are stored in a cookie. You can control how your browser uses cookies.

Use the Help feature in your browser to find out how to control cookies. Try using the keywords "cookie" or "security" when you search the Help index. You will probably find some great tips on how to increase security when working on the Internet.

YOUR TURN Access your browser's cookie policy defaults. Decide if you want to change them.

126 UNIT 9 Lesson 41

Keyboarding Connection

Inedible Cookies

Discuss cookies with students. Ask them whether they accept or reject cookies when they visit Web sites on their personal computers. Cookies can be located using the Find feature and then selected and deleted.

YOUR TURN If time permits, ask students to complete the Your Turn activity.

Reports in APA Style

Goals

- Type at least 36wpm/3′/3e
- Format reports in APA style
- Format author/year citations

A. Type 2 times.

A. WARMUP

```
     The giant-size trucks, all carrying over 600 bushels,   11
were operating "around the clock"; quite a few of them had   23
dumped their boxes at Joe's during the last 18 to 20 hours.  35
| 1 | 2 | 3 | 4 | 5 | 6 | 7 | 8 | 9 | 10 | 11 | 12
```

SKILLBUILDING

B. PROGRESSIVE PRACTICE: ALPHABET

If you are not using the GDP software, turn to page SB-7 and follow the directions for this activity.

C. Type the paragraph 2 times, using your right thumb to press the SPACE BAR in the center.

C. TECHNIQUE PRACTICE: SPACE BAR

```
     Dale is it. Adam is there. Mark is home. Eve was lost.
Helen can see. Faith can knit. Gayle can fly. Hal can type.
Fly the kite. Swim a mile. Close the door. Lift the weight.
```

D. Take two 3-minute timed writings. Review your speed and errors.

Goal: At least 36wpm/3′/3e

D. 3-MINUTE TIMED WRITING

```
     The size of their first paycheck after they finish      10
college seems quite high to a few young men and women. They  22
rent a place to live that is just too much to pay, or they   34
may buy a car with a huge monthly payment. For some, it      45
takes a while to learn that there are other items in the     57
monthly budget.                                              60
     Some other budget items are food, student loans, car    71
insurance, renters' insurance, credit card debt, health      82
insurance, utilities, and miscellaneous expenses. A good     93
goal is to put a regular amount from each paycheck into a   105
savings account.                                            108
| 1 | 2 | 3 | 4 | 5 | 6 | 7 | 8 | 9 | 10 | 11 | 12
```


Lesson 42

FOCUS

TIME MANAGEMENT

Suggested Schedule:

Warmup	2′
Skillbuilding	18′
Formatting	6′
Document Processing	24′
Total	**50′**

TEACH

SKILLBUILDING

LESSON 42-B Students take repeated timed writings on a passage containing the exact number of words for their speed goal until they can complete the passage with no errors. Then they move to the next more difficult passage and start again.

LESSON 42-C Caution students not to hold the SPACE BAR down too long or press it too hard. These actions could result in extra spaces being added.

LESSON 42-D All timed writings contain all letters of the alphabet, no numbers or symbols, and a syllabic intensity (SI, or average number of syllables per word) of 1.30 to 1.40.

TEACHING THE ADULT LEARNER

REDUCE STRESS Provide the following tips to help your adult learners take tests with minimal stress.

- Read instructions carefully.
- Answer the questions they know first.
- Type the portions of a hands-on Skills Assessment that they are most comfortable doing.
- Return to unanswered questions.
- Review test items—especially the items that caused hesitation.
- Proofread all written and typed work.

Lesson 42

FORMATTING

Reference Manual

Ask students to review the APA report style in the **Reference Manual, R-10A** and **R-10B,** before they begin typing.

VISUAL INSTRUCTION

APA Style. Review the formatting for a report in APA style:

- Margins
- Title format
- Report spacing
- Header placement and format
- Paragraph indent

LESSON 42-E Discuss with students how to choose the two or three most important words of the main heading for the short title in the header.

LESSON 42-F Show students how to cite sources with a variety of elements, such as several authors, an editor instead of an author, and a Web site.

LESSON 42-G Observe students to see that they can correctly adjust margins and create headers and footers.

Reference Manual

Refer to page R-10A of the Reference Manual for additional guidance.

E. REPORTS FORMATTED IN APA STYLE

In addition to the traditional academic style, academic reports may also be formatted in APA (American Psychological Association) style. In the APA style, format the report as follows:

1. Use the default 1-inch top and bottom margins and change the left and right margins to 1 inch.
2. Double-space the entire report.
3. Insert a header for all pages; type a shortened title and insert an automatic page number that continues the page-numbering sequence from the previous page right-aligned inside the header.
4. Center and type the title and byline using upper- and lowercase letters. (Do not bold either the title or the byline.)
5. Indent all paragraphs 0.5 inch.
6. Type main headings centered, using upper- and lowercase letters. Press ENTER 1 time before and after the main heading.
7. Type subheadings at the left margin in italics using upper- and lowercase letters. Press ENTER 1 time before and after the subheading.

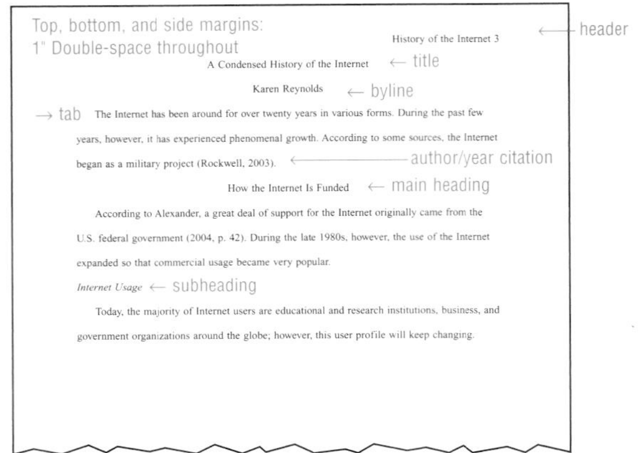

History of the Internet 3

A Condensed History of the Internet

Karen Reynolds

The Internet has been around for over twenty years in various forms. During the past few years, however, it has experienced phenomenal growth. According to some sources, the Internet began as a military project (Rockwell, 2003).

How the Internet Is Funded

According to Alexander, a great deal of support for the Internet originally came from the U.S. federal government (2004, p. 42). During the late 1980s, however, the use of the Internet expanded so that commercial usage became very popular.

Internet Usage

Today, the majority of Internet users are educational and research institutions, business, and government organizations around the globe; however, this user profile will keep changing.

F. AUTHOR/YEAR CITATIONS

Any information based on other sources and used in a report must be documented or cited. The author/year method of citation includes the source information in parentheses at the appropriate point within the text. For more detailed information on APA citations, refer to the illustrations in this book or consult the current APA style guide.

Word Processing Manual

L. 27: Page Numbering

G. WORD PROCESSING: MARGINS, HEADERS, AND FOOTERS

Study Lesson 42 in your word processing manual. Complete all of the shaded steps while at your computer. Then format the jobs that follow.

Technology Tips

HEADERS AND FOOTERS

If time permits, review the following Header and Footer toolbar buttons:

- **Insert Auto Text**
- **Insert Page Number**
- **Format Page Number**
- **Insert Date**
- **Page Setup**
- **Switch Between Header and Footer**
- **Show Previous**
- **Show Next**

When students choose the Different First Page option, it may be necessary to navigate between the header panes. To do this, click the **Show Previous** or **Show Next** buttons.

Report 42-15

Report in APA Style

Remember to add a short title and page number right-aligned in a header.

Computer Generations 3

A Brief History of Computer Generations

Joshua T. Reynolds

¶ The invention of the computer did not occur in the past two centuries; in fact, the first computer was probably the abacus, which was used about 5,000 years ago in Asia Minor. As we know them today, computers were first used just after the Second World War, around 1945. Since then, several computer advancements have occurred that make it possible to classify computer power by one of the significant advancements that can be associated with particular time periods or generations. The following paragraphs summarize the major developments that occurred in each of these generations.

First-Generation Computers

¶ The first generation of computers generally runs from 1945 to 1956. During this time, the first vacuum tube computer, the ENIAC, was invented. The first commercial computer was called the UNIVAC, and it was used by the U.S. Census Bureau. It was also used to predict President Eisenhower's victory in the 1952 presidential election (Baker, 2003).

Second-Generation Computers

¶ During this period, 1956 to 1963, computers were run by transistors. These computers were known for their ability to accept instructions for a specific function that could be stored within the computer's memory. This is also the period when COBOL and FORTRAN were used for computer operations. The entire software industry began in this generation.

Third-Generation Computers

¶ This computer generation ran from 1964 to 1971, and it is characterized by the use of integrated circuits to replace the transistors from the previous generation. As a result of this invention, computers became smaller, faster, and more powerful (Diaz & Moore, 2004).

(Continued on next page)

DOCUMENT PROCESSING

Reference Manual

Ask students to review the format for APA-style reports in the **Reference Manual, R-10A,** before they begin typing.

REPORT 42-15 Remind students that the first page of this APA style report is numbered page 3. Pages 1 and 2 of the report are the title page and the abstract.

Also remind them that APA-style reports require a brief title to accompany the page number as a right-aligned header on each page.

Technology Tips

FIFTH-GENERATION COMPUTER LANGUAGES

Fifth-generation computer languages (5GLs) are actually something of a mystery. Depending on which expert you ask, they may or may not even agree that 5GLs exist. Some experts consider the more advanced development environments to be 5GLs, and others do not. In principle, a 5GL would use artificial intelligence to create software based on your description of what the software should do. This type of system is proving difficult to invent, but attempts at a true 5GL continue to be made.

If the class includes a computer "guru," ask him or her what is known about the latest versions of a 5GL.

Lesson 42

DOCUMENT PROCESSING

REPORT 42-16 Remind students to spell-check, proofread, and preview their documents before printing them.

ASSESS

www.mhhe.com/gdp to download a copy of the Technique Evaluation Form.

TECHNIQUE EVALUATION FORM Walk around the room to observe student technique.

Review results of timed writings.

Review the formatting of Report 42-15.

Extending the Lesson

Encourage students to speculate on what might characterize the next generation of computers.

CLOSE

Have volunteers make and share with the class posters that illustrate the differences in format between business reports and academic reports in APA style.

Fourth-Generation Computers

¶ This generation is placed in the 1971 to 1999 time category. Again, computers became smaller and faster, and the Intel chip was responsible for most of the changes taking place in this 29-year period. Because of the rapid miniaturization that took place with the chip, the CPU, memory, and input/output controls could now be placed on a single chip. Computers were becoming faster and faster; and they were being used in everyday items such as microwave ovens, televisions, and automobiles.

Fifth-Generation Computers

¶ According to Allen, the turn of the century marks this generation, and it will be associated with artificial intelligence, spoken word instructions, and superconductor technology, which allows electricity to flow with little or no resistance (2005, p. 130).

Report 42-16

Report in APA Style

Open the file for Report 42-15 and make the following changes:

1. Place the insertion point at the end of the second sentence in the Fourth-Generation Computers paragraph, and press ENTER 1 time.
2. Type the subheading `Enhancements in Speed` in italics at the left margin; press ENTER 1 time.
3. Press TAB to indent the paragraph.
4. Move the insertion point to the end of the last sentence just above the Fifth-Generation Computers heading; press ENTER 1 time.
5. Type the subheading `Commercial Applications` in italics at the left margin; press ENTER 1 time.
6. Press TAB and type the following text as a paragraph under the new subheading:

```
Word processing and
spreadsheet applications
made their debut in this
generation, as did home
and video game systems.
Names such as Pac-Man and
Atari were very popular
with computer users.
```


Meeting Special Needs

THE KINESTHETIC SENSE Have students place in front of them several of the letters and envelopes of different sizes they collected. Ask them to pick up one of the envelopes and then close their eyes and concentrate on how this size feels in their hands. Repeat this exercise with different sizes.

Reports in MLA Style

Goals

- Improve speed and accuracy
- Refine language arts skills in composing sentences
- Format reports in MLA style

A. Type 2 times.

A. WARMUP

```
     "Baxter & Heimark, Inc., sold 82 new vehicles (47 cars  11
and 35 trucks) during June," the sales manager reported.     23
This is 16.9% of quarterly sales, an amazing achievement!    34
| 1 | 2 | 3 | 4 | 5 | 6 | 7 | 8 | 9 | 10 | 11 | 12
```

SKILLBUILDING

B. PROGRESSIVE PRACTICE: NUMBERS

If you are not using the GDP software, turn to page SB-11 and follow the directions for this activity.

C. Take a 1-minute timed writing on the first paragraph to establish your base speed. Then take four 1-minute timed writings on the remaining paragraphs. As soon as you equal or exceed your base speed on one paragraph, advance to the next, more difficult paragraph.

C. SUSTAINED PRACTICE: SYLLABIC INTENSITY

```
     Taking care of aging parents is not a new trend. This    11
issue has arisen more and more, since we are now living       22
longer. Companies are now trying to help out in many ways.    34
     Help may come in many ways, ranging from financial aid   12
to sponsoring hospice or in-home respite care. Workers may    24
find it difficult to work and care for aging parents.         35
     Why are employers so interested in elder care? Rising    11
interest is the result of a combination of several things.    23
The most notable is a marked increase in life expectancy.     34
     Another trend is the increased participation of women,   11
the primary caregivers, in the workforce. Businesses are      22
recognizing that work and family life are intertwined.        33
| 1 | 2 | 3 | 4 | 5 | 6 | 7 | 8 | 9 | 10 | 11 | 12
```


Technology Tips

ENFORCING A (DOWN) LOAD LIMIT

As computer users, your students need to understand software licensing. Buying a copy of Microsoft Office gives a person permission to install it on only one computer. The licensing agreement does not allow someone to install it on his or her computer and then pass it along to friends and family. In the past, there has been much informal copying. Microsoft Office XP makes unauthorized copying almost impossible. The price of the software includes a preset number of installations, after which the password that activates the software will no longer work.

Lesson 43

FOCUS

TIME MANAGEMENT 

Suggested Schedule:

Warmup	2′
Skillbuilding	17′
Language Arts	6′
Formatting	5′
Document Processing	20′
Total	**50′**

TEACH

SKILLBUILDING

LESSON 43-B Students take repeated timed writings on a passage containing the exact number of words for their speed goal until they can complete the passage with no errors. Then they move to the next longer passage and start again.

LESSON 43-C Each paragraph is more difficult than the preceding one—based on syllabic intensity (SI, or average number of syllables per word):

Paragraph 1: SI = 1.35
Paragraph 2: SI = 1.47
Paragraph 3: SI = 1.62
Paragraph 4: SI = 1.88

Lesson 43

LANGUAGE ARTS

LESSON 43-D Check students' answers to be sure they are composing complete sentences.

FORMATTING

VISUAL INSTRUCTION

MLA Style. Review the formatting for a report in MLA style:

- Margins
- Heading and date format
- Title format
- Report spacing
- Header placement and format
- Paragraph indent

Reference Manual

Refer students to the **Reference Manual, R-10C** and **R-10D,** for the format of reports in MLA style.

LESSON 43-E Have students point out the differences between dates in military style and dates in the usual American style. Which style seems more sensible to students?

LANGUAGE ARTS

D. Answer each question with a complete sentence.

D. COMPOSING SENTENCES

16 What are your best traits that you will bring to your job when you graduate?
17 Would you like to work for a small company or a large company?
18 How much money will you expect to earn each month in your first job?
19 Would you like that first job to be in a small town or a large city?
20 As you begin your first job, what career goal will you have in mind?

FORMATTING

Reference Manual

Refer to page R-10C of the Reference Manual for additional guidance.

E. REPORTS FORMATTED IN MLA STYLE

In addition to the traditional academic style and APA style, academic reports may also be formatted in MLA (Modern Language Association) style. If citations are used, usually the author's last name and page number are cited inside parentheses. For more detailed information on MLA style, refer to the illustrations in this book or consult the current MLA style guide.

In the MLA style, format the report as follows:

1. Use the default 1-inch top and bottom margins and change the left and right margins to 1 inch.
2. Double-space the entire report.
3. Insert a header for all pages; type the author's last name and the page number right-aligned inside the header and positioned 0.5 inch from the top of the page.
4. Type each element of the heading information (your name, your instructor's name, the class name, and the date) on a separate line at the left margin.
5. Type the date day-month-year style (15 April 20--).
6. Center and type the title using upper- and lowercase letters.
7. Indent all paragraphs 0.5 inch.

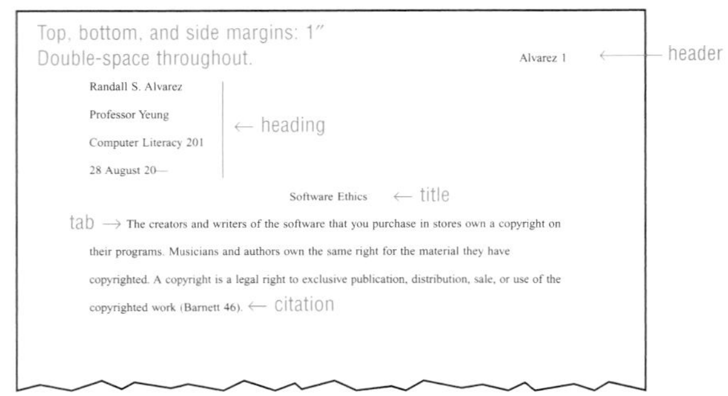

Alvarez 1

Randall S. Alvarez

Professor Yeung

Computer Literacy 201

28 August 20—

Software Ethics

The creators and writers of the software that you purchase in stores own a copyright on their programs. Musicians and authors own the same right for the material they have copyrighted. A copyright is a legal right to exclusive publication, distribution, sale, or use of the copyrighted work (Barnett 46).

EXTENDING LANGUAGE ARTS

Composing To help students write complete sentences, remind them that each sentence must contain a subject and a verb. Ask them to bold the subject of each sentence and to underline the verb of each sentence.

Have students exchange papers with partners and check to see that subjects and verbs agree in number—that is, that both subject and verb are singular or both are plural.

DOCUMENT PROCESSING

Report 43-17

Report in MLA Style

Remember to type the author's last name and page number right-aligned 0.5 inch from the top as a header. Remember to double-space the entire report.

Lee 1

Youn Suk Lee
Dr. Gloria Hernandez
Telecommunications 315
14 September 20--

Judging a Computer System

¶ Judging the effectiveness of a computer system has taken on a new dimension in the past few years, if for no other reason than the wide range of computer systems from which the user can select. It is, therefore, important that we investigate the criteria that should be considered in making this important decision.

¶ Probably the most obvious criterion to be considered when one purchases a computer system is speed. The value of a computer is directly related to its speed, and a computer's speed is typically measured in gigahertz (GHz). A gigahertz is one billion cycles per second, and many of today's microcomputers run in the range of 2 to 5 GHz (Kramer 173).

¶ Flexibility is especially important because of the rapid turnover of hardware and software in the computer industry. The flexibility of a computer system is important for two general reasons: to accommodate a variety of programs and to permit expandability. Hundreds and possibly thousands of software packages are available today to meet the needs of computer users. The computer you purchase must be able to accommodate this variety of software and be flexible enough to change with the increasing sophistication of software packages. Because of the substantial investment you make in a computer, you do not want to commit your resources to a computer that cannot be expanded to handle (1) newer, more powerful operating systems; (2) "memory-hungry" software packages; (3) network interfaces; and (4) additional users (Hartung and Kallock 239).

¶ A third consideration is convenience. Is it easy to learn how to operate your computer? Does the manufacturer stand by its warranty, and is it difficult to obtain repairs? How convenient is it to buy parts for your computer (such as memory boards and drives) if you want to expand your system? These questions need to be answered, and the answers should be weighed carefully before you purchase a new computer system.

DOCUMENT PROCESSING

Reference Manual

Ask students to review the MLA style format in the **Reference Manual, R-10C** and **R-10D,** before they begin typing.

REPORT 43-17 Remind students that the header in an MLA-style report contains the author's last name and the page number.

Students should also be reminded that an MLA-style report is always double-spaced.

INSTRUCTOR STRATEGIES

Updating the Book
You may want to have a volunteer look through a current computer advertising brochure to see if the figures in paragraph 2 of Report 43-17 are still accurate.

ERGONOMICALLY SPEAKING

MONITOR POSITION Students should maintain a comfortable viewing distance from the screen. Most people prefer a viewing distance of around 18 inches to 30 inches, depending on the size of the monitor. The character and size of the text and the available space on the work surface can affect this distance.

Lesson 43

DOCUMENT PROCESSING

REPORT 43-18 Discuss the contents of the report with students. Ask whether any security precautions should be added. Is any material unnecessary?

ASSESS

www.mhhe.com/gdp to download a copy of the Technique Evaluation Form.

TECHNIQUE EVALUATION FORM Walk around the room to observe student technique. Complete a Technique Evaluation Form for each student.

Review the formatting of Report 43-17.

Extending the Lesson

Ask students which report format is the easiest to create and which is the easiest to read. Do students think a reader would evaluate the same report differently depending on its format?

CLOSE

Help students review how business reports, academic reports in APA style, and academic reports in MLA style differ in format.

Report 43-18

Report in MLA Style

Espinoza 1

Christina Espinoza
Professor Sakata
Introduction to E-commerce
9 April 20--

¶ The Internet is dramatically changing the way we shop. In years past, our shopping practices consisted of driving to a local mall or department store, walking through the aisles until we found an item we wished to purchase, and then making the purchase and driving home. Today, it is becoming more common to find shoppers doing their shopping via the Internet. Shopping on the Internet brings with it some cautions that we should observe when we shop. Here are some basic rules to follow when shopping on the Internet.

¶ When you are asked to enter information on your order, do not disclose personal information unless it is needed for shipping your order to you. Be sure you know who is collecting this information, why it is needed, and how it is going to be used. Be certain that the information asked for is actually necessary for the purchase. For example, there are few instances when your password should be disclosed.

¶ You should always verify that the company from whom you are purchasing has secured the purchasing procedures. You will often be asked to enter your credit card number to complete the purchase. Be certain that the transfer of this information is made in a secure environment. Also, be certain that you know the exact cost of the item for which you are being charged. The company from which you are purchasing the item should have a built-in calculator so that you know at all times how much your purchase will cost you, including all necessary shipping and handling charges.

¶ Understand exactly what you should do if you encounter a problem with your purchase online. Is there an easy way to contact the company? Does the company have an e-mail address you can use to contact a customer relations representative? Does the company's order page include a telephone number that you can call if you have questions about your order?

INSTRUCTOR STRATEGIES

Update Your Understanding
Have students conduct online research to find out the number of people who now shop online. Do they think the contents of Report 43-18 are still relevant?

Report Citations

Goals

- Type at least 37wpm/3′/3e
- Format bibliographies, references, and works-cited pages

A. Type 2 times.

A. WARMUP

```
     The prize troops received the following extra gifts:   11
$20 from Larson's Bakery; $19 from Calsun, Ltd.;* $50 from   23
some judges; and quite a number of $5 gift certificates.     34
| 1 | 2 | 3 | 4 | 5 | 6 | 7 | 8 | 9 | 10 | 11 | 12
```

SKILLBUILDING

PPP PRETEST → PRACTICE → POSTTEST

PRETEST
Take a 1-minute timed writing. Review your speed and errors.

B. PRETEST: Vertical Reaches

```
     Kim knew that her skills at the keyboard made her a     11
top rival for that job. About six persons had seen her race  23
home to see if the mail showed the company was aware of it.  34
| 1 | 2 | 3 | 4 | 5 | 6 | 7 | 8 | 9 | 10 | 11 | 12
```

PRACTICE
Speed Emphasis:
If you made 2 or fewer errors on the Pretest, type each *individual* line 2 times.
Accuracy Emphasis:
If you made 3 or more errors, type each *group* of lines (as though it were a paragraph) 2 times.

C. PRACTICE: Up Reaches

```
se seven reset seams sedan loses eases serve used seed dose
ki skids kings kinks skill kitty kites kilts kite kids kick
rd board horde wards sword award beard third cord hard lard
```

D. PRACTICE: Down Reaches

```
ac races pacer backs ached acute laced facts each acre lace
kn knave knack knife knows knoll knots knelt knew knee knit
ab about abide label above abode sable abbey drab able cabs
```

POSTTEST
Repeat the Pretest timed writing and compare performance.

E. POSTTEST: Vertical Reaches

Meeting Special Needs

VISUAL IMPAIRMENTS Students who have visual impairments may prefer using a large font. When a large font is chosen, documents may not fit on 1 page and line breaks will not be the same as those shown in the text. An alternative is to type using the default font and change the Zoom level to a percentage that enables the student to read the document. The **Zoom** button on the Standard toolbar (or **Zoom** from the **View** menu) allows one to change the Zoom percentage.

Lesson 44

FOCUS

TIME MANAGEMENT
Suggested Schedule:

Warmup	2′
Skillbuilding	18′
Formatting	9′
Document Processing	21′
Total	**50′**

TEACH

SKILLBUILDING

PRETEST → PRACTICE → POSTTEST

PPP The Pretest/Practice/Posttest (PPP) routine is designed to build speed and accuracy through a three-step program:

44-B The Pretest is the preliminary effort to determine the learner's initial skill level. Vertical reaches include up and down reaches.

44-C and 44-D The Practice section consists of intensive drills to improve the reaches focused on in the Pretest. Up reaches go from the home row to the upper row and from the bottom row to the home row. Down reaches go from the home row to the lower row and from the upper row to the home row.

44-E The Posttest measures the effect of the Practice.

Lesson 44

SKILLBUILDING

LESSON 44-F Encourage students to type with control, eyes on copy, and correct posture.

FORMATTING

LESSON 44-G Enlarge an example that illustrates a bibliography (as shown on page 137). Point out the characteristics of each part of the bibliography: title, margins, single-spacing, and arrangement of entries of books and articles. Show sample bibliographies that illustrate formatting book entries and journal articles. Using the guidelines given in the textbook, have students write examples of these types of entries on the board.

Reference Manual

Ask students to review the bibliography format in the **Reference Manual, R-9B,** before they begin typing.

INSTRUCTOR STRATEGIES

Finding Journal Articles Ask students why journal articles need a volume number as well as a date in their citations. (A newly published journal article is identified by its date and page, but older journals are bound into annual volumes.)

F. Take two 3-minute timed writings. Review your speed and errors.

Goal: At least 37wpm/3'/3e

F. 3-MINUTE TIMED WRITING

```
     Every business should have its code of ethics. A code     11
contains rules of conduct and moral guidelines that serve      23
the company and its employees. Some general ethics that may    35
be recognized in the code are equal and fair treatment,        46
truth, and zeal on the job.                                    51
     Companies may include a few rules in the code that        62
relate to their type of work. For example, if some laws        73
govern how they conduct business, an owner just might ask      85
employees to conduct all activities in a just and lawful       96
process. The code of business ethics should be equal for      107
all these workers.                                            111
  | 1 | 2 | 3 | 4 | 5 | 6 | 7 | 8 | 9 | 10 | 11 | 12
```

FORMATTING

Reference Manual

Refer to page R-9B of the Reference Manual for additional guidance.

G. BIBLIOGRAPHIES

A bibliography is an alphabetic listing of all sources of facts or ideas used or cited in a report. The bibliography is typed on a separate page at the end of a report. In general, titles of major works like books or magazine titles are italicized, and titles of minor works like articles from magazines are typed in quotation marks. For more detailed information on entries in a bibliography, refer to the illustrations in this book or consult a current style guide.

To format a bibliography:

1. Press ENTER 6 times to begin the first line approximately 2 inches from the top of the page.
2. Center and type `BIBLIOGRAPHY` in all-caps, 14-point font, and bold; then press ENTER 2 times.
3. Set a hanging indent and type the first line. Each entry will begin at the left margin, and the carryover lines will automatically be indented 0.5 inch by the hanging indent.
4. Single-space each entry in the bibliography, and press ENTER 2 times between each entry.

Technology Tips

WEB SEARCH

Have students conduct an online search on the topic of corporate ethics and report to the class on any prominent ethics issues that have been posted on the World Wide Web.

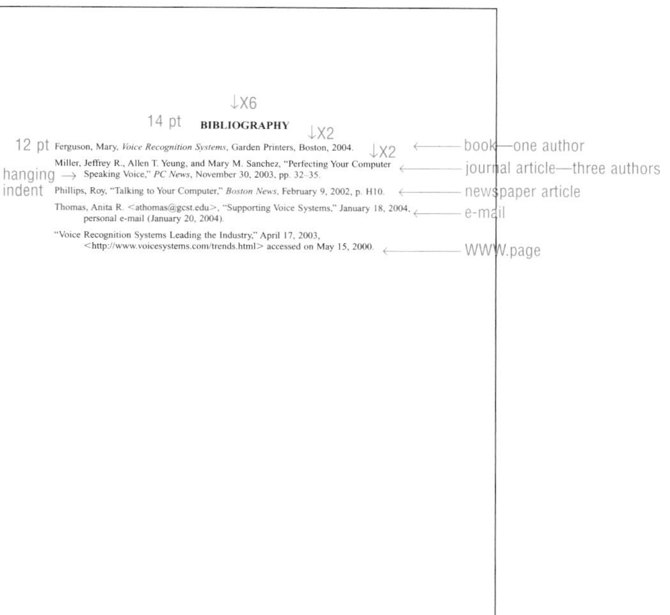

BIBLIOGRAPHY

Ferguson, Mary, *Voice Recognition Systems*, Garden Printers, Boston, 2004.

Miller, Jeffrey R., Allen T. Yeung, and Mary M. Sanchez, "Perfecting Your Computer Speaking Voice," *PC News*, November 30, 2003, pp. 32–35.

Phillips, Roy, "Talking to Your Computer," *Boston News*, February 9, 2002, p. H10.

Thomas, Anita R. <athomas@gcst.edu>, "Supporting Voice Systems," January 18, 2004, personal e-mail (January 20, 2004).

"Voice Recognition Systems Leading the Industry," April 17, 2003, <http://www.voicesystems.com/trends.html> accessed on May 15, 2000.

Refer to Reference Manual

Refer to page R-10B of the Reference Manual for additional guidance.

H. REFERENCE LIST PAGES IN APA STYLE

A reference list is an alphabetic listing of all sources of facts or ideas used or cited in a report formatted in APA style. The reference list is typed on a separate page at the end of a report. For more detailed information on reference list entries, refer to the illustrations in this book or consult a current APA style guide.

To format an APA reference list page:

1. Use the default 1-inch top and bottom margins and change the left and right margins to 1 inch.
2. Double-space the entire page.
3. Insert a header, type a shortened title, and insert an automatic page number that continues the page-numbering sequence from the previous page right-aligned inside the header.
4. Center and type `References` at the top of the page; then press ENTER 1 time.
5. Set a hanging indent and type the first line. Each reference will begin at the left margin, and the carryover lines will automatically be indented 0.5 inch by the hanging indent.

INSTRUCTOR STRATEGIES

Researching APA Style

Visit http://apaguide.net and examine the online style-guide references that are available.

Lesson 44

FORMATTING

VISUAL INSTRUCTION

Bibliography. Review the formatting for a bibliography:

- New page
- Margins
- Title
- Single-spacing of entries with 1 blank line between entries
- Hanging indent for each entry
- Order of book entries and journal entries

Refer to Reference Manual

Ask students to review the format for references in APA style in the **Reference Manual, R-10B,** before they begin typing.

LESSON 44-H Examine some reference list pages in APA style as a class. Discuss the reason for including the publisher's city and state. (These data enable a researcher to contact the publisher and acquire a copy of the source.)

Ask students to point out similarities and differences in APA-style references as compared to the bibliography format.

Provide examples of entries formatted for a reference list in APA style. Have students format these entries using the guidelines in the textbook and the Reference Manual.

Extending the Lesson

Have students do research to find out about the APA (American Psychological Association). Ask them to determine instances in which using the APA style for formatting a reference list may be preferred.

Lesson 44

FORMATTING

VISUAL INSTRUCTION

Reference List in APA Format.
Review the formatting for an APA reference list:

- New page
- Margins
- Title format
- Double spacing
- Hanging indent
- Continuous page numbering
- Order of book entries and periodical entries

Reference Manual

Ask students to review the format for works cited in MLA style in the **Reference Manual, R-10D,** before they begin typing.

Invite students to ask questions regarding the differences in the APA style and the bibliography format. Students need to be comfortable with formatting this type of copy.

LESSON 44-I Provide examples of various types of entries to be formatted for a works-cited list in MLA style. Have students format these entries using the guidelines in the textbook and the Reference Manual.

Have students do research to find out about the MLA (Modern Language Association). Ask them to determine instances in which using the MLA style for formatting a works-cited page may be preferred.

Discuss with students the purpose of a works-cited page. Should it list every source the writer consulted? (No. It should list the sources whose ideas or information the report includes.)

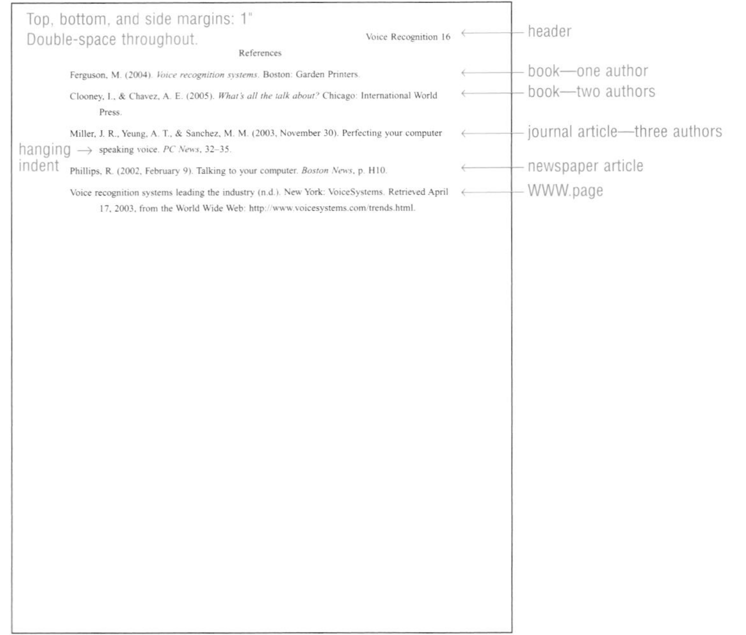

Top, bottom, and side margins: 1"
Double-space throughout.

Voice Recognition 16

References

Ferguson, M. (2004). *Voice recognition systems.* Boston: Garden Printers.

Clooney, I., & Chavez, A. E. (2005). *What's all the talk about?* Chicago: International World Press.

Miller, J. R., Yeung, A. T., & Sanchez, M. M. (2003, November 30). Perfecting your computer speaking voice. *PC News*, 32–35.

Phillips, R. (2002, February 9). Talking to your computer. *Boston News*, p. H10.

Voice recognition systems leading the industry (n.d.). New York: VoiceSystems. Retrieved April 17, 2003, from the World Wide Web: http://www.voicesystems.com/trends.html.

Reference Manual

Refer to page R-10D of the Reference Manual for additional guidance.

I. WORKS-CITED PAGES IN MLA STYLE

A works-cited page is an alphabetic listing of all sources of facts or ideas used or cited in a report formatted in MLA style. This reference list is typed on a separate page at the end of a report. For more detailed information on reference list entries, refer to the illustrations in this book or consult a current MLA style guide.

To format a works-cited page:

1. Use the default 1-inch top and bottom margins and change the left and right margins to 1 inch.
2. Double-space the entire page.
3. Insert a header, type the author's last name, insert an automatic page number that continues the page-numbering sequence from the previous page right-aligned inside the header positioned 0.5 inch from the top of the page, and close the header.
4. Type `Works Cited` centered at the top of the page; then press ENTER 1 time.
5. Set a hanging indent and type the first line at the left margin; the carryover lines will automatically be indented 0.5 inch by the hanging indent.

ERGONOMICALLY SPEAKING

SAVING THEIR NECKS Ask how many students have ever had a sore ear and a stiff neck because they had held a telephone handset between their neck and shoulder for a long time. The solution is a headset. The essential parts are an earplug and a microphone; optional accessories include an over-the-ear headband, an ear clip, a volume control, and a microphone mute switch. A headset leaves both hands free to type or take notes, and at the end of a long day on the phone, there is no stiff neck or sore ear.

Top, bottom, and side margins: 1"
Double-space throughout.

Samson 9 ← header

Works Cited

Ferguson, Mary. *Voice Recognition Systems.* Boston: Garden Printers, 2004. ← book—one author

Miller, Jeffrey R., Allen T. Yeung, and Mary M. Sanchez. "Perfecting Your Computer Speaking Voice." *PC News* 30, Nov. 2003: 32–35. (hanging indent →)

Phillips, Roy. "Talking to Your Computer," *Boston News*, 9 Feb. 2002: p. H10.

Thomas, Anita R. "Supporting Voice Systems." E-mail to the author. 18 Jan. 2004. ← e-mail

"Voice Recognition Systems Leading the Industry." *VoiceSystems.* 17 Apr. 2003. 15 May 2004 <http://www.voicesystems.com/trends.html>. ← WWW page

Word Processing Manual

J. WORD PROCESSING: HANGING INDENT

Study Lesson 44 in your word processing manual. Complete all the shaded steps while at your computer. Then format the jobs that follow.

DOCUMENT PROCESSING

Report 44-19

Bibliography

Italicize publication titles rather than underlining them.

BIBLIOGRAPHY

Bilanski, Charles R., "Corporate Structures in the New Millennium," Modern Management, Vol. 43, June 2003, pp. 43-46.

Calhoun, Josten C., Stockholders' Guide, Missouri Valley Press, St. Louis, 2003.

Dahlman, Leland, and Joyce C. Mahler, Trends for Boards of Directors, Vineyard Press, Boston, 2003.

Hammersmith Institute, Bold Positions of the New Administration, Hammersmith Institute Press, Baltimore, Md., 1999.

"Investing in the Corporate World," March 27, 2003, <http://www.efinance.com/invest/today'sworld.htm>, accessed on May 18, 2003.

Polaski, James S., "Summary of Investment Guide," e-mail message, October 10, 2003.

Lesson 44

FORMATTING

VISUAL INSTRUCTION

Works-Cited Pages in MLA Format. Review the MLA formatting for works cited:

- New page
- Margins
- Title format
- Header format
- Double spacing
- Alphabetic sequence
- Hanging indent

LESSON 44-J Remind students that indents are applied to an entire paragraph. You can select a paragraph by double-clicking in the selection bar, or triple-clicking the paragraph.

DOCUMENT PROCESSING

REPORT 44-19 Point out to students that sources in a bibliography are always alphabetized by the authors' last names.

Before beginning, have students take note of the hanging indents used for return lines. Point out that in this handwritten copy, the titles of books are underlined rather than italicized.

Reference Manual

Ask students to review the bibliography format in the **Reference Manual, R-9B,** before they begin typing.

Enlarge a works-cited page in MLA style. Ask students to point out similarities and differences in the styles used in the work-cited page in MLA style, the reference list in APA style, and the bibliography format.

INSTRUCTOR STRATEGIES

Making Inferences You may want to have students speculate as to the contents of the report associated with this bibliography. What discipline would it fall under? What topic might be discussed?

Lesson 44

DOCUMENT PROCESSING

REPORT 44-20 Remind students that reference page sources are always double-spaced.

Refer to Reference Manual

Ask students to review the format for references in APA style in the **Reference Manual, R-10B,** before they begin typing.

REPORT 44-21 Optional.

Point out to students that sources in a works-cited page are typed with a hanging indent.

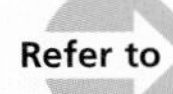
Refer to Reference Manual

Ask students to review the format for works cited in MLA style in the **Reference Manual, R-10D,** before they begin typing.

ASSESS

Go To The Web

www.mhhe.com/gdp to download a copy of the Technique Evaluation Form.

TECHNIQUE EVALUATION FORM Review results of timed writings.

Review the formats for Reports 44-19, 44-20, and 44-21.

Extending the Lesson

Ask students how many and what types of references they use when preparing reports for other classes.

CLOSE

Have students prepare concise 3- by 5-inch cards to use for quick reference on formatting reference materials.

Report 44-20 References in APA Style

The Economy of America 16

References

Chandler, R. D., & Thompson, A. S. (2002). *The evolution of America's economy in the late 1800's*. Westerville, OH: Glencoe/ McGraw-Hill. ~~Chapter 24, pp. 130-145.~~

Deming, W. H. (2003). Economists' guide to economic indicators. *The Economic Review, XVI*, 42-44.

Fortenberry, J. E., Kingston, A.E., & Worthington, S. O. (2004). *The environment of business*. Los Angeles: The University Press.

Meier, T. D., & Hovey, D. H. (2002). *economics on the world wide web*. Toronto: The Northern Press.

Tetrault, G. M. (2003). A guide for selecting economic indicators for the business entrepreneur. ~~*The Southern Economic Forecaster*, 23.~~

Zysmanski, R. J. (2004). *American capitalism and its impact on society*. San Francisco: Bay Press Area.

Report 44-21 Works Cited in MLA Style

Cleaves 14

Works Cited

Abernathy, Thomas R. "Welcome to the Internet." E-mail to the author. 19 Mar. 2005.

Benson, Lisa, et al. "E-commerce on the Net." *Online Observer*. Vol. 17. Sept. 2004: 144–146.

Cooper, Stanley. *Trends for the New Millennium*. Denver: Mountain Press, 2003.

Lawrence, Donna, and Becky Silversmith. *Surfer's Guide to the Internet*. Atlanta: Southern Publishers, 2005.

"Starting a Business on the Internet." *Entrepreneur*. 19 Dec. 2003. 12 June 2005 <http://www.entrepreneur.com/startups.htm>.

Tidwell, Joel, and Jean Swanson. "Things You Don't Know About the Internet." *New York Ledger*, 13 May 2004: C2.

Technology Tips

TOO MANY FONTS?

When a computer seems unusually slow or even crashes, look for the number of fonts installed. In a Microsoft Word document, click the arrow by the Font window, and a list of font names appears. Count them. If there are more than a hundred, you may have discovered why the computer is bogging down.

Before deleting what you think is an unnecessary font, see whether it is one that Windows needs. For this purpose and to get tips on font management, visit About.com's Graphics Software advice pages at **graphicssoft.about.com/compute/graphicssoft/library/weekly/aa072099.htm**.

Preliminary Report Pages

Goals

- Improve speed and accuracy
- Refine language arts skills in proofreading
- Format title pages and tables of contents

A. Type 2 times.

A. WARMUP

```
     Did Kenny and Hazel see the first Sox ball game? I've   11
heard there were 57,268 people there (a new record). Your    23
home crowd was quiet when the game ended with a 4-9 loss.    34
  |  1  |  2  |  3  |  4  |  5  |  6  |  7  |  8  |  9  |  10  |  11  |  12
```

SKILLBUILDING

B. PACED PRACTICE

If you are not using the GDP software, turn to page SB-14 and follow the directions for this activity.

C. DIAGNOSTIC PRACTICE: SYMBOLS AND PUNCTUATION

If you are not using the GDP software, turn to page SB-2 and follow the directions for this activity.

LANGUAGE ARTS

D. Study the proofreading techniques at the right.

D. PROOFREADING YOUR DOCUMENTS

Proofreading and correcting errors are essential parts of document processing. To become an expert proofreader:

1. Use the spelling feature of your word processing software to check for spelling errors; then read the copy aloud to see if it makes sense.
2. Proofread for all kinds of errors, especially repeated, missing, or transposed words; grammar and punctuation; and numbers and names.
3. Use the appropriate software command to see an entire page of your document to check for formatting errors such as line spacing, tabs, margins, and bold.

E. Compare this paragraph with the Pretest on page 137. Edit the paragraph to correct any errors.

E. PROOFREADING

```
     Kim new that her skills at the key board made her a
top rivel for the job. About six persons had scene her race
home to see if the male showd the company was awarre of it.
```


INSTRUCTOR STRATEGIES

Reference Books Direct students to reliable reference books they can consult.

The Gregg Reference Manual, the upfront references found in dictionaries (such as *Webster's New World College Dictionary*), various online references (such as www.ipl.org), and *Roget's Thesaurus* are just a few.

Lesson 45

FOCUS

TIME MANAGEMENT

Suggested Schedule:

Warmup	2′
Skillbuilding	19′
Language Arts	6′
Formatting	6′
Document Processing	17′
Total	**50′**

TEACH

SKILLBUILDING

LESSON 45-B Paced Practice helps students reach individual speed and accuracy goals in 2-wpm increments by pacing them as they strive for a slightly faster rate.

LESSON 45-C Encourage students to push moderately for speed on the Pretest.

LANGUAGE ARTS

LESSON 45-D Demonstrate how to use the bottom of the document window as a visual ruler to help students focus on 1 line at a time.

Have students relate experiences in which they were glad they took the time to proofread. What types of errors and omissions did they find?

Have students compose a 1-page paper in which they discuss the techniques that they use or plan to use for proofreading documents.

Lesson 45

LANGUAGE ARTS

LESSON 45-E If your students are not using the GDP software, have them type a correct version of the paragraph.

SOLUTION: Lines 8–10

8. knew, keyboard
9. rival, seen
10. mail, showed, aware

FORMATTING

VISUAL INSTRUCTION

Title Page. Review the formatting for a title page:

- Vertical centering of text on the page
- Title format
- Subtitle format and placement
- Format and placement of other information

Refer to Reference Manual

Ask students to review the basic parts of a title page in the **Reference Manual, R-7B,** before they begin typing.

LESSON 45-F Show various examples of title pages from textbooks, trade books, hardcover books, paperback books, and reports. Have students point out the type of information found on the title pages.

Have students discuss similarities and differences in each type of book. Have them notice the placement of the title, subtitle, and other information on the page.

FORMATTING

Refer to Reference Manual

Refer to page R-7B of the Reference Manual for additional guidance.

F. TITLE PAGE

Reports may have a title page, which includes information such as the report title, to whom the report is submitted, the writer's name and identification, and the date. To format a title page, follow these steps:

1. Center the page vertically.
2. Center the title in all caps and bold, using a 14-point font.
3. Press ENTER 2 times; then center the subtitle in upper- and lowercase and bold, using a 12-point font.
4. Press ENTER 12 times; then center the words `Submitted to`.
5. Press ENTER 2 times; then center the recipient's name and identification on separate lines, single-spaced.
6. Press ENTER 12 times; then center `Prepared by`.
7. Press ENTER 2 times; then center the writer's name and identification on separate lines, single-spaced.
8. Press ENTER 2 times; then center the date.

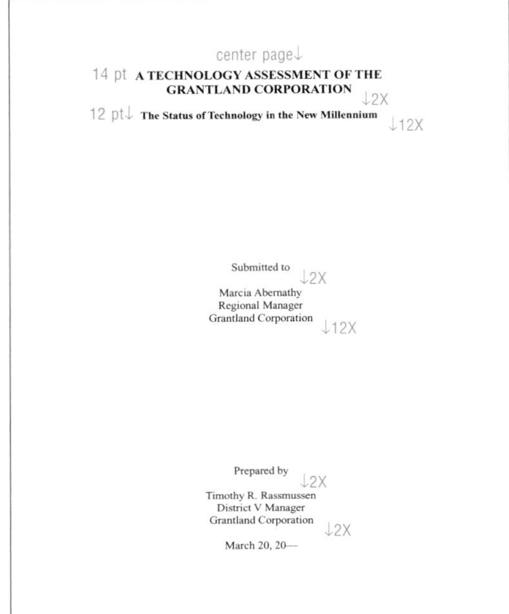

A TECHNOLOGY ASSESSMENT OF THE GRANTLAND CORPORATION

The Status of Technology in the New Millennium

Submitted to

Marcia Abernathy
Regional Manager
Grantland Corporation

Prepared by

Timothy R. Rassmussen
District V Manager
Grantland Corporation

March 20, 20—

EXTENDING LANGUAGE ARTS

Proofreading One of the most effective ways to proofread, especially copy with statistical information, is in pairs. Choose an exercise from the text that contains numbers; have students type the exercise and circle any errors they find. Then have students exchange papers and check each other's work, circling errors in a different color. Generally speaking, the person who did not type the copy will find errors that the typist did not find. You may also have one student read the exercise aloud, while the other student checks the typed copy. This is an excellent way to find errors. Encourage students to read in pairs when proofreading lengthy reports, statistical data, or material containing a number of words specific to a profession, such as medical terminology.

Reference Manual

Refer to page R-7D of the Reference Manual for additional guidance.

G. TABLE OF CONTENTS

A table of contents is usually included in a long report. The table of contents identifies the major and minor sections of a report and includes page numbers preceded by dot leaders. Dot leaders are a series of periods that guide the reader's eye across the page to the page number at the right. To format a table of contents:

1. Press ENTER 6 times to begin the first line approximately 2 inches from the top of the page.
2. Center and type CONTENTS in all-caps, 14-point font, and bold; then press ENTER 2 times.
3. Set a left tab at 0.5 inch; then set a right tab at 6 inches with dot leaders.
4. Change to 12-point font and type the main heading in all-caps.
5. Press TAB 1 or 2 times as needed to insert dot leaders and to move to the right margin; then type the page number, and press ENTER 2 times.
6. Type the next main heading in a similar fashion. If the next item is a subheading, press TAB 1 time to indent the subheading 0.5 inch.
7. Type the subheading, and then press TAB to insert dot leaders and to move to the right margin; then type the page number, and press ENTER 1 time to type the next subheading or 2 times to type a new main heading.
8. Continue in like fashion until the table of contents is complete.

Set left tab at 0.5; right dot-leader tab at 6.

↓6X

14 pt. **CONTENTS**

↓X2

12 pt.↓INTRODUCTION → tab 1

↓X2

SECURITY ON THE INTERNET 3

→ tab Using Passwords → tab 3

Paying by Credit Card 4

Keeping Your Personal Information Private 6

↓X2

IMPLICATIONS OF E-COMMERCE 8

Word Processing Manual

H. WORD PROCESSING: TAB SET—DOT LEADERS

Study Lesson 45 in your word processing manual. Complete all of the shaded steps while at your computer. Then format the jobs that follow.

FORMATTING

Reference Manual

Ask students to review the basic parts of a table of contents in the **Reference Manual, R-7D,** before they begin typing.

VISUAL INSTRUCTION

Table of Contents. Review the formatting for a table of contents:

- Margins
- Tab setting
- Title format
- Major headings format
- Subheadings format
- Page number format

LESSON 45-G Show various examples of tables of contents found in textbooks, trade books, hardcover books, paperback books, and reports. Have students point out the types of information found on tables of contents pages.

Have students discuss similarities and differences in the tables of contents in each type of book. Have them look at margins, title formats, major headings, subheadings, and page numbering formats.

LESSON 45-H Remind students to set a right tab with dot leaders.

ERGONOMICALLY SPEAKING

PREVENTING RSIs One side effect of more and more people spending more and more time sitting at workstations is RSIs (repetitive strain injuries). Some of the more common RSIs are carpal tunnel syndrome, affecting the median nerve in the wrist; cubital tunnel syndrome, affecting the elbow's ulnar nerve; and tendinitis, an inflammation of a tendon (for keyboarders, the thumb tendons may be affected). Prevention? Change positions frequently, and take stretching breaks at least once an hour.

Lesson 45

DOCUMENT PROCESSING

Refer to Reference Manual

Ask students to review the format for a title page and a table of contents in the **Reference Manual, R-7B** and **R-7D,** before they begin typing.

REPORT 45-22 Remind students that they should use the callouts as a guide for producing the title page. The size of the type to be used is shown as 14 point and 12 point; the number of times to press ENTER is shown by ↓12X and ↓2X.

REPORT 45-23 Call attention to the vertical and horizontal spacing formats required to type this table of contents. Remind students to set a custom tab for dot leaders as shown in the copy to be typed.

DOCUMENT PROCESSING

Report 45-22
Title Page

↓center page

14 pt. **DISTANCE LEARNING CLASSROOMS** ↓2X

12 pt.↓ **Using Technology to Reach Students**
at a Distance ↓12X

Prepared by ↓2X

Alicia T. Gonzalez
Technology Coordinator
T-Systems Media, Inc. ↓12X

February 19, 20--

Report 45-23
Table of Contents

Set left tab at 0.5; right dot-leader tab at 6. ↓6X

14 pt. **CONTENTS**

↓X2

12 pt.↓OUR COMPUTER SOCIETY →tab......2
↓X2
HOW COMPUTERS WORK......5
↓X2
→ tab Input →tab......5
Processing......7
Storage......8
Output......12
↓X2
USING COMPUTER SOFTWARE......14

Word Processing......16
Spreadsheet......17
Database......19
Graphics......20

COMPUTERS AND YOUR CAREER......21

Management Information Systems......25
Careers in the Computer Industry......28
Careers in Business and Industry......32
Careers in Government......36

COMPUTERS AND YOUR FUTURE......38

BIBLIOGRAPHY......41

INSTRUCTOR STRATEGIES

Customizing Report Elements Ask students to explain the purpose of title pages and tables of contents.

Students may want to suggest ways to change the look of these reports. What changes do they know how to make at this point? (They know how to change the size and style of type, the font, and the design.) Let them know that when they learn how to use PowerPoint to make slides for presentations, they will know how to add color, sound, and animation.

Report 45-24
Title Page

Create a title page for the report below entitled LOOKING INTO THE 21ST CENTURY and a subtitle that reads Some Predictions for the New Millennium. The report is to be submitted to Alfredo Sanchez, District Manager, Millennium Concepts, Inc. The report is being prepared by Richard P. Morgan, Computer Consultant, Millennium Concepts, Inc. Use a date of May 18, 20--.

Report 45-25
Table of Contents

CONTENTS

Report 45-26
Business Report

Progress and Proofreading Check

Documents designated as Proofreading Checks serve as a check of your proofreading skill. Your goal is to have zero typographical errors when the GDP software first scores the document.

Do not indent paragraphs in a business report.

LOOKING INTO THE 21ST CENTURY
Some Predictions for the New Millennium
Evelyn Hasagawa

¶ It is predicted that computers will alter almost every activity of our lives in the first ten years of this millennium. There is strong evidence to suggest that this prediction will soon become a reality. This report will summarize the changes we will experience in the areas of artificial intelligence and the Internet.

ARTIFICIAL INTELLIGENCE

¶ Artificial intelligence is generally described as a computer's ability to assume an intelligence similar to that of the human brain—thus, its ability to reason and make decisions based on a preassigned set of facts or data.[1] But many experts predict that the computer's power will not stop there. They predict that the computer will soon become much smarter than humans by a process in which "intelligent" computers create even more intelligent computers. What we learn from these computers will have a far greater impact than the combined discoveries of the microscope, telescope, and X-ray machines.

¶ It is also predicted that the power of computers will double every 18 months through the year 2010.[2] With these enhancements, robots will displace humans from farms and factories; we will travel in cars, planes, and trains that are operated solely by computers; and traveling on the interstate highways will be as safe as watching television at home.

(Continued on next page)

Lesson 45

DOCUMENT PROCESSING

REPORT 45-24 The copy for this report is presented in a different format. Before students type the title page, you may wish to discuss the items to be typed for each part. Remind students that they may use the Reference Manual if they need help in formatting the title page.

REPORT 45-25 Before students type the table of contents, you may wish to discuss the horizontal and vertical spacing required. Remind students that they may use the Reference Manual if they need help in formatting the table of contents.

Progress Check/ Proofreading Check:

REPORTS 45-24 through 45-26 Many formatting features presented in this unit are included in these documents. You may want to use these exercises as a short document processing test.

In addition, you may want to inform students that these documents also serve as a check of their proofreading skill. Their goal is to have zero typographical errors when the GDP software first scores the document, in order to earn a satisfactory proofreading grade. If students need a second chance, they should click the **Create** button in the GDP software to retype the document and try again to have zero typos on the first scored attempt. The GDP Portfolio notes how many scored attempts were made when a document is created or re-created to help you track proofreading scores.

Remind students to use the Reference Manual for correct report formatting.

Remind students to spell-check, proofread, and preview their documents before printing them.

MHHE CHAMPIONS

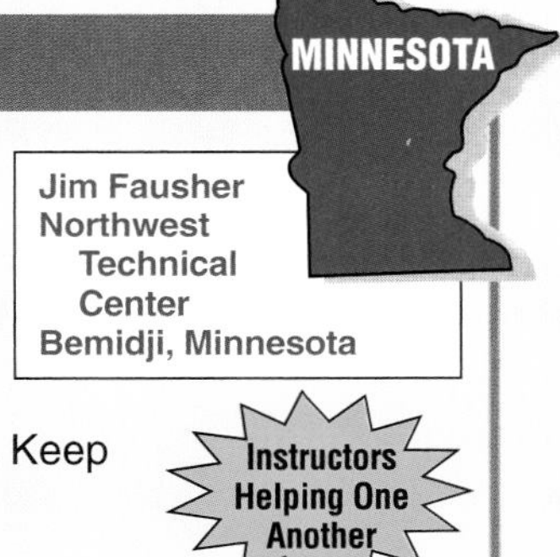

Instructions

When working with the GDP software, go slowly, step by step, through the instructions to be sure all students are keeping up. Keep each step simple.

Jim Fausher
Northwest Technical Center
Bemidji, Minnesota

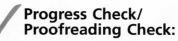

Instructors Helping One Another

Lesson 45

DOCUMENT PROCESSING

Remind students to refer to their Microsoft Word Manual to review footnote formatting.

Remind students to spell-check, proofread, and preview their documents before printing them.

ASSESS

www.mhhe.com/gdp to download a copy of the Technique Evaluation Form.

TECHNIQUE EVALUATION FORM

Review the formats for Report 45-22 and Report 45-23.

Print a report for all skillbuilding exercises for Lessons 41–45.

Extending the Lesson

Have students prepare a title page and a one-page table of contents using the textbook for another class.

CLOSE

Review business report formatting, footnote placement, academic reports in APA style, academic reports in MLA style, references and citations, title pages, and tables of contents.

Encourage students to practice skillbuilding each day.

COMPUTERS AND THE INTERNET

¶ The Internet will continue to expand and proliferate around the world. The speed at which information is transmitted on today's Internet will be considered a "snail's pace" on tomorrow's telemetric system. Most computers will transmit information at gigabit speeds and higher.[3] Computer security will be "foolproof," and most business transactions will be conducted on the Net. Fewer people will travel to foreign countries to vacation since "virtual vacations" will be commonplace.

---

[1] Peter F. Boyd, "Artificial Intelligence," *Journal of Computer Trends*, January 2004, pp. 23–24, 36.

[2] Toshida Doi, "Is Computer Intelligence Better Than the Human Brain?" *Power PC Magazine*, April 2003, pp. 14–17.

[3] Melanie T. Reynolds, "Tomorrow's Brainpower," March 17, 2004, <http://www.businessweek.com/2004/brainpower.htm>, accessed on August 19, 2005.

Strategies for Career Success

Letter of Transmittal

A letter or memo of transmittal introduces a report or proposal. Such letters provide an overview of the report in an informal, conversational writing style.

Let the recipient know what you are sending; for example, "Enclosed is the proposal you requested." If you're submitting an unsolicited report, explain why you've written the report. Include the report topic and identify the person or persons who authorized the report. Recap the main points. Cite any specific information that would help your audience comprehend the material. Is it a draft?

Conclude with a note of appreciation, a willingness to discuss the report, and intended follow-up action. Will you do something? Do you want feedback? If you want the reader to act, explain what you need and provide a deadline; for example, "Please provide your comments by July 15."

YOUR TURN List some ways that a letter of transmittal can promote goodwill between the sender and recipient.

Strategies for Career Success

LETTER OF TRANSMITTAL Ask students whether they have received a letter of transmittal—perhaps as a cover letter for an insurance policy or other important document. Discuss the tone and format of the letter. Ask if the letter of transmittal they received gave a positive or negative impression of the company that sent the letter.

YOUR TURN If time permits, ask students to complete the Your Turn activity.

Correspondence

LESSON 46
Personal Titles and Complimentary Closings in Letters

LESSON 47
Personal-Business Letters

LESSON 48
Memos With Lists

LESSON 49
Letters With Copy Notations

LESSON 50
Letters in Modified-Block Style

January 10, 20--

Mrs. Connie Filstad
4034 Kennedy Lane
Mount Vernon, WA 98274-2340

Dear Mrs. Filstad:

We at Mirror Lake Homes believe that your selection of a SunCity townhouse is just the right choice for you. The SunCity model received three national awards the 12th of last month. You have selected one of the most popular of our six models. As you requested, a brochure of the SunCity model is enclosed. Fifty-four units in the Creekwood site in Mount Vernon, Washington, have been built since December 2000.

I am certain you will agree that the $500 earnest money you put down was a wise decision on your part, and the 6.5 percent loan you received was the best available through our lending agency.

Thank you, Mrs. Filstad, for the opportunity to work with you these past few days. If you have any questions, please let us know.

Sincerely,

(Mrs.) Maria Martinez
Sales Director

urs
Enclosure

November 30, 20--

Sales Manager
Bachmann's Nursery and Landscaping
6823 Oneta Avenue
Youngstown, OH 44500-2175

Dear Sales Manager:

As you requested on the telephone, I am providing the following list of events relating to my tree problem.

1. On April 15, I purchased at your branch in Warren four silver maples for the atrium outside our Riverdale office. We also purchased four Japanese red maples at your branch in Niles later that afternoon.
2. After about six months, one silver maple and one red maple had died. I phoned both the Warren and Niles branches several times on November 1, but no one returned my messages.
3. On November 8, I phoned your nursery in an attempt to have these trees replaced. Again, there was no response.

As these trees were expensive, I expect that you will either replace them or reimburse me for the cost of the trees. I shall look forward to hearing from you.

Sincerely,

Marvin L. Norgaard
Grounds Manager

urs

MEMO TO: Charles A. Cornelius, President

FROM: Alfred A. Long, Convention Director

DATE: September 8, 20--

SUBJECT: Convention Locations

As you know, this year's convention will meet in Jacksonville, Florida. It is the Executive Board's decision to rotate the convention site to each of the districts in our region. Our next three conventions will be held in the following locations:

- Mobile, Alabama
- Atlanta, Georgia
- Myrtle Beach, South Carolina

In May the Board will travel to Mobile to visit the location of our next convention site. When we return, we will draft our convention site proposal for you.

urs

Unit 10

UNIT OVERVIEW

Students will be introduced to personal-business letters and letters in modified-block style. Special features in letters and memos with lists will also be presented. The tab feature of Microsoft Word will be demonstrated.

Did You Know?

Every new word processing feature and every new document processing feature is applied at least two times in the unit in which it is introduced.

Go To The Web

www.mhhe.com/gdp to download a copy of the Technique Evaluation Form.

Name ____ Class ____ Date ____

Technique Evaluation Form

Date	Workstation		Position at the Keyboard		Keystroking	
	Acceptable	Needs Improvement	Acceptable	Needs Improvement	Acceptable	Needs Improvement

Workstation
1. Positions the chair so that the upper and lower legs form a 90-degree angle and the lower back is supported.
2. Positions the keyboard even with the front of the desk.
3. Positions the text on either side of the monitor as close to it vertically and horizontally as possible to minimize head and eye movement and to avoid neck strain.
4. Positions the mouse on a pad at the side of the monitor opposite the text.

Position at the Keyboard
5. Centers the body opposite the keyboard.
6. Leans forward slightly from the hips, with the base of the spine touching the back of the chair and the feet flat on the floor.
7. Keeps the elbows alongside the body in a relaxed position.
8. Curves the fingers naturally over the home position, with the back of the hand at the same angle as the keyboard.

Keystroking
9. Keeps the forearms horizontal and raises the hands slightly when typing so that the wrists do not touch the keyboard while typing. (Hands may rest at the bottom of the keyboard—away from the keys—during nontyping intervals.)
10. Makes quick, snappy strokes using the correct fingers.
11. Returns the finger immediately to the home position or moves to the next position after each stroke.
12. Operates all keys by touch, keeping the eyes on the copy most of the time while typing.

Comments

Use this form to keep track of student progress. Complete a form for each student.

RESOURCE MANAGER

GDP SOFTWARE
- Lessons 46–50
- Software User's Guide
- Instructor Management LAN Version
- Word Processing Manual
- Professional Handbook (IWE*)—Teaching Strategies; Teaching in a Distance-Learning Environment
- MAP 75

ASSESSMENT
- Progress Check—Correspondence 50-35
- Professional Handbook (IWE*)—Assessment Strategies

ON THE WEB
- **www.mhhe.com/gdp**
- Instructor Management Web Version

*Instructor Wraparound Edition

FOCUS

TIME MANAGEMENT

Suggested Schedule:

Warmup	2′
Skillbuilding	18′
Formatting	6′
Document Processing	24′
Total	**50′**

TEACH

SKILLBUILDING

LESSON 46-B Encourage students to push moderately for speed on the pretest.

LESSON 46-C Speed sprints are very motivational. Have students push hard for speed on these easy sentences.

Lesson 46

Personal Titles and Complimentary Closings in Letters

Goals

- Type at least 37wpm/3′/3e
- Format personal titles in letters
- Format complimentary closings in letters

A. Type 2 times.

A. WARMUP

```
     B & Z requested 14 boxes at $37/box. The items they        11
wanted were #6 and #17. A discount of 20% would bring the       22
total to approximately $950. Will you verify that order?        33
 | 1 | 2 | 3 | 4 | 5 | 6 | 7 | 8 | 9 | 10 | 11 | 12
```

SKILLBUILDING

B. DIAGNOSTIC PRACTICE: NUMBERS

If you are not using the GDP software, turn to page SB-5 and follow the directions for this activity.

C. Take three 12-second timed writings on each line. The scale below the last line shows your wpm speed for a 12-second timed writing.

C. 12-SECOND SPEED SPRINTS

```
Nine of those new women were on time for the first session.
She could see that many of those old memos should be filed.
Forty of the men were at the game when that siren went off.
The line at the main hall was so long that I did not go in.
    5    10    15    20    25    30    35    40    45    50    55    60
```

Keyboarding Connection

Evaluating Internet Sources

Are you sure your Internet source has valid information? Because of the broad availability of the Internet and the lack of careful review stages like the ones built into print publishing, you must be cautious about the dependability of information you find on the Internet. Evaluate information on the Internet by the same standards you use to evaluate other sources of information.

The best way to assure that information is valid is to get it from a reputable source. The Internet versions of established, reputable journals in medicine (for example, *Journal of the American Medical Association*), business (for example, *Harvard Business Review*), engineering, computer science, and so forth, warrant the same level of trust as the printed versions.

When you do not use established, reputable Web sites, use caution. Keep in mind that anyone can publish on the Internet. For many sources, there are no editorial review safeguards in place.

YOUR TURN Search the Web for more assessment methods.

Keyboarding Connection

Evaluating Internet Sources

Discuss with students the importance of verifying information on the Internet. Suggest that students rank Web sites from reliable to unreliable. Be sure to include encyclopedic, academic, commercial, government, group, and personal sites. You may want students to find data in at least two different reliable sites to ensure accuracy.

YOUR TURN If time permits, ask students to complete the Your Turn activity.

D. Take two 3-minute timed writings. Review your speed and errors.

Goal: At least 37wpm/3′/3e

D. 3-MINUTE TIMED WRITING

```
     Now is a great time for you to look for a job. Most        11
employers look for people who have mastered a few office        22
skills. For example, if you have acquired good computer         33
skills and are capable of working with people around you        45
and are steadfast, you can find a good job. There are some      56
who will pay top dollar to find and keep good workers.          67
     Your first impression on a prospective employer will       78
be a lasting one. Your resume should list your job skills,      90
your experience, and your personal information. Your zeal      102
when you interview for a job must come through.                111
| 1 | 2 | 3 | 4 | 5 | 6 | 7 | 8 | 9 | 10 | 11 | 12
```

FORMATTING

E. PERSONAL TITLES IN CORRESPONDENCE

Inside Addresses
Always use a courtesy title before a person's name in the inside address of a letter; for example, *Mr., Mrs.,* or *Dr.*

Type a person's title on the same line with the name (separated by a comma), if the title is short, or on the line below. The title and business name may be typed on the same line (separated by a comma) if they are both short.

Personal Titles in Inside Addresses

Mr. Frank R. Yashiro, Manager
Landmark Security Systems

Mrs. Joyce Mansfield
Executive Director
Tanner Hospital

Dr. Carlotta Torres
Manager, Duke Oil Co.

Salutations
When possible, use a person's name in the salutation. The correct form for the salutation is the courtesy title and the last name. If you do not know the name of the person, use a job title or *Ladies and Gentlemen*. A colon is used after the salutation in standard punctuation.

Personal Titles in Salutations

Dear Ms. North:
Dear Dr. Chapman:
Dear Mr. Wagner:
Dear Sales Manager:
Ladies and Gentlemen:

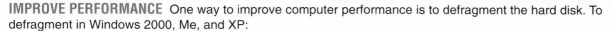

Windows Wizard

IMPROVE PERFORMANCE One way to improve computer performance is to defragment the hard disk. To defragment in Windows 2000, Me, and XP:

- Double-click **My Computer**.
- Right-click the hard drive icon **C:**
- Select **Properties** from the shortcut menu.
- Click the **Tools** tab.
- Click **Defragment Now**.

Lesson 46

SKILLBUILDING

LESSON 46-D Stress correct technique and eyes on copy as they type the 3-minute timed writing.

FORMATTING

LESSON 46-E Writers have some choices when they use personal titles in correspondence. Be sure to review all the variations. Students should understand that if they do not know a person's name, *Ladies and Gentlemen* is an appropriate substitute.

Write the following copy on the board:

Mr. Franklin Pierce
Manager
First National Bank

Miss Gaynell Snow
Executive Director
Riverbend Hospital

Dr. Elizabeth Sharpe
Dean of Education
Walter Community College

After the class discussion, have students demonstrate their understanding of the material by supplying an inside address and salutation for each name.

INSTRUCTOR STRATEGIES

Cultural Differences Invite students of different cultures, if any are present, to tell the class of any salutations or personal titles they know of that differ from the ones explained here. For example, in Chinese usage, the family (last) name precedes the given (first) name.

Lesson 46

LESSON 46-F Remind students that only the first letter of the first word in a complimentary closing is capitalized. Have students supply closing lines for each name used in Lesson 46-E.

DOCUMENT PROCESSING

Refer to Reference Manual

Ask students to review the business letter in block-style format in the **Reference Manual, R-3A,** before they begin typing.

CORRESPONDENCE 46-22 AND 46-23

Observe students' work and technique as they type these business letters. Give guidance as needed.

ASSESS

Go To The Web

www.mhhe.com/gdp to download a copy of the Technique Evaluation Form.

TECHNIQUE EVALUATION FORM

Review results of timed writings.

Review the format of Correspondence 46-22.

Extending the Lesson

Show business letters with nontraditional salutations. Discuss the use of *Ladies and Gentlemen* in a salutation.

CLOSE

Discuss with students the effect of various complimentary closings. Help them understand that the complimentary closing and the writer's identification serve as a frame in which the signature floats.

F. COMPLIMENTARY CLOSINGS IN CORRESPONDENCE

Every letter should end with a complimentary closing. Some frequently used complimentary closings are *Sincerely, Sincerely yours, Yours truly, Cordially*, and *Respectfully yours*.

In the closing lines, do not use a courtesy title before a man's name. A courtesy title may be included in a woman's typed name or her signature. A comma is used after the complimentary closing in standard punctuation.

Closing Lines

Sincerely yours,

Gretchen Day

Miss Gretchen Day
Account Manager

Cordially,

(Ms.) Juanita Ponce

Juanita Ponce
Marketing Director

Yours truly,

Ben R. Cameron

Ben R. Cameron
Regional Supervisor

DOCUMENT PROCESSING

Correspondence 46-22
Business Letter in Block Style

January 10, 20-- | Mrs. Connie Filstad | 4034 Kennedy Lane | Mount Vernon, WA 98274-2340 | Dear Mrs. Filstad:
¶ We at Mirror Lake Homes believe that your selection of a SunCity townhouse is just the right choice for you. The SunCity model received three national awards last month. You have selected one of the most popular of our six models. As you requested, a brochure of the SunCity model is enclosed. Fifty-four units in the Creekwood site in Mount Vernon, Washington, have been built since December 2002.
¶ I am certain you will agree that the $500 earnest money you put down was a wise decision on your part, and the 6.5 percent loan you received was the best available through our lending agency.
¶ Thank you, Mrs. Filstad, for the opportunity to work with you these past few days. If you have any questions, please let us know.
Sincerely, | (Mrs.) Maria Martinez | Sales Director | urs | Enclosure

Correspondence 46-23
Business Letter in Block Style

May 20, 20-- | Mr. Lawrence S. Alwich | 1800 East Hollywood Avenue | Salt Lake City, UT 84108 | Dear Mr. Alwich:
¶ Our radio station would like you to reply to our editorial about the proposed airport site that aired from Provo, Utah, on May 15. Actually, you are 1 of over 27 listeners who indicated your desire for us to air your rebuttal.
¶ Of the more than 100 request letters for equal time, we selected yours because you touched on most of the relevant points of this topic.
¶ We will contact you further about taping your rebuttal on June 4. Please read the enclosed disclaimer that we would like you to sign before airing the rebuttal.
Yours truly, | Peng T. Lim | General Manager | urs | Enclosure

MHHE CHAMPIONS

OHIO

Contributor wishes to remain anonymous.

Instructors Helping One Another

In my keyboarding classes, I emphasize the similarity to other professions in which the presentation must be perfect. In keyboarding, as in many other endeavors, presentation is important. Think of the role of presentation in fine cuisine. Preparing fine documents is worthy of everyone's respect.

Personal-Business Letters

Goals

- Improve speed and accuracy
- Refine language arts skills in number expression
- Format personal-business letters

A. Type 2 times.

A. WARMUP

```
1      "Rex analyzed the supply," Margie said. Based on the    11
2  results, a purchase request for 7# @ $140 (23% of what we   22
3  needed) was issued. Was Jackie surprised by this? Vi was!   34
   | 1 | 2 | 3 | 4 | 5 | 6 | 7 | 8 | 9 | 10 | 11 | 12
```

SKILLBUILDING

B. PACED PRACTICE

If you are not using the GDP software, turn to page SB-14 and follow the directions for this activity.

C. PROGRESSIVE PRACTICE: ALPHABET

If you are not using the GDP software, turn to page SB-7 and follow the directions for this activity.

LANGUAGE ARTS

D. Study the rules at the right.

D. NUMBER EXPRESSION

RULE ▶ # general

In general, spell out numbers zero through ten, and use numerals for numbers above ten.

We rented two movies for tonight.
The decision was reached after 27 precincts sent in their results.

RULE ▶ # figures

Use numerals for

- **Dates. (Use *st*, *d*, or *th* only if the day comes before the month.)**
  The tax report is due on April 15 (*not* April 15th).
  We will drive to the camp on the 23d (or *23rd* or *23rd*) of May.
- **All numbers if two or more *related* numbers both above and below ten are used in the same sentence.**
  Mr. Carter sent in 7 receipts, and Ms. Cantrell sent in 22.
  But: The 13 accountants owned three computers each.
- **Measurements (time, money, distance, weight, and percent).**
  The $500 statue we delivered at 7 a.m. weighed 6 pounds.
- **Mixed numbers.**
  Our sales are up 9½ (or *9 1/2* or *9.5*) percent over last year.

(Continued on next page)

EXTENDING LANGUAGE ARTS

Number Expression Explain that the first rule of number expression is a simple one: in general, spell out numbers zero through ten. If a sentence has two related numbers, with one number above ten and one below ten, show both numbers in figures. Example: Cecily has 6 sweaters and 12 blouses.

Demonstrate how figures are used to express the following: dates, fractions, amounts of money, measurements, decimals and percentages, time, ages, and anniversaries.

Point out that cardinal numbers (*first, second,* and so on) can be written with on-the-line letters (1st, 2nd, and so on) but are usually written with superscripts. Software automatically converts *1st* to *1st*.

FOCUS

TIME MANAGEMENT

Suggested Schedule:

Warmup	2′
Skillbuilding	14′
Language Arts	6′
Formatting	6′
Document Processing	22′
Total	**50′**

TEACH

SKILLBUILDING

LESSON 47-B Paced Practice helps students reach individual speed and accuracy goals in 2-wpm increments by pacing themselves as they strive for a slightly faster rate.

LESSON 47-C Students take repeated timed writings on a passage containing the exact number of words for their speed goal until they can complete the passage with no errors. Then they move to the next longer passage and start again.

LANGUAGE ARTS

LESSON 47-D Numerous number rules are presented in this section. Review thoroughly all the rules presented in Lesson 47-D.

Invite students to compose sentences that have two or more sets of numbers. Help them realize that one set of information should be expressed in figures and the other in words. Example: Eighty-one rookies caught 47 line drives, and thirty-seven veterans caught 117 foul balls.

Lesson 47

LANGUAGE ARTS

SOLUTION: Lines 4–12

4. two
5. *Correct*
6. two
7. 15
8. $3 million
9. June 3, 5 p.m.
10. 2 pounds, 3
11. 12, 21
12. seven 10-page

FORMATTING

LESSON 47-E

Refer to Reference Manual

Ask students to review the basic parts of a personal-business letter in the **Reference Manual, R-3D,** before they begin typing.

DOCUMENT PROCESSING

CORRESPONDENCE 47-24

Be sure students understand the location of the writer's return address.

Typing the return address under the writer's name is becoming an increasingly popular practice because the complete mailing address is positioned in one place. Perhaps the signature block, first used in e-mail, is appearing in other message formats because it makes good sense.

Edit the sentences to correct any errors in number expression.

```
4  On the 3d of June, when she turns 60, 2 of her annuities
5  will have earned an average of 10 3/4 percent.
6  All seven investors were interested in buying 14 condos
7  if they were located within fifteen miles of each other.
8  The credit fee is fifteen dollars, and the interest is set
9  at 8 percent; escrow will close on March 23rd before five p.m.
10 The parcel weighed two pounds. She also mailed three large
11 packages and twelve small packages on June 4.
12 They paid 2.5 points on the loan amount.
```

FORMATTING

E. PERSONAL-BUSINESS LETTERS

Personal-business letters are prepared by individuals to conduct their personal business. To format a personal-business letter:

1. Type the letter on plain paper or personal stationery, not letterhead.
2. Include the writer's address in the letter directly below the writer's name in the closing lines.
3. Since the writer of the letter usually types the letter, reference initials are not used.

DOCUMENT PROCESSING

Correspondence 47-24

Personal-Business Letter in Block Style

Refer to Reference Manual

Refer to page R-3D of the Reference Manual for an illustration of a personal-business letter.

↓6X
October 1, 20-- ↓4X

Ms. Valarie Bledsoe, Director
City Parks and Recreation Department
7034 Renwick Avenue
Syracuse, NY 13210-0475 ↓2X

Dear Ms. Bledsoe: ↓2X

Thank you for the excellent manner in which your department accommodated our family last summer. About 120 Turners attended the reunion at Rosedale Park on August 21. (# general, # figures)

I would like to again request that Shelter 5 be reserved for our next year's family reunion on August 20. A confirmation of the date from your office will be appreciated. ↓2X (# general, # figures)

Sincerely, ↓4X

Blair R. Turner
2410 Farnham Road
Syracuse, NY 13219

TEACHING THE ADULT LEARNER

TIME MODIFICATION Exams may be stressful for the adult learner. Extra effort should be made to make sure that they understand instructions. On their jobs, accuracy has been stressed, and older students tend to bring this emphasis to exams. Accuracy is more important than speed. Therefore, you may want to reconsider the time requirements for exams.

Correspondence 47-25

Personal-Business Letter in Block Style

This personal-business letter is from Roberto G. Trujillo, who lives at 482 22d Street East, Lawrence, KS 66049. Use July 13, 20--, as the date, and supply the appropriate salutation and closing using standard punctuation. The letter is to be sent to Mr. Robert A. Sotherden, Administrator | Glencrest Nursing Home | 2807 Crossgate Circle | Lawrence, KS 66047.

¶ Thanks to you and dozens of other people, the fall crafts sale at Glencrest was highly successful. I am very appreciative of the ways in which you helped.

¶ I particularly wish to thank you for transporting the display tables and chairs to Glencrest and back to the community center. Many people from the community center attended the sale and commented about how nice it was of you and your staff to support such an activity.

¶ Having a parent who is a resident of the home, I am grateful that over 20 people from the Lawrence area volunteer their services to help make life more pleasant for the residents. Please accept my special thanks to you and your staff for supporting the many activities that benefit all Glencrest residents.

general

Correspondence 47-26

Personal-Business Letter in Block Style

June 4, 20-- | Mr. Karl E. Davis | 5270 Rosecrans Avenue | Topeka, KS 67284 | Dear Mr. Davis:

¶ Your presentation at the Sand Hills Country Club was one of the most enjoyable our members have ^ever^ observed. It is always a pleasure to have professionals like you speak on ways college graduates can prepare themselves for future employment. I especially enjoyed the question-and-answer session at the conclusion of your ~~wonderful~~ presentation, and I received many favorable comments from other attendees as well.

¶ Our professor has suggested that we take the information you gave us and prepare a web site that focuses on the ^key^ points 6 you mentioned in your speech. That way, many of our class mates can take advantage of your excellent advice when preparing for ^their^ 1st search job. We have also found ~~several~~ ^at least 20^ other sources to use on the world wide web that we plan to include ~~in~~ ^on^ our web site.

general

figure

(Continued on next page)

Lesson 47

DOCUMENT PROCESSING

CORRESPONDENCE 47-26

Before students begin to type, review the proofreaders' marks used in the letters. Make sure students know how to interpret the rough-draft copy.

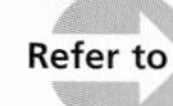

Refer to Reference Manual

Ask students to review the proofreaders' marks in the **Reference Manual, R-14C,** before they begin typing.

INSTRUCTOR STRATEGIES

Evaluating Edits Invite students to explain each handwritten edit in Correspondence 47-26. When they have described the effect of each edit, have them evaluate it. For example, *wonderful* was deleted in line 5 of the body. Why? (It was excessive.)

INSTRUCTOR STRATEGIES

Homophones List If students have not begun a file on their student disks that lists homophones, they can begin their collection with the words *stationary* and *stationery*. Suggest that they include the definition and part of speech of each word, along with a sample sentence showing correct usage.

Lesson 47

ASSESS

www.mhhe.com/gdp to download a copy of the Technique Evaluation Form.

TECHNIQUE EVALUATION FORM

Walk around the classroom to observe students' technique.

Review the format for Correspondence 47-25.

Extending the Lesson

Ask students if they have personal stationery. Discuss the various weights of paper that are suitable for personal-business letters.

CLOSE

Discuss the differences between a business letter and a personal-business letter. Have students brainstorm salutations and complimentary closings that would be appropriate for each.

¶ I believe this is one of the most interesting assignments I have ever been assigned, thank to the excellent information you provided. Members of my project team are excited to see there information on our web site. The project has given other students an incentive to construct their own web sites pertaining to job searches and interviewing techniques.

figure

¶ If you would like to view our Web site, you can do so at the following URL which will be posted by the 10th of the month: www.tamu.edu/comm/abed3600/interview.html. Again, thank you for all your excellent ideas.
Sincerely, | Tamika Yamemoto | 3421 Carlisle Avenue | Topeka, KS 67209

INSTRUCTOR STRATEGIES

Discussing the Photo If your students understand how it is possible for two or more computer workstations to share a printer, then the concept of global networking is within their grasp. Careers in networking are popular—and they pay well.

Network administrators may design and implement networks, set up and manage users' accounts, install and update network software and applications, and back up the network. Information service (IS) managers maintain project lists, oversee project management, perform database administration, and may do some programming. Both careers enable a person to be a member of the global computer community.

Memos With Lists

Goals

- Type at least 38 wpm/3′/3e
- Format lists in correspondence

A. Type 2 times.

A. WARMUP

```
     Three travel agencies (Jepster & Vilani, Quin & Bott,    11
and Zeplin & Wexter) sold the most travel tickets for the     23
past 12 months. They sold 785, 834, and 960 total tickets.    34
  | 1 | 2 | 3 | 4 | 5 | 6 | 7 | 8 | 9 | 10 | 11 | 12
```

SKILLBUILDING

B. DIAGNOSTIC PRACTICE: SYMBOLS AND PUNCTUATION

If you are not using the GDP software, turn to page SB-2 and follow the directions for this activity.

C. Type each sentence on a separate line by pressing ENTER after each sentence.

C. TECHNIQUE PRACTICE: ENTER KEY

```
Debit the accounts. Balance your checkbook. Add the assets.
Take the discount. Send the statements. Compute the ratios.
Review the accounts. Credit the amounts. Figure the totals.
Prepare the statements. Send the catalog. Call the clients.
```

D. Take two 3-minute timed writings. Review your speed and errors.

Goal: At least 38wpm/3′/3e

D. 3-MINUTE TIMED WRITING

```
     Some of us like to use the Internet for shopping. With    11
just a simple click of the mouse, you can shop for almost      23
any type of product. You can purchase books, cars, food,       34
games, toys, zippers, boxes, and even golf clubs by using      46
the computer to shop online.                                   52
     The advantages of using the Web to shop with such ease    63
are many. First, you can shop from any place that has some     75
access to the Internet. Second, you can compare all prices     86
with other places before you make any purchase. Third, you     98
can have your purchases shipped directly to you. All the      110
savings mount quickly.                                        114
  | 1 | 2 | 3 | 4 | 5 | 6 | 7 | 8 | 9 | 10 | 11 | 12
```


ERGONOMICALLY SPEAKING

WRIST POSITION Advise students to keep their hands in a neutral position when using the keyboard, with their forearms, wrists, and hands in a straight line. They should not turn their wrists sideways or more than 10 degrees up or down. They can keep their wrists straight by moving the entire hand and forearm to use the function keys or the numeric keypad.

Visit us on the Web at **www.mhhe.com/gdp** for more information.

Lesson 48

FOCUS

TIME MANAGEMENT

Suggested Schedule:

Warmup	2′
Skillbuilding	18′
Formatting	6′
Document Processing	24′
Total	**50′**

TEACH

SKILLBUILDING

LESSON 48-B Encourage students to push moderately for speed on the Pretest.

LESSON 48-C Remind students to press ENTER at the end of each sentence.

INSTRUCTOR STRATEGIES

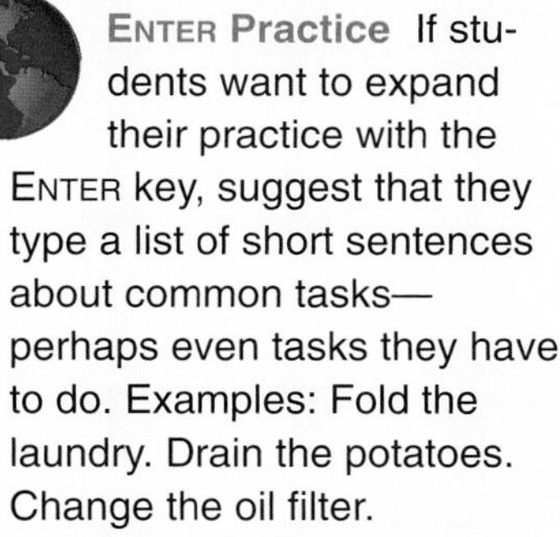

ENTER Practice If students want to expand their practice with the ENTER key, suggest that they type a list of short sentences about common tasks—perhaps even tasks they have to do. Examples: Fold the laundry. Drain the potatoes. Change the oil filter.

LESSON 48-D Remind students to keep eyes on copy and to use proper technique as they strive to meet the goals for this 3-minute timed writing.

Lesson 48

FORMATTING

Reference Manual

Ask students to review the basic parts of bulleted and numbered lists and memos in the **Reference Manual, R-3B, R-3C, R-5B,** and **R-9C,** before they begin typing.

LESSON 48-E Ask students to comment on when and why a bulleted list or numbered list might be used in a document. Explain that a numbered list is often used when the items presented should be read in numerical order. The bulleted list is usually used when sequence isn't important.

Explain how to format bulleted and numbered lists. Point out examples in other illustrations.

DOCUMENT PROCESSING

CORRESPONDENCE 48-27

Guide students step by step through the memo. Remind them to turn off bold formatting at the end of each heading.

Remind students to insert 1 blank line before and after the bulleted list.

The bullets should appear at the left margin in Correspondence 48-27.

FORMATTING

Reference Manual

Refer to pages R-3B, R-3C, and R-5B of the Reference Manual for examples of lists in correspondence. Refer to page R-12C of the Reference Manual for an overview of formatting lists.

E. LISTS IN CORRESPONDENCE

Numbers or bullets may be used in correspondence to call attention to items in a list. If the sequence of the items is important, use numbers rather than bullets.

1. Begin the number or bullet at the left margin for blocked paragraphs.
2. Press ENTER 2 times to insert 1 blank line before and after the list.
3. Within the list, use single spacing as is used in the rest of the document.
4. If all items require no more than 1 line, single-space between the items in the list. If any item requires more than 1 line, single-space each item but press ENTER 2 times to insert 1 blank line between each item.

To format a list in correspondence:

1. Type the list unformatted. (**Note:** If you apply the number or bullet feature at the start of the list, any paragraphs that might follow will usually be indented incorrectly.)
2. Select the items in the list.
3. Apply the number or bullet feature.
4. Decrease the indent to move the position of bullets or numbers to the left margin.

DOCUMENT PROCESSING

Correspondence 48-27

Memo

Refer to Reference Manual

Refer to page R-12C of the Reference Manual for an overview of formatting lists.

↓6X → tab

MEMO TO: Charles A. Cornelius, President ↓2X

FROM: Alfred A. Long, Convention Director ↓2X

DATE: September 8, 20-- ↓2X

SUBJECT: Convention Locations ↓2X

As you know, this year's convention will meet in Jacksonville, Florida. It is the Executive Board's decision to rotate the convention site to each of the districts in our region. Our next three conventions will be held in the following locations: ↓2X

- Mobile, Alabama
- Atlanta, Georgia
- Myrtle Beach, South Carolina ↓2X

In May the Board will travel to Mobile to visit the location of our next convention site. When we return, we will draft our convention site proposal for you. ↓2X

urs

Technology Tips

BULLETS AND NUMBERING

Show students the different numbering systems available in Microsoft Word. Then point out the various bullets available. Ask students to look for unusual bullet forms in newspapers, magazines, and community flyers and bring interesting examples to class. Ask students to cite examples of sequential lists, which should be numbered rather than bulleted.

Correspondence 48-28

Memo

MEMO TO: Marcia Davis | **FROM:** Alex Pera | **DATE:** April 9, 20-- | **SUBJECT:** Program Descriptions

¶As you requested, I have contacted the speakers for our afternoon session discussions. All three speakers have sent me a brief description of their sessions, and they are listed in the order of presentation as follows:

1. Salon A. This session will discuss the advantages of e-commerce and its influence on the economy of the United States.
2. Salon B. This session will introduce several suggestions for enhancing your Web site.
3. Salon C. This session will discuss changes occurring in Internet access and its impact on entrepreneurial ventures.

¶By next Monday I will send you an introduction for each speaker.
urs

Correspondence 48-29

Memo

Open the file for Correspondence 48–27 and make the following changes:

1. Change the three convention sites to Miami, Florida; Raleigh, North Carolina; and Montgomery, Alabama.
2. Change the final paragraph to indicate that the Board will travel to Miami.

Strategies for Career Success

Reducing Bias in Business Communication

Everything we do in business communication attempts to build goodwill. Bias-free language and visuals help maintain the goodwill we work so hard to create.

Bias-free language does not discriminate against people on the basis of sex, physical condition, race, age, or any other characteristic. Do not emphasize gender-specific words in your business vocabulary. Instead, incorporate gender-neutral words (for example, chairman is chairperson) into your business communication.

Organizations that treat people fairly should also use language that treats people fairly. The law is increasingly intolerant of biased documents and hostile work environments. Practice nondiscriminatory behavior by focusing on individual merits, accomplishments, skills, and what you might share in common rather than illustrating differences. Treating every group with respect and understanding is essential to gaining loyalty and future business while cultivating harmonious relationships.

YOUR TURN Review a document that you have recently written. Is the document bias-free?

Strategies for Career Success

REDUCING BIAS IN BUSINESS COMMUNICATION Create a list of words that indicate bias. Create a second list of preferred bias-free words to use as substitutes. Encourage students to add to the lists. Visit **www.ncte.org/about/over/positions/level/gen/107549.htm** to read the National Council of Teachers of English position on bias-free language.

YOUR TURN If time permits, ask students to complete the Your Turn activity.

Lesson 48

DOCUMENT PROCESSING

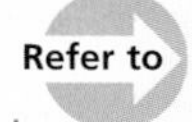

Refer to Reference Manual

Ask students to review the memo format in the **Reference Manual, R-4D** and **R-7C,** before they begin typing.

CORRESPONDENCE 48-28

Be sure students place the numbers in the numbered list at the left margin.

Remind students to refer to their Word Processing Manual to review bulleted and numbered lists.

Remind students to spell-check, proofread, and preview their documents before printing them.

ASSESS

Review results of timed writings.

Review the formatting of Correspondence 48-27.

Extending the Lesson

Have each student decide which memo containing a bulleted or numbered list he or she wants to compose. Have students share their finished memos. Possible memo topics include the following:

How to Build a Birdhouse
How to Teach Tying a Shoelace
How to Give a Haircut
How to Get a Good Job
How to Give a Dog or a Cat a Bath
How to Jump-Start a Battery

CLOSE

Encourage students to review memo formatting by making 3- by 5-inch cards for future reference.

FOCUS

TIME MANAGEMENT 

Suggested Schedule

Warmup	2′
Skillbuilding	15′
Language Arts	6′
Formatting	6′
Document Processing	21′
Total	**50′**

TEACH

SKILLBUILDING

LESSON 49-B 

MAP Do your students seem to think that keystroking accuracy is no longer important since they can backspace-correct errors? What they fail to realize is (1) typists do not recognize many of the errors they make and so do not correct them, and (2) every time students have to stop typing, press the BACKSPACE key, and then press the correct key, their typing speed takes a major hit. In other words, the more accurate your typing, the higher your speed. In that sense, MAP can be considered both a speed and an accuracy builder.

LESSON 49-C Each paragraph is more difficult than the preceding one—based on the number of figures and symbols in each paragraph.

Paragraph 1: none
Paragraph 2: 10
Paragraph 3: 17
Paragraph 4: 26

Letters With Copy Notations

Goals

- Improve speed and accuracy
- Refine language arts skills in spelling
- Format letters with copy notations

A. Type 2 times.

A. WARMUP

```
     "Look at them! Have you ever seen such large birds?"     11
When questioned later on an exam, about 80% to 90% of the     22
junior girls were amazed to learn that they were ospreys.     34
 | 1 | 2 | 3 | 4 | 5 | 6 | 7 | 8 | 9 | 10 | 11 | 12
```

SKILLBUILDING

B. MAP

Follow the GDP software directions for this exercise in improving keystroking accuracy.

C. Take a 1-minute timed writing on the first paragraph to establish your base speed. Then take four 1-minute timed writings on the remaining paragraphs. As soon as you equal or exceed your base speed on one paragraph, advance to the next, more difficult paragraph.

C. SUSTAINED PRACTICE: NUMBERS AND SYMBOLS

```
     The proposed road improvement program was approved       10
by the county commissioners at their last meeting. There      22
were about ten citizens who spoke on behalf of the project.   34

     The plan calls for blacktopping a 14-mile stretch on     11
County Road #2356. This is the road that is commonly called   23
the "roller coaster" because of all the curves and hills.     34

     There will be 116 miles blacktopped by J & J, Inc.       10
(commonly referred to as the Jeremy Brothers*). J & J's       22
office is at 1798 30th Avenue past the 22d Street bridge.     33

     Minor road repair costs range from $10,784 to a high     11
of $163,450 (39% of the total program costs). The "county     23
inspector" is to hold the project costs to 105% of budget!    34
 | 1 | 2 | 3 | 4 | 5 | 6 | 7 | 8 | 9 | 10 | 11 | 12
```


GDP SOFTWARE TIPS

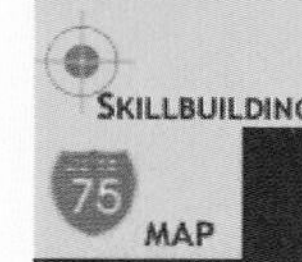

Reference Manual

Encourage students to review the formatting techniques learned in this unit by accessing the Reference Manual for the following documents: personal-business letters, memos, letters with copy notations, and letters in modified-block style.

Lesson 49

LANGUAGE ARTS

D. Type this list of frequently misspelled words, paying special attention to any spelling problems in each word.

D. SPELLING

16 per other receipt present provided commission international
17 service position questions following industrial maintenance
18 well absence support proposal mortgage corporate management
19 upon balance approval experience facilities recommendations
20 paid because premium procedure addition directors currently

Edit the sentences to correct any misspellings.

21 The international comission provided a list of proceedures.
22 That industrial maintainance proposal is curently in place.
23 The directers and management supported the recomendations.
24 Those present raised a question about a corperate morgage.
25 Six of the folowing persons have now given their aproval.
26 In adition, Kris has premium experience at the facilitys.

FORMATTING

E. COPY NOTATIONS

Making file copies of all documents you prepare is a good business practice. At times you may also need copies to send to people other than the addressee of the original document.

A copy notation is typed on a document to indicate that someone else besides the addressee is receiving a copy.

1. Type the copy notation on the line below the reference initials or below the attachment or enclosure notation.
2. At the left margin, type a lowercase *c* followed by a colon.
3. Press the SPACE BAR 1 time and type the name of the person receiving the copy.
4. If more than one person is receiving a copy, type the names on one line separated by a comma and space between each name.

Sincerely, ↓4X

Lester A. Fagerlie
Branch Manager ↓2X

jlt
Enclosure
c: Mrs. Coretta D. Rice, Dr. Thomas Moore

LANGUAGE ARTS

LESSON 49-D Alternate routine: Dictate each word, and have students type the word 1 time. Then have them edit the sentences to correct any misspellings.

SOLUTION: Lines 21–26

21. commission, procedures
22. maintenance, currently
23. directors, recommendations
24. corporate mortgage
25. following, approval
26. addition, facilities

FORMATTING

Refer to Reference Manual

Ask students to review copy notations in the **Reference Manual, R-3C** and **R-5B,** before they begin typing.

VISUAL INSTRUCTION

Copy Notations. Review the formatting for a copy notation:

- Placement
- Text
- Format

EXTENDING LANGUAGE ARTS

Spelling Continue the practice of pronouncing the words for your students; then, have them pronounce the words in unison. Select two or three students to pronounce a line at a time. You may wish to dictate the words prior to having the students type them. Encourage them to look at you while typing and then compare their typed copy with the material in the text.

For each word on which students made an error, ask them to type the word correctly three times.

Have them study particularly difficult words and take the words apart to find smaller words inside to help them remember how they are spelled. For example, *addition* contains the word *add*, which helps one remember to spell it with two *d*'s.

Lesson 49

DOCUMENT PROCESSING

Refer to Reference Manual

Ask students to review the format for a business letter in block style in the **Reference Manual, R-3A,** before they begin typing.

Remind students to spell-check, proofread, and preview their documents before printing them.

CORRESPONDENCE 49-31

Optional. Remind students that multiple copy notations are placed on the same line and separated by commas.

Students should press the ENTER key only 1 time after the reference initials before typing the copy notation.

ASSESS

Evaluate Correspondence 49-30 and Correspondence 49-31.

Extending the Lesson

You may wish to discuss the use of *cc* as a copy notation. This notation originally referred to carbon copies; however, some people continue to use *cc* to denote that *copies* or *courtesy copies* are being sent to other people.

CLOSE

Encourage students to review the list of frequently misspelled words. Have them review their own lists whenever they have a few free minutes.

DOCUMENT PROCESSING

Correspondence 49-30

Business Letter in Block Style

Highlighted words are spelling words from the language arts activities.

May 11, 20-- | Mr. and Mrs. Richard Belson | 783 Wellcourt Lane | Mount Vernon, WA 98273-4156 | Dear Mr. and Mrs. Belson:

¶ Marian Dickenson has informed me that you have several questions pertaining to the maintenance proposal that was submitted by the directors and approved by management. It is our position, based upon the procedures we provided following last week's meeting, that the proposal was submitted to corporate headquarters prior to your inquiry. Therefore, your questions should be directed to Alfred A. Long in our Seattle office.

¶ It has been our experience that inquiries such as yours will receive an immediate response because of the support you have demonstrated during other maintenance negotiations. I would recommend that you call me if you have not heard from Mr. Long by the 13th of the month. In the absence of Mr. Long's response, I am sending you a copy of other materials related to your inquiry.

¶ Thank you for your interest in this matter.

Sincerely, | Theodore A. Gardner | Sales Director | urs | c: Marian Dickenson

Correspondence 49-31

Business Letter in Block Style

Open the file for Correspondence 49-30 and make the following changes:

1. Send the letter to Mr. and Mrs. George Tanner | 105 Royal Lane | Commerce, TX 75428
2. Add the following sentence to the end of the second paragraph:

   `These materials are enclosed for your review.`

3. Include an enclosure notation.
4. Send a copy of this letter to Marian Dickenson and also to Carla Orellano.

INSTRUCTOR STRATEGIES

Discussing the Photo Students should understand what ASCII is. ASCII (pronounced *ASK-key*) is an acronym standing for American Standard Code for Information Interchange. Today the ASCII character set is by far the most commonly used in computers of all types. You may want to compare it to Morse code, which is used by telegraph operators. A telegraph operator can send a signal only by pressing or releasing a key. In a similar way, a computer "recognizes" only two states for a switch: on and off. To a computer, an on switch represents a 1; an off switch represents a 0. By combining 1s and 0s, ASCII and other character sets can represent any data required.

Letters in Modified-Block Style

Goals

- Type at least 38wpm/3′/3e
- Format letters in modified-block style

A. Type 2 times.

A. WARMUP

```
     Mark Kara's quilts down by 25%: #489, #378, and #460.   11
Leave the prices as they are for the remainder of the sizes  23
in that section. Eleven adjoining sections will be next.     34
| 1 | 2 | 3 | 4 | 5 | 6 | 7 | 8 | 9 | 10 | 11 | 12
```

SKILLBUILDING

PRETEST
Take a 1-minute timed writing. Review your speed and errors.

B. PRETEST: Alternate- and One-Hand Words

```
     The chair of the trade committee served notice that     11
the endowment grant exceeded the budget. A million dollars  23
was the exact amount. The greater part might be deferred.   35
| 1 | 2 | 3 | 4 | 5 | 6 | 7 | 8 | 9 | 10 | 11 | 12
```

PRACTICE
Speed Emphasis:
If you made 2 or fewer errors on the Pretest, type each *indivdual* line 2 times.
Accuracy Emphasis:
If you made 3 or more errors, type each *group* of lines (as though it were a paragraph) 2 times.

C. PRACTICE: Alternate-Hand Words

```
amendment turndown visible suspend visual height signs maps
authentic clemency dormant figment island emblem usual snap
shamrocks blandish problem penalty profit thrown chair form
```

D. PRACTICE: One-Hand Words

```
pumpkin eastward plumply barrage greater poplin trade holly
minikin cassette opinion seaweed created kimono union exact
minimum attracts reserve million scatter unhook plump defer
```

POSTTEST
Repeat the Pretest timed writing and compare performance.

E. POSTTEST: Alternate- and One-Hand Words

FOCUS

TIME MANAGEMENT 

Suggested Schedule:

Warmup	2′
Skillbuilding	16′
Formatting	6′
Document Processing	26′
Total	**50′**

TEACH

SKILLBUILDING

PRETEST → PRACTICE → POSTTEST

PPP The Pretest/Practice/Posttest (PPP) routine is designed to build speed and accuracy through a three-step program:

50-B The Pretest is the preliminary effort to determine the learner's initial skill level. Encourage students to push moderately for speed on the Pretest.

50-C and 50-D The Practice section consists of intensive drills to improve the reaches focused on in the Pretest. Alternate-hand words are typed by alternating between the left hand and the right hand. One-hand words are typed either with the left hand or with the right hand.

50-E The Posttest measures the effect of the Practice.

MHHE CHAMPIONS

MINNESOTA

Timed Writings

Mary Hanson
Northwest Technical College
East Grand Forks, Minnesota

Always encourage students to read through a timed writing before beginning to type.

To maximize student performance on timed writings, allow students to choose when to complete their timed writings—after they warm up or later in the class.

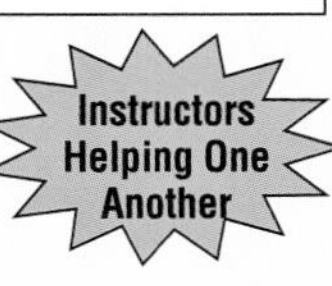

Lesson 50

FORMATTING

LESSON 50-G Discuss the procedures to use to format a letter in modified block style.

Reference Manual

Ask students to review the basic parts of a letter in modified block style in the **Reference Manual, R-3B,** before they begin typing.

Discuss with students which elements begin at the centerpoint. Ask students why they think this letter style is popular. (Perhaps these elements let a reader quickly identify one letter among many.)

F. Take two 3-minute timed writings. Review your speed and errors.

Goal: At least 38wpm/3′/3e

F. 3-MINUTE TIMED WRITING

The Web is a vast source of facts and data on many 10
topics. You can view many newspapers, zip through weather 22
reports, find a tax form and learn how to complete it, and 34
search for a job. You can find answers to health questions 46
and learn about world events almost as soon as they occur. 57
E-mail is another part of the Internet that people are 69
using more often. They use e-mail to keep in touch with 80
friends and family in a quick and efficient way that costs 92
very little. They can write down their thoughts and send 103
messages just as if they were writing a letter or memo. 114

| 1 | 2 | 3 | 4 | 5 | 6 | 7 | 8 | 9 | 10 | 11 | 12

FORMATTING

G. MODIFIED-BLOCK STYLE LETTERS

Modified-block style is a commonly used format for business letters. The date, the complimentary closing, and the writer's identification line(s) are typed at the horizontal centerpoint for each of these lines. Begin the document by first setting a left tab at the centerpoint (usually at 3 inches), and then press TAB 1 time to move to the centerpoint before typing each of these lines. (**Note:** These lines are *not* centered horizontally.)

1. Clear all tabs and set a left tab at the centerpoint (usually at 3 inches).
2. Press ENTER 6 times to begin the letter about 2 inches from the top of the page.
3. Press TAB 1 time to move to the centerpoint, and type the date of the letter.
4. Press ENTER 4 times, and type the inside address at the left margin.
5. Press ENTER 2 times, type the salutation at the left margin, and press ENTER 2 times again.
6. Type the paragraphs blocked at the left margin, and press ENTER 2 times after all paragraphs.
7. After typing the final paragraph, press ENTER 2 times and press TAB 1 time to move to the centerpoint.
8. Type the complimentary closing, and then press ENTER 4 times.
9. Press TAB 1 time to move to the centerpoint, and type the writer's identification. If the writer's identification is to be typed on 2 lines, press TAB 1 time again for any additional line.
10. Press ENTER 2 times, and type the reference initials and remaining letter parts at the left margin.

(Continued on next page)

Technology Tips

EDIT, PASTE SPECIAL

Here are a couple of tips to pass on to students who are frustrated by extra spaces when they have pasted text into Microsoft Word from e-mails or Web pages. Suggest to students that they use one of the following methods to avoid spacing problems.

- Use **Edit, Paste Special** rather than pasting in the standard manner and choose unformatted text. Then the pasted selection can be highlighted and formatted to match the font and font size in the document.
- After text has been pasted in the standard manner, select the text and choose **Format AutoFormat** and click **OK**. The extra spaces should be removed.

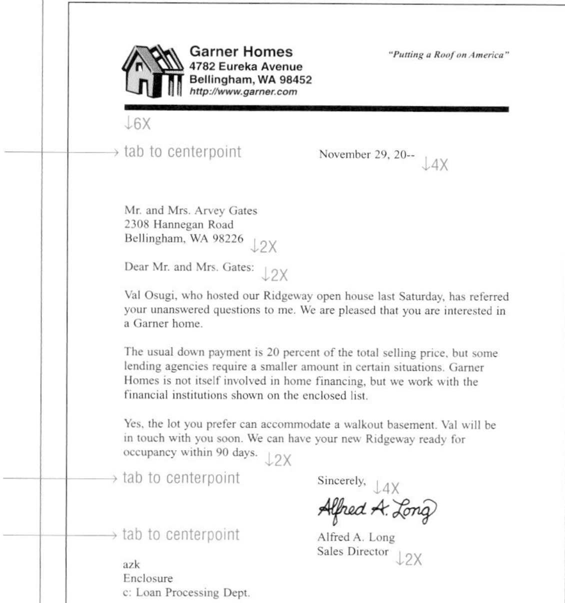
Garner Homes
4782 Eureka Avenue
Bellingham, WA 98452
http://www.garner.com
"Putting a Roof on America"

↓6X
→ tab to centerpoint November 29, 20-- ↓4X

Mr. and Mrs. Arvey Gates
2308 Hannegan Road
Bellingham, WA 98226 ↓2X

Dear Mr. and Mrs. Gates: ↓2X

Val Osugi, who hosted our Ridgeway open house last Saturday, has referred your unanswered questions to me. We are pleased that you are interested in a Garner home.

The usual down payment is 20 percent of the total selling price, but some lending agencies require a smaller amount in certain situations. Garner Homes is not itself involved in home financing, but we work with the financial institutions shown on the enclosed list.

Yes, the lot you prefer can accommodate a walkout basement. Val will be in touch with you soon. We can have your new Ridgeway ready for occupancy within 90 days. ↓2X

→ tab to centerpoint Sincerely, ↓4X

Alfred A. Long

→ tab to centerpoint Alfred A. Long
Sales Director ↓2X

azk
Enclosure
c: Loan Processing Dept.

Word Processing Manual

H. WORD PROCESSING: RULER TABS AND TAB SET

Study Lesson 50 in your word processing manual. Complete all of the shaded steps while at your computer. Then format the jobs that follow.

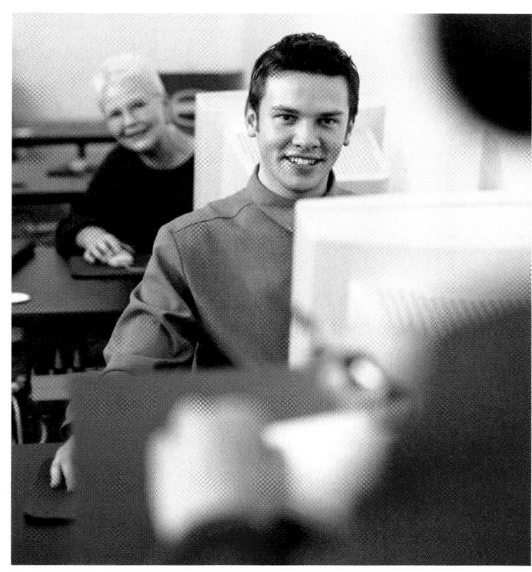

VISUAL INSTRUCTION

Letter in Modified-Block Style. Review the formatting for a letter in modified-block style.

- Margins
- Tab setting
- Date placement
- Spacing before and after each letter part
- Closing lines placement

LESSON 50-H Work closely with students when they learn how to set ruler tabs. Be sure they know the difference between the various tab types: left, center, right, and decimal.

Observe the students while they set tabs, move tabs, and clear tabs as explained in the Word Processing Manual, pp. 106–107. If they make an error, have them use the Undo feature.

Remind students that the insertion point determines where tabs are set. Have them select the paragraph(s) before setting tabs, or set tabs at the beginning of the document.

If students have difficulty seeing the ruler scale settings, tell them to change the Zoom level.

INSTRUCTOR STRATEGIES

Discussing the Photo Network administrators are responsible for managing a company's networking infrastructure. To succeed as a network administrator, a student should gain experience in the major network operating systems, including Novell Netware and Windows 2003 Server.

Information systems (IS) managers are responsible for managing a team of information professionals, including network administrators, software developers, project managers, and other staff. A candidate needs network operating system experience, general operating system experience, relational database knowledge, and staff management abilities.

An early step in either career path is to learn keyboarding.

Lesson 50

DOCUMENT PROCESSING

CORRESPONDENCE 50-32

You may want to conduct speed drills on the opening and closing lines of the letter so that students get accustomed to pressing TAB before typing the date and closing lines.

DOCUMENT PROCESSING

Correspondence 50-32

Business Letter in Modified-Block Style

Reference Manual

Refer to page R-3B of the Reference Manual for additional guidance.

↓6X

→ tab to centerpoint November 29, 20-- ↓4X

Mr. and Mrs. Arvey Gates
2308 Hannegan Road
Bellingham, WA 98226 ↓2X

Dear Mr. and Mrs. Gates: ↓2X

Val Osugi, who hosted our Ridgeway open house last Saturday, has referred your unanswered questions to me. We are pleased that you are interested in a Garner home.

The usual down payment is 20 percent of the total selling price, but some lending agencies require a smaller amount in certain situations. Garner Homes is not itself involved in home financing, but we work with the financial institutions shown on the enclosed list.

Yes, the lot you prefer can accommodate a walkout basement. Val will be in touch with you soon. We can have your new Ridgeway ready for occupancy within 90 days. ↓2X

→ tab to centerpoint Sincerely, ↓4X

Alfred A. Long

→ tab to centerpoint Alfred A. Long
Sales Director ↓2X

urs
Enclosure
c: Loan Processing Dept.

INSTRUCTOR STRATEGIES

Envelopes Ask students to collect envelopes and letters from different businesses and bring them to class. Hold a class discussion about the different formats used by different businesses. Ask students why various sizes of envelopes are used.

GDP SOFTWARE TIPS

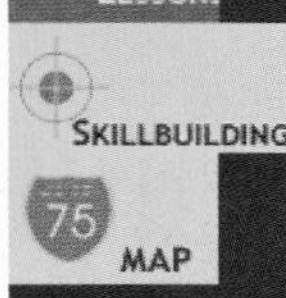

Ruler

Tabs can be set from the menu or the ruler. Settings on the ruler bar are measured from the left margin, not the edge of the page. Therefore, a tab set at the centerpoint is at 3 inches, not 4.25 inches.

Lesson 50

DOCUMENT PROCESSING

Reference Manual

Ask students to review the letter in modified-block style in the **Reference Manual, R-3B,** before they begin typing.

Correspondence 50-33

Business Letter in Modified-Block Style

Use November 30, 20--, as the date as you format this modified-block style letter to be sent to the sales manager at Bachmann's Nursery and Landscaping | 6823 Oneta Avenue | Youngstown, OH 44500-2175

Reference Manual

Refer to page R-12C of the Reference Manual for information on formatting lists and an illustration.

Dear Sales Manager:

¶ As you requested on the telephone, I am providing the following list of events relating to my tree problem.

1. On April 15, I purchased at your branch in Warren four silver maples for the atrium outside our Riverdale office. We also purchased four Japanese red maples at your branch in Niles later that afternoon.
2. After about six months, one silver maple and one red maple had died. I phoned both the Warren and Niles branches several times on November 1, but no one returned my messages.
3. On November 8, I phoned your nursery in an attempt to have these trees replaced. Again, there was no response.

¶ As these trees were expensive, I expect that you will either replace them or reimburse me for the cost of the trees. I shall look forward to hearing from you.

Sincerely, | Marvin L. Norgaard | Grounds Manager | urs

Correspondence 50-34

Business Letter in Modified-Block Style

December 10, 20-- | Mr. Marvin L. Norgaard | 4782 Saranac Avenue | Youngstown, OH 44505-6207 | Dear Mr. Norgaard:

¶ This is in response to your recent letter.

¶ Your trees will be replaced without cost to you. We will make sure that the replacement trees will match the others you purchased in both size and color. I am enclosing a warranty for these new trees so that you can feel confident that we stand behind our product.

¶ The survival rate for trees cannot be perfect; however, we are indeed sorry that you have had to have this temporary setback.

¶ The communication breakdown with our two branch offices should not have occurred. We will take steps to ensure that this will not happen in the future. You can be confident that the appearance of your atrium will be restored and that the beauty of the new trees will add to your property's value. Thank you for shopping at Bachmann's.

Sincerely, | Mrs. Alice G. Schmidt | Co-owner | urs | Enclosure | c: Mr. Raul Cornejo, Co-owner

CORRESPONDENCE 50-33

Remind students to type the text for the numbered list before applying the numbered list format.

CORRESPONDENCE 50-34

Remind students to verify the correct placement of the enclosure and copy notations.

Remind students to spell-check, proofread, and preview their documents before printing them.

INSTRUCTOR STRATEGIES

Effective Response? Students may want to discuss the effectiveness of Correspondence 50-34. What complaints are being addressed? (Dead trees and lack of response to the earlier complaints.) Do students think Correspondence 50-34 will satisfy Mr. Norgaard? How will an error-free letter affect the reader's response?

Technology Tips

MOUSE CARE

Following the manufacturer's instructions, show students the proper procedure for cleaning a mouse. Explain that the mouse must be kept clean so that it will move the insertion point smoothly.

MHHE CHAMPIONS

OHIO

Correctly formatting a letter is a true mark of a good education. It is worthwhile to adhere to long-standing standards and conventions when preparing business correspondence.

Contributor wishes to remain anonymous.

Lesson 50

DOCUMENT PROCESSING

Progress Check/ Proofreading Check

CORRESPONDENCE 50-35

Many formatting features presented in this unit are included in this document. You may want to use this exercise as a short document processing test.

In addition, you may want to inform students that this document also serves as a check of their proofreading skill and that they may have only *one* opportunity to have the GDP software check the document in order for them to receive a satisfactory proofreading grade.

ASSESS

www.mhhe.com/gdp to download a copy of the Technique Evaluation Form.

TECHNIQUE EVALUATION FORM

Review results of timed writings.

Print a report for all skillbuilding exercises for Lessons 46–50.

Review the format of Correspondence 50-33.

Extending the Lesson

Ask students if they have tried to align text in a document using just the SPACE BAR. Did they get the desired results? Point out the difference between nonproportional fonts, such as Courier, and proportional fonts, such as Times Roman, in accomplishing alignment by the SPACE BAR.

CLOSE

Remind students that it is more efficient to set a tab than to press TAB repeatedly.

Correspondence 50-35

Personal-Business Letter in Modified-Block Style

Progress and Proofreading Check

Documents designated as Proofreading Checks serve as a check of your proofreading skill. Your goal is to have zero typographical errors when the GDP software first scores the document.

March 11, 20-- | Ms. Karen Shalicky | Lincoln Travel Center | 2384 Longdale Avenue | Suite 4113 | Boston, MA 02134-3489 | Dear Ms. Shalicky:

¶ I am interested in taking a cruise in one of the following regions:

- Alaska Inland Passageway
- Caribbean Islands
- Greek Isles

¶ Could you please send me some promotional materials for these cruises? My financial resources are such that I would like to limit my cruise package to $5,000 and would prefer a cruise no longer than ten days in length. I will be accompanied by my friend Bonnie Davis, and I assume that any quotes you give me could apply to both of us.

¶ We would like to do sightseeing in some of these locations. Do you have special excursions available to passengers? I am enclosing a list of the sites we would like to visit in each of these regions.

¶ The best time for us to travel is between June 1 and June 20, and we would like you to schedule our trip around those dates. I hope to hear from you soon.

Yours truly, | Rita Wright | 678 Ardale Avenue | Milton, MA 02186-2190 | Enclosure | c: Bonnie Davis

Keyboarding Connection

Avoid E-Mail Flame Wars

Don't fan the flames! A flame is an offensive e-mail that expresses anger, criticism, or insults. If flames are transmitted to a mailing list, they can produce a long list of flames and counter flames known as flame wars.

You may be tempted to join in, but this is a waste of everyone's time. Often the initial offense was merely a poorly worded e-mail that a reader interpreted as an insult. There are those who intentionally send inflammatory e-mails called flame bait. Resist the urge to send a cutting response, and consider whether the writer's intent was to provoke you.

If your reader misjudges something you wrote and becomes offended, just apologize. A timely apology can thwart a potential fire. Avoid miscommunication by watching how you word your e-mails.

YOUR TURN Have you ever been insulted by an e-mail? What was your response?

Keyboarding Connection

E-Mail Flame Wars

Discuss e-mail flame wars and ask if students have been involved in this type of communication. Discuss words or phrases that might be considered offensive and how they can be changed to avoid flaming. Encourage students to save their response to an e-mail about a sensitive topic as a draft and review the response again before sending it.

YOUR TURN If time permits, ask students to complete the Your Turn activity.

Employment Documents

LESSON 51
Traditional Resumes

LESSON 52
Electronic Resumes

LESSON 53
Letters of Application

LESSON 54
Follow-Up Letters

LESSON 55
Integrated Employment Project

PATSY R. ROTHEL

2525 Hickory Ridge Drive, Plant City, FL 33567
Phone: 813-555-0704; e-mail: prothel@netmail.com

OBJECTIVE To continue my career in computer graphics by securing a position related to graphic design.

EDUCATION Central Florida Business College, Valrico, Florida
Two years of related courses in graphic design

Plant City High School, Plant C
Graduated: May 2005

EXPERIENCE *Graphic Designer, NetView, Inc*
Orlando, Florida
October 2004–Present
Designed Web pages for
central Florida. Edited p
database for Web-based

Copy Editor, The Plant City Pre
Plant City, Florida
May 2000–September 2004
Assisted the news editor
editing copy for daily ne
from local businesses. C
the Week forum.

ACTIVITIES
- Spanish Honor Society, 2001
- Member, Phi Beta Lambda, 2
- Newsletter Editor, *CFBC Ne*
- President, FBLA Chapter, 19
- Treasurer, FBLA Chapter, 19

REFERENCES References available upon reque

August 10, 20--

Personnel Director
Arlington Communications
2403 Sunset Lane
Arlington, TX 76015-3148

Dear Personnel Director:

Please consider me as an applicant for a position with Arlington Communications. My strengths have always been in the communication arts, as you can see on the enclosed resume, which lists a number of courses in English, speech, and communication technology. The two part-time jobs I held during the summer months at your company convinced me that Arlington Communications is the place where I want to work.

If you would like to interview me for any possible openings this summer or fall, please
d to hearing from you.

April 7, 20--

Ms. Kay Brewer, Personnel Director
Blanchard Computer Systems
2189 Dace Avenue
Sioux City, IA 51107

Dear Ms. Brewer:

Thank you for the opportunity of interviewing yesterday with Blanchard Computer Systems. Please express my appreciation to all of those who were involved.

The interview gave me a good feeling about the company. The positive description that you shared with me convinced me that Blanchard is indeed a company at which I would like to work. I was greatly impressed with the summary of social service programs that are sponsored by Blanchard for citizens throughout the community.

You may recall that I have had experience with all of the equipment that is used. It appears to me that my strengths in computer application software and office systems would blend in well with your company profile.

I look forward to hearing from you soon regarding your decision on the position of data records operator.

Sincerely,

Arlene F. Jefferson
1842 Amber Road
Wayne, NE 68787

Unit 11

UNIT OVERVIEW

Students will be introduced to employment documents including traditional and electronic resumes, letters of application, and follow-up letters. The last lesson in the unit includes an integrated employment project. The following Microsoft Word features will be presented: fonts, saving in text-only format, and changing column width.

Did You Know?

Employment forms or other forms with lines should be completed using a typewriter that has a variable line spacer. It is very difficult to align forms on the computer.

www.mhhe.com/gdp to download a copy of the Technique Evaluation Form.

Name Class Date

Technique Evaluation Form

Date	Workstation		Position at the Keyboard		Keystroking	
	Acceptable	Needs Improvement	Acceptable	Needs Improvement	Acceptable	Needs Improvement

Workstation
1. Positions the chair so that the upper and lower legs form a 90-degree angle and the lower back is supported.
2. Positions the keyboard even with the front of the desk.
3. Positions the text on either side of the monitor as close to it vertically and horizontally as possible to minimize head and eye movement and to avoid neck strain.
4. Positions the mouse on a pad at the side of the monitor opposite the text.

Position at the Keyboard
5. Centers the body opposite the keyboard.
6. Leans forward slightly from the hips, with the base of the spine touching the back of the chair and the feet flat on the floor.
7. Keeps the elbows alongside the body in a relaxed position.
8. Curves the fingers naturally over the home position, with the back of the hand at the same angle as the keyboard.

Keystroking
9. Keeps the forearms horizontal and raises the hands slightly when typing so that the wrists do not touch the keyboard while typing. (Hands may rest at the bottom of the keyboard—away from the keys—during nontyping intervals.)
10. Makes quick, snappy strokes using the correct fingers.
11. Returns the finger immediately to the home position or moves to the next position after each stroke.
12. Operates all keys by touch, keeping the eyes on the copy most of the time while typing.

Comments

Use this form to keep track of student progress. Complete a form for each student.

RESOURCE MANAGER

GDP SOFTWARE
- Lessons 51–55
- Software User's Guide
- Instructor Management LAN Version
- Word Processing Manual
- Professional Handbook (IWE*)—Teaching Strategies; Teaching in a Distance-Learning Environment
- MAP 

*Instructor Wraparound Edition

ASSESSMENT
- Test Booklet—Alternate Test 3
- Progress Check—Correspondence 55-44 
- Professional Handbook (IWE*)—Assessment Strategies 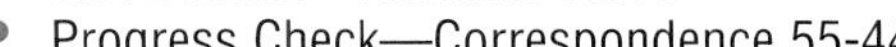

ON THE WEB
- **www.mhhe.com/gdp**
- Instructor Management Web Version

FOCUS

TIME MANAGEMENT 

Suggested Schedule:

Warmup	2′
Skillbuilding	15′
Language Arts	6′
Formatting	6′
Document Processing	21′
Total	**50′**

TEACH

SKILLBUILDING

LESSON 51-B  **MAP** Remind students that unless their straight-copy keyboarding skills are top quality, they will never even get an opportunity to demonstrate to potential employers their high-level word processing or desktop publishing skills. This is because nearly three-fourths of employers still require all entry-level clerical workers to pass a straight-copy timed writing for employment. MAP builds these high-level keyboarding skills.

LESSON 51-C Each paragraph is more difficult than the preceding one—based on the number of capital letters.

Paragraph 1: 2
Paragraph 2: 6
Paragraph 3: 9
Paragraph 4: 12

Lesson 51

Traditional Resumes

Goals

- Improve speed and accuracy
- Refine language arts skills in the use of commas
- Format traditional resumes

A. Type 2 times.

A. WARMUP

```
     Janice had sales of over $23,000; Kathy's sales were    11
only $17,368 for the same quiet period. Craig agreed that    22
some inventory sizes were wrong and should be exchanged.     34
|  1  |  2  |  3  |  4  |  5  |  6  |  7  |  8  |  9  |  10  |  11  |  12
```

SKILLBUILDING

B. MAP

Follow the GDP software directions for this exercise in improving keystroking accuracy.

C. Take a 1-minute timed writing on the first paragraph to establish your base speed. Then take four 1-minute timed writings on the remaining paragraphs. As soon as you equal or exceed your base speed on one paragraph, advance to the next, more difficult paragraph.

C. SUSTAINED PRACTICE: CAPITALIZATION

```
     There are several different approaches that one can      11
take when considering a major purchase. Some people make      22
the mistake of simply going to a store and making a choice.   34

     When one couple decided to buy a chest-type freezer,     11
they looked at a consumer magazine in the library. The        22
Sears, Amana, and General Electric were shown as best buys.   34

     That same issue of their magazine compared electric      11
ranges. Jonathan and Mary Anne found that the Maytag, Magic   23
Chef, Amana, and Gibson were determined to be best buys.      34

     Best buys for full-size microwave ovens were the Sharp   11
Carousel, Panasonic, and GoldStar Multiwave. Good midsize     23
models were the Frigidaire, Panasonic, and Sears Kenmore.     34
|  1  |  2  |  3  |  4  |  5  |  6  |  7  |  8  |  9  |  10  |  11  |  12
```


Technology *Tips*

RESUME TIPS

Encourage students to search the Internet for Web sites that offer tips on resume writing. Allow some class time for students to share the tips.

If you would like your class to learn about resume templates at this point, take them to the Microsoft site at **http://officeupdate.microsoft.com/templates.** Templates are taught in Lesson 101 and Lesson 102.

LANGUAGE ARTS

D. Study the rules at the right.

D. COMMAS

RULE ▶ , date

Use a comma before and after the year in a complete date.

We will arrive on June 2, 2005, for the conference.

But: We will arrive on June 2 for the conference.

But: Work should be submitted between November 2005 and December 2005.

RULE ▶ , place

Use a comma before and after a state or country that follows a city (but not before a ZIP Code).

Joan moved to Vancouver, British Columbia, in May.

Send the package to Douglasville, GA 30135, by Express Mail.

But: Send the package to Georgia by Express Mail

Edit the sentences to correct any errors in the use of commas.

```
16 The warehouse building will be ready in September, 2004.
17 The attorney told a clerk to use June 30, 2005 as the date.
18 The books were sent to Los Angeles, CA, 90029 on July 13, 2005
   and will arrive soon.
19 The move to Toledo, Ohio, was scheduled for November, 2004.
```

FORMATTING

E. TRADITIONAL RESUMES

When you apply for a job, you may be asked to submit a resume. The purpose of a resume is to convey your qualifications for the position you are seeking. A resume should include the following:

- Personal information (name, address, telephone number, and e-mail address).
- Your career objective (optional).
- A summary of your educational background and special training.
- Previous work experience.
- Any activities or personal achievements that relate to the position for which you are applying.
- References (optional). If an employer requests references, you should have at least three people who can tell a prospective employer what kind of worker you are.

Often, your resume creates the first impression you make on a prospective employer; be sure it is free of errors.

Various styles are acceptable for formatting a resume. Choose a style (or design one) that is attractive and that enables you to get all the needed information on one or two pages. The first page of a resume should start about 2 inches from the top of the page.

To format a traditional resume:

1. Press ENTER 6 times.
2. Insert an open table with 2 columns and 1 row for each section of the resume. **Note:** In the example that follows, you would use 6 rows.
3. Merge the cells in Row 1.
4. Change to center alignment.
5. Type your name in all caps in Arial Bold 14 pt. in Row 1, and press ENTER 2 times.
6. Change to Arial Bold 12 pt; then type your street address followed by a comma and 1 space; type your city followed by a comma and 1 space; then type your state followed by 1 space and your ZIP Code; press ENTER 1 time.

(Continued on next page)

EXTENDING LANGUAGE ARTS

Comma, Date Point out that the year is set off with commas when there is a complete date. Examples: Helene signed the first contract on May 12, 2004. Helene signed the first contract in May 2004.

Comma, Place Explain that when a state or a country follows a city, the state or country is set off with commas. Examples: He traveled to Minneapolis, Minnesota, in the summer. He traveled to Minnesota in the summer.

Lesson 51

LANGUAGE ARTS

LESSON 51-D If students are not using the GDP software, have them type a correct version of the sentences.

SOLUTION: Lines 16–19

16. September 2004
17. 2005,
18. Japan,
19. November 2004

FORMATTING

LESSON 51-E To begin class discussion, ask how many students have a current resume they can use when applying for a job. Ask those who have resumes to comment on the procedure they followed to prepare them.

Some students may be familiar with the practice of submitting resumes online. Formats for electronic resumes will be discussed in the next lesson.

Allow about 5 minutes for students to note personal information they would include on their resumes, using the list shown in the text.

Display a variety of resume styles.

Emphasize to students that they must obtain permission from the people they want to use as references.

INSTRUCTOR STRATEGIES

Resume Point out that *resume*, a verb meaning "to begin again after a pause," is pronounced (re ZOOM). *Resume*, a noun meaning "a description of one's work and education history," is pronounced (reh ZOO may). Sometimes it is written *résumé*.

Lesson 51

FORMATTING

VISUAL INSTRUCTION

Traditional Resume. Review the formatting for a traditional resume:

- Format and placement of personal information
- Margins
- Table format
- Heading format

Refer to Reference Manual

Ask students to review the basic parts of a traditional resume in the **Reference Manual, R-12A,** before they begin typing.

LESSON 51-F Show samples of serif and sans serif fonts. Help students identify each type of font.

Have students experiment with both kinds of fonts in various kinds of documents. Which fonts do students prefer for which uses? Which do they see most often?

7. Type `Phone:` followed by 1 space; then type your area code and phone number followed by a semicolon and 1 space.
8. Type `e-mail:` followed by 1 space and your e-mail address.
9. Press ENTER 1 time.
10. Apply a bottom border to Row 1.
11. Move to Row 2, Column A; and press ENTER 1 time.
12. Type the entry in Column A in all caps and bold in Times New Roman 12 pt., and press TAB to move to Column B.
13. Press ENTER 1 time, and type the information related to the Column A heading in Column B.
14. Press ENTER as needed in each section to insert 1 blank line between sections. **Note:** Type job titles and business names in italics.
15. Continue typing all entries until you are finished. **Note:** For any job descriptions, increase the indent to reposition the information. For any lists, decrease the indent until the list is positioned at the left of the column.
16. Decrease the width of Column A to about 1.25 inch to accommodate the longest entry and provide a small amount of space after the longest entry.

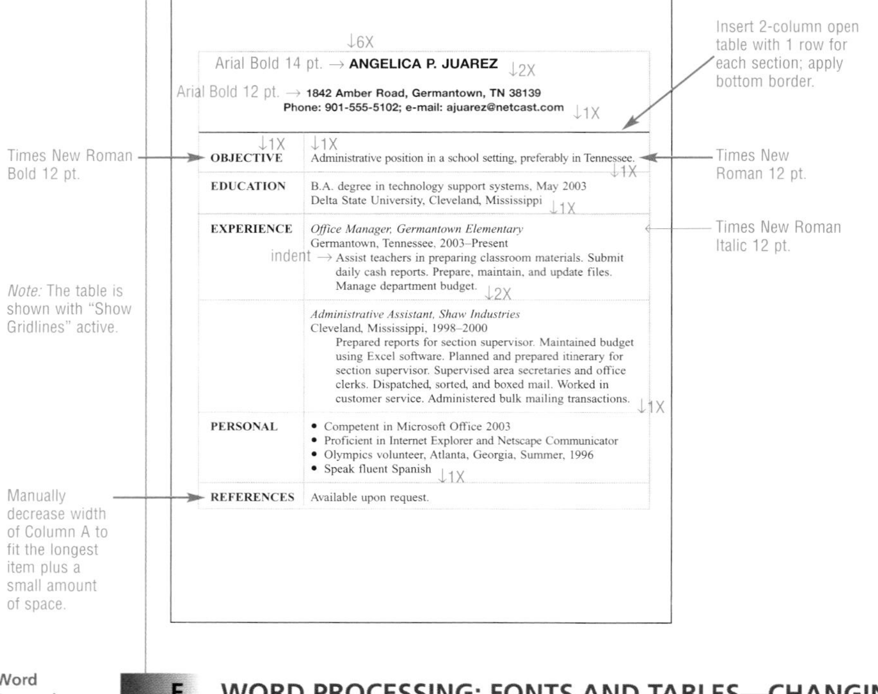

ANGELICA P. JUAREZ

1842 Amber Road, Germantown, TN 38139
Phone: 901-555-5102; e-mail: ajuarez@netcast.com

OBJECTIVE	Administrative position in a school setting, preferably in Tennessee.
EDUCATION	B.A. degree in technology support systems, May 2003 Delta State University, Cleveland, Mississippi
EXPERIENCE	*Office Manager, Germantown Elementary* Germantown, Tennessee, 2003–Present Assist teachers in preparing classroom materials. Submit daily cash reports. Prepare, maintain, and update files. Manage department budget.
	Administrative Assistant, Shaw Industries Cleveland, Mississippi, 1998–2000 Prepared reports for section supervisor. Maintained budget using Excel software. Planned and prepared itinerary for section supervisor. Supervised area secretaries and office clerks. Dispatched, sorted, and boxed mail. Worked in customer service. Administered bulk mailing transactions.
PERSONAL	• Competent in Microsoft Office 2003 • Proficient in Internet Explorer and Netscape Communicator • Olympics volunteer, Atlanta, Georgia, Summer, 1996 • Speak fluent Spanish
REFERENCES	Available upon request.

Go To Word Processing Manual

F. WORD PROCESSING: FONTS AND TABLES—CHANGING COLUMN WIDTH

Study Lesson 51 in your word processing manual. Complete all of the shaded steps while at your computer. Then format the jobs that follow.

Windows Wizard

TASKBAR CLOCK The time display in the Taskbar is very important because every time you save or modify a file, the exact date and time become a part of the file information. To adjust the clock in Windows 2000, Me, and XP:

- Double-click the time display in the Taskbar to open the **Date/Time Properties** dialog box.
- Click the **Date & Time** tab to adjust the month, year, day, and time settings.
- Click the **Time Zone** tab to select a time zone.
- Click **OK** to close the dialog box.

DOCUMENT PROCESSING

Report 51-27

Resume in Traditional Style

Times New Roman Bold 12 pt.

Note: The table is shown with "Show Gridlines" active.

Manually decrease width of Column A to fit longest item.

↓6X

Arial Bold 14 pt. → **PATSY R. ROTHEL** ↓2X

Insert 2-column open table with 1 row for each section; apply top border.

Arial Bold 12 pt. → **2525 Hickory Ridge Drive, Plant City, FL 33567**
Phone: 813-555-0704; e-mail: prothel@netmail.com ↓1X

↓1X **OBJECTIVE**	↓1X To continue my career in computer graphics by securing a position related to graphic design. ↓1X (Times New Roman 12 pt.)
EDUCATION	Central Florida Business College, Valrico, Florida A.A. degree in graphics design Graduated: May 2005 ↓2X Plant City High School, Plant City, Florida Graduated: May 2003 ↓1X
EXPERIENCE	*Graphic Designer, NetView, Inc.* ← Times New Roman Italic 12 pt. Orlando, Florida October 2005–Present indent → Designed Web pages for Internet-connected companies in central Florida. Edited page copy for Web sites. Created a database for Web-based users. ↓2X *Copy Editor, The Plant City Press* Plant City, Florida May 2003–September 2005 Assisted the news editor with typing, proofreading, and editing copy for daily newspaper. Solicited subscriptions from local businesses. Conducted interviews for Citizens of the Week forum. ↓1X
ACTIVITIES	• Member, Phi Beta Lambda, 2004–2005 • Newsletter Editor, *CFBC News*, 2004 • President, FBLA Chapter, 2002 • Treasurer, FBLA Chapter, 2001 ↓1X
REFERENCES	References available upon request.

Lesson 51

DOCUMENT PROCESSING

REPORT 51-27 The resume heading information (name, address, phone, and e-mail address) is always in bold.

Before students begin typing this document, point out the font and spacing requirements that are suggested by the callouts.

Work with the students to be sure they know how to create the table border between the heading and the body of the resume.

Remind students that they must adjust the width of the left column to accommodate the section headings.

Be sure that students type all sections in the resume using individual table rows. Students should add hard returns as needed to obtain the necessary vertical spacing in Column B.

Remind students that they can use either bullets or indentions to highlight various sections of their resumes.

INSTRUCTOR STRATEGIES

Pinpointing an Objective If possible, invite a placement specialist or other employment professional to visit the class to speak briefly about fine-tuning one's objective. How should a resume objective be phrased? What do employers look for in the objective?

Lesson 51

DOCUMENT PROCESSING

REPORT 51-28

Reference Manual

Remind students to use the **Reference Manual, R-12A,** for correct resume formatting.

ASSESS

The Web

www.mhhe.com/gdp to download a copy of the Technique Evaluation Form.

TECHNIQUE EVALUATION FORM

Walk around the room to observe the students' technique.

Review the formatting for Report 51-27.

Extending the Lesson

Show samples of resume formats and provide handouts of the various formats. Discuss why a particular format gives a positive or negative first impression.

Encourage students to keep a record of employment dates, descriptions of job responsibilities, and other information they will use to create a resume. Have them consider individuals who might act as their references.

CLOSE

Have the class brainstorm a perfect resume as you write their ideas on the board. Include previous employment positions, advanced degrees, volunteer work, and a list of references who are celebrities in their fields. As you write to their dictation, make occasional formatting mistakes for them to correct.

Report 51-28

Resume in Traditional Style

Open the file for Report 51-27 and make the following changes:

1. Change the name to `JOYCE K. LEE`.
2. Change the address to `10234 Wood Sorrell Lane, Burke, VA 22015`.
3. Change the phone number to `703-555-4902` and the e-mail address to `jklee@netlink.net`.
4. Replace the OBJECTIVE entry with the following:
   `To gain experience in retail sales as a foundation for a retail management position.`
5. Replace both of the EDUCATION entries with the following:
   `Central High School, Burke, Virginia | Graduated: May 2003.`
6. Change the first EXPERIENCE entry to the following:
   Computer Systems Technician, Kramer & Kramer, Inc. | Harrisburg, Virginia | June 2004-Present | Duties include reviewing, installing, and updating software programs used for processing legal documents.
7. Change the second EXPERIENCE entry to the following:
   Salesclerk, Blanchard's Department Store | Richmond, Virginia | May 2002-May 2004 (part-time) | Duties included selling sporting goods and operating Panasonic cash register. Assisted sales manager in completing monthly sales reports.
8. Change the entries for ACTIVITIES to the following:
   `Volunteer for Habitat for Humanity, 2000-Present | Member, Computer Technicians Association, 2000-Present | Senior Class President, 2002-2003 | Member, Intramural Soccer Team, 2001-2003 | Member, Beta Club, 2001-2003.`

Strategies for Career Success

Formatting Your Resume

The format of your resume communicates important skills—neatness and the ability to organize. Make a good first impression by following these guidelines.

Watch the spacing on your resume. A crowded resume implies that you cannot summarize. Leave adequate white space between the section headings of your resume. Use different font sizes, boldface, and italics to separate and emphasize information. Font sizes should be between 10 and 14.

Print your resume on good-quality 8½" × 11" white or off-white bond paper (for example, 20-pound stock). Colored paper doesn't provide enough contrast when your resume is copied or faxed.

Proofread your resume for spelling errors and consistency of format. Ask a few friends to review it and provide feedback.

YOUR TURN Print one copy of your resume on a dark-colored paper and print one copy on white paper. Photocopy each resume. Which provides the better contrast for readability?

Strategies for Career Success

RESUME FORMATTING Discuss with students the importance of creating a professional-looking resume. Ask students if they have a current resume. Stress the importance of this concept—first impressions do count on resumes. Encourage students to visit **www.mhhe.com/gdp.**

YOUR TURN If time permits, ask students to complete the Your Turn activity.

Electronic Resumes

Goals
- Type at least 39wpm/5′/5e
- Format an electronic resume

A. Type 2 times.

A. WARMUP

```
     The new firm, Kulver & Zweidel, will be equipped to    11
handle from 1/6 to 1/4 of Martin's tax needs after they     22
move to the new location at 1970 Gansby, just east of Main. 34
| 1 | 2 | 3 | 4 | 5 | 6 | 7 | 8 | 9 | 10 | 11 | 12
```

SKILLBUILDING

B. Take three 12-second timed writings on each line. The scale below the last line shows your wpm speed for a 12-second timed writing.

B. 12-SECOND SPEED SPRINTS

```
Pat went back to the store where she had seen the red book.
The good girl was sure that she had not seen that old door.
There was a huge change when he walked into the same class.
Pat was met at the door with one red rose and a giant cake.
5 | 10 | 15 | 20 | 25 | 30 | 35 | 40 | 45 | 50 | 55 | 60
```

C. PROGRESSIVE PRACTICE: ALPHABET

If you are not using the GDP software, turn to page SB-7 and follow the directions for this activity.

Lesson 52

FOCUS

TIME MANAGEMENT 

Suggested Schedule:

Warmup	2′
Skillbuilding	22′
Formatting	6′
Document Processing	20′
Total	**50′**

TEACH

SKILLBUILDING

LESSON 52-B Remind students to type at a fast pace during the 12-second timed writing. At the end of the first and second timed writings, encourage students to type just one or two strokes faster on the next timed writing.

LESSON 52-C Students take repeated timed writings on a passage containing the exact number of words for their speed goal until they can complete the passage with no errors. Then they move to the next longer passage and start again.

INSTRUCTOR STRATEGIES

Discussing the Photo

Present students with one example of software that makes global business possible: enterprise software. Enterprise applications often meet the needs of many users at the same time, sometimes over a wide area. It is possible for two users with the same software to access the same data source and perform the same tasks, even if they are on opposite sides of town—or opposite sides of the world. For instance, during a construction project, a site supervisor can print out the blueprint of a new structure while an engineer in another office uses the same software to prepare the list of materials needed and a purchasing agent back at headquarters tracks inventory as it is consumed.

Lesson 52

SKILLBUILDING

LESSON 52-D This is the first 5-minute timed writing for the students. Remind them that they will be typing for 2 additional minutes and that they are allowed a total of 5 errors on a 5-minute timed writing.

FORMATTING

LESSON 52-E Take time to compare the differences between a traditional resume and an electronic resume.

Emphasize that no special font or graphic features should be used in an electronic resume; explain why these characters and images will not be transmitted accurately.

Point out that special symbols should not be used to highlight selected sections in an electronic resume.

D. Take two 5-minute timed writings. Review your speed and errors.

Goal: At least 39wpm/5′/5e

D. 5-MINUTE TIMED WRITING

```
     Have you completed your education when your graduate   11
from high school or finish your college work? Most people   22
look forward to reaching milestones, such as graduation or  34
completing a course. Have they learned everything they will 46
need to know to be successful in the real world? The answer 58
is not so simple.                                           62
     Learning continues to occur long after you leave the   72
classroom. No matter what job or career you pursue, you     84
will learn something new every day. When you investigate    95
new ideas, ask questions, or find a different way to do a  107
job, you are continuing to learn. In the process, you gain 118
additional experience, develop new skills, and become a    130
better worker.                                             133
     Getting along with your peers, for example, is not    143
something that you learn from studying books. You learn to 155
be a team player when you listen to your coworkers and     166
share your ideas with them. Do not hesitate to acquire new 178
skills or to initiate new ideas. Be zealous in your efforts 190
to continue your education.                                195
| 1 | 2 | 3 | 4 | 5 | 6 | 7 | 8 | 9 | 10 | 11 | 12
```

FORMATTING

E. ELECTRONIC RESUMES

An electronic resume is a resume that has been formatted for display on the Internet and for electronic transmission via e-mail. Format an electronic resume as follows:

1. Use a monospaced font like Courier New, and use the default font size.
2. Use left alignment.
3. Use a line length of 60 characters maximum.
4. Do not hyphenate words at the end of a line.
5. Do not press TAB to indent lines. Instead, space 5 times.
6. If any lines wrap to a second line, press ENTER immediately after the last word of the first line, space 5 times if the turnover line should be indented, and continue typing the lines in this way until all lines for a section are completed.
7. Do not use any special formatting features (bold, italic, or underline) or graphic features (rules, bullets, pictures, boxes, tables, or columns).
8. Use all-caps as a substitute for bold or underline.
9. To create a bulleted list, space 5 times, and type an asterisk; space 1 time and type the line. On the wraparound line, space 7 times and continue typing in this way until all lines for the bulleted list are completed.
10. Save the resume as a text-only file (one that has a .txt extension).

GDP SOFTWARE TIPS

3-Minute Timed Writings or 5-Minute Timed Writings

This lesson presents the first 5-minute timed writing. If the class would benefit from continuing to take 3-minute timed writings, that option is available.

A dialog box will allow the students to select the time limit for the timed writing when the exercise is accessed from the **Lesson** menu.

Go To Word Processing Manual

F. WORD PROCESSING: SAVING IN TEXT-ONLY FORMAT

Study Lesson 52 in your word processing manual. Complete all of the shaded steps while at your computer. Then format the jobs that follow.

DOCUMENT PROCESSING

Report 52-29

Resume in Electronic Style

Type the electronic resume as shown in the illustration below according to these guidelines:

- Change to 12 pt. Courier New.
- Press the SPACE BAR 5 times to indent lines.
- Press the SPACE BAR 5 times, type an asterisk, and type a space, as shown, to create a bulleted list.
- If any lines wrap to a second line, press ENTER immediately after the last word of the first line, space 5 times if the turnover line should be indented or 7 times if the turnover line is part of a bulleted list, and continue typing the lines in this way until all lines for a section are completed.
- Save the resume as a text-only file.

```
BRENDA COTTON ↓2X

→ 5 spaces  1611 Amherst Way
     Emporia, KS 66801
     Phone: 316-555-1384
     E-mail: bcotton@plains.net
     Home page: http://www.esc.org/staff/cotton.htm ↓2X

OBJECTIVE

→ 5 spaces  Staff-level accounting position in an educational ↓1X
→ 5 spaces  institution or public accounting firm.

EDUCATION

→ 5 spaces, *, 1 space  * B.B.A. degree in accounting from Emporia State ↓1X
→ 7 spaces  University, Emporia, Kansas, May 2004 ↓2X

     * High school diploma from Central High School,
       Wichita, Kansas, June 2000

EXPERIENCE

     * STAFF ACCOUNTANT, Gateway Properties
       Emporia, Kansas
       December 2003-Present
       Responsible for budget control. Prepare variance
       report and annual business plan. Generate fixed-
       asset inventory. Prepare consolidated monthly
       financials.

     * ACCOUNTS RECEIVABLE CLERK, Aris Corporation
       Salina, Kansas
       January 2002-December 2003
       Posted cash receipts, prepared bank deposits, and
       processed tax requests.

PERSONAL

     *  Proficient in Microsoft Office desktop tools
     *  Member of AICPA
     *  Graduated summa cum laude from Emporia State

REFERENCES

     Available upon request.
```


INSTRUCTOR STRATEGIES

Scanning a Resume Students might benefit from experimenting. Have a volunteer open a dummy account with an online agency such as **hotjobs.com** and cut and paste an existing resume into the (html-only) format. Print out the resume for the class to examine the corrupted resume. Be sure the volunteer closes the dummy account.

FORMATTING

VISUAL INSTRUCTION

Electronic Resumes. Review the formatting for an electronic resume:

- No tabs
- No bold, italics, or underlining
- No boxes, bullets, tables, or columns
- No pictures
- No end-of-line hyphenation
- Only left alignment
- Only 12-point Courier New font
- Maximum 60-character line length
- Save as text-only file

DOCUMENT PROCESSING

REPORT 52-29 Demonstrate how students can use the SPACE BAR to create the effect of a tab in an electronic resume. Remind them to use a nonproportional font, such as Courier New.

Remind students that an electronic resume should be saved as a text file (.txt) so that it will be transmitted accurately to the World Wide Web or as an e-mail attachment.

Remind students that they must monitor the alignment and special effects they use in the sections as they type. Because they may be using asterisks, all-caps, and the SPACE BAR to help them achieve the desired effect, students must be diligent in proofreading electronic resumes.

Lesson 52

DOCUMENT PROCESSING

REPORT 52-30

Answer any questions students may have about typing an electronic resume.

Remind students that, if they are typing a two-page resume, they need to consider where the page break will occur. If possible, make the page break after a major section in the resume.

Remind students to save the document as a text file.

ASSESS

www.mhhe.com/gdp to download a copy of the Technique Evaluation Form.

TECHNIQUE EVALUATION FORM

Review results of timed writings.

Review the formatting of Report 52-29.

Extending the Lesson

Ask students if they have used the Internet to locate a job. Did they submit an electronic resume?

CLOSE

Have students experiment with a Web site such as **hotjobs.com** or **monster.com**.

Report 52-30

Resume in Electronic Style

Type an electronic resume in correct format for ALLEN P. HUNTER, 10234 Wood Sorrell Lane, Burke, VA 22015; Phone: 703-555-4902; E-mail, aphunter@netlink.net.

1. Type this OBJECTIVE entry: Retail management entry-level position with a midsize | department store.
2. Type these two EDUCATION entries as a bulleted list:
   * Central Virginia Business College, Burke, Virginia, | December 2004
   * High school diploma from Central High School, Burke, | Virginia, May 2002
3. Type these EXPERIENCE entries as a bulleted list:
   * COMPUTER SYSTEMS TECHNICIAN, Kramer & Kramer, Inc. | Harrisburg, Virginia | June 1999-Present | Duties include reviewing, installing, and updating | software programs used for processing legal | documents and monitoring computer network system for | branch offices.
   * SALESCLERK, Blanchard's Department Store | Richmond, Virginia | May 2000-May 2002 (part-time) | Duties included selling sporting goods and operating | Panasonic cash register. Assisted sales manager in | completing monthly sales reports generated by Word | and Excel software programs.
4. Type PERSONAL entries as a bulleted list:
   * Volunteer for Habitat for Humanity, 2000-Present |
   * Senior Class President, 1999 |
   * Member, Intramural Soccer Team, 1997-1999
5. Type this REFERENCES entry: Available upon request.
6. Save the resume as a text-only file.

```
ALLEN P. HUNTER

     10234 Wood Sorrell Lane
     Burke, VA 22015
     Phone: 703-555-4902
     E-mail: aphunter@netlink.net

OBJECTIVE

     Retail management entry-level position with a midsize
     department store.

EDUCATION

     * Central Virginia Business College, Burke, Virginia,
       December 2004

     * High school diploma from Central High School, Burke,
       Virginia, May 2002

EXPERIENCE

     * COMPUTER SYSTEMS TECHNICIAN, Kramer & Kramer, Inc.
       Harrisburg, Virginia
       June 1999-Present
       Duties include reviewing, installing, and updating
       software programs used for processing legal
       documents and monitoring computer network system for
       branch offices.

     * SALESCLERK, Blanchard's Department Store
       Richmond, Virginia
       May 2000-May 2002 (part-time)
       Duties included selling sporting goods and operating
       Panasonic cash register. Assisted sales manager in
       completing monthly sales reports generated by Word
       and Excel software programs.

PERSONAL

     * Volunteer for Habitat for Humanity, 2000-Present
     * Senior Class President, 1999
     * Member, Intramural Soccer Team, 1997-1999

REFERENCES

     Available upon request.
```

Keyboarding Connection

Creating a Scannable Resume

Many companies scan the paper resumes they receive into a database. When a position becomes available, the company searches for resumes that include keywords such as *managerial experience.*

So include only scannable material in your resume—don't use bullets, pictures, bold, and so on—and always include industry buzzwords that apply to your skills.

Letters of Application

Goals

- Improve speed and accuracy
- Refine language arts skills in composing paragraphs
- Format letters of application

A. Type 2 times.

A. WARMUP

```
     Prices were quickly lowered (some by as much as 50%) @  11
Julia's garage sale. She could see that extra sales would    24
not be over the 9%* she had projected to finance the prize.  36
| 1 | 2 | 3 | 4 | 5 | 6 | 7 | 8 | 9 | 10 | 11 | 12
```

SKILLBUILDING

PRETEST → PRACTICE → POSTTEST

PRETEST
Take a 1-minute timed writing. Review your speed and errors.

B. PRETEST: Common Letter Combinations

```
     They formed an action committee to force a motion for   11
a ruling on your contract case. This enabled them to comply  24
within the lawful time period and convey a common message.   36
| 1 | 2 | 3 | 4 | 5 | 6 | 7 | 8 | 9 | 10 | 11 | 12
```

PRACTICE
Speed Emphasis:
If you made 2 or fewer errors on the Pretest, type each *individual* line 2 times.
Accuracy Emphasis:
If you made 3 or more errors, type each *group* of lines (as though it were a paragraph) 2 times.

C. PRACTICE: Word Beginnings

```
for forget formal format forces forums forked forest formed
per perils period perish permit person peruse perked pertly
com combat comedy coming commit common compel comply comets
```

D. PRACTICE: Word Endings

```
ing acting aiding boring buying ruling saving hiding dating
ble bubble dabble double enable feeble fumble tumble usable
ion action vision lesion nation bunion lotion motion legion
```

POSTTEST
Repeat the Pretest timed writing and compare performance.

E. POSTTEST: Common Letter Combinations

F. PROGRESSIVE PRACTICE: NUMBERS

If you are not using the GDP software, turn to page SB-11 and follow the directions for this activity.

ERGONOMICALLY SPEAKING

HAND POSITION Remind students that when they are using a mouse or other input device, such as a stylus or light pen with a graphics tablet, they should not grip it tightly. Tell them to keep their hands and fingers relaxed. Keep hands, wrists, and forearms in a straight line.

Visit us on the Web at **www.mhhe.com/gdp** for more information.

Lesson 53

FOCUS

TIME MANAGEMENT 

Suggested Schedule:

Warmup	2′
Skillbuilding	19′
Language Arts	6′
Formatting	5′
Document Processing	18′
Total	**50′**

TEACH

SKILLBUILDING

PRETEST → PRACTICE → POSTTEST

PPP The Pretest/Practice/Posttest (PPP) routine is designed to build speed and accuracy through a three-step program:

53-B The Pretest is the preliminary effort to determine the learner's initial skill level. Some letter combinations occur so frequently that students eventually learn to type them automatically without having to "spell out" each letter in their minds. These drills help develop this fast typing response. Encourage students to push moderately for speed on the Pretest.

53-C and 53-D The Practice section consists of intensive drills to improve the reaches focused on in the Pretest.

53-E The Posttest measures the effect of the Practice.

Lesson 53

LANGUAGE ARTS

LESSON 53-G Check students' answers to be sure they are composing paragraphs consisting of three or four complete sentences.

FORMATTING

Reference Manual

Ask students to review the format for an application letter in the **Reference Manual, R-12B,** before they begin typing.

LESSON 53-H To begin the discussion, mention that a letter of application is an introduction of you (the candidate) to the prospective employer that describes why you are an excellent candidate for the position. You can use more descriptive words in a letter of application to express yourself than you can in a resume, where you simply list your qualifications.

Discuss the information typically included in a letter of application. Include in the discussion that the letter of application should be addressed to a specific person, if possible. Also mention that a resume is usually enclosed with the application letter.

DOCUMENT PROCESSING

CORRESPONDENCE 53–36

Reference Manual

Encourage students to refer to the personal-business letter in modified-block style in the **Reference Manual, R-3D,** and the application letter in the **Reference Manual, R-12B.**

LANGUAGE ARTS

G. Choose one of the phrases at the right; then compose a paragraph of three to four sentences on that topic.

G. COMPOSING PARAGRAPHS

My computer was working fine until it . . .
The Internet has helped me complete my class assignments by . . .
Several of us decided to take the cruise because . . .
I have several skills, but my best skill is . . . .

FORMATTING

Reference Manual

Refer to page R-12B of the Reference Manual for additional guidance.

H. LETTERS OF APPLICATION

A letter of application is sent along with a resume to a prospective employer. Together, the letter and the resume serve to introduce a person to the organization.

The letter of application should be no longer than one page and should include (1) the job you are applying for and how you learned of the job, (2) the highlights of your enclosed resume, and (3) a request for an interview.

DOCUMENT PROCESSING

Correspondence 53-36

Personal-Business Letter in Modified-Block Style

September 15, 20-- | Ms. Kay Brewer, Personel Director | Blanchard Computer Systems | 2189 Dace Ave. | Sioux City, IA 51107 | Dear Ms. Brewer:

¶ Please consider me as an applicant for the position of Data Records Operator advertized in the September 13th edition of the Sioux City Press.

¶ In May I will graduate with an A.A. degree in Systems Office from West Iowa Business College. My enclosed resume shows that I have completed courses in Excel, Access, and Microsoft word. I also have ~~significant~~ considerable experience in working on the internet. The skills I gained in using these software packages and in accessing the Internet will be ~~extremely~~ useful to your branch office in Sioux City.

¶ The position with your company is very appealing to me. If you wish to interview me for ~~the~~ this position, please call me at 402-555-7265.

Sincerely, | Arlene F. Jefferson | 1842 Amber Road | Wayne, Ne 68787 | Enclosure

EXTENDING LANGUAGE ARTS

Composing Generally speaking, paragraphs that contain no more than four to eight lines give a "visual break" to the reader. This makes it possible for the reader to understand the content of one paragraph before moving on to the next.

Each paragraph should have a specific topic, expressed in the first sentence. The rest of the sentences in the paragraph develop the topic.

The following sentences provide topics from which paragraphs can be developed:

- The second meeting of Professional Business Leaders will be held in September.
- The Spring Fling event is scheduled for April 25.

Each of these sentences provides a topic from which a paragraph can be developed.

Correspondence 53-37

Personal-Business Letter in Block Style

August 10, 20-- | Personnel Director | Arlington Communications | 2403 Sunset Lane | Arlington, TX 76015-3148 | Dear Personnel Director:
¶ Please consider me as an applicant for a position with Arlington Communications. My strengths have always been in the communication arts, as you can see on the enclosed resume, which lists a number of courses in English, speech, and communication technology. The two part-time jobs I held during the summer months at your company convinced me that Arlington Communications is the place where I want to work.
¶ If you would like to interview me for any possible openings this summer or fall, please call me at 903-555-2340. I look forward to hearing from you.
Sincerely, | Kenneth R. Diaz | 105 Royal Lane | Commerce, TX 75428 | Enclosure

Strategies for Career Success

Writing a Job Application Letter

What's the goal of the letter that accompanies your resume? The goal is to get the interview. No two letters of application are alike.

In the opening paragraph, state your purpose (for example, the position applied for, how you became aware of it).

In the middle section, sell yourself. Convince the reader that you are the best match for the job. If you respond to a job posting, match your qualifications to the job description. If you send an unsolicited letter, specify how the employer will benefit from your qualifications. Also, refer to your resume.

In the closing paragraph, show confidence in your abilities (for example, "I'm certain I can meet your needs for a . . ."). Then state a specific time you will call to schedule an interview.

YOUR TURN Obtain a job description for which you believe you are qualified. List the job requirements, and then list your qualifications that match.

DOCUMENT PROCESSING

CORRESPONDENCE 53-37

Before students begin typing, have them read the copy and visualize how the letter should be formatted in block style. Encourage them to use the examples in the Reference Manual for help in formatting the letter.

ASSESS

www.mhhe.com/gdp to download a copy of the Technique Evaluation Form.

TECHNIQUE EVALUATION FORM

Walk around the room to observe student technique. Complete a Technique Evaluation Form for each student.

Review the formatting of Correspondence 53-36.

Extending the Lesson

Discuss different types of information that would belong in either a resume or a letter of application.

CLOSE

Show students a letter of application that is poorly written and poorly formatted. Have students make suggestions for improvement.

Strategies for Career Success

APPLICATION LETTER

Discuss the content requirements for a letter of application. Provide sample introductory paragraphs and discuss whether or not the paragraphs would create an interest in the reader. Rewrite introductory paragraphs that do not state the purpose of writing.

YOUR TURN If time permits, ask students to complete the Your Turn activity.

Lesson 54

FOCUS

TIME MANAGEMENT 

Suggested Schedule:

Warmup	2′
Skillbuilding	17′
Formatting	6′
Document Processing	25′
Total	**50′**

TEACH

SKILLBUILDING

LESSON 54-B Encourage students to push moderately for speed on the Pretest.

Follow-Up Letters

Goals

- Type at least 39wpm/5′/5e
- Format follow-up letters

A. Type 2 times.

A. WARMUP

```
     Quite a night! All sixty senior citizens (including      11
the handicapped) really enjoyed that play. Over 3/4 of the    22
tickets were sold; most had been sold by Frank's workers.     34
 |  1  |  2  |  3  |  4  |  5  |  6  |  7  |  8  |  9  |  10  |  11  |  12
```

SKILLBUILDING

B. DIAGNOSTIC PRACTICE: SYMBOLS AND PUNCTUATION

If you are not using the GDP software, turn to page SB-2 and follow the directions for this activity.

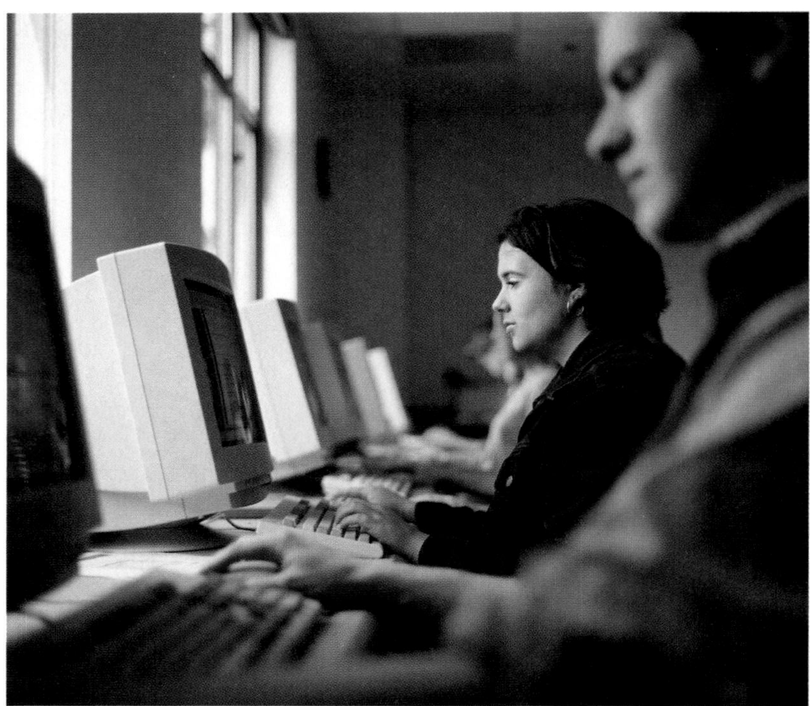

INSTRUCTOR STRATEGIES

Discussing the Photo

The keyboard was one of the first peripherals to be used with computers, and it is still the primary input device for entering text and numbers. A relatively simple device, the standard keyboard contains about 100 keys, each of which sends a different message to the central processing unit.

Keyboard designers realized that a flat keyboard is not well suited to the shape of our hands. Have students relax their hands on the desk in front of them; they should note that their thumbs tend to point up. Logically, then, keyboards should be designed with two sides, one for each hand. Observations like this have influenced the designs of the ergonomic keyboards we use today.

C. Take two 5-minute timed writings. Review your speed and errors.

Goal: At least 39wpm/5'/5e

C. 5-MINUTE TIMED WRITING

```
     In the past, typing was a skill that was used only by    11
those who were secretaries, students, and office workers.     23
High school students who were in school with plans for        34
going on took a typing class so that they could type their    45
work with ease and skill. Often students who wanted to be     57
hired for office jobs would make a plan to take advanced      68
courses in typing.                                            72
     As prices drop and as we have more and more advances     83
in technology of all types, people are recognizing that       94
they need keyboarding skills. From the top executive to the  106
customer service representative, everyone needs to be able   118
to use a computer keyboard. Workers in almost any kind of    130
business use their keyboarding skills to perform their       141
daily tasks.                                                 143
     Employers are looking for skilled workers who type      154
with consistent speed and accuracy. People who can type      165
documents accurately and enter data quickly are needed for   177
many types of careers. Skills in keyboarding are important   188
assets for several types of jobs.                            195
| 1 | 2 | 3 | 4 | 5 | 6 | 7 | 8 | 9 | 10 | 11 | 12
```

FORMATTING

D. FOLLOW-UP LETTERS

As soon as possible after your interview (preferably the next day), you should send a follow-up letter to the person who conducted your interview. In the letter you should:

- Use a positive tone.
- Thank the person who conducted the interview.
- Mention some specific information you learned during the interview.
- Highlight your particular strengths.
- Restate your interest in working for that organization and mention that you look forward to a favorable decision.

Meeting Special Needs

MOBILITY IMPAIRMENTS Mobility impairments can be caused by a variety of illnesses or accidents. Examples include arthritis, stroke, cerebral palsy, Parkinson's disease, multiple sclerosis, and loss of limbs or digits. You may wish to consider using a special keyboarding program designed for teaching students with impairments. If your student's impairment is caused by loss of limbs or digits, *Typing for the Physically Handicapped* by Jack Heller is available from Glencoe/McGraw-Hill.

Visit us on the Web at **www.mhhe.com/gdp** for more information.

SKILLBUILDING

LESSON 54-C Encourage students to type with correct posture, good technique, and eyes on copy. Encourage students to push toward achieving the goals for this 5-minute timed writing.

FORMATTING

LESSON 54-D Share samples of follow-up letters with students.

INSTRUCTOR STRATEGIES

Follow-Up Letters
Begin the discussion of follow-up letters by asking the obvious: When, why, and to whom should follow-up letters be sent? Ask students if they have written and sent follow-up letters. Invite them to share the responses they received from the person who received the letter.

Review the bulleted items presented in the text. Ask students to discuss why a follow-up letter is a good action to take immediately following an interview.

Elicit a response that suggests that follow-up letters give you (the job applicant) another opportunity to put your best foot forward.

Provide some samples of follow-up letters that you have prepared or collected. Invite students to comment on them in light of the bulleted items listed in the text.

Suggest to students that follow-up letters should be brief and convey a positive tone.

Lesson 54

DOCUMENT PROCESSING

CORRESPONDENCE 54-38

Before students begin typing, have them read the handwritten copy to make sure they understand the copy and can envision the letter typed in block style.

Suggest to students that a follow-up letter should be fairly brief, not more than three paragraphs.

Remind students that a follow-up letter should have a very positive tone.

Refer to Reference Manual

Ask students to review the letter in modified-block style in the **Reference Manual, R-3B,** before they begin typing.

CORRESPONDENCE 54-39

Before students begin typing, have them review the rough-draft copy to be typed and visualize the letter in modified-block format.

DOCUMENT PROCESSING

Correspondence 54-38

Personal-Business Letter in Block Style

September 12, 20-- | Ms. Carole Rothchild | Personnel Director | Arlington Communications | 2403 Sunset Lane | Arlington, TX 76015-3148 | Dear Ms. Rothchild:

¶ It was a real pleasure meeting with you yesterday and learning of the wonderful career opportunities at Arlington Communications. I enjoyed meeting all the people, especially those working in the Publications Division. Thank you for taking the time to tell me about the interesting start-up history of the company and its location in Arlington.

¶ I believe my experience and job skills match nicely with those you are seeking for a desktop publishing individual, and this position is exactly what I have been looking for. You may recall that I have had experience with all of the equipment and software that are used in your office.

¶ Please let me hear from you when you have made your decision on this position. I am very much interested in joining the professional staff at Arlington Communications.

Sincerely yours, | Kenneth R. Diaz | 105 Royal Lane | Commerce, TX 75428

Correspondence 54-39

Personal-Business Letter in Modified-Block Style

April 7, 20-- | Ms. Kay Brewer, Personnel Director | Blanchard Computer Systems | 2189 Dace Avenue | Sioux City, IA 51107 | Dear Ms. Brewer:

¶ Thanks [you] for the opportunity of interviewing with Blanchard computer Systems (yesterday). Please express my appreciation to all of those who were involved.

¶ The interview gave me a ~~very~~ good feeling about the company. The [positive] description that you shared (me) (with) convinced me that blanchard is in deed a company at which I would like to work. I was greatly impressed with the summary of social service programs for citizens throughout the community (that are sponsored by Blanchard).

(Continued on next page)

INSTRUCTOR STRATEGIES

Follow-Up Letters

Ask students to conduct a Web search using the keywords *follow-up letters.* Encourage students to share the examples found. Discuss characteristics common to the good examples of follow-up letters.

¶ You may recall that I have had experience with all of the equipment that is used. It appears to me that ^my strengths in ~~software~~ ^computer application soft ware ^and office systems would blend in well with your ~~company~~ profile.

¶ I look forward to hearing you from soon regarding you^r decision on the position of data records operator.

Sincerely, | Arlene F. Jefferson | 1842 Amber Road | Wayne, NE 68787

Correspondence 54-40

Personal-Business Letter in Modified-Block Style

Open the file for Correspondence 54-39, and make the following changes:

- Change the date of the letter to August 7, 20--.
- Send the letter to Mr. William E. Takashi | Personnel Director | Hawkeye Computers, Inc. | 5604 Melrose Avenue | Sioux City, IA 51105.
- Replace "Blanchard Computer Systems" with Hawkeye Computers in both the first and the second paragraphs.
- Change "yesterday" in the first paragraph to August 5.
- Change the complimentary closing to Yours truly.
- Change "data records operator" to technology support assistant in the final paragraph.

Strategies for Career Success

Interview Thank-You Letter

Expressing your appreciation is a very important follow-up step in your job search. Send a thank-you letter or e-mail within 24 hours after your interview.

In the opening paragraph, thank the interviewer for taking time to meet with you. Make a positive statement about the company or interview feature (for example, meeting potential coworkers).

In the middle paragraph, close the sale. Address any qualifications you neglected to mention. Turn around an interview weakness (for example, reconsider your statement that you wouldn't travel). Strengthen your relationship with the interviewer (for example, refer the interviewer to a good article on a topic in which he or she expressed interest).

In the closing paragraph, ask to be notified when the decision is made. A thank-you letter ensures that your last impression is a positive one.

YOUR TURN After your next interview, send a thank-you letter that effectively closes the sale.

Strategies for Career Success

INTERVIEW THANK-YOU LETTER Ask students if they have ever written a thank-you letter following an interview. Discuss sample interview thank-you letters and appropriate content.

YOUR TURN If time permits, ask students to complete the Your Turn activity.

Lesson 54

DOCUMENT PROCESSING

CORRESPONDENCE 54-40
Optional. Remind students to proofread the copy to make sure that the revisions they made to the letter were done correctly and made sense.

ASSESS

www.mhhe.com/gdp to download a copy of the Technique Evaluation Form.

TECHNIQUE EVALUATION FORM
Review results of timed writings.

Review the formatting of Correspondence 54-38. Check the placement and spacing for each part of the letter.

Extending the Lesson

Ask students to verbalize the importance of follow-up letters that are well written. Have them give at least three important reasons.

CLOSE

Remind students to create a file folder to save samples of each employment document they have created. The file will be a valuable reference.

Lesson 55

FOCUS

TIME MANAGEMENT 

Suggested Schedule:

Warmup	2′
Skillbuilding	14′
Language Arts	6′
Formatting	6′
Document Processing	22′
Total	**50′**

TEACH

SKILLBUILDING

LESSON 55-B Review the use of the Tab key when typing columns. Observe whether students use the A finger on the Tab key and whether they keep their eyes on the copy when they tab.

LESSON 55-C Paced Practice helps students reach individual speed and accuracy goals in 2-wpm increments by pacing them as they strive for a slightly faster rate.

LANGUAGE ARTS

LESSON 55-D If your students are not using the GDP software, have them type a correct version of the paragraph.

The copy to be proofread is an excellent activity with which students can recognize the types of unintentional errors that can be made when typing paragraph copy.

 **SOLUTION: Lines 8–13**

8. Smiths, pleased
9. coverage, on a
10. *Delete* policy, $20,000
11. [New paragraph indent], They, premium
12. their, tapped
13. additional, the

Integrated Employment Project

Goals

- Improve speed and accuracy
- Refine language arts skills in proofreading
- Format employment documents

A. Type 2 times.

A. WARMUP

```
1      Lex was quite pleased with his travel plans; the trip   11
2  to Bozeman was on Flight #578 on July 30, and the return is 23
3  on August 12 on Flight #643. The ticket will cost $1,090.   34
   | 1 | 2 | 3 | 4 | 5 | 6 | 7 | 8 | 9 | 10 | 11 | 12
```

SKILLBUILDING

B. Type the columns 2 times. Press Tab to move from column to column.

B. TECHNIQUE PRACTICE: TAB

```
4  J. Barnes      P. Varanth    S. Childers   M. Christenson
5  F. Gilsrud     J. Benson     D. Bates      M. Jordan
6  B. Harringer   J. Suksi      J. Lee        P. North
7  V. Hill        A. Budinger   T. Gonyer     S. Kravolec
```

C. PACED PRACTICE

If you are not using the GDP software, turn to page SB-14 and follow the directions for this activity.

LANGUAGE ARTS

D. Edit this paragraph to correct any typing or formatting errors.

D. PROOFREADING

```
8       The Smith were please to learn from their insurance
9   agent that the covrage ona $50,000 life insurance policy
10  policy would be increased by $ 20,000 at no extra cost.

11  The continued to pay the same premum, not knowing that the
12  cash value of there original policy was being taped each
13  month to pay an addition premium for hte new coverage.
```


EXTENDING LANGUAGE ARTS

Proofreading Proofreading a document is not a one-step task.

1. Read the whole document for content. Do the statements make sense? Does everything add up? Example: We sent them five products: L6007, D3991, R1109, and W2341. (As proofreader, first check the copy you were given to type from to see if you omitted a product number or if *five* should be *four*. If you typed what you were given, check with the writer.)
2. Read each sentence for grammar. Is each sentence complete? Do subjects and verbs agree?
3. Check the spelling of each individual word.
4. Check punctuation. Does each sentence have correct end punctuation? Do parentheses and quotation marks appear correctly in pairs?

DOCUMENT PROCESSING

In this unit you have learned how to prepare a resume, an application letter, and a follow-up letter—all of which are frequently used by job applicants. You will now use these skills in preparing the documents necessary to apply for the job described in the newspaper ad illustrated below.

Desktop Publisher

NetJobs, a worldwide leader in employment and job searches, has an immediate opening for a desktop publisher. This person will work in the ad production and Web page design office.

This is an entry-level position within the Advertising Department in our San Francisco office. Applicant must have experience in using Word, FrontPage, and PageMaker. Creative ability and typing skills are a must. Candidate must be able to work in a fast-paced team environment and be highly self-motivated.

Excellent company benefits are available, and they include a comprehensive medical and dental program, disability insurance, and a credit union.

If interested, send a letter of application and resume to:

Ms. Danielle E. Rose
HRM Department
NetJobs, Inc.
9350 Kramer Avenue
San Francisco, CA 94101

NetJobs Is an Equal Opportunity Employer

Report 55-31
Resume in Traditional Style

Prepare a resume for yourself as though you are applying for the job described in the ad above. Use actual data in the resume. Assume that you have just graduated from a postsecondary program. Include school-related activities, courses you have completed, and any part-time or full-time work experience you may have acquired. Make the resume as realistic as possible, and provide as much information as you can about your background.

Correspondence 55-41
Personal-Business Letter in Block Style

Prepare an application letter to apply for the position described in the ad. Date your letter March 10. Emphasize the skills you have acquired during your years in school and while working in any part-time or full-time positions. Use Correspondence 53-37 as a guide for your letter.

DOCUMENT PROCESSING

REPORT 55-31 and CORRESPONDENCE 55-41

This lesson brings together all the employment documents students have learned in this unit. You may wish to generate a discussion in which students review the points relevant to producing each type of document.

Have available examples of each type of document. Review the parts and/or the formats about which students seem to be unclear.

Have students read the newspaper ad illustrated on the page. Then have them summarize the information in terms of the types of information they need to know in order to compose a resume, an application letter in block style, and a follow-up letter.

You may wish to refer students to the appropriate pages in the Reference Manual.

All major formatting features presented in this unit are included in these documents. You may want to use these activities for a document processing test.

MHHE CHAMPIONS

Technique

Jeanette Parker
Southern Union State Community College
Opelika, Alabama

ALABAMA

Practice technique over and over again for better performance.

Remind students to monitor their progress electronically through the use of the Performance Chart in the GDP software.

Instructors Helping One Another

Lesson 55

DOCUMENT PROCESSING

CORRESPONDENCE 55-42

Be sure students include the essential points in the follow-up letter:

- Use a positive tone
- Thank the interviewer
- Mention specific information learned during the interview
- Highlight the strengths of the applicant
- Restate an interest in working in the position
- Express desire for a positive decision

Have students check their follow-up letters before they print them or submit them for checking. In addition to proofreading for errors in grammar, punctuation, and formatting, they should check to be sure that all pertinent information has been included and that the letter has a positive tone.

CORRESPONDENCE 55-43

Before students type the letter, have them read the copy to determine whether it includes the type of information that should be included in an application.

Reference Manual

Ask students to review the format for an application letter in the **Reference Manual, R-12B,** before they begin typing.

Correspondence 55-42

Personal-Business Letter in Modified-Block Style

Assume that your interview was held on March 25 and that you would very much like to work for NetJobs. It is now the day after your interview. Prepare a follow-up letter expressing your positive thoughts about working for NetJobs. Use Correspondence 54-39 as a guide for your letter.

Correspondence 55-43

Personal-Business Letter in Block Style

April 15, 20-- | Mr. Blair N. Scarborough | Wyatt Insurance
Agency | 2834 International Blvd. | Fort Worth, TX 76390 |
Dear Mr. Scarborough:
¶ My adviser, Dr. Bonnie Allworth, mentioned to me that you
have an opening for a computer specialist in your Denton office.
I would like to be considered as an applicant for that position.
¶ My extensive training and experience in using various
software programs are ideal for the position you have open. As a
student at Texas State University, I won two national awards in
computer programming competition. Also, as my enclosed
resume indicates, I have completed several computer courses
that uniquely qualify me for the computer specialist position at
Wyatt Insurance Agency.
¶ At Texas State University I took an active leadership role as
president of the local chapter of Phi Beta Lambda. In my
junior year I was treasurer of my campus fraternity, and
during my senior year I was elected class president. These
activities have provided me with valuable leadership and
teamwork skills that I hope to demonstrate at Wyatt.
¶ I am very interested in working for Wyatt Insurance
Company. I will telephone your office later this week to
arrange an interview with you at your convenience. If
you would like to speak to me prior to that time, please
telephone me at my home number, 901-555-3203, after 5 p.m.
or e-mail me at pmcclean@stu.edu.
Sincerely, | Pat R. McClean | 894 Cremans Avenue | Fort
Worth, TX 76384 | Enclosure

INSTRUCTOR STRATEGIES

Avoid Job-Hopping What is job-hopping, and why should people avoid doing it?

Job-hopping is changing jobs every year or so for several years in a row. Downsizing or promotion isn't counted as job-hopping. Being fired for poor performance, however, or quitting because the job is unfulfilling is job-hopping.

Most employers don't like to see evidence of job-hopping on resumes. That's natural: Why should they spend time training employees who will leave soon?

It is wise to stay with one employer for at least a few years. That way, an employee has time to develop needed skills and to become part of a team.

Correspondence 55-44

Personal-Business Letter in Modified-Block Style

Assume that you have interviewed for the position mentioned in the previous letter and that you would now like to send a follow-up letter dated June 15, 20--, to Mr. Blair N. Scarborough, thanking him for the interview. Use the inside address, salutation, and closing lines shown in Correspondence 55-43 to create the follow-up letter below:

Progress and Proofreading Check

Documents designated as Proofreading Checks serve as a check of your proofreading skill. Your goal is to have zero typographical errors when the GDP software first scores the document.

¶ Thank you for the time you spent with me, telling me about the Computer Specialist position with Wyatt. My interview with you reafirmed my interest in working for Wyatt.

¶ I was very impresed with work done in your Information Processing department. The hardware and software you use for writing computer code and the people working in that department are very apealing to me.

¶ I believe my particular background and skills blend perfectly with the position. I hope to hear from you by the end of next week for a positive decision on my employment. Thank you for bringing me in for the interview.

Strategies for Career Success

Looking for a Job

Don't waste time! Start your job search early. Scan the Help Wanted section in major Sunday newspapers for job descriptions and salaries. The Internet provides electronic access to worldwide job listings. If you are interested in a particular company, access its home page.

Ask a reference librarian for handbooks (for example, *Occupational Outlook Handbook*), government publications (for example, *Federal Career Opportunities*), and journals or magazines in your field. Visit your college placement office. Sign up for interviews with companies that visit your campus.

Talk with people in your field to get advice. Look for an internship or join a professional organization in your field. Attend local chapter meetings to network with people in your chosen profession.

Taking the initiative in your job search will pay off!

YOUR TURN Visit the Internet site for the *National Business Employment Weekly* at http://www.employmentguide.com, which provides more than 45,000 national and international job listings online.

Strategies for Career Success

LOOKING FOR A JOB Discuss various ways to learn about job openings. Be sure students do not overlook networking and how to enlarge their network. Review acronyms and abbreviations found in employment want ads.

YOUR TURN If time permits, ask students to complete the Your Turn activity.

Lesson 55

DOCUMENT PROCESSING

Progress Check/ Proofreading Check

CORRESPONDENCE 55-44

You may want to use this exercise as a document processing test. In addition, you may want to inform students that this document also serves as a check of their proofreading skill and that they may have only one opportunity to have the GDP software check the document in order for them to receive a satisfactory proofreading grade.

Remind students to spell-check, proofread, and preview their documents before printing them.

ASSESS

www.mhhe.com/gdp to download a copy of the Technique Evaluation Form.

TECHNIQUE EVALUATION FORM

Walk around the room to observe student technique.

Print a report for all skillbuilding exercises for Lessons 51–55.

Extending the Lesson

Ask students to comment on the value of composing employment documents such as the ones they did in Report 55-31, Correspondence 55-42, and Correspondence 55-42. What elements were hardest? Easiest?

CLOSE

Suggest that students compose similar employment documents (resume, application letter, follow-up letter) for filing in a folder to guide them in creating documents they might need when applying for a job.

Unit 12

UNIT OVERVIEW

Students will continue skillbuilding and will prepare documents related to the following areas: insurance, hospitality, retail, non-profit, and manufacturing.

Did You Know?

This program takes a systematic, spiral approach to instruction: the student spirals upward through tasks of increased difficulty and complexity. Therefore, the student always experiences skillbuilding and applications in appropriate balance.

www.mhhe.com/gdp to download a copy of the Technique Evaluation Form.

Name ______ Class ______ Date ______

Technique Evaluation Form

Date	Workstation		Position at the Keyboard		Keystroking	
	Acceptable	Needs Improvement	Acceptable	Needs Improvement	Acceptable	Needs Improvement

Workstation
1. Positions the chair so that the upper and lower legs form a 90-degree angle and the lower back is supported.
2. Positions the keyboard even with the front of the desk.
3. Positions the text on either side of the monitor as close to it vertically and horizontally as possible to minimize head and eye movement and to avoid neck strain.
4. Positions the mouse on a pad at the side of the monitor opposite the text.

Position at the Keyboard
5. Centers the body opposite the keyboard.
6. Leans forward slightly from the hips, with the base of the spine touching the back of the chair and the feet flat on the floor.
7. Keeps the elbows alongside the body in a relaxed position.
8. Curves the fingers naturally over the home position, with the back of the hand at the same angle as the keyboard.

Keystroking
9. Keeps the forearms horizontal and raises the hands slightly when typing so that the wrists do not touch the keyboard while typing. (Hands may rest at the bottom of the keyboard—away from the keys—during nontyping intervals.)
10. Makes quick, snappy strokes using the correct fingers.
11. Returns the finger immediately to the home position or moves to the next position after each stroke.
12. Operates all keys by touch, keeping the eyes on the copy most of the time while typing.

Comments

Use this form to keep track of student progress. Complete a form for each student.

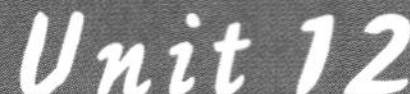

Skillbuilding and In-Basket Review

RESOURCE MANAGER

GDP SOFTWARE
- Lessons 55–60
- Software User's Guide
- Instructor Management LAN Version
- Word Processing Manual
- Professional Handbook (IWE*)—Teaching Strategies; Teaching in a Distance-Learning Environment
- MAP 75

* Instructor Wraparound Edition

ASSESSMENT
- Test Booklet—Alternate Test 3
- Progress Check—Correspondence 60-52, Table 60-22
- Professional Handbook (IWE*)—Assessment Strategies

ON THE WEB
- **www.mhhe.com/gdp**
- Instructor Management Web Version

In-Basket Review (Insurance)

Goals

- Type at least 40wpm/5′/5e
- Format insurance documents

A. Type 2 times.

A. WARMUP

```
     Kyu Choi jumped at the opportunity to assume 40% of      11
the ownership of your restaurant. Alverox & Choi Chinese      22
Cuisine will be opening quite soon at 1528 Waysata Street.    34
| 1 | 2 | 3 | 4 | 5 | 6 | 7 | 8 | 9 | 10 | 11 | 12
```

SKILLBUILDING

B. DIAGNOSTIC PRACTICE: NUMBERS

If you are not using the GDP software, turn to page SB-5 and follow the directions for this activity.

C. Take three 12-second timed writings on each line. The scale below the last line shows your wpm speed for a 12-second timed writing.

C. 12-SECOND SPEED SPRINTS

```
Kay Sue is on her way to that new show to take some photos.
Most of the ones who go may not be able to make it on time.
When they got to their seats, they were glad they had come.
Both men and women might take some of their pets with them.
''''5''''10''''15''''20''''25''''30''''35''''40''''45''''50''''55''''60
```

Keyboarding Connection

Creating an E-Mail Signature File

Creating a signature file saves you time and adds a personal touch to your e-mail messages! A signature file is a tag of information at the end of your e-mail. It may include your signature, a small graphic, your address, your phone number, or a quotation. The signature file appears on every e-mail message you send. Use the following guidelines to create a signature file.

Open your e-mail software. Open the menu item that allows you to create a signature file. Type the information you want to include in your signature file. Close the file.

YOUR TURN Create a signature file. Then address an e-mail to yourself. Type "Test" in the Subject box. In the body, type "This is a test of the signature file." Send the e-mail. Open the test e-mail and locate your signature file at the bottom of the e-mail message.

Keyboarding Connection

Creating an E-Mail Signature File

Ask students what percentage of e-mail they receive contains a signature file. Do students think the signature files are too long, too short, necessary, unnecessary? What do students recommend as "required" information for a signature file? Ask students to compose a signature file.

YOUR TURN If time permits, ask students to complete the Your Turn activity.

Lesson 56

FOCUS

TIME MANAGEMENT

Suggested Schedule:

Warmup	2′
Skillbuilding	22′
Document Processing	26′
Total	**50′**

TEACH

SKILLBUILDING

LESSON 56-B Encourage students to push moderately for speed on the Pretest.

LESSON 56-C Check to see whether students are increasing their wpm speeds as they complete each of the 12-second timed writings.

Lesson 56

SKILLBUILDING

LESSON 56-D Encourage students to type with concentration and correct technique. Encourage them to strive to meet the goals for this 5-minute timed writing.

Before they begin typing, have students read the assignment and the copy to make certain they know how to complete the assignment.

INSTRUCTOR STRATEGIES

Job? Career? Discuss with students the differences between a job and a career. What characteristics do students see as important for their ideal careers? For instance, would their ideal career include or exclude business travel? Would students like their careers to make a difference to our society? Would they want to make life-and-death decisions?

DOCUMENT PROCESSING

CORRESPONDENCE 56-45

Reference Manual

You may want to review letters in block style in the **Reference Manual, R-3A** before students begin typing.

Check for the following: correct date, double-spacing before and after the salutation and between paragraphs, format of bulleted items, and appropriate closing lines.

Remind students to refer to their Word Processing Manual to review the bulleted and numbered list feature.

D. Take two 5-minute timed writings. Review your speed and errors.

Goal: At least 40wpm/5'/5e

D. 5-MINUTE TIMED WRITING

When you begin to think about a career, you should 10
assess your personal abilities and interests. Do you have a 22
natural aptitude in a certain area? Do you have special 34
interests or hobbies that you would like to develop into a 45
career? Do you enjoy working with other people, or do you 57
like to work on your own? Would you like to work in a large 69
office, or do you prefer to work outdoors? These questions 81
are important to consider when you think about your career. 93
Your quest to find the perfect career will be more 103
successful if you try to maximize the opportunities that 115
are available. For example, you might consider working with 127
an organization that offers you career counseling. A career 139
counselor is trained to help you determine your aptitudes 150
and interests. You may contact people who work in a career 162
that interests you and ask to shadow them on their jobs and 174
ask them questions. You might find an online service to 185
help you find a very interesting career that will meet each 197
of your goals. 200

| 1 | 2 | 3 | 4 | 5 | 6 | 7 | 8 | 9 | 10 | 11 | 12

DOCUMENT PROCESSING

Correspondence 56-45

Business Letter in Block Style

Situation: You are employed in the office of All-City Insurance of Columbia, Missouri. Their offices are located at 17 North Eighth Street, Columbia, MO 65201-7272. All-City handles auto, home, and life insurance coverage in Iowa, Kansas, and Missouri. You work for Ellen B. Boldt, executive vice president. Ms. Boldt prefers the letter in block style and *Sincerely* as the complimentary closing. Add your reference initials as appropriate.

October 16, 20-- | Mr. Brandon T. Wright | District Manager | 206 South Rock Road | Wichita, KS 67210 | Dear Mr. Wright:

¶ Several of our service representatives have indicated on our Web site chat room that new clients are becoming increasingly interested in the criteria to consider when evaluating their insurance carriers. All-City has prided itself in years past on its reputable service record with its policyholders, and the service representatives have undoubtedly shared this record with prospective customers. However, we want to be certain that other characteristics about

(Continued on next page)

Windows Wizard

RUN COMMAND To use the **Run** command to start a program in Windows 2000, Me, and XP:

- Click the **Start** button on the Taskbar and choose **Run**.
- Type the location and name of the program you want to start in the **Open** text box.
- Click **OK**.
- You can click the **Browse** button to select the location or name of the program.
- The **Run** command remembers the program commands you have entered. To see the list of commands, click the Down arrow in the **Open** text box.
- Type an Internet address in the **Open** text box to connect to the Internet.

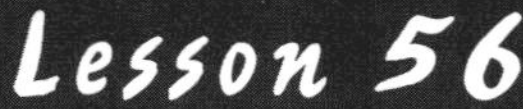

DOCUMENT PROCESSING

CORRESPONDENCE 56-46

Before students begin typing, have them review the rough-draft copy. If necessary, clarify any questions they may have.

Remind students of the proper format for bulleted items with multiple lines. Be sure students single-space the bulleted items and double-space before and after each bulleted item.

Ask students to review the memo format in the **Reference Manual, R-4D,** before they begin typing.

Refer to Reference Manual

Refer to page R-12C of the Reference Manual for information on formatting lists.

Provide suitable closing lines.

All-City are also shared with these potential policyholders.

¶ Please be sure that your representatives share the following service characteristics with potential customers:

- Our claims are handled quickly and with a minimum of "red tape."
- Our ratio of number of policies to number of complaints is the highest in the industry.
- No disciplinary actions have been taken against All-City in the past 50 years.

¶ Please share this information with your service representatives and inform them that updated information on our services is provided on our home page for their use or for their policyholders' use.

Correspondence 56-46

Memo

Ms. Boldt has dictated the following memo for you to transcribe. As you can see, there are several rough-draft changes that you will have to make to the memo.

MEMO TO: Sheila Parsons, Training Director

FROM: Ellen B. Boldt, Executive Vice President

DATE: October 17, 20--

SUBJECT: Training seminar

¶ Our new agent training seminar will be held on December 10, and we plan again ~~this year as we have in the past~~ to conduct separate sessions for auto and life insurance policies. You will be in charge of the auto insurance seminars, and Victor Samuels will conduct the life insurance seminars.

¶ I expect that this years auto insurance seminars will present our ⑥ basic coverage areas using the latest presentation demo software for the following:

(Continued on next page)

INSTRUCTOR STRATEGIES

Bouncing Back After Losing a Job

Admittedly, it's tough to get a new job. However, some people seem to bounce back easily from being fired or downsized.

Martin Yate, a career-guidance specialist in New York, has identified eight critical behaviors found in people who recovered quickly from losing their jobs.

- Goal orientation (motivated to achieve goals)
- Optimism
- Ability to make smart decisions
- Persuasiveness (ability to influence others)
- Organizational action (getting things done)
- Informed risk taking
- Flexible thinking
- Emotional adaptability (open to new ideas)

Lesson 56

DOCUMENT PROCESSING

TABLE 56-17 Review the elements of formatting tables with students before they begin typing.

Check to see that both columnar entries are left-aligned, the table headings are in bold type and centered, and the column headings are centered in their respective cells.

Remind students to press ENTER 1 time after typing the subtitle.

Remind students to press ENTER 1 time before typing the heading for Column A.

ASSESS

www.mhhe.com/gdp to download a copy of the Technique Evaluation Form.

TECHNIQUE EVALUATION FORM Review results of timed writings and review the formatting of each document.

Extending the Lesson

Ask students to identify vocabulary words in the lesson documents that are unique to the insurance industry. Have them make a short glossary that includes a definition and an example sentence for each term.

CLOSE

Have students prepare concise 3- by 5-inch cards telling how to format memos and business letters in block style.

Refer to page R-12C of the Reference Manual for information on formatting lists.

- Bodily injury liability
- Medical payments or personal injury protection
- Property damage liability
- Collision
- Comprehensive
- Uninsured Motorist

We are the market leaders in bodily injury liability and property damage liability coverages. Therefore you should plan to spend at least one-half of your presentation discussing our strengths in these coverages. You might want to include in your presentation the fact that our coverages in these areas have more than surpased those of our competitors for the past 7 years ~~or so~~.

¶ Use Table 1, which is enclosed, to be sure that we explain the variety of discounts offered for Iowa, Kansas, and missouri.

urs | Enclosure

Table 56-17
Boxed Table

Prepare Table 56-17 on a full sheet of paper in correct table format as an enclosure for the memo to Ms. Parsons. Press ENTER to create the 1- and 2-line column headings, as shown, before automatically adjusting the table width.

DISCOUNT PROGRAMS (For Selected States)	
Available Discounts	**Discount Amount (%)**
Air Bag	Up to 8.5
Antitheft Device	Up to 18
Claims Cost Reduction	Up to 1.8
Driving Course	Up to 4.5
Good Driver	20
Good Student	Up to 16
Mature Driver	Up to 1.8
Multipolicy	2 up to 7
Multivehicle	Up to 25
New Driver	Up to 10
Select Professionals Program	4.5 up to 14

Technology Tips

EXTENSIONS

A **.com** extension is a commercial site; **.mil** is a military address; **.gov** is a government site; **.edu** is an educational address; **.net** is an Internet administration site; **.org** is a professional or nonprofit organization site.

INSTRUCTOR STRATEGIES

The Home Office Technology has spurred a major business trend—home offices. Employees work out of their homes sending information to clients and receiving information from clients via computer modems and fax machines. Have students discuss the advantages and disadvantages of a home office, including the need for equipment, records, and self-discipline.

In-Basket Review (Hospitality)

Goals

- Improve speed and accuracy
- Refine language arts skills in number expression and in the use of the hyphen
- Format hospitality documents

A. Type 2 times.

A. WARMUP

```
    Dexter gave an ultimatum: Quit driving on the lawn or  11
I will call the police. A fine of $100 (or even more) may  23
be levied against Kyle, who lives at 2469 Zaine in Joplin.  34
| 1 | 2 | 3 | 4 | 5 | 6 | 7 | 8 | 9 | 10 | 11 | 12
```

SKILLBUILDING

B. PROGRESSIVE PRACTICE: ALPHABET

If you are not using the GDP software, turn to page SB-7 and follow the directions for this activity.

C. PACED PRACTICE

If you are not using the GDP software, turn to page SB-14 and follow the directions for this activity.

LANGUAGE ARTS

D. Study the rules at the right.

D. NUMBER EXPRESSION AND HYPHENATION

RULE ▶ # word

Spell out

- **A number used as the first word of a sentence.**
  Seventy-five people attended the conference in San Diego.
- **The shorter of two adjacent numbers.**
  We have ordered 3 two-pound cakes and one 5-pound cake for the reception.
- **The words *million* and *billion* in round numbers (do not use decimals with round numbers).**
  Not: A $5.00 ticket can win $28,000,000 in this month's lottery.
  But: A $5 ticket can win $28 million in this month's lottery.
- **Fractions.**
  Almost one-half of the audience responded to the question.

Note: When fractions and the numbers twenty-one through ninety-nine are spelled out, they should be hyphenated.

(Continued on next page)

EXTENDING LANGUAGE ARTS

Number Expression Write a sentence on the board to illustrate that when the first word of a sentence is a number, it should be spelled out. Example: Twenty-five people were on the bus.

Point out that when a sentence has two adjacent numbers, the smaller number is spelled out. Example: Katrina baked 6 four-pound packages.

Explain that fractions are spelled out when they stand alone and are not accompanied by a whole number. Use a hyphen with fractions that are spelled out. Example: Manuel is two-thirds of the way through his project.

Lesson 57

FOCUS

TIME MANAGEMENT

Suggested Schedule:

Warmup	2′
Skillbuilding	14′
Language Arts	6′
Formatting	6′
Document Processing	22′
Total	**50′**

TEACH

SKILLBUILDING

LESSON 57-B Students take repeated timed writings on a passage containing the exact number of words for their speed goal until they can complete the passage with no errors. Then, they move to the next longer passage and start again.

LESSON 57-C Paced Practice helps students reach individual speed and accuracy goals in 2-wpm increments by pacing them as they strive for a slightly faster rate.

LANGUAGE ARTS

LESSON 57-D Review the rules for number expression and hyphenation introduced in this lesson. Offer additional examples to clarify the rules if needed.

INSTRUCTOR STRATEGIES

Number Dictation Have volunteers dictate sentences using numbers. Have other volunteers write the dictated material on the board, and let the rest of the class check their work.

Lesson 57

LANGUAGE ARTS

SOLUTION: Lines 4–11

4. two
5. $3 million, one-half
6. five, two-thirds
7. 17 million
8. *Correct*
9. Fifty-nine, one-half
10. eight 20-pound
11. one-fourth

DOCUMENT PROCESSING

This is the second lesson in a series of five in which students complete in-basket assignments that review many of the formatting rules introduced in Part 3.

You may want to preview the jobs to be completed. Discuss the formatting rules for the jobs and identify the lessons in which those formatting rules were introduced.

Remind students to refer to their Word Processing Manual to review table formatting.

TABLE 57-18 Before students type the table, have them review the particulars of formatting this open table.

Remind them that columns consisting of words are left-aligned, and columns consisting of numbers are right-aligned.

Remind them to press ENTER 1 time before typing column headings consisting of one line. Press ENTER 1 time after typing the subtitle of the title heading.

Remind them of the process to use for removing borders from the table.

Reference Manual

Ask students to review the basic parts of tables in the **Reference Manual, R-13** before they begin typing.

RULE ▶ - number

Hyphenate compound numbers between twenty-one and ninety-nine and fractions that are expressed as words.

Twenty-nine recommendations were approved by at least three-fourths of the members.

Edit the sentences to correct any errors in number expression.

4 Seven investors were interested in buying 2 15-unit condos.
5 The purchase price for the buildings will be $3,000,000.00 each, which is 1/2 the total.
6 The computers were mailed in 5 40-pound boxes for 2/3 of the price paid yesterday.
7 Our food chain sold hamburgers for $3.00 each last year.
8 I can sell nearly one-half of all the tickets at the gate on November 13.
9 59 parking spaces are located within 1/2 mile of the city center.
10 We must place our mailing pieces in 8 twenty-pound bags for the mail clerk.
11 I don't believe more than 1/5 of the drivers have insurance.

DOCUMENT PROCESSING

Situation: Today is August 21, and you are employed in the office of Suite Retreat, a group of vacation resorts in Naples, Florida. Your employer, the general manager, is Mr. Aaron Hynes. Mr. Hynes is attending a meeting in Miami and has left the following jobs for you to complete. Press ENTER to create the 1- and 2-line column headings as displayed before automatically adjusting the table width.

Table 57-18
Open Table

SUITE RETREAT PROPERTIES
Selected Beach Rentals

Property	Rooms	Rental Rate In Season	Rental Rate Off Season
Carriage House	4	$3,500	$2,400
Naples Hideaway	5	2,750	2,100
Ocean Breeze	5	3,850	2,700
Princeton Palace	4	3,200	2,550
Seville Landings	6	4,250	3,100
The Vanderbilt	5	3,475	2,575
Westover Estates	6	5,250	4,150

TEACHING THE ADULT LEARNER

CLASSROOM INTERACTION Older students tend to be cautious when interacting with other students or responding to questions in the classroom. They are inclined to provide no response to a question rather than risk a mistake. Reward their responses, even if a comment is incorrect, to help build their confidence in classroom interactions.

Many instructors of adult learners come to rely upon them to provide a mature and realistic point of view in discussions.

It is important to stimulate some classroom interaction in the keyboarding classrooms or labs so that your older students do not feel isolated and uncomfortable.

Correspondence 57-47

Business Letter in Modified-Block Style

August 21, 20-- | Mr. Leland Mott | 243 Worth Street | Raleigh, NC 27603 | Dear Mr. Mott:

¶ We were pleased to hear of your interest in renting one of our prime beach units in Naples, Florida. I have enclosed a listing of all our current properties in the Naples area. We have 14 two-bedroom rentals, 15 three-bedroom rentals, and 11 four-bedroom rentals. Five of our three-bedroom units have already been rented for this season; one-half of the other thirty-four units are still available.

word

word

≡ number

¶ Let me review a few of the particulars of each unit with you. Our Carriage House and Naples Hideaway have Gulf Coast views and garage facilities. The Ocean Breeze and Princeton have lake views and tennis courts. The Seville, Vanderbilt, and Westover have a Gulf Coast view and a private golf course.

¶ If you plan to rent one of our units, please be sure to notify us by writing or by calling our toll-free number at 1-800-555-1348.

Sincerely, | Aaron Hynes | General Manager | urs | Enclosure | c: Theresa McDonald, Celeste Binghamton

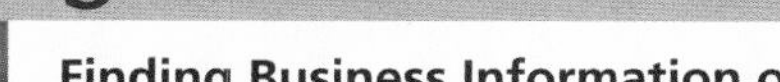

Keyboarding Connection

Finding Business Information on the Internet

To begin research on a business-related topic, try one of the following sites:

Business Resources on the Web at www.cio.com/bookmark provides links to Cable News Network (CNN) Business News, the Wall Street Journal Money and Investing Update, and other news sources. It includes information about careers, Electronic Data Interchange (EDI) and the Internet, general business sources, training, marketing, and resources for entrepreneurs.

Business Administration Internet Resources at www.acad.sunytccc.edu/library/busman.htm provides links to news and financial market updates, the Securities and Exchange Commission (SEC), Thomas Register, U.S. Census Bureau, U.S. Economic and Labor Statistics, and World Bank reports.

Selected Business Resources on the Web at www.bls.gov provides information about marketing, finance, small business, business law, international business, stock markets, and a link to the Small Business Administration.

YOUR TURN Access one of the business information sites listed above and explore its offerings.

Lesson 57

DOCUMENT PROCESSING

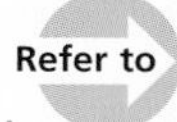

Refer to Reference Manual

Ask students to review the format for letters in modified-block style in the **Reference Manual, R-3B,** before they begin typing.

Before students type the letter in modified-block style, have them read the handwritten copy. Point out the instances in which the language arts rules for number expression and fractions have been applied.

CORRESPONDENCE 57-47

Remind students to spell-check, proofread, and preview their documents before printing them.

Have students examine Correspondence 57-47 and explain its use of number words and figures.

You may want to dictate an additional paragraph to students for them to insert. Use phrases such as *two 3-person couches* and *a four-seater porch swing* in order to help them practice number expression and hyphenation.

Keyboarding Connection

Finding Business Information on the Internet

The Web sites named in this feature have information on business in general, not just e-business. Ask students to suggest instances when they might use each of the Web sites and describe the type of information they would expect to find on that Web site.

YOUR TURN If time permits, have students complete the Your Turn activity and report their findings to the class.

Lesson 57

DOCUMENT PROCESSING

REPORT 57-32 Remind students to type the copy in the format for a business report. Point out that the bulleted list should align at the left margin.

ASSESS

www.mhhe.com/gdp to download a copy of the Technique Evaluation Form.

TECHNIQUE EVALUATION FORM Walk around the room to observe student technique. Complete a Technique Evaluation Form for each student.

Have students type and exchange multiple-choice questions that reinforce the language arts rules presented—number expression and hyphenation.

Extending the Lesson

Ask students to identify vocabulary words in the lesson documents that are related to the hospitality field.

Have them define the terms as a new section in the glossary they began in the Extending the Lesson activity of Lesson 56.

CLOSE

Encourage students to review the Reference Manual for document formatting. They may want to highlight topics they have already learned.

Mr. Hynes has recently purchased a fishing resort on Lake Okeechobee, Florida, and plans to open it on September 1. Type the following report and send it to the *Naples Press* so that it will appear in this Sunday's special *Travel and Tourism* section. Use a standard business format to prepare the report.

Report 57-32
Business Report

FISHING PARADISE SCHEDULED TO OPEN | Suite Retreat | Naples, Florida

¶ Suite Retreat is celebrating the grand opening of its newest fishing resort, Kamp Kellogg, located on the northwest corner of Lake Okeechobee, on the banks of the Kissimmee River.

GENERAL INFORMATION

¶ The following information will give you an overview of our policies and accommodations:

¶ **Reservations**. The reservation desk will open on September 1 to reserve your cabin at our beautiful resort. You can reach reservations via the Internet by logging on to our Web site at http://www.kampkellogg.com.

¶ **Accommodations.** Whether you're looking for deluxe accommodations or rustic surroundings, Kamp Kellogg has it all. You have a choice of rustic cabins nestled in the woods or large chalets overlooking Lake Okeechobee. If you enjoy an evening of relaxation, each cabin includes a gazebo, out near the water's edge, that is screened in for a perfect evening of comfort.

¶ **Amenities.** Your lodging choice includes full kitchens for those who want to do their own cooking, or you can order a full meal through our catering service. Each unit has a game room with a large-screen television, VCR, videotapes, and computer workstation with Internet connection. Outside the sliding glass door is a covered deck, equipped with a barbecue grill and hot tub.

LAKE OKEECHOBEE

¶ Lake Okeechobee lies geographically in the center of the state of Florida. The name "Okeechobee" was given to the lake by the Seminole Indians, and it means "big water." Lake Okeechobee is the largest freshwater lake in the United States occurring in one state. It is approximately 37 miles long and 30 miles wide, with an average depth of almost 10 feet. The lake produces more bass over 8 pounds than any other lake in the United States. It is famous for bass, crappie, and bluegill fishing. Several species of wildlife also thrive around the lake, such as the bald eagle, blue heron, egret, white ibis, sand hill crane, turkey, vulture, owl, alligator, bobcat, turkey, and panther.

Refer to Reference Manual

Refer to page R-12C of the Reference Manual for information on formatting lists.

PRICING INFORMATION

¶ We are offering a special introductory rate of $250 through November 1. This rate includes the following:

- Two-night stay for a family of four (# word)
- Two half days of fishing (# word)
- One USCG-licensed fishing guide (# word)
- Tackle and bait

¶ A full refund will be made if the fishing excursion is canceled because of inclement weather or failure of equipment (boat, trailer, or vehicle). If only a partial day of fishing is completed, one-half of the charges will be refunded. (- number)

INSTRUCTOR STRATEGIES

Hospitality Careers Have students research Web sites related to careers in the hospitality industry. How will their keyboarding skills be used in these careers (for example, reception desk at a hotel)?

Encourage students to visit **www.mhhe.com/gdp** for additional information on careers.

In-Basket Review (Retail)

Goals

- Type at least 40wpm/5′/5e
- Format retail documents

A. Type 2 times.

A. WARMUP

```
1      Do you think 1/3 of the contents of the five quart-     11
2 sized boxes would be about right? I do! If not, they can     22
3 adjust the portions by adding 6 or 7 gallons of warm water.  34
  | 1 | 2 | 3 | 4 | 5 | 6 | 7 | 8 | 9 | 10 | 11 | 12
```

SKILLBUILDING

B. DIAGNOSTIC PRACTICE: SYMBOLS AND PUNCTUATION

If you are not using the GDP software, turn to page SB-2 and follow the directions for this activity.

C. Type each line 2 times. Change every singular noun to a plural noun, and change every plural noun to a singular noun.

C. TECHNIQUE PRACTICE: CONCENTRATION

```
4 Debit the accounts. Balance your checkbook. Add the assets.
5 Take the discount. Send the statements. Compute the ratios.
6 Review the accounts. Credit the amounts. Figure the totals.
7 Prepare the statements. Send the catalog. Call the clients.
```

Meeting Special Needs

KEYBOARD CONFIGURATION Students can adjust their keyboard configuration to make the keyboard more accessible. If a person cannot release a key quickly after pressing it, a setting called Filter Keys tells the computer to ignore repeated keystrokes. In newer versions of Windows, the user can set the keyboard's cursor-movement keys to control the mouse pointer.

Modern operating systems also provide various alert methods. Hearing-impaired users can set their PCs to display visual alerts instead of sounding audible alerts.

Lesson 58

FOCUS

TIME MANAGEMENT 

Suggested Schedule:

Warmup	2′
Skillbuilding	22′
Formatting	6′
Document Processing	20′
Total	**50′**

TEACH

SKILLBUILDING

LESSON 58-B Encourage students to push moderately for speed on the Pretest.

LESSON 58-C The Technique Practice is designed to encourage students to concentrate as they type.

After students have followed instructions, if time permits, have them type to your dictation as you change some of the commands into negatives. Example: Do not debit the accounts. Do not balance your checkbook. Do not add the assets.

 **SOLUTION: Lines 4–7**

4. account, checkbooks, asset
5. discounts, statement, ratio
6. account, amount, total
7. statement, catalogs, client

INSTRUCTOR STRATEGIES

Discussing the Photo Ask students to think about instances when their keyboarding skills are important when working with their computers.

Lesson 58

DOCUMENT PROCESSING

LESSON 58-D Remind students to maintain good posture and use correct technique as they work toward meeting the goals for this 5-minute timed writing.

FORMATTING

Reference Manual

Refer students to these pages in the **Reference Manual: R-3A** (business letter in block style), **R-4D** (memo), and **R-13A** (boxed table) before they start typing the jobs for this in-basket assignment.

CORRESPONDENCE 58-48

Have students read the material that establishes the situation for the in-basket activities. You may wish to make a list on the board as students provide you a summary of their information.

Remind students to spell-check, proofread, and preview their documents before printing them.

D. Take two 5-minute timed writings. Review your speed and errors.

Goal: At least 40wpm/5'/5e

D. 5-MINUTE TIMED WRITING

Most workers will learn about their success on the job 11
at least once a year. The person in charge will be the one 23
to conduct these reviews. Even though the job review is 34
important, either party might not look forward to such a 46
meeting. Frequently, an employee and a boss can view these 57
meetings as a time to discuss everything that this person 69
has done wrong in the last year. Such a negative approach 81
can add a lot of stress and tension between the employee 92
and management. In the long run, work performance suffers. 104
A good manager must learn a new way to conduct more 114
positive job reviews. Such a meeting might start by sizing 126
up what the employee has done to help improve things in the 138
past year. Positive comments may include coming to work on 150
time, working well with others, and being willing to pitch 162
in whenever needed. Next, the areas for improvement may be 174
discussed. Then the employee should be given the chance to 185
ask questions, write a response to the appraisal, and get 197
other feedback. 200

| 1 | 2 | 3 | 4 | 5 | 6 | 7 | 8 | 9 | 10 | 11 | 12

DOCUMENT PROCESSING

Situation: You are employed as an administrative assistant for Good Sports, a retailer for sports equipment and clothing in Denver, Colorado. Your employer is Mr. Kevin Hite, marketing director for Good Sports. Upon arriving at your office on Monday morning, you notice that Mr. Hite has left several jobs that need to be completed for his signature. He prefers a letter in block style in his correspondence and uses *Sincerely* as the complimentary closing.

Correspondence 58-48
Business Letter in Block Style

January 10, 20-- | Mr. Alex R. Chaney, Principal | Madison Heights High School | 1839 East Colfax Avenue | Denver, CO 80212 | Dear Mr. Chaney:
¶ Thank you for your invitation to advertise on your school's Web site. We were delighted to have the opportunity to sponsor last week's Marathon Mile at Madison Heights High School and hope that all the participants enjoyed the competition and spectator activities.
¶ This week my office staff will be putting together a Web page that we would like to display on the Web space you have so generously provided. It is my understanding that the Web site will remain online throughout this school year. We will be certain to maintain it on a regular basis so that our products and prices always remain current.

(Continued on next page)

INSTRUCTOR STRATEGIES

Employers and Employees Discuss with students the employer-employee relationship. What does each side owe the other? Do students think performance appraisals should be mutual—that is, should employees appraise the employer's performance?

Add the closing lines to Mr. Hite's letter. Send copies of this letter to Ardele Stevens, Jennifer Smits, and Randall Campbellton.

¶ The Marathon Mile has certainly become one of the county's most popular school events. We look forward to the opportunity of cosponsoring next year's Marathon Mile at Madison Heights.

Correspondence 58-49

Memo

MEMO TO: Blanche O. Pruitt | **FROM:** Kevin Hite | **DATE:** January 11, 20-- | **SUBJECT:** District Meetings

¶ As you know, each year we rotate the location of our district meetings to one of our regional offices. This year our meeting will be held in your region, preferably in Albuquerque. Would you please contact the hotels in Albuquerque and select a suitable site for this year's meeting, which will be held on March 7 and 8.

¶ We decided at our last regional managers' meeting that this year's meeting would highlight our Internet sales campaign. Specifically, we want to focus on the following issues:

1. How can we improve our Web page design to attract a higher percentage of the market?
2. How can we improve our e-commerce procedures so that our order-processing routine is easier and faster for the average Web visitor?
3. What links can we add to our home page to encourage visitors to view a greater percentage of our product line?

¶ Please let me know when you have made arrangements for our meeting site. I look forward to meeting with all of you in March. | urs

Refer to Reference Manual

Refer to page R-12C of the Reference Manual for information on formatting lists.

Table 58-19

Boxed Table

WEEKLY BICYCLE SPECIALS January 13, 20--		
Model	**Price**	**Special Features**
Comanche	$270	15" Y-frame; 18-speed drivetrain; adjustable seat
Cyclone	375	Our lightest bike; preassembled; wired blue color
Duster	480	Front suspension fork; semislick tires; 24-speed
Trail Blazer	725	Titanium frame; aluminum seat post; two bottle mounts

ERGONOMICALLY SPEAKING

NOT JUST FINGER EXERCISES You may want to stage an exercise that consists of real exercise for a change. At a certain point, have students get up out of their seats and circle their row before sitting down and continuing to type.

Lesson 58

DOCUMENT PROCESSING

CORRESPONDENCE 58-49

Reference Manual

Have students study the **Reference Manual, R-3B,** to review how to format the numbered list.

Remind students to spell-check, proofread, and preview their documents before printing them.

TABLE 58-19 Before they begin typing, have students review the information to be formatted in the table. They should determine how to format the table heading, the column headings, and the column entries before they begin typing.

Students need to AutoFit the contents so that the third column extends to accommodate the longest entry in that column.

ASSESS

www.mhhe.com/gdp to download a copy of the Technique Evaluation Form.

TECHNIQUE EVALUATION FORM Walk around the classroom to observe student technique.

Review results of timed writings.

Review the formatting of all documents.

Extending the Lesson

Assist students who are having difficulties completing the in-basket assignments. Encourage students to use the Reference Manual and the textbook to find answers.

CLOSE

Encourage students to practice skillbuilding exercises.

FOCUS

TIME MANAGEMENT 

Suggested Schedule:

Warmup	2′
Skillbuilding	15′
Language Arts	6′
Formatting	6′
Document Processing	21′
Total	**50′**

TEACH

SKILLBUILDING

LESSON 59-B  **MAP** In Misstroke Analysis and Prescription (MAP), the material typed by each student is analyzed and specific drills are prescribed to help the student correct errors; over 75 different kinds of typed errors are included in the analysis.

LESSON 59-C Each paragraph is more difficult than the preceding one—based on the number of punctuation marks.

Paragraph 1: 2
Paragraph 2: 4
Paragraph 3: 6
Paragraph 4: 8

Lesson 59

In-Basket Review (Nonprofit)

Goals

- Improve speed and accuracy
- Refine language arts skills in spelling
- Format government documents

A. Type 2 times.

A. WARMUP

```
     Crowne and Metzner, Inc., employees* joined with 68      11
youngsters to repair the brick homes of 13 elderly persons;   23
several became very well acquainted with six of the owners.   35
| 1 | 2 | 3 | 4 | 5 | 6 | 7 | 8 | 9 | 10 | 11 | 12
```

SKILLBUILDING

B. MAP

Follow the GDP software directions for this exercise in improving keystroking accuracy.

C. Take a 1-minute timed writing on the first paragraph to establish your base speed. Then take four 1-minute timed writings on the remaining paragraphs. As soon as you equal or exceed your base speed on one paragraph, advance to the next, more difficult paragraph.

C. SUSTAINED PRACTICE: PUNCTUATION

```
     The men in the warehouse were having a very difficult    11
time keeping track of that inventory. Things began to go      22
much more smoothly for them when they got the new computer.   34

     Whenever something was shipped out, a computer entry     11
was made to show the changes. They always knew exactly what   23
merchandise was in stock; they also knew what to order.       34

     Management was pleased with that improvement. "We        10
should have made the change years ago," said the supervisor   22
to the plant manager, who was in full agreement with him.     34

     This is just one example (among many) of how the work    11
areas can be improved. Workers' suggestions are listened      22
to by alert, expert managers. Their jobs are better, too.     34
| 1 | 2 | 3 | 4 | 5 | 6 | 7 | 8 | 9 | 10 | 11 | 12
```


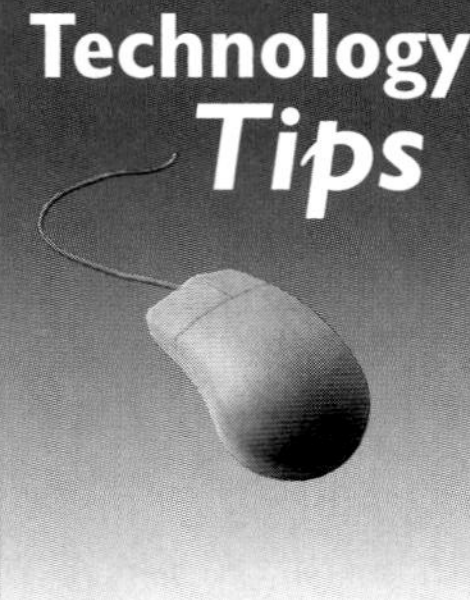

Technology *Tips*

NONPROFIT ORGANIZATIONS

Encourage students to search for Web sites that discuss careers in nonprofit organizations. Discuss advantages and disadvantages of working for nonprofit organizations.

LANGUAGE ARTS

D. Type this list of frequently misspelled words, paying special attention to any spelling problems in each word.

D. SPELLING

```
16 development determine enclosed complete members recent site
17 permanent personal facility medical library however purpose
18 representative implementation electrical discussed eligible
19 organization performance minimum discuss expense areas next
20 professional arrangements separate changes reason field pay
```

Edit the sentences to correct any misspellings.

```
21 Members of the medicle and profesional group discussed it.
22 The development of the seperate cite will be completed.
23 A recent representive said the libary facility may be next.
24 A perpose of the electricle organization is to get changes.
25 However, the implimentation of changes will be permenant.
26 Arrangments for the enclosed eligable expenses are listed.
```

DOCUMENT PROCESSING

Situation: Today is October 10. You work for Quick Trip, a ride-share company located in Windsor, Connecticut.

Your company is a nonprofit commuter company that provides the following services: move people to and from work, conduct parking studies, match people with available rides, and publish a commuter ride-share weekly report.

Your job responsibilities include preparing reports that summarize weekly commuter news, typing correspondence to advertise and promote Quick Trip's services, and communicating with area commuters who subscribe to Quick Trip's services.

Today, you must (1) prepare a report that summarizes services offered by Quick Trip, and (2) create a table that lists new additions to the weekly report.

Report 59-33
Business Report

QUICK TRIP

Windsor's Premier Ride- Share

¶ If you're tired of driving that one- to two hour commute into Connecticuts busy metropolitan areas, then let us take that burden ~~on for you.~~ off your shoulders. Quick Trip, the metro's premier ride-share company, is a convenient economical way to get to & from work. All you have to do is get on board!

(Continued on next page)

Lesson 59

LANGUAGE ARTS

LESSON 59-D Alternate routine: Dictate each word, and have students type the word 1 time. Then have them edit the sentences to correct any misspellings.

INSTRUCTOR STRATEGIES

Mnemonics Encourage students to develop memory clues, or mnemonics, to help them remember difficult spellings. For example, There is *a rat* in *separate.*

SOLUTION: Lines 21–26

21. medical, professional
22. separate, site
23. representative, library
24. purpose, electrical
25. implementation, permanent
26. Arrangements, eligible

DOCUMENT PROCESSING

Refer to Reference Manual

Ask students to review the format for APA-style reports and proofreaders' marks in the **Reference Manual, R-8A**, **R-8B,** and **R-14C** to help them in formatting the business report.

Help students become familiar with the facts that pertain to the situation. You may wish to have students outline the information to help them prepare the in-basket assignments.

REPORT 59-33 Before students type the report, have them read the rough-draft copy to make sure they know the meaning of the proofreaders' marks and how to apply them to the copy.

EXTENDING LANGUAGE ARTS

Spelling Choose one or more of the following activities to do prior to having your students type the exercise:

- Pronounce each word.
- Have the class pronounce the words in unison.
- Have two or three students pronounce a line of words.
- Provide a simple definition for each word.
- Dictate the words while students look at you, not at the monitor or their hands, as they type.
- Have students circle any errors and type at least 3 times any word on which they made an error.
- For homework, have students prepare a list of definitions of these words.

Lesson 59

DOCUMENT PROCESSING

REPORT 59-33 (continued)
Remind students to type the text for the bulleted list before they apply the bulleted list format.

Remind students to spell-check, proofread, and preview their documents before printing them.

INSTRUCTOR STRATEGIES

Ride-Share Business
Discuss the content of Report 59-33 with students. Do they think such a service would succeed in their area? Which parts do they like best? Would they need any other benefits in order to use the service?

Refer to Reference Manual

Refer to page R-12C of the Reference Manual for information on formatting lists.

Costs of Commuting

¶ A recent article showed that commuting just 15 miles each way can cost a minimum of $1,200 per year; sharing the ride with some one else can cut your comuting expenses in half.[1] In addition to the cost of gas, you must also figure in other costs of transportation such as maintenance on your vehicle, insurance premiums, depreciation, and finance charges.[2] ~~When you consider all these costs, ride-sharing takes on a whole new significance.~~ You should also consider how you are helping the trafic congestion and air pollution problems by ride-sharing. And don't forget about the possibility of being involved in an accident. Finally you can reduce stress by ride-sharing because you can choose to leave the driving to someone else.

RESERVATIONS AND BENEFITS

¶ If you want to reserve a seat on a Quick Trip route, just call one of our professional service representatives at 1-800-555-Trip. Our representatives in the field have information on routes, schedules, rides availability, and other benefits. For example, we have an E-ride available for you if there is an emergency that requires you to get home. Here are some special benefits with Quick Trip:

- A free commute for every 500 comuting miles.
- Separate insurance and medical coverage.
- Flexible payment policies.
- A free commute for every 500 commuting miles.
- Full insurance coverage.
- Flexible payment policies.
- 4 free taxi rides home per year in the event of illness or personal emergency.

SERVICE AREAS

¶ Quick Trip serves the cities of Plainville, Rocky Hill, Manchester, Windsor, New Haven, and Sufield. Next month we open routes to Avon, Glastonbury,

(Continued on next page)

Meeting Special Needs

HEARING IMPAIRMENTS Arranging your classroom properly can be of great help to the hearing-impaired student.

- Arrange seating so that the student can read your lips (or provide an interpreter).
- Write instructions on the board or use an overhead projector.
- Avoid standing in front of windows or other light sources so that glare will not affect the student's ability to see you clearly.

Visit us on the Web at **www.mhhe.com/gdp** for more information.

Durham, and Middletown. In all, we have over 300 regular routes statewide, and service is expanding monthly. Easy access is guaranteed with all our routes. To view our entire service area, go to our Web site, http://www.qt.com, and link to the Quick Trip regional service area map. The map details all our routes, highlights specific pickup points, and identifies our regional service facilities. Visit our site today and become a ride-share enthusiast!

---

[1] Erica Sommers, "Ride-Sharing for the Environment," *Environmental Planning*, February 21, 2004, p. 18.

[2] Joshua R. Blake, *Cleaning Up America*, New Haven Publishing, Manchester, Connecticut, 2005, p. 138.

Table 59-20

Boxed Table

QUICK TRIP COMMUTER BULLETIN For October			
From	To	Name	Telephone
Manchester	Rocky Hill	S. Baskin	860-555-5581
Manchester	Windsor	E. Lindholm	203-555-4684
Manchester	Suffield	P. Mack	860-555-4322
New Haven	Plainville	T. Thompson	203-555-1249
Rocky Hill	Windsor	J. Kiczuk	860-555-1842
Suffield	Manchester	M. Duprey	203-555-9339
Suffield	New Haven	B. Huebner	203-555-0442
Suffield	New Haven	M. Mac	203-555-1844
Windsor	Manchester	L. Smith	203-555-8893
Windsor	Rocky Hill	R. McCaffrey	203-555-7782

ERGONOMICALLY SPEAKING

STRETCH BREAK If you sit in front of your computer too long, you may develop aching muscles and stiff joints. An informational software program is available to help increase circulation, relieve tension, and guard against repetitive strain injuries. To learn more about this program and to obtain information on how to download the software, visit **www.pcworld.com/downloads**. Type "stretch break" in the **Search** box and click the link to **Stretch Break Pro**. Allow students to practice some of the stretching exercises.

DOCUMENT PROCESSING

REPORT 59-33 (continued) Remind students to refer to their Word Processing Manual to review the procedure to insert footnotes.

Reference Manual

Ask students to review the boxed table format in the **Reference Manual, R-13A,** before they begin typing.

TABLE 59-20 Optional. Remind students to use the AutoFit feature for correct horizontal placement of all row entries.

Open the **Page Setup** dialog box to center the table vertically.

ASSESS

www.mhhe.com/gdp to download a copy of the Technique Evaluation Form.

TECHNIQUE EVALUATION FORM Review the format for the documents created as part of this lesson. Review any parts that may have been difficult for students to complete.

Extending the Lesson

Discuss the results of the MAP skillbuilding exercise.

CLOSE

Remind students to save their documents according to the established procedure.

Have them go over their work for this course to see what documents they might want to include in a job interview portfolio.

FOCUS

TIME MANAGEMENT 

Suggested Schedule:

Warmup	2′
Skillbuilding	16′
Formatting	6′
Document Processing	26′
Total	**50′**

TEACH

SKILLBUILDING

PRETEST ➔ PRACTICE ➔ POSTTEST

PPP The Pretest/Practice/Posttest (PPP) routine is designed to build speed and accuracy through a three-step program:

60-B The Pretest is the preliminary effort to determine the learner's initial skill level. Encourage students to push moderately for speed on the Pretest. Close reaches include adjacent keys and consecutive-finger reaches.

60-C and 60-D The practice section consists of intensive drills to improve the reaches focused on in the Pretest. Adjacent keys are side by side on the same row. Consecutive-finger reaches are two consecutive keys that are typed with the same finger.

60-E The Posttest measures the effect of the Practice.

In-Basket Review (Manufacturing)

Goals

- Type at least 40wpm/5′/5e
- Format manufacturing documents

A. Type 2 times.

A. WARMUP

```
     "Fay's #6 report shows 26 pens @ .49 each and 37 pens   11
@ .79 each," the CEO announced. Mrs. Bailey's reaction was   23
quite amazing as 80 jobs were validated with checked boxes.  35
| 1 | 2 | 3 | 4 | 5 | 6 | 7 | 8 | 9 | 10 | 11 | 12
```

SKILLBUILDING

PPP **PRETEST ➔ PRACTICE ➔ POSTTEST**

PRETEST
Take a 1-minute timed writing. Review your speed and errors.

B. PRETEST: Close Reaches

```
     Sally took the coins from the pocket of her blouse   10
and traded them for seventy different coins. Anyone could   22
see that Myrtle looked funny when extra coins were traded.  34
| 1 | 2 | 3 | 4 | 5 | 6 | 7 | 8 | 9 | 10 | 11 | 12
```

PRACTICE
Speed Emphasis:
If you made 2 or fewer errors on the Pretest, type each *individual* line 2 times.
Accuracy Emphasis:
If you made 3 or more errors, type each *group* of lines (as though it were a paragraph) 2 times.

C. PRACTICE: Adjacent Keys

```
as asked asset based basis class least visas ease fast mass
we weary wedge weigh towel jewel fewer dwell wear weed week
rt birth dirty earth heart north alert worth dart port tort
```

D. PRACTICE: Consecutive Fingers

```
sw swamp swift swoop sweet swear swank swirl swap sway swim
gr grade grace angry agree group gross gripe grow gram grab
ol older olive solid extol spool fools stole bolt cold cool
```

POSTTEST
Repeat the Pretest timed writing and compare performance.

E. POSTTEST: Close Reaches

MHHE CHAMPIONS

Grading

Create a transparency for each document in a lesson. Use the transparency to review the correct format for each document. Place each transparency in a binder for use next term.

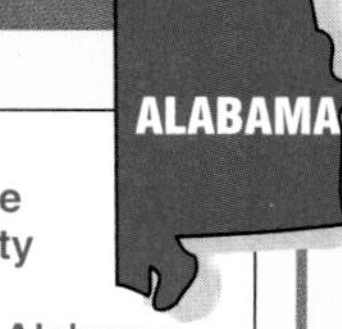

Pam Strong
Shelton State Community College
Tuscaloosa, Alabama

Instructors Helping One Another

F. Take two 5-minute timed writings. Review your speed and errors.

Goal: At least 40wpm/5'/5e

F. 5-MINUTE TIMED WRITING

Information technology is among the fastest-growing 11
job fields today and is also one of the fields to change 22
the quickest. The goal of many schools is to try to prepare 34
students to be specialists in a workplace that continues to 46
be challenging and will need to change quickly as advances 58
are made in technology. 63
Those who wish to work in a field that will not stand 74
still need to know all about the systems with which they 85
labor. Network administrators, for example, will often take 97
courses to certify that they have a sound knowledge of any 109
of the new hardware. They must also learn about specific 120
equipment and have an understanding of how new software 131
will function with hardware. 137
Those who wish to pass certification exams must have 148
the zeal, determination, and drive to complete all of the 160
requirements. They know that it will not be long before the 172
current systems will be upgraded or new software will be 183
released. They need to learn the latest systems and review 195
their certification again. 200

| 1 | 2 | 3 | 4 | 5 | 6 | 7 | 8 | 9 | 10 | 11 | 12

DOCUMENT PROCESSING

Situation: You are an administrative assistant, and you work for Disk Drives, Etc., in Phoenix, Arizona. Your supervisor is Ms. Nancy Mendez, sales and marketing director. Ms. Mendez has asked you to prepare the following documents for her while she is in a staff meeting this morning. The letter is to be prepared for her signature, the table will be enclosed with the letter, and she will initial the memo before sending it out this afternoon.

Correspondence 60-50

Business Letter in Block Style

September 13, 20-- | Ms. Nancy Luo | 1387 Rim Drive | Flagstaff, AZ 86001-3111 | Dear Ms. Luo:

¶ We were pleased to see that you have used our Web site at www.tosabi.com to inquire about our online catalog. We specialize in computer drives of all types: CD-ROM, DVD, Zip, Jaz, floppy, and hard drives. I have enclosed a listing of our most popular CD-ROM writers that will appear online next week in our catalog. As a new customer, you are invited to visit our catalog and place your order at these special prices.

(Continued on next page)

Meeting Special Needs

COGNITIVE OR LANGUAGE IMPAIRMENT Keyboard filters such as word prediction utilities and add-on spell checkers can help students who have cognitive or language disabilities. These utilities, compatible with Microsoft, are made by independent companies.

INSTRUCTOR STRATEGIES

Keeping Up With Technology Discuss with students the disciplines in your college that teach information technology (IT). If possible, invite an IT teacher to address the class briefly on the subject of keeping up with technology.

Lesson 60

SKILLBUILDING

LESSON 60-F Remind students to keep eyes on copy and use correct technique.

Encourage them to concentrate on meeting the goals for this 5-minute timed writing while maintaining correct technique.

DOCUMENT PROCESSING

Ask students to review and become familiar with the material stated in the Situation paragraph. Students may find it helpful to make an itemized list, outlining the tasks to be completed in this in-basket.

CORRESPONDENCE 60-50

Reference Manual

Ask students to review the letter in block style in the **Reference Manual, R-3A,** before they begin typing.

Students will need to know how to type a bulleted list and add an enclosure notation and copy notation.

Ask students whether they expect Ms. Mendez to look over their work carefully, or whether they think she will merely sign it and return it to them for mailing. Solicit the opinions of the adult learners in the class, along with those of any younger students who have actually worked in an office. After the discussion, ask, "For which type of employer should you proofread very carefully? Why?" (Both. If an employer proofreads, you don't want him or her to see mistakes in your work. If an employer doesn't proofread, you don't want clients to think the office staff isn't careful about details.)

Lesson 60

DOCUMENT PROCESSING

TABLE 60-21

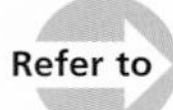
Refer to Reference Manual

Ask students to review the table features in the **Reference Manual, R-13,** before they begin typing.

Before typing the table, students should be aware of how they will format the table heading, the column headings, and the column entries of the four-column table.

Refer to Reference Manual

Ask students to review memo and list formatting in the **Reference Manual, R-4D** and **R-3B,** before they begin typing.

CORRESPONDENCE 60-51

Remind students to spell-check, proofread, and preview their documents before printing them.

¶ Our online customers receive the same privileges as our hard-copy catalog shoppers. These online privileges include:

- No shipping charges.
- Toll-free customer support line.
- Discounts on 10 or more purchases.
- Ninety-day warranties (parts and labor) on all purchases.

¶ We look forward to many years of doing business with you. Please e-mail me at nmendez@tosabi.net if you have any questions or would like additional information.
Sincerely, | Nancy Mendez | Sales and Marketing Director | urs | Enclosure | c: S. Choi, W. Matson

Table 60-21
Boxed Table

Your finished table will have different line endings for Column D when you resize the column widths to fit the contents.

CD-ROM WRITERS
(Effective Dates September 18-23)

Model No.	Part No.	Price	Specifications
460RW	841120	$199	4x speed write, 16x speed read, CD recording software
2600E	841111	235	4x speed write, 24x speed read, 4x speed rewrite, stores up to 650 MB per disk
9282E	841415	415	Rewritable. 4x speed write, 8x speed read, Direct CD software
8428S	842013	595	Rewritable. 8x speed write, 24x speed read, 2x speed erase, Direct CD software
93422R	841712	658	Rewritable. 4x speed write, 6x speed read, 2x speed rewrite, Direct CD software, CDR-DJ

Correspondence 60-51
Memo

MEMO TO: Claudia Crenshaw | Publications Department | **FROM:** Nancy Mendez | Sales and Marketing Director | **DATE:** September 13, 20-- | **SUBJECT:** Ad in the *Arizona Daily Sun*
¶ Claudia, please include the following criteria in our ad that will run in the *Arizona Daily Sun* this Sunday:

1. Quarter-page ad
2. Run-time: 2 weeks
3. Location: Business Section as well as Classified Section
4. Contact: Include telephone, fax, and e-mail numbers

¶ This is our first ad piece in the *Sun* since we ran that special promotion last March. Let's add some graphics to make this one an "eye-catcher." | urs

TEACHING THE ADULT LEARNER

ESSAY QUESTIONS Suggest the following to help adult learners answer essay test items:

- Outline major points you will address in your answer.
- Explain technical terms.
- Provide examples to support your points.
- Conclude the essay by summarizing the major points.
- Proofread your answer.

Correspondence 60-52

Business Letter in Modified-Block Style

September 15, 20-- | Ms. Rolanda L. Farmer | 203 Grand Avenue | Bozeman, MT 59715 | Dear Ms. Farmer:

¶ Your order for Internet service has been processed, and you can enjoy surfing the Web immediately! As a customer of Global Communications, a subsidiary of Disk Drives, Etc., you will enjoy several benefits:

1. You will receive 24/7 customer service when using our service hotline at 1-800-555-3888.
2. You will be protected by E-Protect, Global's virus protection software. This software is updated weekly, and you can download weekly updates at www.gc.net.
3. You will receive 10 Mbytes of Web page space.
4. You will receive automated credit card billing, as requested.

¶ A complete listing of all our services is enclosed for your perusal.

¶ Thank you for joining Global Communications. Please e-mail us at support@gc.net if you have any questions, or call us on our service hotline. We expect the coming months of providing Internet service to you to be a very enjoyable experience for both of us.

Sincerely, | Nancy Mendez | Sales and Marketing Director | urs | Enclosure

Refer to Reference Manual

Refer to page R-12C of the Reference Manual for information on formatting lists.

Lesson 60

DOCUMENT PROCESSING

CORRESPONDENCE 60-52

Reference Manual

Ask students to review the format for a business letter in modified-block style in the **Reference Manual, R-3B,** before they begin typing.

Have students review the handwritten copy before they begin to type. They will need to know how to format a numbered list and an enclosure notation.

INSTRUCTOR STRATEGIES

Discussing the Photo Ask if any students are familiar with designing Web pages, or if anyone is interested in pursuing a career as a Web master. Invite a person who is associated with the Web design industry to speak with the class about career opportunities.

INSTRUCTOR STRATEGIES

Discussing the Photo Corporate Web, intranet, and extranet sites are developed, designed, and maintained by experienced designers and Web masters. Web designers bring various traditional design skills to the table—such as experience with graphics, text design, and layout—but they are also skilled with hypertext markup language (HTML) tools and scripting languages (languages written so that one computer can communicate with another computer). Web masters often have the more technical skills required for high-level technical support.

Programmers are finding all sorts of opportunities in Internet development because Web sites are commonly used to support high-level functions such as interactivity, searches, and data mining.

Lesson 60

DOCUMENT PROCESSING

Progress Check/ Proofreading Check

In formatting Table 60-22, students will use many of the table formatting features. You may want to use this document as a document processing test. This document also serves as a check of your students' proofreading skill. Their goal is to have zero typographical errors when the GDP software first scores the document in order to earn a satisfactory proofreading grade. If students need a second chance, they should click the **Create** button in the GDP software to retype the document and try again to have zero typos on the first scored attempt. The GDP Portfolio notes how many scored attempts were made when a document is created or re-created to help you track proofreading scores.

ASSESS

www.mhhe.com/gdp to download a copy of the Technique Evaluation Form.

TECHNIQUE EVALUATION FORM

Review results of timed writings and print a report for all skillbuilding exercises for Lessons 56–60.

Extending the Lesson

Ask students to identify the documents with which they felt confident and those for which they need more practice.

CLOSE

Remind students to follow the steps for saving documents.

Table 60-22

Boxed Table

Progress and Proofreading Check

Documents designated as Proofreading Checks serve as a check of your proofreading skill. Your goal is to have zero typographical errors when the GDP software first scores the document.

Your finished table will have different line endings for all columns when you resize the column widths to fit the contents.

CUSTOMER SERVICES **(Effective October 1, 20--)**		
Service	**Description/Comments**	**Representative**
24/7 Service	Call 1-800-555-3888; wait time is usually less than 1 minute.	M. R. Osumi, mrosumi@global.net
Virus-Protection Service	E-Protect software is downloaded automatically to your computer when service is installed.	W. N. Gauthier, wngauth@global.net
Web Space	10 MB of Web page space is standard; an additional 10 MB can be obtained on an as-needed basis.	M. J. Martinez, mjmartinez@global.net
Credit Card Billing	When requested by the customer, we automatically send your monthly bill to a credit card of your choice.	L. T. Matthews, ltmatt@global.net

Strategies for Career Success

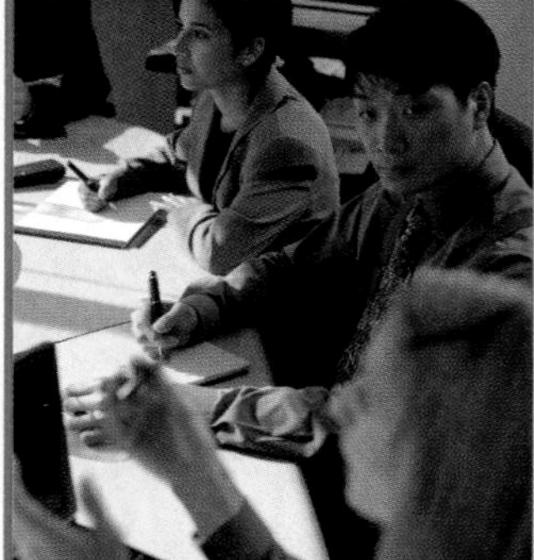

Successful Interviewing Techniques

The interview is a useful tool for researching information. Here are some steps to effective interviewing.

Conduct preliminary research so you can ask intelligent questions and make efficient use of the interview time. Prepare a list of questions (for example, an interview script) to use in the interview. Make sure the questions are open-ended, unbiased, and geared toward gathering insights you can't gain through reading. Be prepared to take notes, listen actively, and ask follow-up questions, as needed.

Greet the interviewee by name and thank him or her for taking time to talk with you. Explain why you are interested in interviewing him or her. Stay within the scheduled time limits. In closing the interview, thank the interviewee again, and ask if you can get in touch if other questions come to mind.

YOUR TURN Prepare a list of questions you might use in interviewing someone concerning the current U.S. immigration policies.

Strategies for Career Success

SUCCESSFUL INTERVIEW TECHNIQUES Create a list of questions students should be prepared to answer during an interview. Discuss appropriate answers for the questions. Distribute the questions to the students.

YOUR TURN If time permits, ask students to complete the Your Turn activity.

Skills Assessment on Part 3

5-Minute Timed Writing

People are often the most prized assets in a business. 11
Excellent firms know that having well-qualified workers is 23
an important step to ensure the success of the company. The 35
people in charge can play a huge part in how much success a 47
firm will have when they provide a workplace that is meant 59
to support teams of people who can work together to achieve 71
a common goal. When people know they are being encouraged 82
to work toward achieving their own goals as well as the 94
goals of the company, they will respond by working to their 106
highest potential with ardor and zeal. 113
Managers need to show that they value the hard work 124
and long hours that employees put in to ensure the success 136
of the business. People thrive on compliments that show 147
their work is appreciated. They like to be rewarded in some 159
way when they have done an exceptional job. When those in 171
charge are successful in motivating the employees to work 182
to their full potential, their company will prosper. The 194
result is that each person wins. 200

| 1 | 2 | 3 | 4 | 5 | 6 | 7 | 8 | 9 | 10 | 11 | 12

Correspondence Test 3-53

Business Letter in Block Style

Add an envelope to the letter, and omit the return address.

July 13, 20-- | Mr. Anthony Gillespie | Goddard Properties | 1808 Augusta Court | Lexington, KY 40505-2838 | Dear Mr. Gillespie:

¶ Let me introduce myself. I am committee chair of a group that monitors development projects in Lexington, Kentucky. It was brought to my attention that your proposal to construct 100 three- and four-bedroom homes was approved by the city council last night. As a resident in a neighboring community, I wish to share with you the stipulations

(Continued on next page)

INSTRUCTOR'S NOTES/INTERNET BOOKMARKS

Visit us on the Web at www.mhhe.com/gdp.

Test 3

ASSESS

An alternate Progress Test (similar to this one) is included in the Tests and Solution Keys booklet. Because of time constraints, you may want to administer this test over two class meetings.

To save class time, be sure to have appropriate clip art and templates readily available in your word processing software. See the Instructor's Manual for suggested grading standards for Test 3.

CORRESPONDENCE TEST 3-53 Review the format for a business letter in block style in Lesson 31-F, Basic Parts of a Business Letter, on page 85. Also review the format for a business letter and an envelope on pages R-3A and R-6 in the Reference Manual.

Review the format of a bulleted list in correspondence, Lesson 48-E, on page 156.

Review the format of a copy notation in Lesson 49-E, on page 159.

Test 3

ASSESS

CORRESPONDENCE TEST 3-54 Review the format for a memo in Lesson 34-E, on page 97. Also review the memo on page R-4D in the Reference Manual.

Review the format of a bulleted list in correspondence, Lesson 48-E, on page 156.

Review the format of an attachment notation in Lesson 35-E, page 100.

we would like you to incorporate into your development project:
- The new homes should have no less than 2,700 square feet of living space.
- All structures should have brick frontage.
- No external, unattached buildings should be constructed.

¶ Following these stipulations will ensure that your homes adhere to our community building codes. Sincerely, | Dora H. Hayes | Committee Chair | urs | c: S. Benefield, T. Grace

Correspondence Test 3-54
Memo

MEMO TO: Ana Pacheco
FROM: Liang Quan
DATE: June 26, 20--
SUBJECT: Desktop Publishing Certificate
¶ Our DTP certificate seminar will be held in St. Louis on August 14. Upon request of last year's participants, we want to be sure to include the following topics:
- Integrated Computer Applications
- Advanced Desktop Publishing
- Introduction to Computer Graphics
- Graphic Design A and B

¶ These were the four most popular topics at last year's seminar. Let's use a brochure design similar to the one we used at the Denver meeting last year. A copy of that brochure is attached for you to review. | urs | Attachment

INSTRUCTOR'S NOTES/INTERNET BOOKMARKS

Visit us on the Web at www.mhhe.com/gdp.

Report Test 3-34

Business Report

AIR POLLUTION

¶ When we hear about pollution, we tend to think of smog, traffic congestion, acid rain, and other pollutant-related terms. However, we also need to consider the air we breathe as we work.

AIR QUALITY AND POLLUTANTS

¶ We need to be concerned about indoor air because it can affect the health, comfort, and productivity of workers.[1]

¶ **Strategies to Improve Air Quality.** The three basic approaches to improving air quality include the use of air pressure to keep the pollutants "at bay," the use of ventilation systems to remove the pollutants, and the use of filters to clean the air. The pollutants can appear in various forms but are typically biological contaminants, chemical pollutants, or particles.

¶ **Pollutant Descriptions.** Biological contaminants can include viruses, molds, bacteria, dust mites, pollen, and water spills. These contaminants cause allergic reactions that trigger asthma attacks for an estimated 16 million Americans.[2] Chemical pollutants include tobacco smoke and accidental chemical spills. Particles include such pollutants as dust and dirt from drywall, carpets, copying machines, and printing operations.[3]

MANAGERS' RESPONSIBILITIES

¶ Office managers should help by reviewing records pertaining to air conditioning and ventilation systems. They should also provide training sessions for employees to learn about maintaining clean air. Finally, they should keep a record of reported health complaints related to polluted air and aid in resolving these complaints.

AIR QUALITY IS A TEAM EFFORT

¶ All workers can have a positive impact on improving the quality of the air they breathe. For example, simply making sure that air vents and grilles are not blocked will help improve the quality of air. People who smoke should do so only in areas designated as smoking areas for employees.

---

[1] Karen Scheid, "Pollution at Work," *Los Angeles Times*, May 4, 2004, p. C8.

[2] "Dirty Air in Today's Offices," March 12, 2004, <http://www.airamerica.com/dirty.htm>, accessed on May 13, 2004.

[3] Carlos Sanchez, *Pollutants in America*, Southwest Press, Albuquerque, 2003.

INSTRUCTOR'S NOTES/INTERNET BOOKMARKS

Visit us on the Web at www.mhhe.com/gdp.

ASSESS

REPORT TEST 3-34 Review the format for a business report with footnotes in Lessons 41-E and 41-G on page 124. Also review page R-8A in the Reference Manual.

Review the format for side headings and paragraph headings in a report in Lesson 26-E and 26-G, on pages 64 and 65.

SKILLBUILDING

Diagnostic Practice: Symbols and Punctuation

The Diagnostic Practice: Symbols and Punctuation program is designed to diagnose and then correct your keystroking errors. You may use this program at any time throughout the course after completing Lesson 19.

Directions

1. Type one of the three Pretest/Posttest paragraphs 1 time, pushing *moderately* for speed. Review your errors.
2. Note your results—the number of errors you made on each symbol or punctuation key. For example, if you typed *75&* for *75%*, you would count 1 error on the % key.
3. For any symbol or punctuation key on which you made 2 or more errors, type the corresponding drill lines 2 times. If you made only 1 error, type the drill line 1 time.
4. If you made no errors on the Pretest/Posttest paragraph, type one set of the Practice: Symbols and Punctuation lines on page SB-4.
5. Finally, retype the same Pretest/Posttest, and compare your performance with your Pretest.

PRETEST/POSTTEST

Paragraph 1

```
Price & Joy stock closed @ 5 1/8 yesterday; it was up 13%
from yesterday. If we had sold our "high-demand" shares*
(*300 of them) before 3:30 p.m., we'd have made $15,000,
wouldn't we? Oh, well! I'll be in my office (#13C) crying.
```

Paragraph 2

```
The Time/CNN poll had the slate of Myers & Bassey ahead by
just 5%. Weren't you surprised? I was; after all, "they"*
(*meaning the crew) had ordered 60# of food @ $9.50 a pound
for a victory party at 3:30 p.m. today. What a sad mix-up!
```

Paragraph 3

```
Didn't my colleague* (*Elsa Jones-Salizar) send in $50 as a
10% deposit for reserving Room #5B on Friday and/or Monday?
Attached to her deposit was a note that said, "Call Tibby,
& me @ 10:30 a.m."; I was surprised. She sounded desperate!
```

PRACTICE: Individual Reaches

Ampersand

```
juj ju7j j7j j7&j j&&j j&&j juj ju7j j7j j7&j j&&j j&&j &&&
Alma & Bill & Carr & Dern & Epps & Farr & Gary & Horn & Ing
Jack & Kyle & Mann & Nash & Okum & Parr & Rand & Star & Tua
Uber & Vern & Will & Xang & Year & Zack & Sons & Bros & Inc
```

Apostrophe

```
;;; ;'; ;'; ';' ';' ''' Al's Bo's Di's it's Jo's Li's Moe's
you'd he'll she'd it'll she'll they'd aren't you're they're
we're we've we'll can't you've you'll hasn't didn't they've
she's don't isn't won't hadn't wasn't here's that's what'll
```

Asterisk

kik ki8k k8*k k8*k k**k k**k ki8k k8*k k8*k k**k k**k Note*
Ames* Beck* Carr* Dern* Epps* Farr* Gary* Horn* Iago* Jack*
Kyle* Mann* Nash* Okum* Parr* Rand* Star* Teri* Uber* Vern*
Will* Xang* Year* Zack* Note* Star* Also* List* Text* Cite*

At Sign

sws sw2s s2@s s2@s s@s s@@s and sws sw2s s2@s s2@s s@s s@@s
138 @ 34 and 89 @ 104 and 18 @ 458 and 89 @ 10 and 18 @ 340
162 & 31 and 48 & 606 and 81 @ 923 and 69 @ 42 and 54 @ 128
277 @ 89 and 57 & 369 and 70 @ 434 and 50 @ 15 and 37 @ 512

Colon

;;; ;:; ;:; :;: ::: and :/: and :?: and :p: and :-: and :::
From: Name: City: Madam: 4:30 Bill to: Address: To: cc: PS:
Date: Rank: Time: Dept.: 27:1 Subject: Time in: Hi: Re: Cf:
Sirs: Ext.: Apt.: State: 1:00 Ship to: Acts 4:2 FY: ID: OS:

Comma

kkk k,k k,k and ,k, and ,i, and ,8, and I,I and K,K and ,,,
Ava, ebb, lac, had, foe, elf, hug, ugh, poi, raj, ink, gal,
bum, Ben, ago, cop, req, far, has, dot, tau, env, wow, sax,
I am, you are, he is, we are, they are, Al, Ty, Hy, Jo, Ann

Diagonal

;;; ;/; /// and p/p and /p/ and 0/0 ;;; ;/; /// and p/p ///
a/c c/o B/L ft/s ac/dc and/or he/she cad/cam due/dew 1/2005
I/O n/a B/S n/30 AM/FM ob/gyn on/off lay/lie fir/fur 2/2006
p/e m/f w/o km/h d/b/a ad/add to/too set/sit him/her 3/2007

Dollar Sign

frf fr4 f4f f$f f$f f$f $40 $44 $44 f$f f4f $ff $45 $54 $$$
$40 and $82 and $90 and $13 and $33 and $56 and $86 and $25
$214 plus $882 plus $900 plus $718 plus $910 plus $112 plus
$1,937.53 plus $337.89 tax $3,985.43 minus $150.75 discount

Exclamation Mark

aqa aqla aq!a a!!a a!!a aqa aqla aq!a a!!a a!!a Go! Hi! Lo!
Oh! Wow! Gas! Dig! Yes! Sit! Rats! Darn! Well! Drat! Shoot!
So! Eat! Air! Out! Not! Aim! Whoa! Wait! Whee! Oops! Yahoo!
No! Yea! Eek! Run! Boo! Buy! Look! Help! Duck! Alas! There!

Hyphen

;;; ;p; ;-; -;- --- and -;- and -;- and -/- and -:- and -P-
add-on be-all F-stop H-bomb A-frame age-old all-day boo-boo
how-to in-out jam-up log-in come-on cop-out end-all fade-in
mix-up no-win say-so tie-up one-act pig-out rip-off T-shirt

Number/Pound

de3d de3#d d3#d d3#d d##d d##d #33 #33 #333 de3d de3#d d3#d
45# of #245 and 837# of #013 and 31# of #981 and 2# of #013
12# of #883 and 345# of #328 and 67# of #112 and 8# of #109
54# of #542 and 378# of #310 and 13# of #189 and 6# of #657

Parentheses

1o91 1o91 lo(1 lo(1 1((1 1((1 ;p0; ;p0; ;p); ;p); ;)); ;));
(a) (b) (c) (d) (e) (f) (g) (h) (i) (j) (k) (l) (m) (n) (o)
(p) (q) (r) (s) (t) (u) (v) (w) (x) (y) (z) (1) (2) (3) (4)
(5) (6) (7) (8) (9) (0) (@) (#) ($) (&) (*) (-) (;) (,) (:)

Percent

ftf ft5f f5f f5%f f%%f f%%f ftf ft5f f5f f5%f f%%f f%%f %%%
40% and 82% and 90% and 13% and 33% and 56% and 86% and 25%
21% and 48% and 82% and 90% and 70% and 18% and 91% and 10%
34.5% off 89% increase 12% credit 67% finished 10% discount

Period

1.1 ... and .l. and .o. and .9. and .(. and .O. and L.L ...
Jan. Feb. Mar. Apr. Jun. Jul. Aug. Sep. Oct. Nov. Dec. a.m.
Sun. Mon. Tue. Wed. Thu. Fri. Sat. Mrs. Esq. Mex. Can. D.C.
I am. I see. We do. He is. I can. Do not. Help me. Go slow.

Question Mark

;;; ;/; ;?; ??? ?;? and p?p and ?0? and ?)? and ?-? and ???
So? Who? What? Can I? Why not? Who does? Stop here? Is she?
Me? How? When? May I? Who, me? Says who? Do it now? For me?
Oh? Why? Am I? Do we? Am I up? How much? Who knows? Will I?

Quotation Mark

;'; ;"; ;"; ";" """ and ;'; ;"; ;"; ";" """ and ;"; ";" """
"Eat" "Sit" "Rest" "Stay" "Roll" "Hello" "Look" "Pet" "Dry"
"Yes" "Lie" "Halt" "Next" "Move" "Write" "Type" "Ink" "Sew"
"Beg" "See" "Walk" "Wave" "Stop" "Speak" "File" "Run" "Cry"

Semicolon

;;; ;:; and ;'; and ;"; and ;p; and ;-; and ;/; and ;?; ;;;
tea; ebb; Mac; mid; lie; arf; hug; nth; obi; Taj; ark; Hal;
dim; man; bio; hop; seq; our; Gus; let; you; Bev; row; lax;
do not cry; that is Liz; see to it; I am sad; we do; I can;

PRACTICE: SYMBOLS AND PUNCTUATION

Doe & Fry sued May & Ito; Ho & Fox sued Doe & Lee for M&Ms.
Ann's dad said he's happy she's out of school; she'd agree.
Yesterday* (*April 9), the rock star said **** right on TV.
E-mail them at glyden@sales.com to buy 3 @ $89 or 9 @ $250.

Hi, Ross: Place odds of 3:1 on the game at 10:30 and 11:15.
Tom gave Ava, Jo, Al, and Tyson a red, white, and blue car.
On 3/1/2008, he will receive a pension and/or a big buyout.
The $80 skirt was cut to $70 and then $55 for a $25 saving.

What! No ice! I'm mortified! Run, order some more. Quickly!
Jones-Lynch built an all-season add-on to her A-frame home.
Please order 500# of #684, 100# of #133, and 200# of #1341.
The answer is (a) 1, (b) 4, (c) 7, or (d) all of the above.

The car was cut 15% and then 25% for a final saving of 40%.
Mr. R. J. Dix ordered from L. L. Bean on Dec. 23 at 11 a.m.
Who? Me? Why me? Because I can type? Is that a good reason?
"Look," he said, "see that sign?" It says, "Beware of Dog."
Stop here; get out of your car; walk a foot; begin digging.

Diagnostic Practice: Numbers

The Diagnostic Practice: Numbers program is designed to diagnose and then correct your keystroking errors. You may use this program at any time throughout the course after completing Lesson 14.

Directions

1. Type one of the three Pretest/Posttest paragraphs 1 time, pushing *moderately* for speed. Review your errors.
2. Note your results—the number of errors you made on each key and your total number of errors. For example, if you type *24* for *25*, you would count 1 error on the number *5*.
3. For any number on which you made 2 or more errors, select the corresponding drill lines and type the drills 2 times. If you made only 1 error, type the drill 1 time.
4. If you made no errors on the Pretest/Posttest paragraph, type 1 set of the drills that contain all numbers on page SB-6.
5. Finally, retype the same Pretest/Posttest, and compare your performance with your Pretest.

PRETEST/POSTTEST

Paragraph 1

```
     The statement dated May 24, 2004, listed 56 clamps; 15
batteries; 169 hammers; 358 screwdrivers; 1,298 pliers; and
1,475 files. The invoice numbered 379 showed 387 hoes, 406
rakes, 92 lawn mowers, 63 tillers, and 807 more lawn items.
```

Paragraph 2

```
     My inventory records dated May 31, 2004, revealed that
we had 458 pints; 1,069 quarts; and 8,774 gallons of paint.
We had 2,953 brushes; 568 scrapers; 12,963 wallpaper rolls;
897 knives; 5,692 mixers; 480 ladders; and 371 step stools.
```

Paragraph 3

```
     Almost 179 hot meals were delivered to the 35 shut-ins
in April, 169 in May, and 389 in June. Several workers had
volunteered 7,564 hours in 2004; 9,348 hours in 2003; 5,468
in 2002; and 6,577 in 2001. About 80 people were involved.
```

PRACTICE: INDIVIDUAL REACHES

```
1 aq aq1 aq1qa 111 ants 101 aunts 131 apples 171 animals a1
They got 11 answers correct for the 11 questions in BE 121.
Those 11 adults loaded the 711 animals between 1 and 2 p.m.
All 111 agreed that 21 of those 31 are worthy of the honor.

2 sw sw2 sw2ws 222 sets 242 steps 226 salads 252 saddles s2
The 272 summer tourists saw the 22 soldiers and 32 sailors.
Your September 2 date was all right for 292 of 322 persons.
The 22 surgeons said 221 of those 225 operations went well.

3 de de3 de3ed 333 dots 303 drops 313 demons 393 dollars d3
Bus 333 departed at 3 p.m. with the 43 dentists and 5 boys.
She left 33 dolls and 73 decoys at 353 West Addison Street.
The 13 doctors helped some of the 33 druggists in Room 336.
```

4 fr fr4 fr4rf 444 fans 844 farms 444 fishes 644 fiddles f4
My 44 friends bought 84 farms and sold over 144 franchises.
She sold 44 fish and 440 beef dinners for $9.40 per dinner.
The 1954 Ford had only 40,434 fairly smooth miles by May 4.

5 fr fr5 fr5rf 555 furs 655 foxes 555 flares 455 fingers f5
They now own 155 restaurants, 45 food stores, and 55 farms.
They ordered 45, 55, 65, and 75 yards of that new material.
Flight 855 flew over Farmington at 5:50 p.m. on December 5.

6 jy jy6 jy6yj 666 jets 266 jeeps 666 jewels 866 jaguars j6
Purchase orders numbered 6667 and 6668 were sent yesterday.
Those 66 jazz players played for 46 juveniles in Room 6966.
The 6 judges reviewed the 66 journals on November 16 or 26.

7 ju ju7 ju7uj 777 jays 377 jokes 777 joists 577 juniors j7
The 17 jets carried 977 jocular passengers above 77 cities.
Those 277 jumping beans went to 77 junior scouts on May 17.
The 7 jockeys rode 77 jumpy horses between March 17 and 27.

8 ki ki8 ki8ik 888 keys 488 kites 888 knives 788 kittens k8
My 8 kennels housed 83 dogs, 28 kids, and 88 other animals.
The 18 kind ladies tied 88 knots in the 880 pieces of rope.
The 8 men saw 88 kelp bass, 38 kingfish, and 98 king crabs.

9 lo lo9 lo9ol 999 lads 599 larks 999 ladies 699 leaders 19
All 999 leaves fell from the 9 large oaks at 389 Largemont.
The 99 linemen put 399 large rolls of tape on for 19 games.
Those 99 lawyers put 899 legal-size sheets in the 19 limos.

0 ;p ;p0 ;p0p; 100 pens 900 pages 200 pandas 800 pencils ;0
There were 1,000 people who lived in the 300 private homes.
The 10 party stores are open from 1:00 p.m. until 9:00 p.m.
They edited 500 pages in 1 book and 1,000 pages in 2 books.

All numbers

a1a s2s d3d f4f f5f j6j j7j k8k l9l ;0; Add 6 and 8 and 29.
That 349-page script called for 10 actors and 18 actresses.
The check for $50 was sent to 705 Garfield Street, not 507.
The 14 researchers asked the 469 Californians 23 questions.

All numbers

a1a s2s d3d f4f f5f j6j j7j k8k l9l ;0; Add 3 and 4 and 70.
They built 1,299 houses on the 345-acre site by the canyon.
Her research showed that gold was at 397 in September 2004.
For $868 extra, they bought 15 new books and 61 used books.

All numbers

a1a s2s d3d f4f f5f j6j j7j k8k l9l ;0; Add 5 and 7 and 68.
A bank auditor arrived on May 26, 2004, and left on May 27.
The 4 owners open the stores from 9:30 a.m. until 6:00 p.m.
After 1,374 miles on the bus, she must then drive 185 more.

Progressive Practice: Alphabet

This skillbuilding routine contains a series of 30-second timed writings that range from 16wpm to 104wpm. The first time you use these timed writings, take a 1-minute timed writing on the Entry Timed Writing paragraph. Note your speed.

Select a passage that is 2wpm higher than your current speed. Then take six 30-second timed writings on the passage.

Your goal each time is to complete the passage within 30 seconds with no errors. When you have achieved your goal, move on to the next passage and repeat the procedure.

Entry Timed Writing

Bev was very lucky when she found extra quality in the 11
home she was buying. She quietly told the builder that she 23
was extremely satisfied with the work done on her new home. 35
The builder said she can move into her new house next week. 47

| 1 | 2 | 3 | 4 | 5 | 6 | 7 | 8 | 9 | 10 | 11 | 12

16wpm The author is the creator of a document.

18wpm Open means to access a previously saved file.

20wpm A byte represents one character to every computer.

22wpm A mouse may be used when running Windows on a computer.

24wpm Soft copy is text that is displayed on your computer screen.

26wpm Memory is the part of the word processor that stores information.

28wpm A menu is a list of choices to direct the operator through a function.

30wpm A sheet feeder is a device that will insert sheets of paper into a printer.

32wpm An icon is a small picture that illustrates a function or an object in software.

34wpm A window is a rectangular area with borders that displays the contents of open files.

36wpm To execute means to perform an action specified by an operator or by the computer program.

38wpm Output is the result of a word processing operation. It can be either printed or magnetic form.

40wpm Format refers to the physical features which affect the appearance and arrangement of your document.

42wpm A font is a style of type of one size or kind which includes all letters, numbers, and punctuation marks.

44wpm Ergonomics is the science of adapting working conditions or equipment to meet the physical needs of employees.

46wpm Home position is the starting position of a document; it is typically the upper left corner of the display monitor.

48wpm The mouse may be used to change the size of a window and to move a window to a different location on the display screen.

50wpm An optical scanner is a device that can read text and enter it into a word processor without the need to type the data again.

52wpm Hardware refers to the physical equipment used, such as the central processing unit, display screen, keyboard, printer, or drives.

54wpm A peripheral device is any piece of equipment that will extend the capabilities of a computer system but is not required for operation.

56wpm A split screen displays two or more different images at the same time; it can, for example, display two different pages of a legal document.

58wpm When using Windows, it's possible to place several programs on a screen and to change the size of a window or to change its position on a screen.

60wpm With the click of a mouse, one can use a button bar or a toolbar for fast access to features that are frequently applied when using a Windows program.

62wpm An active window can be reduced to an icon when you use Windows, enabling you to double-click another icon to open a new window for formatting and editing.

64wpm Turnaround time is the length of time needed for a document to be keyboarded, edited, proofread, corrected if required, printed, and returned to the originator.

66wpm A local area network is a system that uses cable or another means to allow high-speed communication among many kinds of electronic equipment within particular areas.

68wpm To search and replace means to direct the word processor to locate a character, word, or group of words wherever it occurs in the document and replace it with newer text.

70wpm Indexing is the ability of a word processor to accumulate a list of words that appear in a document, including page numbers, and then print a revised list in alphabetic order.

72wpm When a program needs information from you, a dialog box will appear on the desktop. Once the dialog box appears, you must identify the option you desire and then choose that option.

74wpm A facsimile is an exact copy of a document, and it is also a process by which images, such as typed letters, graphs, and signatures, are scanned, transmitted, and then printed on paper.

76wpm Compatibility refers to the ability of a computer to share information with another computer or to communicate with some other apparatus. It can be accomplished by using hardware or software.

78wpm Some operators like to personalize their desktops when they use Windows by making various changes. For example, they can change their screen colors and the pointer so that they will have more fun.

80wpm Wraparound is the ability of a word processor to move words from one line to another line and from one page to the next page as a result of inserting and deleting text or changing the size of margins.

82wpm It is possible when using Windows to evaluate the contents of different directories on the screen at the very same time. You can then choose to copy or move a particular file from one directory to another.

84wpm List processing is a capability of a word processor to keep lists of data that can be updated and sorted in alphabetic or numeric order. A list can also be added to any document that is stored in one's computer.

86wpm A computer is a wondrous device, which accepts data that are input and then processes the data and produces output. The computer performs its work by using one or more stored programs, which provide the instructions.

88wpm The configuration is the components that make up your word processing system. Most systems include the keyboard that is used for entering data, a central processing unit, at least one disk drive, a monitor, and a printer.

90wpm

Help for Windows can be used whenever you see a Help button in a dialog box or on a menu bar. Once you finish reading about a topic that you have selected, you will see a list of some related topics from which you can choose.

92wpm

When you want to look at the contents of two windows when using Windows, you will want to reduce the window size. Do this by pointing to a border or a corner of a window and dragging it until the window is the size that you want.

94wpm

Scrolling means to display a large quantity of text by rolling it horizontally or vertically past the display screen. As the text disappears from the top section of the monitor, new text will appear at the bottom section of the monitor.

96wpm

The Windows Print Manager is used to install and configure printers, join network printers, and monitor the printing of documents. Windows requires that a default printer be identified, but you can change the designation of it at any point.

98wpm

A stop code is a command that makes a printer pause while it is printing to permit an operator to insert text, change the font style, or change the kind of paper in the printer. To resume printing, the operator must use a special key or command.

100wpm

A computerized message system is a class of electronic mail that enables any operator to key a message on any computer terminal and have the message stored for later retrieval by the recipient, who can then display the message on his or her terminal.

102wpm

Many different graphics software programs have been brought on the market in recent years. These programs can be very powerful in helping with a business presentation. If there is any need to share data, using one of these programs could be quite helpful.

104wpm

Voice mail has become an essential service that many people in the business world use. This enables anyone who places a call to your phone to leave a message if you cannot answer it at that time. This special feature helps lots of workers to be more productive.

Progressive Practice: Numbers

This skillbuilding routine contains a series of 30-second timed writings that range from 16wpm to 80wpm. The first time you use these timed writings, take a 1-minute timed writing on the Entry Timed Writing paragraph. Note your speed.

Select a passage that is 4 to 6wpm *lower* than your current alphabetic speed. (The reason for selecting a lower speed goal is that sentences with numbers are more difficult to type.) Take six 30-second timed writings on the passage.

Your goal each time is to complete the passage within 30 seconds with no errors. When you have achieved your goal, move on to the next passage and repeat the procedure.

Entry Timed Writing

Their bags were filled with 10 sets of jars, 23 cookie 11
cutters, 4 baking pans, 6 coffee mugs, 25 plates, 9 dessert 23
plates, 7 soup bowls, 125 recipe cards, and 8 recipe boxes. 35
They delivered these 217 items to 20487 Mountain Boulevard. 47

| 1 | 2 | 3 | 4 | 5 | 6 | 7 | 8 | 9 | 10 | 11 | 12

16wpm There were now 21 children in Room 2110.

18wpm Fewer than 12 of the 121 boxes arrived today.

20wpm Maybe 12 of the 21 applicants met all 15 criteria.

22wpm There were 34 letters addressed to 434 West Cranbrooke.

24wpm Jane reported that there were 434 freshmen and 43 transfers.

26wpm The principal assigned 3 of those 4 students to Room 343 at noon.

28wpm Only 1 or 2 of the 34 latest invoices were more than 1 page in length.

30wpm They met 11 of the 12 players who received awards from 3 of the 4 trainers.

32wpm Those 5 vans carried 46 passengers on the first trip and 65 on the next 3 trips.

34wpm We first saw 3 and then 4 beautiful eagles on Route 65 at 5 a.m. on Tuesday, June 12.

36wpm The 16 companies produced 51 of the 62 records that received awards for 3 of 4 categories.

38wpm The 12 trucks hauled the 87 cows and 65 horses to the farm, which was about 21 miles northeast.

40wpm She moved from 87 Bayview Drive to 657 Cole Street and then 3 blocks south to 412 Gulbranson Avenue.

42wpm My 7 or 8 buyers ordered 7 dozen in sizes 5 and 6 after the 14 to 32 percent discounts had been bestowed.

44wpm There were 34 men and 121 women waiting in line at the gates for the 65 to 87 tickets to the Cape Cod concert.

46wpm Steve had listed 5 or 6 items on Purchase Order 241 when he saw that Purchase Requisition 87 contained 3 or 4 more.

48wpm Your items numbered 278 will sell for about 90 percent of the value of the 16 items that have code numbers shown as 435.

50wpm The managers stated that 98 of those 750 randomly selected new valves had about 264 defects, far exceeding the usual 31 norm.

52wpm Half of the 625 volunteers received over 90 percent of the charity pledges. Approximately 83 of the 147 agencies will have funds.

54wpm Merico hired 94 part-time workers to help the 378 full-time employees during the 62-day period when sales go up by 150 percent or more.

56wpm Kaye only hit 1 for 4 in the first 29 games after an 8-game streak in which she batted 3 for 4. She then hit at a .570 average for 6 games.

58wpm The mail carrier delivered 98 letters during the week to 734 Oak Street and also took 52 letters to 610 Faulkner Road as he returned on Route 58.

60wpm Pat said that about 1 in 5 of the 379 swimmers had a chance of being among the top 20. The best 6 of those 48 divers will receive the 16 best awards.

62wpm It rained from 3 to 6 inches, and 18 of those 20 farmers were fearful that 4 to 7 inches more would flood about 95 acres along 3 miles of the new Route 78.

64wpm Those 7 sacks weighed 48 pounds, more than the 30 pounds that I had thought. All 24 believe the 92-pound bag is at least 15 or 16 pounds above its true weight.

66wpm They bought 7 of the 8 options for 54 of the 63 vehicles last month. They now own over 120 dump trucks for use in 9 of the 15 new regions in the big 20-county area.

68wpm Andy was 8 or 9 years old when they moved to 632 Glendale Street away from the 1700 block of Horseshoe Lane, which is about 45 miles directly west of Boca Raton, FL 33434.

70wpm Doug had read 575 pages in the 760-page book by March 30; Darlene had read only 468 pages. Darlene has read 29 of those optional books since October 19, and Doug has read 18.

72wpm That school district has 985 elementary students, 507 middle school students, and 463 high school students; the total of 1,955 is 54, or 2.84 percent, over last year's grand total.

74wpm Attendance at last year's meeting was 10,835. The goal for this year is to have 11,764 people. This will enable us to plan for an increase of 929 participants, a rise of 8.57 percent.

76wpm John's firm has 158 stores, located in 109 cities in the West. The company employs 3,540 males and 2,624 females, a total of 6,164 employees. About 4,750 of those employees work part-time.

78wpm Memberships were as follows: 98 members in the Drama Guild, 90 members in Zeta Tau, 82 members in Theta Phi, 75 in the Bowling Club, and 136 in the Ski Club. This meant that 481 joined a group.

80wpm The association had 684 members from the South, 830 members from the North, 1,023 members from the East, and 751 from the West. The total membership was 3,288; these numbers increased by 9.8 percent.

Paced Practice

The Paced Practice skillbuilding routine builds speed and accuracy in short, easy steps by using individualized goals and immediate feedback. You may use this program at any time after completing Lesson 9.

This section contains a series of 2-minute timed writings for speeds ranging from 16wpm to 96wpm. The first time you use these timed writings, take the 1-minute Entry Timed Writing.

Select a passage that is 2wpm higher than your current typing speed. Then use this two-stage practice pattern to achieve each speed goal: (1) concentrate on speed, and (2) work on accuracy.

Speed Goal. To determine your speed goal, take three 2-minute timed writings in total. Your goal each time is to complete the passage in 2 minutes without regard to errors. When you have achieved your speed goal, work on accuracy.

Accuracy Goal. To type accurately, you need to slow down—just a bit. Therefore, to reach your accuracy goal, drop back 2wpm from the previous passage. Take consecutive timed writings on this passage until you can complete the passage in 2 minutes with no more than 2 errors.

For example, if you achieved a speed goal of 54wpm, you should then work on an accuracy goal of 52wpm. When you have achieved 52wpm for accuracy, move up 4wpm (for example, to the 56-wpm passage) and work for speed again.

Entry Timed Writing

If you can dream it, you can live it. Follow your 10
heart. There are many careers, from the mundane to the 21
exotic to the sublime. Start your career planning now. 32
Prepare for the future by exploring your talents, skills, 44
and interests. 47

| 1 | 2 | 3 | 4 | 5 | 6 | 7 | 8 | 9 | 10 | 11 | 12

16wpm

Your future is now. Seize each day. After you have explored your personal interests, study the sixteen career clusters for a broad range of job possibilities.

18wpm

While exploring various job options, think about what a job means to you. A job can mean something you do simply to earn money or something you find more rewarding and challenging.

20wpm

If you have a job you enjoy, work means more than just receiving wages. It means using your talents, being among people with like interests, making a contribution, and gaining a sense of satisfaction.

22wpm

What is the difference between a job and a career? Think carefully. A job is work that people do for money. A career is a sequence of related jobs built on a foundation of interests, knowledge, training, and experiences.

24wpm

Learn more about the world of work by looking at the sixteen career clusters. Most jobs are included in one of the clusters that have been organized by the government. During your exploration of careers, list the clusters that interest you.

26wpm

Once you identify your career clusters of interest, look at the jobs within each cluster. Find out what skills and aptitudes are needed, what education and training are required, what the work environment is like, and what is the possibility for advancements.

28wpm

Use your career center and school or public libraries to research career choices. Search the Internet. Consult with professionals for another perspective of a specific career. As you gather information about career options, you may discover other interesting career possibilities.

30wpm

Gain insights into a career by becoming a volunteer, participating in an internship, or working a part-time or temporary job within a chosen field. You will become more familiar with a specific job while developing your skills. You'll gain valuable experience, whether you choose that career or not.

32wpm

Whichever path you choose, strive for a high level of pride in yourself and your work. Your image is affected by what you believe other people think of you as well as by how you view yourself. Evaluate your level of confidence in yourself. If you have self-doubts, begin to build up your self-confidence and self-esteem.

34wpm

Self-esteem is essential for a positive attitude, and a positive attitude is essential for success in the world of work. While you cannot control everything that happens at work, you can control how you react. Your attitude matters. Becoming more confident and cultivating positive thoughts can bring you power in your life and on the job.

36wpm

Several factors lead to success on the job. People who have studied the factors say that it is the personal traits that often determine who is promoted or who is not. One of the finest traits a person can possess is the trait of being likable. Being likable means a person is honest, courteous, loyal, thoughtful, pleasant, kind, and most assuredly, positive.

38wpm

If you are likable, probably you relate well with others. Your kindness serves you well in the workplace. Developing good interpersonal relationships with coworkers will make work more enjoyable. After all, think of all the hours you will spend together. By showing that you are willing to collaborate with your coworkers, most likely you will receive their cooperation in return.

40wpm

Cooperation begins on the first day of your new job. When you work for a company, you become part of the team. Meeting people and learning new skills can be exciting. For some people, however, any new situation can trigger anxiety. The best advice is to remain calm, do your job to the best of your ability, learn the workplace policies, be flexible, avoid being too critical, and always be positive.

42wpm

When you begin a new job, even if you have recently received your college diploma, chances are you will start at the bottom of the organizational chart. Each of us has to start somewhere. But don't despair. With hard work and determination, soon you will be climbing up the corporate ladder. If you are clever, you will embrace even the most tedious tasks, take everything in stride, and use every opportunity to learn.

44wpm

If you think learning is restricted to the confines of an academic institution, think again. You have plenty to learn on the job, even if it is a job for which you have been trained. As a new worker, you won't be expected to know everything. When necessary, do not hesitate to ask your employer questions. Learn all you can about your job and the company. Use the new information to enhance your job performance and to prepare for success.

46wpm

Begin every valuable workday by prioritizing all your tasks. Decide which tasks must be done immediately and which can wait. List the most important tasks first; then determine the order in which each task must be done. After you complete a task, triumphantly cross it off your priority list. Do not procrastinate; that is, don't put off work you should do. If a task needs to be done, do it. You will be on top of your task list if you use your time wisely.

48wpm

Prevent the telephone from controlling your time by learning to manage your business phone calls. Phone calls can be extremely distracting from necessary tasks. When making an outgoing call, organize the topics you want to discuss. Gather needed materials such as pencils, papers, and files. Set a time limit, and stick to business. Give concise answers, summarize the points discussed, and end the conversation politely. Efficient telephone usage will help you manage your time.

50wpm

As with anything, practice makes perfect, but along the way, we all make mistakes. The difference between the successful people and those who are less successful is not that the successful people make fewer mistakes. It's that they don't give up. Instead of letting mistakes bring them down, they use their mistakes as opportunities to grow. If you make a mistake, be patient with yourself. You might be able to fix your mistake. Look for more opportunities for success to be just around the corner.

52wpm

Be patient with yourself when handling problems and accepting criticism. Handling criticism gracefully and maturely may be a challenge. Still, it is vital in the workplace. Criticism presented in a way that can help you learn and grow is constructive criticism . When you see criticism as helpful, it's easier to handle. Believe it or not, there are some employees who welcome criticism. It teaches them better ways to succeed on the job. Strive to improve how you accept constructive criticism, and embrace your growth.

54wpm

People experience continuous growth during a career. Goal setting is a helpful tool along any career path. Some people believe that goals provide the motivation needed to get to the place they want to be. Setting goals encourages greater achievements. The higher we set our goals, the greater the effort we will need to reach these goals. Each time we reach a target or come closer to a goal, we see an increase in our confidence and our performance, leading to greater accomplishments. And the cycle continues to spiral onward and upward.

56wpm

One goal we should all strive for is punctuality. When employees are tardy or absent from the workplace, it costs the company money. If you are frequently tardy or absent, others have to do their own work and cover for you. If you are absent often, your peers will begin to resent you, causing everyone stress in the department. Being late and missing work can damage the relationship with your manager and have a negative effect on your career. To avoid these potential problems, develop a personal plan to assure that you arrive every day on time or early.

58wpm

Holding a job is a major part of being an adult. Some people begin their work careers as adolescents. From the beginning, various work habits are developed that are as crucial to success as the actual job skills and knowledge that a person brings to the job. What traits are expected of workers? What do employers look for when they evaluate their employees? Important personal traits include being confident, cooperative, positive, and dependable. If you are organized, enthusiastic, and understanding, you have many of the qualities that employers value most in their employees.

60wpm

Being dependable is a desirable trait. When a project must be completed by a specific time, a manager will be reassured to know that reliable workers are going to meet the deadline. Workers who are dependable learn to utilize their time to achieve maximum results. Dependable workers can always be counted on, have good attendance records, are well prepared, and arrive on time ready to work. If a company wants to meet its goals, it must have a team of responsible and dependable workers. You, your coworkers, your supervisors, and your managers are all team members, working to reach common goals.

62wpm

The ability to organize is an important quality for the employee who wishes to display good work habits. The worker should have the ability to plan the work that needs to be completed and then be able to execute the plan in a timely manner. An employer requires a competent worker to be well organized. If an office worker is efficient, he or she handles requests swiftly and deals with correspondence without delay. The organized worker does not allow work to accumulate on the desk. Also, the organized office worker returns all phone calls immediately and makes lists of the activities that need to be done each day.

64wpm

Efficiency is another work habit that is desired. An efficient worker completes a task quickly and begins work on the next project eagerly. He or she thinks about ways to save steps and time. For example, an efficient worker may plan a single trip to the copier with several copying jobs rather than multiple trips to do each separate job. Being efficient also means having the required supplies to successfully complete each job. An efficient employee zips along on each project, uses time wisely, and stays focused on the present task. With careful and thorough planning, a worker who is efficient can accomplish more tasks in less time.

66wpm

Cooperation is another ideal work habit. As previously mentioned, cooperation begins on the first day on the job. Cooperation is thinking of all team members when making a decision. A person who cooperates is willing to do what is necessary for the good of the whole group. For you to be a team player, it is essential that you take extra steps to cooperate. Cooperation may mean being a good sport if you are asked to do something you would rather not do. It may mean you have to correct a mistake made by another person in the office. If every employee has the interests of the company at heart and works well as a team player, then cooperation is at work.

68wpm

Enthusiasm is still another work trait that is eagerly sought after by employers. Being enthusiastic means that a person has lots of positive energy. This is reflected in actions toward your work, coworkers, and employer. It has been noted that eagerness can be catching. If workers show they are eager to attempt any project, they will not only achieve the highest praise but will also be considered for career advancement. How much enthusiasm do you show at the workplace? Do you encourage people or complain to people? There will always be plenty of good jobs for employees who are known to have a wealth of zeal and a positive approach to the projects that they are assigned.

70wpm

Understanding is also a preferred work habit for every excellent worker. In today's world, virtually all business includes both men and women of different religions, races, cultures, work ethic, abilities, aptitudes, and attitudes. You'll interact with various types of people as customers, coworkers, and owners. Treat everyone fairly, openly, and honestly. Any type of prejudice is hurtful, offensive, and unacceptable. Prejudice cannot be tolerated in the office. Each employee must try to understand and accept everyone's differences. Because so many diverse groups of people work side by side in the workplace, it is essential that all coworkers maintain a high degree of mutual understanding.

72wpm

It can be concluded that certain work habits or traits can play a major role in determining the success of an employee. Most managers would be quick to agree on the importance of these traits. It is most probable that these habits would be evaluated on performance appraisal forms. Promotions, pay increases, new responsibilities, and your future with the company may be based on these evaluations. You should request regular job performance evaluations even if your company does not conduct them. This feedback will improve your job performance and career development by helping you grow. If you continually look for ways to improve your work habits and skills, then you will enjoy success in the workplace and beyond.

74wpm

You can be certain that no matter where you work, you will use some form of computer technology. Almost every business is dependent upon computers. Companies use such devices as voice mail, fax machines, cellular phones, and electronic schedules. Technology helps to accomplish work quickly and efficiently. A result of this rapidly changing technology is globalization, which is the establishment of worldwide communication links between people. Our world is becoming a smaller, global village. We must expand our thinking beyond the office walls. We must become aware of what happens in other parts of the world. Those events may directly affect you and your workplace. The more you know, the more valuable you will become to the company.

76wpm

Technological advancements are affecting every aspect of our lives. For example, the advent of the Internet has changed how we receive and send information. It is the world's largest information network. The Internet is often called the information superhighway because it is a vast network of computers that connect people and resources worldwide. It is an exciting medium to help you access the latest information. You can even learn about companies by visiting their Web sites. Without any doubt, we are all globally connected, and information technology services support those necessary connections. This industry offers many different employment opportunities. Keep in mind that proficiency in keyboarding is beneficial in this field and in other fields.

78wpm

It is amazing to discover the many careers in which keyboarding skill is necessary today, and the use of the computer keyboard by executive chefs is a prime example. The chefs in major restaurants must prepare parts or all of the meals served while directing the work of a staff of chefs, cooks, and other kitchen staff. The computer has become a necessary tool for a variety of tasks, including tracking inventories of food supplies. By observing which items are favorites and which items are not requested, the chef can calculate food requirements, order food, and supervise the food purchases. Additionally, the computer has proven to be a very practical tool for such tasks as planning budgets, preparing purchase orders for vendors, creating menus, and printing out reports.

80wpm

Advanced technology has opened the doors to a wider variety of amazing new products and services to sell. It seems the more complex the products, the higher the price of the products, or the greater the sales commission, the stiffer the competition. Selling these technical products requires detailed product knowledge, good verbal skills, smooth sales rapport, and proficient keyboarding skills. Business favors people with special training. For example, a pharmacy company may prefer a person with knowledge in chemistry to sell its products. Selling is for people who thrive on challenges and changes in products and services. Sales is appealing to people who enjoy using their powers of persuasion to make the sales. The potential for good earnings is very high for the well-trained salesperson.

82wpm

As you travel about in your sales job or type a report at the office or create Friday night's pasta special for your five-star restaurant, always remember to put safety first. Accidents happen, but they don't have to happen regularly or to have such serious consequences. Accidents cost businesses billions of dollars annually in medical expenses, lost wages, and insurance claims. A part of your job is to make certain you're not one of the millions of people injured on the job every year. You may believe you work in a safe place, but accidents occur in all types of businesses. A few careless people cause most accidents, so ensure your safety on the job. Safety doesn't just happen. Safety is the result of the careful awareness of many people who plan and put into action a safety program that benefits everyone.

84wpm

In today's market, you need more than the necessary skill or the personal qualities described above to succeed in the workplace. Employers also expect their employees to have ethics. Ethics are the principles of conduct governing an individual or a group. Employees who work ethically do not lie, cheat, or steal. They are honest and fair in their dealings with others. Employees who act ethically build a good reputation for themselves and their company. They are known to be dependable and trustworthy. Unethical behavior can have a spiraling effect. A single act can do a lot of damage. Even if you haven't held a job yet, you have had experience with ethical problems. Life is full of many opportunities to behave ethically. Do the right thing when faced with a decision. The ethics you practice today will carry over to your workplace.

86wpm

Now that you know what is expected of you on the job, how do you make sure you will get the job? Almost everyone has experienced the interview process for a job. For some, the interview is a traumatic event, but it doesn't have to be stressful. Preparation is the key. Research the company with whom you are seeking employment. Formulate a list of questions. Your interview provides you the opportunity to interview the organization. Don't go empty-handed. Take a portfolio of items with you. Include copies of your resume with a list of three or more professional references, your academic transcript, and your certificates and licenses. Be sure to wear appropriate business attire. The outcome of the interview will be positive if you have enthusiasm for the job, match your qualifications to the company's needs, ask relevant questions, and listen clearly.

88wpm

How can you be the strongest candidate for the job? Be sure that your skills in reading, writing, mathematics, speaking, and listening are solid. These basic skills will help you listen well and communicate clearly, not only during a job interview, but also at your workplace. The exchange of information between senders and receivers is called communication. It doesn't matter which occupation you choose; you will spend most of your career using these basic skills to communicate with others. You will use the basic skills as tools to gain information, solve problems, and share ideas. You will use these skills to meet the needs of your customers. The majority of jobs available during the next decades will be in the industries that will require direct customer contacts. Your success will be based upon your ability to communicate effectively with customers and coworkers.

90wpm

Writing effectively can help you gain a competitive edge in your job search and throughout your career. Most of[1] us have had occasion to write business letters whether to apply for a job, to comment on a product or service, or[2] to place an order. Often it seems easy to sit and let our thoughts flow freely. In other cases, we seem to struggle[3] to find the proper wording while trying to express our thoughts in exactly the right way. Writing skill can[4] improve with practice. Implement the following principles to develop your writing skill. Try to use language that[5] you would be comfortable using in person. Use words that are simple, direct, kind, confident, and professional.[6] When possible, use words that emphasize the positive side. Remember to proofread your work. Well-organized thoughts[7] and proper grammar, spelling, and punctuation show the reader that you care about the quality of your work.[8]

92wpm

Listening is an essential skill of the communication process. It is crucial for learning, getting along, and forming[1] relationships. Do you think you are an active or passive listener? Listening is not a passive activity. Conversely,[2] active listening is hearing what is being said and interpreting its meaning. Active listening makes you a more[3] effective communicator because you react to what you have heard. Study the following steps to increase your listening[4] skills. Do not cut people off; let them develop their ideas before you speak. If a message is vague, write down[5] your questions or comments, and wait for the entire presentation or discussion to be finished. Reduce personal and[6] environmental distractions by focusing on the message. Keep an open mind. Be attentive and maintain eye contact whenever[7] possible. By developing these basic communication skills, you will become more confident and more effective.[8]

94wpm

Speaking is also a form of communication. In the world of work, speaking is an important way in which to share information. Regardless of whether you are speaking to an audience of one or one hundred, you will want to make sure that your listeners get your message. Be clear about your purpose, your audience, and your subject. A purpose is the overall goal or reason for speaking. An audience is anyone who receives information. The subject is the main topic or key idea. Research your subject. Using specific facts and examples will give you credibility. As you speak, be brief and direct. Progress logically from point to point. Speak slowly and pronounce clearly all your words. Do people understand what you say or ask you to repeat what you've said? Is the sound of your voice friendly and pleasant or shrill and off-putting? These factors influence how your message is received. A good idea is worthless if you can't communicate it.

96wpm

Developing a career is a process. You have looked at your interests, values, skills, aptitudes, and attitudes. Your exploration into the world of work has begun. The journey doesn't stop here, for the present is the perfect place to start thinking about the future. It's where you begin to take steps toward your goals. It's where you can really make a difference. As you set personal and career goals, remember the importance of small steps. Each step toward a personal goal or career goal is a small victory. That feeling of success encourages you to take other small steps. Each step builds onto the next. Continue exploring your personal world as well as the world you share with others. Expect the best as you go forward. Expect a happy life. Expect loving relationships. Expect success in life. Expect fulfilling and satisfying work in a job you truly love. Last but not least, expect that you have something special to offer the world, because you do.

Supplementary Timed Writings

Supplementary Timed Writing 1

All problem solving, whether personal or academic, 10
involves decision making. You make decisions in order to 21
solve problems. On occasion, problems occur as a result of 33
decisions you have made. For example, you may decide to 44
smoke, but later in life, you face the problem of nicotine 56
addiction. You may decide not to study mathematics and 67
science because you think that they are too difficult. 78
Because of this choice, many career opportunities will be 90
closed to you. There is a consequence for every action. Do 102
you see that events in your life do not just happen, but 113
that they are the result of your choices and decisions? 124

How can you prepare your mind for problem solving? A 135
positive attitude is a great start. Indeed, your attitude 147
affects the way in which you solve a problem or make a 158
decision. Approach your studies, such as science and math 170
courses, with a positive and inquisitive attitude. Try to 182
perceive academic problems as puzzles to solve rather than 192
homework to avoid. 198

Critical thinking is a method of problem solving that 209
involves decoding, analyzing, reasoning, evaluating, and 220
processing information. It is fundamental for successful 231
problem solving. Critical thinking is a willingness to 242
explore, probe, question, and search for answers. Problems 254
may not always be solved on the first try. Don't give up. 266
Try, try again. Finding a solution takes sustained effort. 278
Use critical thinking skills to achieve success in today's 290
fast-paced and highly competitive world of business. 300

| 1 | 2 | 3 | 4 | 5 | 6 | 7 | 8 | 9 | 10 | 11 | 12

Supplementary Timed Writing 2

For many, the Internet is an important resource in 10
their private and professional lives. The Internet provides 22
quick access to countless Web sites that contain news, 33
products, games, entertainment, and many other types of 44
information. The Web pages on these sites can be designed, 56
authored, and posted by anyone, anywhere around the world. 68
Utilize critical thinking when reviewing all Web sites. 79

Just because something is stated on the radio, printed 90
in the newspaper, or shown on television doesn't mean that 102
it's true, real, accurate, or correct. This applies to 113
information found on the Internet as well. Don't fall into 125
the trap of believing that if it's on the Net, it must be 137
true. A wise user of the Internet thinks critically about 149
data found on the Net and evaluates this material before 160
using it. 162

When evaluating a new Web site, think about who, what, 173
how, when, and where. Who refers to the author of the Web 185
site. The author may be a business, an organization, or a 197
person. What refers to the validity of the data. Can this 209
data be verified by a reputable source? How refers to the 221
viewpoint of the author. Is the data presented without 232
prejudice? When refers to the time frame of the data. Is 244
this recent data? Where refers to the source of the data. 256
Is this data from an accurate source? By answering these 267
critical questions, you will learn more about the accuracy 279
and dependability of a Web site. As you surf the Net, be 290
very cautious. Anyone can publish on the Internet. 300

| 1 | 2 | 3 | 4 | 5 | 6 | 7 | 8 | 9 | 10 | 11 | 12

Supplementary Timed Writing 3

Office employees perform a variety of tasks during 10
their workday. These tasks vary from handling telephone 21
calls to forwarding personal messages, from sending short 33
e-mail messages to compiling complex office reports, and 44
from writing simple letters to assembling detailed letters 56
with tables, graphics, and imported data. Office workers 67
are a fundamental part of a company's structure. 77

The office worker uses critical thinking in order to 88
accomplish a wide array of daily tasks. Some of the tasks 100
are more urgent than other tasks and should be completed 111
first. Some tasks take only a short time, while others take 123
a lot more time. Some tasks demand a quick response, while 135
others may be taken up as time permits or even postponed 147
until the future. Some of the tasks require input from 158
coworkers or managers. Whether a job is simple or complex, 170
big or small, the office worker must decide what is to be 182
tackled first by determining the priority of each task. 193

When setting priorities, critical thinking skills are 204
essential. The office worker evaluates each aspect of the 216
task. It is a good idea to identify the size of the task, 228
determine its complexity, estimate its effort, judge its 239
importance, and set its deadline. Once the office worker 250
assesses each task that is to be finished within a certain 262
period of time, then the priority for completing all tasks 274
can be set. Critical thinking skills, if applied well, 285
can save the employer money or, if executed poorly, can 296
cost the employer. 300

| 1 | 2 | 3 | 4 | 5 | 6 | 7 | 8 | 9 | 10 | 11 | 12

Supplementary Timed Writing 4

Each day business managers make choices that keep 10
businesses running smoothly, skillfully, and profitably. 21
Each decision regarding staff, finances, operations, and 32
resources often needs to be quick and precise. To develop 44
sound decisions, managers must use critical thinking. They 56
gather all the essential facts so that they can make good, 68
well-informed choices. After making a decision, skilled 79
managers review their thinking process. Over time, they 90
refine their critical thinking skills. When they encounter 102
similar problems, they use their prior experiences to help 114
them solve problems with ease and in less time. 124

What type of decisions do you think managers make that 135
involve critical thinking? Human resources managers decide 147
whom to employ, what to pay a new employee, and where to 158
place a new worker. In addition, human resources managers 170
should be unbiased negotiators, resolving conflict between 182
other employees. Office managers purchase copy machines, 194
computers, software, and office supplies. Finance officers 206
prepare precise, timely financial statements. Top managers 218
control business policies, appoint mid-level managers, and 230
assess the success of the business. Plant supervisors set 242
schedules, gauge work quality, and evaluate workers. Sales 254
managers study all of the new sales trends, as well as 265
provide sales training and promotion materials. 275

Most managers use critical thinking to make wise, well- 286
thought-out decisions. They carefully check their facts, 297
analyze these facts, and make a final judgment based upon 309
these facts. They should also be able to clearly discern 320
fact from fiction. Through trial and error, managers learn 332
their own ways of solving problems and finding the most 343
effective and creative solutions. 350

| 1 | 2 | 3 | 4 | 5 | 6 | 7 | 8 | 9 | 10 | 11 | 12

Supplementary Timed Writing 5

In most classes, teachers want students to analyze 10
situations, draw conclusions, and solve problems. Each 21
of these tasks requires students to use thinking skills. 32
How do students acquire these skills? What is the process 44
students follow to develop thinking skills? 53

During the early years of life, children learn words 63
and then combine these words into sentences. From there, 74
they learn to declare ideas, share thoughts, and express 85
feelings. Students learn numbers and simple math concepts. 97
They may learn to read musical notes, to keep rhythm, to 108
sing songs, and to recognize many popular and classical 119
pieces of music. Students learn colors, identify shapes, 130
and begin drawing. During the early years, students learn 142
the basic problem-solving models. 149

One way to solve problems and apply thinking skills 159
is to use the scientific approach. This approach requires 171
the student to state the problem to be solved, gather all 183
the facts about the problem, analyze the problem, and pose 195
viable solutions. Throughout this process, teachers ask 206
questions that force students to expand their thinking 217
skills. Teachers may ask questions such as these: Did you 229
clearly state the problem? Did you get all the facts? Did 241
you get the facts from the right place? Did you assume 252
anything? Did you pose other possible solutions? Did you 263
keep an open mind to all solutions? Did you let your bias 275
come into play? Did you listen to others who might have 286
insights? Did you dig deep enough? Does the solution make 298
sense to you? 301

This simple four-step process for solving problems 311
gives students a model to use for school, for work, and 322
for life. While the process may not be used to solve every 334
problem, it does provide a starting point to begin using 345
critical thinking skills. 350

| 1 | 2 | 3 | 4 | 5 | 6 | 7 | 8 | 9 | 10 | 11 | 12

Supplementary Timed Writing 6

A major goal for nearly all educators is to teach 10
critical thinking skills to a class. Critical thinking, 21
which is the process of reasonably or logically deciding 32
what to do or believe, involves the ability to compare and 44
contrast, resolve problems, make decisions, analyze and 55
evaluate, and combine and transfer knowledge. These skills 67
benefit the student who eventually becomes a part of the 78
workforce. Whether someone is in a corporate setting, is 89
in a small business, or is self-employed, the environment 101
of today is highly competitive and skilled employees are in 113
great demand. 116

One factor in achieving success in the workforce is 127
having the ability to deal with the varied demands of the 139
fast-paced business world. Required skills are insightful 150
decision making, creative problem solving, and earnest 162
communication among diverse groups. These groups could be 174
employees, management, employers, investors, customers, 185
or clients. 187

In school, we learn the details of critical thinking. 198
This knowledge extends far beyond the boundaries of the 209
classroom. It lasts a lifetime. We use critical thinking 220
throughout our daily lives. We constantly analyze and 231
evaluate music, movies, conversations, fashion, magazine 242
or newspaper articles, and television programs. We all had 254
experience using critical thinking skills before we even 265
knew what they were. So keep on learning, growing, and 276
experimenting. The classroom is the perfect setting for 287
exploration. Take this opportunity to see how others solve 299
problems, give each other feedback, and try out new ideas 311
in a safe environment. 316

A person who has learned critical thinking skills is 327
equipped with the essential skills for achieving success 338
in today's workforce. There are always new goals to reach. 350

| 1 | 2 | 3 | 4 | 5 | 6 | 7 | 8 | 9 | 10 | 11 | 12

Supplementary Timed Writing 7

Use your unique creativity when applying critical 10
thinking skills. One of the first steps in unlocking your 22
creativity is to realize that you have control over your 33
thinking; it doesn't control you. Creativity is using new 45
or different methods to solve problems. Many inventions 56
involved a breakthrough in traditional thinking, and the 67
result was an amazing experience. For example, Einstein 78
broke with tradition by trying lots of obscure formulas 89
that changed scientific thought. Your attitude can form 100
mental blocks that keep you from being creative. When you 112
free your mind, the rest will follow. 120

Do your best to unleash your mind's innate creativity. 131
Turn problems into puzzles. When you think of a task as a 143
puzzle, a challenge, or a game instead of a difficult 154
problem, you open your mind and encourage your creative 165
side to operate. Creative ideas often come when you are 176
having fun and are involved in an unrelated activity. 187
You will find that when your defenses are down, your brain 199
is relaxed and your subconscious is alive; then creative 210
thoughts can flow. 214

Habit often restricts you from trying new approaches 225
to problem solving. Remember, there is usually more than 237
one solution. Empty your mind of the idea of only one way 249
of looking at a problem and strive to see situations in a 261
fresh, new way. How many times have you told yourself that 273
you must follow the rules and perform tasks in a certain 284
way? If you want to be creative, look at things in a new 295
way, break the pattern, explore new options, and challenge 307
the rules. If you are facing a difficult problem and can't 319
seem to find a solution, take a quick walk or relax for 330
a few minutes; then go back to the problem renewed. When 341
working on homework or taking a test, always work the 352
easiest problems first. Success builds success. 362

A sense of humor is key to being creative. Silly and 373
irrelevant ideas can lead to inventive solutions. Humor 384
generates ideas, puts you in a creative state of mind, 395
and makes work exciting! 400

| 1 | 2 | 3 | 4 | 5 | 6 | 7 | 8 | 9 | 10 | 11 | 12

Supplementary Timed Writing 8

Keyboarding is a popular business course for many 10
students. The major objectives of a keyboarding course are 22
to develop touch control of the keyboard and proper typing 34
techniques, build basic speed and accuracy, and provide 45
practice in applying those basic skills to the formatting 57
of letters, reports, tables, memos, and other kinds of 68
personal and business communications. In the early part of 80
a keyboarding course, students learn to stroke by touch 91
using specific techniques. They learn to hit the keys in a 103
quick and accurate way. After the keys are learned and 114
practiced, students move into producing documents of all 125
sizes and types for personal and vocational use. 135

When you first learn keyboarding, there are certain 145
parameters, guidelines, and exercises to follow. There are 157
rules intended to help you learn and eventually master the 169
keyboard. Creating documents requires students to apply 180
critical thinking. What format or layout should be used? 191
What font and font size would be best? Are all the words 202
spelled correctly? Does the document look neat? Are the 213
figures accurate? Are punctuation and grammar correct? 224

There is a lot to learn in the world of keyboarding. 235
Be persistent, patient, and gentle with yourself. Allow 246
failure in class and on the job; that's how we learn. It's 258
okay to admit mistakes. Mistakes are stepping-stones for 269
growth and creativity. Being creative has a lot to do with 281
risk taking and courage. It takes courage to explore new 292
ways of thinking and to risk looking different, being 303
silly and impractical, and even being wrong. Your path to 315
creativity is such a vital component of your critical 326
thinking skills. Allow your creative thoughts to flow 337
freely when producing each of your keyboarding tasks. 348

Keyboarding skill and personal creativity are valuable 359
attributes for life and on the job. The worker who can see 371
situations and problems in a fresh way, reason logically, 383
explore options, and come up with inventive ideas is sure 395
to be a valuable employee. 400

| 1 | 2 | 3 | 4 | 5 | 6 | 7 | 8 | 9 | 10 | 11 | 12

Supplementary Timed Writing 9

One of the most important decisions we all have to 10
face is choosing a career. The possibilities can appear 21
overwhelming. Fear not! Your critical thinking skills will 33
save you! Start your career planning today. Begin with 44
self-assessment. What are your interests? Do you enjoy 55
working indoors or outdoors? Do you prefer working with 66
numbers or with words? Are you the independent type or 77
would you rather work with a group? What are your favorite 89
academic studies? Think about these questions and then 100
create a list of your interests, skills, aptitudes, and 111
values. What you discover about yourself will help you in 123
finding the career that is right for you. 131

After you have explored your personal interests, look 142
at the sixteen career clusters for a wide range of job 153
prospects. Most jobs are included in one of these clusters 165
that have been organized by the government. During your 176
exploration, make a note of the clusters that interest you 188
and investigate these clusters. 194

Gather as much information as possible by using all 205
available resources. Scan the Help Wanted section in the 216
major Sunday newspapers for job descriptions and salaries. 228
Search the Net. The Internet provides electronic access to 240
worldwide job listings. If you want to know more about a 251
specific company, access its home page. Go to your college 263
placement office. Sign up for interviews with companies 274
that visit your campus. Visit your local school or county 286
library and ask the reference librarian for occupational 297
handbooks. Talk with people in your field of interest to 308
ask questions and get advice. Attend chapter meetings of 319
professional organizations to network with people working 331
in your chosen profession. Volunteer, intern, or work a 342
part-time or temporary job within your career choice for 353
valuable, first-hand insight. Taking an initiative in your 365
job search will pay off. 370

A career search requires the use of critical thinking 381
skills. These skills will help you to choose the career 392
that will match your skills and talents. 400

| 1 | 2 | 3 | 4 | 5 | 6 | 7 | 8 | 9 | 10 | 11 | 12

Ten-Key Numeric Keypad

Goal

- To control the ten-key numeric keypad keys.

Some computer keyboards have a separate ten-key numeric keypad located to the right of the alphanumeric keyboard. The arrangement of the keypad enables you to type numbers more rapidly than you can when using the top row of the alphanumeric keyboard.

To input numbers using the ten-key numeric keypad, you must activate the Num Lock (Numeric Lock) key. Usually, an indicator light signals that the Num Lock is activated.

On the keypad, 4, 5, and 6 are the home keys. Place your fingers on the keypad home row as follows:

- First finger (J finger) on 4
- Second finger (K finger) on 5
- Third finger (L finger) on 6

The keypad keys are controlled as follows:

- First finger controls 1, 4, and 7
- Second finger controls 2, 5, and 8
- Third finger controls 3, 6, 9, and decimal point
- Right thumb controls 0
- Fourth finger controls ENTER

Since different computers have different arrangements of ten-key numeric keypads, study the arrangement of your keypad. The illustration shows the most common arrangement. If your keypad is arranged differently from the one shown in the illustration, check with your instructor for the correct placement of your fingers on the keypad.

NEW KEYS

A. THE 4, 5, AND 6 KEYS

A. Use the first finger to control the 4 key, the second finger to control the 5 key, and the third finger to control the 6 key.

Keep your eyes on the copy.

Before beginning, check to be sure the Num Lock key is activated.

Type the first column from top to bottom. Next, type the second column; then type the third column. Press ENTER after typing the final digit of each number.

444	456	454
555	654	464
666	445	546
455	446	564
466	554	654
544	556	645
566	664	666
644	665	555
655	456	444
456	654	456

B. Use the 4 finger to control the 7 key, the 5 finger to control the 8 key, and the 6 finger to control the 9 key.

Keep your eyes on the copy.

Press ENTER after typing the final digit of each number.

B. THE 7, 8, AND 9 KEYS

474	585	696
747	858	969
774	885	996
447	558	669
744	855	966
477	588	699
444	555	666
747	858	969
774	885	996
747	858	969

C. Use the 4 finger to control the 1 key, the 5 finger to control the 2 key, and the 6 finger to control the 3 key.

Keep your eyes on the copy.

Press ENTER after typing the final digit of each number.

C. THE 1, 2, AND 3 KEYS

444	555	666
111	222	333
144	225	336
441	552	663
144	255	366
411	522	633
444	555	666
414	525	636
141	252	363
411	525	636

D. Use the right thumb to control the 0 key.

Keep your eyes on the copy.

Press ENTER after typing the final digit of each number.

D. THE 0 KEY

404	470	502
505	580	603
606	690	140
707	410	250
808	520	360
909	630	701
101	407	802
202	508	903
303	609	405
505	401	506

E. Use the 6 finger to control the decimal key.

Keep your eyes on the copy.

Press ENTER after typing the final digit of each number.

E. THE . KEY

4.5	7.8	1.2
6.5	9.8	3.2
4.4	7.7	1.1
4.4	7.7	1.1
5.5	8.8	2.2
5.5	8.8	2.2
6.6	9.9	3.3
6.5	9.9	3.3
4.5	7.8	1.2
6.5	8.9	1.3

INDEX

NOTE: Page numbers preceded by A- indicate material in Appendix; page numbers preceded by R- indicate material in Reference Manual; page numbers preceded by SB- indicate material in Skillbuilding supplement.

B

C

D

E

F

G

H

I

J

K

L

M

N

O

P

Q

R

S

T

U

V

W

Y

McGraw-Hill/Irwin and the GDP author team would like to acknowledge the participants of the 2004 Focus Group for their efforts in making the 10th edition the best it can be:

Special thanks goes to Ken Baker for his work as the tech editor on GDP.

Kim Aylett
Branford Hall Career Institute
Southington, CT

Ken Baker
Sinclair Community College
Dayton, OH

Lenette Baker
Valencia Community College
Orlando, FL

Joyce Crawford
Central Piedmont Community College
Charlotte, NC

Martha Gwatney
Northern Virginia Community College
Annandale, VA

Marijean Harmonis
Community College of Philadelphia
Philadelphia, PA

Mary Hedberg
Johnson County Community College
Overland Park, KS

Kay Ono
Leeward Community College
Pearl City, HI

Marcia Polanis
Forsyth Tech Community College
Winston-Salem, NC

Photo Credits
Steve Cole/Getty Images 95; Adam Crowley/Getty Images 163; Jack Hollingsworth/Getty Images 66; Jeff Maloney/Getty Images 173; Ryan McVay/Getty Images iii, iv, R-23, 42, 56, 91, 154, 180; Royalty Free/Corbis vi, 120, 197, 207; Royalty Free/Getty Images R-2; Royalty Free/PhotoDisc 160; Jack Star/ Photo Link/Getty Images 117